Principles of External Auditing

Third edition

Principles of External Auditing

Third edition

Brenda Porter
Jon Simon
David Hatherly

WILEY

A John Wiley & Sons, Ltd., Publication

Copyright © 2008   Brenda Porter, Jon Simon, David Hatherly
Published by   John Wiley & Sons, Ltd
                      The Atrium, Southern Gate, Chichester,
                      West Sussex PO19 8SQ, England

                      Telephone +44 (0) 1243 779777

Email (for orders and customer service enquiries): cs-books@wiley.co.uk
Visit our Home Page on www.wiley.com

First edition published 1996 by John Wiley & Sons, Ltd
Second edition published 2003 by John Wiley & Sons, Ltd

Reprinted February 2009, August 2010

Other Wiley Editorial Offices
John Wiley & Sons Inc., 111 River Street, Hoboken, NJ 07030, USA
Jossey-Bass, 989 Market Street, San Francisco, CA 94103-1741, USA
Wiley-VCH Verlag GmbH, Boschstr. 12, D-69469 Weinheim, Germany
John Wiley & Sons Australia Ltd, 42 McDougall Street, Milton, Queensland 4064, Australia
John Wiley & Sons (Asia) Pte Ltd, 2 Clementi Loop #02-01, Jin Xing Distripark, Singapore 129809
John Wiley & Sons Canada Ltd, 6045 Freemont Blvd, Mississauga, ONT, L5R 4J3

Wiley also publishes its books in a variety of electronic formats. Some content that appears in print may not be available in electronic books.

Library of Congress Cataloging-in-Publication Data

Porter, Brenda.
  Principles of external auditing / Brenda Porter, David Hatherly, Jon Simon. – 3E.
    p. cm.
  Includes bibliographical references and index.
    ISBN 978-0-470-01825-5 (pbk. : alk. paper) 1. Auditing. 2. Auditing–Law and legislation. 3. Auditors' reports. 4. Auditing–Automation.
I. Hatherly, David J. II. Simon, Jon. III. Title.
  HF5667.P633 2008
  657'.45–dc22   2008013168

A catalogue record for this book is available from the British Library

ISBN: 978-0-470-018255 (P/B)

Typeset by SNP Best-set Typesetter Ltd., Hong Kong
Printed and bound in Great Britain by CPI Antony Rowe, Chippenham, Wiltshire

Contents

Preface

The third edition of *Principles of External Auditing* follows the first and second editions, which were published in 1996 and 2002, respectively. Like its predecessors, this edition describes and explains, in readily comprehensible, non-technical language, the nature of the audit function and the principles of the audit process. The book is designed for *anyone* who is interested in understanding the principles that underlie external auditing. It also provides an ideal foundation for all those studying auditing, and is particularly suitable as a text for introductory courses in universities and for professional examinations such as the ACCA's *Audit and Assurance* and *Advanced Audit and Assurance*. For more advanced auditing courses, the book may be supplemented by specialist articles and other reading material drawn from professional and academic journals. Some suitable references are indicated in the 'Additional Reading' provided at the end of each chapter.

Since 2002 and the collapse of Enron and Arthur Andersen, followed by debacles such as WorldCom, Tyco, Parmalat, HIH and Ahold, the auditing environment has been transformed. Formerly a self-regulating profession, auditing has become subject to stringent external regulation in the United Kingdom (UK), as in many other parts of the world. The Financial Reporting Council, the UK's independent regulator for corporate reporting and governance, oversees the auditing profession, ethical and technical auditing standards, the monitoring of auditors' performance, and the disciplining of those who do not perform to expected standards. Additionally, auditing in the UK has been impacted significantly by the European Union's *8th Directive on the statutory audits of annual accounts and consolidated accounts* and the Companies Act 2006. Another very significant change in the auditing arena is the general worldwide acceptance, apart from in the United States of America, of *International Standards on Auditing*.

Notwithstanding the changes in the auditing environment, the basic principles of auditing have remained unchanged. However, in this third edition of the book, we have incorporated important developments. These include:
- the increased emphasis on:
  - audit quality and monitoring of auditors' performance,
  - understanding the client, its business, industry, key personnel, internal and external environment, and so on, as a basis for assessing the risk of the financial statements being materially misstated;

- the auditing profession's response to society's increased concern about corporate fraud;
- the tightening of requirements in respect of auditors' independence and the debate over audit firm rotation;
- enhanced responsibilities for external auditors in relation to communicating with those charged with audit clients' governance;
- developments in the realm of limiting auditors' liability to their clients and to third parties;
- developments in respect of environmental (or, now more commonly, corporate responsibility) reporting and the independent assurance of such reports.

The fundamental principles of auditing, as set out in *The Auditors' Code*, were revised by the Auditing Practices Board (APB) in 2008. As in the earlier editions, they are reproduced on the inside cover of this book. These fundamental principles are all-pervasive but we have identified the chapter where each principle seems to have greatest application and have highlighted this principle at the beginning of the relevant chapter.

A feature of this third edition is that it incorporates the International Standards on Auditing (ISAs) issued by the International Auditing and Assurance Standards Board (IAASB). As is explained in more detail in the '*Important Note on Auditing Standards referred to in this book*' on page xv, during the past couple of years, the IAASB has been undertaking a 'clarity project' and re-issuing all of the ISAs in 'Redrafted' form. In order to ensure that this text is as up to date as possible, we have referred to the latest version of each ISA (including some in Exposure Draft form) that was available at the time the book went to print in June 2008.

This book commences with six chapters that form the backdrop for an understanding of the audit process. Given the importance of the conceptual framework which underpins audit practice, a separate chapter (Chapter 3) is devoted to this topic. Similarly, a separate chapter explores the important and topical issue of auditors' independence (Chapter 4). Chapter 5 provides an overview of the legal, regulatory and professional requirements which govern the work of auditors – including those specified in the Companies Act 2006, and Chapter 6 examines the topical and controversial issue of auditors' responsibility for detecting and reporting corporate fraud and other illegal acts committed by auditees or their directors and/or senior executives.

Chapter 7 constitutes an introduction to auditing practice in that it provides an overview of the audit process and its staffing, documentation and administration. In the following seven chapters (Chapters 8 to 14), the reader is taken step by step through the audit process – from conducting engagement procedures and gaining an initial understanding of the audit client, to issuing reports to users of financial statements and to those charged with the entity's governance. It should be noted that legally a company's board of directors (comprising both executive and non-executive directors) is responsible for the company's governance. However, the board relies on senior executives (who may or may not be directors) to implement its policies and to ensure the smooth running of the company on a day-to-day basis. In this book we use the term 'management' to embrace executive and non-executive directors and non-director senior executives.

In Chapter 15 we discuss the important issue of auditors' liability – in particular, how auditors' duty of care to third parties has evolved up to, and since, the landmark *Caparo* case. Chapter 16 follows on from the examination of auditors' liability in Chapter 15. It describes measures auditing firms and engagement partners are required to take, and regulators have adopted, in order to ensure high-quality audits are conducted – thereby helping auditors to avoid exposure to liability. The chapter provides an analysis of the findings of the units that have monitored auditors' performance in the UK and Ireland since monitoring was introduced in 1992. It also provides an update on other measures that have been proposed or adopted as a means of limiting auditors' liability, namely, the use of limited liability companies and limited liability partnerships, the imposition of a statutory cap on damages, the introduction of proportionate liability, and the Companies Act 2006 provision which enables auditors to make limitation of liability agreements with their audit clients.

As preparation for the third edition of this book we conducted extensive consultations with representatives of major auditing firms and academic colleagues. Those we consulted were extremely helpful in providing constructive feedback on the second edition and how it should be revised. In this, and in other respects, our sincere thanks go to Warren Allen of Ernst & Young, Fred Hutchings of PricewaterhouseCoopers, Graeme Mitchell of Deloitte and Ross Buckley of KPMG. These and other colleagues in the profession advised us that, notwithstanding the significant changes which characterise the auditing environment, in particular the adoption of ISAs – "which are becoming progressively more prescriptive and exacting" (quoting one of the audit partners) – the place of auditors and the audit function in society and the audit process, as reflected in this book, remain intact.

Academic colleagues whom we consulted, who teach auditing courses in various universities in the UK and elsewhere, stressed the importance in today's environment of providing material on environmental audits and the independent assurance of environmental, environmental and social, or wide-ranging corporate responsibility, reports (whichever version of these reports companies publish). Accordingly, in this edition of the book, we have included two chapters (Chapters 17 and 18) on these topics.

In addition to the academic and professional colleagues who provided us with invaluable feedback and guidance for this third edition, we would like to thank the numerous students whose insightful feedback on the second edition has been extremely helpful. We would also like to express special thanks to Rhys Barlow of BDO Spicers, Robert Elms and Paolo Ryan of Martin Jarvie PKF, Brent Kennerly of Grant Thornton, Geoff Lane of PricewaterhouseCoopers, Steve Leonard of the Auditing Practices Board, Sha Ali Khan of the Association of Chartered Certified Accountants and Arisa Kishigami of FTSE4Good, for the valuable information they have provided for various chapters of the book. Thanks are also due to our families, friends and colleagues for their patience, understanding and support.

Brenda Porter
Jon Simon
David Hatherly

Important Note on Auditing Standards Referred to in this Book

As noted in the Preface, in this book we have sought to include the latest version of each International Standard on Auditing (ISA) issued by the International Auditing and Assurance Standards Board (IAASB). The IAASB is an independent standards setting body established by the International Federation of Accountants (IFAC). IFAC, a global organisation for the accountancy profession, has 163 member bodies in 120 countries, including the United Kingdom (UK). In the UK, the Auditing Practices Board (APB) has responsibility, delegated by the Financial Reporting Council, to set, *inter alia*, auditing standards that apply in the UK and Ireland. The APB has issued a UK and Ireland version of each ISA which replicates the relevant ISA but includes additional requirements. Where the additional UK and Ireland requirements are significant they are highlighted in this book.

During the past couple of years, the IAASB has been engaged in a 'Clarity Project' through which the ISAs are being redrafted to improve their clarity. Their content is essentially the same as the relevant predecessor but the format differs: all of the 'Standards' (or 'rules') with which auditors must comply are presented in the first part of each ISA, and guidance on the application of the Standards is provided in a second section. (In the first section, the paragraphs are numbered 1, 2, 3, etc.; in the second part, A1, A2, A3, and so on.) The full set of redrafted ISAs will be available towards the end of 2008 and they all become effective on 15 December 2009.

In order to ensure we have incorporated the most up-to-date information possible in this book, and assuming that an Exposure Draft of a 'Redrafted ISA' is closer to its final version than its pre-redrafted predecessor, where the final version of an ISA is not available we have used its Exposure Draft. Where a post-Exposure Draft version of an ISA has been included in the agenda papers of the IAASB (at its meetings in March or June 2008) but the final version of the ISA had not been issued when this book went to print in June 2008, we have used the post-Exposure Draft version of the ISA.

On the first page of each chapter we identify ISAs that are particularly relevant to that chapter. The version of the ISA referred to in the chapter is indicated as follows:

- ISA XXX – the ISA used in the chapter was issued in final form in the year indicated;
- ISA XXX* – the Exposure Draft of the ISA is used in the chapter; it was issued by the IAASB in the year indicated;
- ISA XXX** – the post-Exposure Draft version of the ISA, as included in the agenda papers of the IAASB, is used in the chapter. The IAASB meeting at which the post-Exposure draft version was discussed is indicated.

We use similar notation for ISAs included in the References of any chapter.

We should make special mention of ISA 250: *Consideration of Laws and Regulations in an Audit of Financial Statements*, ISA 510: *Initial Audit Engagements – Opening Balances*, ISA 550: *Related Parties*, and ISA 570: *Going Concern*. We have shown each of these ISAs as issued in 2008. In fact, in June 2008, although the ISAs were in their 'final form', they still awaited confirmation from IFAC's Public Interest Oversight Board that due process was followed in the development. The Standards will be formally published by IFAC once IAASB received this confirmation.

1   What is Auditing?

LEARNING OBJECTIVES

After studying the material in this chapter you should be able to:
- explain the general nature of the audit function;
- distinguish between financial statement audits, compliance audits and operational audits;
- distinguish between external and internal audits;
- describe how auditing differs from accounting;
- explain why financial statement audits are necessary;
- discuss the benefits which arise from the external audit function for:
  - users of financial statements,
  - the auditee (i.e., the entity whose financial statements are audited),
  - society as a whole.

The following fundamental principle of external auditing included in *The Auditors' Code*[1] is particularly relevant to this chapter: Providing value

---

[1] The fundamental principles of external auditing are reproduced on the inside of the front cover of this book.

1.1 INTRODUCTION

In general, United Kingdom (UK) legislation requires all but small companies, and virtually all public sector entities, to produce annually, audited financial statements. The audits of these financial statements frequently involve considerable time, effort and resources. As shown in Figure 1.1, in 2006, the audit fees of the 10 largest companies listed on the London Stock Exchange alone amounted to nearly £149 million.[2] From this it is evident that the statutory audits of UK corporate entities as a whole involve a substantial amount of the nation's resources. But, what is an audit? Why are they needed – and, indeed, are so important that they are required by law? Do they provide benefits which are commensurate with their cost?

We address these questions in this chapter. More specifically, we examine the nature of the audit function and distinguish between financial statement audits, compliance audits and operational audits, and also between external and internal audits. We consider the factors that make financial statement audits necessary and discuss their value for users of financial statements, for auditees (that is, the entities whose financial statements are audited), and for society as a whole.

Figure 1.1:   Audit and non-audit fees paid to the auditors of the 10 largest (by market capitalisation) companies listed on the London Stock Exchange in 2006[3]

| Company | Audit fees | Non-audit fees paid to auditors | | Auditor |
		Audit related	Other	
	£million	£million	£million	
Royal Dutch Shell plc*	26.4	2.5	1.0	PricewaterhouseCoopers
BP plc*	23.4	7.6	43.2	Ernst & Young
HSBC Holdings plc*	22.7	20.8	4.2	KPMG
GlaxoSmithKline plc	7.7	4.4	3.8	PricewaterhouseCoopers
Vodafone Group plc	4.0	1.0	3.0	Deloitte & Touche
Royal Bank of Scotland Group plc	11.6	5.9	5.5	Deloitte & Touche
Barclays Bank plc	28.0	5.0	11.0	PricewaterhouseCoopers
HBOS plc	6.9	1.4	3.0	KPMG
AstraZeneca plc*	4.6	2.1	1.1	KPMG
Anglo American plc*	13.4	3.8	2.4	Deloitte & Touche
Total	**£148.7**	**£54.5**	**£78.2**	
*Figures stated in annual reports in $US. Converted at the closing rate on 31 December 2005: $US1.967 = £1				

Source: Relevant companies' annual reports

---

[2] The 10 largest companies by market capitalisation on 31 December 2006.

[3] The fees shown include worldwide audit and non-audit fees paid by the relevant company (or group).

1.2 WHAT IS AN AUDIT?

Anderson (1977) captured the essence of auditing when he stated:

> The practice of auditing commenced on the day that one individual assumed stewardship over another's property. In reporting on his stewardship, the accuracy and reliability of that information would have been subjected to some sort of critical review [i.e., an audit]. (p. 6)

The term 'audit' is derived from the Latin word meaning 'a hearing'. Auditing originated over 2,000 years ago when, firstly in Egypt, and subsequently in Greece, Rome and elsewhere, citizens (or sometimes slaves) entrusted with the collection and disbursement of public funds were required to present themselves publicly, before a responsible official (an auditor), to give an oral account of their handling of those funds.

In order to understand what an audit is, and how it is conducted in the modern context, we need a definition. A comprehensive definition of auditing with general application is as follows:

> Auditing is a systematic process of objectively gathering and evaluating evidence relating to assertions about economic actions and events in which the individual or organisation making the assertions has been engaged, to ascertain the degree of correspondence between those assertions and established criteria, and communicating the results to users of the reports in which the assertions are made.[4]

This definition conveys that:
- auditing proceeds by means of an ordered series of steps (a systematic process);
- auditing primarily involves gathering and evaluating evidence;
- in pursuing this activity the auditor maintains an objective unbiased attitude of mind;
- the auditor critically examines assertions made by an individual or organisation about economic activities in which they have been engaged;
- the auditor assesses how closely these assertions conform to the 'set of rules' which govern how the individual or organisation is to report to others about the economic events that have occurred. This 'set of rules' comprises the established criteria which enable the auditor to evaluate whether the assertions fairly represent the underlying events;
- the auditor communicates the results of this evaluation in a written report. The report is available to all users of the document(s) in which the assertions are made.

The major features of an audit are presented diagrammatically in Figure 1.2 below.

---

[4] Adapted from the definition provided by the Committee on Basic Auditing Concepts (1973, p. 8).

Figure 1.2:   Major features of an audit

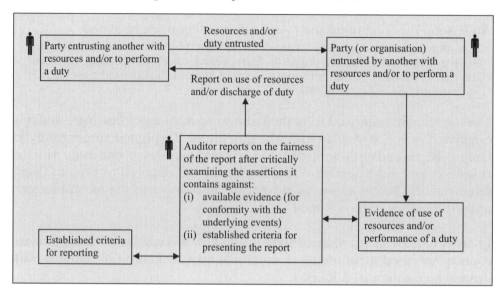

1.3   TYPES OF AUDIT

Audits may be classified in various ways. They may, for instance, be classified according to:
*   the primary objective of the audit; or
*   the primary beneficiaries of the audit.

1.3.1   Classification by primary audit objective

Based on primary audit objective, three main categories of audits may be recognised:
(i)   financial statement audits,
(ii)   compliance audits,
(iii) operational audits.

(i)   Financial statement audits

A financial statement audit is an examination of an entity's financial statements, which have been prepared by the entity's management/directors[5] for shareholders and other interested parties outside the entity, and of the

---

[5] In the Preface to this book we note that the term 'managers' is defined to mean a company's executive directors, non-executive directors, and non-director executives (that is, all executives and directors). Under the Companies Act 2006 (s. 394), a company's directors are responsible for the preparation of its annual financial statements.

evidence supporting the information contained in those financial statements. It is conducted by a qualified, experienced professional,[6] who is independent of the entity, for the purpose of expressing an opinion on whether or not the financial statements provide a true and fair view of the entity's financial performance and financial position, and comply with relevant statutory and/or other regulatory requirements. The major features of a financial statement audit are presented in Figure 1.3.

Figure 1.3: Major features of a financial statement audit

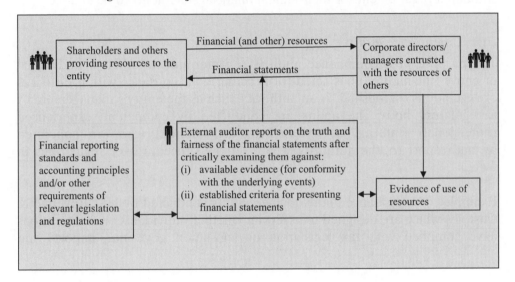

The Companies Act (CA) 2006 (ss. 396, 404) requires the directors of all companies to prepare annually, financial statements which include:
- a balance sheet, showing a true and fair view of the company's financial position (or 'state of affairs') as at the last day of the financial year;
- a profit and loss account, showing a true and fair view of the company's profit or loss for the financial year.

Additionally, under CA 2006, s. 495, auditors are required to report on these financial statements.[7] Thus, *prima facie*, all companies must, by law, subject their financial statements to an external audit. However, companies which qualify as small [that is, whose turnover is no more than £5.6 million and

---

[6] The term 'an auditor' usually refers to an audit firm. Although one person in the firm (known under the Companies Act 2006, s. 504, as 'the senior statutory auditor') is responsible for the audit and signs the audit report the audit is usually conducted by an audit team. We explain this further in Chapter 7.

[7] The statutory and regulatory requirements applying to the audited financial statements of companies are discussed in detail in Chapter 5.

balance sheet total (total assets) is no more than £2.8 million, during the financial year] are generally exempt from a statutory audit (CA 2006, s. 477).[8]

Companies taking advantage of the audit exemption, and also partnerships and sole traders (which are not legally required to have their financial statements audited),[9] may still require financial statement audits for specific purposes. For example, if one of these entities approaches a bank for a loan, the bank may require audited financial statements as a basis for deciding whether or not to grant the loan. Further, it is usual for clubs and societies to include in their constitution a requirement for their annual financial statements to be audited.

(ii) Compliance audits

The purpose of a compliance audit is to determine whether an individual or entity (the auditee) has acted (or is acting) in accordance with procedures or regulations established by an authority, such as the entity's management or a regulatory body. The audits are conducted by competent, experienced professionals (internal or external to the auditee) who are appointed by, and report to, the authority which set the procedures or regulations in place.

Examples of compliance audits include audits conducted by HM Revenue & Customs which are designed to ascertain whether individuals or organisations have complied with tax legislation or legislation governing imports and

---

[8] Even if a company qualifies as 'small', it is not exempt from an audit if, at any time during the financial year, it was:
   - a public company (CA 2006, s. 384),
   - a company entitled to carry on a regulated activity (such as banking and insurance market activities), or is an appointed representative, under the Financial Services and Marketing Act 2000 (CA 2006, s. 384),
   - a parent or subsidiary company (unless the group qualifies as a small group: that is, the group's aggregate turnover in the financial year is not more than £5.6 million net, or £6.72 million gross, and its balance sheet total is not more than £2.8 million net, or £3.36 million gross (CA 2006, s. 479). ('Net' refers to any set-offs or other adjustments made to eliminate group transactions; 'gross' means without those set-offs or adjustments: CA 2006, s. 383), or
   - if members holding not less than 10 per cent of the nominal value of the company's issued share capital, or a class thereof, request an audit (CA 2006, s. 476).

The directors of any company taking advantage of the audit exemption provisions are required to state on the company's balance sheet:
   – the fact they have taken advantage of the audit exemption provisions;
   – that the members of the company have not required an audit of the financial statements for the year in question; and
   – that they acknowledge their responsibilities for complying with the provisions of CA 2006 with respect to accounting records and the preparation of financial statements (CA 2006, s. 475).

[9] Limited liability partnerships, but not ordinary partnerships, are legally required to have their annual financial statements audited. We explain this in relation to audit firms in Chapter 16.

exports. They also include audits conducted within companies, or other entities, to ascertain whether the entity's employees are complying with the system of internal control established by management.[10]

(iii) Operational audits

An operational audit involves a systematic examination and evaluation of an entity's operations which is conducted with a view to improving the efficiency and/or effectiveness of the entity. Such audits are usually initiated by the entity's management or, sometimes, if there is one, by its audit committee.[11] They are conducted by competent, experienced professionals (internal or external to the organisation) who report their findings to the party which initiated the audit. An operational audit may apply to the organisation as a whole or to an identified segment thereof, such as a subsidiary, division or department. The objectives of the audit may be broad, for example, to improve the overall efficiency of the entity, or narrow and designed, for example, to solve a specific problem such as excessive staff turnover.[12]

1.3.2 Classification by primary audit beneficiaries

Based on primary audit beneficiaries (that is, those for whom the audit is conducted), audits may be classified as:
  (i) external audits, or
  (ii) internal audits.

(i) External audits

An external audit is an audit performed for parties external to the auditee. Experts, independent of the auditee and its personnel, conduct these audits in accordance with requirements which are defined by, or on behalf of, the parties for whose benefit the audit is conducted. Probably the best-known, and most frequently performed, external audits are the statutory audits of the financial statements of companies and public sector entities (that is, financial statement audits). However, compliance audits conducted, for instance, by HM Revenue & Customs are also examples of external audits.

---

[10] Internal control is discussed in Chapter 10.

[11] An audit committee is a subgroup of the board of directors (or its equivalent).

[12] In public sector entities, broadly based operational audits (or value for money audits) are generally required as part of the statutory audit function. However, additional more specific operational audits may also be initiated by the entity's management and conducted along the lines of those undertaken in private sector entities.

(ii) Internal audits

In contrast to external audits, internal audits are performed for parties (usually management) internal to the entity.[13] They may be performed by employees of the entity itself or by personnel from an outside source (such as an accounting firm). However, in either case, the audit is conducted in accordance with management's requirements. These may be wide-ranging or narrowly focused, and they may be continuous (on-going) or one-off in nature. They may, for example, be as broad as investigating the appropriateness of, and level of compliance with, the organisation's system of internal control, or as narrow as examining the entity's policies and procedures for ensuring compliance with health and safety regulations.

1.3.3   Common characteristics of audits

It should be noted that although different categories and types of audit may be recognised all audits possess the same general characteristics. Whether they are financial statement, compliance or operational audits, and whether they are conducted for parties external or internal to the entity, they all involve:
- the systematic examination and evaluation of evidence which is undertaken to ascertain whether statements by individuals or organisations fairly represent the underlying facts and comply with established criteria; and
- communication of the results of the examination, usually in a written report, to the party by whom, or on whose behalf, the auditor was appointed.

1.4   AUDITING VS ACCOUNTING

This book is primarily concerned with the external financial statement audits of public companies and, unless indicated otherwise, when we refer to 'audit' or 'auditor', these terms should be understood in that context. However, before focusing attention on these audits we need to distinguish between auditing and accounting.

Accounting data, and the accounting systems which capture and process these data, provide the raw materials with which auditors work. In order to understand these systems, and the data they process, an auditor must first be a qualified accountant. However, the processes involved in auditing and accounting are rather different. Accounting is primarily a *creative* process which involves

---

[13] Within companies, internal audits are usually initiated by senior executives or, if there is one, the audit committee. Those conducting the audit usually report their findings to the party which initiated the audit.

identifying, organising, summarising and communicating information about economic events. Auditing, on the other hand, is primarily an *evaluative* process. It involves gathering and evaluating audit evidence, and communicating conclusions based on this evidence, about the fairness with which the communication resulting from the accounting process (that is, the financial statements) reflects the underlying economic events.

1.5 WHY ARE EXTERNAL FINANCIAL STATEMENT AUDITS NEEDED?

1.5.1 The need to communicate financial information

Over the last 160 or so years, 'large' business organisations have changed from being owner-operated entities with a small number of employees, many of whom were family members, to vast multinational companies staffed by very many thousands of employees. The growth of such organisations has been made possible by channelling financial resources from innumerable investors, through financial markets and credit-granting institutions, to the growing companies.

As companies have grown in size, their management has passed from shareholder-owners to small groups of professional managers. Thus, company growth has been accompanied by the increasing separation of ownership interests and management functions. As a consequence, a need has arisen for company managers to report to the entity's owners, and other providers of funds such as banks and other lenders, on the financial aspects of their activities. Those receiving these reports (external financial statements) need assurance that they are reliable. Therefore, they wish to have the information in the reports 'checked out' or audited.

1.5.2 The need to have the communication examined

Three questions arise in relation to the 'checking out' of management's reports:
1. Why might the information in their reports not be reliable?
2. Why is it so important to the receivers of the reports that the information is reliable?
3. Why do the receivers of the reports not audit the information for themselves?

The answers to these questions may be found in four main factors:
(i) a conflict of interests,
(ii) consequences of error,

(iii) remoteness, and

(iv) complexity.

We discuss each of these below.

(i) Conflict of interests

As noted earlier, a company's financial statements are prepared by its directors; these directors are essentially reporting on their own performance. Users of the financial statements want the statements to portray the company's financial position and financial performance as accurately as possible but they perceive that the directors may bias their report so that it reflects favourably on their management of the company's affairs.

Thus, there is a potential conflict of interest between the preparers and users of the financial statements. The audit plays a vital role in helping to ensure that directors provide, and users are confident in receiving, information which is a fair representation of the company's financial affairs.

(ii) Consequences of error

If users of a company's external financial statements base decisions (such as whether to invest in, buy from, supply to, or accept employment with the company) on unreliable information, they may suffer serious financial loss as a result. Therefore, before basing decisions on financial statement information, they wish to be assured that the information is reliable and 'safe' to act upon.

(iii) Remoteness

In general, as a consequence of legal, physical and economic factors, users of a company's external financial statements are not able to verify the reliability of the information contained in the financial statements for themselves. Even if, for example, they are major shareholders in a company, they have no legal right of access to the company's records. Further, they may be many miles distant from the company which prevents easy access to it, and/or they may not be able to afford the time and expense which would be involved in checking the information personally, should they have the legal right to do so.[14]

---

[14] However, it should be noted that many financial institutions (including pension funds, insurance companies and unit and investment trusts), which are significant shareholders of major UK companies, visit companies in which they have, or are considering, investment and question their managements. These institutions have considerable influence over the investee companies, especially if, in the view of the relevant financial institution(s), they are under-performing.

As a result of legal, physical and economic factors preventing users of external financial statements from examining personally the information provided by a company's directors, an independent party is needed to assess the reliability of the information on their behalf.

(iv) Complexity

As companies have grown in size, the volume of their transactions has increased. Further, especially in recent years, economic transactions, and the accounting systems which capture and process them, as well as the 'rules' governing their measurement and disclosure, have become very complex. As a result of these changes, errors are more likely to creep into the financial statements. Additionally, with the increasing complexity of economic transactions, accounting systems and financial reports, users of external financial statements are less able to evaluate the quality of the information for themselves. Therefore, there is a growing need for the financial statements to be examined by an independent qualified auditor who has the necessary competence and expertise to understand the entity's business, its transactions and its accounting system.

1.6 BENEFITS DERIVED FROM EXTERNAL FINANCIAL STATEMENT AUDITS

In section 1.5 above, we noted that external financial statement audits are necessary because the ownership and management functions of companies have become increasingly separated, and because of factors such as a potential conflict of interest between preparers and users of financial statements and the inability of financial statement users to verify the information for themselves. In this section we consider the benefits derived from external financial statement audits by financial statement users, auditees and society as a whole. These benefits are reflected in the fundamental principle of external auditing – *Providing value*:

> Auditors add to the reliability and quality of financial reporting [to external parties]; they [also] provide to directors and officers [of the auditee] constructive observations arising from the audit process; and thereby contribute to the effective operation of business capital markets and the public sector. (Auditing Practices Board, 2008, Appendix 2)

1.6.1 Financial statement users

The value of an external audit for financial statement users is the credibility it gives to the financial information provided by the reporting entity. This credibility arises from three forms of control which an audit provides:

(i) *Preventive control*: Employees involved in the capture and processing of accounting data and/or the preparation of the entity's financial statements, who know their work will be subject to the scrutiny of an auditor, are likely to work more carefully than they would in the absence of an audit. It is probable that the extra care taken by employees prevents at least some errors from occurring.

(ii) *Detective control*: Even if employees in the auditee entity process the accounting data and prepare the financial statements carefully, errors may still occur. The auditor may detect these errors during the audit and draw them to management's attention. They may then be corrected prior to publication of the financial statements.

(iii) *Reporting control*: If the auditor detects material errors in the financial statements and refers them to management, but management refuses to correct them, the auditor draws attention to the errors by qualifying the audit report (that is, the auditor states that all is not well, giving reasons for this conclusion). In this way, users of the financial statements are made aware that, in the auditor's opinion, the information provided is not reliable.

It is interesting to note that, while UK legislation is silent on the qualifications of those who may prepare a company's financial statements, the Companies Act 2006 (s. 1212) specifies that the auditor of these statements must be a member of a recognised supervisory body. To be a member of such a body, an individual (or firm) must be appropriately qualified and be subject to the rules and supervision of that body: the rules include those governing "the conduct of statutory audit work" (s. 1217).[15] Thus, although the preparer of the financial statements need not be a qualified accountant, as a consequence of the Companies Act provisions, the auditor must be a well qualified, competent and experienced professional. It therefore seems that Parliament looks to auditors to protect the interests of financial statement users by giving assurance that the financial statements are reliable or providing a warning that they are not.

1.6.2 Auditees

During the course of an external financial statement audit, the auditor becomes very familiar with the organisation, its business, its accounting system and all aspects of its financial affairs. Added to this, the auditor is a qualified and experienced individual who comes to the auditee as an independent objective outsider, divorced from the day-to-day running of the entity.

These factors place the auditor in an ideal position to observe where improvements can be made. (S)he is able to advise the auditee on matters such as

---

[15] The required qualifications and supervision of auditors are discussed in Chapter 5.

strengthening internal control; the development of accounting or other management information systems; and tax, investment and financial planning. In addition (in cases where the issue arises for the auditee), the auditor is able to provide advice on matters such as how to proceed with a share float, business acquisition or divestment, or liquidation. The provision of these 'additional services' by the auditor is very valuable for the auditee. Indeed, as Anderson (1977) pointed out:

> In many cases, it is the presence of these collateral services which makes the audit an economical package from management's point of view. The professional auditor must always be alert for opportunities to be of service to his or her client while at the same time discharging conscientiously his or her responsibilities to the users of the audited financial statements. (p. 6)

Notwithstanding the value of these advisory services for the auditee, largely as a result of investigations following alleged audit failures in the early 2000s at Enron, WorldCom and Xerox (amongst others) in the United States of America (USA), Parmalat in Italy, HIH in Australia and similar failures in other parts of the world, serious disquiet was expressed by politicians, regulators and the public about the extent of the provision by auditors of non-audit services to their audit clients. Indeed, by the early years of the 21st century, fees paid by audit clients to their auditors for non-audit services had grown to such an extent that, in many instances, they exceeded the audit fee by a very significant margin.[16] This led to concerns that the provision of such services to auditees had resulted in auditors compromising their independence; in order to avoid upsetting the entity's management and consequently losing lucrative non-audit work, auditors had not been sufficiently critical when performing their auditing duties. As a consequence, laws and regulations have been enacted in many parts of the world to prohibit or curtail the provision of non-audit services by auditors to their audit clients. Probably the most far-reaching and stringent restrictions have been enacted in the USA in the Sarbanes-Oxley Act of 2002.[17]

1.6.3 Society as a whole

The benefits flowing from audits for society as a whole fall into two broad groups:

---

[16] For example, in the USA in 2001, Enron paid Arthur Andersen $25 (£17.9) million in audit fees and a further $27 (£19.3) million in non-audit fees; and Disney paid PricewaterhouseCoopers $8.7 (£6.2) million in audit fees and a staggering $32 (£22.9) million for non-audit services. In the UK in the same year, BP paid Ernst & Young £16.7 million for audit, and an additional £41 million for non-audit, services; Vodafone paid Deloitte & Touche £3 million for its audit, and a further £22 million for non-audit, work; and Astra-Zeneca paid KPMG £2 million in audit, and another £5.6 million in non-audit, fees.

[17] The dangers to auditors' independence of providing non-audit services to audit clients, and measures taken in recent years to reduce those dangers, are discussed in Chapter 4.

   (i) those relating to the smooth functioning of financial markets; and

   (ii) those relating to securing the accountability of corporate managements.

(i) Smooth functioning of financial markets

The benefits – and importance – of audits in helping to ensure the smooth functioning of financial markets was aptly conveyed by Turner (2001) when he was Chief Accountant of the Securities and Exchange Commission (SEC) in the USA. He stated:

> The enduring confidence of the investing public in the integrity of our capital markets is vital. In America today, approximately one out of every two adults has invested their savings in the securities markets, either [directly] through the purchase of individual stocks or [indirectly through investment] in a mutual fund or . . . pension plan. . . . These investments have provided trillions of dollars in capital for companies in the United States and around the globe. That capital is providing the fuel for our economic engine, funding for the growth of new businesses, and providing . . . job opportunities for tens of millions of workers. But . . . the willingness of investors to continue to invest their money in the markets cannot be taken for granted. . . . Public trust begins, and ends, with the integrity of the numbers the public uses to form the basis for making their investment decisions. . . . Accordingly, investors in the U.S. capital markets have depended for over a hundred years on an independent third party, an external auditor, to examine the books and financial reports prepared by management. (pp. 1–2)

Thus, in the USA – and similarly in the UK, as in most other countries – continued investment in capital markets is essential to the well-being of the economy – and to the financial well-being of those who invest directly or indirectly in those markets. Continued investment in financial markets rests on investors having confidence in the financial information on which they base their investment decisions. This confidence, in turn, is derived from their having confidence in the external audit function. Although not referred to by Turner, indirect investment includes investment by local authorities, and other public sector bodies, of funds (derived in the form of taxes of one type or another) provided by the vast majority of the public. Therefore, most members of society – directly or indirectly – benefit from external financial statement audits.

(ii) Securing the accountability of corporate managements

Over the last 160 or so years, as financial, human and other non-financial resources have been channelled by individuals and groups in society to companies, so these entities have been able to grow in size. As they have become larger, they have gained significant social, economic and political power. Today, large national and multinational companies dominate the lives, and control the well-being, of whole communities and have a major impact on society in general. However, in a democratic society, power is not absolute. Mindful of Lord Acton's dictum that "power tends to corrupt, and absolute power corrupts absolutely", society has set in place checks and balances designed to prevent possible abuse of power. As one of the checks designed to ensure that company managements do not abuse the power bestowed upon them through the provision of resources, they are held accountable for the responsible use of the resources entrusted to them. This accountability is secured primarily by requiring company directors:

- to provide publicly available annual financial statements which report on their use of resources;[18]
- to submit these financial statements to a critical examination by an independent expert (that is, to an audit).

Thus, auditors may be seen as an integral part of the process of securing the accountability of company managements who control and use the financial and non-financial resources of various groups in society such as shareholders, debt-holders, creditors, employees, suppliers, customers and the general public. Legally in the UK, a company's auditor is appointed by, and reports to, the shareholders. In reality, however, all stakeholders who provide resources to company managements (or who are otherwise affected by company managements' decisions) have an interest in the accountability process of which auditing is a part.

Therefore, in addition to protecting the interests of financial statement users by giving credibility to the financial statements, and providing ancillary services to auditee entities, by helping to ensure the smooth functioning of financial markets, and by functioning as an element of social control within the corporate accountability process, the external audit is also of value to society as a whole.

1.6.4 Failure to secure the potential benefits of the audit function

While the external audit function can – and does – provide important benefits for financial statement users, auditees and society as a whole, the manner in which auditors have performed their function has, on occasion, been the subject of criticism – some of it justifiably scathing. Indeed, some critics go so far

---

[18] As we will see in Chapter 5, the audited information directors are required to provide in their company's annual report has increased quite markedly since the mid-1990s. This 'additional' information, like the financial statements, is designed to help secure the accountability of company managements.

as to argue that the 'Big' accounting firms[19] use their extensive power and knowledge to facilitate doubtful financial practices that help a few wealthy clients, who can afford to pay "exorbitant consultancy fees", to exploit the capital system for their own benefit. They assert that these firms are at the centre of a web of conspiracies to "operate cartels, launder money, facilitate tax avoidance/evasion, [engage in] bribery and obstruct enquiries into frauds and deliver shoddy audits" (Mitchell and Sikka, 2002, p. 50).

While few would adopt quite such an extreme view, many commentators have noted the failings of some auditors and the adverse impact of 'shoddy audits' on investors and society in general. Some have also noted the reluctance of audit firms and/or the profession to acknowledge that the fault might lie with them and to recognise the need to improve their practices. For example, in 1994 Shields noted:

> The Big Six firms[20] have been key players in a recent spate of audit failures around the world which are beginning to undermine the internal system of accountability on which the business world relies. But instead of focusing on improving their practices and regaining the public's trust, the Big Six have launched a full-scale campaign to reduce their liability for failed audits. (Shields, 1994, p. 1)

A decade later, Sarup (2004) observed:

> [T]he audit profession . . . is increasingly under attack as the profession attracts, fairly or unfairly, some of the blame for the recent corporate failures and the consequent losses to the investing public, the thousands of innocent employees and suppliers, and a multitude of other stakeholders. At Enron . . . the profession tried, unsuccessfully, to rationalize the patently failed audit. . . . [T]he circumstances of the multibillion-dollar fraud at WorldCom are hard to even attempt to rationalize. . . . People are asking, given [the] basic nature [of the fraud] and its magnitude, how could it have been missed. The alleged frauds at Tyco International, Adelphia Communications, HealthSouth Corp, and Dutch retailing giant Ahold NV all beg the same questions: What were the auditors doing? Is the audit approach fundamentally flawed? (pp. 1–2)

The adverse consequences of substandard auditing were also highlighted by Schuetze (former Chief Accountant of the SEC) when he testified to the US Senate Committee on Banking, Housing and Urban Affairs (chaired by Sarbanes) in 2002, following the collapse of Enron. He stated:

> The public's confidence in financial reports of and by Corporate America, and in the audits of those financial reports by the public accounting profession, has been shaken badly by the recent surprise collapse of Enron, by recent restatements of

---

[19] During the 1980s there were 'the Big 8' global accounting firms – Arthur Andersen, Arthur Young, Coopers & Lybrand, Deloitte Haskins & Sells, Ernst & Whinney, Peat Marwick, Price Waterhouse and Touche Ross. During the 1990s 'the Big 8' became 'the Big 5' – Arthur Andersen, Deloitte & Touche, Ernst & Young, KPMG and PricewaterhouseCoopers. With the demise of Arthur Andersen in 2002, 'the Big 5' became 'the Big 4' firms.

[20] Arthur Andersen, Ernst & Young, Coopers & Lybrand, Deloitte & Touche, KPMG and Price Waterhouse.

financial statements by the likes of Enron, Waste Management, Sunbeam, Cendant, Livent, and MicroStrategy, and the SEC's assertion of fraud by Arthur Andersen in connection with its audits of Waste Management's financial statements in the 1990s ... The public's confidence needs to be regained and restored ... [otherwise] ... investors will bid down the price of stocks and bonds issued by both US and foreign corporations; ... This will reduce the market capitalization of corporations, which in turn will negatively affect capital formation, job creation and job maintenance, and ultimately our standard of living. (Schuetze, 2002, pp. 1–2)

Poor-quality auditing has also had adverse consequences for the culpable auditors. As we discuss in Chapter 15 when exploring the topic of auditors' legal liability, a significant number of auditors have faced court action and hefty financial penalties as a consequence of performing defective audits. For example, as Shields (1994) reports:

[In the USA in 1994] Deloitte & Touche agreed to pay $312 million to settle $1.8 billion in lawsuits and other claims brought by US bank regulators. ... In Ireland, Ernst & Whinney (now Ernst & Young) reached an out-of-court settlement for $118 million with AIB Group, Ireland's largest bank and administrator of the Insurance Corporation of Ireland ... [and] KPMG was accused of faulty auditing which contributed to the $2.1 billion crash of Tricontinental, the merchant-banking arm of the State Bank of Victoria in Australia. The firm reached an out-of-court settlement for $106 million. ... (pp. 1–2)

In other cases, the activity of audit firms has been curtailed as a consequence of poor auditing. For example, in the 1980s in the USA, the deficient auditing of many savings and loan (S&L) institutions[21] prompted "Government regulators [to bar] several Big Six accounting firms' partners from auditing banks and S&L's, [and] the courts ordered others to take professional training courses before engaging in additional audits of financial institutions" (Saeed, Lee and Ray, 1994, p. 1). Along similar lines, in August 2004, Ernst & Young in the USA was barred from:

accepting new public audit clients for six months because of the firm's "blatant" disregard and "utter disdain" for rules that require accountants to be independent from the companies whose books they review. [It was also] ordered to return $1.7 million in audit fees it collected from PeopleSoft Inc. from 1994 to 1999 and to hire an outside consultant to overhaul independence policies that the judge called a "sham". (Johnson, 2004, p. 1)

Likewise, in May 2006, the Japanese Financial Services Agency ordered Chuo Aoyama, PricewaterhouseCoopers' Japanese affiliate, to:

halt auditing services for two months. The regulator specifically cited Chuo Aoyama's audit of cosmetics company Kanebo Ltd, in which three of the [audit]

---

[21] In the USA in the 1980s, more than 1,000 S&L institutions failed unexpectedly – and many auditors were found to be guilty of substandard auditing. The total cost of what is known as 'the savings and loan crisis' is estimated to be about $150 billion, of which about $125 billion was directly borne by the US Government (Wikipedia, 2006).

firms' partners allegedly assisted with accounting fraud and boosted earnings for the company by about $1.9 billion over the course of five years. (Answers.com, 2006, p. 4)

In other cases the adverse financial consequences of poor auditing have been so severe that the audit firm concerned has been unable to survive. Probably the most dramatic demise was that of Arthur Andersen in 2002, as a consequence of its misdeeds in relation to its energy giant client, Enron. However, in 1990, Laventhol & Horwath, then the seventh largest accounting firm in the USA, was forced into bankruptcy and, at the time, this sent shock waves throughout the accounting profession similar to those resulting from Andersen's collapse 12 years later. According to Richards (2002):

> In the years leading up to 1990, Laventhol was frequently hauled into court to settle allegations of sloppy work. At its end, the firm had 115 legal actions against it, [almost entirely related to failed savings and loan institutions], seeking a total of $362 million. (p. 1)

Although, as we have seen, some auditors have attracted criticism – and penalties – as a result of shoddy audit work, and the reputation of, and the public's confidence in, the auditing profession has suffered as a consequence, it should be remembered that:

> Commentary in the media tends to focus on the few, high profile audit failures, rather than the huge number of successful audits. . . . The overwhelming majority of audits conducted by the major accounting firms are highly professional, effective and valuable. (Accountancy Age, 2005, p. 1)

This conclusion is supported by the findings of Francis (2004), who reviewed empirical research conducted during the last quarter of the 20th century. His findings suggest that audit failure is infrequent although there is some indication of a decline in audit quality during the 1990s.

When considering the failings of auditors, it should be noted that the deficiencies relate, not to the audit function *per se*, but to how that function is fulfilled by a few substandard auditors. In Chapter 16 we explore the steps the profession and regulators have taken, and/or proposed, to ensure that auditors perform their audits to the highest standard thus enabling the audit function to deliver its potential benefits to the users of audited financial statements, auditees and society as a whole.

1.7 SUMMARY

In this chapter we have considered the nature of the audit function and distinguished between financial statement audits, compliance audits and operational audits, and between external and internal audits. We have also noted the difference between accounting and auditing and discussed why external financial statement audits are needed. In the final section of the chapter we have examined some of the benefits derived from these audits by financial statement users, auditees and society as a whole – and discussed some of the consequences of auditors failing to perform their audits with the rigour that the beneficiaries of the audit function have a right to expect.

In the next chapter we trace the development of auditing, noting in particular how auditing has responded over time to changes in its socio-economic environment.

SELF-REVIEW QUESTIONS

1.1 Explain briefly the following words and phrases included in the definition of auditing given in this chapter:
  (i) systematic process,
  (ii) objectively gathering and evaluating evidence,
  (iii) assertions,
  (iv) degree of correspondence between assertions and established criteria,
  (v) communicating the results.

1.2 List the major elements which are present in all audits.

1.3 Explain briefly the key differences between the following types of audits:
  (i) financial statement audits,
  (ii) compliance audits,
  (iii) operational audits.

1.4 Under the provisions of the Companies Act 2006 an auditor's report must be attached to a company's financial statements. Is this true for all companies? Explain.

1.5 Distinguish between:
  (i) auditing and accounting, and
  (ii) internal and external audits.

1.6 Explain briefly why external financial statement audits are needed.

1.7 The value of an audit for financial statement users lies, at least in part, in the credibility it gives to the financial statements which are prepared by management. Explain briefly the three types of control which help an audit to give credibility to audited financial statements.

1.8   Explain briefly the benefits which an external financial statement audit provides for an auditee. Also explain any dangers which may result from auditors providing 'additional services' to auditees.

1.9   Explain briefly the value of external financial statement audits for society as a whole.

1.10   Explain briefly how high-profile audit failures damage the reputation of the auditing profession.

REFERENCES

Accountancy Age. (2005, 5 August). Audit failure? Don't blame us. *Accountancy Age,* www.accountancyage.com/accountancyage/comment/214085.

Anderson, R.J. (1977). *The External Audit.* Toronto: Cropp Clark Pitman.

Answers.com. (2006). *PricewaterhouseCoopers,* www.answers.com/topic/pricewater-housecoopers.

Auditing Practices Board (APB). (2008). *The Auditing Practices Board – Scope and Authority of Pronouncements (Revised).* London: Financial Reporting Council.

Committee on Basic Auditing Concepts. (1973). *A Statement of Basic Auditing Concepts.* Florida, Sarasota: American Accounting Association.

Francis, J. (2004). What do we know about audit quality? *British Accounting Review* **36**, 345–368.

Johnson, C. (2004, 17 April). Ernst & Young barred from taking new public audit clients. *Washington Post*, E01.

Mitchell, A., and Sikka, P. (2002). *Dirty Business: The unchecked power of major accountancy firms.* Basildon: Association for Accountancy & Business Affairs.

Richards, G. (2002, 2 August). 1990: The other big accounting firm meltdown Laventhol & Horwath's final days: a 'sad tragedy to watch'. *Philadelphia Business Journal*, www.bizjournals.com/philadelphia/stories/2002/08/05/focus9.html.

Saeed, R., Lee, K., and Ray, K. (1994). S&L crisis: a learning experience for accountants. *The Journal of Bank Cost & Management*, www.findarticles.com/p/articles/mi_qa3682/ is_199401.

Sarup, D. (2004). The watchdog or bloodhound? The push and pull toward a new audit model. *Information Systems Control Journal* **1**, 1–2.

Schuetze, W. (2002, 26 February). Hearing on 'Accounting and investor protection issues raised by Enron and other public companies: Oversight of the accounting profession, audit quality and independence, and formulation of accounting principles'. *Testimony of Walter Schuetze to the US Senate Committee on Banking, Housing and Urban Affairs.*

Shields, J. (1994). *A Worldwide Trail of Failures*, www.multinationalmonitor.org/hyper/ issues/1994/12/mm1294.

Turner, L.E. (2001, 28 June). *Independence: A Covenant for the Ages.* Speech at the International Organisation of Securities Commissions, Stockholm, Sweden.

Wikipedia. (2006). *Savings and loan crisis*, www.reference.com/browse/wiki/Savings _and_Loan_crisis.

ADDITIONAL READING

Benston, G. (1985). The market for public accounting services: Demand, supply and regulation. *Journal of Accounting and Public Policy* **4**, 33–79.

Collis, J., Jarvis, R., and Skerratt, L. (2004). The demand for the audit in small companies in the UK. *Accounting & Business Research* **34**(2), 87–100.

Commission on Auditors' Responsibilities. (1978). *Report, Conclusions and Recommendations* (The Cohen Commission), pp. 3–12. New York: American Institute of Certified Public Accountants (AICPA).

Cousins, J., Mitchell, A., and Sikka, P. (2004). *Race to the bottom: The case of the Accountancy Firms.* Basildon: Association for Accountancy and Business Affairs.

Flesher, D.L., and Zarzeski, M.T. (2002). The roots of operational (value for money) auditing in English-speaking nations. *Accounting & Business Research* **32**(2), 93–104.

Institute of Chartered Accountants in England and Wales (ICAEW, Audit and Assurance Faculty). (2000). *Investing in an Audit.* London: ICAEW.

Lee, T.A. (1998). A stakeholder approach to auditing. *Critical Perspectives on Accounting* **9**(2), 217–226.

Newman, D. (2005). The role of auditing in investor protection. *The Accounting Review* **80**(1), 289–314.

Quick, C. (2006). Audit aftershock. *Accountancy* **138**(1360), 84–85.

Woolfe, E. (2007). How reliable are unaudited accounts? *Accountancy* **139**(1362), 18.

2 The Development of Auditing and Audit Objectives

> **LEARNING OBJECTIVES**
>
> After studying the material in this chapter you should be able to:
> - describe and explain the changes which have taken place in audit objectives in the English-speaking world over the last 160 or so years;
> - explain the relationship between changes in the external audit function and changes in the socio-economic environment of the English-speaking world over the last 160 or so years;
> - discuss the differences between the audit risk and business risk approach to auditing;
> - describe, and explain the reasons for, significant changes which have occurred in the auditing arena in the 21st century.

The following fundamental principle of external auditing included in *The Auditors' Code*[1] is particularly relevant to this chapter: Accountability

---

[1] The fundamental principles of external auditing are reproduced on the inside of the front cover of this book.

2.1 INTRODUCTION

In this chapter we discuss the evolution of audit objectives in the English-speaking world, and examine the ways in which the external audit function has responded (and is responding) to changes in its socio-economic environment.

2.2 THE DEVELOPMENT OF AUDITING

2.2.1 An overview

Auditing, like all professions, exists to satisfy an identified need of society. It is therefore to be expected that auditing changes as the needs and demands of society change. Figure 2.1 shows the close link between auditing and the socio-economic environment it serves in the English-speaking world. In particular, it shows:
- how audit objectives have changed in response to changes in the socio-economic environment (in particular, to changes in the characteristics, and the accountability expected, of business enterprises);
- how the main centre of auditing development shifted from the United Kingdom (UK) to the United States of America (USA) as the centre of economic development moved across the Atlantic and, during the past couple of decades, has become increasingly global in focus;
- how the procedures adopted by auditors accord with the objectives auditing is trying to meet.

Figure 2.1 also shows that the development of auditing can be considered conveniently in five phases:
- period up to 1844,
- 1844–1920s,
- 1920s–1960s,
- 1960s–1990s,
- 1990s–present.

2.2.2 Period up to 1844

During this earliest and longest phase in its development, auditing was primarily concerned with public accounts. Evidence, mainly in the form of markings on tablets and buildings, shows that over 2,000 years ago the Egyptians, Greeks and Romans all used systems to check the accounting of officials entrusted with public funds. In the old Greek and Roman empires, those responsible

Figure 2.1: The interrelationships of external auditing

Period	Main centre of audit development	Main characteristics of business enterprises and audit environment	Accountability of business enterprises — To Whom	Accountability of business enterprises — For What?	Audit objectives	Major characteristics of auditing techniques
Medieval times to 1844	United Kingdom	• Cottage industries • Individual trading ventures. Emergence of industrial organisations (with the Industrial Revolution).	• Owners (Shareholders)	Honest, authorised use of funds	Detection of fraud (Only Balance Sheet audited)	• Detailed checking of transactions and account entries • Concern for arithmetical accuracy and agreement between accounts and Balance Sheet
1844–1920s	United Kingdom	• Growth in number and size of companies • Separation of ownership and management (Emergence and increase in the number of professional accountants and auditors)	• Shareholders • Creditors	Honest, authorised use of funds	• Detection of fraud • Detection of errors • Determination of solvency/insolvency (Only Balance Sheet of importance)	• Detailed checking of transactions and account entries • Little physical observation of assets or use of external evidence • Concern for arithmetical accuracy and agreement between accounts and Balance Sheet
1920s–1960s	Shift from United Kingdom to United States of America in the early 1920s	• Wall Street Crash (1929) and the Great Depression • Increasing concentration of capital in, and growth of, large corporations • Increasing separation of ownership and professional managers • Emergence of institutional investors	• Shareholders • Creditors • Investors in general	• Honest, authorised use of funds • Profitable use of resources	• Lending credibility to financial statements prepared by management • Fraud and error detection lost significance as audit objectives and became of minor importance (Emphasis gradually shifted to Profit and Loss Statement but Balance Sheet remained important)	• Gradual change to reliance on internal controls combined with test checking of samples • Physical observation of external and other evidence outside the 'books of account' • Concern for the truth and fairness of financial information provided by management
1960s–1990s	United States of America	• Continued growth of large corporations (with many takeovers and mergers) • Companies increasingly multinational in nature • Dominance of professional management divorced from ownership interests • Increasing importance of taxation • Dominance of institutional investors • Increasing competition between businesses and between audit firms • Stock Market Crash (1987)	• Shareholders • Creditors • Investors • Customers • Suppliers • Society in general	• Honest, authorised use of funds • Profitable use of resources • Wider social responsibilities (e.g. pollution, product and employee safety)	• Lending credibility to financial statements prepared by management • Provision of management advisory services	• Examination of evidence from a wide variety of sources internal and external to the entity • Emergence and increasing significance of auditing by, and of, computers • Emergence and reliance placed on statistical sampling • Risk-based auditing – based on: - thorough understanding of the client, its business and its industry - identification of audit risk through analytical review - assessment of reliance that can be placed on internal controls
1990s–present	Primarily United States of America but increasingly global in focus	• Dominance of western economies by global businesses and audit firms • Technological advances affecting all aspects of the corporate/business environment • Increasing regulatory concern about corporate governance • Increasing societal pressure for companies to be socially responsible • Increasing concentration of auditing as the 'Big 8' audit firms reduced to the 'Big 4' • Increasing regulation of external auditing (especially since 2002) • Widespread adoption of international accounting and auditing standards	• Shareholders • Creditors • Investors • Customers • Suppliers • Society in general	• Honest, authorised use of funds • Profitable use of resources • Responsible corporate governance • Wider social and environmental responsibilities	• Lending credibility to financial and non-financial information provided by management in annual reports • Provision of management advisory services (but largely removed as audit objective since 2002) • Increased responsibility for detecting, and reporting corporate fraud and doubts about an auditee's status as a 'going concern' • Increasing expectation of regulatory authorities that auditors will report to them matters of concern • Helping to secure responsible corporate governance • Some auditing of sustainability reports	• Adoption of audit methodologies focusing on clients' business risk (risk of audits not meeting their objectives) • Audit based on: - thorough understanding of the client, its business, its industry and (especially) its risks - identification of audit risk through analytical review • Adaptation of auditing to the e-commerce/e-business environment (including emergence of continuous auditing)

for public funds were required to appear periodically before a government official to give an oral presentation of their accounts. As noted in Chapter 1, the word 'audit' (derived from the Latin for 'a hearing') dates from these times.

Similarly, in medieval times in England, government officials visited the various manors and estates to check the accounts (now in written form) to ensure that the funds collected and disbursed on behalf of the Crown were properly accounted for. Interestingly, as the following quotation reveals, the information collected for the Domesday Book in 1085 (which formed the initial basis for assessing the amounts due to the Crown from the manors and estates) was subject to audit.

> *The Anglo-Saxon Chronicle* records that in 1085 at Gloucester,
>> ...at midwinter...the King [William the Conqueror] had deep speech with his counsellors...and sent men all over England to each shire...to find out...what or how much each landowner held...in land and livestock, and what it was worth. The returns were brought to him.
>
> William was thorough.... [H]e also sent a second set of Commissioners to shires they did not know, where they themselves were unknown, to check their predecessors' survey, and report culprits to the King. (Reported and cited by Morris, 1977, p. 1, from Domesday Book, 20 Bedfordshire).

Prior to the industrial revolution (which began in the late 18th century), auditing had little commercial application. Industry was primarily based in cottages and small mills, located where water power was available. Individuals both owned and managed these small businesses and therefore there was no need for the business managers to report to the owners on their management of resources – and no need for such reports to be audited.

However, especially during the 18th century, overseas trading ventures became important. The captains of the ships engaged in these commercial ventures were required to account for the funds and cargos entrusted to their care, to those who had financed the undertaking. These accounts were subject to audit. Indeed, private commercial venture audits originate in the audits of the accounts of trading ships returning to Britain from the East and the New World.

During this pre-1844 period, concern centred on the honest authorised use of funds by those to whom the funds had been entrusted. Correspondingly, the main audit objective was the detection of fraud. In order to meet this objective, the accounts under audit were subjected to a detailed and thorough examination, with special emphasis on arithmetical accuracy and compliance with the authority given to the custodian of the funds.

2.2.3 1844–1920s

(i) Socio-economic developments

As in the latter stages of the pre-1844 period, economic and auditing development during the period from 1844 to the 1920s was centred in the UK. This period, which followed the industrial revolution, saw far-reaching changes in the socio-economic environment. In particular, it witnessed the emergence of large-scale industrial and commercial enterprises and the displacement of individual (one-off) joint ventures by continuing corporations. Accompanying these changes, the period also witnessed a significant advancement in auditing.

In the late 18th century, the Industrial Revolution, with its associated large factories and machine-based production, led to a demand for vast amounts of capital. At the same time, a new 'middle class' emerged, with small amounts of surplus funds available for investment. As a result, small amounts of capital were contributed by many people, and these were channelled by financial entrepreneurs into the growing industrial and commercial undertakings. However, in the 18th and early 19th centuries, the sharemarket was unregulated and highly speculative, and the rate of financial failure was high. At this time, liability was not limited and the treatment of debtors, including innocent investors who became debtors when 'their' business venture failed, was very harsh. Given this environment, it was clear that the growing number of small investors needed some protection.

(ii) Statutory developments

As a result of these socio-economic developments in the UK, the Joint Stock Companies Act was enacted in 1844. This Act enabled companies to be formed and officially recognised merely by registration. Previously, companies could only become recognised as such by means of a Royal Charter or a special Act of Parliament. The first option was very expensive; the latter very slow.

In return for gaining recognition through registration, companies had to comply with certain regulations. These included the following:
- Each company's directors had to provide an annual balance sheet to their shareholders setting out the state of affairs (in particular, the assets and liabilities) of the company.
- An auditor had to be appointed by the company's shareholders. The auditor was empowered to examine the company's records at reasonable intervals throughout the year and was required to report to the company's shareholders whether, in his opinion, the balance sheet gave a 'full and fair' view of the company's state of affairs. Unlike today, the auditor was

not required to be independent of the company's management, or a qualified accountant. In practice, a shareholder was usually appointed as auditor by his fellow members.

In 1856, the statutory provisions requiring compulsory audits were repealed. Subsequent events proved this move to be ill-advised: of 88,000 companies registered between 1862 and 1904, over 50,000 had come to an end by 1904 (Brown, 1905, p. 325). Not surprisingly, compulsory audits were re-introduced in the Companies Act of 1900. Under the auditing provisions of this Act, an auditor was still not required to be a qualified accountant but the need for auditors to be independent of management was recognised. The Act provided that neither a director nor an officer of the company (that is, any of the company's management) could be appointed as auditor. The Act also provided that:

- auditors were to be given access to all of the company's books and records they required to enable them to perform their duties as auditors. This included access to documents such as contracts and the minutes of directors' meetings;
- auditors were to append a certificate to the foot of the audited balance sheet stating that all of their requirements as auditors had been met;
- in addition to the above certificate, auditors were to report to shareholders on the balance sheet stating whether, in their opinion, it conveyed a 'true and correct' view of the state of affairs of the company.

The Institute of Chartered Accountants in England and Wales (ICAEW) sought legal advice on the form the required certificate and report should take. This resulted in the adoption of a standard form of certificate and audit report that were reported in an Editorial in *The Accountant's Magazine* (1901, p. 47) as follows:

Auditor's Certificate

In accordance with the provisions of the Companies Act 1900, I certify that all my requirements as auditor have been complied with.

Auditor's Report

I have audited the above balance sheet and, in my opinion, such a balance sheet is properly drawn up, so as to exhibit a true and correct view of the state of affairs of the company, as shown by the books of the company.

The Companies Act 1900 was a prominent milestone in the history of company auditing. It established compulsory audits, the independence of auditors from company managements and a standard form of audit report.

(iii) Corporate accountability and audit objectives

During the period from 1844 to the 1920s, companies, in general, remained relatively small, and company managers were generally regarded as accountable only for the safe custody and honest, authorised use of funds entrusted to them. In accordance with society's needs and expectations of the time, audit objectives were designed to protect principally shareholders, but secondarily lenders/bankers, from unscrupulous acts by company managers who had custody of their funds. Hence the main audit objectives were:

- the detection of fraud and error; and
- the proper portrayal of the company's solvency (or insolvency) in the balance sheet.

During most of this period, company managers were usually considered to be accountable only to the company's shareholders although, after the turn of the century, their accountability to creditors also came to be recognised. The primacy of managers' accountability to shareholders is reflected in the fact that the balance sheet was regarded as a private communication between the company's management and its shareholders. Indeed, there was much debate in accounting circles about the auditor's report on the balance sheet. The Act only required the report to be read at the shareholders' annual general meeting, and many professional accountants apparently thought it was wrong also to attach it to the published balance sheet. They feared that the auditor might have something to say in the report which, should it become public knowledge, might be injurious to the company; for example, comments which might cause creditors to panic and to demand that their claims be met immediately, causing the company to collapse. Others considered that, logically, the report should be combined and published with the auditor's certificate. In the event, the Companies Act 1908 settled the debate by supporting the latter view and requiring the auditor to provide just one (combined) report (Lee, 1970, p. 366).

(iv) Development of auditors' duties

The decisions of the courts during the period from 1844 to 1920 served to clarify auditors' duties. The two most notable cases were those of *London and General Bank* (1895) and *Kingston Cotton Mill* (1896).

- In the renowned case of *Re London and General Bank (No. 2)* [1895] 2 Ch. 673, the auditor had discovered errors in the balance sheet. He had reported the facts to the directors but failed to report the matter to the shareholders. In his summing up, Lindley L J stated that it was not the duty of the auditor to see that the company and its directors acted prudently or imprudently, profitably or unprofitably, in performing their business activities, but it was the auditor's duty to report to shareholders any dishonest acts which had occurred and which affected the propriety of the information contained in the balance sheet. However, he also said that the auditor could not be expected to find every fraud and error committed within the company. That would be asking too much; the auditor was not an insurer or guarantor. What was expected of him was reasonable skill and care in the circumstances.

- In *Re Kingston Cotton Mill Co Ltd (No. 2)* [1896] 2 Ch. 279, Lopes, L J elaborated on the remarks of Lindley L J (above). He stated:

  It is the duty of an auditor to bring to bear on the work he has to perform that skill, care and caution which a reasonably competent, careful and cautious auditor would use. What is reasonable skill, care and caution must depend on the particular circumstances of each case. An auditor is not bound to be a detective or . . . to approach his work with suspicion or with a foregone conclusion that there is something wrong. He is a watchdog not a bloodhound. If there is anything to excite suspicion he should probe it to the bottom; but in the absence of anything of that kind he is only bound to be reasonably cautious and careful.

These two cases reinforced the audit objectives of detecting fraud and error and established the general standard of work expected of auditors. They established that auditors are not expected to ferret out every fraud but they are required to use reasonable skill and care in examining the relevant books and records.

Corresponding with the primary audit objective of detecting fraud and error, from 1844 to the 1920s, auditing procedures involved close examination of the accounting entries and related internal documentary evidence, and detailed checking of the arithmetical accuracy of the accounting records. However, towards the end of the period, judgments by the courts made it clear that auditors were required to do more than merely check the company's books and records. In the case of *London Oil Storage Co Ltd* v *Seear, Hasluck & Co.* [1904] 31 Acct. LR 1, it was held that the auditor was liable for damage sustained by a company which resulted from his omission to verify the existence of assets stated in the balance sheet. It was established that the auditor, in ensuring that the information given in the audited balance sheet corresponded with the company's books and records, was not merely required to check the arithmetical accuracy of the entries. He was also required to ensure that the data in the books represented fact rather than fiction. This case made it clear, for the first time, that the auditor was required to go beyond the internal books and records of the company for evidence to support his audit opinion.

This position was confirmed and extended in *Arthur E. Green & Co.* v *The Central Advance and Discount Corporation Ltd* [1920] 63 Acct LR 1. In this case the court held that the auditor was negligent in accepting a schedule of bad debts provided by a responsible officer of the company when it was apparent that other debts not included in the schedule were also irrecoverable. The case established that the auditor was not only required to go beyond the company's internal documentary evidence but he was also required to relate evidence obtained from different sources.

These cases indicate that, by the 1920s, auditing was rapidly developing into a technical process, requiring the skills of qualified accountants. However, many auditors were still laymen: frequently, they were merely shareholders chosen to be auditors by their fellow members. This reflects the key to this early period in the development of company audits. Company managers were regarded as accountable for the safe custody and honest, authorised use of the funds entrusted to them, primarily by shareholders. Audits were required to protect the interests of, and secure managers' accountability to, the company's shareholders.[2]

2.2.4   1920s–1960s

(i)   Socio-economic developments

During this period the centre of economic and auditing development shifted from the UK to the USA. The period was marked by the continued growth of

---

[2] Chandler, Edwards and Anderson (1993) present a contrary view of audit objectives for the period from 1844 to the 1920s. They provide evidence to support the notion that verifying financial statements prepared by company managements, rather than fraud detection, was the chief audit objective during the second and third quarters of the 19th century. However, they limit this suggestion to banking, railway and insurance companies which:

> were generally much larger and possessed a much more widely dispersed shareholder group than the majority of industrial and manufacturing companies. [These] shareholders ... tended to view themselves not so much as owners but as investors looking for the best return ... For the generality of companies, which remained relatively small, it was the auditor's fraud detection role which remained predominant. (Chandler *et al.,* 1993, pp. 444–445)

Thus, it seems that between 1844 and the 1870s the shareholders of banking, railway and insurance companies were similar to the typical investors of the 1920s to 1960s period – investors who required reliable (verified) information for their investment decisions. However, Chandler *et al.* (1993) note that during the latter part of the 19th century the primary audit objective, even for "sectors of the economy where large (usually quoted) companies predominated" (p. 445), became fraud detection. They suggest the change can be traced to leading professional accountant-auditors (who were beginning to replace the amateur shareholder-auditors) becoming obsessed with fraud detection as a consequence of the frequency of corporate bankruptcy in the 1860s and 1870s, with fraud featuring as a major factor in the demise of the companies (p. 447). Professional accountants at this time were heavily involved in bankruptcy and insolvency work and thus many gained insight into the causes and adverse effects of fraud. The dominance of fraud detection as the chief audit objective at the turn of the century is reflected in Spicer and Pegler's (1911) textbook:

> In the minds of the public at large, and of the majority of clients, the discovery of fraud is so far the principal function of the Auditor as to overshadow his other duties entirely, and there can be no question that it is of primary importance. (p. 5)

companies and the development of sophisticated securities markets and credit-granting institutions, designed to serve the financial needs of the growing economic entities.

In the years of recovery following the 1929 Wall Street Crash and ensuing depression, investment in business entities grew rapidly and became widespread. Company ownership became highly diffused and a new class of small investors emerged. Unlike the shareholders of earlier years, who were few in number but closely bound to the companies they partially owned, the new breed of investors were little interested in the management or fortunes of 'their' companies *per se*. They were primarily concerned with the return they could earn on their investment and, if they perceived better returns could be earned elsewhere, they readily switched their allegiance to another company. With these developments, ownership interests and management functions of companies became increasingly separated. The management and control of companies gradually passed to small groups of qualified, professional managers (directors and executives) who frequently owned no shares in the companies they managed (Porter, 1989).

In this new economic environment, the accountability of company managers was extended from the honest, authorised use of shareholders' funds to include the profitable use of those funds; business managers became accountable for generating a reasonable return on the financial resources entrusted to them.

At the same time as shareholders became increasingly divorced from their companies and companies grew in size and extended their influence in society, it came to be recognised that the survival and growth of companies rested not only on the financial resources provided by shareholders but on the joint contribution of all stakeholders, that is, all those with a particular 'stake' or interest in the company – shareholders, debtholders, employees, suppliers, customers and the government. As a consequence, many in society came to regard company managers as accountable to all of their company's stakeholders and as having an obligation to ensure that each stakeholder group is sufficiently rewarded for its contribution so as to ensure it maintained its 'stake' in the company.

The trend towards society expecting increased accountability from company managers was reinforced by events such as the 1929 Wall Street Crash and the questionable or downright dishonest acts of company directors which resulted in cases such as the *Royal Mail* case (1932) in the UK (discussed in the next sub-section) and the *McKesson & Robbins* case (1938) in the USA (see Chapter 5, section 5.3).

(ii) Developments in auditing

During the period from the 1920s to the 1960s, in response to changes in the socio-economic environment, auditing changed in four main ways. These are as follows.

(a) *Review of internal control and development of sampling techniques*: As companies grew in size, the volume of transactions in which they engaged made it progressively less feasible for auditors to check in detail all of the entries in the accounting records.

At the same time as companies grew in size, their managers found it necessary to delegate accounting and other duties to employees. With the growth in the volume of transactions and the delegation of responsibilities, errors in the company's records and also fraud became more likely. In order to prevent and/or detect errors and fraud, managements introduced systems of internal control.[3]

As a result of these changes, auditing procedures changed from meticulous checking of accounting records to testing samples of transactions and accounting entries, combined with a review and evaluation of the company's system of internal control.

(b) *Increased emphasis on external audit evidence*: Particularly as a result of decisions in cases such as *London Oil Storage Co. Ltd* v *Seear Hasluck and Co.* (1904; see section 2.2.3 above) and the *McKesson & Robbins* case (1938), new emphasis was given to the physical observation of assets such as cash and inventory, and to the use of external evidence (for example, confirmation of debtors). These duties came to be recognised as of equal importance to the auditor's traditional task of examining the company's internal books, records and documents.

(c) *Auditing the profit and loss statement*: As return on investment became the factor of prime importance for investors, and as companies' stakeholders focused their attention on receiving adequate compensation for their contribution to joint performance, so the emphasis of financial statement users shifted away from the balance sheet and ideas of solvency towards the profit and loss statement and ideas of earning power.

This shift in emphasis was led from the USA but was reinforced dramatically in the UK by the *Royal Mail* case (*Rex* v *Kyslant* [1932] I KB

---

[3] Systems of internal control are discussed in Chapter 10.

442; [1931] All ER 179) which, in the words of De Paula, "fell like an atom bomb and changed the face of the world of accounting" (as reported, Johnston, Edgar and Hays, 1982, p. 9). Similarly, Chandler *et al.* (1993) refer to it as: "perhaps the single most significant 20th century case in terms of its impact on the development of accounting thought and practice" (p. 454). They also attribute "the transition from fraud detection to [financial] statement verification" as the primary audit objective in the 1930s "mainly to the effects of the Royal Mail case" (p. 457).

The case principally revolved around the Royal Mail Steam Packet Company, which published profit and loss accounts between 1921 and 1928 that failed to show whether profits had or had not been earned. During these years, the company also paid dividends amounting to £5 million, funded largely from undisclosed transfers from secret reserves. Additionally, in 1928, the company published:

> a prospectus inviting the public to subscribe to the issue of debenture stock ... which ... concealed the true position of the company, with intent to induce persons to entrust or advance property to the company. (Mr Justice Wright, presiding Judge)

The profit and loss accounts and prospectus disclosed 'surpluses' for the years 1921 to 1928, ranging from £628,535 to £779,114 – implying that the company was profitable and a sound investment opportunity. In fact, the company made significant losses in each year from 1921 to 1928 ranging from £95,614 to £779,153.

The *Royal Mail* case, more than any other, highlighted the need for the profit and loss statement to be audited. Not surprisingly, the legislators introduced mandatory auditing of the profit and loss statement – in the USA in 1934 under the Securities and Exchange Commission Act, and in the UK in the Companies Act 1948.

(d) *Change in audit objectives*: Although the other changes which occurred in auditing between the 1920s and 1960s were significant, the greatest single change which took place was that in audit objectives. The focus of auditing shifted away from preventing and detecting fraud and error towards assessing the truth and fairness of the information presented in companies' financial statements.

As noted earlier, as companies grew in size, their ownership and management functions became increasingly separated. In order to ensure that funds continued to flow from investors to companies, and that financial markets functioned smoothly, it was essential that participants in the financial markets were confident that company financial statements provided a true and fair portrayal of the relevant company's financial position and financial performance. Responding to these needs, auditors accepted as their primary audit objective, providing credibility to the financial statements prepared by company managers[4] for their share-holders, which essentially reported on their own (that is, the managers') performance.

At the same time as providing credibility to externally reported financial information emerged as the chief audit objective, that of detecting fraud and error declined in importance. As Spicer and Pegler (1936) noted:

> The main object of an audit is the verification of accounts and statements prepared by a client or client's staff. Although of great importance the detection of fraud and error must be regarded as incidental to such main object. (p. 5)

The decline in the importance of fraud and error detection as the primary audit objective corresponded with the fact that, as companies grew in size:

- their managements established systems of internal control designed to prevent and detect fraud and error; and
- auditing procedures changed from detailed checking of the company's books and records to testing samples of transactions and accounting entries, combined with a review and evaluation of the company's system of internal control. This change reduced the likelihood of discovering fraud during an audit at the transaction and account level.

The changes indicated above also provided new opportunities for auditors. Through their review of their audit client's accounting system and related internal controls, and through the thorough knowledge of the client entity and its business which auditors gained during the course of their audit, they were ideally placed to offer ancillary services to the entity's managers. They were, for example, in an ideal position to suggest ways in which the efficiency and effectiveness of the accounting system and/or internal controls might be improved, and to offer assistance in areas such as financial and tax planning.

By the mid-1960s, companies had become an increasingly influential element in society and their managers were regarded as accountable to a wide range of interested parties, not only for the honest, authorised use of resources entrusted to their care, but also for the profitable use of those resources.

---

[4] Readers are reminded that in this book we use the term 'managers' to mean a company's executive directors, non-executive directors, and non-director executives (that is, all executives and directors). Under the Companies Act 2006 (s. 394), a company's directors are responsible for the preparation of its annual financial statements.

Auditing had become well established as a profession and auditors' rights and duties were embodied in statute and case law. Nevertheless, since the 1960s further notable changes have occurred in the audit environment, audit objectives and auditing techniques.

2.2.5   1960s–1990s

(i)   Socio-economic developments

Between the 1960s and 1990s, aided – and accelerated – by technological advances, mergers and takeovers, 'large' companies continued to grow in size and, particularly in the case of national and multinational companies, became extremely powerful and influential forces in society. The extent of the power held by companies during this period is reflected in the enormous share of the nation's financial and non-financial resources which was invested in the corporate sector.

The social and economic influence of companies was also reflected in the effect they had in their local communities. This was not restricted to providing employment and generating a flow of funds in their neighbourhoods; they also had an impact through the presence and appearance of their grounds and buildings. Many provided sporting and cultural facilities. They used the local transport network and affected traffic volumes and flows. They produced goods and services desired by consumers. They purchased goods and services produced by suppliers. Many helped to beautify, or to exploit and pollute, the local environment. When these and other factors are taken into consideration, it is clear that even a moderately sized company could have a significant influence on the economic and social life of the community of which it was a part. Taken as a whole, the corporate sector had an enormous impact on the well-being of society in general. Given this level of power and influence in society, it came to be argued that company managers should be held accountable for behaving in a socially responsible manner. A significant – and increasing – number of commentators advanced the notion that corporate managers had an obligation to consider the impact of their decisions on those who would be affected thereby, at the same time as they sought to accomplish their traditional economic goals, such as profit-making and long-term survival (see, for example, Davis, 1976; Demers and Wayland, 1982).

To an extent, by the 1980s, this wider obligation to society was well established. Company managers were, for example, considered to have an obligation to prevent environmental pollution, to enhance employee and product safety, to adopt equal employment opportunities, and to protect consumers. Parliament had introduced a considerable volume of statutory regulation covering these and similar issues with which company managers had to comply. The necessary compliance auditing was not, however, the responsibility of the company's financial statement auditors; instead, it was usually undertaken by inspectors from a State agency.

Notwithstanding the extension of the accountability expected of company managers since the 1960s, legislation relating to external reporting by companies in the UK (as elsewhere) continued to focus on company managers' accountability to shareholders for financial performance. Nevertheless, the legislators recognised that corporate managers were also accountable to their company's debenture-holders as, under the Companies Act 1985, s. 238, companies were required to provide their debenture-holders, as well as their shareholders, with a copy of their annual financial statements, directors' report and auditor's report.

(ii) Developments in auditing

As shown in Figure 2.1, four significant developments in auditing techniques occurred during the 1960s–1990s period. These are as follows:
- an increased emphasis on examining audit evidence derived from a wide variety of sources, both internal and external to the auditee (this is a continuation of the trend noted in the earlier phases of auditing's development);
- the emergence and increasing significance of computers, both as an audit tool and as an element in auditee entities to be embraced by audit examinations;
- the adoption of statistical sampling techniques as an aid to making difficult audit judgments. These techniques were designed primarily to reduce the variability in auditors' judgments and, to an extent, to place those judgments on a 'scientific' basis which could be justified and defended should they be challenged subsequently – for example, in a court of law;[5]
- the development of risk-based auditing; in essence, assessing the likelihood of material misstatements occurring in the financial statements, identifying the areas where such misstatements appear most likely to occur, and focusing audit effort on those areas.[6] This 'audit risk' approach was designed to reduce to an acceptable level the risk that the auditee's financial statements (to which a 'clean' audit report is attached) contain material misstatements – and to achieve this at minimum cost

---

[5] Statistical sampling is discussed in Chapter 12. In respect of the adoption of such techniques, Bell, Peecher and Solomon (2005) explain:

> During the 1980s some [audit] firms ... developed and implemented a suite of sophisticated mathematical tools ... Auditors used these state-of-the-art statistical sampling and mathematical decision aids to help make difficult audit judgments, including judgments about audit scope, planning materiality, evaluations of internal control and assessment of control risk, and judgments about sample size for tests of details. ... The high level of structure [of audits, including the adoption of statistical sampling,] was an attempt to reduce variation across audits and thereby promote consistently high audit quality. (p. 10)

[6] Risk-based auditing is discussed in detail in Chapter 9.

(an important consideration at a time when audit fees were under severe downward pressure; see below).

Adoption of risk-based auditing resulted in auditors needing to gain a thorough understanding of their audit clients (the organisation, key personnel, policies, procedures, etc.), their business operations and their industries. It also involved auditors understanding their clients' systems of internal financial controls and the extent to which these could be relied upon to prevent misstatements from occurring in the financial statements. Additionally, during the 1960s–1990s period, virtually all companies introduced computer systems to process their financial and other data, and to perform, monitor and/or control many (if not most) of their operational and administrative processes. These changes provided auditors with new opportunities to identify areas within their client companies where improvements could be made – for example, in their internal control, accounting and management information systems, in their tax and financial planning, and in aspects of their operations.

At the same time as changes in auditing presented opportunities for auditors to provide advisory services for management, fierce competition developed between businesses and between audit firms. This was largely prompted by advances in information technology and the phenomenal increase in the speed of information transfer, which meant that companies' (and audit firms') products and services, prices, processes, etc. were quickly known by their competitors and others. In the case of audit firms, increased competition also resulted from company mergers and acquisitions, which reduced the number of potential audit clients. A consequence of the competition – combined with a view held by many company managements that financial statement audits were a commodity and, therefore, should be obtained at minimum cost – was that audit fees came under severe pressure. Auditors seeking to maintain (or increase) their fees emphasised to their clients' managements that, rather than being viewed as 'an evil required by law', an audit should be viewed as a value-adding activity: valuable management advisory services could be provided as an outcome of the audit. As a result, the provision of advisory services for management emerged as a secondary audit objective.

2.2.6 1990s–the present

(i) Socio-economic developments

Since the 1990s, the socio-economic developments which typified the 1960s–1990s period have continued – at an accelerating pace. Today, developed economies are characterised by huge multinational companies, many other businesses are global in nature, and technology (and technical advances) pervades all aspects of the commercial environment. The size of some companies is reflected in an observation by Turley, Chairman and Chief Executive Officer of Ernst &

Young: "We live in a world where scores of individual corporations boast revenue figures that exceed the GDP of whole nations" (Turley, 2004, p. 18).

As large companies have grown to vast sizes, so they have gained enormous power and influence in society. However, this power and influence has not remained unfettered. The aftermath of the 1987 Stock Market Crash and well-publicised company failures such as the Bank of Credit and Commerce International (BCCI) and Barings Bank in the UK, Enron, WorldCom and Tyco in the USA, Parmalat in Italy and HIH in Australia have clearly demonstrated that the demise (or even faltering) of any large company has a major adverse impact on many individuals, groups and organisations in society. As a response to the unheralded failure of a number of large companies during and since the late 1980s, and evidence of misconduct, negligence and/or recklessness by senior company officials which came to light during investigations of the failed companies by agencies such as the Department of Trade and Industry (DTI)[7] in the UK and the Securities and Exchange Commission (SEC) in the USA, regulators have sought to ensure that companies are governed properly. Hence, for example, all companies listed on the London Stock Exchange are required to comply[8] with *The Combined Code on Corporate Governance* [Financial Reporting Council (FRC) 2006a].[9]

At the same time as regulators have been concerned with securing responsible corporate governance, large companies have come under increasing societal, political and media pressure to conduct their business in a socially and environmentally responsible manner. This is reflected in Parliament's introduction, in the Companies Act (CA) 2006 (s. 417), of a requirement for the directors of all quoted[10] companies to include in the business review section of their directors' report:

> to the extent necessary for an understanding of the development, performance
> or position of the company's business . . . information about –

---

[7] In June 2007, the DTI was replaced by the Department for Business, Enterprise and Regulatory Reform (DBERR).

[8] Alternatively, if they do not comply, to disclose the provisions with which they have not complied and explain the reasons for the non-compliance.

[9] This Code incorporates many of the provisions of *The Combined Code* issued by the Committee on Corporate Governance (1998b) and the FRC's *Combined Code on Corporate Governance* (2003). The 1998 Code was developed from a series of earlier corporate governance reports – particularly those of the Cadbury Committee (Committee on the Financial Aspects of Corporate Governance, 1992), the Greenbury Committee (Study Group Examining Directors' Remuneration, 1995), and the Hampel Committee (Committee on Corporate Governance, 1998a). The FRC's 2003 *Combined Code on Corporate Governance* included provisions derived from the Higgs *Review of the Role and Effectiveness of Non-Executive Directors* (Higgs, 2003) and the Smith Report (2003) on *The Effectiveness of Audit Committees*.

[10] A quoted company is defined as one whose equity share capital is listed in accordance with the Financial Services and Markets Act 2000 (that means, in effect, on a stock exchange in any EU Member State), or is officially listed in a European Economic Area State (EEA; comprising Norway, Iceland and Liechtenstein), or is admitted to dealing on either the New York Stock Exchange or NASDAQ (CA 2006, s. 385).

    (i)   environmental matters (including the impact of the company's business on the environment),

    (ii) the company's employees, and

    (iii) social and community issues,

including information about any policies of the company in relation to those matters and the effectiveness of those policies; . . . [And also] include –

    (a) analysis using key financial indicators, and

    (b) where appropriate, analysis using other key performance indicators, including information relating to environmental matters and employee matters.

Auditors are not specifically required to audit this information but they are required to state in the audit report whether "the information given in the directors' report for the financial year for which the accounts are prepared is consistent with those accounts" (CA 2006 s. 496).

Notwithstanding this and other changes introduced in the CA 2006, companies are not (as yet) required to report to stakeholders other than their shareholders and debenture-holders, nor are they required to report fully on their environmental impact or social activities.[11] Nevertheless, many companies undertake such reporting voluntarily and submit at least part of their reports to audit.[12] The essence of the present position is reflected in the fundamental principle of external auditing – *Accountability*:

> Auditors act in the interests of primary stakeholders, whilst having regard to the wider public interest. The identity of primary stakeholders is determined by reference to the statute or agreement requiring an audit: in the case of companies, the primary stakeholder is the general body of shareholders. [Auditing Practices Board (APB), 2008a, Appendix 2]

(ii)   Developments in auditing

As in the earlier periods of auditing's development discussed above, since the early 1990s auditing has adapted and responded to changes in its environment. However, unlike the earlier phases, the post-1990 period can be divided into two distinct parts: during the 1990s, trends evident during the 1980s continued, and culminated in adoption of the business (rather than audit) risk approach to auditing. However, since the early 2000s, following well-publicised company and audit failures, auditing has been subject to increasingly wide-ranging and stringent regulation which, to an extent, has reversed the trends of the 1990s.

The business risk approach to auditing is essentially a development of the audit risk approach which characterised the 1970s and 1980s (Lemon, Tatum and

---

[11] The statutory duties of companies with respect to external financial reporting (including changes introduced in the CA 2006) are discussed in Chapter 5, section 5.2.

[12] Environmental and social reporting by companies – and the audit of this information – is discussed in Chapters 17 and 18.

Turley, 2000). It rests on the notion that a broad range of the client's business risks are relevant to the financial statement audit. Proponents point out that many business risks, if not controlled, will eventually affect the financial statements. They maintain that, by understanding the full range (and potential impact and likelihood of occurrence) of risks facing an auditee, the auditor is better able (than when adopting a narrow approach focusing directly on the financial statements) to identify matters of significance and relevance to the audit. As Lemon *et al.* (2000) note:

> factors such as the business environment, governance issues and the nature of managerial control will ultimately have significance for the financial statements – their accuracy, issues of fraud and going concern (p. 10).

Supporters of the business risk approach also contend that by gaining a full understanding of the business, its operations, governance, financial and non-financial risks – and measures in place to mitigate those risks – auditors are better equipped (than under alternative approaches) to evaluate the significance and veracity of other evidence gathered during the audit. Both the audit risk and business risk approaches to auditing have as their ultimate objective expressing an opinion on the truth and fairness of the financial statements. However, while the audit risk approach seeks to achieve this by focusing on the financial statements (assessing the likelihood of their being materially misstated and identifying the areas where errors seem most likely), the business risk approach adopts a holistic business-wide perspective.

According to Lemon *et al.* (2000), the business risk approach to auditing resulted primarily from two sets of factors, namely, those related to:

(a) the effectiveness and efficiency of the audit;
(b) the 'added value' dimension of the audit.

(a)   Factors related to audit effectiveness and efficiency

Audit firms (especially the large firms) which reviewed the causes of audit failure (that is, expressing a 'clean' audit opinion on financial statements that are materially misstated) concluded that such failure does not generally stem from auditors' failure to detect errors in the recording or processing of accounting data. Rather, it tends to result from matters associated with how the business is managed. As Defliese, Jaenicke, Sullivan and Gnospelius (1985) explain:

> Analyses of past alleged audit failures indicate that such ... factors as failure to understand business situations or risks, errors in interpreting accounting principles, mistakes in interpreting and implementing standards, and misstatements caused by client fraud are among the most significant audit risk factors and sources of auditor liability. (p. 248).

Following such reasoning, firms adopting the business risk approach concluded: "effective auditing [that is, expressing an appropriate audit opinion on the financial statements] requires greater attention to be paid to understanding the risks of the business" (Lemon, *et al.*, 2000, p. 12).

Further, according to the International Auditing and Assurance Standards Board (IAASB: 2003):

> [r]ecent changes in the business environment have included ... the increasing use of judgment and estimates in the preparation of financial statements and significantly increased pressures that may lead to fraudulent financial reporting. (p. 3)

At the same time, advances in computer technology have resulted in auditees' basic accounting records, and the processing of routine data, being inherently less prone to error than formerly. Thus, changes in technology used by both auditors and their audit clients have provided greater scope for less audit effort to be devoted to detailed checking of 'lower-level' information but correspondingly more effort to be devoted to higher-level (less detailed, business- and financial statement-wide) analysis and assessment. According to the proponents of the business risk approach to auditing, this higher-level assessment generates more broadly based evidence about the auditee and this, in turn, provides the auditor with a more broadly – and soundly – based context for making judgments about the truth and fairness of the auditee's financial statements.

(b)   The added-value dimension of the audit

By adopting a holistic, business-wide approach and considering a broad range of issues associated with the risks faced by an auditee's business, auditors increased their opportunities to assist the client to avoid problems which would, if not addressed, threaten achievement of its (the client's) objectives – or even its survival. As Lemon *et al.* (2000) explain:

> Rather than an ex-post exercise to detect misstatement in financial statements, the audit is viewed as a means of influencing the conduct and control of business such that problems with financial statement information are less likely to arise. There is therefore an added-value or client service dimension to ... the business risk audit approaches ... [that is] consistent with a desire to ensure that the audit provides insights and information which is valued by the entity's management and contributes to the enterprise in some positive way. (pp. 10, 12)

Gaining greater knowledge of the client's business and attendant risks also accords with the emphasis placed by regulators and others on the need for responsible corporate governance – and the auditor's role in securing this.[13]

As noted earlier and reflected in Figure 2.2, adoption of the business risk approach does not signal a change in the primary audit objective – that remains

---

[13] This topic is discussed in greater detail in Chapter 5, section 5.5.

providing credibility to the financial statements prepared by management. However, the approach has assisted auditors to develop additional audit objectives, in particular, that of providing advisory services to management. Further, since the early 1990s, in conformity with society's and regulators' increasing concern about corporate governance, the auditing profession has acknowledged increased responsibility for detecting and reporting corporate fraud[14] and for assessing, and reporting more explicitly doubts about, an auditee's ability to continue as a going concern.[15] Adoption of the business risk approach enhances auditors' ability to fulfil these responsibilities. Similarly, the approach assists auditors to fulfil the United Kingdom Listing Authority's (UKLA) requirement that auditors of listed companies review certain corporate governance disclosures in their (listed) clients' annual reports.[16]

Figure 2.2:   Comparison of the audit risk and business risk approach to auditing

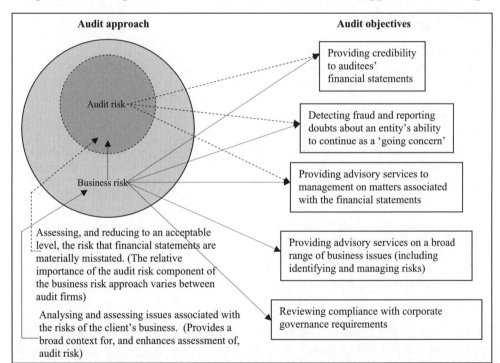

---

[14] The development of auditors' responsibilities for detecting and reporting fraud is discussed in detail in Chapter 6.

[15] The development of auditors' responsibilities in relation to auditees' going concern status is discussed in detail in Chapter 13, section 13.4.

[16] Regulatory responsibility for companies listed on the London Stock Exchange passed from the London Stock Exchange to the Financial Services Authority (FSA) in 2000. The FSA has delegated its responsibilities for listed companies to the United Kingdom Listing Authority (UKLA). We discuss auditors' responsibilities in relation to the UKLA's listing rules in Chapter 5, section 5.5.

Despite the benefits claimed for the business risk approach, it was not without its critics. Perhaps most prominent among these are Levitt and Turner, former Chairman and Chief Accountant, respectively, of the SEC in the USA. Turner (1999), for example, observed:

> Recent events[17] have caused the Commission and other securities regulators around the world to raise questions about the effectiveness of audits and the audit process, in particular, the perceived strengths and weaknesses of a [business] risk-based audit approach.... This approach requires an assessment of business risk within the business itself...[S]ome have argued that this approach...has resulted in less verification of account balances by examining documentation from independent sources.... Instead, the firms are relying on analytical analysis, inquiries of company personnel, and when appropriate control testing.... While some auditors have asserted that changes to their audit processes are responsive to the increased use of technology in financial reporting and accounting, other market participants have indicated a belief that the accounting profession is discarding the techniques that, in the past, made the financial statement audit a tool that enhances the reliability of information provided to investors. (pp. 3–6)

Along similar lines, Levitt observed:

> As firms increasingly have branched out to generate other sources of revenue, the basic audit model, not surprisingly, has undergone changes. In an era that calls for greater risk management, the [audit] industry has migrated to what they call the "[business] risk-based" model. It sounds right on target ... (Levitt, 1999, p. 2)

> [R]ecent headlines of accounting failures have led some people to question the thoroughness of audits.... We rely on auditors to put something like the good housekeeping seal of approval on the information investors receive. The integrity of that information must take priority over a desire for cost efficiencies or competitive advantage in the audit process.... As I look at some of the [audit] failures today, I can't help but wonder if the staff in the trenches of the profession have the training and supervision they need to ensure that audits are being done right. We cannot permit thorough audits to be sacrificed for re-engineered approaches that are efficient [that is, less costly], but less effective [that is, result in expressing an inappropriate opinion on financial statements]. (Levitt, 1998, p. 6)

By the turn of the century, partly as a result of criticism of the business risk approach by influential regulators such as the SEC, and partly in response to doubts being expressed within the auditing profession about its effectiveness

---

[17] 'Recent events' referred, in particular, to some well-publicised audit failures such as Andersen's audit of Waste Management's 1992–1996 financial statements. In June 2001 the SEC settled enforcement actions against Arthur Andersen LLP in respect of its audits of Waste Management amounting to $7 million. The SEC found that "Arthur Andersen's reports on the financial statements for Waste Management Inc were materially false and misleading and that Andersen engaged in improper professional conduct" (SEC Press Release, 19 June 2001).

as an audit approach, some of the larger firms in both the UK and the USA were beginning to retreat from its wholesale adoption. Some of these firms were also beginning to question the efficiency gains claimed for the business risk approach, in particular, those arising from assessing and evaluating business risks that have no direct relationship with the financial statements.[18] Thus, the effectiveness and efficiency factors motivating adoption of the business risk approach to auditing were already being questioned when Enron and Arthur Andersen collapsed in 2001 and 2002, respectively – events that were to trigger a new (regulated) phase in the development of auditing and a sharp curtailment of the provision of non-audit (value added) services by auditors to their audit clients.

Bell *et al.* (2005) provide a succinct account of developments:

> The NASDAQ market index reached its all-time high in March of 2000 and then begun a precipitous slide. . . . As has been the case many times before, when the economy turned down, indications of business improprieties came to light. Some of the alleged improprieties were of enormous scale, appeared to involve the highest levels of business management, and were perpetuated or facilitated, at least in part, by materially misstated financial statements. Quickly, the cry went out – *Where were the auditors*? One of the Big Five [audit] firms[19], Arthur Andersen LLP was the auditor . . . for several of these high-profile cases, including Enron and WorldCom. . . . Andersen was charged with several crimes, convicted of obstructing justice, and ultimately had to discontinue operations.[20] . . . Sweeping standard-setting and regulatory changes followed these and related events. The International Auditing and Assurance Standards Board (IAASB)[21] developed an ambitious action plan and issued several new International Standards on Auditing (ISAs). The U.S. Congress passed . . . the *Corporate and Auditing Accountability, Responsibility, and Transparency Act of 2002*, commonly called the Sarbanes-Oxley (SOX) Act. . . . [R]egulators from across the globe are contemplating or already have introduced legislation, regulations, and/or authoritative auditing guidance that, collectively, represent some of the most significant reforms in 70 years for public company auditing . . . [– reforms] intended to enhance public company financial reporting and thereby elevate investors' confidence. (Preface and pp. 1–2)

---

[18] These assertions are based on discussions between one of the authors and senior audit partners in some of the large accounting firms in the UK.

[19] Arthur Andersen, Deloitte, Ernst & Young, KPMG, and PricewaterhouseCoopers.

[20] On 31 May 2005 the US Supreme Court announced its unanimous decision to reverse the 2002 criminal conviction of Andersen (Bell *et al.*, 2005, p. 1).

[21] The IAASB replaced the International Auditing Practices Committee of the International Federation of Accountants (IFAC) in 2002. It is an independent standard setting body designated by, and operating independently under the auspices of, IFAC. Its goal is to serve the public interest by setting high-quality auditing, assurance, quality control and related services standards and by facilitating the convergence of international and national standards, thereby enhancing the quality and uniformity of practice throughout the world and strengthening public confidence in the global auditing and assurance profession (IFAC, 2006).

To a significant extent, SOX has served as an exemplar for legislation and regulations that have been enacted in many parts of the world since 2002, including the UK and the European Union (EU) more generally.[22] It is likely that this has resulted, in no small measure, from the fact that the SOX provisions relate not only to the audits (and auditors) of public companies registered in the USA but to those of all companies listed on the USA's stock exchanges (irrespective of where they are registered) and, also, to those of all significant subsidiaries of companies registered or listed in the USA irrespective of where those subsidiaries are located. As a result, the tentacles of SOX have extended into many parts of the world and have a significant effect in the UK. Likewise, the EU 8th Company Law Directive (EU, 2006: adopted by Member States in May 2006) has tentacles that extend beyond the boundaries of the EU. Its provisions apply to "third country auditors and audit firms" (including those in the USA) that provide an audit report on a company incorporated outside the EU but whose transferable securities are traded on a regulated market of a Member State. Indeed, the EU 8th Directive has been described as the European equivalent of the Sarbanes-Oxley Act (for example, Turley, 2004, p. 4; Woolf, 2006).

Key elements of SOX that are reflected, at least to an extent, in legislation and/or regulations in the UK and EU include the following:
  (i) the establishment of an authority to oversee and regulate auditors of, in particular, public companies;
  (ii) restrictions on auditors providing non-audit services to their audit clients;
  (iii) reporting on the effectiveness of audit clients' systems of internal control.

(i) Authority to oversee and regulate public company auditors

SOX established a Public Company Accounting Oversight Board (PCAOB) in the USA:

to oversee the audit of public companies that are subject to the securities laws . . . in order to protect the interests of investors and further the public interest in the preparation of informative, accurate and independent audit reports . . .
The Board shall . . .
  (1) register public accounting firms that prepare audit reports for issuers . . .
  (2) establish or adopt, or both, by rule, auditing, quality control, ethics, independence, and other standards relating to the preparation of audit reports for issuers . . .
  (3) conduct inspections of registered public accounting firms . . .

---

[22] Relevant UK and EU legislation and regulations are discussed in detail in Chapter 5, section 5.2.

(4) conduct investigations and disciplinary proceedings concerning, and impose appropriate sanctions where justified upon, registered public accounting firms and associated persons of such firms ... (s. 101)

In the UK, in April 2004, the Government similarly created "a unified regulator with a wide range of functions" by extending the responsibilities and powers of the Financial Reporting Council (FRC, 2006b, p. 1). Like the PCAOB in the USA, the FRC is "an independent regulator ... [with] ... statutory powers derived from Parliament", which operates independently from those whose activities it regulates (p. 3). Its stated aim "is to promote confidence in corporate reporting and governance" and its functions include:

- setting, monitoring and enforcing accounting and auditing standards;
- establishing ethical standards in relation to the independence, objectivity and integrity of external auditors;
- statutory oversight and regulation of auditors;
- operating an independent investigation and discipline scheme for matters which raise, or appear to raise, important issues affecting the public interest;
- overseeing the regulatory activities of the accountancy profession (FRC, 2006b, pp. 2, 11, 14).

Likewise, the EU 8th Directive requires Member States to "designate one or more competent authorities for the purposes of the tasks provided for in this Directive" (Art. 35). A competent authority is one "designated by law [to be] in charge of the regulation and/or oversight of statutory auditors and audit firms"[23] (Art. 2). The tasks for which competent authorities are responsible include the following:

- approving and registering statutory auditors and audit firms;
- ensuring approved statutory auditors and audit firms:
  - meet the standards of education, training and continuing education required by the EU 8th Directive;
  - are subject to principles of professional ethics (including their public interest function, integrity, objectivity, professional competence and due care) and are independent of their audit clients;
  - conduct statutory audits in compliance with international auditing standards adopted by the European Commission;
  - are subject to a system of quality assurance which meets specified minimum requirements and to a system of public oversight;

_____

[23] A statutory auditor is a natural person, and an audit firm is an entity, approved in accordance with the EU 8th Directive by the competent authorities of a Member State to carry out audits that are required by statute (i.e., laws enacted by Parliament) (Art. 2).

- ensuring there are effective systems of investigations and penalties to detect, correct and prevent inadequate performance of statutory audits.

(ii)   Restrictions on auditors providing non-audit services to audit clients[24]

Many commentators attributed much, if not most, of Arthur Andersen's apparent failure to conduct proper audits of Enron's financial statements to the absence of the required level of auditor independence. Reflecting this view, SOX (s. 201) prohibits auditors from providing a wide range of non-audit services to their audit clients. Services that are not explicitly prohibited may be provided but they must be pre-approved by the company's audit committee and disclosed in the company's annual report (s. 202). These provisions apply not only to the auditors of public companies registered in the USA but also to those of all companies listed on the USA's stock exchanges and of all significant subsidiaries of companies registered or listed in the USA.

In the UK, auditors are not prohibited from providing non-audit services to their audit clients (except where the SOX provisions apply because a client is registered or listed in the USA or is a subsidiary of such a company) but they are required to avoid situations:

> which make it probable that a reasonable and informed third party would conclude that objectivity either is impaired or could be impaired. . . . For example, if a third party were aware that the auditor had certain financial, employment, business or personal relationships with the audited entity, that individual might reasonably conclude that the auditor could be subject to undue influence from the directors or would not be impartial or unbiased. (APB, 2008b, paras 12–13)

Similar provisions have been included in the EU 8th Directive. Article 22 prohibits auditors in the EU (including the UK) from involvement in their audit clients' decision-making, and also from carrying out a statutory audit if there is any financial, business, employment or other relationship (including the provision of additional non-audit services) with the audit client from which a reasonable and informed party would conclude that the auditor's independence is compromised. Article 22 also provides that auditors must document all significant threats to their independence and safeguards they have applied to mitigate those threats. Further, the auditors of public-interest clients are required to disclose annually to the client's audit committee any additional services provided to the client, and to discuss with the audit committee threats to their independence and safeguards applied to mitigate those threats. In the UK, if an auditor has provided a listed company client with non-audit services,

---

[24] Auditors' provision of non-audit services to audit clients is discussed in detail in Chapter 4.

the directors of the company are required by *The Combined Code on Corporate Governance* (FRC, 2006a) to provide, in their company's annual report, an explanation of how the auditor's objectivity and independence have been safeguarded.

Additionally, regulations made by the Secretary of State under powers conferred on him by CA 2006, s. 494, and the EU 8th Directive, Art. 49, require companies to disclose in the notes to their audited annual financial statements total fees paid to the auditor for: (i) the statutory audit, (ii) other assurance services, (iii) tax advisory services and (iv) other non-audit services.[25] This enables users of a company's financial statements to judge for themselves whether, and if so the extent to which, the auditor's independence may have been compromised.

(iii) Reporting on the effectiveness of audit clients' systems of internal control

The issue of auditors reporting on the effectiveness of auditees' systems of internal control was first raised in the UK by the Cadbury Committee (Committee on the Financial Aspects of Corporate Governance, 1992) and was examined in some detail by the Turnbull Committee (Working Party on Internal Control, 1999). Since then, it has been a hotly debated issue in auditing circles. In the USA, the debate has been largely resolved as SOX (s. 404) requires the annual report of all public companies registered or listed in the USA (and significant subsidiaries of such companies) to contain a report that sets out management's responsibility for, and its assessment of, the effectiveness of the company's internal control structure and procedures for financial reporting. It also requires the auditors of these companies to "attest to, and report on, the assessment made by the management" (s. 404). This provision applies to the auditors of any UK (or, indeed, of any other country's) company that is listed on a USA stock exchange or is a significant subsidiary of such a company.

In the UK, the requirements have not gone as far as those in the USA but steps have been taken in that direction. *The Combined Code on Corporate Governance* (FRC, 2006a, Provision C.2.1) requires the directors of companies

---

[25] The Companies (Disclosure of Auditor Remuneration) Regulations 2005, which came into force on 1 October 2005, require more detailed disclosures than the EU 8th Directive. The Regulations were originally made by the Secretary of State in accordance with powers conferred on him by the Companies Act (CA) 1985, s. 390B, as amended by the Companies (Audit, Investigations and Community Enterprise) Act 2004, s. 7. The statutory provision of the CA 1985, s. 390B (as amended), has been incorporated in s. 494 of the CA 2006. Further details of these regulatory requirements are provided in Chapter 4, section 4.3.1.

listed on the London Stock Exchange to include a statement in their company's annual report stating that they have conducted a review of the effectiveness of the company's system of internal controls; this review is to cover all material controls – financial, operational and compliance controls – and also risk management systems. Along related lines, the CA 2006, s. 417, requires the directors of all but small companies to include in the business review section of their directors' report a description of the principal risks and uncertainties facing the company.

Neither *The Combined Code* nor the CA 2006 requires auditors specifically to review and report on the directors' statements relating to their company's internal controls and risks. However, as noted earlier, CA 2006, s. 496, requires auditors to state in the audit report whether, in their opinion, the information given in the directors' report is consistent with the financial statements. Similarly, the UKLA's Listing Rules[26] require the auditors of all companies listed on the London Stock Exchange to review the directors' statement to verify that the company has complied with *The Combined Code's* provision C.2.1 (see above).[27]

The Auditing Practices Board (APB, 2004b) points out that, when assessing the directors' statement on their review of the effectiveness of the company's internal controls, auditors need to:

> obtain an understanding ... of the process defined by the board [of directors] for its review of the effectiveness of all material internal controls and compare that understanding to the statement made by the board in the annual report. ... [They also need to] review the documentation prepared by or for the directors to support their statement made in connection with Code provision C.2.1 and assess whether or not it provides sound support for that statement. (para 39)

However, as auditors in the UK explain in their audit reports, they:

> are not required to consider whether the board's statements on internal control cover all risks and controls, or form an opinion on the effectiveness of the company's corporate governance procedures or its risk and control procedures. (APB, 2004b, para 43)

2.3 FUTURE DEVELOPMENTS

Given the extent and nature of the legal and regulatory changes to the audit environment since 2002, it seems unlikely that there will be any major change to auditors' approach to auditing, or their responsibilities, in the near future. As

---

[26] See footnote 16.

[27] Or disclosed that it has not so complied and explained the reasons for the non-compliance.

noted earlier, by 2002 the audit effectiveness and efficiency arguments for adopting the business risk approach to auditing were already being challenged. With the subsequent curtailment of auditors' provision of non-audit services to their audit clients, the 'added value' motivation was also undermined. This, combined with the new regulatory environment and the promulgation of more prescriptive International Standards on Auditing (ISAs) by the IAASB since 2002, has resulted in auditors moving back towards the audit risk approach to auditing that typified the 1980s. Nevertheless, the business risk approach's emphasis on auditors gaining an in-depth understanding of their audit clients – their business, industry and key personnel, and on identifying and assessing relevant internal and external risks, has remained – and, indeed, has been enshrined in ISA 315: *Identifying and assessing the risks of material misstatement through understanding the entity and its environment* (IAASB, 2006).

Considering the changes that have occurred since 2002, specific developments in auditors' responsibilities might include the following:

1. *Reporting on the effectiveness of auditees' systems of internal controls and risk management*: Changes to the legal and regulatory requirements of auditors with respect to auditees' systems of internal control and risk management since 2002 (described in section 2.2.6 above) have resulted in auditors edging towards assessing the effectiveness of their audit clients' systems of internal control and risk management, and reporting thereon. With the requirements of SOX (s. 404) providing an example – and affecting auditors of UK companies listed on the USA's stock exchanges (or significant subsidiaries of such companies) – it does not seem unlikely that, in the not-too-distant future, UK auditors will be required to undertake the responsibilities in respect of auditees' internal controls and risks that they currently point out (in their audit reports) they are not required to perform (see quotation in section 2.2.6).

2. *Examining, and expressing an opinion about, the truth and fairness of all the information (financial and non-financial) provided in companies' annual reports*: A number of steps in this direction already seem to have been taken. For example:
   - Auditing Standards require auditors to explicitly acknowledge in their audit reports that they "read other information contained in the annual report and consider whether it is consistent with the audited financial statements".[28]

---

[28] Audit reports are discussed in detail in Chapter 14.

- The CA 2006 (s. 497) requires the auditors of quoted companies[29] to state in their audit reports whether, in their opinion, the auditable part of the Directors' Remuneration Report has been properly prepared in accordance with the CA 2006. If the auditors are of the opinion that information required to be included in the Directors' Remuneration Report is not provided, they are required to include in their audit report, "so far as they are reasonably able to do so, a statement giving the required particulars" (s. 498).
- The CA 2006 (s. 496) requires auditors to state in their audit reports whether, in their opinion, the information given in the directors' report (including the business review) is consistent with the financial statements. The information directors must provide in their business review includes:
  - a fair review of the company's business, and
  - a description of the principal risks and uncertainties facing the company.

  For quoted companies, the business review must also include information about:
  - environmental matters (including the impact of the business of the company on the environment),
  - the company's employees, and social and community issues,
  - analysis using financial and, where appropriate, other key (non-financial) performance indicators, including information relating to environmental and employee matters.

Given the evidence of disclosure and auditing requirements introduced in recent years (indicated above), it seems likely that, in the future, directors will be required to provide in their company's annual reports, and auditors will be required to examine and express an opinion thereon, an increasing amount of information on a widening range of matters.

3. *Expressing an audit opinion on auditees' financial statements published on the Internet*: Many companies publish their financial statements on their website voluntarily; however, the CA 2006, s. 430, requires quoted companies[30] to ensure that their annual reports (including their audited financial statements) are made available on their company's website and remain there until the next year's annual report is available.

The auditor's report on the annual financial statements must be included in a quoted company's annual report published on its website (CA 2006,

---

[29] These companies are required to include a Directors' Remuneration Report in their annual report.

[30] See footnote 10.

s. 434). However, given the public's quest for 'instant information', it seems likely that, in the not-too-distant future, companies will be required to provide up-to-date audited financial information on their websites far more frequently than annually. As a 'Big Four audit firm'[31] audit partner in the USA stated:

> [S]omeday soon the market will expect much more rapid reporting from the best-performing companies. The benefit of this information being audited is the integrity of the data. I believe this will be a requirement in the very near future. (as reported, Searcy and Woodroof, 2003, p. 1)

It is only one short step from frequent publishing of audited financial information to continuous reporting.

4. *Continuous auditing*: Continuous auditing was defined in a research report jointly published by the American Institute of Certified Public Accountants (AICPA) and the Canadian Institute of Chartered Accountants (CICA) as: "a methodology that enables independent auditors to provide written assurance on a subject matter using a series of auditors" reports issued simultaneously with, or a short period of time after, the occurrence of events underlying the subject matter' (AICPA and CICA, 1999). To external auditors, financial statement users and professional bodies such as the AICPA and CICA, the 'subject matter' and 'events' are understood to relate to accounting data.

Searcy and Woodroof (2003) explain the process of continuous auditing in the following terms:

> [It] leverages technology and opens database architecture to enable auditors to monitor a company's systems over the Internet using sensors and digital agents. Any discrepancies between the records and the rules defined in the digital agents are transmitted via e-mail to the client and the auditor. At that point the auditor can determine the appropriate action to take. For example, a digital agent performing analytical procedures on the accounts [receivable] would e-mail the auditor an exception report on those accounts [receivable] that fluctuate outside the parameters defined in the digital agent. Once an account trigger has occurred, the digital agent moves to the transactional level to identify the problem and e-mail the auditor. Once the transaction is identified, a digital agent would verify the sale with the customer and e-mail the confirmation to the auditor.
>
> All of the audit routines described above are done electronically and automatically. The audit routines are performed not only at year-end but quarterly, monthly, daily, or in real time. The only constraints are the performance limitations of the client's system and the update frequency of the client's records. (pp. 1–2)

The AICPA/CICA (1999) research report concluded that continuous audits are viable providing certain interrelated conditions are met. For example,

---

[31] Deloitte, Ernst & Young, KPMG and PricewaterhouseCoopers.

the processes audit clients use to capture, manipulate and store data, and report information, need to be largely automated and the automated processes need to be very reliable; similarly, highly automated audit procedures need to be implemented to provide the required audit evidence. The report also concluded that research by academics, experimentation by practitioners and guidance from standard setters are all needed to help continuous audit services to evolve. Additionally, the report noted that the demand for more reliable, relevant and timely decision-making information is likely to create a need for continuous audits but the auditing profession needs to ready itself to respond to this demand. A 'Big Four audit firm' audit partner in the USA conveyed the current readiness of – at least his firm – when he stated:

> The process we have is good but is designed for the annual audit. . . . We will need the ability to push a button at any point in time and have the system summarize for the [audit] engagement team process issues identified to date that can lead to risk that the financial statements are inaccurate, rather than rely only on a traditional review of workpapers, manual summarizations of issues, and follow-up. (as cited, Searcy and Woodroof, 2003, p. 1)

Before leaving the topic of continuous auditing it should be noted that the term is used with a slightly different (but related) meaning by internal auditors. Coderre (2005) provides a succinct view of the current audit environment and internal auditors' interpretation of the term 'continuous auditing':

> The need for timely and ongoing assurance over the effectiveness of risk management and control systems is critical. Organizations are continually exposed to significant errors, frauds or inefficiencies that can lead to financial loss and increased levels of risk. An evolving regulatory environment, increased globalization of businesses, market pressure to improve operations, and rapidly changing business conditions are creating the need for more timely and ongoing assurance that controls are working effectively and risk is being mitigated. . . . Traditionally, internal auditing's testing of controls has been performed on a retrospective and cyclical basis, often many months after business activities have occurred. . . . Continuous auditing is a method used to perform control and risk assessments automatically on a more frequent basis. . . . A continuous audit approach allows internal auditors to fully understand critical control points, rules, and exceptions. With automated frequent analyses of data, they are able to perform control and risk assessments in real time or near real time. (p. 1)

2.4 SUMMARY

In this chapter we have reviewed the development of auditing – more particularly, its development since the first introduction of compulsory audits in 1844 – and we have highlighted the close link between changes in the socio-economic environment of the English-speaking world and changes in audit objectives and techniques. We have noted that auditing continually evolves as it responds to, and utilises opportunities provided by, changes in its environment. We have also highlighted the relationship between auditing and the accountability expected of corporate managers.

We have noted that current legislation, which governs the preparation and audit of companies' financial statements and other reports, may not be attuned to the level of accountability now expected of company managers. However, particularly since 2002, new reporting and auditing requirements have been introduced and it seems likely that in the future large national and multinational companies, at least, will be required to produce, and external auditors will be required to audit, more comprehensive accountability (i.e., annual) reports. Nevertheless, if legislators and, more particularly, regulators seek to extend the role and responsibilities of auditors, they will need to be mindful of the costs associated with securing greater corporate accountability in this way, and ensure that the costs do not outstrip the benefits derived therefrom. Although the business risk approach to auditing described in this chapter appeared to provide the auditing profession with a cost-effective means of fulfilling a wider set of responsibilities, critics noted – and well-publicised audit failures seem to have confirmed – that it carried the risk that the financial statement audit, which remains the essence of auditors' role in society, might be compromised.

Following the unheralded collapse of Enron and Andersen in 2001 and 2002, respectively, auditing has become highly regulated and auditors have moved back towards the audit risk approach to auditing. Nevertheless, a fundamental attribute of the business risk approach has been retained – that of gaining a thorough understanding of the business and its internal control and risk management systems. Given the extensive legislative and regulatory changes since 2002, further major changes in the auditing arena in the near future seem unlikely. Perhaps, in the current era of rapid technological advancement and 'real time information', the most significant change will be a move towards continuous reporting and auditing.

SELF-REVIEW QUESTIONS

2.1 Briefly describe the audit environment in each of the following periods:
    (i)   pre-1844,
    (ii) 1844–1920s,
    (iii) 1920s–1960s,
    (iv) 1960s–1990s,
    (v) 1990s–present.

2.2   Outline the major audit objectives in each of the following periods:
       (i)   pre-1844,
       (ii) 1844–1920s,
       (iii) 1920s–1960s,
       (iv) 1960s–1990s,
       (v)   1990s–present.

2.3   State the major changes which have occurred in auditing techniques
       during the last 160 years. Explain briefly how changes in technology
       have impacted on the changes in auditing techniques.

2.4   Explain briefly the significance of the Joint Stock Companies Act 1844
       to the development of auditing.

2.5   The Companies Act 1900 has been referred to as 'a prominent milestone
       in the history of company auditing'. List reasons which help to explain
       why this Act has been given this title.

2.6   Explain briefly the importance of the following cases to the development
       of auditors' responsibilities:
       (i)   *Re London and General Bank (No. 2)* [1895];
       (ii) *Re Kingston Cotton Mill Co. Ltd (No. 2)* [1896].

2.7   'Changes in auditing reflect, and represent a response to, changes in the
       socio-economic environment'.

       Using examples to illustrate your answer, explain briefly the link
       between changes in auditing and changes in the socio-economic
       environment.

2.8   (a) Outline key differences between the audit risk and business risk
           approaches to auditing; and
       (b) Explain briefly why auditing firms have tended to return to the audit
           risk approach since 2002.

2.9   Outline the key legislative and regulatory changes that have affected
       auditing since 2002.

2.10   Explain briefly four likely developments in auditing in the near to
       medium-term future.

REFERENCES

American Institute of Certified Public Accountants (AICPA), & Canadian Institute of Chartered Accountants (CICA). (1999). *Continuous Auditing.* New York: AICPA and Toronto: CICA.

Auditing Practices Board (APB). (2004). *The Combined Code on Corporate Governance: Requirements of auditors under the Listing Rules of the Financial Services Authority.* Bulletin 2004/3. London: Financial Reporting Council.

Auditing Practices Board (APB). (2008a). *The Auditing Practices Board – Scope and Authority of Pronouncements (Revised).* London: Financial Reporting Council.

Auditing Practices Board (APB). (2008b). *APB Ethical Standard 1: Integrity, Objectivity and Independence.* London: Financial Reporting Council.

Bell, T.B., Peecher, M.E., and Solomon, I. (2005). *The 21st Public Company Audit: Conceptual Elements of KPMG's Global Audit Methodology.* Zurich: KPMG International.

Brown, R. (1905). *History of Accounting and Accountants.* London: Jack.

Chandler, R.A., Edwards, J.R., and Anderson, M. (1993). Changing perceptions of the role of the company auditor, 1840–1940. *Accounting and Business Research* **23**(92), 443–459.

Coderre, D. (2005). *Global Technology Audit Guide Continuous Auditing: Implications for Assurance, Monitoring and Risk Management.* Florida: Institute of Internal Auditors.

Committee on Corporate Governance (Hampel Committee). (1998a). *Final Report of the Committee on Corporate Governance.* London: London Stock Exchange.

Committee on Corporate Governance. (1998b). *The Combined Code.* London: London Stock Exchange.

Committee on the Financial Aspects of Corporate Governance (Cadbury Committee). (1992). *Report of the Committee on the Financial Aspects of Corporate Governance.* London: Gee.

Davis, K. (1976). Social responsibility is inevitable. *California Management Review* **XIX**(Fall), 14–20.

Defliese, P.L., Jaenicke, H.R., Sullivan J.D., and Gnospelius, R.A. (1985). *Montgomery's Auditing*, 10th edition (College version). United States of America: Coopers & Lybrand.

Demers, L., and Wayland, D. (1982). Corporate social responsibility: is no news good news? *CA Magazine* **115**(January), 42–46; **115**(February), 56–60.

Editorial. (1901, January). *The Accountant's Magazine.*

European Union (EU). (2006). *Directive 2006/43/EC of the European Parliament and of the Council on the Statutory Audits of Annual Accounts and Consolidated Accounts (8th Directive).* Brussels: European Parliament and Council.

Financial Reporting Council (FRC). (2003). *The Combined Code on Corporate Governance.* London: Financial Reporting Council.

Financial Reporting Council (FRC). (2006a). *The Combined Code on Corporate Governance.* London: Financial Reporting Council.

Financial Reporting Council (FRC). (2006b). *Regulatory Strategy* (Version 2.1). London: Financial Reporting Council.

Greenbury, Sir Richard. (1995). *Directors' Remuneration: Report of a Study Group Chaired by Sir Richard Greenbury.* London: Gee.

Higgs, D. (2003). *Review of the Role and Effectiveness of Non-Executive Directors.* London: Department of Trade and Industry.

International Auditing and Assurance Standards Board (IAASB). (2003). *IAASB Action Plan 2003–2004.* New York: International Federation of Accountants.

International Auditing and Assurance Standards Board (IAASB). (2006). International Auditing Standard (ISA) 315 (Redrafted): *Identifying and assessing the risks of material misstatement through understanding the entity and its environment.* New York: International Federation of Accountants.

International Federation of Accountants (IFAC). (2006). *International Auditing and Assurance Standards Board.* New York: IFAC.

Johnston, T.R., Edgar, G.C., and Hays, P.L. (1982). *The Law and Practice of Company Accounting.* 6th edition. Wellington: Butterworths.

Lee, T.A. (1970). A brief history of company audits: 1840–1940. *The Accountant's Magazine,* **74**(782), 363–368.

Lemon, W.M., Tatum, K.W., and Turley, W.S. (2000). *Developments in the Audit Methodologies of Large Accounting Firms.* London: Auditing Practices Board.

Levitt, A. (1998, 28 September). *The Numbers Game.* Remarks at the NYU Center for Law and Business, New York.

Levitt, A. (1999, 7 October). *Remarks to the Panel on Audit Effectiveness of the Public Oversight Board.* Public Oversight Hearings, New York.

Morris, J. (1977). *Domesday Book 20 Bedfordshire.* Chichester: Philimore & Co. Ltd.

Porter, B.A. (1989). *The Development of Corporate Accountability and the Role of the External Auditor.* Palmerston North: Massey University, Accountancy Department, Discussion Paper Series, No.92.

Searcy, D.L., and Woodroof, J.B. (2003, May). Continuous auditing: leveraging the technology. *The CPA Journal,* www.nysscpa.org/cpajournal/2003/0503/dept/d054603.

Securities & Exchange Commission (SEC). (2001, 19 June). *Arthur Andersen LLP agrees to Settlement Resulting in First Anti-Fraud Injunction in More than 20 Years.* SEC Press Release 2001–62.

Smith, Sir Robert. (2003). *Report on the Effectiveness of Audit Committees.* Financial Services Authority: London.

Spicer, E.E., and Pegler, E.C. (1911). *Practical Auditing.* London: UFL.

Spicer, E.E., and Pegler, E.C. (1936). *Practical Auditing*. 7th edition. edited by Bigg, W.W. London: UFL.

Turley, J.S. (2004, June). Get ready for the EU's 8th Directive. *Directorship*, 18–21.

Turner, L.E. (1999, 7 October). *Speech to the Panel on Audit Effectiveness*. New York.

Woolf, E. (2006). Sarbox in Europe. *Accountancy* **138**(1357), 24.

Working Party on Internal Control (Turnbull Committee). (1999). *Internal Control: Guidance for Directors on the Combined Code*. London: ICAEW.

ADDITIONAL READING

Chandler, R.A. (1997). Judicial views on auditing from the nineteenth century. *Accounting History* **2**(1), 61–80.

Chandler, R.A. (1997). Taking responsibility: the early demand for institutional action to define an auditor's duties. *International Journal of Auditing* **1**(3), 165–174.

Chandler, R.A., and Edwards, J.R. (1996). Recurring issues in auditing: back to the future. *Accounting, Auditing & Accountability Journal* **9**(2), 4–29.

Curtis, E., and Turley, S. (2007). The business risk audit – A longitudinal case study of an audit engagement. *Accounting, Organizations and Society* **32**(4–5), 439–461.

Edwards, R.J., Anderson, M., and Matthews, D. (1997). Accountability in a free-market economy: the British company audit, 1886. *Abacus* **33**(1), 1–25.

Flesher, D.L., Previts, G.J., and Samson, W.D. (2005). Auditing in the United States: a historical perspective. *Abacus* **41**(1), 21–39.

Flint, D. (1971). The role of the auditor in modern society: an exploratory essay. *Accounting and Business Research* **1**(4), 287–293.

Institute of Chartered Accountants of Scotland (ICAS). (1993). *Auditing into the Twenty-first Century*. Edinburgh: ICAS.

Knechel, W.R. (2007). The business risk audit: origins, obstacles and opportunities. *Accounting, Organizations and Society* **32**(3–4), 383–408.

Power, M. (1994). *The Audit Explosion*. London: Demos.

Power, M. (2007). Business risk auditing – debating the history of its present. *Accounting, Organizations and Society* **32**(3–4), 379–382.

Robson, K., Humphrey, C., Khalifa, R., and Jones, J. (2007). Transforming audit technologies: business risk audit methodologies and the audit field. *Accounting, Organizations and Society* **32**(4–5), 409–438.

3 A Framework of Auditing Concepts

LEARNING OBJECTIVES

After studying the material in this chapter you should be able to:
*   explain the meaning of, and relationship between, the social purpose of auditing, postulates of auditing and key concepts of auditing;
*   state seven postulates of auditing;
*   explain and discuss the importance of the concepts relating to:
    *   the credibility of auditors' work (Independence, Competence, Ethical Conduct),
    *   the audit process (Evidence, Materiality, Audit Risk, Judgment, Scepticism),
    *   auditors' communication (Reporting),
    *   the standard of auditors' work (Due Care, Quality control).

The following publications and fundamental principles of external auditing are particularly relevant to this chapter:

Publications:
*   International Standard on Auditing (ISA) 200 (Redrafted): *Overall Objectives of the Independent Auditor, and the Conduct of an Audit in Accordance with International Standards on Auditing* (IFAC, June 2008)**[1]
*   International Standard on Auditing (ISA) 220 (Redrafted): *Quality Control for an Audit of Financial Statements* (IFAC, June 2008)**
*   International Standard on Auditing (ISA) 320 (Redrafted): *Materiality in Planning and Performing an Audit* (IFAC, June 2008)**
*   International Standard on Auditing (ISA) 500 (Redrafted): *Audit Evidence* (IFAC, June 2008)**
*   International Standard on Quality Control (ISQC) 1 (Redrafted): *Quality Control for Firms that Perform Audits and Reviews of Financial Statements, and Other Assurance and Related Services Engagements* (IFAC, June 2008)**
*   International Education Standard (IES) 8: *Competence Requirements for Audit Professionals* (IFAC, 2006)
*   *Code of Ethics for Professional Accountants* (IFAC, 2006) [section 290, 2006][2]

Fundamental principles of external auditing included in *The Auditor's Code:*[3]
*   Objectivity and independence
*   Integrity
*   Clear, complete and effective communication
*   Competence
*   Judgment
*   Rigour

---

[1] The status of ISAs referred to in this chapter is explained in the Important Note following the Preface to this book.

[2] The IFAC *Code of Ethics* was revised in July 2006 but an Exposure Draft (ED) of section 290 (Independence – Audit and Review Engagements) was issued in December 2006. A further ED of some paragraphs of section 290 was issued in July 2007. In this chapter, IFAC (2006*) is used to refer to the ED of section 290 and IFAC (2006) is used to denote the revised *Code of Ethics*.

[3] The fundamental principles of external auditing are reproduced on the inside of the front cover of this book.

3.1 INTRODUCTION

During auditing's long history, dating back some 3,000 years (see Chapter 1) and, more particularly, during the last 160 or so years which witnessed its very rapid development (see Chapter 2), auditing has developed in a very practical way. Perhaps surprisingly, given its importance to the smooth functioning of financial markets and the economy in general, and the effort devoted to developing a coherent theory (or conceptual framework) of *accounting*, relatively little attention has been given to developing a theory of *auditing*. Three notable exceptions to this are the classic works of Mautz and Sharaf (1961), the Committee on Basic Auditing Concepts (1973) and Flint (1988).

Why is a theory of auditing important? According to Mautz and Sharaf (1961, pp. 4–5):

> One reason . . . for a serious and substantial investigation into the possibility and nature of auditing theory is the hope that it will provide us with solutions, or at least clues to solutions, of problems which we now find difficult.

They suggested adopting a philosophical approach and explained (p. 8):

1. Philosophy gets back to first principles, to the rationale behind the actions and thoughts which tend to be taken for granted.
2. Philosophy is concerned with the systematic organisation of knowledge in such a way that it becomes at once more useful and less likely to be self-contradictory.
3. Philosophy provides a basis whereby social relationships may be molded and understood.

Thus, auditing theory helps us to identify (and be cognisant of) basic assumptions which underpin auditing practice, to organise auditing knowledge so that it is useful and internally consistent, and to understand the social role and context of the audit function.

Flint (1988) shed more light on the issue when he stated:

> The purpose of theory in relation to auditing is to provide a coherent set of propositions about the activity which explains its social purpose and objectives, which furnishes a rational foundation and justification for its practices and procedures, relating them to the purposes and objectives, and which explains the place of the activity in the context of the institutions of society and the social, economic and political environment. (p. 9)

From this a three-tier hierarchy of notions may be distilled. At the top is a statement of the social purpose and objectives of auditing. This is followed by the postulates or basic assumptions which underpin the social purpose of the audit function on the one hand and auditing practices and procedures on the other. At the bottom we have a coherent set of concepts which underpin (and help to explain and guide) auditing practice. This 'hierarchy of notions' is presented in outline form in Figure 3.1 and discussed below.

Figure 3.1: Hierarchy of notions underpinning a theory of auditing

Social purpose of auditing							
Auditors are agents of social control in the process of corporate accountability							

Postulates of auditing (Fundamental assumptions or truths)							
Accountability relationship	Subject matter remote, complex, significant	Independence, investigatory and reporting freedom	Verifiable subject matter	Standards of accountability can be set, measured and compared with known criteria	Credibility given to financial and other information can be communicated	Provides an economic or social benefit

Key concepts of auditing										
Credibility of work performed			Audit process					Commu-nication	Standard of performance	
Independence, Objectivity	Competence	Ethical conduct, Integrity	Evidence	Materiality	Audit risk	Judgment	Scepticism	Reporting	Due care	Quality control

In this chapter we do not attempt to provide a comprehensive theory of auditing. For this, reference may be made to the three 'classics' noted above.

Rather, our purpose is to provide a basic framework for, and to discuss, key concepts which underpin auditing practice. We first outline the social purpose and postulates of auditing and provide a framework for the key auditing concepts. We then discuss 11 key concepts – their meaning and relevance for auditing – in greater detail. Most of the concepts have particular significance for material presented in subsequent chapters and these are cross-referenced to, and further developed in, the relevant later chapter.

3.2 SOCIAL PURPOSE, POSTULATES AND FRAMEWORK FOR KEY CONCEPTS OF AUDITING

3.2.1 Social purpose of the audit function

As noted in Chapter 2, the primary objective of statutory company audits is to provide credibility to the financial statements prepared by the company's directors for use by parties external to the entity. In performing this function, auditors are one of the checks and balances imposed by society (through legislation) on company directors as a counter to the power and influence they wield in society. Thus, auditors' social purpose is to act as agents of social control in the process of corporate accountability.

3.2.2 Postulates of auditing

A postulate is defined by the *Concise Oxford Dictionary* as "a thing assumed as a necessary condition especially as a basis for reasoning; a fundamental prerequisite or condition". Mautz and Sharaf (1961) explain that postulates have five general attributes. They state (p. 37):

> Postulates are:
> 1. Essential to the development of any intellectual discipline.
> 2. Assumptions that do not lend themselves to direct verification.
> 3. A basis for inference.
> 4. A foundation for erection of any theoretical structure.
> 5. Susceptible to challenge in the light of later advancement of knowledge.

In the context of auditing, postulates may be defined as fundamental principles, assumed to be truths, which help to explain the social purpose of auditing and/or auditing practices. Flint (1988, pp. 21–23) identifies seven basic postulates. These are as follows:

1. The primary condition for an audit is that there is either:
   (a) a relationship of accountability between two or more parties in the sense that there is a duty of acceptable conduct or performance owed by one party to the other party or parties;
   (b) a need by some party to establish the reliability and credibility of information for which they are responsible which is expected to be used and relied on by a specified group or groups of which the members may not be constant or individually identifiable, producing constructively a relationship of accountability . . .
2. The subject matter of accountability is too remote, too complex and/or of too great a significance for the discharge of the duty to be demonstrated without the process of audit.
3. Essential distinguishing characteristics of audit are the independence of its status and its freedom from investigatory and reporting constraints.
4. The subject matter of audit, for example conduct, performance or achievement, or record of events or state of affairs, or a statement or facts relating to any of these, is susceptible to verification by evidence.
5. Standards of accountability, for example of conduct, performance, achievement and quality of information, can be set for those who are accountable; actual conduct, performance, achievement, quality and so on can be measured and compared with those standards by reference to known criteria; and the process of measurement and comparison requires special skill and the exercise of judgement.
6. The meaning, significance and intention of financial and other statements and data which are audited are sufficiently clear that the credibility which is given thereto as a result of audit can be clearly expressed and communicated.
7. An audit produces an economic or social benefit.

Reviewing these postulates, it may be seen that postulates 1, 2, 5 and 7 correspond with material presented in Chapter 1. The fundamental truth of the other postulates underpins, and should become evident as we discuss, the audit process in later chapters.

3.2.3 Framework for key concepts of auditing

Concepts of auditing are general notions that underlie audit practices and procedures. As indicated in Figure 3.1, the key concepts can usefully be categorised into four main groups, namely, those relating to:

- the credibility of auditors' work [auditors' independence and objectivity, competence and ethical conduct (including integrity)];
- the audit process (evidence, materiality, audit risk, judgment and scepticism);
- the communication of audit conclusions (reporting);
- the standard of auditors' work (due care and quality control).

We discuss each of these concepts below.

3.3 CONCEPTS RELATING TO THE CREDIBILITY OF AUDITORS' WORK

3.3.1 Concept of independence and objectivity

3.3.1a   Independence: the cornerstone of auditing

As may be seen from Figure 3.1, independence has a unique status within auditing. It figures amongst the postulates: it is assumed, as a fundamental truth, that the audit function is independent; it is also a key concept – a characteristic that is essential for ensuring the credibility of auditors' work. Indeed, independence has been referred to as 'the cornerstone [the very heart] of auditing' (Stewart, 1977; Levitt, 2000; Haber, 2005): without independence an audit is virtually worthless.

Let us examine this more closely. Auditors are intermediaries between the directors/senior executives of an entity and external parties interested in the entity. They have a duty to form and express an opinion on, *inter alia*, whether or not the entity's financial statements (prepared by management for use by shareholders and others outside the entity) provide a true and fair view of the entity's financial position and performance. If users of the financial statements are to believe and rely on the auditor's opinion, it is essential that the auditor is, and is perceived to be, independent of the entity, its management and all other influences. This is reflected in the fundamental principle of external auditing – *Objectivity and independence*, which states:

> Auditors are objective and provide impartial opinions unaffected by bias, preju-
> dice, compromise and conflicts of interest. Auditors are also independent; this
> requires them to be free from situations and relationships which would make it
> probable that a reasonable and informed third party would conclude that the
> auditors' objectivity either is impaired or could be impaired. (Auditing Practices
> Board, 2008a, Appendix 2)

If auditors are considered not to be independent of the client entity and its
management, their opinion will carry little credibility and users of the financial
statements will gain little, if any, assurance from the auditor's report about the
truth and fairness (or otherwise) of the financial statements. As a consequence,
the audit will have little purpose or value.

The importance of auditors' independence – to both investors and the wider
economy – was conveyed succinctly by Turner (2001), former Chief Accountant
of the Securities and Exchange Commission (SEC) in the USA, when he
stated:

> The enduring confidence of the investing public in the integrity of our capital
> markets is vital. . . . [The capital they invest] is providing the fuel for our economic
> engine, funding for the growth of new businesses, . . . and job opportunities for
> tens of millions of workers. But . . . the willingness of investors to continue to
> invest their money in the markets cannot be taken for granted. . . . Public trust
> begins, and ends, with the integrity of the numbers the public uses to form the
> basis for making their investment decisions. . . . [I]t is the report of the indepen-
> dent auditor that provides investors with the critical assurance that the numbers
> in the financial statements have been subjected to an impartial, unbiased, and
> rigorous examination by a skilled professional. But in order for that report to
> have credibility with investors, to add value to the process and investors, it must
> be issued by a person or firm that *the investor* perceives is free of all conflicts –
> conflicts that may or will in part, weight on or impair the auditor's judgments
> about the accuracy of the numbers. (pp. 1–2)

3.3.1b Meaning of independence in the auditing context

Given the importance of independence to the audit function, it is clearly important to examine what the concept means. However, as will be seen below, the
auditing profession has been grappling with finding appropriate terms to
explain the concept.

It is well accepted that independence, in the sense of being self-reliant and
not subordinating one's professional judgment to the opinions of others, is
a fundamental hallmark of all professions. However, in auditing the term
means rather more than this. In essence it means maintaining an independent attitude of mind and also avoiding situations which would tend to
impair, or could be perceived as tending to impair, objectivity or to create
personal bias. Until recent years, these two forms of independence were

usually referred to as 'independence in fact' and 'independence in appearance'. The International Federation of Accountants (IFAC) has continued to define the term 'independence' with this dual meaning. In its *Code of ethics for professional accountants* (2006*, Definitions), 'independence' is defined as follows:

> Independence is:
> (a) Independence of mind – the state of mind that permits the expression of a conclusion without being affected by influences that compromise professional judgment, thereby allowing an individual to act with integrity, and exercise objectivity and professional skepticism.
> (b) Independence in appearance – the avoidance of facts and circumstances that are so significant that a reasonable and informed third party would be likely to conclude, weighing all the specific facts and circumstances, that a firm's, or a member of the audit team's, integrity, objectivity or professional skepticism has been compromised.

Seeking to distinguish between the two forms of independence, the Auditing Practices Board (APB), in Ethical Standard (ES) 1: *Integrity, objectivity and independence* (2008b), has adopted two separate terms – 'objectivity' for 'independence in mind' and 'independence' for 'independence in appearance'.[4] It explains:

- Objectivity is a state of mind that excludes bias, prejudice and compromise and that gives fair and impartial consideration to all matters that are relevant to the task in hand, disregarding those that are not. Objectivity requires that the auditors' judgment is not affected by conflicts of interest. (para 9)
- Independence is freedom from situations and relationships which make it probable that a reasonable and informed third party would conclude that objectivity either is impaired or could be impaired. Independence is related to and underpins objectivity. However, whereas objectivity is a personal behavioural characteristic concerning the auditor's state of mind, independence relates to the circumstances surrounding the audit, including the financial, employment, business and personal relationships between the auditor and the audited entity. (para 12)

If interested parties are to rely on the auditor's opinion, it is clearly essential that the auditor is both objective and independent when conducting the audit and expressing an opinion in the audit report. Indeed, to stipulate that auditors must be objective and independent (or independent in both mind and appearance) may seem to be a straightforward and obvious requirement. However,

---

[4] IFAC, in its *Code of Ethics for Professional Accountants* (2006), distinguishes between objectivity and the two forms of independence. It recognises objectivity as a fundamental principle with which all professional accountants are required to comply. It expresses it in the following terms (para 100.4b):

> *Objectivity* – A professional accountant should not allow bias, conflict of interest or undue influence of others to override professional or business judgments.

in practice, such independence may be difficult to achieve and easy to compromise. This issue is explored in detail in Chapter 4.

3.3.2 Concept of competence

If auditors' opinions are to have credibility and be relied upon by users of financial statements, auditors must be regarded as competent. According to Flint (1988): "Audit competence requires both knowledge and skill, which are the products of education, training and experience" (p. 48). The fundamental principle of external auditing – *Competence* – conveys similar ideas but goes a little further in explaining the requirements of auditors' competence. It states:

> Auditors act with professional skill, derived from their qualification, training and practical experience. This demands an understanding of financial reporting and business issues, together with expertise in accumulating and assessing the evidence necessary to form an opinion. (APB, 2008a, Appendix 2)

Both Flint and the fundamental principle (cited above) indicate that 'competence' involves *acquiring*, and *applying*, "knowledge and skill" (Flint) or "professional skills" (fundamental principle). International Education Standard (IES) 8: *Competence requirements for audit professionals*,[5] makes this two-fold notion explicit in its distinction between 'capabilities' and 'competence'. It defines these terms as follows (para 8):
- **Capabilities** The professional knowledge; professional skills; and professional values, ethics, and attitudes required to demonstrate competence.
- **Competence** Being able to perform a work role to a defined standard with reference to real working environments.

From these definitions it is clear that acquiring capabilities is a necessary prerequisite of, and integral to, auditors performing their work competently.

IES 8 expands on its definition of capabilities by outlining the components of the 'knowledge', 'skills' and 'values, ethics and attitudes' required by audit professionals.
- With respect to knowledge, IES 8 (paras 32–40) notes that auditors need to be informed about:
    - (i) best practices employed in the audits of historical financial information;

---

[5] IES 8 defines an audit professional as:

> a professional accountant who has responsibility, or has been delegated responsibility, for significant audit judgments in an audit of historical financial information. (para 9)

It therefore includes the audit engagement partner (the individual responsible for the audit) and senior members of the audit team.

    (ii)   financial accounting and reporting processes and practices;

    (iii) relevant current issues and developments in audit practices and financial accounting and reporting;

    (iv) International Standards on Auditing (ISAs), the International Standard on Quality Control (ISQC) 1, International Auditing Practice Statements (IAPs) and International Financial Reporting Standards (IFRS);

    (v)   other applicable auditing and accounting standards or laws;

    (vi) information technology (IT) systems for financial accounting and reporting, and related current issues and developments;

    (vii) IT frameworks for evaluating controls and assessing risks in accounting and reporting systems as appropriate for the audit of historical financial information.

- As regards professional skills, IES 8 (para 42) specifies that auditors need to be able to:

  (a) apply the following in the audit environment:
  - (i)   identifying and solving problems;
  - (ii) undertaking appropriate technical research;
  - (iii) working in teams effectively;
  - (iv) gathering and evaluating evidence;
  - (v) presenting, discussing, and defending views effectively through formal, informal, written, and spoken communication; and

  (b) develop the following skills to an advanced level in an audit environment:
  - (i)   applying relevant audit standards and guidance;
  - (ii) evaluating applications of relevant financial reporting standards;
  - (iii) demonstrating capacity for inquiry, abstract logical thought, and critical analysis;
  - (iv) demonstrating professional skepticism;
  - (v) applying professional judgment; and
  - (vi) withstanding and resolving conflict.

- With respect to professional values, ethics and attitudes, auditors need to be able to:

  (a) apply the fundamental principles that constitute the foundation of IFAC's *Code of Ethics* (2006), namely, integrity, objectivity, professional competence and due care, confidentiality, and professional behaviour, and

  (b) understand the consequences of unethical behaviour and how to resolve ethical dilemmas.

  In relation to this component of auditors' capabilities, IES 8 explains:

  > It is important that audit professionals are
  > (a) aware of potential new ethical dimensions and conflicts in their work; and

(b) keep current on the expectations of their professional accounting bodies and the public in terms of professional ethics. (para 53)

Having outlined the capabilities auditors require to enable them to be competent, we need to consider how they acquire these capabilities. Broadly, they are acquired through a combination of general and technical accounting education, on-the-job training and work experience. Flint (1988), observing that "auditing is intellectually demanding, requiring a trained mind and the capacity for exercise of judgement" (p. 48), gives particular emphasis to the contribution of general education to auditors' competence. He notes:

> A broad general education cultivating the habit of systematic thinking and mental discipline, combined with a basic understanding of the principal fields of knowledge and ability for expression and communication orally and in writing, are an essential foundation. . . . [A]uditing requires much more than a knowledge of its own theory or philosophy and the principles of its peculiar investigative process: it requires an understanding of the nature, structure, institutions and law of the society in which it is applied. And in relation to particular audits it requires a knowledge of the activity in respect of which the conduct, performance or information has to be addressed. (pp. 48–49)

International Standard on Quality Control (ISQC) 1: *Quality control for firms that perform audits and reviews of financial statements, and other assurance and related services engagements* also provides guidance on how auditors acquire their required capabilities and competence. It explains (para A24):

> Capabilities and competence can be developed through a variety of methods, including the following:
> • Professional education.
> • Continuing professional development, including training.
> • Work experience.
> • Coaching by more experienced staff, for example, other members of the engagement team.
> • Independence education for personnel who are required to be independent.

Although auditors acquire their capabilities and competence by a number means, the process is not haphazard. As Flint (1988, p. 51) points out, if auditors are to gain the public's confidence in the credibility of their work, they must be able to demonstrate that they have obtained a recognised reputable qualification – one that requires them to successfully complete a formalised programme of education, training and experience. Flint further notes:

> Audit is a matter of such social importance that the state has a responsibility to be satisfied in the public interest that appropriate standards of knowledge, training and experience are prescribed and that an adequate standard of proficiency is achieved. (p. 51)

As will be seen in Chapter 5 (section 5.2.3), in the United Kingdom (UK) this is achieved through legislation that requires the auditors of companies to be 'registered', and specifies, among other things, that in order to be registered, auditors must be suitably qualified and supervised.

However, acquiring capabilities and competence is not the end of the story for auditors (or for other professional accountants). IFAC, in its *Code of ethics for professional accountants* (2006), when explaining the fundamental principle of competence, states:

> A professional accountant has a *continuing duty to maintain professional knowledge and skill* at the level required to ensure that a client or employer receives competent professional service based on current developments in practice, legislation and techniques. (para 100.4c; emphasis added).

Expanding on this principle, the *Code of ethics* notes:

> Competent professional service requires the exercise of sound judgment in applying professional knowledge and skill in the performance of such service. Professional competence may be divided into two separate phases:
> (a) Attainment of professional competence; and
> (b) Maintenance of professional competence. (para 130.2)
> The maintenance of professional competence requires a continuing awareness and an understanding of relevant technical professional and business developments. (para 130.3)

ISQC 1, which relates to audit firms[6] rather than professional accountants in general, similarly underlines the importance of maintaining professional competence. It also expands on how this may be achieved. It explains:

> The continuing competence of the [audit] firm's personnel depends to a significant extent on an appropriate level of continuing professional development so that personnel maintain their knowledge and capabilities. Effective policies and procedures emphasize the need for continuing training for all levels of firm personnel, and provide the necessary training resources and assistance to enable personnel to develop and maintain the required capabilities and competence. (para A25)

It should be noted that most professional accounting bodies, including those in the UK, require their members to undertake continuing professional development as a condition of continued membership. Further, for all statutory auditors in the European Union (EU) continuing education is a compulsory requirement. The EU 8th Directive states:

> Member States shall ensure that statutory auditors are required to take part in appropriate programmes of continuing education in order to maintain their theoretical knowledge, professional skills and values at a sufficiently high level, and that failure to respect the continuing education requirements is subject to appropriate penalties. (Art. 13)

---

[6] Also to firms that perform reviews of historical financial information and other assurance and related services engagements.

The concept of competence is particularly relevant to the topics of 'staffing an audit' and 'controlling the quality of audit work'. These are discussed in Chapters 7 and 16, respectively.

3.3.3   Concept of ethical conduct and integrity

As shown in Figure 3.1, the credibility of auditors' work rests on auditors being regarded as independent, competent and adhering to ethical conduct. But what is ethical conduct? And how does it impact on the credibility of auditors' work?

Flint (1988) provides an answer when he observes:

> Public trust and confidence in auditors are dependent on a continuing belief in their unqualified integrity, objectivity, and, in appropriate circumstances, acceptance of a duty to the public interest, with a consequential subordination of self-interest. Creating and retaining trust and confidence, therefore, requires auditors to show certain characteristics, which are those commonly associated with employments which are recognised and sanctioned by society as professions. (p. 87)

Thus, in order to retain the public's confidence in the credibility of their work, auditors must adhere to standards of ethical conduct: standards of conduct that embody and demonstrate integrity, objectivity and concern for the public (rather than self-) interest.

As for all other professions, the conduct expected of members of the auditing profession is set out in a Code of Ethics.[7] In 1996 IFAC published its first *Code of ethics for professional accountants*. This was revised in 1998, 2001, 2004, 2005 and 2006. In the Preface to its 2006 *Code*, IFAC explains:

> The mission of the International Federation of Accountants (IFAC) ... is "to serve the public interest, IFAC will continue to strengthen the worldwide accountancy profession and contribute to the development of strong international economics by establishing and promoting adherence to high quality professional standards, furthering the international convergence of such standards and speaking out on public interest issues where the profession's expertise is most relevant". In pursuing this mission, the IFAC Board has established the Ethics Standards Board for Accountants to develop and issue ... high quality ethical standards ... for professional accountants for use around the world.

> This *Code of Ethics for Professional Accountants* establishes ethical requirements for professional accountants. A member body of IFAC [including, the Institutes

---

[7] A Code of Ethics may have various titles, for example, a Guide to Ethical Conduct, Code of Professional Conduct, Guide to Professional Ethics, etc. but, in essence, the content is the same. It sets out the conduct expected of members of the profession (or of the professional body) in question.

of Chartered Accountants in England and Wales, of Scotland, and of Ireland, and the Association of Chartered Certified Accountants] . . . may not apply less stringent standards than those stated in this Code.[8]

Central to the Code are five fundamental principles with which professional accountants are required to comply, and a conceptual framework for applying those principles. The five principles relate to professional accountants' integrity, objectivity, professional competence and due care, confidentiality, and professional behaviour. The principles of objectivity and professional competence were cited above in sections 3.3.1b and 3.3.2, respectively, and the principle of due care (which IFAC combines with professional competence) is discussed in section 3.6.1 below. IFAC (2006) defines the fundamental principles of integrity, confidentiality and professional behaviour in the following terms (para 100.4):

(a) *Integrity*: A professional accountant should be straightforward and honest in all professional and business relationships.

(d) *Confidentiality*: A professional accountant should respect the confidentiality of information acquired as a result of professional and business relationships and should not disclose any such information to third parties without proper and specific authority unless there is a legal or professional right or duty to disclose. Confidential information . . . should not be used for the personal advantage of the professional accountant or third parties.[9]

(e) *Professional Behavior*: A professional accountant should comply with relevant laws and regulations and should avoid any action that discredits the profession.

In relation to the principle of integrity, the Code explains: "Integrity also implies fair dealing and truthfulness" (para 110.1).

Although the IFAC *Code of ethics* applies to all professional accountants (not just to auditors), the essence of its fundamental principles of integrity and confidentiality are embodied in the fundamental principle of external

---

[8] In the UK and Ireland, each professional accounting body has issued its own Code of Ethics (with varying titles) based on the IFAC *Code of ethics for professional accountants*. However, in January 2003, following the Enron, WorldCom and similar debacles, the UK government, as part of its measures to reform regulation of the accounting profession, determined that the APB should take over responsibility for setting standards for the independence, objectivity and integrity of auditors. From April 2004, the APB became one of six 'operating bodies' of the Financial Reporting Council (FRC: see footnote 35 for more details about the FRC). To date, the APB has issued five Ethical Standards (ES1 to ES5) in relation to the independence, objectivity and integrity of auditors. (These are discussed in detail in Chapter 4.) The APB explains that, in developing these standards, it "sought to ensure that the Ethical Standards adhere to the principles of the IFAC Code" (APB, 2008a, para 10). Ethical issues other than those covered by ES1 to ES5 remain the responsibility of the individual professional bodies (ES1, para 5).

[9] The topic of client confidentiality is discussed in Chapter 6, section 6.5.

auditing – *Integrity* – included in the APB's Auditors' Code.[10] This principle states:

> Auditors act with integrity, fulfilling their responsibilities with honesty, fairness, candour, courage and confidentiality. Confidential information obtained in the course of the audit is disclosed only when required in the public interest, or by operation of law. (APB, 2008a, Appendix 2)

In addition to specifying five fundamental ethical principles, the IFAC *Code of ethics* also provides a conceptual framework for applying those principles. It recognises the impossibility of trying to define every situation in which accountants might find themselves which poses a threat to their compliance with one or more of the fundamental principles and, similarly, the impossibility of identifying appropriate measures to mitigate the particular threat(s). So, instead of trying to achieve the impossible, the Code provides a conceptual framework "to assist a professional accountant to identify, evaluate and respond to threats to compliance with the fundamental principles" (para 100.5). It also explains:

> If identified threats are other than clearly insignificant, a professional accountant should, where appropriate, apply safeguards to eliminate the threats or reduce them to an acceptable level, such that compliance with the fundamental principles is not compromised. (para 100.5)

3.4 CONCEPTS RELATING TO THE AUDIT PROCESS

3.4.1 Concept of evidence

3.4.1a Necessity of sufficient appropriate evidence for an audit

It was shown in Chapter 2 that the primary objective of an audit is to provide credibility to an auditee's financial statements (which are prepared by the auditee's management), by the auditor expressing an opinion on the truth and fairness (or otherwise) of the financial statements. Auditors can only express such an opinion if they are able to examine sufficient appropriate evidence to form an opinion. If no evidence exists in relation to the subject matter on which an auditor is to express an opinion, then there can be no audit. The fundamental necessity of the existence of evidence for an audit to take place is reflected in postulate 4 cited in section 3.2.2 above, that is:

> The subject matter of audit, for example conduct, performance or achievement, or record of events or state of affairs, or a statement of facts relating to any of these, is susceptible to verification by evidence.

---

[10] *The Auditors' Code* is reproduced on the inside of the front cover of this book.

The key task of the auditor is to obtain sufficient appropriate audit evidence on which to base an audit opinion. International Standard on Auditing (ISA) 500: *Audit evidence* (para 5) defines the terms 'sufficient' and 'appropriate' as follows:

> Sufficiency of audit evidence – The measure of the quantity of audit evidence. The quantity of audit evidence needed is affected by the auditor's assessment of the risks of material misstatement[11] and also by the quality of such audit evidence.

> Appropriateness of audit evidence – The measure of the quality of audit evidence; that is, its relevance and its reliability in providing support for the conclusions on which the auditor's opinion is based.

From these definitions it is clear that the sufficiency and appropriateness of audit evidence are interrelated. All other things being equal, the more appropriate the audit evidence, the less that is required (and *vice versa*).[12]

ISA 500 makes it clear that there is a direct relationship between audit procedures (the means of gathering audit evidence), audit evidence *per se*, and the auditor's opinion; the auditor performs audit procedures to gather evidence, evaluates that evidence and, based on that evaluation, forms and expresses an opinion about the truth and fairness of the financial statements. This relationship is presented diagrammatically in Figure 3.2.

Figure 3.2: Relationship between audit procedures, evidence and the auditor's opinion

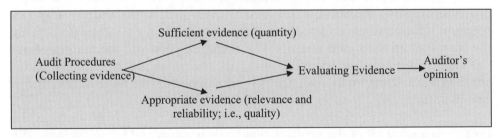

Having established the necessity of sufficient appropriate evidence for an audit to take place, we need to consider the meaning and nature of audit evidence.

3.4.1b Definition of audit evidence

ISA 500 defines audit evidence in the following terms:

---

[11] 'Risks of material misstatement' refers to the likelihood of material errors being present in the financial statements. The concept of materiality is discussed in section 3.4.2.

[12] The relationship between the sufficiency and appropriateness of audit evidence is discussed in detail in Chapter 7, section 7.4.4.

> Audit evidence – Information used by the auditor in arriving at the conclusions on which the audit opinion is based. Audit evidence includes both information contained in the accounting records underlying the financial statements and other information. (para 5)

The second part of this definition seems rather to limit its scope and, as a result, it does not convey the all-embracing nature of audit evidence. A rather more useful definition has been provided by Anderson (1977). To him, audit evidence is:

> any perceived object, action or condition relevant to the formation of a knowledgeable opinion on the financial statements. Perceived objects may include certain tangible assets (such as cash funds, inventories, and fixed assets), various documents, accounting records and reports, and written representations. Perceived actions generally consist of certain procedures performed by the client's employees. Perceived conditions may include the observed quality of assets, the apparent competence of employees met, the care with which procedures were seen to be performed, or an identified logical relationship with other facts known to the auditor. (p. 251)

Thus, in auditing, 'evidence' means all of the facts, information and impressions auditors acquire which help them to form an opinion about, *inter alia*, the truth and fairness of the financial statements under review and their compliance (or otherwise) with relevant legislation and regulations.

3.4.1c   The nature of audit evidence

Unlike scientific evidence, audit evidence does not consist of hard facts which prove or disprove the accuracy of financial statements. Instead, it comprises pieces of information and impressions which are gradually accumulated during the course of an audit and which, taken together, persuade the auditor about the truth and fairness (or otherwise) of the financial statements under consideration. Thus, audit evidence is generally persuasive rather than conclusive in nature.

Furthermore, not all of the available evidence is examined by an auditor. The purpose of an audit is not to *prove* or *disprove* the accuracy of the financial statements. If it were, auditors would have to collect and evaluate as much evidence as possible. Instead, the objective is to form an *opinion* as to whether or not the financial statements under review give a true and fair view of the financial position and performance of the reporting entity. To accomplish this, auditors need only gather sufficient appropriate evidence to support their opinion. Thus, for example, rather than examining all of the evidence which is available, auditors usually test only samples of data.

Although only part, rather than all, of the available evidence is examined, when evidence derived from different sources is consistent, it has a reinforcing effect. Conversely, when evidence is inconsistent, it has an undermining effect. For example, an auditor may wish to reach a conclusion about a particular financial statement assertion (for example, about the ownership or value of an asset) using evidence from different sources and/or of different types. When such evidence is consistent, the auditor gains cumulative assurance about the assertion in question. (That is, the assurance the auditor gains regarding the truth and fairness of the assertion is greater than that obtained from the individual pieces of evidence by themselves.) However, when evidence from different sources or of different types is inconsistent, further evidence usually needs to be obtained in order to resolve the inconsistency.

The procedures used to gather audit evidence, and the various types and sources of evidence available to auditors, are discussed in detail in Chapter 7.

3.4.2 Concept of materiality

3.4.2a *Meaning of materiality in the auditing context*

ISA 200: *Overall objectives of the independent auditor, and the conduct of an audit in accordance with International Standards on Auditing*, states:

> The purpose of an audit is to enhance the degree of confidence of intended users in the financial statements. This is achieved by the expression of an opinion by the auditor on whether the financial statements are prepared, in all *material* respects, in accordance with an applicable financial reporting framework. (para 4, emphasis added)

From this statement it is clear that the term 'material' is of critical importance in the auditing context. But, what does the term mean?

ISA 320: *Materiality in planning and performing an audit*, explains:

> - Misstatements, including omissions, are considered to be material if they, individually or in the aggregate, could reasonably be expected to influence the economic decisions of users taken on the basis of the financial statements;
> - Judgments about materiality are made in light of surrounding circumstances, and are affected by the size or nature of a misstatement, or a combination of both; and
> - Judgments about matters that are material to users of the financial statements are based on a consideration of the common financial information needs of users as a group. The possible effect of misstatements on specific individual users, whose needs may vary widely, is not considered. (para 2)

From this explanation it may be seen that the term 'materiality' needs to be understood in the context of users of the financial statements as a group. ISA 320 (para 4) explains this further as follows:

> The auditor's determination of materiality is a matter of professional judgment, and is affected by the auditor's perception of the financial information needs of the users of the financial statements. In this context, it is reasonable for the auditor to assume that users:

(a) Have a reasonable knowledge of business and economic activities and accounting and a willingness to study the information in the financial statements with reasonable diligence;

(b) Understand that financial statements are prepared, presented and audited to levels of materiality;

(c) Recognize the uncertainties inherent in the measurement of amounts based on the use of estimates, judgment and the consideration of future events; and

(d) Make reasonable economic decisions on the basis of the information in the financial statements.

From ISA 320, paras 2 and 4 (cited above), it is clear that, when auditors determine the materiality to apply during an audit, they need to consider how users, with the characteristics outlined above, may reasonably be expected to be influenced by misstatements (including omissions) in the financial statements when making economic decisions based on those financial statements.

3.4.2b Characteristics of materiality

Having considered the meaning of materiality, and noted the importance of users of the financial statements in determining what is to be judged 'material', we can turn our attention to the characteristics of the concept. In the auditing context, materiality has a number of characterising features. These include the following:

(i) Deciding what is, and what is not, material in any given circumstance is a matter of professional judgment.

(ii) An item may be material by virtue of its size or its nature.

(iii) Materiality needs to be considered at two levels:
  – the financial statements as a whole, and
  – individual classes of transactions, account balances or disclosures.

We examine each of these characteristics below.

(i) A matter of professional judgment

ISA 320 (para A3) notes: "Determining materiality involves the exercise of professional judgment". However, the paragraph also provides guidance to auditors on how materiality for the financial statements as a whole[13] may be established. It explains:

> A percentage is often applied to a chosen benchmark as a starting point in determining materiality for the financial statements as a whole. Factors that may affect the identification of an appropriate benchmark include the following:

---

[13] *Prima facie*, if omissions and/or misstatements in the financial statements as a whole exceed this level (or amount) determined for materiality, the auditor will conclude that the financial statements are materially misstated and, unless the auditee's directors rectify the error(s), the auditor cannot issue a 'clean' audit report on the financial statements. (The various types of audit report are explained in Chapter 14.)

- The elements of the financial statements (for example, assets, liabilities, equity, income and expenses);
- Whether there are items on which the attention of the users of the particular entity's financial statements tends to be focused (for example, for the purpose of evaluating financial performance users may tend to focus on profit, revenue or net assets);
- The nature of the entity, where the entity is in its life cycle, and the industry and economic environment in which the entity operates;
- The entity's ownership structure and the way it is financed (for example, if an entity is financed solely by debt rather than equity, users may put more emphasis on assets, and claims on them, than on the entity's earnings); and
- The relative volatility of the benchmark. (para A3)

> Examples of benchmarks that may be appropriate, depending on the circumstances of the entity, include categories of reported income such as profit before tax, total revenue, gross profit and total expenses, total equity or net asset value. (para A4)

In Chapter 9 (Figure 9.1), we will see that the benchmarks selected by various audit firms, and the percentages applied to those benchmarks, vary quite widely. But, whatever the benchmarks and percentages used to establish materiality, it is important to recognise that the exercise does not generate a 'magic number' such that any errors or omissions greater than that number will be adjudged 'material', and errors or omissions smaller than that number are considered to be 'immaterial'. In every case, auditors must exercise their professional judgment when determining materiality and when deciding whether, in the particular circumstances, omissions and/or misstatements are material.

(ii)   Size vs nature of an omission or misstatement

When determining whether an omission or misstatement is material, it is not only its size which is relevant; its nature is also significant. As ISA 320 observes:

> Judgments about materiality ... are affected by the size or nature of a misstatement, or a combination of both; ... Although it is not practicable to design audit procedures to detect misstatements that could be material solely because of their nature, the auditor considers not only the size but also the nature of uncorrected misstatements, and the particular circumstances of their occurrence, when evaluating their effect on the financial statements. (paras 2, 6)

Factors relating to the nature of items that may affect the auditor's judgment as to their materiality include the following:

- Whether law, regulations or the applicable financial reporting framework affect users' expectations regarding the measurement or disclosure of certain items (for example, related party transactions, and the remuneration of management and those charged with governance).
- The key disclosures in relation to the industry in which the entity operates (for example, research and development costs for a pharmaceutical company).
- Whether attention is focused on a particular aspect of the entity's business that is separately disclosed in the financial statements (for example, a newly acquired business). (ISA 320, para A10)

Thus, a misstatement of directors' remuneration may be very small relative to the entity's profit and *prima facie* would be considered immaterial. However, the nature of the item may be of such sensitivity that even a small inaccuracy would be material. Similarly, the omission of a financial statement amount or disclosure that is required by law, regulation, and/or accounting standards will normally be regarded as material. For example, disclosure of audit fees is required by the Companies Act 2006, s. 494,[14] and disclosure by lessees of finance lease liabilities, classified into the amounts of minimum lease payments at balance sheet date and the present value thereof (i) for the next year, (ii) years two to five inclusive (as a combined total) and (iii) beyond five years, is required by International Accounting Standard (IAS) 17, para 31. In most cases, failure to disclose such item(s) will be regarded by the auditor as a material omission. Along similar lines, if an accounting policy or other financial statement disclosure is described so inadequately or inaccurately that it is likely that financial statement users could be misled by the description, the auditor would judge this to be a material misstatement.

(iii) Materiality at overall (financial statement) and account balance or disclosure level

Overall materiality refers to the maximum amount of error (through omission and/or misstatement) the auditor is prepared to accept in the financial statements as a whole while still concluding that they provide a true and fair view of the auditee's financial performance and financial position. It is the amount of error the auditor considers may be present in the financial statements without affecting the economic decisions of reasonable users of those financial statements.

---

[14] The Companies (Disclosure of Auditor Remuneration and Liability Limitation Agreements) Regulations 2008, came into force on 6 April 2008. These regulations replaced The Companies (Disclosure of Auditor Remuneration) Regulations 2005, which became effective on 1 October 2005. The latter were made by the Secretary of State in accordance with powers originally conferred on him by the Companies Act (CA) 1985, s. 390B, as amended by the Companies (Audit, Investigations and Community Enterprise) Act 2004, s. 7. The statutory provision of the CA 1985, s. 390B (as amended), has been incorporated in s. 494 of the CA 2006.

Account balance or disclosure level materiality refers to the maximum amount of error an auditor will accept in a particular class of transactions, account balance or financial statement disclosure before concluding that the relevant financial statement account balance or disclosure may mislead reasonable financial statement users. In this book, we adopt the term 'tolerable error' to denote this level of materiality.

As for establishing materiality for the financial statements as a whole, auditors may determine the tolerable error for a class of transactions or account balance by applying a percentage to a benchmark. For example:
- tolerable error for income (or profit and loss) statement accounts may be calculated based on a percentage (say, five or 10 per cent) of profit before tax and exceptional items for continuing operations for the current year, or the average pre-tax profit for continuing operations for the last, say, three years (including the current year), whichever is the more relevant measure of profit (or loss) having regard to the trend of business over the period; and
- tolerable error for balance sheet accounts may be based on a percentage of the lower of:
  - total shareholders' funds, and
  - the appropriate balance sheet class total, for example, current assets, fixed assets, current liabilities, long-term liabilities.

It should be noted that materiality established for the financial statements as a whole or for individual classes of transactions or account balances is only a starting point. Even where omissions and/or misstatements fall below materiality, their nature must be considered, as must the circumstances surrounding the omission(s) or misstatement(s), the reporting entity and the users of the entity's financial statements. These issues are discussed in detail in Chapter 9.

3.4.3 Concept of audit risk

3.4.3a Definition of audit risk

The International Auditing and Assurance Board's (IASSB) *Glossary of terms* (2007) states:

> Audit risk is the risk that the auditor expresses an inappropriate audit opinion when the financial statements are materially misstated.

Technically speaking, this is only half of the story. Audit risk is more correctly defined as 'the risk that the auditor may issue an inappropriate opinion on financial statements'. Expressed in this way, it is evident that audit risk has two forms:

- α risk: the risk that the auditor may express a *qualified* opinion (say something is amiss) on financial statements that are *not* materially misstated; and
- β risk: the risk that the auditor may express an *unqualified* ('clean') opinion on financial statements that *are* materially misstated.

The risk of an auditor expressing a qualified opinion on financial statements that are not materially misstated is very unlikely. Before qualifying the audit report, the auditor will need good reasons for doing so, and such reasons will need to be justified to the relevant company's directors. If the auditor has drawn invalid conclusions about the financial statements, these are likely to come to light during this 'justification process'. Thus, as may be deduced from the extract from the IAASB's *Glossary of terms* quoted above, the term 'audit risk' is commonly used to mean β risk. Ultimately, to the auditor, audit risk amounts to exposure to legal liability if, as a result of issuing a 'clean' audit report on financial statements which are materially misstated, a user of the financial statements is misled and suffers a loss as a consequence. However, as we noted in section 3.4.1 above, auditors are required to *express an opinion* on the financial statements, not to *certify* their truth and fairness. As a result, some degree of audit risk is always present. Consequently, legal action against an auditor is likely to succeed only if the auditor deliberately or negligently accepts an unreasonably high level of audit risk (that is, the auditor fails to conduct an adequate audit before issuing a 'clean' audit report on materially misstated financial statements).

3.4.3b Components of audit risk

Audit risk comprises two main components, namely:

(i) the risk that, prior to the audit, the financial statements are materially misstated. This risk of material misstatement occurring results from inherent risk and internal control risk;

(ii) the risk that the auditor will fail to detect material misstatement which is present in the financial statements prior to the audit. This component is referred to as detection risk and comprises sampling risk and quality control risk.[15]

These components of audit risk are shown in Figure 3.3 and discussed below.

---

[15] IAASB's *Glossary of terms* recognises as separate audit risk components, inherent risk, control risk and detection risk. Control risk, as defined in the *Glossary*, equates with what we term internal control risk, and detection risk embraces both sampling risk and quality control risk.

Figure 3.3: The components of audit risk

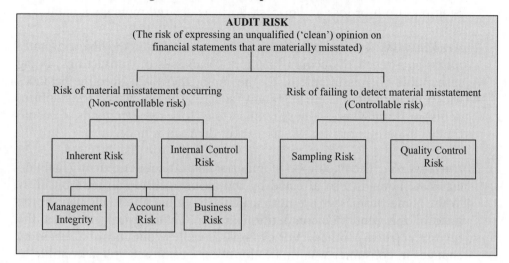

(i) *The risk that material misstatement is present (risk of misstatement occurring)*

The likelihood of material misstatement occurring in the financial statements prior to the audit is, for the most part, beyond the auditor's control. This component of audit risk results from two factors, inherent risk and internal control risk.

- **Inherent risk**: This is the risk or likelihood of material misstatement being present in the financial statements in the absence of internal controls (that is, controls designed to prevent misstatements from occurring). As may be seen from Figure 3.3, inherent risk derives from three main sources. These are as follows:

  1. *Management integrity*: The likelihood of material misstatement being present in the financial statements prior to the audit is strongly influenced by the integrity of the auditee's management. This integrity has two aspects:
     (a) *inherent integrity*, that is, management's moral and ethical stance; its 'natural' tendency towards being honest or dishonest; and
     (b) *situational integrity*, that is, management's ability to withstand temptation to misrepresent the company's financial position, profit or loss and/or its cash flows in situations of pressure. For example, when the entity has failed to meet profit forecasts, or when there are plans to float new shares and the year's profit has been small, management may be tempted to 'artificially improve' the entity's reported profit.
     Where a company's management lacks integrity, the information presented in the financial statements prior to the audit may well be

manipulated to the extent necessary to portray the company's financial position, profit or loss and/or cash flows as desired by management.

2. *Account risk*: Material misstatement may also occur in the financial statements as a result of account balances (or classes of transactions) being susceptible to misstatement. In the main, these are account balances which involve significant judgment (such as the allowance for doubtful debts) or those where values are uncertain (for example, stands of unsold timber in plantations for which market demand is uncertain).

3. *Business risk*: The likelihood of material misstatement occurring in financial statements is also affected by the nature of the auditee's business. While some businesses are not particularly vulnerable to changes in the state of the economy, competition and/or technological advances, the reverse is true for others. For example, jewellery outlets are affected by changes in consumer wealth; fashion-wear businesses are susceptible to changes in customer 'fads'; businesses in the electronics industry are prone to changes in technology and those in the oil industry are exposed to rapid and large changes in oil prices in world markets. In each case, a high risk attaches to the entity's inventory valuation and possibly also to its ability to sustain operating cash flow at a level necessary to meet its debt obligations. In the latter instance, business risk may generate a situation in which management's integrity is put under pressure.

- **Internal control risk**:[16] This is the risk that material misstatement will occur in the auditee's accounting data (and hence in its financial statements) because it is not prevented, or detected and corrected on a timely basis, by the company's internal controls. Some internal control risk will always be present because any internal control system has inherent limitations.[17] However, the more effective a company's internal controls, the greater the likelihood that material misstatement(s) occurring in its financial statements prior to the audit will be reduced.

In relation to the likelihood of material misstatement being present in an auditee's financial statements, it is pertinent to note that, although auditors have little or no direct control over inherent risk and internal control risk, they can and should be aware of the circumstances in which these risks are likely to be high. They can perform procedures to ascertain whether these circumstances are present in any given audit and adjust their audit effort and techniques

---

[16] As noted in footnote 15, IAASB's *Glossary of terms* refers to this type of risk as 'control risk'.

[17] The inherent limitations of internal control systems are discussed in Chapter 10.

accordingly. (Evaluating the integrity of the client's management and evaluating internal control risk are discussed in Chapters 8 and 10, respectively.)

(ii) The risk that material misstatement will not be detected (detection risk)

Unlike the risk of material misstatement occurring in the financial statements prior to the audit, the risk of auditors failing to detect such misstatement is subject to their direct control. As Figure 3.3 shows, this component of audit risk derives from sampling risk and quality control risk.[18]

- **Sampling risk**: This is the risk that the auditor may fail to detect material misstatement present in the financial statements because not all of the available evidence is examined and those particular transactions or account balances which include a material misstatement are not included in the samples of transactions or balances examined during the audit. Alternatively stated, sampling risk:

    Arises from the possibility that the auditor's conclusion, based on a sample may be different from the conclusion reached if the entire population were subjected to the same audit procedure. (IAASB, *Glossary of terms,* 2007)

  When statistical sampling techniques are used, sampling risk is quantifiable and controllable. As explained in Chapter 12, statistical sampling techniques enable sample sizes to be adjusted so that the level of audit (sampling) risk the auditor is prepared to accept may be achieved.

- **Quality control risk**:[19] This is the risk that the auditor will fail to detect material misstatements which are present in the financial statements because sufficient appropriate audit evidence is not collected and/or is not evaluated properly. The IAASB's *Glossary of terms* explains that non-sampling risk:

    Arises from factors that cause the auditor to reach an erroneous conclusion for any reason not related to the size of the sample. For example, most audit evidence is persuasive rather than conclusive, the auditor might use inappropriate procedures, or the auditor might misinterpret evidence and fail to recognize an error.

As with internal control risk, some quality control risk will always be present simply because audits are conducted by humans (who are fallible) and they involve a considerable amount of judgment. Audit staff cannot be expected

---

[18] As indicated in the text which follows, IAASB's *Glossary of terms* distinguishes between sampling and non-sampling risk. In our view, as the latter can be assumed to be proportional to the standard of quality control applied during an audit, the title 'quality control risk' provides a better description than 'non-sampling risk'.

[19] The concept of quality control is discussed in Section 3.6.2 below.

to make optimal judgments, and to perform with perfection, on every occasion throughout an audit. Some human error is inevitable![20]

As noted above, the risk of auditors failing to detect material misstatement present in the financial statements is under their direct control. They should therefore seek to reduce sampling risk and quality control risk (that is, detection risk) to the level it is economically feasible to do so. As explained in Chapter 9, this level varies inversely with the auditor's assessment of inherent risk and internal control risk.

3.4.4 Concept of judgment

Judgment is a fundamental characteristic of all professions – including auditing. The concept encapsulates the notion of evaluating the circumstances and/or available evidence relevant to a known objective and forming an opinion based on that evaluation. It contrasts with achieving an objective by means of following an established set of rules or procedures.

In order for a professional judgment to be sound it is essential that the person exercising it (for example, an auditor) has integrity, is competent, and maintains an objective, unbiased attitude of mind – concepts, as we have already seen, that are central to the credibility of auditors' work.

Judgment pervades every stage of the audit process. As Bell, Peecher and Solomon (2005) observe:

> Professional judgment is the very essence of auditing; it pervasively influences audit quality from beginning to end, and it can be both the primary means by which auditors control non-sampling [i.e., quality control] risk and a major source of it. (p. 18)

ISA 200: *Overall objectives of the independent auditor, and the conduct of an audit* ... (para A22) provides some insight into what the concept involves:

> Professional judgment is essential to the proper conduct of an audit. This is because interpretation of relevant ethical requirements and ISAs and the decisions required throughout the audit cannot be made without the application of relevant knowledge and experience to the facts and circumstances. Professional judgment is necessary in particular regarding decisions about:
> • Materiality and audit risk.
> • The nature, timing, and extent of audit procedures used to meet the requirements of the ISAs and gather audit evidence.
> • Evaluating whether sufficient appropriate audit evidence has been obtained, and whether more needs to be done to achieve the objectives of the ISAs and thereby, the overall objectives of the auditor.

---

[20] In relation to quality control risk, Bell, Peecher and Solomon (2005) state:
> In our view, given today's complex business environment as well as the subjectivity both featured in applicable financial reporting frameworks and associated with the assessment of audit risk components, non-sampling risk is a significant, if not the major, source of DR [detection risk]. Further, the auditor cannot accurately assess and manage sampling risk (e.g., determine a sufficient sample size and draw implications from sample findings to the population of interest) unless he or she properly assesses and manages non-sampling risk. (p. 10)

- The evaluation of management's judgment in applying the entity's applicable financial reporting framework.
- The drawing of conclusions based on the audit evidence obtained, for example, assessing the reasonableness of the estimates made by management in preparing the financial statements.

More specifically, judgment must be exercised in relation to questions such as:
- how much effort (time and expertise) should be devoted to the audit in question?
- who should constitute the audit team (in terms of numbers of staff and their level of competence and experience)?
- where should audit effort be focused?
- how much, what, and from where, should evidence be gathered?
- what conclusions about the truth and fairness of the financial statements (and each segment thereof) are supported by the evidence gathered?
- has sufficient appropriate audit evidence been collected and evaluated to form an opinion?
- what opinion should be expressed in the audit report?

These, and numerous other questions that arise in any audit, do not have clear-cut answers that apply routinely in a given situation. Each audit is unique, and the circumstances of the particular audit must be considered when auditors exercise their judgment. However, one general factor that impacts on, and to some extent limits, the exercise of auditors' judgment in all audits is the materiality of the matter in question. As the fundamental principle of external auditing *Judgment* explains:

> Auditors apply professional judgment taking account of materiality in the context of the matter on which they are reporting. (APB, 2008a, Appendix 2).

Whether or not something is material is itself a matter for the auditor's judgment and, as noted in section 3.4.2 above, varies according to the circumstances and characteristics of the auditee (for example, its size, business and ownership structure) and its financial statements.

The exercise of auditors' judgment is not only unique to the circumstances of each audit: it is also unique to each auditor. The ability of auditors to arrive at professional decisions and opinions, and the cognitive process by which they do so, varies according to a wide range of environmental and personal factors. These include such things as the social, cultural and political environment in which the auditor (and auditee) operates as well as the auditor's general and professional education, professional training and experience, problem-solving ability, the extent and detail of guidance provided by Auditing Standards and other professional promulgations, and the policies and culture of the auditor's firm. Nevertheless, as ISA 200, para A23, explains, auditors' training, knowledge and experience should result in reasonable consistency in their judgments. It states:

The distinguishing feature of the professional judgment expected of an auditor is that it is exercised by an auditor whose training, knowledge and experience have assisted in developing the necessary competencies to achieve reasonable consistency of judgment.

3.4.5 Concept of scepticism

The first part of the fundamental principle of external auditing – *Rigour* – states:

> Auditors approach their work with thoroughness and with an attitude of professional scepticism. (APB, 2008a, Appendix 2)

However, this leaves open the question of what is meant by 'professional scepticism'.

ISA 200, explains the concept as follows:

> Professional skepticism – An attitude that includes a questioning mind, being alert to conditions which may indicate possible misstatement due to error or fraud, and a critical assessment of audit evidence. (para 13)

The Standard further explains:

> Professional skepticism includes being alert to, for example:
> * Audit evidence that contradicts other audit evidence obtained.
> * Information that brings into question the reliability of documents and responses to inquiries to be used as audit evidence.
> * Conditioins that may indicate possible fraud.
> * Circumstances that suggest the need for audit procedures in addition to those required by the ISAs. (para A17)

The APB, in its Consultation Paper: *Fraud and Audit: Choices for Society* (1998) notes that "scepticism is a personal quality that relates to the attitude of individual auditors: it is characterised by a questioning, probing – almost suspicious – approach being applied throughout the audit" (para 3.7). It should be noted that the APB refers to an *almost* suspicious approach: there is a fine but clear line between auditors adopting a 'suspicious' rather than 'sceptical' approach to an audit. As indicated by Lopes, L J in the *Kingston Cotton Mill* case [1896] 2 Ch. 279,[21] auditors are *not* required to "approach [their] work with suspicion or with a foregone conclusion that there is something wrong". This is beyond the concept of professional scepticism. Rather, auditors should be neutral in their approach: they should neither assume that the auditee's directors, executives and other employees are dishonest, nor should they assume unquestioned honesty – even if they have found them to be honest and to have integrity in the past. Auditors need to be alert to the possibility that circumstances have changed. They need to carefully evaluate (rather than merely accept) the audit evidence they gather and the information and explanations obtained from

---

[21] The key principles to emerge from this case are discussed in Chapter 5, section 5.3.

auditee personnel, with an objective, unbiased attitude of mind.[22] They need to ask themselves: "Given my knowledge of this auditee, its business, its circumstances and its operations, does the evidence (or information or explanations) obtained make sense?" If not, they should seek further evidence and ask probing questions to satisfy themselves as to the validity or otherwise of the evidence, information or explanations obtained.

Auditors' ability and propensity to evaluate evidence gathered and information provided, and to ask probing questions, is affected by a variety of environmental and personal factors. These factors tend to coincide with those (noted in section 3.4.4 above) that impact auditors' ability to, and the manner in which they, exercise judgment.

3.5 CONCEPTS RELATING TO AUDITORS' COMMUNICATION

3.5.1 Concept of reporting

Given that the key objective of an audit is to form and express an opinion (in an audit report) on the truth and fairness of the auditee's financial statements, reporting is clearly a concept that goes to the very heart of the audit function. However, it is not just a case of auditors completing their audit and issuing a report without regard to the readers of that report. Rather, it involves *communicating* essential information to users of the audited financial statements. As the first part of the fundamental principle of external auditing – *Clear, complete and effective communication* explains:

> Auditors' reports contain clear expressions of opinion and set out information necessary for a proper understanding of the opinion. (APB, 2008a, Appendix 2)

When preparing their reports, auditors need to bear in mind that the users of the financial statements on which they are expressing an opinion, unlike themselves, do not have access to the auditee's accounting and other data, records and information, and frequently they have little (if any) technical accounting or auditing knowledge. Thus, they rely on auditors to report their opinion about the financial statements in which they are interested – and to do so in a manner that enables them to comprehend the opinion expressed, and the level of assurance it provides.

Flint (1988) explains the importance of auditors' reports:

---

[22] In the closely regulated, post-Enron, post-2002, era (discussed in Chapter 2, section 2.2.5), the concept of professional scepticism has moved a notch or two along an imaginary continuum from auditors assuming management's honesty towards assuming dishonesty. Bell *et al.* (2005) note: "the concept of professionalism [has shifted] from *neutrality* toward *presumptive doubt*" (p. 21; emphasis in original).

> Audit reports have potentially serious consequences for all parties involved. The inadequacy of a report and the failure to communicate successfully could result in consequences which were not justified by the facts, with injustice and damage to the interests of the parties. (p. 117)

This conveys the idea that, if users of financial statements rely on the auditor's report and make, for example, investment decisions based on their understanding of the message it contains, if their understanding is erroneous, their investment decisions could be unwise and they could suffer serious adverse financial consequences as a result.

Flint's statement also indicates that, to be effective, auditors' reports need to meet two key criteria: they need to (a) be adequate in content and (b) communicate successfully with users of the audited financial statements. We will examine each of these criteria a little more closely.

(a) Adequacy: To be of value to financial statement users, audit reports must contain sufficient information for them (the users) to be left in no doubt about the opinion (and any reservations) the auditor is ex-pressing. Audit reports must be explicit and complete. As Flint (1988) observes:

> Auditors are rarely in a position to engage in a dialogue with the parties who will use their report, and once released the report is frequently public information. . . . An audit report must be complete and explicit so that the reader at any time in the future knows fully and exactly what the auditors had to communicate as the outcome of the audit. It must be complete within itself, not requiring the reader to refer to any other document to understand its terms. (pp. 117–118)

(b) Successful communication: In order to communicate a message to financial statement users, audit reports need to be explicit, precise and comprehensible. However, meeting these requirements is no easy task. Flint (1988) highlights some of the difficulties when he explains:

> The matters which are the subject of audit are frequently complex and highly specialised, and auditing itself is an advanced professional specialism. Auditors face the dilemma that they must communicate effectively with persons with limited or no technical understanding and at the same time must express themselves with sufficient technical precision to define precisely the terms and limits of the responsibility they undertake. . . .

> However desirable it may be, it is unrealistic . . . to expect an audit report which discharges an auditor's professional obligations to be understandable to the least knowledgeable of the recipients. [However] the audit report must be in terms which enable the knowledgeable[23] to be informed . . . whether or not accounts, reports or other statements provide the information which they should, and in what respects, if any, there have been failures or

---

[23] Similarly, the IAASB assumes financial statement users "have a reasonable knowledge of business and economic activities and accounting and a willingness to study the information in the financial statements with reasonable diligence" (ISA 320, para 4: see section 3.4.2a above).

> defaults or any description in relation to matters with which the recipients of the audit report are concerned. (pp. 118–119)

Since 1988 (when the 'extended' audit report was first adopted in the USA; it was adopted in the UK in 1993), the auditing profession has made efforts to ensure that audit reports are adequate in content, explicit, precise and comprehensible. The International Standard on Auditing relating to auditors' reports on financial statements (as well as similar Auditing Standards issued in various countries around the world) has been revised on a number of occasions since 1988 with this objective in view.[24]

As we discuss in detail in Chapter 14, auditors' reports, amongst other things:
- identify the financial statements which have been audited and about which the auditor is expressing an opinion;
- explain the respective responsibilities of the auditee's directors and auditors as regards the financial statements;
- outline the audit process which forms the basis for the opinion expressed;
- express an opinion about the truth and fairness (or otherwise) of the financial statements and their compliance (or otherwise) with legal requirements and the relevant financial reporting framework (such as International Financial Reporting Standards).

In addition to reporting to the users of the audited financial statements, ISA 260: *Communication with those charged with governance* requires auditors to, *inter alia*: "[p]rovide those charged with governance with timely observations arising from the audit that are significant and relevant to their responsibility to oversee the financial reporting process" (para 5c). This responsibility of auditors is also conveyed in the second part of the fundamental principle of external auditing – *Clear, complete and effective communication*. It states:

> Auditors communicate audit matters of governance interest arising from the audit of financial statements with those charged with governance of an entity. (APB, 2008a, Appendix 2)

ISA 260 defines 'those charged with governance' in the following terms:

> The person(s) ... with responsibility for overseeing the strategic direction of the entity and obligations related to the accountability of the entity. This includes overseeing the financial reporting process. ... (para 6a)

The Standard (paras 10–13) also details the matters auditors are to communicate to those charged with governance. They include the following:

---

[24] The development of audit reports as means of communication is discussed in Chapter 14, section 14.7. The latest revision to the wording of auditors' reports on financial statements, contained in ISA 700: *The independent auditor's report on general purpose financial statements* and ISA 705: *Modifications to the opinion in the independent auditor's report* was published in 2006. (The Exposure Draft of Redrafted ISA700 and ISA705 were issued in 2007. In June 2008 the IAASB proposed changing the title of ISA700 to *Forming an opinion and reporting on financial statements*.)

- The auditor's responsibilities in relation to the financial statement audit.
- An overview of the planned scope and timing of the audit.
- Significant findings from the audit, including:
  - the auditor's views about significant qualitative aspects of the entity's accounting practices, including accounting policies, accounting estimates and financial statement disclosures;
  - significant difficulties, if any, encountered during the audit;
  - other matters, if any, arising from the audit that, in the auditor's professional judgment, are significant to the oversight of the financial reporting process.
- In the case of listed entities, assurances with respect to the audit firm's, and audit team's independence.[25]

As might be expected, the key principles that constitute the concept of reporting, and which underlie auditors' communication to users of financial statements, similarly apply to their communications with those charged with governance. To be effective, these communications must be adequate in content, explicit, precise and comprehensible. Also like audit reports on financial statements, unless auditors' reports to those charged with governance meet these criteria, those who rely on those reports might be misled and, as a result, make erroneous decisions. These, in turn, could cause serious adverse consequences for the entity. For example, if the auditor of a financial institution such as a bank encounters serious deficiencies in the internal controls relating to foreign exchange dealings and does not communicate his or her findings in an unequivocal and comprehensible manner to the board of directors (or, possibly, the audit committee),[26] a dealer may exploit the internal control deficiencies and engage in unauthorised trading activities undetected for an extended period of time. This (as the collapse of Barings Bank in 1995[27] demonstrates) can result in devastating financial consequences.

Notwithstanding the similarities in the concept of reporting in the context of auditors reporting to users of the auditee's financial statements and to those charged with the entity's governance, there are two important differences. One relates to dialogue, the other to knowledge.

(a) *Dialogue*: It was noted above, citing Flint (1988, p. 117), that "auditors are rarely in a position to engage in a dialogue with the parties who will use their report". While this is true of an auditor reporting to users of

---

[25] These, and other matters auditors are required to report to those charged with governance (including internal control deficiencies and unadjusted misstatements) are discussed in detail in Chapter 14, section 14.8.

[26] Audit committees are discussed in Chapter 4, section 4.4.5.

[27] This case is discussed in Chapter 15, section 15.4.3.

the auditee's audited financial statements,[28] it does (or should!) not apply in the case of an auditor reporting to those charged with the entity's governance. Today, it is normal practice for the auditor to meet with the entity's audit committee (or board of directors) at the conclusion of the audit to discuss the audit findings and any matters relating to the audit.[29] This provides an opportunity for those charged with the entity's governance to ask the auditor probing questions about a wide range of issues; for example, the adequacy of the entity's systems of internal control, errors detected in the financial statements during the audit, and any disagreements with management about, for example, the choice of accounting policies or the validity of accounting estimates included in the financial statements.

(b) *Knowledge*: Also unlike users of financial statements who rely on the auditor's report, those charged with the entity's governance have access to the entity's internal information such as its accounting and other data, records, minutes of executive and other meetings, correspondence and other information. Thus, while the auditor's communication to those charged with the entity's governance is extremely important, it is only one source of information available to the entity's directors (or audit committee). Of equal importance, in terms of assisting the board to fulfil its governance responsibilities, is the communication between the directors (or audit committee) and the entity's internal auditors (or those who fulfil the internal audit function).[30]

3.6 CONCEPTS RELATING TO THE STANDARD OF AUDITORS' PERFORMANCE

3.6.1 Concept of due care

In order for an auditor's opinion to be respected and valued, those relying on that opinion must be able to assume it has been formed by an auditor who has conducted the underlying audit diligently, competently and with *due care*. But what does the term 'due care' mean in the auditing context?

---

[28] For shareholders of quoted companies there is a limited opportunity for additional communication with the company's auditor. The Companies Act 2006, s. 527, provides that members of such companies can require the company to publish on its website a statement setting out any matters relating to the audit of the company's accounts [financial statements] (including the audit report and the conduct of the audit) that are to be laid before the next accounts meeting (in most cases this will be the next Annual General Meeting). It can be assumed that the auditor will be present at the next accounts meeting to answer such questions.

[29] Such meetings are recommended in 'The Smith Guidance' (*Report on the Effectiveness of Audit Committees*; Smith, 2003) which *The Combined Code on Corporate Governance* (FRC, 2006a) points out "suggests means of applying this part of the Code", that is, Provision C.3 Audit Committees and Auditors.

[30] Audit committee communications with internal auditors is discussed in Chapter 4, section 4.4.5.

Court decisions from the 19th and 20th centuries shed some light on the meaning. For example, in *Re Kingston Cotton Mill (No. 2)* [1896] 2 Ch 279, Lopes L J explained:

> It is the duty of an auditor to bring to bear on the work he has to perform, that skill, care and caution which a reasonably competent, careful and cautious auditor would use. What is reasonable skill, care and caution must depend on the particular circumstances of each case.

Pennycuick, J in the case of *Re Thomas Gerrard & Son Ltd.*, [1967] 2 All ER 525, further clarified the issue. He stated:

> I am not clear that the quality of the auditor's duty has changed in any relevant respect since 1896. Basically that duty has always been to audit the company's accounts with reasonable care and skill. The real ground on which Re Kingston Cotton Mill Co. (No. 2) is I think capable of being distinguished, is that the standards of reasonable care and skill are ... more exacting today than those which prevailed in 1896.

Similar ideas were expressed by Moffit, J in *Pacific Acceptance Corporation Ltd.* v *Forsyth and Others* (1970) 92 WN (NSW) 29:[31]

> It is beyond question that when an auditor ... enters into a contract to perform certain tasks as auditor, he promises to perform such tasks using that degree of skill and care as is reasonable in the circumstances as they then exist.... The legal duty, namely, to audit the accounts with reasonable skill and care remains the same, but ... reasonable skill and care calls for changed standards to meet changed conditions or changed understanding of dangers and in this sense standards are more exacting today than in 1896.

Moffit, J goes on to observe that the auditing profession, by changing the guidance it has given to auditors, has recognised that changed conditions require changed audit procedures. However, he also gives a warning:

> [The] standards and practices adopted by the profession to meet current circumstances provide a sound guide to the court in determining what is reasonable....
> [However,] when the conduct of an auditor is in question in legal proceedings it is not the province of the audit profession itself to determine ... what reasonable skill and care require to be done in a particular case. [This is the province of the court.]

So, what can we distil from the judges' statements in the cases cited above about the concept of due care? It may be seen that it has four significant characteristics, namely:

(i) It embodies the notion of auditors exercising reasonable skill, care and caution.

(ii) What is 'reasonable skill, care and caution' in any audit depends on the particular circumstances of the case.

---

[31] This case is also reported in Chapter 5, section 5.3.

(iii) The standard of 'reasonable skill, care and caution' has become more exacting over the past 110 or so years, as society, and more particularly the commercial and corporate worlds, have become more complex and dynamic.

(iv) Although Auditing Standards and other professional promulga-tions provide guidance to the court on what may reasonably be expected of auditors, it is up to the court, not the auditing profession, to determine whether an auditor has taken due care in any particular audit.

This concept is discussed further in Chapter 5, section 5.3, and in Chapter 15.

3.6.2 Concept of quality control

If the public is to have confidence in auditors' work, it is essential that measures (or controls) are put in place to ensure their work is consistently of high quality. Flint (1988) conveys succinctly the importance of quality control for auditing:

> Auditors have both a legal duty and a professional obligation to work to the highest standard which can reasonably be expected to discharge the responsibility that is placed on them. ... In a profession whose authority is dependent among other things on public confidence ... a demonstrable concern, individually and collectively on the part of the members of the profession, to control and maintain the highest quality in its work, is a matter of basic principle. The basis of continuing public confidence and trust in professional competence is a belief that the standards of the members of the profession will be maintained and can be relied on. (pp. 159, 161)

The issue of ensuring high-quality audit work has been tackled in two main ways, namely:

(i) embodying quality control requirements in two professional standards – International Standard on Quality Control (ISQC) 1: *Quality control for firms that perform audits and reviews of financial statements, and other assurance and related services engagements* and ISA 220: *Quality control for an audit of financial statements*; and

(ii) implementing external monitoring/inspection of auditors' compliance with legal, regulatory and professional requirements (including compliance with Auditing and Ethical Standards).

(i) Quality control standards

ISQC 1 and ISA 220 implicitly recognise that responsibility for securing high quality audit work lies at all levels of audit firms. While ISQC 1 relates to quality control at audit firm level, ISA 220 addresses quality control at audit engagement (individual audit) level. The need for controls at both firm and engagement level derives from the fact that audit firms frequently have many offices and each office has a number of audit partners. Further, apart from the smallest audit clients, audits are conducted by audit teams ranging from two or three members for fairly small auditees, to some 20 or more members for large clients. It is only by implementing quality control processes and procedures at both firm and engagement level that the auditing profession can ensure that all audits are conducted with the same high quality of work.

At firm level, an important element in securing high quality audit work is embedding quality in the firm's policies and procedures and monitoring the results of audit work. Thus, ISQC 1 requires each audit firm to establish a system of quality control designed to provide it with reasonable assurance that:

(a) The firm and its personnel comply with professional standards and regulatory and legal requirements; and

(b) Reports issued by the firm or engagement partners are appropriate in the circumstances. (para 11)

ISQC 1 (para 15) expands on the requirements of a firm's system of quality control. It is to include:

policies and procedures that address each of the following elements:

(a) Leadership responsibilities for quality within the firm.

(b) Relevant ethical requirements.

(c) Acceptance and continuance of client relationships and specific engagements.

(d) Human resources.

(e) Engagement performance.

(f) Monitoring.

The Standard (para 16) also requires the firm's quality control policies and procedures to be documented and communicated to the firm's personnel. It explains that the communication:

May include, for example, a description of the quality control policies and procedures and the objectives they are designed to achieve, and the message that each individual has a personal responsibility for quality and is expected to comply with these policies and procedures. (para A3)

Although establishing and maintaining a system of quality controls that applies to the firm as a whole is a necessary element of the auditing profession's measures for ensuring that audit work is consistently of a high quality, it is not sufficient. Audits are conducted by individual audit teams and, therefore, quality controls are also needed that apply at the audit engagement level. These are addressed in ISA 220. This Standard places primary responsibility on the audit engagement partner (the partner responsible for the particular audit)[32] for engendering a quality culture within the audit team and for ensuring that audit team members adhere to procedures designed to ensure high quality audit work. More specifically, the engagement partner has responsibility for matters such as:

---

[32] The Companies Act 2006, s. 504, uses the term 'senior statutory auditor' for the engagement partner for a statutory audit (i.e., one required by the Companies Act).

- ensuring that the audit engagement complies with legal and professional requirements relating to independence, and that members of the engagement team comply with the profession's ethical requirements;
- ensuring the audit team has the appropriate capabilities, competence and time to perform the audit in accordance with professional standards and regulatory and legal requirements;
- directing, supervising and reviewing the audit work performed;
- ensuring the audit team undertakes appropriate consultation during the audit, especially where difficult or contentious matters are encountered;
- ensuring that, by the conclusion of the audit, sufficient appropriate evidence has been collected, that it supports the conclusions reached and is adequate for the auditor's report to be issued.

(ii)   External monitoring/inspection of registered auditors

Not only has the profession sought to ensure that all audits are performed to a high standard, Parliament too, recognising the importance of the audit function to society,[33] has taken steps in this direction. As we explain in Chapter 5, under the provisions of the Companies Act 2006, only 'registered auditors' may be appointed as auditors of companies. To become 'registered', an individual or firm must register with a Recognised Supervisory Body (RSB). One of the conditions of becoming an RSB is that procedures must be in place for monitoring the performance of registrants. Thus, since 1991, monitoring units established by the five RSBs[34] have been responsible for monitoring registered auditors' compliance with all of the RSBs' requirements. These include performing audit work in accordance with legal, regulatory and professional requirements – including complying with Auditing Standards and Ethical Standards. The monitoring activities of the RSBs are overseen and reviewed by the Professional Oversight Board (POB).[35]

Since June 2004, the monitoring arrangements for registered auditors of companies of significant public interest have been modified. Under the Companies (Audit, Investigations and Community Enterprise) Act 2004, auditors of

---

[33] See Chapter 1, section 1.6.3.

[34] As we explain in Chapter 5, section 5.2.3, the five RSBs are the Institutes of Chartered Accountants in England and Wales (ICAEW), of Scotland (ICAS), and of Ireland (ICAI), and the Associations of Chartered Certified Accountants (ACCA), and of Authorised Public Accountants.

[35] The POB is an 'operating body' of the Financial Reporting Council (FRC). The FRC was established as an integrated independent regulator of the accountancy profession in the UK in April 2004 following the UK Government's post-Enron review of the regulation of the UK's accountancy profession. The functions of the FRC are exercised by six operating bodies (the Accounting Standards Board, Auditing Practices Board, Board for Actuarial Standards, the POB, Financial Reporting Review Panel, and the Accountancy Investigation and Discipline Board) and the Council (FRC, 2006b).

companies with listed (equity or non-equity) securities, and other companies considered to be of major public interest, are required to be monitored by an independent Audit Inspection Unit (AIU). The AIU has been established as a unit of, and reports to, the POB. The AIU also issues formal reports to the RSBs on the results of its monitoring of auditors registered with the RSB in question. If registered auditors are found not to be complying with all of the RSB's (and, in appropriate cases, the POB's) requirements, they are subject to sanction – including the ultimate sanction of de-registration.

We discuss the requirements of ISQC 1, ISA 220 and the monitoring of auditors' work in detail in Chapter 16.

3.7 SUMMARY

In this chapter we have laid the theoretical foundation for our study of the practice of auditing. We have noted the interrelationship between the social purpose, the postulates and the concepts of auditing. We have also described seven postulates and examined the meaning and importance to auditing of 11 concepts. We have seen that these concepts fall into four groups – the credibility of auditors' work (independence, competence, ethical conduct), the audit process (evidence, materiality, audit risk, judgment, scepticism), communication (reporting), and standard of performance (due care, quality control) – and that each is of fundamental importance to the audit function. We will study most of these concepts in greater detail in their relevant contexts in subsequent chapters. However, we devote all of the next chapter to the critically important issue of auditors' independence.

SELF-REVIEW QUESTIONS

3.1 State the social purpose of auditing and how this relates to the postulates and concepts of auditing.

3.2 (a) Explain briefly what is meant by a 'postulate'.
    (b) List four postulates of auditing.

3.3 Define and explain the importance of the concept of independence as it relates to auditing. [Your definition should refer to both independence in mind (or in fact) and independence in appearance.]

3.4 Explain briefly the meaning and importance to auditing of the concept of competence.

3.5   Explain briefly the meaning and importance to auditing of the concept of ethical conduct.

3.6   Explain briefly the meaning and importance to auditing of the concept of evidence.

3.7   Explain briefly the meaning and importance to auditing of the concept of materiality.

3.8   Explain briefly the meaning and importance to auditing of the concept of audit risk.

3.9   (a) Distinguish between 'non-controllable' and 'controllable' risk.
      (b) Explain briefly the components of non-controllable and controllable risk.

3.10 Explain briefly the meaning and importance to auditing of the concepts of due care and quality control.

REFERENCES

Anderson, R.J. (1977). *The External Audit.* Toronto: Cropp Clark Pitman.

Auditing Practices Board (APB). (1998). *Fraud and Audit: Choices for Society.* Consultation Paper. London: APB.

Auditing Practices Board (APB). (2008a). *The Auditing Practices Board – Scope and Authority of Pronouncements (Revised).* London: Financial Reporting Council.

Auditing Practices Board (APB). (2008b). *APB Ethical Standard (ES) 1: Integrity, Objectivity and Independence.* London: Financial Reporting Council.

Bell, T.B., Peecher, M.E. and Solomon, I. (2005). *The 21st Public Company Audit: Conceptual Elements of KPMG's Global Audit Methodology.* KPMG International.

Committee on Basic Auditing Concepts. (1973). *A Statement of Basic Auditing Concepts.* Sarasota, FL: American Accounting Association.

European Union (EU). (2006). *Directive 2006/43/EC of the European Parliament and of the Council on the Statutory Audits of Annual Accounts and Consolidated Accounts (8th Directive).* Brussels: European Parliament and Council.

Financial Reporting Council (FRC). (2006a). *The Combined Code on Corporate Governance.* London: Financial Reporting Council.

Financial Reporting Council (FRC). (2006b). *Regulatory Strategy* (Version 2.1). London: Financial Reporting Council.

Flint, D. (1988). *Philosophy and Principles of Auditing: An Introduction.* Basingstoke: Macmillan Education.

Haber, J.R. (2005). Does being the auditor impair independence? *CPA Journal* **LXXV**(6), 12.

International Auditing and Assurance Standards Board (IAASB). (2007). *Glossary of Terms.* New York: International Federation of Accountants.

Levitt, A. (2000, 18 September). *A Profession at the Crossroads.* Speech by SEC Chairman to National Association of State Boards of Accountancy, Boston, MA.

Mautz, R.K. and Sharaf, H.A. (1961). *The Philosophy of Auditing.* New York: AAA.

Smith, Sir Robert. (2003). *Report on the Effectiveness of Audit Committees.* London: Financial Services Authority.

Stewart, R.E. (1977). Independence: the auditor's cornerstone. *Accountants' Journal* **56**(9), 333–337.

Turner, L.E. (2001, 28 June). *Independence: A Covenant for the Ages.* Speech by SEC Chief Accountant to International Organization of Securities Commissions, Stockholm, Sweden.

ADDITIONAL READING

Duff, A. (2004). *Dimensions of Audit Quality.* Edinburgh: Institute of Chartered Accountants of Scotland.

Fédération des Experts Comptables Européens (FEE). (2007). *Selected issues relating to financial statement audits – inherent limitations, reasonable assurance, professional judgement and its documentation and enforceability of auditing standards.* Brussels: FEE.

Hayward, J. (2003). *Thinking not Ticking: Bringing competition to the public interest audit.* London: Centre for the Study of Financial Innovation (CSFI).

Iselin, E.R. and Iskandar, T.M. (2000). Auditors' recognition and disclosure materiality thresholds: their magnitude and the effects of industry. *British Accounting Review* **32**, 289–309.

O'Sullivan, H. (2007). A question of ethics. *Accountancy* **140**(1372), 86–87.

Velayutham, S. (2003). The accounting profession's code of ethics: is it a code of ethics or a code of quality assurance. *Critical Perspectives on Accounting* **14**(4), 483–503.

4   Threats to, and Preservation of, Auditors' Independence

LEARNING OBJECTIVES

After studying the material in this chapter you should be able to:

- explain the critical importance to the audit function of auditors being independent of mind (or in fact) and in appearance;
- describe the circumstances in which auditors' independence may, or may appear to be, compromised;
- discuss measures introduced by legislation, regulation and/or the auditing profession which are designed to ensure auditors are (and remain) independent of their audit clients;
- distinguish between two forms of auditor rotation;
- outline arguments for and against (i) auditors' appointment by the State (or a State agency), (ii) auditors' appointment by a shareholder panel, and (iii) mandatory auditor rotation, as means of strengthening auditors' independence;
- explain the development, importance and principal responsibilities of audit committees – with particular reference to auditors' independence.

The following publications and fundamental principle of external auditing are particularly relevant to this chapter:

Publications:
- APB Ethical Standard (ES) 1: *Integrity, Objectivity and Independence* (FRC, 2008)
- APB Ethical Standard (ES) 2: *Financial, Business, Employment and Personal Relationships* (FRC, 2008)
- APB Ethical Standard (ES) 3: *Long Association with the Audit Engagement* (FRC, 2008)
- APB Ethical Standard (ES) 4: *Fees, Remuneration and Evaluation Policies, Litigation, Gifts and Hospitality* (FRC, 2008)
- APB Ethical Standard (ES) 5: *Non-audit Services Provided to Audit Clients* (FRC, 2008)
- *Code of Ethics for Professional Accountants* (IFAC, 2006) [section 290 (IFAC, 2007)]*[1]

Fundamental principle of external auditing included in *The Auditors' Code*:[2] Objectivity and independence

---

[1] The IFAC *Code of Ethics* was revised in July 2006 but an Exposure Draft (ED) of section 290 (Independence – Audit and Review Engagements) was issued in December 2006. A further ED of some paragraphs of section 290 was issued in July 2007. In this chapter, IFAC (2006*) is used to refer to the ED of section 290 and IFAC (2006) is used to denote the revised *Code of Ethics*.

[2] The fundamental principles of external auditing are reproduced on the inside of the front cover of this book.

4.1 INTRODUCTION

The fundamental principle of external auditing *Objectivity and independence*[3] explains:

> Auditors are objective and provide impartial opinions unaffected by bias, prejudice, compromise and conflicts of interest. Auditors are also independent, this requires them to be free from situations and relationships which would make it probable that a reasonable and informed third party would conclude that the auditors' objectivity either is impaired or could be impaired. (Auditing Practices Board, 2008a, Appendix 2)

As we observe in Chapter 3, auditors being independent of their audit clients, their clients' managements, and any other influences which might impair their objectivity and impartiality, is of critical importance to the audit function. If auditors are not perceived to be independent by those who use and rely on audited financial statements, their opinion on those financial statements will lack credibility and, as a result, the audit will be of little or no value.

Given the importance of auditors' independence to the audit function, stipulating that auditors must be independent both of mind (or in fact) and in appearance may seem to be an obvious requirement. However, in practice, such independence may be difficult to achieve and easy to compromise. This was demonstrated all too clearly as an outcome of the Enron, WorldCom, Tyco and similar debacles in the early years of the 21st century. Although, as the related court cases revealed, the unexpected corporate failures resulted from a number of contributing factors, the (apparent) lack of auditor independence was highlighted as a key reason for warning bells not being sounded by the auditors.

Cognisant of the importance of the audit function (and investors' confidence in the integrity of that function) to the smooth functioning of capital markets, Governments in the United Kingdom (UK), the United States of America (USA) and elsewhere have enacted legislative provisions designed to strengthen auditors' independence. Similarly, regulatory and professional bodies such as the Auditing Practices Board (APB) and the International Federation of Accountants (IFAC) have promulgated standards or other 'rules' with the same objective.

---

[3] As we note in Chapter 3 (section 3.3.1b), the two forms of independence which auditors must maintain were, until recently, referred to as 'independence in fact' and 'independence in appearance'. While IFAC, in its *Code of Ethics for Professional Accountants*, has used the terms 'independence of mind' and 'independence in appearance' for these two forms of independence, the UK's Auditing Practices Board (APB) has adopted two separate terms – 'objectivity' for 'independence in fact (or of mind)' and 'independence' for 'independence in appearance'.

In this chapter we discuss threats to auditors' independence – and steps taken, or proposed, which are designed to mitigate those threats and preserve and/or strengthen auditors' independence.

4.2 FACTORS THAT MAY COMPROMISE AUDITORS' INDEPENDENCE

For many years, politicians (such as Congressman Dingell in the USA and Austin Mitchell, Member of Parliament in the UK), regulators [such as the Department of Trade and Industry (DTI)[4] in the UK and the Securities and Exchange Commission (SEC) in the USA] and various commentators (such as Briloff, 1986; Mitchell and Sikka, 1993; and Jeppesen, 1998) have raised questions about auditors' ability to remain independent of their audit clients. They note that auditors are, in practice, hired, fired and paid by their clients' managements;[5,6] they also work closely with them as they conduct their audits and, as a result, after a number of years of acting as auditor for the client they become very familiar with them. Further, as noted in Chapter 2, from the 1960s until the turn of the century, auditors were frequently (and increasingly) engaged to provide non-audit, as well as audit, services for their clients. They often still provide such services but, since enactment of the Sarbanes-Oxley Act of 2002 in the USA, to a far more limited extent than formerly.

During the 1990s the SEC, in particular, became very concerned about possible impairment of auditors' independence as a consequence of auditors providing non-audit services to their audit clients.[7] In its Proposed Rule on Auditor Independence (SEC, 2000a), the SEC noted:

> We have become increasingly concerned that the dramatic increase in the nature, number, and monetary value of non-audit services that accounting firms provide to audit clients may affect their independence. (p. 3)

It reported that, in 1999, the Big Five audit firms[8] earned revenues from management advisory and similar services of more than $15 billion in the USA alone and, between 1993 and 1999, the average annual growth rate in revenues from these services was 26 per cent compared with nine per cent for audit, and

---

[4] In June 2007, the DTI was replaced by the Department for Business, Enterprise and Regulatory Reform (DBERR).

[5] Readers are reminded that in the Preface to this book we note that we use the term 'management' to embrace directors (executive and non-executive) and senior executives (directors and non-directors).

[6] The statutory provisions relating to the appointment, remuneration and resignation of auditors is discussed in Chapter 5, section 5.2.

[7] It should be noted that concerns about possible impairment of auditors' independence were already being expressed by the SEC and others in the years before Enron and Andersen collapsed.

[8] Arthur Andersen, Deloitte & Touche, Ernst & Young, KPMG, PricewaterhouseCoopers.

13 per cent for tax, services (SEC, 2000a, p. 9).[9] Levitt (2000), former Chairman of the SEC, also observed:

> I could not help but notice the many advertisements for the big accountancy firms. They seem to always extol their IT talents, corporate finance capabilities, and financial planning tools. But rarely do I see an advertisement that conveys to the public and their clients their passion for living up to their public mandate of keeping the sanctity of the numbers inviolate – never a mention of the public interest. (p. 7)

> [A]uditors who also provide consulting services for their audit clients must now serve *two* masters: a public obligation to shareholders, and a professional duty to management. And when the two come into conflict, the independent audit – dwarfed by the more lucrative consulting businesses – too often may be compromised. (p. 2, emphasis in original)

Given the story of Enron's demise – and the extent of the non-audit services provided to the company by its auditor, Arthur Andersen – it seems that the SEC's fears were not unfounded.[10]

While the SEC has focused on the provision of non-audit services to audit clients as the key threat to auditors' independence, the APB, in Ethical Standard (ES) 1: *Integrity, objectivity and independence*, has identified six broad 'threats' to auditors' objectivity and independence.[11] These are explained in the following terms (para 28):

---

[9] Similarly, a study of the Financial Times Stock Exchange (FTSE) 100 companies by the Financial Director magazine, published in January 2002, found that the average audit fee for these companies was £2.21 million; they also paid their auditors an average in excess of £6.5 million for non-audit services. However, in a number of cases the ratio of audit to non-audit fees was 12:1 and in two extreme cases were 48:1 and 78:1 respectively (Hermes, 2002).

[10] In 2000, Enron paid Andersen $25 million for the audit of its financial statements and a further $27 million for non-audit services (Hirsch, 2002). Not only was the fee for non-audit work exceptionally high, so too was the audit fee. As Hirsch (2002, p. 1) reported:

> The average charge [audit fee] among the blue chips was just $9 million . . . [Enron's audit fee] was also large compared with the fees other energy companies paid their accountants, even Andersen. In a review of fees listed in Securities and Exchange Commission filings, The Times found that audit contracts averaged $3 million at nine large energy companies, including Andersen clients Mirant Corp., UtiliCorp United Inc., Dynegy Inc. and Calpine Corp. Andersen's fee was a red flag to some experts and critics who say it could have clouded the company's judgment as it examined Enron's tangled financial structure. . . . Indeed, Andersen executives debated internally whether the audit and other fees would be perceived as a breach of the firm's independence.

However, the extent of the provision of non-audit services to Enron was not the only problematic element of Andersen maintaining its independence from this audit client. Enron Watchdog (2002, p. 2) observed that Andersen's audit and other accounting staff

> had permanent offices in Enron's building. Its staff wore Enron golf shirts, attended Enron parties and ski trips and generally were difficult to tell from Enron staff. Enron's Chief Accounting Officer and Chief Financial Officer were both Andersen alums (i.e. former Andersen partners).

Squires *et al.* (2003) further noted that Duncan (Andersen's engagement partner for the Enron audit) and Causey (Enron's Chief Financial Officer) "were virtually inseparable. They worked together, went to lunch together, and played golf together. Their families even went on vacations together" (p. 2).

[11] Or, as termed by IFAC in its *Code of Ethics for Professional Accountants*; independence of mind and independence in appearance (see footnote 3).

- *self-interest threat*
  A self-interest threat arises when the auditor has financial or other interests which might cause it to be reluctant to take actions that would be adverse to the interests of the audit firm or any individual in a position to influence the conduct or outcome of the audit (for example, where the auditor has an investment in the audited entity, is seeking to provide additional services to the audited entity or needs to recover long-outstanding fees from the audited entity).
- *self-review threat*
  A self-review threat arises when the results of a non-audit service performed by the auditor or by others within the audit firm are reflected in the amounts included or disclosed in the financial statements (for example, where the audit firm has been involved in maintaining the accounting records, or undertaking valuations that are incorporated in the financial statements). In the course of the audit, the auditor may need to re-evaluate the work performed in the non-audit service. As, by virtue of providing the non-audit service, the audit firm is associated with aspects of the preparation of the financial statements, it may be (or may be perceived to be) unable to take an impartial view of relevant aspects of those financial statements.
- *management threat*
  [P]artners and employees of the audit firm [are prohibited] from taking decisions on behalf of the management of the audited entity. However, a management threat can also arise when the audit firm undertakes an engagement to provide non-audit services in relation to which management are required to make judgments and take decisions based on that work (for example, the design, selection and implementation of a financial information technology system). In such work, the audit firm may become closely aligned with the views and interests of management and the auditor's objectivity and independence may be impaired, or may be perceived to be, impaired.
- *advocacy threat*
  An advocacy threat arises when the audit firm undertakes work that involves acting as an advocate for an audited entity and supporting a position taken by management in an adversarial context (for example, by acting as a legal advocate for the audited entity in litigation or a regulatory investigation). In order to act in an advocacy role, the audit firm has to adopt a position closely aligned to that of management. This creates both actual and perceived threats to the auditor's objectivity and independence.
- *familiarity (or trust) threat*
  A familiarity (or trust) threat arises when the auditor is predisposed to accept or is insufficiently questioning of the audited entity's point of view (for example, where close personal relationships are developed with audited entity's personnel through long association with the audited entity).
- *intimidation threat*
  An intimidation threat arises when the auditor's conduct is influenced by fear or threats (for example, where the auditor encounters an aggressive and dominating individual).

The Standard further explains (para 32):
These categories may not be entirely distinct: certain circumstances may give rise to more than one type of threat. For example, where an audit firm wishes to

retain the fee income from a large audited entity, but encounters an aggressive and dominating individual, there may be a self-interest threat as well as an intimidation threat.

It should be noted that the European Union (EU) Commission's Recommendation: *Statutory Auditors' Independence in the EU: A Set of Fundamental Principles* (2002) similarly recognises: "auditors" independence can be affected by different types of threats, including self-interest, self-review, advocacy, familiarity or trust, and intimidation' (section A.3.1). IFAC, in its *Code of ethics for professional accountants* (2006, para 100.10), recognises these same five broad threats. However, although the essence of the 'threats' is the same, IFAC sets them in a broader context than the APB's ES1 and the EU Recommendation: they are signalled as threats, not just to auditors maintaining, and being perceived as maintaining, their independence, but as threats to professional accountants' compliance with the five fundamental principles of professional ethics – integrity, objectivity, professional competence and due care, confidentiality, and professional behaviour.[12]

Examples of specific circumstances in which an auditor may find it difficult (or may be perceived as likely to find it difficult) to maintain an unbiased, objective attitude of mind (additional to those cited in ES1, para 32) include circumstances in which the auditor, the audit firm, or a senior member of the audit engagement team:

- has some financial involvement with the audit client as a shareholder, debtholder or creditor;[13]
- participates (or plans to participate) in the affairs of a client in a capacity other than that of auditor (for example, as a director of, or consultant to, the client);
- has a mutual business interest with the audit client, or with a director or senior executive of the client (for example, by being engaged in a joint

---

[12] These five fundamental principles of professional ethics for professional accountants are discussed in Chapter 3, sections 3.3.1 to 3.3.3.

[13] An example of such involvement is provided by KPMG in the USA. An SEC (2002) Press Release reported that it had:

> censured KMPG ... for engaging in improper professional conduct because it purported to serve as an independent accounting firm for an audit client at the same time that it had made substantial financial investments in the client. ... [F]rom May through December 2000, KPMG held a substantial investment in the Short-Term Investment Trust ("STIT"), a money market fund within the AIM family of funds.... KPMG opened the money market account with an initial deposit of $25 million on May 5, 2000, and at one point the account balance constituted approximately 15% of the fund's net assets.... [T]he SEC found that KPMG audited the financial statements of STIT at a time when the firm's independence was impaired, and that STIT included KPMG's audit report in 16 separate filings it made with the SEC on November 9, 2000. (p. 1)

venture with one of the client's directors or executives, or involved in a business that is a major supplier or customer of the client);

- receives favourable treatment from the client in the form of goods, services or hospitality;[14]
- is actually or potentially involved in litigation on behalf of, or against, the client;
- has a close family or personal relationship with a director or senior executive of the client;[15]
- depends on the audit client for a substantial portion of total fee income and/or provides significant (in terms of total fee income) non-audit services to the audit client. (This latter point is discussed in detail in section 4.3.3 below.)

4.3 STEPS TAKEN BY PARLIAMENT, REGULATORS AND THE PROFESSION TO SECURE AUDITORS' INDEPENDENCE FROM THEIR AUDIT CLIENTS

4.3.1 Overview of the measures taken by Parliament and regulators

From the above, it is clear that a wide range of circumstances may cause auditors' independence to be impaired – in appearance if not of mind (or in fact). However, conscious of the importance of independence to the credibility of the audit function, Parliament, regulators [such as the Financial Reporting Council (FRC)] and the accounting profession have established measures designed to ensure that auditors are, and remain, independent of their audit clients. The Companies Act (CA) 2006, s. 1214, for example, stipulates that a person may not be the auditor of a company if that person is:

(i) an officer or employee of the company, or of a parent or subsidiary undertaking of the company; or

(ii) a partner or employee of such a person as in (i) above, or a partnership in which such a person is a partner.

Further, a person may not be the auditor of a company if there exists between that person, or an associate of that person, and the company (or a parent or subsidiary undertaking of the company), a connection of any such description as may be specified by regulations made by the Secretary of State.

---

[14] For example, when arriving to conduct the audit of a ski company client just before the start of the skiing season, one of the authors was offered (and declined!) a free ski pass for the entire season.

[15] As illustrated by the relationship between Duncan (Andersen's audit engagement partner) and Causey (Enron's Chief Financial Officer) (see footnote 10).

These provisions are designed to ensure that the auditor is not exposed to a conflict of interest as a result of a direct or indirect relationship with the auditee company in a capacity other than that of auditor.

Additionally, the CA 2006, s. 494, empowers the Secretary of State to make regulations that require companies to disclose in their annual reports information about the nature of any services provided to the company or its associates (for example, subsidiaries and pension funds) by the auditor, or an associate of the auditor, and the remuneration received or receivable by the auditor (or the auditor's associates) for such services. The relevant regulations, entitled The Companies (Disclosure of Auditor Remuneration and Liability Limitation Agreements) Regulations (Statutory Instrument, 2008), came into force on 6 April 2008.[16] Under the Regulations two sets of rules apply – (i) those for small and medium-sized companies, and (ii) those for all other companies.

(i) *Small and medium-sized companies* (i.e., those which meet at least two of the following criteria: turnover of not more than £22.8 million, balance sheet total of not more than £11.4 million, and not more than 250 employees: CA 2006, ss. 382, 465) are required to disclose in the notes to their annual audited financial statements the remuneration[17] receivable by the auditor for the audit of the company's financial statements (Reg. 4).

(ii) *All other companies* are required to disclose in the notes to their annual audited financial statements the amount receivable by the auditor (and any associates of the auditor) for (i) the audit of the financial statements, and (ii) all other services provided to the company, its subsidiaries and its associated pension funds. Each type of service specified in Schedule 2 to the Regulations and the associated remuneration must be disclosed separately. Similarly, services to the company and its subsidiaries on the one hand, and to associated pension schemes on the other, must be disclosed separately (Reg. 5). Consolidated group financial statements (except those of small or medium-sized groups) must disclose the audit fee and the types of services specified in Schedule 2 (and the associated fees for each service) as if the group were a single

---

[16] Regulations requiring disclosure of auditors' remuneration were originally made by the Secretary of State in accordance with powers conferred on him by the CA 1985, s. 390B, as amended by the Companies (Audit, Investigations and Community Enterprise) Act 2004, s. 7. These regulations, entitled The Companies (Disclosure of Auditor Remuneration) Regulations 2005 (Statutory Instrument, 2005) came into force on 1 October 2005. The statutory provision of the CA 1985, s. 390B (as amended), was incorporated in s. 494 of the CA 2006 and new regulations were promulgated in February 2008.

[17] 'Remuneration' is defined to include:"payments in respect of expenses and benefits in kind"(Reg. 3). Reg. 4, relating to small and medium-sized companies, and Reg. 5, relating to all other companies, specifies: "where the remuneration includes benefits in kind, the nature and estimated money-value of those benefits must also be disclosed in a note [to the financial statements]".

company. If that is done, the individual companies within the group need not make the disclosures (Reg. 6).

The services specified in Schedule 2 for which separate disclosure is required are:

1. The auditing of accounts of associates of the company pursuant to legislation ...
2. Other services supplied pursuant to such legislation.
3. Other services relating to taxation.
4. Services relating to information technology.
5. Internal audit services.
6. Valuation and actuarial services.
7. Services relating to litigation.
8. Services relating to recruitment and remuneration.
9. Services relating to corporate finance transactions entered into or proposed to be entered into on behalf of the company or any of its associates.
10. All other non-audit services. (Statutory Instrument, 2008)

These disclosure requirements ensure that financial statement users are provided with information which enables them to assess the likelihood of the auditor's independence being compromised as a consequence of too great an involvement with the audit client through the provision of non-audit services. As the *Explanatory Notes to Companies (Audit Investigations and Community Enterprise) Act 2004* explains:

> The aim [of the provision which resulted in the Auditor Remuneration Disclosure Regulations] is to address concerns about possible conflicts of interest between the audit firm in its role as auditor and in its role as provider of other services to the company. More detailed disclosure requirements should allow stakeholders and others to identify particular features of the company/ auditor relationship that may cause concerns over the auditor's independence. (para 33)

The CA 2006, s. 1212, also specifies that, to be eligible for appointment as a company auditor, an individual or firm must be a member of a recognised supervisory body (RSB)[18] and eligible for appointment under the rules of that body. To qualify for recognition as such, a RSB must, *inter alia*, participate in arrangements for the setting of standards relating to professional integrity and independence. These standards (the setting of which is to be done independently of the RSBs) are to govern rules and practices designed to ensure all members of the RSBs:

---

[18] There are five RSBs, namely, the Institutes of Chartered Accountants in England and Wales (ICAEW), of Scotland (ICAS), and of Ireland (ICAI), and the Associations of Chartered Certified Accountants (ACCA), and of Authorised Public Accountants. The requirement for company auditors to be registered with a RSB, and the requirements professional accounting bodies must meet in order to be recognised as a supervisory body, are discussed in Chapter 5, section 5.2.3.

- conduct their audit work properly and with integrity;
- are not appointed as a company's auditor in circumstances in which they have an interest likely to conflict with the proper conduct of the audit;
- comply with the professional integrity and independence standards (CA 2006, Schedule 10, paras 9, 21).

The FRC, the integrated independent regulator of accounting and auditing in the UK, has delegated to the APB responsibility for setting ethical (i.e., integrity and independence) standards with which all registered auditors must comply.

The APB has issued five Ethical Standards (ESs) that apply to financial statement audits. It explains (APB, 2008a, para 10) that, when preparing the ESs, it sought to ensure that they adhered to the principles of the *Code of ethics for professional accountants* (IFAC, 2006) and also to the EU Commission's Recommendation: *Statutory Auditors' Independence in the EU: A Set of Fundamental Principles* (EU Commission, 2002). Like the Code and the EU Commission's Recommendation, the APB uses what the Fédération des Experts Comptables Européens (FEE, 2004) calls "a conceptual framework, sometimes referred to as the 'threats and safeguards approach'" (p. 7). Circumstances which could adversely affect the auditors' independence are termed 'threats', and procedures to eliminate or to reduce identified threats to an acceptable level[19] are referred to as 'safeguards'.

The ESs detail 'safeguards' (similar in nature to rules) that are designed to prevent auditors' objectivity and independence[20] from being compromised. The safeguards are of two types, namely, those that relate to:
- the general audit environment and audit engagements;
- specific situations where auditors' objectivity or independence may be at risk.

4.3.2 Safeguards relating to the general audit environment and audit engagements

ES1: *Integrity, objectivity and independence* details requirements that seek to ensure the audit environment is conducive to auditors maintaining their

---

[19] An 'acceptable level' in this context is "a level at which it is not probable that a reasonable and informed third party would conclude that the auditors' objectivity is impaired or is likely to be impaired" (ES1, para 27).

[20] The ESs are designed to prevent auditors' integrity, objectivity and independence from being compromised. In this chapter we are concerned with auditors' objectivity and independence ('independence of mind' and 'independence in appearance'). We discuss auditors' integrity in Chapter 7.

objectivity and independence. In some cases responsibility is assigned to the audit firm, in others to the audit engagement partner.[21]

(a) Audit firm responsibilities

Audit firms are required to establish, document and communicate policies and procedures designed to ensure, for each audit engagement, that the audit firm and all those in a position to influence the conduct and outcome of the audit:[22]

- act with objectivity and independence;
- are constantly alert to circumstances that might reasonably be considered threats to their objectivity and/or the perceived loss of independence; and
- where such circumstances are identified, to report them to the audit engagement or ethics partner, as appropriate (ES1, paras 15, 28).

The ethics partner is the partner in the audit firm who has responsibility for:

- the adequacy of the firm's policies and procedures relating to objectivity and independence, the firm's, compliance with the APB's Ethical Standards, and the effectiveness of its communication to partners and staff (including coverage in induction programmes, professional training and continuing professional development) to all partners and staff within the firm;
- providing guidance on matters referred to them, or of which they otherwise become aware, where a difficult and objective judgment needs to be made or a consistent position reached (ES1, paras 21, 22).

Audit firms are also required to promote a strong control environment within the firm that places adherence to ethical principles and compliance with the Ethical Standards above commercial considerations. More particularly, they are to establish appropriate policies and procedures that include:

- requiring audit partners and staff to report matters that affect their objectivity or independence with respect to any particular audit client (such as past, present or planned personal, financial or employment relationships with the client or its management);
- monitoring of compliance with the firm's policies and procedures relating to objectivity and independence;
- requiring prompt communication to the relevant audit engagement partner of possible or actual breaches of the firm's policies and procedures;

---

[21] The audit engagement partner is the partner in the audit firm who is responsible for the particular audit engagement and who issues the audit report on behalf of the firm.

[22] This includes audit partners, audit managers and audit staff; professional personnel from other disciplines who are involved with the audit (for example, actuaries, lawyers, IT and tax and treasury management specialists); and those responsible for the quality control of the audit (ES1, para 16). Quality control is discussed in Chapter 16.

- requiring audit engagement partners to evaluate the implications of possible or actual breaches of the form's policies and procedures that are reported to them;
- empowering and encouraging staff members to communicate to senior levels within the firm any issue of objectivity or independence that concerns them (ES1, paras 18, 20).

(b) Engagement partner responsibilities

Audit engagement partners (rather than the audit firm) are responsible for, *inter alia*, identifying and assessing the significance of threats to the audit firm's, their own, or members of the audit team's objectivity and independence, especially when:

- considering whether to accept or retain an audit engagement;
- planning the audit;
- forming an opinion on the financial statements;
- considering whether to accept or retain an engagement to provide non-audit services to the audit client;
- potential threats are reported to him or her.

When identifying and assessing the significance of threats to objectivity or independence, the engagement partner is to consider the firm's, and members of the audit team's, current, past and likely future relationships with the audit client (including the provision of non-audit services) as such relationships may be perceived as likely to impair the audit firm's, or one or more audit team member's, objectivity and independence (ES1, paras 34, 36).

Having identified threats to the audit firm's, or the audit team's, objectivity or independence, audit engagement partners are required to identify and assess the effectiveness of available safeguards, and to apply sufficient safeguards to eliminate or reduce identified threats to an acceptable level.[23] If the threats cannot be reduced to this level, the engagement partner must not accept, or continue with, the engagement (as applicable). Additionally, at the conclusion of the audit, when forming an opinion on the financial statements but before issuing the audit report, the engagement partner is to reach an overall conclusion that any threats to objectivity and independence have been properly addressed. If such a conclusion cannot be formed, the engagement partner is to consult with the ethics partner and, if necessary, the audit firm is to refrain from issuing an audit report and to resign as auditors (ES1, paras 38, 44, 48, 49).

Audit engagement partners are also responsible for ensuring that those charged with the audit client's governance (i.e., the directors or, more usually, the audit committee on the directors' behalf) are appropriately informed on a timely

---

[23] See footnote 19.

basis of all significant facts and matters that bear upon the audit firm's, the engagement partner's and the audit team's objectivity and independence. The matters to be communicated include:

- the principal threats to objectivity and independence that have been identified, including any relevant relationships between the audit firm, engagement partner or members of the audit team on the one hand, and the audit client, its affiliates (such as subsidiaries) and its management on the other;
- any safeguards adopted to mitigate the threats and the reasons why they are considered to be effective;
- the overall assessment of threats and safeguards;
- information about the general policies and processes within the audit firm for maintaining objectivity and independence (ES1, paras 56, 58).

Audit engagement partners are further required to ensure that their consideration of the firm's, their own and members of the audit team's objectivity and independence is appropriately documented on a timely basis. Matters to be documented include all of the key elements of the assessment process and any significant judgments concerning:

- threats identified and the process used to identify them;
- safeguards adopted and the reasons why they are considered to be effective;
- overall assessment of threats and safeguards;
- communication of identified threats and related safeguards to those charged with the audit client's governance (ES1, paras 64, 66).

There are two additional requirements when an audit client is a listed company. These are as follows:

(i) The engagement quality control reviewer is required to be involved in the process of ensuring that objectivity and independence are preserved.[24] This partner is required to:
- consider the audit firm's compliance with the APB's Ethical Standards on objectivity and independence in relation to the audit engagement;
- form an independent opinion as to the appropriateness and adequacy of the safeguards applied;

---

[24] An 'engagement quality control reviewer' is:

A partner, other person in the firm, suitably qualified external person, or a team made up of such individual, with sufficient and appropriate experience and authority to objectively evaluate, before the report is issued, the significant judgments the engagement team made and the conclusions they reached in formulating the report. (APB, 2008b)

ISA 220: *Quality control for an audit of financial statements* requires the audit engagement partner to appoint an independent quality control reviewer for the audit of a listed company. The quality control review includes consideration of the engagement team's evaluation of the independence of the audit firm. Thus, when an audit client is a listed company, the 'independent partner' and the 'engagement quality control reviewer' are one and the same. The requirements of ISA 220 are discussed in Chapter 16.

- consider the adequacy of the documentation of the audit engagement partner's consideration of the auditors' objectivity and independence.

(ii) The audit engagement partner is to disclose in writing to those charged with the client's governance (or, more usually, its audit committee):

- details of all relationships between (including all services provided by) the audit firm, associates of the audit firm, the engagement partner or audit team members on the one hand and the client, its affiliates, or its management on the other, that the engagement partner considers may reasonably be thought to bear on their objectivity and independence;
- the related safeguards that are in place;
- the total amount of fees the audit firm (and its related firms) have charged the client and its affiliates for the provision of services during the reporting period, analysed into appropriate categories, for example, statutory audit services, tax advisory services and other non-audit services;
- the audit firm, and all those involved in the audit, have complied with the APB's Ethical Standards and that, in the engagement partner's professional judgment, they are independent and their objectivity has not been impaired (ES1, paras 46, 59–62).

4.3.3 Safeguards relating to specific situations where objectivity or independence may be at risk

While ES1 sets out standards designed to ensure the audit environment is conducive to auditors maintaining their objectivity and independence, ES2 to ES5 are concerned with specific circumstances that may create threats to auditors' independence, and safeguards to eliminate or reduce such threats to an acceptable level.

The specific circumstances that may impair auditors' independence may conveniently be considered under the following headings:
  (i)   financial involvement with an audit client;
  (ii)   business, employment or personal relationships with an audit client;
  (iii) long association with an audit client;
  (iv)   undue dependence on an audit client for fee income;
  (v)   threatened or actual litigation;
  (vi)   gifts and hospitality from an audit client;
  (vii) provision of non-audit services to an audit client.

(i) Financial involvement with an audit client

Financial involvement with an audit client may arise through a share- or debenture-holding in, or loan to or from, the client, or through any other direct or indirect financial interest in the client: this includes a financial interest arising through a trust (as trustee or beneficiary) or a pension scheme which has the audit client among its investments.

ES2: *Financial, business, employment and personal relationships* contains a number of safeguards (or 'rules') that seek to prevent auditors' independence from being compromised as a result of financial involvement with an audit client. These include the following:

1. No audit firm, partner of the firm, or person in a position to influence the conduct and outcome of the audit,[25] or an immediate family member[26] thereof if that family member is in a position to influence the conduct and outcome of the audit or control the investment concerned, may hold:
   (a) any direct financial interest in an audit client or its affiliates; or
   (b) any indirect financial interest (that is, a financial interest owned through an intermediary such as a pension scheme) in an audit client or its affiliates if:
      – the investment is material to the audit firm or to the financial interest owner and the intermediary; or
      – the financial interest owner has both the ability to influence the investment decisions of the intermediary and knowledge of the underlying investment in the audit client (ES2, para 7).

   Where such financial interests exist, no safeguards are able to eliminate, or reduce to an acceptable level, the threat to auditors' objectivity and independence. Thus, they are prohibited (ES2, para 8).

   If a financial interest, like those outlined above, is acquired unintentionally (for example, through inheritance, gift, or merger of audit firms or companies), it is to be disposed of as soon as possible after the person has knowledge, and the right to dispose, of it. If this cannot be effected immediately, the audit firm is to adopt safeguards to ensure the firm's objectivity is preserved until the financial interest is disposed of. Similarly, if a partner of the audit firm, or person in a position to influence the conduct and outcome of the audit, becomes aware that a close family member holds a direct or indirect financial interest of a type specified above, that individual is to report the matter to the engagement partner so that appropriate action can be taken. If the close family member is that of the audit engagement partner, or if the audit engagement partner is unsure about the action to be taken, (s)he is to consult the firm's ethics partner (ES2, paras 12, 13, 16).

---

[25] See footnote 22.

[26] An "immediate family member' is 'a spouse (or equivalent) or dependent" (APB, 2008b).

2. If a person in a position to influence the conduct and outcome of the audit is a shareholder of an audit client because of shareholding requirements, the audit firm is to ensure that:
    - only the minimum number of shares needed to comply with the requirements are held;
    - this shareholding is not material to either the audit client or the individual concerned; and
    - the shareholding is disclosed to those charged with the audit client's governance (or, as is usually the case, the audit client's audit committee) (ES2, para 11).

3. No partner of the audit firm, person in a position to influence the conduct and outcome of the audit, or an immediate family member thereof, may hold a direct or indirect financial interest in the audit client, or its affiliates, as a trustee unless all of the following conditions are met:
    - the person concerned is not an identified potential beneficiary of the trust;
    - the trust's financial interest in the audit client is not material to the trust;
    - the trust is not able to exercise significant influence over the audit client or its affiliates;
    - the person concerned does not have significant influence over the investment decisions of the trust in so far as they relate to the financial interest in the audit client or its affiliates.

Unless these conditions are met, a self-interest threat may be created because the trustee interest may influence the conduct of the audit or the trust may influence the actions of the audit client (ES2, para 18).

4. No audit firm may have as an audit client an organisation in which the firm's pension scheme has a financial interest and the firm is able to influence the investment decisions of the pension scheme's trustees. In such a case, no safeguards can eliminate, or reduce to an acceptable level, the self-interest threat that would result. However, where the relationship between the firm's pension scheme and the audit client is less direct (for example, where the pension fund is invested through a collective investment scheme and the firm's influence is limited to investment policy decisions, such as the allocation of the pension fund between, say, debt and equity investments), the firm's ethics partner is to consider whether or not the indirect investment in the client (or its affiliates) is acceptable (ES2, para 21).

5. No audit firm, person in a position to influence the conduct and outcome of the audit, or an immediate family member thereof may:

      (a) make a loan to, or guarantee the borrowings of, an audit client or its affiliates; or

      (b) accept a loan from, or have borrowings guaranteed by, an audit client or its affiliates

unless three conditions are met, namely:

      – the audit client is a bank or similar deposit-taking institution;

      – the loan or guarantee is made in the ordinary course of business on normal business terms; and

      – in the case of a loan from, or guarantee of borrowings by, the audit client or its affiliates, the loan or guarantee is not material to the audit client or the audit firm (ES2, paras 23–25).

(ii) *Business, employment and personal relationships with an audit client*

A business relationship (i.e., a common commercial interest) between an audit firm, those in a position to influence the conduct and outcome of the audit, and/or their immediate family members, on the one hand, and the audit client, its affiliates, and/or its management, on the other, may, like financial involvement, impair auditors' objectivity and independence. An example of such an interest is afforded by Ernst & Young's profit-sharing agreement with the travel unit of its audit client, American Express Company, in the 1990s. During 2004, the SEC investigated this apparent breach of auditor independence and, as a consequence, in November 2004, American Express Company appointed PricewaterhouseCoopers as auditor in place of Ernst & Young (a position Ernst & Young, and its predecessor firm Arthur Young, had held since 1975) (Raiborn, Schorg and Massoud, 2006). Other examples of business relationships with audit clients include arrangements whereby an audit firm acts as a distributor or marketer of an audit client's products or services; a joint venture between a senior member of the audit team and a director or executive of the audit client; and a transaction which involves the audit firm leasing office space from (or to) an audit client (ES2, para 27).

To counter the self-interest, advocacy or intimidation threat to auditors' objectivity and independence that may arise from such arrangements, ES2 prohibits audit firms, and persons in a position to influence the conduct and outcome of the audit and their immediate family members, from entering business relationships with an audit client or its affiliates. An exception to this is the purchase of goods and services from the audit firm or the audit client (as applicable) in the ordinary course of business on an arm's-length basis where the value involved is not material to either party.

Like business relationships, family, personal and employment relationships between audit firm members and the audit client (or audit client members and the audit firm) can endanger auditors' independence through, in particular, self-interest, self-review, familiarity and/or intimidation threats. Pertinent examples include the infamous personal and employment relationships between Arthur Andersen's audit staff, partners, and former partners, and its audit client, Enron, cited in section 4.2 above (see footnote 10); and the 'personal-service' agreement between an independent director of Best Buy Company in the USA and the company's auditor, Ernst & Young. This relationship resulted in the company replacing Ernst & Young (Best Buy's auditor since 1994) with Deloitte & Touche in December 2004 (Raiborn et al., 2006).

In order to eliminate, or reduce to an acceptable level, threats to auditors' independence from family, personal and employment relationships, ES2 includes the following provisions:

1. Audit firms should establish policies and procedures that ensure:
   (a) the firm is notified of potential employment:
       – by any partner within the firm with any of the firm's audit clients;
       – by any member of an audit engagement team with the audit client concerned;
   (b) where such notice is given, the person concerned is excluded from the relevant audit engagement team and their work on the current and, if appropriate, the most recent audit is reviewed;
   (c) any partner or professional staff member in the audit firm who has an immediate or close family, or other personal, relationship involving an audit client, which the partner or staff member considers might create a threat to auditors' objectivity or independence, reports this fact to the audit firm;
   (d) relevant audit engagement partners are notified promptly of any such reported relationships (paras 44, 62).

2. Where a family or personal relationship involving an audit client is reported to the relevant audit engagement partner, that partner is required to assess the resulting threat to auditors' objectivity and independence and to apply appropriate safeguards to eliminate or reduce the threat to an acceptable level. If unsure of the situation, (s)he is to consult the firm's ethics partner (para 63).

3. If a former audit firm partner joins an audit client, the audit firm is to take prompt action (before any further work is done for the audit client) to ensure that no significant connections remain between the firm and the individual. Further, if the partner joins the client as a director or senior executive and, at any time in the two years prior to the appointment, (s)he played a significant role in that client's audit, the firm is to resign as auditors and not accept re-appointment for two years following the former partner ceasing to be involved with the client's audit or, if sooner, until (s)he ceases to be employed by the former client (paras 42, 48).

4. If an audit client wishes a partner or employee of the audit firm to work for it (or one of its affiliates) temporarily, the audit firm may only agree to this if the client agrees:
   - the agreement is for a short period of time and does not involve staff or partners performing non-audit services prohibited by ES5;
   - the individual concerned will not hold a management position;
   - it is responsible for directing and supervising the work to be performed;
   - the work will not involve making management decisions or exercising discretionary authority to commit the audit client to a particular position or accounting treatment.

   Upon returning to the audit firm, the individual concerned is not to be given an audit role that involves any function or activity that (s)he performed or supervised while working for the client (paras 37, 40).

5. No partner or employee of the audit firm may accept appointment to the board of directors (or a subcommittee thereof) of any client for which the partner or employee undertakes audit work. Similarly, they may not accept a directorship in any entity which holds more than 20 per cent of the voting rights in the audit client (or in which the audit client holds more than 20 per cent of the voting rights). If an immediate or close family member of a person in a position to influence the conduct and outcome of the audit holds such a directorship, that person is to be removed from a position where they can influence the audit. If any partner or employee of the audit firm who is not a member of the audit engagement team has an immediate or close family member who holds such a directorship, that person is to report the fact to the relevant audit engagement partner. The engagement partner is to consider whether the relationship might be regarded by a reasonable and informed third party as impairing the audit firm's objectivity and, if so, the partner is to consult the firm's ethics partner to determine whether appropriate safeguards are in place; if they are not, the firm is to withdraw from the audit (paras 53–55).

6. Where a former director or employee of an audit client, who was in a position to exert significant influence over the preparation of the financial statements, joins the audit firm, that individual is not to be assigned to a position in which (s)he is able to influence the conduct and outcome of the audit for that client, or its affiliates, for a period of at least two years after leaving the client (para 57).

(iii) Long association with an audit client

For many years, the long association of audit firms with particular audit clients has been of major concern to politicians, regulatory and professional committees, and the business press, as a threat to auditors' independence (Arel,

Brody and Pany, 2005; Institute of Chartered Accountants in England and Wales, 2002). Arel *et al.,* (2005) report, for example:

> In 1985, Congressman Richard Shelby asked on the floor of the House of Representatives, "How can an audit firm remain independent ... when it has established long-term personal and professional relationships with a company by auditing that company for many years, some 10, 20 or 30 years?". (p. 2)

They also note that a study released in 2003 by the Fulcrum Financial Group "found that the average auditor tenure for Fortune 1000 companies is 22 years ... [and that] 10% of the companies in the study were found to have had the same auditor for 50 years, with the average tenure of this group being 75 years" (Arel *et al.*, 2005, p. 2).

In 1976 in the USA, auditor rotation was proposed by a Senate Subcommittee chaired by Metcalf as a possible solution to the self-interest, self-review and familiarity threats to auditors' independence that may result from a long association of auditors with particular audit clients (Metcalf, 1976).[27] Since then, arguments for and against two alternative forms of auditor rotation – the rotation of senior members of audit engagement teams and the rotation of audit firms – have been hotly debated in professional and regulatory circles. (These arguments are discussed in section 4.4.4 below.) However, the APB in ES3: *Long association with the audit engagement* (like IFAC's *Code of Ethics*, the EU Commission, 2002, and the Sarbanes-Oxley Act of 2002) has adopted the rotation of senior audit team members as a 'safeguard' but distinguishes between the audits of listed companies and those of other reporting entities.

For listed companies, ES3 requires audit firms to establish policies and procedures that ensure:

   (a) in the absence of special circumstances, no one acts as the audit engagement partner or engagement quality control reviewer[28] for the audit (or holds a combination of these positions) for a continuous period of more than five years, and does not hold a position of responsibility in relation to the audit engagement for at least the following five years (para 12);

   (b) no one acts as a key audit partner,[29] or key audit partner and engagement partner, for a period longer than seven years, and does not hold

---

[27] The Committee was highly critical of the accounting profession and, in a 1,769 page report, made numerous recommendations on how the accounting (including auditing) profession should be regulated (see, for example, Arens and Loebbecke, 1980, p. 26). It is interesting to note that many of the Metcalf Committee's recommendations have been enacted in the Sarbanes-Oxley Act of 2002.

[28] See footnote 24.

[29] A 'key audit partner' is:

> An audit partner ... of the engagement team (other than the engagement partner) who is involved at the group level and is responsible for key decisions or judgments on significant matters, such as on significant subsidiaries or divisions of the audit client, or on significant risk factors that relate to the audit of that client. (APB, 2008b)

a position of responsibility in relation to the audit engagement for at least the following two years (para 18);

(c) where partners (other than key partners) and/or staff have been involved in the audit in senior positions, for a continuous period of more than seven years, the audit engagement partner reviews the safeguards put in place to address the resulting threats to auditors' objectivity and independence and discusses those situations with the engagement quality control reviewer. If issues remain unresolved, these are referred to the firm's ethics partner (para 19).

For reporting entities other than listed companies, ES3 is rather less restrictive. It requires audit firms who have audit engagement partners, key audit partners, and/or staff in senior positions, who have a long association with an audit client, to assess the resulting threats to auditors' objectivity and independence, and to apply safeguards to reduce the threats to an acceptable level. The safeguards may include:

– rotating audit partners and other senior members of the engagement team after a pre-determined number of years;
– involving an additional partner who is not, and has not recently been, a member of the audit engagement team, to review the work of the audit partners and other senior members of the engagement team and to advise them as necessary;
– applying independent internal quality reviews to the engagement in question.

If appropriate safeguards cannot reduce the threat to auditors' independence to an acceptable level, the firm is to resign or not seek reappointment, as applicable (paras 6, 8).

ES3 notes that if an individual has been an audit engagement partner for a continuous period of ten years, careful consideration is to be given to the likely conclusion of a reasonable and informed third party about impairment of the audit firm's objectivity and independence. Further, in any case where an engagement partner is not rotated after ten years, it is important that appropriate safeguards are applied, and reasons for the individual remaining as the audit engagement partner are documented and communicated to those charged with the audit client's governance (or the audit committee if it has one).

(iv) Undue dependence on an audit client for fee income

ES4: *Fees, remuneration and evaluation policies, litigation, gifts and hospitality* recognises that the objectivity of auditors may be compromised if the audit firm is, to any significant extent, economically dependent on an audit client.

Such dependence may inhibit the engagement partner's willingness "to express a qualified opinion on the financial statements, since this could be viewed as likely to lead to [the firm] losing the audit engagement and the entity as a client" (para 30). An audit firm is deemed to be economically dependent on a client if the total fees (for audit and non-audit services) derived from that client and its subsidiaries represent 10 per cent of the audit firm's total fees if it is a listed client, or 15 per cent if it is a non-listed client (para 25, 26).

Following from this reasoning, ES4 prohibits audit firms from acting as auditors for a client if they expect the total fees from that client and its subsidiaries to regularly exceed 10 per cent of the firm's annual fee income if it is a listed client, or 15 per cent if a non-listed client.[30] If necessary, the firm is to resign from the audit or not seek re-appointment, as applicable (paras 23, 24).

Where the regularly expected total fee income from a listed client and its sub-sidiaries is between 5 and 10 per cent of the firm's annual fee income, or between 10 and 15 per cent for a non-listed client, the audit engagement partner is to:
(a) disclose that expectation to the firm's ethics partner and also to those charged with the audit client's governance (or its audit committee), and either:
(b) (i) for a listed client, consider whether appropriate safeguards (such as reducing non-audit work or referring the matter to the engage-ment quality control reviewer) need to be applied in order to reduce the threat to auditors' objectivity and independence to an accept-able level; or
(ii) for a non-listed client, arrange for an external independent quality control review of the audit engagement to be conducted before the audit report is finalised (paras 29, 33).

ES4 (para 34) explains:
A quality control review [whether by the engagement quality control reviewer or an external party], involves discussion with the audit engagement partner, a review of the financial statements and the auditor's report, and consideration of whether the report is appropriate. It also involves a review of selected working papers relating to the significant judgments the engagement team has made and the conclusions they have reached.[31]

_____

[30] If a firm's profits are not shared on a firm-wide basis, the 10 per cent and 15 per cent of fees from a listed or non-listed client, respectively, is to be calculated by reference to the part of the firm on which the audit engagement partner's profit share is calculated. In these cases it may be possible to reassign the client to another part of the firm (ES4, paras 25–27).

[31] Quality control reviews are discussed in greater detail in Chapter 16.

As for economic dependence on an audit client, overdue fees may create a self-interest threat to auditors' objectivity and independence. If a significant part of the previous year's fee is not paid before the audit report on the current year's financial statements is due to be issued, a firm may lean towards issuing an unqualified audit report as this may enhance the firm's prospects of securing payment of the overdue fees. To guard against such eventualities, ES4 requires the basis for calculating the audit fee to be agreed with the audit client each year before significant audit work is undertaken. It also notes that, ordinarily, any outstanding fees for the previous audit period are paid before the audit firm commences any new work (paras 13, 19).

If fees from the audit client are overdue, especially if they are in dispute and the amount involved is not trivial, the audit engagement partner, in consultation with the ethics partner, is to consider whether the firm can continue as auditors or whether the threat to auditors' objectivity and independence is such that no safeguards can eliminate or reduce it to an acceptable level and, therefore, it is necessary to resign. In any case where the audit firm does not resign, the amount of the audit fee for the previous audit, and arrangements for its payment, are to be agreed with the client before the audit firm formally accepts appointment as auditors in respect of the following period (ES4, paras 18, 20, 22).

Economic dependence on an audit client (or group of connected clients), and overdue (and/or disputed) fees from an audit client, although serious, are not the only threats to auditors' objectivity and independence arising from audit fees. The Companies Act 2006, s. 492, provides that, in general, auditors' remuneration is to be fixed by the company's shareholders "by ordinary resolution or in such manner as the [shareholders] may by ordinary resolution determine". However, in practice, auditors' fees have traditionally been settled through direct negotiation between the client's management and the auditors, and it is a widely held view that while this situation continues auditors are unlikely to be truly independent of their clients. They are perceived as unlikely to bite the hand that feeds them!

A significant proposal designed to divorce company officials from negotiating the audit fee with their auditors is that of having audit fees determined according to a fixed scale. The main difficulty with this proposal is identifying a suitable base for developing a scale of fees. The most common suggestion has been the size of the audit client, but there is no consensus as to the appropriate indicator of size. Should it be, for example, total assets? total revenue? total profits? – and, if so, before or after exceptional items? before or after tax? etc.

Even if agreement could be reached on the 'best' indicator of size, this may not be an appropriate basis for determining audit fees. The time, effort and skills required for an audit frequently depend on factors other than size; for example, whether the audit is an initial or subsequent engagement (an initial audit requires additional time to become familiar with the client, its business, its accounting system, etc.); the complexity (or simplicity) of the client's organisational structure, business operations and industry; the quality of the client's internal controls; the expertise of the client's accountancy staff; the presence (or absence) of circumstances which might motivate client-personnel to manipulate the financial statements (for example, plans to float shares or issue debentures during the ensuing accounting period, or managers' bonuses being tied to reported profits).

Further, even if a satisfactory scale of fees could be developed which accommodated factors recognised as affecting the time and skills needed for audits, there is a danger that auditors would be tempted to tailor individual audits to the set fees rather than to the particular circumstances of the audit. In some cases this could result in over-auditing: that is, auditors conducting audit tests beyond those which are strictly necessary because additional time is 'available' under the set fee. In other cases, under-auditing may result: auditors failing to perform tests which are required because the fee is insufficient to cover the time needed.

Direct negotiation of audit fees between auditors and audit-client managements is a serious obstacle to securing and maintaining auditors' objectivity and independence, and it is an obstacle that is difficult to overcome. However, a mechanism that ensures executives who are responsible for the day-to-day management of the entity are not involved in negotiating audit fees with the auditors is that of assigning this responsibility to the audit committee (where the reporting entity has one). Audit committees are discussed in section 4.4.5 below.

(v)   Threatened or actual litigation

Where litigation between an auditor and audit client is in progress, or is likely to take place, it seems most unlikely that the auditor will be able to maintain an independent attitude of mind when evaluating the client's financial statements and supporting evidence. Even if the auditor is, in fact, able to maintain his or her objectivity, independence in appearance will almost certainly be impaired. This applies whether the client has sued the auditor (for example, for negligence), or the auditor has brought a case against the client for occurrences such as deceit or overdue fees.

ES4 explains that where litigation (in relation to audit or non-audit services) takes place between the audit client and audit firm (or any person able to influence the conduct and outcome of the audit), or where litigation is threatened and is likely to proceed, self-interest, advocacy and intimidation threats to the auditors' objectivity and independence are created and the auditor should resign from, or not accept, the audit engagement. This is because the audit firm will be (or will be perceived to be) concerned with achieving a favourable outcome to the litigation; additionally, with the audit team and the audit client on opposing adversarial sides, it seems unlikely that the client's management will feel disposed to make full and frank disclosure to the audit team – a necessary requirement for an effective audit to be performed (paras 41, 42).

(vi) Gifts and hospitality

A self-interest and familiarity threat to auditors' independence may arise if gifts or hospitality are received from an audit client; similarly, a familiarity threat may arise if gifts or hospitality are offered to a client. ES4 observes that the relevant test is not whether auditors consider accepting or offering a gift or hospitality impairs their independence but whether a reasonable and informed third party is likely to conclude that it is impaired (para 50).

In order to avoid their independence from being compromised as a result of gifts and/or hospitality being accepted from, or offered to, an audit client, ES4 (para 49) requires audit firms to establish policies on the nature and value of gifts and hospitality that may be accepted or offered. However, it prohibits audit firms, and those in a position to influence the conduct and outcome of the audit and their immediate family members, from accepting gifts from an audit client unless the value is clearly insignificant (para 44). Nevertheless, ES4 is rather more permissive in respect of hospitality. It observes:

> Hospitality is a component of many business relationships and can provide valuable opportunities for developing an understanding of the audited entity's business and for gaining the insight on which an effective and successful working relationship depends. Therefore, the auditors' objectivity and independence is not necessarily impaired as a result of accepting hospitality from the audited entity, provided it is reasonable in terms of its frequency, its nature and its cost. (para 48)

(vii) Provision of non-audit services to an audit client

The possible impairment of auditors' objectivity and/or independence through the provision of non-audit services to audit clients has been a highly contentious issue for many years. The Commission on Auditors' Responsibilities (1978), commentators such as Cowen (1980) and organisations like Hermes

(2002) have asserted that there is little or no empirical evidence to suggest that the provision of non-audit services to audit clients impairs auditors' independence. However, others from both inside the auditing profession, such as Briloff (1986), and from outside, such as Congressman Dingell (a vocal critic of auditors in the USA) and Austin Mitchell MP (a vocal critic of auditors in the UK), are adamant that the provision of non-audit services to audit clients must, and does, impair auditors' independence. The latter view now generally prevails and many – especially in the USA, where, as noted in Chapter 2, Arthur Andersen provided extensive non-audit services to its audit client Enron – regard the provision of non-audit services to audit clients as posing one of the greatest threats to auditors' independence. Nevertheless, the issue may be viewed from two different perspectives. These are as follows:

1. As explained in Chapter 2, during the course of an audit, the auditor becomes familiar with all aspects of the audit client – its industry, business operations, organisation, accounting system, internal controls, significant risks, key personnel, etc. This familiarity places the auditor in an ideal position to provide financial and management advice to the audit client. The auditor, unlike other outside consultants, does not have to spend time getting to know the client. This clearly reduces the costs involved. Furthermore, because the auditor is familiar with all aspects of the client's organisation, (s)he is able to anticipate the likely impact of any advice given to management, on all parts of the organisation. An outside consultant is likely to become familiar only with the aspect of the entity related to the particular task in hand. This consultant may not, therefore, appreciate wider ramifications within the organisation of advice given to the entity's management. A further benefit to be derived from the auditor providing non-audit services to an audit client is that, during the process of providing those services, the auditor gains greater insight into one or more areas of the client, its business, its risks, its operations, etc. than (s)he would acquire through the audit process – knowledge that is valuable in conducting the audit, assessing the evidence gathered, and forming an opinion on the truth and fairness of the financial statements.[32]

2. While it is generally agreed that auditors are well placed to provide financial and management advice to their audit clients more efficiently and effectively than other outside consultants, and frequently there are beneficial 'spill-overs' from non-audit services to the audit, providing these services is likely to be at the cost of at least some of the auditor's objectivity and independence. The threat to independence comes from

---

[32] The importance of knowledge of the client, its business, risks, personnel, etc. to the audit is discussed in detail in Chapter 8, section 8.4.

four main sources: self-interest, self-review of non-audit work, becoming indistinct from management, and adopting an advocacy role.

– *Self-interest threat*: ES5: *Non-audit services provided to audit clients* reports: "In relation to non-audit services, the main self-interest threat concerns fees and economic dependence" (para 17). If the provision of non-audit services is lucrative, auditors may be tempted to bias the opinion expressed in the audit report in the client's favour rather than risk losing the client – and the associated lucrative non-audit service work. The limitation imposed by ES4 on the proportion of the firm's annual fee income that may be derived from any one client and its subsidiaries [noted in (iv) above] has, to some extent, limited this danger but it cannot, by itself, eliminate the threat to auditors' independence from this source, or reduce it to an acceptable level.

– *Self-review threat*: If an auditor (or audit firm) advises an audit client on, say, a new accounting system and the client, acting on that advice, installs the new system, in any subsequent audit the auditor (or members of the audit firm) will review the outcome of their own (or their firm's) advice. In this circumstance, it is difficult to believe that the auditor will evaluate the system with the same level of objectivity as (s)he would apply had the advice on the system come from an outside consultant. Even if the auditor is, in fact, able to maintain an objective and unbiased attitude of mind, it may be difficult for a reasonable and informed outside observer to accept that this is the case and so, as a minimum, independence in appearance will be impaired.

A similar situation exists when an auditor provides a non-audit service and the results of that service impact on the financial statements. An extreme example is afforded by an auditor both preparing and auditing a set of financial statements. Even if the auditor manages to maintain an impartial attitude of mind whilst performing the audit, it may be difficult for a reasonable and informed third party to conclude that this is the case. Other examples include auditors providing valuation services for audit clients, where the valuation amounts have a material effect on the financial statements, and internal audit services, where the auditors place reliance on the internal audit work performed.

The situation might be helped if some other person or group within the audit firm compiles the financial statements or provides the advisory service. However, independence in appearance, if not in fact, is still at a lower level than would apply if the audit firm were not involved in providing the service concerned to the audit client. Further, ES5 notes that in cases where the non-audit service involves a significant degree of subjective judgment, and/or the results of the advisory service have a material effect on the preparation or presentation of the financial statements, it is unlikely that safeguards can be applied that would reduce the self-review threat to an acceptable level (para 23).

- *Management threat*: If an auditor provides non-audit services to an audit client that involve making judgments or decisions that are properly the responsibility of management, then the distinction between the auditor and the client becomes blurred. ES5 warns that, if auditors become closely aligned with the views and interests of management, this may impair or call into question their ability to apply a proper degree of professional scepticism when auditing the financial statements (para 25). This may occur, for example, if an auditor (or audit firm) designs and implements information technology systems (including financial information systems) for an audit client and the client's management lacks the expertise to take responsibility for the system(s) concerned. In this situation, the auditor, in essence, is contracted by the client as an expert and is relied upon to make significant decisions in respect of the system(s). If these relate to internal control or financial reporting systems, it is unlikely that any safeguards can reduce the threats to auditors' independence to an acceptable level (ES5, para 53).

- *Advocacy threat*: If an auditor agrees to provide non-audit services that involve adopting an advocacy role for the audit client, (s)he will, of necessity, support a position aligned to that of the client. This could make it difficult for the auditor to adopt an objective, unbiased attitude of mind when conducting the audit – or, at the very least, it would be difficult for a reasonable and informed third party to conclude that the auditor can, and will, adopt such an attitude. For example, if the auditor agrees to provide tax advice to an audit client and this involves (or results in) the auditor acting as an advocate for the client before Commissioners of HM Revenue & Customs (or another tax tribunal), it is likely that the auditor's objectivity and independence will be impaired, at least to an extent. ES5 (para 30) notes that, if a non-audit service requires an auditor to act as an advocate for an audit client in relation to matters that are material to the financial statements, it is unlikely that any safeguards can eliminate or reduce the advocacy threat to an acceptable level.

Notwithstanding the benefits that may be derived from auditors providing non-audit services to their audit clients, during the 1990s, the SEC in the USA became so concerned about the growth in the provision of non-audit services by auditors to their audit clients, and the consequential likely impairment of auditors' independence, that it introduced strict new independence rules (SEC, 2000b) limiting the services auditors could provide to their SEC registrant audit clients (essentially, all US public companies). The SEC's Chief Accountant, Turner (2001), explained that, in formulating the rules, the SEC was guided by four principles that indicate a breach of auditors' independence:

> The four principles specify an auditor would not be considered independent when the auditor:
> 1. Has a mutual or conflicting interest with the audit client.
> 2. Is placed in the position of auditing his or her own work.
> 3. Acts as management or an employee of the audit client, or
> 4. Is in the position of being an advocate for the client. (p. 5)

These principles coincide with the threats to auditors' independence resulting from auditors providing non-audit services to audit clients identified in ES5 (outlined above). They also underlie the activities the Sarbanes-Oxley Act of 2002 (SOX; s. 201) prohibits auditors from providing to their SEC registrant audit clients, namely:[33]

> (1) bookkeeping or other services related to the accounting records or financial statements of the audit client;
> (2) financial information systems design and implementation;
> (3) appraisal or valuation services, fairness opinions, or contribution-in-kind reports;[34]
> (4) actuarial services;
> (5) internal audit outsourcing services;
> (6) management functions or human resources;
> (7) broker or dealer, investment adviser, or investment banking services;
> (8) legal services and expert services unrelated to the audit; and
> (9) any other service that the [Public Company Accounting Oversight] Board determines, by regulation, is impermissible.

Auditors may provide any non-prohibited non-audit service to their audit clients, including tax services, but before doing so the client's audit committee must approve their provision of the service in question (SOX, s. 201).[35]

---

[33] The activities prohibited by SOX reflect those prohibited by the SEC's Independence Rule (SEC, 2000b). Similarly, many of the provisions of IFAC's *Code of ethics for professional accountants*, in so far as they relate to auditors' independence, reflect those in the SEC's Independence Rule. These, in turn, are reflected in the APB's Ethical Standards.

[34] The SEC (2000b) explains:

> Appraisal and valuation services include any process of valuing assets, both tangible and intangible, or liabilities. Fairness opinions are opinions that an accounting firm provides on the adequacy of consideration in a transaction . . . . [I]f an audit firm provides these services to an audit client, when it is time to audit the financial statements the accountant could well end up reviewing his or her own work. . . . (p. 55)

[35] In April 2008, the Public Company Accounting Oversight Board (PCAOB) adopted a rule which requires auditors of public companies listed or registered in the USA (or subsidiaries thereof), before accepting a new or continuing audit engagement, to describe in writing to the audit committee all relationships between the audit firm (and its affiliates) and the company (or persons in a financial reporting oversight in the company) that may reasonably be thought to bear on the audit firm's independence. The audit firm is also required to hold discussions with the audit committee about the potential effects any such relationships may have on the audit firm's independence (PCAOB, 2008).

ES5 does not directly prohibit auditors from providing specified non-audit services to audit clients in a manner akin to SOX;[36] however, as we noted above, in its explanation of the self-interest, self-review, management and advocacy threats to auditors' independence that may result from auditors providing non-audit services to their audit clients, ES5 observes that, in certain circumstances, it is unlikely that safeguards are able to reduce the threat(s) to auditors' independence to an acceptable level. In these circumstances, the audit firm must relinquish or decline (as applicable) the provision of either audit or non-audit services to the client: it cannot provide both.

For other circumstances, ES5 specifies safeguards that audit firms or engagement partners are required to adopt in order to eliminate, or reduce to an acceptable level, threats to auditors' independence resulting from the provision of non-audit services to audit clients. These include the following:

1. Audit firms are to establish policies and procedures that require partners or staff of the firm or its associated firms, when considering whether to accept a proposed engagement to provide a non-audit service to an audit client or any of its affiliates (or a proposed significant change to an existing engagement), to communicate details of the proposed (or changed) engagement to the audit engagement partner (ES5, para 8).[37]

2. Before an audit firm accepts a proposed engagement to provide a non-audit service to an audit client, the audit engagement partner is to:
    (a) consider whether a reasonable and informed third party is likely to regard the objectives of the proposed engagement as inconsistent with those of the audit of the financial statements;
    (b) identify and assess the significance of any related threat(s) to the auditors' objectivity and independence; and
    (c) identify and assess the effectiveness of available safeguards to eliminate or reduce the identified threat(s) to an acceptable level (ES5, para 11).
  If the audit engagement partner concludes that:
    (i) a reasonable and informed third party is likely to regard the objectives of the proposed non-audit service engagement as inconsistent with those of the financial statement audit; or

---

[36] It should be recalled from Chapter 2 (section 2.2.6) that the SOX provisions relate not only to the audits (and auditors) of public companies registered in the USA but also to those of all companies listed on a USA stock exchange (irrespective of where they are registered) and, also, to those of all significant subsidiaries of companies registered or listed in the USA irrespective of where those subsidiaries are located.

[37] The Combined Code on Corporate Governance (FRC, 2006) requires the audit committees of companies listed on the London Stock Exchange to develop their company's policy on engaging the company's external auditors to supply non-audit services. ES5 (para 10) requires, in the case of listed companies the group audit engagement partner to establish that the company has communicated its policy to its subsidiaries and other affiliates, and to obtain confirmation that the auditors of the affiliates will comply with this policy.

(ii) no appropriate safeguards are available to eliminate or reduce the related threat(s) to auditors' independence to an acceptable level,

(s)he is to inform relevant others within the firm of that conclusion. The audit firm is then to decline the non-audit work or not accept, or resign from, the audit engagement. If the audit engagement partner is in doubt as to the appropriate action to be taken, (s)he is to resolve the matter through consultation with the firm's ethics partner (ES5, paras 13, 33).

3. If an audit firm decides to accept an engagement to provide non-audit services to an audit client, the audit engagement partner is to ensure that relevant matters, including significant judgments, are appropriately documented. The matters to be documented include:
   (a) the reasoning underlying the decision to accept the engagement to provide non-audit services;
   (b) identified threats to the auditors' objectivity and independence;
   (c) safeguards adopted and the reasons why they are considered to be effective; and
   (d) the communication of these matters to those charged with the client's governance (ES5, paras 37, 38).

4. The audit engagement partner is to ensure that those charged with the audit client's governance (or, in most cases, its audit committee) are appropriately informed on a timely basis of:
   (i) all significant matters related to the provision of non-audit services that impact on the auditors' objectivity and independence, and the safeguards the audit firm has applied; and
   (ii) for listed companies, any inconsistencies between the APB's ESs and the company's policy on the provision of non-audit services by the audit firm, and any apparent breach of that policy (ES5, para 35).

   ES5 (para 36) explains the importance of this communication:

   > Transparency is a key element in addressing the issues raised by the provision of non-audit services by audit firms to the entities audited by them. This can be facilitated by timely communication with those charged with governance of the audited entity.

4.4 OTHER PROPOSALS FOR STRENGTHENING AUDITORS' INDEPENDENCE

4.4.1 Key objectives of other proposals

Many politicians, investors, financial journalists and others have recognised the importance of auditors' independence to the value of the audit function. They have also drawn attention to the dangers posed to that independence, particularly as a result of auditors becoming too familiar with their audit clients' managements, and being dependent on those managements for their continued appointment. From the measures discussed in section 4.3, it is clear that, especially since the turn of the century, significant legislative and regulatory changes have been introduced to try to ensure that auditors avoid situations where threats to their independence cannot be eliminated or reduced to an acceptable level. However, since the mid-1970s and the unexpected collapse of Penn Central in the USA, concern about the apparent impairment of auditors' independence in high-profile cases such as Johnson Matthey Bankers, Ferranti, Bank of Credit & Commerce International (BCCI), and Barings Bank in the UK, Enron, World-Com, Tyco and Xerox in the USA, Parmalat in Italy and HIH in Australia, has resulted in a number of proposals designed, in particular, to prevent:

(i) audit client managements from being involved in the appointment of their company's auditor; and/or
(ii) auditors from becoming too familiar with their audit client managements.

We examine four such proposals in the sub-sections which follow, namely:
- the appointment of auditors by the State or a State agency;
- the appointment of auditors by a shareholder or stakeholder panel;
- mandatory auditor rotation;
- audit committees.

4.4.2 Appointment of company auditors by the State or a State agency

It is a widely held view that auditors will not be truly independent of their audit clients' managements while those managements are influential in the auditors' appointment and remuneration. This has given rise to the suggestion that auditors' independence would be strengthened if company auditors were appointed by the State, a State agency or an independent oversight body. Haber (2005), for example, notes:

> Coverage and discussion of the Enron scandal tends to focus on the length of the relationship between Andersen and Enron and the additional services rendered by Andersen to Enron ... [however,] Andersen's independence would be questioned simply because ... the client paid a fee to the auditor. ... Auditors are hired and paid by the client, but their product is really for use by the public, ... Having the stock exchanges (or the SEC or another oversight body) be responsible for hiring and paying the auditors would remove the potential for independence impairment. If the goal is to increase the public's perception of auditor independence, then the company being audited can no longer be the client. Another party must contract for the audit, pay the auditor, and become the client. Then there would be no perceived or actual impairment of independence. All other solutions ... leave open the potential for questioning independence, and therefore for undermining the usefulness of the audit process (pp. 1–2)

However, this 'solution' to the auditor independence problem is not without significant difficulties. For example, if the State, a State agency, or an oversight body such as the Public Company Accounting Oversight Body (PCAOB) in the USA or the Financial Reporting Council (FRC) in the UK were to control auditors' appointment and remuneration, then the State could, in effect, also control the audit function. This would introduce the possibility of auditors becoming susceptible to the political agenda of the day and of the audit profession losing its professional independence. Further, if auditors were appointed by the State, a State agency, or an oversight body, they would be accountable to the entity that appointed them. If, at the same time, the directors of companies remained accountable to their shareholders, a conflict between the directors' and auditors' accountabilities could arise, with consequential difficulties for the achievement of an effective audit.

4.4.3 Shareholder/stakeholder panel

The potential conflict of directors' and auditors' accountabilities (resulting from auditors being appointed by the State, a State agency, or an oversight body) could be avoided if auditors were accountable to an independent panel of shareholders or shareholder representatives. Rather than the company's shareholders as a body being legally responsible for appointing the auditor and, for pragmatic reasons, delegating this responsibility to the company's management (as is currently the position),[38] the shareholders could appoint a panel (which would exclude the company's directors) to represent their interests in respect of appointing, remunerating, monitoring and appraising the company's auditor. In this way, both the directors and the auditor would be separately accountable to the company's shareholders.

The idea of a shareholder panel was mooted by the APB (1992, 1994) and it was also suggested that, in time, it might develop into a stakeholder panel. Such a panel would represent a wider group of interests – those of the company's stakeholders (including the shareholders) – rather than those of the shareholders alone (Hatherly, 1995).[39] However, a possible criticism of the stakeholder panel idea is that, by involving a wider set of stakeholders in the auditor appointment and monitoring process, some conflict in the accountability of the auditor and the directors would be re-introduced. While the auditor would be accountable to the company's stakeholders (through the stakeholder panel) the directors would legally be accountable only to the shareholders.

From the perspective of strengthening auditors' independence, the shareholder/stakeholder panel is conceptually superior to the audit committee, which is discussed in section 4.4.5 below. This is because, unlike stakeholders

---

[38] The existing position is discussed in Chapter 5, section 5.2.4.

[39] The notion of a stakeholder panel accords with the idea discussed in Chapter 1 (section 1.6.3) that the audit is an integral element of securing corporate accountability.

(or shareholders) who are outside – and independent of – the auditee's governance structure, the audit committee is a committee of the board of directors and it cannot therefore appraise, or support, the auditor independently of the board. Although the audit committee should comprise mainly (or wholly) non-executive directors (who are independent of the day-to-day management of the company), it is the board as a whole (including executive as well as non-executive directors) which is legally responsible for the overall performance, direction and conduct of the company.

Although the shareholder/stakeholder panel idea may have conceptual superiority over alternative proposals for securing auditors' independence, its implementation presents serious difficulties. For example, if the shareholder or stakeholder panel is to be responsible for the appointment, remuneration and monitoring of the company's auditor, its members would gain detailed knowledge of the company, its financial performance and its prospects that would not be available (at least at the same time) to all other shareholders and investors. As a consequence, there is a danger that, if some members of the panel traded in the company's shares, they would be open to allegations of insider trading.

There is also the difficulty of the appointment of the shareholder or stakeholder panel. Should, for example, the shareholder panel comprise, or be elected or appointed by, only shareholders who intend, or guarantee, to hold their shares in the company for, say, the next 12 months? Should the panel comprise, or be elected or appointed by, only those who have been shareholders in the company for a specified number of years? If so, what period should be specified? and so on. The appointment criteria are even more problematic for a stakeholder panel. For example, how are the stakeholder groups to be represented on the panel to be identified? How are the representatives of disparate groups such as customers, suppliers and the local community to be selected? How large should the panel be? How are the places on the panel to be allocated to the various stakeholder groups, each of which has a distinct relationship with the company?

Notwithstanding its conceptual merit, largely as a consequence of implementation difficulties, to date the idea of a shareholder/stakeholder panel as a mechanism for divorcing company managements from the auditor appointment process has not attracted much support.

4.4.4 Mandatory auditor rotation

As noted in section 4.3.3(iii) above, the merits and demerits of two alternative forms of auditor rotation – the rotation of senior members of audit teams (but retaining the audit within the firm) and the rotation of audit firms responsible for a particular audit client – have been debated in professional and regulatory circles since Senator Metcalf (1976) suggested auditor rotation as a means of preventing auditors from becoming too familiar with their clients and of increasing competition within the auditing market.

Support for, and opposition to, both proposals has been expressed from time to time in many countries of the world. (The key arguments for and against mandatory rotation are discussed below.) However, as noted in section 4.3.3(iii) above, notwithstanding arguments to the contrary, the rotation of audit engagement partners, independent partners, key audit partners and audit staff in senior positions has been mandated for the audits of listed companies in the UK by APB Ethical Standard 3 since 2004, and similar provisions are contained in IFAC's *Code of ethics for professional accountants* and the EU Commission's *Recommendation on Auditors' Independence* (EU Commission, 2002). Likewise, in the USA, SOX, s. 203, prohibits "the lead (or coordinating) audit partner (having primary responsibility for the audit), or the audit partner responsible for reviewing the audit" (equivalent to the audit engagement partner and engagement quality control reviewer[40] in the UK) from providing audit services to a public company for more than five years. These requirements may appear to be a reaction by regulators to the audit failures associated with the Enron, WorldCom, Tyco, Parmalat and similar debacles. However, in reality, they are a formalisation, and extension, of measures previously introduced by the professional accounting bodies. For example, in 1985, the American Institute of Certified Public Accountants (AICPA) required all firms joining its Securities and Exchange Commission (SEC) Practice Section[41] to rotate the audit engagement partner of an SEC registered audit client every seven years. Similarly, in 1994, the Institutes of Chartered Accountants in England and Wales (ICAEW), of Scotland (ICAS) and in Ireland (ICAI) introduced a requirement for the engagement partner responsible for the audit of a public listed company to be rotated every seven years.

Thus, by the turn of the 21st century, the rotation of audit engagement partners (if not of other senior audit personnel) was generally accepted both as a concept and as a practice. The same does not apply to the rotation of audit firms. However, according to Pajuelo (2003), in Brazil (where audit firm rotation was introduced in 1999), the securities regulator (CVM):

> believes that audit firm rotation would provide a better safeguard against improper accounting than mere rotation of the engagement partners. An auditor may be less likely to go easy on a client's audit for the sake of retaining the relationship if the engagement will end after several years.

---

[40] See footnote 24.

[41] See Chapter 16, section 16.2.3.

Nevertheless, the issue remains open to debate, at least in the USA. In 2002, SOX, s. 207, required the "Comptroller General of the United States [to] conduct a study and review of the potential effects of requiring the mandatory rotation of registered public accounting firms". The General Accounting Office (GAO) reported the results of the study[42] in November 2003. It concluded that "mandatory audit firm rotation may not be the most efficient way to enhance auditor independence and audit quality considering the additional financial costs and the loss of institutional knowledge of a public company's previous auditor of record" (GAO, 2003, p. 8). It recommended that, given the provisions of SOX that are designed to strengthen auditors' independence, the best course of action is for the SEC and the PCAOB to monitor the effectiveness of the SOX requirements before any further measures are introduced.

The conclusion of the GAO report, namely, that the costs associated with mandatory rotation of audit firms are likely to exceed the benefits, reflects that reached by earlier investigations of the issue. These include those conducted by the Commission on Auditors Responsibilities (CAR; 1978); the National Commission on Fraudulent Financial Reporting (Treadway Commission, 1987) and the SEC Practice Section of the AICPA (AICPA; 1992) in the USA; Arrunada and Paz-Ares (1997) in Spain; the Review Group on Auditing (2000) in Ireland; Ramsay (2001) in Australia; and the Committee on the Financial Aspects of Corporate Governance (CFACG; Cadbury Committee, 1992), the Institute of Chartered Accountants in England and Wales (ICAEW; 2002) and the Co-ordinating Group on Audit and Accounting Issues (CGAA; 2003) in the UK.[43]

These investigations were able to consider, *inter alia*, evidence from countries that practised mandatory audit firm rotation. For example, in Italy, three-year mandatory audit firm rotation (with a maximum of two re-appointments, i.e., a total of nine years) has applied to firms auditing public listed companies since 1974. In Spain, mandatory audit firm rotation for firms auditing listed clients was introduced in 1988 (with a minimum period of appointment of three years and a maximum of nine years); it was abolished in 1995 by the Limited Liability Partnership Act. The Czech Republic introduced mandatory audit firm rotation (with a four-year maximum period of appointment) in 1989 but abolished

---

[42] In addition to reviewing prior research, the GAO surveyed 97 large public accounting firms with at least 10 public clients registered with the SEC, 330 of the Fortune 1000 public companies, 450 other domestic companies and mutual funds, and 391 foreign companies registered with the SEC (GAO, 2003).

[43] An anonymous article in *The Finance Professional* (Anon., 2006) reports:
> [I]nternational research shows a general lack of investor support for mandatory audit rotation. Virtually every group that has studied the suggestion has found that the perceived benefits are outweighed by the costs, including the potential costs to shareholders. . . . The conclusion is a compelling one: mandatory audit firm rotation is a bad idea.

it in 1992. In 1996, the system was introduced in the Slovak Republic for all audits (with a maximum period of appointment of three years) but it was abolished in 2000. A two-year audit firm rotation was briefly introduced into Latvia for banks but was dropped in 2001 "following complaints from two of the country's largest banks that they were unable to find an international accounting firm prepared to undertake the audit" (FEE, 2004, p. 6). In 1999, Brazil introduced a five-year mandatory audit firm rotation requirement for all listed companies "following the bankruptcy of two major banks" (ICAEW, 2002, p. 10); the first mandated rotation of audit firms commenced in May 2004 (Pajuelo, 2003). In 2002, Singapore introduced a five-year mandatory audit firm rotation for banking engagements as "part of an ongoing effort to enhance the independence and effectiveness of external auditors" (Harian, 2002).

From the conclusions of detailed studies of the merits and demerits of mandatory audit firm rotation, together with the experience of a significant number of countries which have introduced and subsequently abolished the system, there is clear evidence that, at least at this point of time, mandatory rotation of audit firms is generally believed not to be cost-effective. Nevertheless, a number of strong arguments have been advanced in its favour. We consider some of these below and then consider some of the contrary arguments.

(a) *Arguments in favour of mandatory audit firm rotation*

(i) The quality and competence of auditors' work tends to decline over time as auditors become over-familiar with their audit clients and, as a consequence, begin to lose their professional scepticism and to make unjustified assumptions. An auditor may, for example, make assumptions about the effectiveness of certain internal controls and the reliability of management's representations based on the findings of previous audits, instead of objectively evaluating current evidence. Arel *et al.* (2005) explain this situation and the benefit of audit firm rotation in the following terms:

> Auditors may become stale and view the audit as a simple repetition of earlier engagements. This staleness fosters a tendency to anticipate results rather than keeping alert to ... changes in circumstances ... [R]epeat audit engagements [also] allow auditors to rely on the judgments of prior auditors in deciding whether a management estimate is in accordance with GAAP [Generally Accepted Accounting Principles]. Mandatory audit firm rotation will periodically force new auditors to review management's representation for compliance with GAAP and may force management to adopt more-conservative accounting practices. (p. 37)

Similarly FEE (2004, p. 9), citing Arrunada and Paz-Ares (1997), notes:

> A long period working with the same client can lead the auditor to put too much trust in the previous years' work and ... to treat the work as a repetition of the reviews performed in prior years.... [T]his creates a tendency

> to anticipate results instead of being alert to subtle and often surreptitious, though important, anomalies. A similar effect [applies to] "self revision" cases, those in which the auditor must report negatively on his previous work. . . . [B]y bringing a "fresh view" and forcing an in-depth review, rotation might attenuate these problems.

(ii)   A long-term relationship with an audit client is likely to result in the development of a close personal relationship between the auditor and the client's management. This may result in auditors identifying too closely with management and reducing their objectivity and impartial attitude of mind when conducting the client's audits. Mandatory audit firm rotation prevents long-term relationships with audit clients from developing.

(iii) As a consequence of the financial rewards associated with maintaining a long-term relationship with an audit client, auditors may be tempted to 'overlook' or to 'accommodate' management's viewpoint on financial reporting issues. As Bazerman, Loewenstein and Moore (2002) observe: "auditors have strong business reasons to remain in clients' good graces and are thus highly motivated to approve their clients' accounts" (p. 99). Mandatory audit firm rotation nullifies auditors' desire to 'remain in clients' good graces' and 'frees up' audit firms to challenge questionable client practices. The auditee will be a client for a limited period only so the audit firm does not risk future revenue streams if it challenges aggressive accounting practices, dubious judgments or unorthodox recording of business transactions.

(iv)   Mandatory audit firm rotation increases the public's perception of auditors' independence as it provides a distancing between audit firm and audit client personnel. An unpublished study by the SDA Università Bocconi (2002) in Milan provides support for this proposition. It reports:

> [T]he results of the empirical research performed indicates that many respondents (internal auditors, managers of Italian listed companies, financial analysts . . . [and] Big 5 audit firm partners . . .) believed that the current mandatory audit rotation rule in Italy constitutes a potential mechanism to improve auditor independence. (cited by FEE, 2004, p. 8)

(v)   The costs associated with mandatory rotation are significantly less than the costs associated with audit failures. Healey (2004), for example, notes that Morgan Stanley estimates the loss in market capitalisation resulting from the failures of WorldCom, Tyco, Qwest, Enron and Computer Associates alone to be about $460 billion. He compares this with his estimate of the annual cost of rotation by the Big 4 accounting firms, assuming rotation occurs every five years, of approximately $1.2 billion.

(vi) A consequence of mandatory rotation is that a successor audit firm will, at some future time, review the financial statement judgments made by the current audit firm. The successor firm will bring 'fresh eyes' to the engagement and any financial statement errors or irregularities that may have been overlooked, or acquiesced to, by the predecessor auditor are likely to come to light. Awareness of this eventuality reduces the likelihood of the current auditor overlooking accounting irregularities or signing off on controversial accounting procedures. Support for this benefit of auditor rotation has been provided by the Executive Counsel of the Accountants' Joint Disciplinary Scheme (JDS).[44] According to the ICAEW (2002):

> [He] has expressed his opinion that an auditor will perform a more thorough and sceptical audit and will be more inclined to fix any problems encountered, if they know that there will be a new auditor scrutinising their work in the near future. (p. 14)

(vii) Mandatory audit firm rotation promotes greater competition amongst audit firms. As Raiborn et al. (2006) explain: "[M]andatory rotation puts all audit firms on some degree of level footing and could encourage smaller firms to grow and develop niche specializations that would allow greater competition with the Big Four" (p. 40). Support for the notion that mandatory audit firm rotation increases competition in the audit market is provided by Arrunada and Paz-Ares (1995). They note that, following the introduction of mandatory rotation in Spain in 1988, the non-Big (then) six audit firms' share of the statutory audit market increased from 28 per cent to 40 per cent (as reported, ICAEW, 2002, p. 18).

The key arguments in favour of mandatory audit firm rotation are succinctly summarised by the Co-ordinating Group on Audit and Accounting Issues (CGAA, 2003) as follows:

> In a long-term audit relationship, the auditors will tend to identify too closely with management, their proper professional scepticism will be diluted and they will be more likely to smooth over areas of difficulty in order to preserve the relationship and in particular the long-term income which flows from it. In other words, the longer their tenure, the more likely that the auditors will be less rigorous, more inclined to rely on what they are told by management and less likely to press on difficult issues. All these factors suggest that rotation would enhance audit effectiveness and quality. (para 1.26)

---

[44] The JDS conducts independent investigations of the work and conduct of Chartered Accountants in the UK in cases of public concern. Cases are referred to the JDS by the ICAEW and ICAS, and the investigations are led by the Executive Counsel, a barrister employed by the JDS. Where he finds sufficient evidence, he lays complaints against firms and/or individual Chartered Accountants.

Reviewing the arguments advanced in favour of mandatory auditor rotation, it can be seen that many apply equally to the rotation of senior audit team personnel (while retaining the audit within the firm) and to the rotation of audit firms. The benefits to be derived from the mandatory rotation of audit firms, but not from the rotation of senior audit team personnel, are the removal of the lure of continued financial rewards flowing to the audit firm, the public's perception of increased independence and increased competition amongst audit firms [(iii), (iv) and (vii) above].

Although the arguments in favour of mandatory auditor rotation may seem compelling, opponents of the system support their position with equally strong contrary arguments.

(b) Arguments against mandatory audit firm rotation

(i)   During the course of an audit, the audit team gains a thorough knowledge of the client's industry, business, policies, operations, accounting system, internal controls, key personnel, and so on – an essential requirement for an effective audit in today's environment. However, as a consequence of the increasing complexity and size of many modern businesses in terms of their organisational structure, business processes, financial controls, technology and geographical spread, it takes auditors an increasing amount of time to thoroughly understand a client and its operations. Additionally, as a result of the increasing complexity and continued development of accounting standards, auditors need to gain an in-depth understanding of their client's business complexities in order to ensure they are able to assess the impact of changes to financial reporting requirements on the client's financial statements. The AICPA (1992) observed that newly appointed auditors need to climb a steep learning curve if they are to become, not simply acquainted or conversant with, but deeply knowledgeable about the client's operating environment, risks, and technical accounting policies and procedures. It estimated that auditors require two to three years on an engagement in order to fully understand the business, procedures and structure of a complex client.

Under a mandatory rotation system, the institutional knowledge of the incumbent auditor is lost with each change of audit firm. Following from this, opponents of mandatory rotation assert that a new auditor's lack of knowledge of the client's operations, financial information systems, and financial reporting practices dramatically reduces audit quality.

(ii)   In order to perform an effective audit, auditors must build a co-operative relationship with the client regardless of the period of the auditor–client relationship. As Arel *et al.* (2005) explain:

> [A] client must feel comfortable with an auditor and be willing to share information and discuss problems when they exist. . . . An auditor must be able to gauge when the client is not revealing all available information, and this often comes from knowing the client and its management. Auditors from a new firm are faced with a "getting to know each other" stage and are unlikely to have the necessary open, respectful professional relationship that builds over time. . . . The familiarity the auditor has with a [client] provides a better understanding of the issues and a better appreciation for the changes that have taken place from one year to the next. (p. 37)

Raiborn *et al.* (2006) add to this by observing:

> In all instances of relationship change [such as when a new auditor is appointed under a system of rotation], there is a high potential for misunderstanding, uncertainty, and ambiguity – all of which could have critical impacts on the level of audit risk. (p. 41)

(iii)   Audit failure rates are higher during the first few years of an engagement when the auditors have yet to develop the institutional and personnel knowledge necessary for the early discovery and resolution of audit problems. Evidence for this assertion is provided by, for example, the AICPA (1992), which analysed 406 cases of alleged audit failure and found that such allegations are nearly three times more likely when the auditing firm is conducting its first or second audit of a client. The study cites John Burton, former Chief Accountant of the SEC, who stated:

> In the overwhelming majority of situations . . . the problem in these cases arose from too little involvement by the auditors in the activities of their clients, rather than too much. A significant proportion of cases arose in initial audits where the main pattern was normally one of the client misleading the auditor rather than conspiring with him. (as cited, ICAEW, 2002, pp. 15–16)

Similarly, George (2004), who studied audit failures between 1996 and 2001, found that audit failures in aggregate and by type occurred most often in the first three years, and in seven years or more, of auditor tenure. He concluded that the risk of audit failure increases with each change of audit firm and that a reduction in audit quality results when a new auditor is unfamiliar with the client's business and operations. This implies that new audit engagements are riskier than continuing engagements; as mandatory rotation of audit firms increases the number of new engagements, it also increases the risk of audit failures.

(iv)   Audit firm rotation results in significantly increased costs for both audit firms and their clients. During the initial years of any audit, auditors must devote considerable time and effort to becoming familiar with the client, its business and its systems. Research by the SDA Università Bocconi in Italy found that up to 40 per cent more working hours, and more qualified resources, were required in the first year of an audit and that the "'training period' is never less than two to three years for complex international groups" (as reported, ICAEW, 2002, p. 19).

There are also additional costs for the client in terms of selecting new auditors and familiarising them with the company's business, operations and systems. The SDA Università Bocconi researchers (2002) found that an auditor change results in an "increased burden on managers, personnel and internal auditors in supplying necessary information about corporate governance, internal control systems, organizational structure, market relations, and so on" (as cited, ICAEW, 2002, p. 20).

Some commentators (for example, Arrunada and Paz-Ares, 1995) have further noted that mandatory rotation of audit firms reduces competition in the audit market and that this, in turn, results in increased audit costs. As audit engagements are for a limited period only, and as audits become available on a regular basis, audit firms have little incentive to be efficient or to compete intensively (as reported, ICAEW, 2002, p. 19).

(v)   Mandatory auditor rotation results in lower audit quality as audit firms, aware that a particular audit engagement is to be terminated after a limited number of years, have little incentive to invest in the development of the audit process to achieve increased effectiveness and efficiencies. Arrunada and Paz-Ares (1995) contend that, where audit firms are subject to mandatory rotation, they are unlikely to invest in either new audit technologies or in training audit staff. The lack of investment in audit staff results in lower-quality auditors and this, combined with reduced investment in new technologies, results in lower-quality audits (as reported, ICAEW, 2002, p. 17).

A further adverse impact on audit quality from mandatory audit firm rotation results from audit firms transferring audit partners and staff from one client to another as a rotation period nears its end. Respondents to the GAO survey (2003)[45] indicated that they would shift their most knowledgeable and experienced audit personnel from the current engagement to another audit client towards the end of the rotation period – even though they believed that re-assigning these individuals would increase the risk of audit failure.

(vi) Companies in specialised industries, such as banking, insurance and mining, are particularly vulnerable to a reduction in audit quality as a result of mandatory rotation. Only a small number of firms are likely to

---

[45] See footnote 42.

have the required complement of audit personnel with specialist knowledge and expertise in these industries. One of these firms may provide a company in a specialised industry with non-audit services that are considered incompatible with the provision of audit services [as specified by, for example, SOX, the APB's Ethical Standards, IFAC's *Code of ethics*, or the EU Commission's Recommendation (2002)]. When the company is forced to change its auditors under an audit firm rotation system, it may be forced to engage an audit firm that lacks the desired depth of industry expertise. This is likely to increase the risk of audit failure and potentially harm the company and its shareholders.[46] FEE (2004, p. 12), quoting Arrunada and Paz-Ares (1997), sums up the position as follows:

> [M]andatory rotation can seriously impair auditor specialization. In a static perspective, it does not allow pre-existing economies of scale to be exploited. From a dynamic perspective, given that it substantially reduces the incentive to invest in specialized resources, the rule will lessen the future degree of specialization and with it the level of auditor competence.

(vii) Mandatory rotation of audit firms may result in an inadequate supply of competent audit firms to meet the demand for audits. This extends beyond the specialised industries to the audit market more generally. Raiborn *et al.* (2006), for instance, point out that, in the USA, there is a limited "number of audit firms that have the quantity of personnel, depth and breadth of industry expertise, or merely the name recognition to satisfy large domestic and international client companies" (p. 41). They note that, in 2001, there were approximately 18,000 domestic and foreign entities registered with the SEC, 10,500 of which were audited by the Big 4 auditing firms (an average of 2,625 companies per firm). The remaining 7,500 companies were audited by about 700 other accounting firms (an average of fewer than 11 companies per firm). Therefore, if a public company, currently audited by a Big 4 firm, wishes to continue to be audited by a Big 4 firm but engages another Big 4 firm to provide non-audit services that are incompatible with conducting an independent audit, the choice of a new firm, required by mandatory audit firm rotation, is extremely limited. The situation applies equally to large companies in the UK.

Further, since the demise of Enron and Arthur Andersen, the Big 4 firms' engagement procedures have become far more stringent and, according to Raiborn *et al.* (2006), these firms have been "shedding

---

[46] The 'new' audit firm may, however, be able to overcome its lack of industry expertise by recruiting knowledgeable audit staff from the outgoing audit firm – an activity which, anecdotal evidence suggests, is fairly common in countries such as Italy, where mandatory rotation of audit firms has been required for public listed companies since 1974.

clients at almost three times the rate they did in 2002" – generally those clients that are "too small to be worth the extra work and those judged too risky to work with under the new accounting rules" (p. 42).[47] Given this scenario, there might be a shortage of firms willing to accept some audit engagements when they become available at the end of their rotation period.

(viii) Audit firm rotation negates the signalling effect of auditor switches. Without mandatory rotation, a change of auditors tends to be an unusual event and suggests that, for reasons worth probing, there is a breakdown in the auditor-client relationship. A study by Schwartz and Menon (1985), in which they compared 132 failing with 132 matched non-failing companies, found that failing companies had a greater tendency to switch auditors than healthy companies. They concluded that financially distressed companies tend to seek to appoint more compliant or less knowledgeable auditors who are more likely than the incumbent auditors to express a 'clean' opinion on the company's financial statements. Mandatory rotation masks the valuable informational effect that a change of auditor gives to the market.

The key arguments against mandatory audit firm rotation are succinctly expressed by Wyman (2005). He observes:

> [T]he Italian experience [since mandatory rotation was introduced in 1974] provides evidence that mandatory rotation increases costs to businesses, creates problems with audit quality in the period immediately after the change of audit firms, and leads to further consolidation of audit work amongst the largest audit firms. (as cited, Raiborn et al., 2006, p. 42)

Similarly, the Ramsay Report (2001) notes: "the anticipated cost, disruption and loss of experience to companies [resulting from audit firm rotation] is considered unacceptably high, as is the unwarranted restriction on the freedom of companies to choose their own auditors [as and when they please]" (para 6.100).

Reviewing the arguments against mandatory rotation, it may be seen that, at least to some extent, those relating to decreased quality and increased audit costs resulting from lack of knowledge about the client and the lack of a personal relationship between senior audit personnel and the audit client [(i), (ii), (iii) and (iv) above] apply to the rotation of senior audit personnel as well as to the rotation of audit firms. However, with the rotation of senior audit

---

[47] During interviews with senior audit partners of the Big 4 firms in both the UK and New Zealand, one of the authors of this textbook was informed that the strengthening of audit engagement procedures and the "shedding of clients that are no longer considered acceptable" is a global phenomenon for each Big 4 audit firm. It applies in the UK as elsewhere in the world.

personnel, the institutional and client personnel knowledge is available within the audit firm and therefore the impact on audit quality and cost is likely to be significantly less than that resulting from the rotation of audit firms.

While mandatory auditor rotation has attracted significant support as a means of strengthening auditors' independence, a number of commentators, audit firms and professional bodies maintain that it is unnecessary because client managements and audit personnel change naturally over time. The AICPA (1992), for example, reported that a review of executives of the largest 100 industrial concerns in the 1991 Fortune 500 companies, and the 50 largest bank holding companies in the USA at 31 December 1990, showed that the turnover of executives is sufficiently high to ensure the relationship between client managements and audit personnel is continually changing without mandatory rotation (as reported, ICAEW, 2002, p. 21). Similarly, Larkin (2004), focusing on audit firms rather than their clients, observed: "slow rotation occurs naturally within a firm as staff members are promoted, retire, change assignments, etc., thus bringing new personnel to every audit over time".

Others contend that mandatory rotation is not necessary as more effective, less costly alternatives are available. PricewaterhouseCoopers (2002) and the SDA Università Bocconi study (2002), for example, point to the importance of:
  (i)   independent second partner reviews of audit firms' and audit team members' independence;
  (ii) audit firms' quality controls and governance mechanisms; and
  (iii) effective oversight (or inspections) by regulatory bodies,
as effective means of ensuring the maintenance of auditors' objectivity and independence.[48] The significance of the latter means of enhancing auditors' independence is indicated in the following observation by FEE (2004):

> In Italy ... a study by the Bocconi University [SDA Università Bocconi] ... in 2002, has identified a number of disadvantages from [audit] firm rotation. However the Galgano Committee, formed in response to the scandals in the USA, concluded that mandatory rotation should continue. The Galgano report ... does not set out the basis for its conclusions nor why the earlier report has been disregarded. (It should be noted that Italy has not so far instituted external inspection of auditors of the type described in the European Commission Recommendation [2002] ... and widely in force elsewhere. Mandatory rotation of firms may therefore have been considered, to some degree at least, an alternative safeguard). The Eighth Directive on Statutory Audit [EU 2006] will make external inspection a requirement [throughout the EU] for the first time [by mid-2008]. (p. 5)

---

[48] These three mechanisms for securing auditor independence and audit quality are discussed in detail in Chapter 16.

Another significant mechanism that helps to ensure the maintenance of auditors' independence and, according to some commentators, renders mandatory rotation unnecessary is that of the audit committee. As the GAO (2003) observed:

> [I]f audit committees ... are actively involved in helping to ensure audit independence and audit quality, many of the intended benefits of audit firm rotation could be realized at the initiative of the audit committee rather than through a mandatory requirement. (p. 52)

It is to this topic that we now turn our attention.

4.4.5 Audit committees

An audit committee is a committee of the board of directors (or its equivalent) which has delegated responsibility from the board for, *inter alia*, overseeing the external financial reporting process – including the external audit. The committee usually comprises at least three members, of whom all, or the majority, are independent non-executive directors.[49]

Over the past four or so decades, the value of audit committees as a means of enhancing external financial reporting and ensuring the independence of external auditors has been increasingly recognised and these committees have become a normal feature of corporate life, especially of public companies, in many parts of the world. Their development has varied from country to country but, interestingly, in each case it has been stimulated by unexpected corporate failure and/or reports of misconduct by senior executives or directors. It seems that politicians and the public believe that, if the auditors had been properly independent of their audit client's managements, and had

---

[49] The Combined Code (FRC, 2006) requires publicly listed companies in the UK to establish audit committees with at least three (or in the case of smaller companies two) members, all of whom are independent non-executive directors (or to disclose that they have not done so and provide reasons therefor). Non-executive directors are directors who are not involved in the day-to-day management of the company (or other entity). According to the Combined Code (provision A.3.1), it is a matter for the Board of Directors to determine whether a director:

> is independent in character and judgement and whether there are relationships or circumstances which are likely to affect, or could appear to affect, the director's judgement. The Board should state its reasons if it determines that a director is independent notwithstanding the existence of relationships or circumstances which may appear relevant to its determination, including if the director:
> - has been an employee of the company or group within the last five years;
> - has, or has had within the last three years, a material business relationship with the company either directly, or as a partner, shareholder, director or senior employee of a body that has such a relationship with the company;
> - has received or receives additional remuneration from the company apart from a director's fee, participates in the company's share option or a performance-related pay scheme, or is a member of the company's pension scheme;
> - has close family ties with any of the company's advisers, directors or senior employees;
> - holds cross-directorships or has significant links with other directors through involvement in other companies or bodies;
> - represents a significant shareholder; or
> - has served on the board for more than nine years from the date of their first election.

performed their duties with due skill and care, then warning bells would have been sounded in at least some of the cases. Following on from this, it is generally reasoned that if audit committees are established solely (or with at least a majority) of independent non-executive directors, to oversee the appointment of external auditors and the external audit function, then unexpected corporate failure and undetected misconduct by senior officials will be significantly reduced, if not eliminated. In the next two sections we examine (a) the development and (b) the duties of audit committees.

(a) Development of audit committees

Audit committees made their first significant appearance in Canada (the first country to introduce a legal requirement for public companies to establish audit committees) and the USA. During the 1970s, audit committees were established in these countries largely as a result of "several well-publicised instances of corporate wrongdoing and questionable conduct that severely tarnished the image of big business in North America" (CICA, 1981, p. 1). Prompted by the collapse of Atlantic Acceptance Corporation Ltd in Canada in 1965, in 1971 audit committees became a legal requirement for public companies incorporated in Ontario. In 1973, a similar requirement became effective for public companies incorporated in British Columbia, and in 1975 for federally incorporated companies. Since then audit committees have become a universally accepted feature of corporate life in Canada.

In the USA, audit committees received their first major endorsement, from both the New York Stock Exchange (NYSE) and the SEC in the late 1930s, as a result of the infamous *McKesson & Robbins* case. However, few audit committees were established until the 1970s, when interest in them was revived as a result of several factors, including a number of legal decisions (including the *BarChris Construction Corporation* case) which emphasised that executive and non-executive directors are equally responsible for their company's affairs, and equally liable for misleading financial statements. Other factors included the unexpected collapse of Penn Central Company, the notorious Equity Funding fraud and the widespread instances of corporate misconduct which came to light during the enquiries which led to the enactment of the Foreign Corrupt Practices Act in 1977 (CICA, 1981, pp. 98–99).

In June 1978, primarily as a result of pressure from politicians and the SEC for public companies to be required to establish audit committees, they became a listing requirement of the NYSE. Adoption of audit committees was further encouraged in 1987 when the National Commission on Fraudulent Financial Reporting (Treadway Commission, 1987) recommended that they be established by all public companies. Since the enactment of SOX in 2002, all companies registered with the SEC (virtually all public companies registered or listed in the USA and their significant subsidiaries) have been required to establish audit committees comprised solely of independent directors.[50]

In the UK, adoption of audit committees did not begin in earnest until the late 1980s. Indeed, until 1987, neither the professional accountancy bodies nor the regulatory agencies (such as the Bank of England and the Department of Trade and Industry[51]) seemed to give these committees serious consideration. However, in 1987, stimulated by the serious and growing size and incidence of corporate fraud, the ICAEW recommended that public companies be required to establish audit committees, and the Bank of England and PRO-NED[52] also urged these companies to adopt such committees. These moves were followed in 1988 by the introduction of a Private Member's Bill to Parliament which, if enacted, would have required large public listed companies in the UK to establish audit committees. The adoption of audit committees by all UK public companies received a further boost in 1992, when the Committee on the Financial Aspects of Corporate Governance (the Cadbury Committee) included in its *Code of Best Practice* the establishment of an audit committee comprising non-executive directors, with at least three members (CFACG, 1992, *Code of Best Practice*, clause 4.3).[53] Today, the UK Listing Authority (UKLA)[54] requires all companies listed on the London Stock Exchange to comply with *The Combined Code on Corporate Governance* (FRC, 2006) or to disclose that they have not done so and provide reasons therefor. Code provision C.3.1 requires listed companies to establish audit committees of at least three (or in the case of smaller companies two) members, all of whom are independent non-executive directors.[55] One member of the

---

[50] According to SOX, s. 301, in order to be considered independent, audit committee members may not, other than in their capacity as directors:
    (i) accept any consulting, advisory, or other compensatory fee from the issuer [i.e., public company];
    (ii) be an affiliated person of the issuer or any subsidiary thereof.

[51] See footnote 4.

[52] An organisation established in 1982 by the Stock Exchange, the Confederation of British Industry, the Bank of England and other financial institutions to promote the appointment of non-executive directors to Boards of Directors.

[53] In April 1993, the London Stock Exchange made it a listing requirement for companies to include in their annual reports a statement as to whether or not they had complied with the *Code of Best Practice* during the reporting period. If they had not done so, they were required to explain the respects in which they had not complied and the reasons why.

[54] In 2001, responsibility for the UKLA (and hence for the listing rules) passed from the London Stock Exchange to the Financial Services Authority (FSA). The FSA has delegated responsibility for *The Combined Code on Corporate Governance* to the Financial Reporting Council (FRC).

[55] See footnote 49.

committee is also required to possess "recent and relevant financial experience" (provision C.3.1).

Audit committees are a normal feature of corporate life not only in Canada, the USA and the UK; they are similarly legally required and/or generally accepted in many other countries of the world. These include Australia, New Zealand, South Africa, Singapore, Malaysia and, as a consequence of the EU's 8th Directive on Statutory Audit (EU, 2006), all countries within the European Union. However, although there has been a noticeable trend in recent years towards regulators requiring companies' audit committees to comprise, or include, independent non-executive directors, the precise form and composition of audit committees varies between countries. This also applies between EU member states: Article 41(1) of the EU 8th Directive states:

> Each public-interest entity[56] shall have an audit committee. The Member State shall determine whether audit committees are to be composed of non-executive members of the administrative body [i.e., Board of Directors] and/or members of the supervisory body [in States, such as Germany, which have a two-tier board structure] of the audited entity and/or members appointed by the general meeting of shareholders of the audited entity. At least one member of the audit committee shall be independent and shall have competence in accounting and/or auditing.

(b) Duties of audit committees

Particularly during the early 1970s, the principal duties of audit committees were generally confined to matters related to external financial reporting and the external audit. They were, for example, typically expected to:

- select (and recommend to shareholders for approval) the company's external auditors;
- oversee the external financial reporting process – including the external audit; and
- review the external financial statements prior to their submission to the full board of directors for approval.

Since the mid-1970s, the value of audit committees to fulfil a much broader function has been recognised – that of securing responsible corporate governance.[57] This broader function is reflected in the duties audit committees are now typically expected to perform. They include, for example:

---

[56] 'Public-interest entities' are defined in Article 2(13) as:
   entities governed by the law of a Member State whose transferable securities are admitted to trading on a regulated market of any Member State ..., credit institutions ... and insurance undertakings ... Member States may also designate other entities as public-interest entities, for instance entities that are of significant public relevance because of the nature of their business, their size or the number of their employees.

[57] For a full discussion of the development of audit committees and the change of their role in the mid-1970s see Porter and Gendall (1997).

- helping to establish an environment in which internal controls can operate effectively;
- ensuring that an effective accounting system and related internal controls are maintained;
- reviewing the company's accounting policies and reporting requirements;
- assessing the adequacy of management reporting;
- selecting and recommending for appointment the external auditor(s), and recommending their remuneration;
- appointing the chief internal auditor;
- discussing with the chief internal auditor and external audit engagement partner the intended scope of the internal and external audit, respectively, and satisfying itself that no unjustified restrictions have been imposed by executive management;
- reviewing the findings and recommendations of the internal and external auditors;
- reviewing the entity's financial statements and annual report prior to their submission to the full board of directors;
- reviewing public announcements relating to financial matters prior to their release;
- reviewing, and monitoring compliance with, the company's code of conduct;
- reviewing the company's compliance with legal and regulatory requirements.

As audit committees have become more commonplace, and their value in fulfilling a broad corporate governance role has come to be recognised, so regulators have sought to specify not only the requirements of audit committees' composition but also their role and responsibilities. The first step in this direction was taken in the USA in 1999, with the establishment of the Blue Ribbon Committee on Improving the Effectiveness of Corporate Audit Committees, by the NYSE and the National Association of Securities Dealers (NASD). The Blue Ribbon Committee's (1999) report and recommendations set out five Guiding Principles for audit committee best practices (pp. 37–44). These may be summarised as follows:

- *Principle 1* discusses the audit committee's pivotal role in monitoring the other components of the audit. In particular, it notes that the audit committee oversees:
  - (i) management which has primary responsibility for the financial statements;
  - (ii) the external auditors on whom investors rely to provide an impartial, robust examination of the financial statements to ensure their credibility; and

(iii) where they exist, internal auditors who provide a source of advice on information on the processes and safeguards that exist.

- *Principle 2* highlights the importance of independent communication and information flow between the audit committee and the company's internal auditors.
- *Principle 3* notes the need for independent communication and information flow between the audit committee and the external auditors.[58]
- *Principle 4* emphasises the need for candid discussions between the audit committee and, respectively, management, the internal auditors, and external auditors, regarding issues concerned with judgments used in, and the quality of, the company's financial statements.
- *Principle 5* underscores the need for effective audit committees, comprised of diligent and knowledgeable audit committee members.

In 2000, building on the work and recommendations of the Blue Ribbon Committee, the Panel on Audit Effectiveness (2000) [established in the USA in 1998 by the Public Oversight Board (POB)[59] in response to a request by the SEC] published its Final Report. This recommended, *inter alia*, that audit committees:

- obtain annually from management a written report on how effectively the company's internal controls are operating;
- review annually the performance of the external and internal auditors;
- be advised of plans to hire personnel of the external audit firm into high-level positions within the company;
- be proactive in ensuring factors such as time pressures on auditors are addressed so as not to negatively impact the credibility of audits;
- pre-approve non-audit services to be provided by the external auditor above a specified threshold.

In 2002, SOX took the Blue Ribbon Committee's and Panel on Audit Effectiveness' recommendations further and enshrined certain audit committee responsibilities in legislation. Section 301, for example, specifies that the audit committee of each issuer of securities that are listed on a stock exchange in the USA is to:

- be directly responsible for the appointment, compensation, and oversight of the work of any registered public accounting firm employed by that issuer

---

[58] This topic is discussed in Chapter 14, Section 14.8.

[59] The POB was created as an independent, autonomous body in 1977 by the AICPA. Its primary role was to oversee and report on the programmes of the SEC Practice Section of the AICPA. (This is explained in Chapter 16.) In 2002, SOX, s. 101, created the Public Company Accounting Oversight Board and this, in effect, replaced the POB.

(including resolution of disagreements between management and the auditor regarding financial reporting) for the purpose of preparing or issuing an audit report or related work, . . .

- establish procedures for
  - the receipt, retention, and treatment of complaints received by the issuer regarding accounting, internal accounting controls, or auditing matters; and
  - the confidential, anonymous submission by employees of the issuer of concerns regarding questionable accounting or auditing matters;
- have the authority to engage independent counsel and other advisers, as it determines necessary to carry out its duties;
- [be provided with] appropriate funding as determined by the audit committee . . . for payment of compensation
  - to the registered public accounting firm employed [to provide audit services]; and
  - to any advisers employed by the audit committee . . .

Under s. 204, the auditor is required to report in a timely manner to the issuer's audit committee:

- all critical accounting policies and practices to be used;
- all alternative treatments of financial information within generally accepted accounting principles that have been discussed with management . . . , ramifications of the use of such alternative disclosures and treatments, and the treatment preferred by the [auditor]; and
- other material written communications between the [auditor] and the management of the issuer, such as any management letter or schedule of unadjusted differences.[60]

Additionally, in accordance with SOX, s. 202, the audit committee of the issuer must pre-approve all audit and non-audit services provided to the issuer by the auditor unless the aggregate fees for non-audit services amount to not more than five per cent of the total fees paid by the issuer to the auditor.

The responsibilities of audit committees specified in the EU 8th Directive (2006) are similar to those contained in SOX but focus rather more exclusively on those relating to the external financial reporting process. For example, Article 41 states:

The audit committee [of a public-interest entity] shall, *inter alia*:
(a) monitor the financial reporting process;
(b) monitor the effectiveness of the company's internal control, internal audit where applicable, and risk management systems;
(c) monitor the statutory audit of the annual and consolidated accounts;
(d) review and monitor the independence of the statutory auditor . . . , and in particular the provision of additional [non-audit] services to the audited entity.

---

[60] Management letters and schedules of unadjusted differences are explained in Chapter 13.

[T]he proposal of the [Board of Directors] or supervisory body for the appointment of a statutory auditor ... shall be based on a recommendation made by the audit committee.

The statutory auditor ... shall report to the audit committee on key matters arising from the statutory audit, and in particular on material weaknesses in internal control in relation to the financial reporting process.

The provisions of the EU 8th Directive apply to the audit committees of public-interest entities in the UK as in all other EU countries. However, listed companies in the UK must also comply with the requirements of *The Combined Code on Corporate Governance* (FRC, 2006) – and, as can be seen from the Code provisions C.3.2 to C.3.4 set out below, these are somewhat broader than those contained in the EU 8th Directive:[61]

C.3.2 The main role and responsibilities of the audit committee should be set out in written terms of reference and should include:
- to monitor the integrity of the financial statements of the company, and any formal announcements relating to the company's financial performance, reviewing significant financial reporting judgements contained in them;
- to review the company's internal financial controls and ... [its] internal control and risk management systems;
- to monitor and review the effectiveness of the company's internal audit function;
- to make recommendations to the board, ... in relation to the appointment, re-appointment and removal of the external auditor and to approve the remuneration and terms of engagement of the external auditor;
- to review and monitor the external auditor's independence and objectivity and the effectiveness of the audit process, taking into consideration relevant UK professional and regulatory requirements;
- to develop and implement policy on the engagement of the external auditor to supply non-audit services, taking into account relevant ethical guidance regarding the provision of non-audit services by the external audit firm; ...

C.3.3 The terms of reference of the audit committee ... should be made available [for example, on the Internet, or in the annual report]. A separate section of the annual report should describe the work of the audit committee in discharging those responsibilities.

C.3.4 The audit committee should review arrangements by which staff of the company may, in confidence, raise concerns about possible improprieties in matters of financial reporting or other matters. The audit committee's objective should be to ensure that arrangements are in place for the proportionate and independent investigation of such matters and for appropriate follow-up action.

---

[61] The audit committee provisions of *The Combined Code on Corporate Governance* are derived from the Smith Committee's report to the FRC on Audit Committees (Smith, 2003). Other provisions relating to audit committees are presented in Chapter 5, section 5.5.

4.5 SUMMARY

The issue of auditors' independence seems to be aptly summarised by Turner (2001):

> The independence of auditors of public companies has been and continues to be an issue of paramount importance. . . . It is a subject that cannot be a question, but rather must be a given. But all too often today, the question is being asked, "Did the auditors provide an unbiased and truly independent report on the numbers?" To maintain their value to the capital markets and regain the confidence of investors, auditors around the globe must renew their covenant with investors; a covenant that says each auditor will remain . . . free from a web of entanglements or arrangements that threaten the appearance of his or her objectivity; that with the auditor's stamp, the numbers speak the truth. (pp. 7–8)

Since Turner expressed these words in 2001, as we have seen in this chapter, regulators around the world have introduced measures designed to ensure that auditors "remain free from a web of entanglements and arrangements that threaten . . . [their] objectivity".

Maintaining auditors' independence, both in fact (or of mind) and in appearance, is clearly crucial to the credibility of the opinion expressed by auditors in their audit reports and, thus, to the future of the audit function and the smooth functioning of financial markets. However, it is equally evident that a number of factors serve to undermine (or threaten) this independence – in particular, financial, business, employment and personal involvement with an audit client; long association with an audit client; undue dependence on a client for fee income; gifts and hospitality received from, or offered to, a client; the provision of non-audit services to an audit client; and the influence of executive directors over the auditor's appointment and remuneration.

Regulators (such as the APB) and professional bodies (like IFAC) have sought to prevent the impairment of auditors' independence by promulgating ethical standards and guidance. These identify threats, or perceived threats, to auditors' independence, and require auditors to consider their exposure to such threats and, when necessary, to introduce appropriate safeguards. Nevertheless, shaken by well-publicised audit failures in the early years of the 21st century, and mindful of the importance of auditors' independence to the well-being of financial markets, regulators and/or legislators in many countries have introduced additional safeguards. These include the mandatory rotation of senior audit personnel (specifically, the engagement and key audit partners and the engagement quality control reviewer) and requiring public (especially listed) companies to establish audit committees to oversee the external financial reporting process (including the external audit function). However, in the view of a significant number of commentators, all the time auditors are appointed and remunerated by their clients (even if this is 'controlled' by the company's audit committee comprised solely of independent non-executive directors) they will not be truly independent. To overcome this difficulty, two key proposals have been advanced, namely, to make (i) the State (or a State agency) and (ii) a panel comprising representatives of the client's shareholders or stakeholders responsible for the appointment and remuneration of auditors. At the present time, the appointment of auditors through either of these means seems to entail implementation hurdles that are difficult to overcome and, to date, neither has gained widespread support. Another proposal, designed to distance auditors from their clients – the mandatory rotation of audit firms (rather than senior audit personnel) – has been the subject of widespread debate but, currently, the costs attaching to the proposal are adjudged to outweigh the benefits to be derived from the resulting increase in auditor independence.

SELF-REVIEW QUESTIONS

4.1 Explain briefly the importance of auditors being independent both in fact (or of mind) and in appearance.

4.2 List six 'threats' to auditors' independence and provide an example of each.

4.3 Outline four 'safeguards' to auditor's independence that may be provided by the general audit environment – two for which audit firms, and two for which audit engagement partners, are responsible.

4.4 (a) List seven specific circumstances that are likely to endanger auditors' independence.
     (b) For each circumstance, outline one safeguard that might prevent auditors' independence from being compromised.

4.5 List the four principles that underpin the SEC's auditor independence rules.

4.6 List nine services that the Sarbanes-Oxley Act of 2002 prohibits auditors from providing to audit clients who are SEC registrants.

4.7 (a) Discuss briefly how auditors being appointed by:
         (i) the State or by a State agency, or
         (ii) a shareholder panel, may help strengthen auditors' independence.
     (b) Briefly explain the key obstacles to auditors' independence being strengthened through these means.

4.8 (a) Explain briefly two forms of 'mandatory rotation of auditors'.
    (b) Outline seven arguments in favour and seven arguments against mandatory auditor rotation.
    (c) Outline the auditor rotation requirements that apply in (i) the UK and (ii) the USA.

4.9 Explain briefly what is meant by an audit committee. (What is it and what is its usual composition?)

4.10 Outline the principal responsibilities of audit committees and explain briefly how audit committees may help to strengthen auditors' independence.

REFERENCES

American Institute of Certified Public Accountants (AICPA). (1992). *Statement of Position Regarding Mandatory Rotation of Audit Firms of Publicly Held Companies.* New York: AICPA.

Anon. (2006). Mandatory rotation of audit firms: world's worst practice? *The Finance Professional*, www.indiainitiative.com/articles_mandaterot.htm.

Arel, B., Brody, R., and Pany, K. (2005). Audit firm rotation and audit quality. *The CPA Journal* **LXXV**(1), 36–39.

Arens, A.A., and Loebbecke, J.K. (1980). *Auditing an Integrated Approach* (2nd edn.). Englewood Cliffs, NJ: Prentice-Hall.

Arrunada, B., and Paz-Ares, C. (1995). *Economic Consequences of Mandatory Auditor Rotation* (as quoted in ICAEW, 2002).

Arrunada, B., and Paz-Ares, C. (1997). Mandatory rotation of company auditors: a critical examination. *International Review of Law and Economics* **17**(1), 31–61.

Auditing Practices Board (APB). (1992). *Future Development of Auditing.* London: APB.

Auditing Practices Board (APB). (1994). *The Audit Agenda.* London: APB.

Auditing Practices Board (APB). (2008a). *The Auditing Practices Board – Scope and Authority of Pronouncements (Revised).* London: Financial Reporting Council.

Auditing Practices Board (APB). (2008b). *APB Ethical Standards Glossary of Terms.* London: Financial Reporting Council.

Bazerman, M.H., Loewenstein, G., and Moore, D.A. (2002). Why good accountants do bad audits. *Harvard Business Review* **80**(11), 97–102.

Blue Ribbon Committee on Improving the Effectiveness of Corporate Audit Committees. (1999). *Report and Final Recommendations of the Blue Ribbon Committee.* New York: New York Stock Exchange and National Association of Securities Dealers.

Briloff, A.J. (1986, April). *Corporate Governance and Accountability: Whose Responsibility?* Unpublished address delivered at the University of Connecticut, Storrs, Connecticut.

Canadian Institute of Chartered Accountants (CICA). (1981). *Audit Committees: A Research Study.* Toronto: CICA.

Commission on Auditors' Responsibilities (CAR). (1978). *Report, Conclusions and Recommendations* (The Cohen Commission). New York: American Institute of Certified Public Accountants.

Committee on the Financial Aspects of Corporate Governance (CFACG, Cadbury Committee). (1992). *Report of the Committee on the Financial Aspects of Corporate Governance.* London: Gee.

Co-ordinating Group on Audit and Accounting Issues (CGAA). (2003, 29 January). *Final Report to the Secretary of State for Trade and Industry and the Chancellor of the Exchequer.* London: Her Majesty's Stationery Office; Crown Copyright.

Cowen, S.S. (1980). Non-audit services: how much is too much? *Journal of Accountancy* **150**(6), 51–56.

Enron Watchdog. (2002). *Why accountants should be banned from providing consulting services to audit clients*, www.enronwatchdog.org/topreforms/topreforms1.

European Union (EU). (2006). *Directive 2006/43/EC of the European Parliament and of the Council on the Statutory Audits of Annual Accounts and Consolidated Accounts (8th Directive).* Brussels: European Parliament and Council.

European Union (EU) Commission. (2002, May). *Recommendation: Statutory Auditors' Independence in the EU: A Set of Fundamental Principles.* Brussels: EU: 2002/590/EC.

Fédération des Experts Comptables Européens (FEE). (2004). *Mandatory rotation of Audit Firms.* Brussels: FEE.

Financial Reporting Council (FRC). (2006). *The Combined Code on Corporate Governance.* London: Financial Reporting Council.

General Accounting Office (GAO). (2003, November). *Public Accounting Firms: Required study on the potential effects of mandatory audit firm rotation.* Report to the Senate Committee on Banking, Housing, and Urban Affairs and the House Committee on Financial Services. Washington: GAO-04-216.

George, N. (2004). Auditor rotation and the quality of audits. *The CPA Journal* **74**(12), 22–27.

Haber, J.R. (2005). Does being the auditor impair independence? *CPA Journal* **LXXV**(6), 12.

Harian, U. (2002, 16 March). Singapore banks to rotate audit firms under new rules. *Suara Merdeka*, www.suaramerdeka.com/harian/0203/16/eng8.htm.

Hatherly, D.J. (1995). The case for the shareholder panel in the U.K. *The European Accounting Review* **4**(3), 535–553.

Healey, T. (2004, 12 March). The best safeguard against financial scandal. *Financial Times.* London.

Hermes. (2002). *Auditor Independence*. www.hermes.co.uk/pdf/corporate_governance/commentary/comment_on_ auditor independence.

Hirsch, J. (2002, 23 January). Enron audit fee raises some brows. *Los Angeles Times.* Los Angeles.

Institute of Chartered Accountants in England and Wales (ICAEW). (2002, July). *Mandatory Rotation of Audit Firms: Review of current requirements, research and publications.* London: ICAEW.

Jeppesen, K.K. (1998). Reinventing auditing, redefining consulting and independence. *The European Accounting Review* **7**(3), 517–539.

Larkin, D. (2004). Mandatory auditor rotation. *Nonprofit Alert* (6), 4. USA: BDO Seidman, LLP.

Levitt, A. (2000, 18 September). *A Profession at the Crossroads*. Speech by SEC Chairman to National Association of State Boards of Accountancy, Boston, MA.

Metcalf, L. (1976). *The Accounting Establishment: A Staff study*. A Report of the Senate Subcommittee on Reports, Accounting and Management of the Committee on Government Operations, Chaired by Senator Lee Metcalf. Washington: US Government Printing Office.

Mitchell, A., and Sikka, P. (1993). Accounting for change: the institutions of accountancy. *Critical Perspectives on Accounting* **4**(1), 29–52.

National Commission on Fraudulent Financial Reporting. (Treadway Commission). (1987). *Report of the National Commission on Fraudulent Financial Reporting.* New York: American Institute of Certified Public Accountants.

Pajuelo, J. (2003, 21 November). Brazil reaffirms tougher auditor rule than U.S. *The ISS Friday Report*, p. 6. USA: Maryland: Institutional Shareholders Services, Inc., www.issueatlas.com/content/subscription/fridayreportfiles/fridayreport11212003.

Panel on Audit Effectiveness. (2000). *Report and Recommendations.* New York: Public Oversight Board.

Porter, B.A., and Gendall, P.J. (1997). *Audit Committees in Private and Public Sector Corporates: An Empirical Investigation.* Paper presented at the 20th Annual Congress of the European Accounting Association, Graz, Austria.

PricewaterhouseCoopers. (2002, 11 November). Maintaining Auditor Independence. *The Edge.* PricewaterhouseCoopers International Limited.

Public Company Accounting Oversight Board (PCAOB). (2008, 24 April). *Board Adopts New Ethics and Independence Rule concerning Communications with Audit Committees and an Amendment to its Existing Tax Services Rule.* Washington: PCAOB.

Raiborn, C., Schorg, C.A., and Massoud, M. (2006). Should Auditor Rotation Be Mandatory? *Wiley InterScience*, www.interscience.wiley.com, 37–49.

Ramsay, I. (2001, 21 October). *Independence of Australian Company Auditors: Review of Current Australian Requirements and Proposals for Reform.* Report to the Minister from Financial Services and Regulation. Australia, Canberra: Treasury.

Review Group on Auditing. (2000, July). *The Report of the Review Group on Auditing.* Report to the Department of Enterprise, Trade and Employment (Ireland). Ireland: Dublin: Department of Enterprise, Trade and Employment.

Sarbanes-Oxley Act of 2002. (2002). Congress of the United States of America.

Schwartz, K.B., and Menon, K. (1985). Auditor switches by failing firms. *The Accounting Review* **60**(2), 248–261.

SDA Università Bocconi (Bocconi University). (2002). *The impact of mandatory audit rotation on audit quality and on audit pricing: The case of Italy.* Milan: SDA Università Bocconi, Corporate Finance and Real Estate Department and Administration and Control Department. (Unpublished.)

Securities and Exchange Commission (SEC). (2000a). Proposed Rule: *Revision of the Commission's Auditor Independence Requirements.* Washington: SEC. Ref 34-42994.

Securities and Exchange Commission (SEC). (2000b). Final Rule: *Revision of the Commission's Auditor Independence Requirements.* Washington: SEC. Ref 33-7919.

Securities and Exchange Commission (SEC). (2002, 14 January). *SEC Censures KPMG for Auditor Independence Violation.* Press Release 2002-4. Washington: SEC.

Smith, Sir Robert. (2003). *Audit Committees: Combined Guidance.* A report and proposed guidance by an FRC-appointed group chaired by Sir Robert Smith. London: Financial Reporting Council.

Squires, S.E., Smith, C.J., McDougall, L., and Yeack, W.R. (2003). *Inside Arthur Andersen: Shifting values, unexpected consequences.* Upper Saddle River, NJ: Prentice-Hall, Financial Times.

Statutory Instrument 2005 No. 2417: *The Companies (Disclosure of Auditor Remuneration) Regulations 2005.*

Statutory Instrument 2008 No. 489: *The Companies (Disclosure of Auditor Remuneration and Liability Limitation Agreements) Regulations 2008.*

Turner, L.E. (2001, 28 June). *Independence: A Covenant for the Ages.* Speech by SEC Chief Accountant to International Organization of Securities Commissions, Stockholm, Sweden.

Wyman, P. (2005, 21 March). How do Europe's 8th Directive and Sarbanes-Oxley compare? *Gtnews.com*, www.gtnews.com/article/5847.

ADDITIONAL READING

Ashbaugh, H., LaFond, R., and Mayhew, B.W. (2003). Do non-audit services compromise auditor independence? Further evidence. *The Accounting Review* **78**(3), 611–640.

Auditing Practices Board (APB). (2007). *APB Research into Ethical Standards for Auditors.* London: Financial Reporting Council.

Bamber, E.M., and Iyer, V.M. (2007). Auditors' identification with their client and its effect on auditors' objectivity. *Auditing: A Journal of Practice & Theory* **26**(2), 1–24.

Bedard, J., Chtourou, S.M., and Courteau, L. (2004). The effect of audit committee expertise, independence, and activity on aggressive earnings management. *Auditing: A Journal of Practice & Theory* **23**(2), 13–35.

Carcello, J.V., and Neal, T.L. (2000). Audit committee composition and auditor reporting. *The Accounting Review* **75**(4), 453–467.

Carey, P., and Simnett, R. (2006). Audit partner tenure and audit quality. *The Accounting Review* **81**(3), 653–677.

Falk, H., Lynn, B., Mestelman, S., and Skehata, M. (1999). Auditor Independence, self-interested behaviour and ethics: some experimental evidence. *Journal of Accountancy and Public Policy*, **18**, 395–428.

Fearnley, S., and Beattie, V. (2004). The reform of the UK's auditor independence framework after the Enron collapse: An example of evidence based policy making. *International Journal of Auditing* **8**(2), 117–138.

Fédération des Experts Comptables Européens (FEE). (2003). *Auditor Independence.* Brussels: FEE.

Gavious, I. (2007). Alternative perspectives to deal with the auditors' agency problem. *Critical Perspectives on Accounting* **18**(4), 451–467.

Gendron, Y., Bedard, J., and Gosselin, M. (2004). Getting inside the black box: a field study of practices in 'effective' audit committees. *Auditing: A Journal of Practice & Theory* **23**(1), 153–171.

Gendron, Y., and Bedard, J. (2006). On the constitution of audit committee effectiveness. *Accounting, Organizations and Society* **31**(3), 211–239.

Gietzmann, M.B., and Sen, K. (2002) Improving auditor independence through selective mandatory rotation. *International Journal of Auditing* **6**(2), 183–210.

Huang, H-W., Mishra, S., and Raghunandan, K. (2007). Types of nonaudit fees and financial reporting quality. *Auditing: A Journal of Practice & Theory* **26**(1), 133–145.

International Organization of Securities Commissions (IOSCO). (2002). *Principles of Auditor Independence and the Role of Corporate Governance in Monitoring an Auditor's Independence.* A Statement of the Technical Committee of IOSCO.

Institute of Internal Auditors – UK and Ireland. (IIA). (2007). *A view from the Audit Committee.* London: IIA.

Myers, J.N., Myers, L.A., and Omer, T.C. (2003). Exploring the term of the auditor–client relationship and the quality of earnings: a case for mandatory auditor rotation? *The Accounting Review* **78**(3), 779–800.

Raghunandan, K., Read, W.J., and Rama, D.V. (2001). Audit committee composition, "grey directors," and interaction with internal auditors. *Accounting Horizons* **15**(2), 105–118.

Reynolds, J.K., and Francis, J.R. (2000). Does size matter? The influence of large clients on office-level auditor reporting decisions. *Journal of Accounting and Economics* **30**(3), 375–400.

5 Legal and Professional Duties of Auditors

LEARNING OBJECTIVES

After studying the material in this chapter you should be able to:
- state which companies are required to have an audit;
- list the rights, responsibilities and duties of external auditors under:
    - (a) legislation,
    - (b) decisions of the courts,
    - (c) auditing standards,
    - (d) regulatory requirements;
- describe the relationship between auditors and their clients;
- explain both auditors' and company directors' responsibility for audited annual financial statements;
- discuss the meaning, importance and structure of the audit expectation–performance gap.

The following publications are particularly relevant to this chapter:

- Companies Act 2006
- *The Auditing Practices Board – Statement of Scope and Authority of APB Pronouncements* (APB, 2008)
- *Preface to the International Standards on Quality Control, Auditing, Review, Other Assurance and Related Services* (IFAC, 2005)
- *The Combined Code on Corporate Governance* (FRC, 2006)
- *The Combined Code on Corporate Governance: Requirements of Auditors under the Listing Rules of the Financial Services Authority and the Irish Stock Exchange*, Bulletin 2006/5 (APB, 2006)
- *Auditor's Reports on Financial Statement in the United Kingdom*, Bulletin 2006/6 (APB, 2006).

5.1 INTRODUCTION

Broadly speaking, the rights, responsibilities and duties of auditors are defined by four 'levels' of institution, namely:
- Parliament – in legislation (or statute law);
- the courts – in case (or common) law;
- regulators – in various forms of regulation which may have general or limited application. The regulations may, for example, apply to the auditors (and audits) of all companies or just to those of companies in a particular industry or of a particular type (for example, public listed companies);
- the profession – in 'requirements' and guidance issued by professional accountancy bodies. These apply to the members of the body in question, for example, the Institutes of Chartered Accountants in England and Wales (ICAEW), of Scotland (ICAS), or in Ireland (ICAI), or the Association of Chartered Certified Accountants (ACCA).

The impact of these institutions on auditors' duties in the United Kingdom (UK) is cumulative in the sense explained below.
- *Parliament* enacts legislation (for example, the Companies Act 2006) that specifies the entities whose financial statements must be audited and sets out the administrative details of auditors' appointment, removal and remuneration. It also defines the criteria that determine who may be appointed as a company's auditor, and outlines auditors' rights and duties.[1]
- *The courts* create case (or common) law that expands on statute law by deciding cases that come before them. Since the late 19th century, by hearing cases that have involved auditors, the courts have helped to clarify the standard of work expected of auditors in the performance of their statutory duties.
- *Regulators* put 'flesh on the bones' of auditors' duties as defined in statute and common law. Exercising powers delegated to them by legislation, they promulgate regulations which set out detailed requirements with which all, or a limited set of, auditors (as applicable) must comply. As we shall see in this and subsequent chapters, the Auditing Practices Board

---

[1] Some of the legislation enacted by the UK Parliament incorporates the provisions of European Union (EU) Regulations and Directives. EU Regulations have legal effect in all Member States, irrespective of whether they are also enacted in a State's legislation. Directives, in general, indicate the outcomes Member States are required to achieve but, to an extent, leave each Member State to determine how the outcomes are to be achieved. Nevertheless, for 'maximum harmonisation' Directives, Member States have little or no flexibility as to the manner in which the outcomes are to be achieved. However, unlike EU Regulations, all Directives require each Member State to enact measures to implement the Directive in that State (i.e., to give the Directive legal effect).

(APB)[2] issues Auditing and Ethical Standards with which all registered auditors in the UK and Ireland must comply when performing their audits. Along similar lines, the Recognised Supervisory Bodies (RSBs),[3] with which, in general, all UK company auditors must be registered, detail the criteria auditors must meet in order to qualify for appointment as a company auditor. Other regulators, such as those responsible for the regulation of particular industries or types of company, specify requirements that apply only to the auditors of those companies. For example, the Financial Services Authority (FSA)[4] specifies requirements that apply to the audits of financial institutions.

- *The profession*: Until a couple of decades ago, the accounting profession was, in general, self-regulating and the criteria for becoming an accountant (and auditor), and auditing and ethical standards, were set and enforced by the profession itself. Over the past 20 or so years, the profession has become increasingly regulated – a move that accelerated markedly following the Enron, WorldCom, Parmalat, Tyco, HIH and similar debacles in the dawn years of the 21st century. Today, in the international arena, the profession, represented by the International Federation of Accountants (IFAC), develops and promulgates International Standards on Auditing (ISAs) and the Code of Ethics for Professional Accountants. However, as noted above, in the UK, the APB is responsible for setting auditing and ethical standards. Thus, responsibility for setting and enforcing the requirements which govern the work of auditors in the UK has passed from the profession to regulators. Similarly, in order to be appointed as a company auditor, the individual or firm must be a member of an RSB and eligible for appointment under its rules. Although the RSBs coincide with UK professional bodies such as the ICAEW, ICAS, ICAI and the ACCA, in their role as RSBs they function as regulators rather than as representatives of the profession. The professional bodies do, however, each produce a Code of Ethics for their members for matters not covered by the APB's Ethical Standards. Further, members of the profession are intimately involved (usually as advisors or committee members) in developing and/or promulgating the regulations that affect auditors.

The relationship between the institutions defining auditors' duties and those duties is presented diagrammatically in Figure 5.1.

---

[2] The composition and functions of the APB are discussed in section 5.4.

[3] The RSBs are discussed in section 5.2.3.

[4] The FSA is an independent, non-governmental body, established under the Financial Services and Markets Act 2000, that is responsible for regulating the financial services industry in the UK.

Figure 5.1: Defining auditors' duties

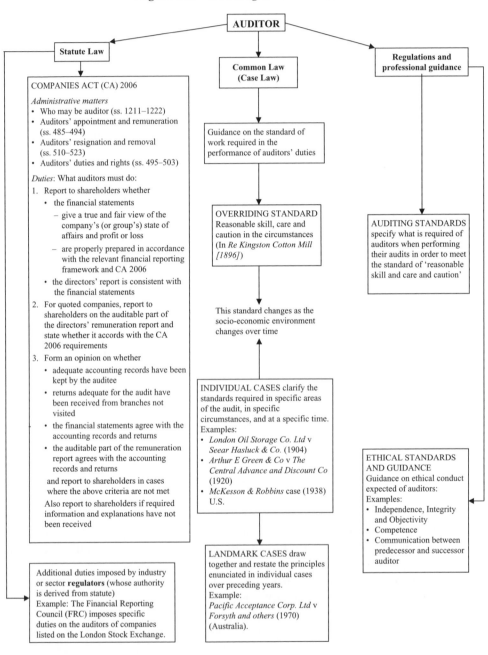

In this chapter, we discuss the statutory requirement for companies' financial statements to be audited, and the rights and responsibilities of auditors. We also consider auditors' relationship with their clients, examine auditors' (*vis-à-vis* directors') responsibility for the audited financial statements, and discuss the audit expectation–performance gap – the gap between the duties society expects auditors to perform and what society perceives auditors actually deliver. This gap has serious consequences for the auditing profession as it helps to fuel criticism of auditors and to undermine confidence in their work.

5.2 AUDITS AND AUDITORS' DUTIES UNDER STATUTE LAW[5]

5.2.1 Overview

The main statutory provisions governing the audits of companies' financial statements are contained in the Companies Act 2006 (CA 2006). This Act specifies the companies that are required to have their financial statements audited and also sets out:
- who may be an auditor;
- who is responsible for appointing, and determining the remuneration of, auditors;
- how auditors may resign or be removed;
- the statutory duties and rights of auditors.

Each of these matters is discussed below.

5.2.2 Requirement for audited financial statements

The CA 2006 distinguishes between two types of company, namely:
(i) public companies – companies that are registered as public companies, have a certificate of incorporation that states they are a public company, and a name which ends with 'public limited company' (or plc)[6] (ss. 4, 58);

---

[5] We restrict our discussion to companies whose financial statements are subject to audit. Other private sector organisations such as building societies, trade unions and employer associations, housing associations, certain charities and unincorporated investment businesses, and also public sector entities, are subject to specific financial reporting and auditing requirements. These are usually enshrined in separate legislation.

[6] Any company in which the liability of its members (shareholders) is limited by shares or by guarantee must include the word 'limited' in its name. In most companies, the liability of shareholders is limited by shares and their exposure to liability is limited to any unpaid portion of their shareholding.

(ii) private companies – companies that are not public companies. In most cases, the name of these companies ends with the word 'limited' (or ltd) (ss. 4, 59).

Only a public company may issue shares or loan stock (such as bonds) to the general public.

The Act (s. 385) also distinguishes between:
(i) quoted companies – companies with transferable securities[7] that are traded on a regulated market in a Member State of the European Union (EU; including the UK) or the European Economic Area (EEA),[8] or on the New York Stock Exchange (NYSE) or NASDAQ;[9] and
(ii) unquoted companies – companies that are not quoted companies.

It further distinguishes small and medium-sized companies (and groups).[10] These are companies (or groups) that meet at least two of the criteria shown in Figure 5.2[11] (ss. 382–383; 465–466).

Figure 5.2: Qualifying criteria for small and medium-sized companies

Criteria	Small		Medium-sized	
	Company	Group	Company	Group
Company or group turnover not more than	£5.6 million	£5.6 million net £6.72 million gross	£22.8 million	£22.8 million net £27.36 million gross
Company or group balance sheet total not more than	£2.8 million	£2.8 million net £3.36 million gross	£11.4 million	£11.4 million net £13.68 million gross
Employees not more than	50	50	250	250
'Net' means turnover or balance sheet total (as applicable) after any set-offs or other adjustments have been made to eliminate intra-group transactions.				

---

[7] Transferable securities are primarily shares and bonds or other forms of securitised debt.

[8] The EEA comprises Norway, Iceland and Liechtenstein. It has an agreement with the EU whereby it participates in the 'internal market' of the EU (i.e., it participates in the freedom of movement of goods, services, people and capital across EU and EEA Member States). The EEA States also adopt EU legislation relating to social policy, consumer protection, the environment, company law and statistics.

[9] In this text we use the word 'quoted' with the meaning indicated above, and 'listed' to mean companies listed on the London Stock Exchange. 'NASDAQ' was originally the acronym for National Association of Securities Dealers Automated Quotations system. It is now the largest screen-based electronic stock exchange in the USA (Wikipedia).

[10] A group comprises a parent company and one or more subsidiary companies.

[11] A company or group is ineligible to qualify as small or medium-sized if, at any time during the financial year, it (or one of the members of the group) was a public company, a banking or insurance company, an e-money issuer, it had permission under the Financial Services and Market Act 2000 to carry on a regulated activity, or its shares were admitted to trading on a regulated market (CA 2006, ss. 384, 467).

The directors of all companies (whether public or private, quoted or unquoted and irrespective of size) must prepare a balance sheet and profit and loss account for each financial year.[12] These must comply with either International Financial Reporting Standards (IFRSs) or regulations issued by the UK's Secretary of State. The CA 2006 refers to financial statements prepared in accordance with these two reporting frameworks as 'IAS accounts' and 'Companies Act accounts', respectively[13,14] (CA 2006, ss. 394–396, 403–405). The board of directors is required to approve the company's (and, in applicable cases, the group's) annual financial statements, and at least one director must sign the company's (or group's) balance sheet on behalf of the company (s. 414). This approval and signing signifies acceptance by the board of its responsibility for the financial statements. However, the directors may not approve the relevant financial statements unless they are satisfied that they give a true and fair view of the assets, liabilities, financial position and profit or loss of the company or group concerned (CA 2006, s. 393).[15] This requirement for financial statements to give a true and fair view, in addition to complying with IFRSs or the Secretary of State's regulations [i.e., UK Generally Accepted Accounting Practice (GAAP)], as applicable, is frequently referred to as the 'true and fair view override'.

The CA 2006 (ss. 396, 404) explicitly requires 'Companies Act accounts' to present a true and fair view of the company's (or group's) state of affairs as at

---

[12] In general, companies with subsidiaries (i.e., parent companies) are also required to prepare and submit group (consolidated) financial statements (i.e., financial statements which treat the parent company and its subsidiaries as a single entity). However, for groups that qualify as 'small', preparing group financial statements is optional rather than compulsory (CA 2006, ss. 398, 399).

[13] CA 2006 refers to international accounting standards (IAS) rather than IFRSs. Financial statements prepared in accordance with this framework ('IAS accounts') must state in a note to the financial statements that they have been prepared on this basis (CA 2006, ss. 397, 406). The parent company of a group that includes an entity whose securities are traded on a regulated market of any EU Member State *must* prepare 'IAS accounts' and comply with EU Regulation (EC) No. 1606/2002 *on the application of international accounting standards* [CA 2006, s. 403; EU Regulation (EC) No. 1606/2002, Article 4]. For other companies and groups, after the first financial year in which they have (voluntarily) prepared IAS accounts, their financial statements must be prepared on the same basis in all subsequent years unless there is a relevant change of circumstances; (given the definition of 'relevant change', this will occur rarely) (CA 2006, ss. 395, 403).

[14] In essence, Companies Act accounts are required to be prepared in accordance with UK Generally Accepted Accounting Practice (GAAP) (i.e., applicable law and UK accounting standards). However, small and medium-sized companies that prepare Companies Act accounts are permitted to file with the Registrar of Companies 'abbreviated accounts', that is, a profit and loss account and balance sheet in which specified items may be combined or omitted. Further, small companies have the option (rather than compulsion) of filing a profit and loss account (in full or abbreviated form) (CA 2006, ss. 444–445). In this text we refer to 'Companies Act accounts' as being prepared in accordance with UK GAAP (rather than in accordance with the Secretary of State's regulations).

[15] It is interesting to observe that CA 2006, s. 393, refers to, *inter alia*, the company's *financial position*. In ss. 396 and 404 (which specify the requirements of financial statements) and s. 495 (relating to auditors' duties), the term *state of affairs* is used instead. In this book we use the terms 'financial position' and 'state of affairs' interchangeably as, apparently, does CA 2006.

the end of its financial year and its profit or loss for the financial year. 'True and fair' is not defined in the Act but it recognises that financial statements prepared in accordance with UK GAAP may not give the required true and fair view. It provides that, if compliance with UK GAAP is insufficient to present a true and fair view of the company's (or group's) state of affairs and profit or loss, additional information is to be provided so that the required true and fair view is given. Further, if, in special circumstances, compliance with any GAAP provision is inconsistent with the requirement for the financial statements to give a true and fair view, the relevant provision is to be departed from to the extent necessary for a true and fair view to be presented. Reasons for, and the particulars and effect of, any such departure must be provided in a note to the financial statements (CA 2006, ss. 396, 404).

Along similar (but rather more prescriptive) lines, 'IAS accounts' are required by IAS 1: *Presentation of financial statements* (IASB, 2003) to:

> present fairly the financial position, financial performance and cash flows of [the company or group]. Fair presentation requires the faithful representation of the effects of transactions, other events and conditions in accordance with the definitions and recognition criteria for assets, liabilities, income and expenses set out in the *Framework*.[16] The application of IFRSs, with additional disclosure when necessary, is presumed to result in financial statements that achieve a fair presentation.... In the extremely rare circumstances in which management concludes that compliance with a requirement in [an IFRS or IAS] would be so misleading that it would conflict with the objective of financial statements set out in the *Framework*, the entity shall depart from that requirement. ...(paras 13, 17)[17]

As for 'Companies Act accounts', if, in the preparation of 'IAS accounts', an IFRS or IAS is departed from, full details of the departure and the reasons therefor, and effect thereof, must be disclosed in a note to the financial statements.

Companies must not only prepare annual financial statements; CA 2006, s. 475, requires that they be audited.[18] However, in general, this requirement does not apply to companies that, during the relevant financial year, have a turnover of not more than £5.6 million and a balance sheet total of not more than £2.8 million. Similarly, it does not, in general, apply to groups that have an aggregate turnover of not more than £5.6 million net (or £6.72 million gross) and an aggregate balance sheet total of not more than £2.8 million net (or £3.36

---

[16] International Accounting Standards Board (IASB) *Framework for the preparation and presentation of financial statements* (IASB, 2001).

[17] Although neither CA 2006 nor IAS 1 explicitly refers to financial statements prepared in accordance with IAS 'giving a true and fair view', in a legal Opinion, Martin Moore QC has "confirmed the centrality of the true and fair requirement to the preparation of financial statements in the UK, whether they are prepared in accordance with international or UK accounting standards" (Financial Reporting Council, 2008).

[18] Certain aspects of the directors', and directors' remuneration, report are also subject to audit: see section 5.2.6.

million gross) (CA 2006, ss. 477, 479).[19] Nevertheless, the audit exemption does not apply to a company or group if, at any time during the financial year:
- it (or one of the members of the group) was a public company, a banking or insurance company, or an e-money issuer; or
- members holding an aggregate of 10 per cent or more of the nominal value of the company's issued capital, or any class of it (or, in the absence of a share capital, at least 10 per cent of the company's members) request that the company's financial statement be audited (ss. 476, 478).

Where a company (or group) takes advantage of the audit exemption provisions, the company's directors are required to include in the balance sheet (above the directors' signatures) a statement to the effect that:
(a) the members (i.e., shareholders) have not required the company to have an audit for the year in question; and
(b) the directors acknowledge their responsibilities for complying with the requirements of CA 2006 with respect to accounting records and the preparation of the financial statements (s. 475).

In addition to preparing annual financial statements, the directors of each company are also required to prepare a directors' report for each financial year of the company. (In the case of groups, the directors of the parent company are required to prepare a 'group directors' report'.) Their report must contain the information specified in CA 2006, ss. 416–418. This includes the names of persons who were directors of the company during the financial year, the principal activities of the company and, unless the company qualifies as 'small', the amount of dividend (if any) the directors recommend should be paid. Additionally, unless the company qualifies as 'small', the directors' report must include a business review which contains, *inter alia*:
(i) a fair review of the development and performance of the company's business during the year, and its position at the end of the year;
(ii) a description of its principal risks and uncertainties;
(iii) if the company is a quoted company, to the extent necessary for readers to understand the development, performance and position of the company's business:
   (a) the main business trends and factors likely to affect the future of the company's business;
   (b) information about:
      - environmental matters (including the impact of the company's business on the environment),
      - the company's employees, and
      - social and community issues.

---

[19] The financial statements of most dormant companies are also exempt from the audit requirement, that is, companies which have not undertaken any significant accounting transactions during the financial year (CA 2006, s. 480).

Further, unless the company is exempt from an audit requirement, the directors' report must contain a statement to the effect that, as far as each director is aware:
- there is no relevant audit information of which the company's auditor is unaware; and
- (s)he has taken all necessary steps to become aware of any relevant audit information, and to establish that the company's auditor is aware of that information.

The directors of quoted companies must also prepare a directors' remuneration report which provides the information required by CA 2006, s. 421. The directors' report and, in the case of a quoted company, the directors' remuneration report must be approved by the board of directors and signed on behalf of the board by a director or the secretary of the company. If the directors' report does not comply with the requirements of CA 2006, every director who knew it did not comply, or was reckless as to whether or not it complied, and failed to take reasonable steps to secure compliance with the requirements or prevent the report from being approved, commits an offence. Such offence may result in imprisonment for up to two years or a fine up to an unlimited maximum amount.

The board of directors must send a copy of the company's (and, in applicable cases, the group's) annual financial statements, the auditor's report (unless the company is exempt from audit), the directors' report and, for quoted companies, the directors' remuneration report to the Registrar of Companies. The audit report must state the name of the auditor and, where the auditor is a firm, the name of the person who signed it as senior statutory auditor;[20] the directors' and directors' remuneration report must state the name of the person who signed the report on behalf of the company. The documents must be filed with the Registrar within six or nine months (for public and private companies, respectively) of the end of the company's financial year (CA 2006, ss. 442–447).

The audited annual financial statements and reports must also be sent to the company's shareholders, debenture holders, and all those entitled to receive notice of general meetings:[21] for a private company, this should be effected when the documents are filed with the Registrar of Companies; for public

---

[20] The senior statutory auditor is, in effect, the audit engagement partner – the partner (or other person) in the firm who is responsible for the audit engagement and its performance, and also for the audit report that is issued on behalf of the firm (APB, 2008).

[21] In many cases, a company may send summary financial statements in place of the full set of audited annual financial statements to shareholders, debenture holders, and those entitled to receive notice of general meetings.

companies, not less than 21 days before the general meeting at which copies of the documents are to be laid (the 'accounts meeting': see section 5.2.4) (CA 2006, ss. 423, 424). A quoted company must additionally make their audited annual financial statements and reports available on a website (s. 430).

5.2.3 Who may be an auditor of a company?

CA 2006 includes provisions designed to ensure that only people (or firms) who are appropriately qualified and properly supervised are appointed as statutory (including company) auditors, and that audits are carried out properly, with integrity and with the proper degree of independence (s. 1209). In order to be eligible for appointment in the UK as a statutory auditor, an individual must hold an appropriate qualification [which generally means qualifying with one of the six Recognised Qualifying Bodies (RQBs)],[22] be a member of (or registered with) one of the five Recognised Supervisory Bodies (RSBs),[23] and be eligible for appointment as a statutory auditor under the rules of that RSB.

In order to become an RSB, a professional body must have, *inter alia*:
  (a) rules to the effect that:
    (i) an individual is not eligible for appointment as a statutory auditor unless (s)he holds an appropriate qualification; and
    (ii) a firm is not eligible for such an appointment unless:
      – each individual responsible for statutory audit work on behalf of the firm is eligible for appointment as a statutory auditor, and
      – the firm is controlled by qualified persons (i.e., the majority of its members with voting rights, or who are otherwise able to direct its overall policy, are eligible for appointment as statutory auditors in the UK, or for a corresponding appointment as an auditor under the law of any EU Member State);
  (b) rules and practices relating to statutory auditors being fit and proper persons, conducting their audit work properly and with integrity, and not being appointed as auditors in circumstances in which their independence may be compromised;

---

[22] The six RQBs are the Institutes of Chartered Accountants in England and Wales (ICAEW), of Scotland (ICAS), and in Ireland (ICAI), and the Associations of Chartered Certified Accountants (ACCA), of Authorised Public Accountants (AAPA), and of International Accountants (AIA). The requirements relating to recognised professional qualifications are detailed in CA 2006, Schedule 11.

[23] The five RSBs are the ICAEW, ICAS, ICAI, ACCA and AAPA. Although most individuals qualify and register with the same professional body, they may, if they wish, qualify with one body and register as an auditor with another. It should be noted that qualified persons who are members of AAPA are only eligible for appointment as an auditor of an unquoted company (CA 2006, s. 1222).

(c) rules and practices regarding the technical standards to be applied in audit work and the manner in which the standards are to be applied in practice;

(d) rules and practices for admitting, disciplining and excluding members, and for ensuring that those eligible for appointment as statutory auditors maintain an appropriate level of competence;

(e) adequate arrangements for the effective monitoring and enforcement of compliance with its rules, investigating complaints about its members or itself (as an RSB), and meeting claims arising out of audit work (professional indemnity insurance).

(The requirements for recognition as an RSB are set out in CA 2006, Schedule 10, Part 2.)

Each RSB is also required to participate in arrangements for:

(i) setting technical auditing standards and standards relating to statutory auditors' integrity and independence;

(ii) independent monitoring of the audits of listed companies and other bodies in which there is major public interest;

(iii) independent investigation for disciplinary purposes of public interest cases (i.e., those which raise, or appear to raise, important issues affecting the public interest).

The Government has assigned overall responsibility for these activities to the Financial Reporting Council (FRC). The FRC discharges this responsibility through its operating bodies, in particular, the APB, the Professional Oversight Board (POB) and the Accountancy Investigation and Discipline Board, respectively, with input from, and working collaboratively with, the RSBs.

5.2.4 Who is responsible for appointing, and setting the remuneration of, an auditor?

CA 2006 specifies that both private and public companies must appoint an auditor (or auditors) for each financial year, unless the audit exemption provisions apply and the company's directors reasonably resolve that an auditor not be appointed on the ground that audited financial statements are unlikely to be required (ss. 485, 489). However, the timing and the period of the auditor's appointment differ between private and public companies. In each case, CA 2006 provides for the relevant company's shareholders to appoint an auditor (or auditors) by ordinary resolution but:

- for a private company, this should be effected before the end of the 'period for appointing auditors', that is, within 28 days of the earlier of:

    (i)   the end of the nine-month period following the end of the company's financial year during which the company must file its annual financial statements with the Registrar of Companies;

    (ii) the date on which the company actually files its annual financial statements with the Registrar (s. 485);

- for a public company, the auditor should be appointed before the end of the members' general meeting at which the audited financial statements for the previous financial year are presented (the 'accounts meeting') (s. 489).

In either case, if no auditor is appointed before the end of the specified period for appointing an auditor, the shareholders may appoint the auditor subsequently by ordinary resolution. However, if no auditor is appointed within a week of the end of the 'period for appointing auditors' or the 'accounts meeting' (as applicable), the company is required to inform the Secretary of State. The Secretary of State may then appoint one or more persons to fill the vacancy (ss. 486, 490).

The directors of both private and public companies are permitted to appoint the company's auditor any time before the company's first 'period for appointing auditors' or first 'accounts meeting' (as applicable), or to fill a casual vacancy which may arise if (for whatever reason) the auditor ceases to hold office before the end of his/her term of appointment (ss. 485, 489).

Auditors of both private and public companies hold office in accordance with the terms of their appointment subject to the requirement that:

    (i)   they do not take office until the predecessor auditor has ceased to hold office; and

    (ii) their appointment ceases at the end of the next 'period for appointing auditors' or 'accounts meeting' (as applicable) unless they are re-appointed.

In the case of a private, but not a public, company, if no auditor is appointed by the end of the next 'period for appointing auditors', the incumbent auditor is deemed to be re-appointed. However, this does not apply if the company's articles require actual re-appointment, or the shareholders have resolved that the auditor not be re-appointed, or shareholders holding at least five per cent of the voting rights of all members have given notice that the auditor should not be re-appointed (CA 2006, s. 487).

The party who appoints the company's auditor has responsibility for fixing their remuneration.[24] Thus, when the company's shareholders appoint the

---

[24] For the purposes of CA 2006, s. 492, the term 'remuneration' is defined to include "sums paid in respect of expenses' and 'benefits in kind' ".

auditor they must also, by ordinary resolution, either fix the associated remuneration or determine the manner in which it is to be fixed. Similarly, when
the auditor is appointed by the directors or by the Secretary of State, the
party concerned is also responsible for fixing the remuneration (CA 2006,
s. 492).

Notwithstanding the legal provisions empowering the shareholders to appoint,
and fix the remuneration of, their company's auditor, in practice the company's
directors usually decide who they wish to be appointed and their decision is
merely ratified by the shareholders. Normally, the shareholders also delegate
to the directors responsibility for fixing the auditor's remuneration. However,
as noted in Chapter 4, for companies with audit committees, it is usually a
responsibility of that committee to make recommendations to the board
of directors regarding, *inter alia*, the appointment, re-appointment or removal
of the auditor, and to approve the auditor's remuneration and terms of
engagement.[25]

Further (as also noted in Chapter 4, section 4.3.1), in order to secure 'transparency' with respect to the remuneration paid to, and the services provided by,
auditors, all but small and medium-sized companies are required to disclose in
a note to their financial statements details about the amounts paid to their
auditor (or any associates of the auditor) for the audit and all other services
provided to the company, its subsidiaries and its associated pension funds
[*Companies (Disclosure of Auditor Remuneration and Liability Limitation
Agreements) Regulations 2008*, Statutory Instrument 2008].[26]

5.2.5   How may an auditor resign or be replaced?

Auditors may resign simply by depositing a written notice to this effect at the
company's registered office. However, to be effective, it must be accompanied
by a 'statement of circumstances' or of 'no circumstances' (these statements
are explained below) (CA 2006, s. 516). Alternatively, the company may remove
the auditor at any time by passing an ordinary resolution at a general meeting
(s. 510). If a company wishes to appoint another auditor in place of the auditor

---

[25] As noted in Chapter 4 (section 4.4.5), *The Combined Code on Corporate Governance* (FRC, 2006a)
requires companies listed on the London Stock Exchange to establish audit committees and to include
amongst their responsibilities, making recommendations to the board about the auditor's appointment,
re-appointment or removal, and approving their remuneration – or to disclose that they have not done
so and the reasons therefor (provisions C.3.1, C.3.2). Similarly the EU 8th Directive on Statutory Audit
(EU, 2006), Article 41, requires the board of directors' recommendation to shareholders regarding the
auditor's appointment to be based on a recommendation of the audit committee.

[26] See Chapter 4, footnote 16. Most small and medium-sized companies are required to disclose only the
remuneration paid to the auditor for the audit of their financial statements.

whose term of appointment is ending (the 'outgoing auditor'), it must pass a resolution to appoint the 'replacement auditor' in accordance with the auditor's appointment provisions explained in section 5.2.4 above. However, resolutions to remove an auditor may not be passed at a general meeting unless at least 28 days' notice of the resolution has been given to both the shareholders and the incumbent auditor, and the latter has been given the opportunity to make representations to the shareholders on the intended resolution to remove him or her (s. 511). The same applies to a resolution, proposed to be passed at a general meeting of the company:

- to appoint another auditor in place of the outgoing auditor if no 'period for appointing auditors' has ended or 'accounts meeting' has been held (for a private and public company, respectively) since the outgoing auditor ceased to hold office; or
- no auditor was appointed during the relevant 'period for appointing auditors' or 'accounts meeting'.

The 'replacement auditor' must also be given at least 28 days' notice of the resolution (s. 515).[27]

The provisions enabling outgoing auditors to inform shareholders of the reasons they believe explain their removal or replacement are particularly important where company directors wish to remove auditors for the wrong reasons – for example, because they have uncovered questionable acts by the directors or senior managers of which the shareholders are not aware and of which they would not approve. Directors lacking integrity may wish the company to engage less diligent auditors!

Whenever auditors cease to hold office (whether it be through resignation, removal or replacement), they are required to deposit at the relevant company's registered office, a statement of the circumstances connected with their ceasing to hold office. However, in the case of unquoted companies, auditors are excused from making this statement if they consider there are no circumstances that should be brought to the attention of the company's shareholders or creditors. In this event, the auditor is required to deposit at the company's

---

[27] CA 2006 (Part 13, Ch. 2) provides for a private company to propose and pass written resolutions with the same effect as those passed in a general meeting. In general, such a resolution is passed when the required majority of eligible shareholders have signified their agreement to it. Unless the company's articles provide otherwise, the resolution lapses if it is not passed within 28 days of its circulation (ss. 296–297). If a private company proposes to appoint another auditor in place of the outgoing auditor by written resolution, rather than in a general meeting, in place of the 28 days' notice of the resolution that would otherwise be required, the company must send a copy of the proposed resolution to both the 'replacement' and 'outgoing auditor' and the latter must be given the opportunity to make written representations to the company and request that these be circulated to the shareholders. The auditor must be given 14 days from receiving the notice, and the company must circulate the proposed resolution and the outgoing auditor's representations within 28 days (s. 514).

registered office a statement that there are no such circumstances[28] (CA 2006, s. 519).

When a company receives a statement of circumstances, unless it applies to the court for a judgment on whether the auditor is seeking needless publicity for defamatory matter and the court decides in the company's favour, it must send a copy of the auditor's statement to all those entitled to receive copies of the company's annual financial statements. If the company makes application to the court, the auditor must be notified accordingly. In the absence of such notice, the auditor must send a copy of his or her statement to the Registrar of Companies (CA 2006, ss. 520, 521).

Auditors are also required to notify the 'appropriate audit authority' of their ceasing to hold office (whatever the reason therefor), and to send with their notice, a 'statement of circumstances' or of 'no circumstances': in the latter case, the auditor is also required to provide a statement setting out the reasons for ceasing to hold office. The 'appropriate audit authority' to which auditors should give notice, and the notification requirements, differ according to whether the audit from which the auditor has ceased to hold office is, or is not, a 'major audit'.[29]

- For 'major audits', the appropriate audit authority is the Secretary of State, or the body to whom the Secretary of State delegates the relevant function.[30] Auditors must notify the authority whenever they cease to hold office and they are required to do this at the same time as they deposit their 'statement of circumstances' (or of 'no circumstances') at the relevant company's registered office.
- For 'not major audits', the appropriate audit authority is the RSB with which the auditor is registered. In these cases, auditors are required to inform the authority of their ceasing to hold office only when this occurs before the end of their term of appointment, and they must do this "at such time as the appropriate audit authority may require" (CA 2006, s. 522).

When auditors cease to hold office before the end of their term of appointment, the relevant company (in addition to the auditor) is required to notify the 'appropriate audit authority' (s. 523). The notice must be accompanied by:

(i) a statement of the company's reasons for the auditor ceasing to hold office; and

---

[28] In this book we refer to these statements as 'statements of circumstances' and 'statements of no circumstances', respectively.

[29] A 'major audit' is the audit of a company listed on the London Stock Exchange or in whose financial condition there is major public interest.

[30] In effect, it is the FRC's Public Oversight Board (POB).

(ii) if the auditors' 'statement of circumstances' contains circumstances in connection with their ceasing to hold office that need to be brought to the attention of the company's members (i.e., shareholders) or creditors, a copy of that statement.

5.2.6 Auditors' statutory duties

Auditors' primary statutory duties are set out in CA 2006, ss. 495–498. These provisions require auditors to report to the company's shareholders on the company's annual financial statements. Their report is to include:

(i) an introduction identifying the financial statements that are the subject of the audit and the financial reporting framework adopted for their preparation;

(ii) a description of the scope of the audit, identifying the auditing standards in accordance with which the audit was conducted;

(iii) a clear statement as to whether, in the auditor's opinion, the company's financial statements:

- give a true and fair view of the company's state of affairs as at the end of the financial year and its profit or loss for the financial year;[31]
- have been properly prepared in accordance with the relevant financial reporting framework (i.e., IAS or UK GAAP);
- have been prepared in accordance with the Companies Act 2006 and, for consolidated financial statements of groups traded on the regulated market of an EU Member State, with the EU's IAS Regulation;[32]

(iv) a statement as to whether, in the auditor's opinion, the directors' report for the financial year is consistent with the company's annual financial statements;

(v) for quoted companies, a report on the auditable part of the directors' remuneration report and a statement whether, in the auditor's opinion, that part of the directors' report has been properly prepared in accordance with the Companies Act 2006.[33]

---

[31] In applicable cases, auditors are also required to report whether group financial statements give a true and fair view of the state of affairs and profit or loss of the undertakings included in the consolidated financial statements, so far as concerns the members of the parent company.

[32] EU Regulation (EC) No. 1606/2002 *on the application of international accounting standards*. See footnote 13.

[33] The 'auditable part of the directors' remuneration report' is specified in regulations to be issued by the Secretary of State pursuant to CA 2006, s. 421. Until such regulations are issued, those in Statutory Instrument 2002 No. 1986: *The Directors' Remuneration Report Regulations 2002* apply.

The auditor's report must be either unqualified (when the auditor is satisfied that everything is as it should be) or qualified (when the auditor is not so satisfied) and it must include a reference to any matters to which the auditor wishes to draw attention by way of emphasis without qualifying the report.[34]

In order to prepare their report, auditors are required to carry out such investigations as will enable them to form an opinion whether:
- adequate accounting records have been kept by the company;
- returns, adequate for their audit, have been received from branches of the company not visited by them;
- the financial statements are in agreement with the accounting records and returns;
- in the case of a quoted company, the auditable part of the directors' remuneration report is in agreement with the accounting records and returns.

In any case where auditors consider that one or more of the above requirements has not been met, they are required to state that fact in their audit report. Similarly:
- if auditors fail to obtain all the information and explanations they consider are necessary for the purposes of their audit; and/or
- if the company's directors have prepared the financial statements in accordance with the small companies' provisions and, in the auditors' opinion, they are not entitled to do so,

the auditors are required to state the fact in the audit report.

Additionally, in any case where the directors' remuneration report does not comply with:
(i) the regulations issued pursuant to CA 2006, s. 412 (Information about directors' benefits: remuneration);[35] or
(ii) in the case of a quoted company, the regulations issued pursuant to CA 2006, s. 421 regarding the information constituting the auditable part of the report,

the auditor is to include the required particulars in the audit report, as far as (s)he is reasonably able to do so.

The auditor's report must state the name of, and be signed by, the auditor. Where the auditor is an individual, it is to be signed by him or her; where it is

---

[34] The various types of audit report are discussed in detail in Chapter 14.

[35] Until such regulations are issued, those in Statutory Instrument 2002 No. 1986: *The Directors' Remuneration Report Regulations 2002* apply.

a firm, it is to be signed by the senior statutory auditor[36] in his or her own name, for and on behalf of the audit firm. In general, every copy of the auditor's report that is published by or on behalf of the company must state the name of the auditor and (where the auditor is a firm) the name of the person who signed it as the senior statutory auditor. A company is regarded as publishing the report if it publishes, issues or circulates it, or otherwise makes it available for public inspection in a manner calculated to invite members of the public generally, or any class of members of the public, to read it (CA 2006, ss. 503–505).

5.2.7 Auditors' statutory rights

CA 2006 (ss. 499–502) provides auditors with rights which facilitate the performance of their duties. They are, for example, given a right of access, at all times, to all of the auditee's books, accounts and vouchers, and the right to require directors and employees of the company to provide any information and explanations the auditor considers necessary for the performance of his or her duties as auditor. Similarly, where a parent company has subsidiaries incorporated outside the UK, the auditor of the parent company can require that company to obtain relevant information and explanations from the directors and employees of those subsidiaries. If any person knowingly or recklessly makes a written or oral statement to the company's auditor that:

(i) conveys, or purports to convey, any information or explanations the auditor requires; and

(ii) is misleading, false or deceptive in a material particular,

that person is guilty of an offence. This can result in imprisonment for up to two years or a fine up to an unlimited maximum amount. Along similar lines, if any person fails to provide information or explanations requested by the auditor "without delay" (s. 501), that person commits an offence that may result in a fine of up to £1,000.

Auditors are also entitled to attend any general meeting of the company, to receive notices and other communications relating to any general meeting which a shareholder is entitled to receive, and to be heard at any general meeting on matters that concern them as auditors. In respect of a written resolution proposed to be passed by a private company,[37] the auditor is entitled to receive all the communications relating to the resolution a shareholder may receive.

---

[36] See footnote 20.

[37] See footnote 27.

5.3 AUDITORS' DUTIES UNDER COMMON LAW

While statute law requires the financial statements of companies to be audited and specifies the duties auditors are to perform, the courts have explained what is expected of auditors in the performance of their statutory duties.

The general standard of performance required of auditors was laid down by Lopes L J in *Re Kingston Cotton Mill Co. (No. 2)* [1896] 2 Ch 279, when he said:

> It is the duty of an auditor to bring to bear on the work he has to perform that skill, care and caution which a reasonably competent, careful and cautious auditor would use. What is reasonable skill, care and caution must depend on the particular circumstances of each case.

Clearly, what is regarded as 'reasonable skill, care and caution in the circumstances' will change over time as changes occur in society, in society's attitudes and values, and in the 'technology' of auditing.

As we noted in Chapter 2, until the 1920s, auditors were primarily concerned with detecting fraud and error and ensuring that the solvency position of the reporting entity was fairly portrayed in the balance sheet. Accordingly, during the 19th century, auditors carefully checked the detailed entries in, and arithmetical accuracy of, the company's books and made sure that the amounts shown in the balance sheet corresponded with the ledger account balances. If this was all that auditors did today they would be regarded as grossly negligent. They are now expected to examine sufficient appropriate evidence, drawn from a variety of sources (from both inside and outside the entity), on which to base an opinion about the truth and fairness of the auditee's financial statements – including the profit and loss account and (unless exempt from preparing one) the cash flow statement,[38] in addition to the balance sheet.

Over the years, various parties who have suffered loss after relying on audited financial statements have taken auditors to court on claims of negligence; that is, on grounds that the auditors did not perform their duties properly and, as a result, failed to detect material error(s) in the financial statements. Many of these cases have helped to clarify specific duties of auditors. The following cases serve as examples.

- In *Leeds Estate Building and Investment Co.* v *Shepherd* (1887) 36 Ch D 787, the auditor (a bank clerk) was found to be negligent for failing to ensure that the audited balance sheet was drawn up in accordance with

---

[38] While the CA 2006 requires all companies to produce a balance sheet and profit and loss account, UK GAAP and IASs require all but small companies also to produce a cash flow statement.

the company's Articles of Association (which the auditor had, in fact, never seen). The auditor claimed that his duty was to see that the balance sheet represented, and was a true result of, what appeared in the books of the company, and that his certificate went no further than that. However the judge (Sterling J) thought otherwise. He stated:

> [It is] the duty of the auditor not to confine himself merely to the task of verifying the arithmetical accuracy of the balance sheet, but to enquire into its substantial accuracy, and to ascertain that it contained the particulars specified in the articles of association ... and was properly drawn up so as to contain a true and correct representation of the state of the company's affairs. (at 802)

- As in the *Leeds Estate* case, in *Re London and General Bank (No. 2)* (1895) 2 Ch 677, (which concerned a bank whose loans to other companies were of doubtful recoverability) the auditor, in phrasing his audit report, tried unsuccessfully to limit his duty to a comparison of the balance sheet with the books of account. Lindley L J made it clear that more was expected of auditors. He stated:

> [An auditor's] business is to ascertain and state the true financial position of the company at the time of the audit and his duty is confined to that. But then comes the question: How is he to ascertain such position? The answer is: By examining the books of the company. But he does not discharge his duty by doing this without enquiry, and without taking any trouble to see that the books of the company show the company's true position. He must take reasonable care to ascertain that they do. Unless he does this, his duty will be worse than a farce. (at 682–3)

The *London and General Bank* case, which confirmed the *Leeds Estate* case, is a landmark in that it established that auditors had to examine the auditee's books and records and to form an opinion as to whether they 'truly' reflected the substance of the company's financial position.

- In *The London Oil Storage Co. Ltd* v *Seear, Hasluck & Co.* (1904) Acc LR 30, it was established that auditors are required to verify the existence of assets stated in the balance sheet. In this case, the cash book balance did not agree with the physical cash balance, a fact that the auditors failed to check or discover. The case is particularly significant as it was the first time that the court made it clear that auditors are expected to go beyond the books and records of the client company for evidence to support their opinion about the truth and fairness of the financial statements.

- In *Arthur E Green & Co.* v *The Central Advance and Discount Corporation Ltd* (1920) 63 Acc LR 1, an auditor was held to be negligent for accepting a schedule of bad debts provided by a responsible officer of the company when it was apparent that other debts, not included in the schedule, were also irrecoverable. The case settled that auditors may not blindly accept evidence given to them by officers of the auditee. They must properly relate it to other evidence gathered during the course of the audit.

- In the infamous *McKesson and Robbins* case (US, 1938), the auditor failed to uncover a massive fraud involving fictitious accounts receivable (debtors) and inventory (stock). The court held that auditors have a duty to verify the existence of these assets. This extended the *London Oil Storage Company* case, making it clear that auditors must verify assets stated in the balance sheet, even when those assets are at a distant location.

Occasionally when a case comes before the court, the judge takes the opportunity to bring together the specific duties of auditors that have been settled in a number of previous cases, and to enunciate general principles. One of the most renowned cases of this type is the Australian case *Pacific Acceptance Corporation Limited* v *Forsyth and Others* (1970) 92 WN (NSW) 29.

In his long judgment, Moffit J provided comprehensive guidance on auditors' duties and responsibilities. Among the important legal principles he confirmed or established are the following:

1. When auditors accept an engagement to conduct a statutory financial statement audit they can be taken to have promised, not only to make the report required by legislation (for example, by s. 495 of CA 2006) but also to conduct such examination as is necessary to form their opinion, and to exercise due skill and care in so doing.
2. Auditors' duties are not confined to an examination of the company's books and records at balance sheet date but extend to an audit of the company's financial affairs in general and for the whole of the relevant financial period.
3. The duty to audit involves a duty to pay due regard to the possibility that fraud may have occurred. The audit programme and audit tests should be structured so that the auditor has a reasonable expectation of detecting material fraud if it exists.
4. Auditors have a duty to make prompt and frank disclosure, to the appropriate level of management, of material matters discovered during the course of an audit. This includes a duty to report promptly to the company's directors if suspicious circumstances are encountered.
5. The auditor's duty to report includes a duty to report to shareholders at their general meeting any material matters discovered during the audit. This responsibility cannot be shirked on the grounds that it involves an adverse reflection on the board, a director, or a senior executive, or on the pretext that public disclosure may damage the company.

6. The auditor has a paramount duty to check material matters for him- or herself. However, reliance may be placed on enquiries from others where it is reasonable to do so. Nevertheless, reliance on others is to be regarded as an aid to, and not a substitute for, the auditor's own procedures.
7. The use of inexperienced staff, or the failure to use an adequate audit programme do not, of themselves, establish negligence. However, if audit failure occurs (that is, a material misstatement in the financial statements is not uncovered by the audit), then the use of such staff and/or the absence of a satisfactory audit programme may be taken as evidence that the failure occurred as a result of negligence.

In his judgment, Moffit J noted that professional standards and practice must change over time, to reflect changes in the economic and business environment. He further observed that the courts, in trying to ascertain what qualifies as 'reasonable skill, care and caution', are guided by professional standards and best auditing practices of the time. However, he emphasised that the courts are not bound by these standards and, if they see fit, they will go beyond them. It is the courts, not the profession, which determine, in the light of society's prevailing norms, what is reasonable skill, care and caution in the particular circumstances of the case.[39]

The relevance of these points is evident when it is realised that the duties which Moffit J attributed to auditors were not generally practised at the time (1970). Indeed, Kenley (1971, pp. 153–161) noted that the case brought to light key matters which required the immediate attention of auditors. These included:
1. The need to have an adequate written audit programme, and the need to correlate this with a review of the audit client's system of internal controls, and to modify it as necessary during the course of the audit to ensure that it adequately covers all material aspects of the entity.
2. The need to ensure that audit samples are drawn from records and events that cover the entire financial period, not just the period around the balance sheet date.
3. The need to ensure that audit staff are properly supervised by both partners and managers, and that proper instructions are given to assistants who have limited qualifications and/or experience.
4. The need to carefully assess the level of management from which the auditor seeks information, and the need to record appropriate details of responses to enquiry in the audit working papers.

---

[39] It should be remembered that at the time of the *Pacific Acceptance* case all auditing standards and guidelines (such as they were) were promulgated by the professional accountancy bodies. Enshrining auditing standards in regulations is a 21st century phenomenon.

5. The need to report promptly and forthrightly to the appropriate level of the audit client's management, deficiencies in transactions or accounting records examined by the auditor.

Today all of these matters are regarded as 'usual practice'. Indeed, the *Pacific Acceptance* case has had a profound impact on auditing, as the principles enunciated by Moffit J underlie the Auditing Standards that have been promulgated subsequently by professional accountancy bodies (and, in recent years, by regulators) throughout the world.

5.4 AUDITORS' DUTIES UNDER AUDITING STANDARDS

Until relatively recently, professional accountancy bodies around the world were responsible for setting, monitoring and amending (as appropriate) Auditing Standards that governed the work of their members who were auditors. This still applies in some countries outside the EU and USA – for example, in New Zealand and India. In many, if not most, cases the 'national/professional body standards' were based on (and largely replicated) the International Auditing Standards (ISAs) issued by the International Federation of Accountant's (IFAC) Auditing Practices Committee or its replacement – the International Auditing and Assurance Standards Board (IAASB).[40]

In the UK and Ireland, rather than each of the professional bodies[41] setting its own Auditing Standards, in 1991 the bodies established the Auditing Practices Board (APB) to perform this function on their behalf. In April 2002, the APB became a component (an operating body) of the Financial Reporting Council (FRC) and the status of its Auditing Standards changed from 'professional' (enforceable by the relevant professional body) to regulatory (enforceable by law).[42]

The APB has 15 members and, in order to ensure it is, and is seen to be, independent of the auditing profession, no more than 40 per cent of its members

---

[40] IFAC is a global organisation for the accountancy profession. It has 163 member bodies in 120 countries, including the UK. In April 2002, IFAC established the IAASB as an independent standard setting body. At that time, the IAASB replaced the International Auditing Practices Committee and assumed delegated responsibility from IFAC for setting International Standards on Auditing (ISAs).

[41] Or, more correctly, the RSBs which, as noted in section 5.2.3, coincide with the professional bodies with whom qualified individuals or firms may register as auditors, i.e., the ICAEW, ICAS, ICAI, ACCA, AAPA (see footnote 23).

[42] The FRC explains:
> We are an independent regulator and thus operate independently from those whose activities we regulate.... Our statutory powers derive from Parliament. (FRC, 2006b, p. 3)

As noted in section 5.2.3, the APB has delegated responsibility from the FRC for setting technical auditing standards and standards relating to auditors' integrity and independence.

may be eligible for appointment as company auditors. Of the other 60 per cent, none may be "office holders" or "persons actively involved in the governance of any accountancy body nor be partners in firms authorised to conduct audits" (www.frc.org.uk/apb).

In its *Scope and Authority of Pronouncements* (APB, 2008a), the APB states that its objectives are, *inter alia*, to:

- Establish Auditing Standards which set out the basic principles and essential procedures with which external auditors in the United Kingdom and the Republic of Ireland are required to comply;
- Issue guidance on the application of Auditing Standards in particular circumstances and industries and timely guidance on new and emerging issues; ...
- Establish Ethical Standards in relation to the independence, objectivity and integrity of external auditors and those providing assurance services; ... (para 1)

It also notes that its pronouncements include:

- 'Quality control standards' for firms that perform audits of financial statements ... ;
- A framework of fundamental principles which the APB expects to guide the conduct of auditors;[43]
- 'Engagement standards' for audits of financial statements ... ;
- Guidance for auditors of financial statements ... (para 4)

In relation to its quality control and engagement (i.e., auditing) standards, the APB explains that it has adopted:

the International Standard on Quality Control 1 (ISQC 1) and International Standards on Auditing (ISAs) issued by the International Auditing and Assurance Standards Board (IAASB). Where necessary [the] APB has augmented such international standards by additional standards and guidance ... This additional material is clearly differentiated from the original text of the international standards by the use of grey shading. (APB, 2008a, para 7)

The ISAs have been issued in a structured series which is shown in Figure 5.3.

The adoption of ISAs by the APB results in an interesting situation: the ISAs are developed by a professional body (the IAASB, under the auspices of IFAC, also a professional body) and are, therefore, professional standards; however, through their adoption by the APB they assume the status of regulations.

---

[43] This framework is The Auditors' Code, which "provides a framework of fundamental principles which encapsulate the concepts that govern the conduct of audits and underlie the APB's ethical and auditing standards" (APB, 2008a, para 11). The Auditors' Code is reproduced on the inside of the front cover of this book.

Figure 5.3: Structure of International Standards on Auditing[44]

ISA No	Title
200/299	**General Principles and Responsibilities**
200	Overall objectives of the independent auditor and the conduct of an audit in accordance with International Standards on Auditing
210	Agreeing the terms of audit engagements
220	Quality control for an audit of financial statements
230	Audit documentation
240	The auditor's responsibilities relating to fraud in an audit of financial statements
250	Consideration of laws and regulations in an audit of financial statements
260	Communication with those charged with governance
265	Communicating deficiencies in internal control
300/499	**Risk Assessment and Response to Assessed Risks**
300	Planning an audit of financial statements
315	Identifying and assessing the risks of material misstatement through understanding the entity and its environment
320	Materiality in planning and performing an audit
330	The auditor's responses to assessed risks
402	Audit considerations relating to an entity using a third party service organization
450	Evaluation of misstatements identified during the audit
500/599	**Audit evidence**
500	Audit evidence
501	Audit evidence regarding special financial statement account balances and disclosures
505	External confirmations
510	Initial audit engagements – Opening balances
520	Analytical procedures
530	Audit sampling
540	Auditing accounting estimates, including fair value accounting estimates, and related disclosures
550	Related parties
560	Subsequent events
570	Going concern
580	Written representations
600/699	**Using Work of Others**
600	Special considerations – Audits of group financial statements (including the work of component auditors)
610	Using the work of internal auditors
620	Using the work of an auditor's expert
700/799	**Audit conclusions and reporting**
700	Forming an opinion and reporting on financial statements
705	Modifications to the opinion in the independent auditor's report
706	Emphasis of matter paragraphs and other matter(s) paragraphs in the independent auditor's report
710	Comparative information – Corresponding figures and comparative financial statements
720	The auditor's responsibility in relation to other information in documents containing audited financial statements
800-899	**Specialized areas**
800	Special considerations – Audits of special purpose financial statements and specific elements, accounts or items of a financial statement
805	Engagements to report on summary financial statements

---

[44] Titles of International Standards on Auditing are as adopted or proposed by the IAASB in June 2008. (See Important Note following the Preface to this book.)

In its *Preface to the International Standards*, IFAC (2005) explains:

> IAASB members act in the common interest of the public at large and the world-wide accountancy profession. (para 2)

> The IAASB's pronouncements govern audit ... engagements that are conducted in accordance with International Standards. They do not override the local laws or regulations that govern the audit of historical financial statements ... in a particular country required to be followed in accordance with that country's national standards. In the event that local laws or regulations differ from, or conflict with, the IAASB's Standards on a particular subject, an engagement conducted in accordance with local laws or regulations will not automatically comply with the IAASB's Standards. A professional accountant should not represent compliance with the IAASB's Standards unless the professional accountant has complied fully with all of those relevant to the engagement. (para 3)

Similarly, the APB (2008a) states: "Auditors ... should not claim compliance with APB standards [i.e., ISAs (UK and Ireland)] unless they have complied fully with all of those standards relevant to an engagement" (para 5).

The International Quality Control and Auditing Standards (IQCS 1 and ISAs) contain basic principles and essential procedures together with related guidance. The latter, in the form of explanatory and other material (including appendices), is provided to assist auditors interpret and apply the basic principles and essential procedures. Compliance with the basic principles and essential procedures, which constitute the actual Auditing Standards,[45] is mandatory. If auditors fail to comply with these (mandatory) Standards when performing company audits, disciplinary action may be taken against them by the RSB with which they are registered. Such disciplinary action may result in withdrawal of registration and hence of the auditor's eligibility to perform company audits (APB, 2008a, para 21).

In addition to guidance on the application of particular quality control and auditing standards which is included within the relevant standard, the APB issues guidance to auditors in the form of Practice Notes and Bulletins:

- Practice Notes "assist auditors in applying APB engagement [i.e., auditing] standards to particular circumstances and industries";
- Bulletins "provide timely guidance on new or emerging issues".

---

[45] In common parlance, entire ISAs (Auditing Standards and explanatory material) are referred to as 'Auditing Standards'. In this book we use the terms 'Auditing Standard' and 'the Standard' in a similar manner; i.e., to refer to the relevant ISA in its entirety. In recent years the IAASB has redrafted the ISAs to improve their clarity (the 'clarity project'). Their content is essentially the same as that of their predecessors but, prior to the clarity project, each 'basic principle and essential procedure' was stated in bold type followed by explanatory paragraphs (in ordinary type). In the ISAs' redrafted form, the basic principles and essential procedures are presented together in the first section of each ISA and 'Application and other explanatory matter' is presented in a second section. Each application and explanatory paragraph is identified by the letter A (i.e., A1, A2, etc.). The redrafted ISAs are effective from 15 December 2009.

These Practice Notes and Bulletins "are persuasive rather than prescriptive and are indicative of good practice" (APB, 2008a, para 13).

It is pertinent to observe that, although the explanatory material included in the APB's quality control and auditing standards, as well as its Practice Notes and Bulletins, is persuasive rather than mandatory, the APB notes: "All relevant APB pronouncements and in particular auditing standards are likely to be taken into account when the adequacy of the work of auditors is being considered in a court of law or in other contested situations" (APB, 2008a, para 22).

The quality control and auditing standards serve two important purposes, namely:
   (i)   they inform individual auditors about the standard of work required of them in the performance of their duties; and
   (ii) they help to enhance the reputation of, and increase public confidence in, the profession as a whole.
As auditors' responsibilities are set out in the standards, and as the standards are binding on all members of the profession in the conduct of all audits (and any auditor falling short of the mandatory standards when performing an audit is exposed to disciplinary action), the standards help to ensure that all members of the profession perform their audits in accordance with the standards. If all auditors comply with the standards, high-quality audits should result – to the benefit of users of the audited financial statements, the auditees and society as a whole,[46] as well as the auditing profession.

5.5   AUDITORS' DUTIES UNDER REGULATORY REQUIREMENTS APPLYING TO COMPANIES OF SPECIFIC TYPES OR IN SPECIFIC INDUSTRIES

Certain regulatory bodies, such as the Financial Services Authority (FSA),[47] have been given authority under relevant statutes to impose requirements on entities under their jurisdiction and also on the auditors of these entities. Most of the regulatory requirements are limited in their application to entities within certain industrial sectors (for example, the financial services sector) and it is outside the scope of this book to discuss auditing requirements that are specific to any particular sector. However, the requirements of the United Kingdom

---

[46] See Chapter 1, section 1.6.

[47] Regulatory responsibility for companies listed on the London Stock Exchange passed from the London Stock Exchange to the Financial Services Authority (FSA) in 2000. The FSA has delegated its responsibilities for listed companies to the United Kingdom Listing Authority (UKLA). To all intents and purposes the UKLA constitutes a division of the FSA.

Listing Authority (UKLA) are wide ranging in their application as they apply to all companies listed on the London Stock Exchange.

Under the UKLA's Listing Rules, listed companies are required to comply with (or explain their departure from) *The Combined Code on Corporate Governance* (FRC, 2006a). This Code essentially consolidates the recommendations of a number of earlier reports – in particular, those of the Committee on the Financial Aspects of Corporate Governance (Cadbury Committee; 1992), the Committee on Corporate Governance (Hampel Committee; 1998a), the Study Group on Directors' Remuneration (Greenbury Committee; 1995), Higgs on non-executive directors (2003) and Smith on audit committees (2003). It also supersedes the FRC's 2003 *Combined Code on Corporate Governance* (FRC, 2003) which, in turn, replaced the *Combined Code* of the Committee on Corporate Governance (1998b).

The Combined Code on Corporate Governance (FRC, 2006a) comprises five parts (A to E), each of which contains main and supporting principles, and provisions: the Code's structure is shown in Figure 5.4. The Listing Rules require companies to include in their annual report a two-part disclosure statement describing their application of, and compliance with, the Code's principles and provisions, respectively. The two parts are as follows:
   (i) a narrative part explaining how the company has applied the Code's main and supporting principles;
   (ii) a compliance statement confirming that the company has complied with all of the Code's provisions throughout the reporting period or detailing those with which it has not complied, giving the reasons for the non-compliance.

The Listing Rules also require listed companies to ensure their auditor reviews the compliance statement in so far as it relates to their compliance (or otherwise) with nine of the 10 accountability and audit provisions (see Figure 5.4). The nine are as follows:
   C.1.1 The directors should explain in the annual report their responsibility for preparing the accounts and there should be a statement by the auditors about their reporting responsibilities.
   C.2.1 The board should, at least annually, conduct a review of the effectiveness of the group's system of internal controls and should report to shareholders that they have done so. The review should cover all material controls, including financial, operational and compliance controls and risk management systems.
   C.3.1 The board should establish an audit committee of at least three, or in the case of smaller companies two, members, who should all be independent non-executive directors. The board should satisfy itself that at least one member of the audit committee has recent and relevant financial experience.

Figure 5.4: Structure of *The Combined Code of Corporate Governance*

Section 1 Companies			No. of Provisions
A Directors	A.1	The Board	5
	A.2	Chairman and chief executive	2
	A.3	Board balance and independence	3
	A.4	Appointments to the Board	6
	A.5	Information and professional development	3
	A.6.	Performance evaluation	1
	A.7	Re-election	2
B Remuneration	B.1	The level and make-up of remuneration	6
	B.2	Procedure	4
C Accountability and audit	C.1	Financial reporting	2
	C.2	Internal controls	1
	C.3	Audit committees and auditors	7
D Relations with shareholders	D.1	Dialogue with institutional shareholders	2
	D.2	Constructive use of the AGM	4
Section 2 Institutional shareholders			
E Institutional shareholders	E.1	Dialogue with companies	-
	E.2	Evaluation of governance disclosures	-
	E.3	Shareholder voting	-

C.3.2 The main role and responsibilities of the audit committee should be set out in written terms of reference . . . [The matters to be included are reproduced in Chapter 4, section 4.4.5].

C.3.3 The terms of reference of the audit committee, including its role and the authority delegated to it by the board, should be made available. A separate section of the annual report should describe the work of the committee in discharging those responsibilities.

C.3.4 The audit committee should review arrangements by which staff of the company may, in confidence, raise concerns about possible improprieties in matters of financial reporting or other matters. . . .

C.3.5 The audit committee should monitor and review the effectiveness of the internal audit activities. Where there is no internal audit function, the audit committee should consider annually whether there is a need for an internal audit function and make a recommendation to the board, and the reasons for the absence of such a function should be explained in the relevant section of the annual report.

C.3.6 The audit committee should have primary responsibility for making a recommendation on the appointment, re-appointment and removal of the external auditors. If the board does not accept the audit committee's recommendation, it should include in the annual report . . . a statement from the audit committee explaining the recommendation and should set out reasons why the board has taken a different position.

C.3.7 The annual report should explain to shareholders how, if the auditor provides non-audit services, auditor objectivity and independence is safeguarded. (FRC, 2006a)

It should be noted that the Listing Rules only require auditors to review directors' compliance statements insofar as they relate to the above nine of the Code's 48 provisions; they are not required to review the narrative part of the directors' disclosure statement nor are they required to review the part of the compliance statement that relates to the tenth accountability and audit provision, namely: "The directors should report [in the annual report] that the business is a going concern, with supporting assumptions or qualifications as necessary" (provision C.1.2). This avoids the possible implication that the auditor supports the directors' assessment of the auditee as a going concern. Nevertheless, under different listing rules, the auditor is required to review the directors' 'going concern' statement prior to its publication in the annual report[48] (APB, 2006a, para 10).

The APB, in Bulletin 2006/5: *The Combined Code on Corporate Governance: Requirements of Auditors under the Listing Rules . . .* (APB, 2006a) has provided guidance for auditors in respect of their review of their listed company clients' compliance statement. It states:

In relation to all elements of the corporate governance disclosures relating to the provisions of the Combined Code that are within the scope of the auditor's review, the auditor obtains appropriate evidence to support the compliance statement made by the company. The type of procedures usually performed include:

(a) reviewing the minutes of meetings of the board of directors, and of relevant board committees;
(b) reviewing supporting documents prepared for the board of directors or board committees . . . ;
(c) making enquiries of certain directors . . . and the company secretary to satisfy themselves on matters relevant to those provisions of the Combined Code specified for review by the auditor; and
(d) attending meetings of the audit committee . . . at which the annual report and accounts, including the statement of compliance, are considered and approved for submission to the board of directors. (para 16)

The APB goes on to explain (paras 19–20) that, if an auditor establishes that the company has not complied with a provision that is within the scope of auditors' review, but concludes that the non-compliance and the reasons

---

[48] Auditors' responsibilities with respect to their auditees' status as a 'going concern' are discussed in Chapter 13, section 13.4.

therefor are properly disclosed, the auditor does not refer to the non-compliance in the audit report. However, if the auditor considers that the non-compliance is not fully and properly disclosed, this conclusion should be reported in the audit report on the financial statements.[49]

Although an auditor is not required to review the directors' explanation of how the company has applied the Code's principles, or review the parts of the compliance statement that relate to provisions other than the nine cited above, the APB notes that auditors do not wish to be associated with the directors' disclosure statement if they have reason to believe the statement may be misleading. Auditors, therefore, read both parts of the disclosure statement and consider whether information in either part appears to be misstated or is materially inconsistent with other information they have obtained during the course of their audit or their review of the company's compliance statement. If auditors become aware of a misstatement or inconsistency, they are required to discuss it with the directors in order to establish its significance. If they consider it to be significant, and the directors cannot be persuaded to amend the disclosure to the auditor's satisfaction, they need to consider the implications for their audit report and may need to take legal advice (APB, 2006a, paras 21–22).

5.6 AUDITOR–CLIENT RELATIONSHIP

The legal relationship between the auditor and the client company, and the auditor and the company's shareholders, is somewhat unusual. It was noted in section 5.2 that the Companies Act 2006 gives shareholders responsibility for appointing the auditor and it is implicit in the statutory provisions that the auditor is appointed primarily to protect shareholders' interests. However, after being appointed at the company's general meeting, the auditor has no contact with the shareholders until the audit report is sent to them (after the end of the financial period) together with the audited financial statements.

Notwithstanding that auditors are appointed by the company's shareholders (at least, technically), the contractual arrangement for the audit is between the auditor and the client company. As a result, the auditor owes a contractual

---

[49] Auditors' reports on financial statements are discussed in Chapter 14.

responsibility to the company *per se*, not to its shareholders. Further, in conducting the audit, a close working relationship necessarily develops between the auditor and the company's management,[50] and it is the company's management (or, if it has one, its audit committee), not its shareholders, who receive details of the auditor's findings.[51] The auditor's relationship with the client company and its shareholders is represented diagrammatically in Figure 5.5.

Given auditors' dual relationship with the company and its shareholders, it is essential that they adhere strictly to the fundamental ethical principle of objectivity and independence: that they remain objective and independent of the entity and directors.

Figure 5.5: The auditor's relationship with the client company and its shareholders

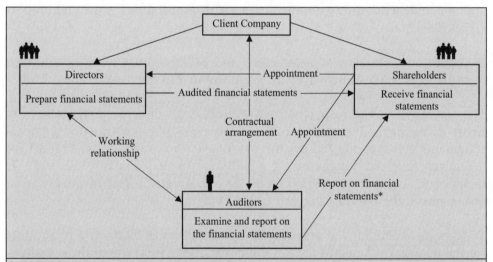

* NOTE: There is no provision for communication between the shareholders and the auditor other than through the audit report and the shareholders' general meeting. Even the communication via the audit report is not direct as the directors are responsible for providing the company's financial statements, complete with the auditor's report, to its shareholders.

---

[50] Readers are reminded that in the Preface to this book we note that the term 'management' is defined to mean a company's executive directors, non-executive directors, and non-director executives (that is, all executives and directors).

[51] Auditors' 'communications of audit matters to those charged with the entity's governance' are discussed in Chapter 14.

5.7 AUDITORS' *VIS-À-VIS* DIRECTORS' RESPONSIBILITY FOR THE FINANCIAL STATEMENTS

Responsibility for the preparation of a company's financial statements lies with the company's directors. As noted in section 5.2, the Companies Act (CA) 2006 requires the directors of all companies to provide financial statements annually to their shareholders and debenture holders. It also requires all companies to keep adequate accounting records. These are records which, among other things, facilitate both the preparation and audit of the company's annual financial statements (CA 2006, s. 386).

The APB, in ISA (UK and Ireland) 700: *The auditor's report on financial statements*,[52] requires auditors, in their audit reports, to distinguish between their responsibilities and those of the directors[53] for the company's audited financial statements. If the directors' responsibilities are described elsewhere in the audited financial statements or accompanying information (i.e., the annual report), auditors are to refer to that description.[54] However, if the information is not provided elsewhere in the financial statements or annual report, auditors are to include a description of the directors' responsibilities in the audit report (APB, 2004, para 9–1).

Representative statements of directors' and auditors' responsibilities, derived from BP plc's 2006 Annual Report, are presented in Figures 5.6 and 5.7.

The statement of the respective responsibilities of directors and auditors in Ernst & Young LLP's audit report on BP plc's 2006 consolidated financial statements substantially follows the wording in the example audit report for the group financial statements of a publicly traded company (Example 7) included in Appendix 1, APB Bulletin 2006/6: *Auditor's Reports on Financial Statements in the United Kingdom* (APB, 2006b).

Statements explaining the respective responsibilities of directors and auditors for the financial statements are helpful in informing users about these matters.

---

[52] ISA (UK and Ireland) 700 (ABP, 2004) is discussed in Chapter 14. For reasons explained in that chapter, the APB has not (yet) adopted the IAASB's ISA 700 (Revised): *The independent auditor's report on general purpose financial statements* (IAASB, 2006). In June 2008, when developing redrafted ISA 700 (Revised) as part of its clarity project, the IAASB proposed changing the title of the Standard to: *Forming an opinion and reporting on financial statements* (see footnote 45 and Figure 5.3).

[53] The standard refers to 'those charged with governance' rather than 'directors' but, in attached footnote 4, the APB (2004) explains: "it is the directors of a company who are required by law to prepare annual accounts which consist of a balance sheet and profit and loss account ... ".

[54] It should be recalled from section 5.5 that *The Combined Code on Corporate Governance* (FRC, 2006a, Prov C.1.1) requires the directors of all listed companies to explain, in their annual reports, their responsibility for preparing the financial statements, and states there should also be a statement by the auditors about their reporting responsibilities.

Figure 5.6: Representative statement of directors' responsibilities in company annual reports

Statement of directors' responsibilities in respect of the consolidated financial statements
The directors are responsible for preparing the Annual Report and the consolidated financial statements in accordance with applicable UK law and those International Financial Reporting Standards (IFRS) adopted by the EU.
The directors are required to prepare financial statements for each financial year which present fairly[55] the financial position of the group and the financial performance and cash flows of the group for that period. In preparing those financial statements, the directors are required to: – Select suitable accounting policies and then apply them consistently. – Present information, including accounting policies, in a manner that provides relevant, reliable, comparable and understandable information. – Provide additional disclosure when compliance with the specific requirements of IFRS is insufficient to enable users to understand the impact of particular transactions, other events and conditions on the group's financial position and financial performance. – State that the company has complied with IFRS, subject to any material departures disclosed and explained in the financial statements.
The directors are responsible for keeping proper accounting records[56] which disclose with reasonable accuracy at any time the financial position of the group and enable them to ensure that the financial statements comply with the Companies Act 1985 and Article 4 of the IAS Regulation.[57] They are also responsible for safeguarding the assets of the group and hence for taking reasonable steps for the prevention and detection of fraud and other irregularities.
The directors confirm that they have complied with these requirements and, having a reasonable expectation that the group has adequate resources to continue in operational existence for the foreseeable future, continue to adopt the going concern basis in preparing the financial statements.
Having made the requisite enquiries, so far as the directors are aware, there is no relevant audit information (as defined [in the] Companies Act 1985) of which the group's auditors are unaware, and the directors have taken all the steps they ought to have taken to make themselves aware of any relevant audit information and to establish that the group's auditors are aware of that information.

Source: BP plc's 2006 Annual Report

Research conducted prior to the inclusion of such explanations in auditors' reports (i.e., prior to 1988[58]) indicated that many financial statement users were not aware that it is the directors, and not the auditors, who are responsible for preparing a company's financial statements. A survey conducted by Lee and Tweedie (1975), for example, found that one quarter of institutional investors and more than half of private investors had little or no understanding of

---

[55] The term 'present fairly' is used in the directors' statement of responsibilities (Figure 5.6) but 'true and fair view' is used in the auditors' statement (Figure 5.7). Under section 262(2A) of the Companies Act 1985, which applied to 2006 Annual Reports, the terms have an equivalent meaning.

[56] The Companies Act 2006 refers to 'adequate accounting records'; the Companies Act 1985 (which applied to 2006 Annual Reports) used the term "proper accounting records".

[57] 'IAS Regulation' refers to EU Regulation (EC) No. 1606/2002 *on the application of international accounting standards*: see footnote 13.

[58] In the USA; 1993 in the UK. The development of audit reports and the change from the 'short' to the 'expanded' report is discussed in Chapter 14, section 14.7.

Figure 5.7:   Representative statement of 'respective responsibilities of directors and auditors' included in auditors' reports

Respective responsibilities of directors and auditors
The directors are responsible for preparing the Annual Report and the consolidated financial statements in accordance with applicable United Kingdom law and International Financial Reporting Standards (IFRS) as adopted by the European Union as set out in the Statement of directors' responsibilities in respect of the consolidated financial statements.
Our responsibility is to audit the consolidated financial statements in accordance with relevant legal and regulatory requirements and International Standards on Auditing (UK and Ireland).
We report to you our opinion as to whether the consolidated financial statements give a true and fair view and whether the consolidated financial statements have been properly prepared in accordance with the Companies Act 1985 and Article 4 of the IAS Regulation. We also report to you whether in our opinion the information given in the directors' report, including the business review, is consistent with the financial statements.
In addition we report to you if, in our opinion, we have not received all the information and explanations we require for our audit, or if information specified by law regarding directors' remuneration and other transactions is not disclosed.
We review whether the governance board performance report [Corporate Governance Statement] reflects the company's compliance with the nine provisions of the 2006 Combined Code Principles of Good Governance and Code of Best Practice specified for our review by the Listing Rules of the Financial Services Authority, and we report if it does not. We are not required to consider whether the board's statements on internal control cover all risks and controls, or form an opinion on the effectiveness of the group's corporate governance procedures or its risk and control procedures.
We read other information contained in the Annual Report and consider whether it is consistent with the audited consolidated financial statements. The other information comprises the Additional information for US reporting, the Supplementary information on oil and natural gas, the Directors' Report and the Governance: Board performance report. We consider the implications for our report if we become aware of any apparent misstatements or material inconsistencies with the consolidated financial statements. Our responsibilities do not extend to any other information.

Source: Ernst & Young LLP's audit report in BP plc's 2006 Annual Report

who is legally responsible for the preparation of company financial statements. However, even with the inclusion of an explanation in auditors' reports, a significant proportion of society still seems to believe that auditors are responsible for preparing company financial statements: Porter and Gowthorpe (2003) found that, in the UK in 2000, 14 per cent of financial community, and 30 per cent of non-financial community, audit beneficiaries held such an opinion.

5.8   THE AUDIT EXPECTATION–PERFORMANCE GAP

5.8.1   Importance of the audit expectation–performance gap

Although auditors explain their responsibilities in their audit reports, there is a mismatch between what society expects of auditors and what it perceives they deliver. This phenomenon, known as the audit expectation–performance gap, is not new, nor is it confined to the UK. It has existed for more than 100 years (Chandler and Edwards, 1996) and it has been recognised and studied in many countries of the world – for example, in the USA, Canada, South Africa, China, New Zealand, Australia, Singapore, Denmark, the Netherlands, Spain and Finland.

Why has this gap attracted so much attention? And why is it of concern to the auditing profession? It is because auditors' failure to meet society's expectations of them has resulted in severe criticism of, and litigation against, auditors and this in turn has served to undermine confidence in the audit function. This loss of confidence was all too evident in the aftermath of the Enron, WorldCom, Tyco, HIH and similar failures that marred the early years of the 21st century.

Nearly 80 years ago, Limperg (1932) explained:

> The [audit] function is rooted in the confidence that society places in the effectiveness of the audit and in the opinion of the accountant [i.e., auditor] . . . if the confidence is betrayed, the function, too, is destroyed, since it becomes useless. (as reproduced in Limperg Instituut, 1985, p. 16)

He went on to explain that auditors have a dual responsibility: not to arouse "in the sensible layman" greater expectations than can be fulfilled by the work done, and to carry out the work in a manner that does not betray the expectations evoked. In other words, it is the responsibility of auditors to ensure that society does not have unreasonable expectations of them and to satisfy its reasonably held expectations.

If the auditing profession is to narrow the audit expectation–performance gap (and thereby reduce criticism and loss of confidence in its work), it needs to ascertain:

(i)   the duties society expects auditors to perform;
(ii) which of these duties are reasonable to expect of auditors;
(iii) the extent to which society's reasonable expectations are satisfied (or, more pertinently, not satisfied) by auditors.

This brings us to examining the structure and composition of the audit expectation–performance gap.

5.8.2   Structure and composition of the audit expectation–performance gap

Analysis of the audit expectation–performance gap reveals that it has two major components (Porter 1991, 1993):

1. The *reasonableness gap* – the gap between the duties society expects auditors to perform and those it is reasonable to expect of auditors. This

component comprises the duties that society *un*reasonably expects auditors to perform.

2. The *performance gap* – the gap between the duties society reasonably expects of auditors and what it perceives auditors actually accomplish. This component may be subdivided into:

   (a) the *deficient standards gap* – the gap between the duties reasonably expected of auditors and auditors' existing duties as defined by the law, auditing standards, other regulations and professional promulgations;

   (b) the *deficient performance gap* – the gap between the standard of performance of auditors' existing duties expected by society and auditors' performance of those duties as perceived by society.

The structure of the audit expectation–performance gap is depicted in Figure 5.8.

Figure 5.8: Structure of the audit expectation–performance gap

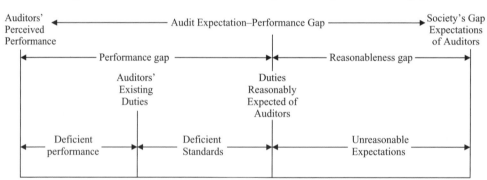

(i) *Reasonableness gap*

Research conducted in the UK, as well as elsewhere in the world, has established that society expects auditors to perform a very wide range of duties. These constitute the right end of the gap depicted in Figure 5.8 and include auditors' actual existing duties, duties which are reasonably expected of auditors (even though they are not required by the law, regulations or professional promulgations) and those that are unreasonably expected of auditors.

It seems logical that, in order for duties to be reasonably expected of auditors, they should be cost-beneficial for auditors to perform:[59] the benefits derived by financial statement users, auditees and society as a whole from auditors performing a duty should be equal to, or greater than, the cost of auditors so

---

[59] The surrogate for cost-benefit analysis is explained in Porter and Gowthorpe (2003).

doing. Research by Porter and Gowthorpe (2003) suggests that, in the UK in 2000, society expected auditors to perform 46 duties[60] and that half of these (23 of the 46[61]) were not cost-beneficial for auditors to perform; that is, half of the duties were unreasonably expected of auditors. These duties, which constitute the reasonableness gap, fall into two broad groups:

(a) those that are not economically feasible for auditors to perform – for example, *guaranteeing* the accuracy of the auditee's financial statements and/or its solvency, detecting and reporting minor theft of auditee assets, and detecting other illegal acts by the company's directors/senior managers that only indirectly impact on the financial statements;

(b) those relating to issues that only recently emerged as significant in the corporate arena – for example, examining and reporting (in the audit report) on the auditee's IT systems, the adequacy of its risk management procedures, the effectiveness of its internal non-financial controls, and the efficiency and effectiveness of its management; examining and reporting on the reliability of all of the information contained in the auditee's annual report, in particular, about its equal employment opportunities, product safety, and occupational health and safety. In time, as these emerging issues become more commonplace, it may be that benefits to be derived from auditors performing related duties will be more widely recognised and, thus, the duties will cross the cost-benefit threshold to be reasonably (rather than unreasonably) expected of auditors.[62]

(ii) Deficient standards gap

Porter and Gowthorpe (2003) found that 13 of the 23 duties reasonably expected of auditors were existing duties. The other 10 duties were reasonably expected but not required of auditors: these constitute the deficient standards gap. Like the duties comprising the reasonableness gap, the deficient standards gap duties tend to fall into two broad groups:

---

[60] Identified from a list of 51 actual and potential duties of auditors listed in the survey instrument.

[61] The number of duties at each boundary, and comprising each component, of the audit expectation–performance gap, are shown in Figure 5.9.

[62] In the post-Enron era, some of these duties, such as reporting on the effectiveness of auditees' internal controls, have become required by law or regulation in some jurisdictions (for example, in the USA). In the UK, as we noted earlier in this chapter, preliminary steps have been taken to expand auditors' duties (especially for listed companies) to include, for example, reviewing:

– the directors' report – including its business review which is required to provide information about, *inter alia*, the company's principal risks and uncertainties and, to the extent necessary for readers to understand the company's business, information about environmental matters, employees and community issues (see section 5.2.2); and

– the directors' statement on their review of the effectiveness of the company's system of internal controls and its risk management system (see section 5.5).

(a) those that involve disclosing in the audit report and/or to an appropriate authority, matters of concern that are uncovered during an audit. These include reporting theft of a material amount of the auditee's assets, other illegal acts by the company's directors/senior managers which directly impact on the financial statements, deliberate distortion of the financial statements, and doubts about the entity's continued existence;[63]

(b) those that relate to corporate governance issues; for example, examining and reporting (in the audit report) on the effectiveness of the company's internal financial controls, and its compliance with the UKLA's corporate governance requirements; and also examining and reporting (to the company's directors) on the adequacy of the auditee's risk management procedures.[64]

(iii) Deficient performance gap

How well does society consider that auditors perform their existing duties? Porter and Gowthorpe (2003) found that society in the UK was of the view that, of the 13 existing duties of auditors, six were performed well or satisfactorily. However, seven were adjudged to be performed deficiently, and these duties constitute the deficient performance gap. They include detecting the theft of a material amount of the company's assets by the entity's directors or senior managers; reporting, to an appropriate authority, illegal acts by the entity's directors or senior managers; and disclosing in the audit report doubts about the company's continued existence.

5.8.3 Relative extent of the gap's components

If auditors fail to perform a duty expected of them by society, or they fail to perform an existing duty to society's satisfaction, society has unfulfilled expectations with respect to the duty concerned. Based on a measure of 'unfulfilled expectations' attaching to each duty contributing to the audit expectation–performance gap,[65] it appears that, in the UK in 2000, about 50 per cent of the

---

[63] In most cases, in 2000 auditors had an existing duty to report the particular 'matter of concern' which came to light during the audit either in the audit report or to an appropriate authority, but not both. Reporting to an appropriate authority suggests that corrective action might be imposed on the company and/or its directors.

[64] As noted in section 5.5, since 2006, auditors have been required to review nine of the 48 provisions of *The Combined Code on Corporate Governance* with which listed companies must comply (or disclose and explain their non-compliance). Auditors *may* report to the directors on the effectiveness of the company's risk management procedures, but they are under no obligation to do so.

[65] The measure of unfulfilled expectations attaching to each duty was derived from the proportion of the society group (auditees, financial community audit beneficiaries and non-financial community audit beneficiaries) who signified that the duty in question should be performed by auditors (in the case of the reasonableness gap and deficient standards gap duties) or that auditors perform the duty poorly (in the case of the deficient performance gap duties) (Porter and Gowthorpe, 2003).

audit expectation–performance gap resulted from society having unreasonable expectations of auditors, 42 per cent from auditors not being required to perform duties that are reasonably expected of them, and 8 per cent from auditors' deficient performance. These proportions are shown in Figure 5.9.

Figure 5.9: Composition of the audit expectation–performance gap in the UK in 2000

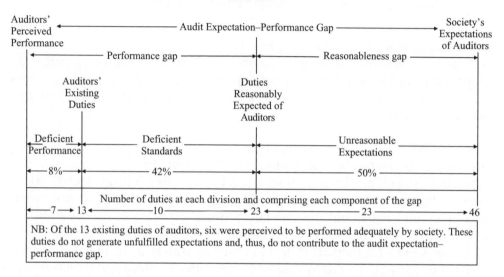

NB: Of the 13 existing duties of auditors, six were perceived to be performed adequately by society. These duties do not generate unfulfilled expectations and, thus, do not contribute to the audit expectation–performance gap.

5.8.4 Changes in the composition of the gap between 1989 and 2000

Although the audit environment in the UK and New Zealand (NZ) is not identical, the two countries are very similar culturally, socially, politically and economically. As a consequence, by comparing the findings of Porter's study of the audit expectation–performance gap in NZ in 1989 with those of Porter and Gowthorpe in the UK in 2000 (Porter, 1993; Porter and Gowthorpe, 2003), we can gain some insight into how the gap changed over the period from 1989 to 2000.

The most striking change is in the relative contribution of the gap's components: while the performance gap decreased from 69 per cent in 1989 in NZ to 50 per cent in the UK in 2000 (with the deficient performance and deficient standards components falling from 11 per cent to eight per cent, and 58 per cent to 42 per cent, respectively), the reasonableness gap increased from 31 per cent to 50 per cent. Thus, while it appears that auditors' performance (in terms of the duties required of them and the standard of their work) improved between 1989 and 2000, the resultant narrowing of the audit expectation–performance gap was offset by an increase in society's (unreasonable) expectations of auditors. Indeed, Porter and Gowthorpe found that, despite the marked reduction in the performance gap, as a result of increased expectations of auditors the overall audit expectation–performance gap in the UK in 2000 was 34 per cent wider than that pertaining in NZ in 1989.[66] Society's increased expectations of auditors are primarily associated with corporate governance matters that were not significant in the auditing arena in 1989.

5.8.5   Narrowing the audit expectation–performance gap

Knowledge of the structure and composition of the audit expectation–performance gap enables us to determine how the gap might be narrowed. The more auditors' performance is aligned to society's expectations, the greater the reduction in society's unfulfilled expectations – and the less criticism auditors will face: as a corollary, the greater the confidence of society in auditors and the audit function.

Reviewing the three components of the audit expectation–performance gap, appropriate corrective action is almost self-evident. In order to narrow the deficient performance gap, auditors need to be better informed about their existing duties under statute and case law, regulations and professional promulgations,[67] and also about the standard of work expected of them. Additionally, improved quality control procedures are needed in order to ensure that all auditors perform their work to the required standard. In this they should be assisted by ISQC 1: *Quality control for firms that perform audits and reviews of financial statements . . .* and ISA 220: *Quality control for an audit of financial statements*, which were issued in 2004.[68]

In order to narrow the deficient standards gap, auditing standards need to embrace the duties that are not required of auditors but are cost-effective for auditors to perform. Most of the duties constituting the deficient standards gap in the UK in 2000 have featured prominently in corporate governance or other similar debates since the mid-1990s and, as is noted in this and other chapters of this book, significant changes have been made to auditors' duties since 2002 (through changes in the law, auditing standards and other regulations): some of the duties contributing to the deficient standards gap in 2000 are now required of auditors.[69] It might be anticipated that, in the future,

---

[66] These findings were based on measures of society's unfulfilled expectations in 1989 in NZ and 2000 in the UK.

[67] Porter and Gowthorpe (2003) found that, in the UK in 2000, some 13 per cent of auditors were uncertain or incorrect about their existing duties.

[68] The concept and application of quality control are discussed in Chapters 3, 7 and 16. In 2008, ISA 220 (IAASB, 2008a) was revised and redrafted, and ISQC 1 (IAASB, 2008b) was redrafted, as part of the IAASB's 'clarity project' (see footnote 45).

[69] See footnote 62 for examples.

further deficient standards gap duties will change from being reasonably expected but not required, to existing duties of auditors.

The effect of improving quality control over auditors' work and of developing new auditing standards is reflected in the marked narrowing of the deficient performance and deficient standards components of the gap between 1989 and 2000. Since 1989, monitoring of auditors' work has been introduced in both the UK[70] and NZ, and it seems likely that this is responsible, at least in part, for the apparent improvement in auditors' performance. This conclusion accords with the opinions of the Joint Monitoring Unit (JMU) and ACCA monitoring unit in the UK – as reflected in their annual reports to the Department of Trade and Industry. Similarly, since 1989, new auditing standards have been responsible for changing the status of two duties that were reasonably expected but not required of auditors in 1989 into existing duties. These are reporting fraud, and other illegal acts, by company officials discovered during an audit to an appropriate authority when it is in the public interest to do so. Additionally, SAS 130: *The Going Concern Basis in Financial Statements* was issued in the UK in 1994 (i.e., post 1989)[71] and this provided much clearer guidance to auditors than its predecessor as to what is required of them in this regard. It is notable that society's dissatisfaction with auditors' performance of their duty 'to disclose in the audit report doubts about the continued existence of the auditee' declined significantly over the period 1989 to 2000. (In 1989 in NZ, 37 per cent of the society group expressed dissatisfaction with auditors' performance of this duty; this compares with 23 per cent in the UK, and 20 per cent in NZ, in 2000).

Although further improvement in auditors' performance would help to narrow the audit expectation–performance gap, the greatest challenge facing the auditing profession is reducing the reasonableness gap: reducing society's unreasonable expectations of auditors by educating members of society about the audit function and what it can – and cannot – be reasonably expected to achieve. As indicated above, the set of duties comprising the reasonableness gap has expanded as new issues, particularly those related to corporate governance, have moved into the domain where society expects auditors to play a part.

---

[70] In the UK, the RSBs are required to monitor the work of auditors registered with them (see section 5.2.3). Between 1991 and 2004, the Joint Monitoring Unit (JMU) performed this function for the ICAEW, ICAS and ICAI; the ACCA monitoring unit performed the same function for the ACCA and AAPA. Since January 2005, the Audit Inspection Unit of the FRC's Professional Oversight Board has been responsible for monitoring the audits of all listed and other major public interest entities and the RSBs have monitored the work of their other registrants. Monitoring of auditors is discussed in Chapter 16.

[71] SAS 130 was superseded in 2004 by ISA (UK and Ireland) 570: *Going Concern.*

As explained in section 5.7, the profession has taken steps to educate financial statement users about the respective responsibilities of auditors and directors for auditees' financial statements, and also about the audit process.[72] However, it seems that more is needed – particularly in educating indirect (non-financial community) audit beneficiaries who seem unlikely to read auditors' reports.[73] It is perhaps pertinent to note that, should auditors be taken to court for apparently failing to perform their duties to the expected standard, the jury will almost certainly comprise a cross-section of society. Those both with, and without, knowledge of the audit function and what is reasonable to expect of auditors are likely to be represented. Similarly, when a company fails unexpectedly, particularly if the failure is accompanied by allegations of fraud or other forms of misconduct by the company's senior officials, the cry will (almost certainly) be heard: 'Where were the auditors?'. This will reflect unfulfilled expectations of auditors which will, in turn, fuel criticism of auditors and undermine confidence in their work.

5.9 SUMMARY

In this chapter we have discussed auditors' legal and professional duties. We have shown that auditors' duties are derived from statute law, case law, and regulatory and professional promulgations. Statute law (primarily embodied in the Companies Act 2006) provides that (subject to certain exemptions) companies' financial statements are to be audited, and it sets out the administrative framework for the auditor's appointment, remuneration, rights, duties and resignation or removal. Statute law is silent on the standard expected of auditors in the performance of their statutory duties but case law provides guidance on what is required. Auditing standards and other guidance, issued by the IAASB in the international arena and the APB in the UK, provide further and more detailed guidance to auditors on what is required of them when conducting an audit.

In this chapter we have also explained the somewhat unusual three-way relationship between auditors, the client company and the company's shareholders, and emphasised that responsibility for a company's financial statements lies

---

[72] As we note earlier in this chapter, the first step towards explaining the respective responsibilities of directors and auditors for financial statements was taken in the expanded audit report in the USA in 1988 (1993 in the UK). Since 1992 in the UK, successive Codes of Corporate Governance have recommended or required information about the directors' responsibilities for the financial statements to be provided in listed companies' annual reports.

[73] Most members of society benefit indirectly from company audits – for example, they may contribute to pension funds and/or pay central or local government taxes; the accumulated funds (from pension contributions or taxes) are invested in companies whose financial statements are audited.

with its directors, not with the auditors. The auditor's responsibility is limited to forming and expressing an opinion on the truth and fairness of the company's financial statements and their compliance (or otherwise) with relevant legislation. We have also noted that the directors' and auditors' responsibilities are required to be spelt out clearly in the company's annual report and/or audit report.

Notwithstanding the explanation of auditors' responsibilities which is provided in each audit report, there is a gap between what society expects from auditors and what it perceives it receives from them (i.e., an audit expectation–performance gap). We have described the structure and composition of the gap as it existed in the UK in 2000 and compared this with the composition of the gap that pertained in NZ in 1989. We reported that, although society appears to perceive that auditors' performance improved quite markedly over the decade 1989–2000, its (unreasonable) expectations of auditors grew to a greater extent. Thus, although the 'performance gap' narrowed between 1989 and 2000, this was more than offset by a widening of the 'reasonableness gap'.

In the next chapter we turn our attention to auditors' responsibility to detect and report corporate fraud and other illegal acts. As we will see, this issue has long been very controversial and, over the years, it has witnessed quite remarkable changes.

SELF-REVIEW QUESTIONS

5.1 State the institutions which define the rights and responsibilities of auditors and the particular part played by each.

5.2 (a) State who may, and who may not, be appointed as an auditor of a company.
   (b) List those parties who may:
      (i) appoint the auditor,
      (ii) remove the auditor from office,
      and the circumstances in which these parties can exercise their rights.

5.3 List the items which the Companies Act 2006 requires auditors to include in their reports to shareholders.

5.4 State the fundamental standard required of auditors in the performance of their duties as laid down in the *Kingston Cotton Mill* case (1896).

5.5 Explain briefly:
   (i) the purpose and benefits of Auditing Standards;
   (ii) how the APB's Auditing Standards differ from its Practice Notes and Bulletins.

5.6 Explain briefly the legal relationship between the shareholders and auditor of a company.

5.7 Explain the responsibilities of a company's:
(i) directors, and
(ii) its auditors,
with respect to the company's financial statements.

5.8 Explain briefly the duties of auditors under the requirements of the United Kingdom's Listing Authority's (UKLA) Listing Rules.

5.9 Explain briefly what is meant by 'the audit expectation–performance gap' and explain why it is of importance to the auditing profession.

5.10 Describe the basic structure of the audit expectation–performance gap and outline how each of its component gaps might be narrowed.

REFERENCES

Auditing Practices Board (APB). (2004). International Standard on Auditing (ISA) (UK and Ireland) 700: *The Auditor's report on financial statements*. London: Financial Reporting Council.

Auditing Practices Board (APB). (2006a). *The Combined Code on Corporate Governance: Requirements of Auditors under the Listing Rules of the Financial Services Authority and the Irish Stock Exchange*, Bulletin 2006/5. London: Financial Reporting Council.

Auditing Practices Board (APB). (2006b). *Auditor's Reports on Financial Statement in the United Kingdom*, Bulletin 2006/6. London: Financial Reporting Council.

Auditing Practices Board (APB). (2008a). *The Auditing Practices Board* – Scope and Authority of Pronouncements. London: Financial Reporting Council.

Auditing Practices Board (APB). (2008b). *Glossary*. London: Financial Reporting Council.

Chandler, R., and Edwards, J.R. (1996). Recurring issues in auditing: back to the future? *Accounting, Auditing & Accountability Journal* **9**(2), 4–29.

Committee on the Financial Aspects of Corporate Governance. (1992). *Report of the Committee on the Financial Aspects of Corporate Governance* (Cadbury Committee). London: Gee.

Committee on Corporate Governance. (1998a). *Final Report of the Committee on Corporate Governance* (Hampel Committee). London: London Stock Exchange.

Committee on Corporate Governance. (1998b). *The Combined Code*. London: London Stock Exchange.

European Union (EU). (2002). Regulation (EC) No. 1606/2002 *on the application of international accounting standards*. Brussels: European Parliament and Council.

European Union (EU). (2006). *Directive 2006/43/EC of the European Parliament and of the Council on statutory audits of annual accounts and consolidated accounts (8th Directive).* Brussels: European Parliament and Council.

Financial Reporting Council (FRC). (2003). *The Combined Code on Corporate Governance.* London: FRC.

Financial Reporting Council (FRC). (2006a). *The Combined Code on Corporate Governance.* London: FRC.

Financial Reporting Council (FRC). (2006b). *Regulatory strategy.* London: FRC.

Financial Reporting Council (FRC). (2008, 19 May). *Relevance of 'True and Fair' concept confirmed.* London: FRC.

Higgs, D. (2003). *Review of the role and effectiveness of non-executive directors.* London: Department of Trade and Industry.

International Accounting Standards Board (IASB). (2001). *Framework for the preparation and presentation of financial statements.* London: IASB.

International Accounting Standards Board (IASB). (2003). International Accounting Standard (IAS) 1: *Presentation of Financial Statements.* London: IASB.

International Auditing and Assurance Standards Board (IAASB). (2006). International Standard on Auditing (ISA): 700 (Revised): *The independent auditor's report on general purpose financial statements.* New York: IFAC.

International Auditing and Assurance Standards Board (IAASB). (2008a,** June).[74] International Standard on Auditing (ISA): 220: *Quality Control for an Audit of Financial Statements.* New York: IFAC.

International Auditing and Assurance Standards Board (IAASB). (2008b,** June). International Standard on Quality Control (ISQC) 1: *Quality Control for Firms that Perform Audits and Reviews of Financial Statements, and Other Assurance and Related Services Engagements.* New York: IFAC.

Kenley, W.J. (1971). Legal decisions affecting auditors. *The Australian Accountant* **41**(4), 153–161.

Lee, T.A., and Tweedie, D.P. (1975). Accounting information: An investigation of private shareholder usage, *Accounting and Business Research* **5**(20), 289–291.

Limperg, T. (1932). *The Social Responsibility of the Auditor*, reproduced in Limperg Instituut (1985). The Netherlands: Limperg Institute.

Porter, B.A. (1991). Narrowing the expectation-performance gap: A contemporary approach. *Pacific Accounting Review* **3**(1), 1–36.

Porter, B.A. (1993). An empirical study of the audit expectation-performance gap. *Accounting and Business Research* **24**(93), 49–68.

Porter, B.A., and Gowthorpe, C. (2003). *Audit expectation-performance gap in the United Kingdom in 1999 and comparison with the gap in New Zealand in 1989 and 1999.* Edinburgh: Institute of Chartered Accountants of Scotland.

---

[74] The status of ISA 220 and ISQC1 is explained in the Important Note following the Preface to this book.

Smith, Sir Robert. (2003). *Audit Committees: Combined Guidance*. A report and proposed guidance by an FRC-appointed group chaired by Sir Robert Smith. London: Financial Reporting Council.

Statutory Instrument 2002 No. 1986: *The Directors' Remuneration Report Regulations 2002*.

Statutory Instrument 2005 No. 2417: *Companies (Disclosure of Auditor Remuneration) Regulations 2005*.

Study Group on Directors' Remuneration. (1995). *Report of the Study Group on Directors' Remuneration* (Greenbury Committee). London: Gee.

ADDITIONAL READING

Lin, Z.J., and Chen, F. (2004). An empirical study of audit 'expectation gap' in The People's Republic of China. *International Journal of Auditing* **8**(2), 93–115.

Martinis, M.D., and Kim, E. (2000). An examination of the audit expectation gap in Singapore. *Asian Review of Accounting* **8**(1), 59–82.

Morrison, M.A. (2004). Rush to Judgment: The lynching of Arthur Andersen & Co. *Critical Perspectives on Accounting* **15**(3), 335–375.

Sikka, P., Puxty, A., Willmott, H., and Cooper, C. (1998). The impossibility of eliminating the expectations gap: some theory and evidence. *Critical Perspectives on Accounting* **9**(3), 299–330.

Willekens, M., and Simunic, D.A. (2007). Precision in auditing standards: effects on auditor and director liability and the supply and demand for audit services. *Accounting and Business Research* **37**(3), 217–232.

6 Auditors' Duties with Respect to Fraud and Non-compliance with Laws and Regulations

LEARNING OBJECTIVES

After studying the material in this chapter you should be able to:

- explain the meaning of 'fraud' and 'non-compliance with laws and regulations' in the auditing context;
- discuss changes in the level of responsibility for detecting fraud acknowledged by the auditing profession between 1844 and the present;
- explain the importance of the components of the 'fraud triangle';
- outline the procedures auditors are required to perform to detect material misstatement in the financial statements due to (i) fraud or (ii) non-compliance with laws and regulations;
- describe auditors' responsibility to report actual or suspected instances of fraud or non-compliance with laws or regulations;
- discuss auditors' duty of confidentiality to their clients.

The following publications and fundamental principle of external auditing are particularly relevant to this chapter:

Publications:

- International Standard on Auditing (ISA) 240 (Redrafted*): The Auditor's Responsibilities Relating to Fraud in an Audit of Financial Statements* (IFAC, 2006)[1]
- International Standard on Auditing (ISA) 250 (Redrafted): *Consideration of Laws and Regulations in an Audit of Financial Statements* (IFAC, 2008)
- International Standard on Auditing (ISA) (UK and Ireland) 250: *Section A – Consideration of Laws and Regulations in an Audit of Financial Statements* (APB, 2004)
- *Code of Ethics for Professional Accountants* (IFAC, 2006), Section 140: Confidentiality

Fundamental principle of external auditing included in *The Auditors' Code:*[2]
Integrity

---

[1] The status of ISAs referred to in this chapter is explained in the Important Note following the Preface to this book.

[2] The fundamental principles of external auditing are reproduced on the inside of the front cover of this book.

6.1 INTRODUCTION

In Chapter 5 we discussed the legal, regulatory and professional framework within which auditors' duties are defined. We also examined the audit expectation–performance gap, the gap between what society expects from auditors and what it perceives they deliver. The issue which, over the years, has witnessed the greatest 'gap' between society's and auditors' expectations regarding auditors' duties is that of detecting and reporting corporate fraud (Porter, 1997). It is also an issue which, for many years, has been hotly debated both inside and outside the auditing profession.

A closely related issue – that of auditors' duty to detect and report auditees' non-compliance with laws and regulations – has not had as high a profile as their duties in respect of fraud, nor has it been as controversial. However, misstated financial statements resulting from non-compliance with applicable laws and regulations can have an effect, as equally devastating, as that resulting from fraud – on the auditee *per se* and on those who invest in, are employed by, supply to, or buy from the entity. Some laws and regulations (including accounting standards) directly affect the form and content of entities' financial statements, the amounts recorded, and the disclosures made in the financial statements or elsewhere in the annual report. Others relate more generally to a company's operations – for example, being properly registered or holding a required licence to trade in a particular industry, and complying with health and safety, equal opportunity and environmental regulations. Although these laws and regulations may seem far removed from the financial statements, non-compliance with any law or regulation that applies to an entity can result in financial consequences, such as fines or litigation, that are likely to impact on amounts and/or other disclosures in the entity's financial statements and, in some cases, may lead to the entity's demise.

Clearly management[3] (not the auditor) is responsible for ensuring that the company's operations are conducted in accordance with relevant laws and regulations and that appropriate steps are taken to prevent and detect fraud and other instances of non-compliance with applicable laws and regulations. However, auditors are responsible for expressing an opinion on, *inter alia*, the truth and fairness of the financial statements, and in order to do this they need to ascertain, with reasonable certainty, whether or not the financial statements are materially misstated as a result of, amongst other things, fraud or non-compliance with other relevant laws and regulations.

---

[3] Readers are reminded that in the Preface to this book we note the term 'management' is defined to mean a company's executive directors, non-executive directors and non-director executives (that is, all executives and directors).

In this chapter we first explore the thorny issue of auditors' responsibility to detect and report corporate fraud, and how – and why – the level of responsibility acknowledged by the auditing profession in this regard has changed so markedly over the period since compulsory audits were first introduced in 1844 to the present day. We then turn our attention to auditors' responsibility to detect and report non-compliance with other applicable laws and regulations. It should be noted that, unlike many of the auditors' duties which we examine in subsequent chapters of this book, auditors' duty to detect fraud and non-compliance with laws and regulations is not associated with any particular part of the audit process but extends to every aspect of the audit: auditors must be constantly alert, throughout an audit, to the possibility that fraud or non-compliance with other laws and regulations may have caused the financial statements to be materially misstated.

When discussing auditors' duty to report fraud and non-compliance with laws and regulations, we will observe that, in some circumstances, this includes overriding their duty of confidentiality to their clients and reporting the matter in question to parties external to the entity. So that this reporting duty may be understood in context, in the final section of this chapter we discuss auditors' duty of confidentiality to their clients and the circumstances in which it may be overridden.

6.2 AUDITORS' RESPONSIBILITY TO DETECT AND REPORT FRAUD

6.2.1 Fraud defined

Before considering auditors' duties with respect to fraud, we need to establish what is meant by 'fraud' in the auditing context. International Standard on Auditing (ISA) 240: *The auditor's responsibilities relating to fraud in an audit of financial statements* defines fraud as follows:

> An intentional act by one or more individuals among management, those charged with governance [i.e., the directors], employees, or third parties, involving the use of deception to obtain an unjust or illegal advantage. (para 11)

The Standard also explains:

> [T]he auditor is concerned with fraud that causes a material misstatement in the financial statements. Two types of intentional misstatements are relevant to the auditor – misstatements resulting from fraudulent financial reporting and misstatements resulting from misappropriation of assets. (para 3)

Let us examine these two types of fraud more closely:

(i) *Fraudulent financial reporting*: The International Auditing and Assurance Standards Board's (IAASB) *Glossary of terms* (2007) explains that this type of fraud: "Involves intentional misstatements, including omissions of amounts or disclosures in financial statements, to deceive financial statement users". It is intended to result in financial statements which give a misleading impression of the entity's financial affairs. It is almost always perpetrated by management but, rather than being committed for direct personal financial gain, it is usually motivated by what the individual concerned considers to be in his or her own best interests in terms of reporting the company's financial position or (more commonly) its performance in a particularly favourable (or in some cases, unfavourable) light. Management may, for instance, feel pressured to report earnings (or net profit after tax) in line with the financial market's expectations when the 'actual' earnings figure is significantly below those expectations. This may occur, for example, when the company has announced a rather optimistic earnings forecast and/or plans to raise new share or debt finance during the next financial year and the 'actual' earnings figure is unlikely to encourage further outside investment in the company.[4]

(ii) *Misappropriation of corporate assets*: According to the IAASB's *Glossary of terms* (2007), this type of fraud:

> Involves the theft of an entity's assets and is often perpetrated by employees in relatively small and immaterial amounts. However, it can also involve management who are usually more capable of disguising or concealing misappropriations in ways that are difficult to detect.

Misappropriation of assets includes such things as stealing physical assets or intellectual property (for example, items of inventory (stock), laptop computers, computer hardware and/or software, technological and/or customer data), stealing cash (through, for example, payments to fictitious employees or suppliers, and kickbacks paid by suppliers in return for inflating prices) and using entity assets for personal use (for example, using entity assets as security for a personal loan). Unlike fraudulent financial reporting, theft of a company's assets is usually undertaken for personal gain and is an action against the company.

6.2.2 An evolving and controversial issue

The stance of the auditing profession in relation to auditors' responsibility for detecting fraud has changed markedly over the years. As noted in Chapter 2, from the time compulsory audits were first introduced in the United Kingdom (UK) in 1844 until about the 1920s, the prevention and detection of fraud and error were regarded as primary audit objectives. Nevertheless, as also noted in Chapter 2, it was decided in the *Kingston Cotton Mill* case (1896) that

---

[4] As explained in section 6.3, fraudulent financial reporting often develops from aggressive earnings management.

auditors are not required to ferret out every fraud (auditors are 'watchdogs not bloodhounds') but they are expected to exercise reasonable skill, care and caution appropriate to the particular circumstances. Further, if anything comes to their attention which arouses their suspicion, they are expected to 'probe the matter to the bottom' and to report it promptly to the appropriate level of management.

Between the 1920s and 1960s, the importance of fraud detection as an audit objective was steadily eroded. During this period companies grew in size and complexity and, as a consequence, company managements set in place accounting systems to capture and process accounting data. These systems incorporated internal controls designed to prevent or detect both error and fraud and, thus, to protect the integrity of the accounting information. At the same time, growth in the volume of company transactions made it impractical, within the limits of reasonable time and cost constraints, for auditors to check every entry in auditees' accounting records. Auditing procedures changed accordingly, from meticulous checking of every transaction to techniques based on testing samples of transactions, combined with a review and evaluation of the effectiveness of the accounting system and its internal controls (see Chapter 2, section 2.2.4).

Given this environment, the auditing profession argued that fraud prevention and detection are the responsibility of management and are best achieved through the maintenance of an effective system of internal control. It also argued that auditing procedures are not designed, and cannot be relied upon, to detect fraud. The general attitude of the profession from the 1940s to 1960s is reflected in the American Institute of Certified Public Accountants' (AICPA) *Codification of statements on auditing procedure*, published in 1951. It states:

> The ordinary examination incident to the issuance of an opinion respecting financial statements is not designed and cannot be relied upon to disclose defalcations and other similar irregularities, although their discovery frequently results. In a well-organized concern reliance for the detection of such irregularities is placed principally upon the maintenance of an adequate system of accounting records with appropriate internal control. If an auditor were to discover defalcations and similar irregularities he would have to extend his work to a point where its cost would be prohibitive. (paras 12–13)

By the 1960s, the profession's position on detecting fraud was subject to criticism from both inside and outside the profession and, by 1970, it seems that the judiciary was also adopting a stance that contrasts with that reflected in the AICPA's statement (cited above). As we observed in Chapter 5, section 5.3, in his long judgment on the *Pacific Acceptance* case (1970), Moffit J noted, *inter alia*, that the duty to audit involves a duty to pay due regard to the possibility that fraud may have occurred and the audit programme and audit tests should be structured so that the auditor has a reasonable expectation of detecting material fraud if it exists.

Nevertheless, the position of the auditing profession appears to have remained unchanged and, as the size and incidence of corporate frauds continued to grow, so dissatisfaction with the extent of the responsibility acknowledged by auditors increased. In 1978, for example, the Commission on Auditors' Responsibilities (CAR; 1978; the Cohen Commission), reported:

> Court decisions, criticism by the financial press, actions by regulatory bodies, and surveys of users indicate dissatisfaction with the responsibility for fraud detection acknowledged by auditors. Opinion surveys . . . indicate that concerned segments of the public expect independent auditors to assume greater responsibility in this area. Significant percentages of those who use and rely on the auditor's work rank the detection of fraud among the most important objectives of an audit. (p. 31)

The level of discontent with auditors' denial of responsibility for detecting fraud in the 1970s and 1980s is evident from the following illustrations:

- Woolf (1978) drew attention to the pertinent question raised by the investment analyst whose solo efforts were responsible for exposing the notorious *Equity Funding* fraud in the USA in the early 1970s:

    > If routine auditing procedures cannot detect 64,000 phony insurance policies [two-thirds of the total number], $25 million in counterfeit bonds, and $100 million in missing assets, what is the purpose of audits? (p. 62)

- In similar vein, Carty (1985), a member of the Auditing Practices Committee (the predecessor of the Auditing Practices Board), observed:

    > [T]he public do not readily accept the limitations on the scope of an audit that the auditors inevitably build into their approach. Whenever there is a revelation in the press of a fraud, there is public outcry and the usual question, 'Why didn't the auditors pick this up years ago?' (p. 30)

In the UK, as in most other parts of the world, corporate fraud continues to be an increasingly worrying issue. KPMG (1997, 2001) reported that, in the UK between 1987 and 2000, there were 855 major fraud cases, each involving more than £100,000 and totalling some £4,177 million. Among these frauds were the well-publicised cases of the Bank of Credit and Commerce International (BCCI), Ferranti, Guiness Peat, and Maxwell Communications. Since 2000, the situation has worsened. KPMG's annual surveys of fraud cases exceeding £100,000 in the UK court system have found, for example, that in 2004 there were 174 fraud cases involving a total of £329 million; in 2005 there were 222 cases involving £942 million, and in 2006 there were 277 cases involving £837 million (KPMG, 2006; Yirrell, 2007). However, what is even more startling than the number and value of major frauds is that, according to Ernst and Young (2000), 82 per cent of all identified corporate fraud is committed by employees and almost one-third of this is committed by management. In 2006, KPMG similarly found that 40 per cent of all fraud by value (£350 million) was perpetrated by companies' own managers (Yirrell, 2007). This proportion of management fraud is lower than that noted by Turner in the USA (see quotation below) but is still very high – and is particularly worrying, given auditors' reliance on management's responses to enquiries in relation to many aspects of the audit.

6.2.3   Increased responsibility for auditors to detect and report corporate fraud

Since the early 1980s, perhaps not surprisingly given the size and incidence of corporate fraud, auditors have come under mounting pressure from politicians, the media and influential commentators to play a more active role in combating corporate fraud. In the mid-1980s, for example, faced by the rising wave of corporate fraud in the UK, Fletcher and Howard, successive Ministers of Corporate and Consumer Affairs, made it clear that they viewed auditors as being in the front line of the public's defences in the fight against fraud, and they called upon auditors to extend their duties in this regard. Their stance was supported by fraud investigators, who stated that they considered it both practical and desirable, within the limits of cost and auditing procedures, for auditors to accept a general responsibility to detect fraud (Smith, 1985, p. 10).

Similar opinions were expressed in the United States of America (USA) by senior staff of the Securities and Exchange Commission (SEC). For example, Walker (1999a), former Director of the SEC's Division of Enforcement, stated:

> The Commission looks to auditors to combat fraud. . . . The Commission, with its small staff and limited resources . . . necessarily must rely heavily on the accounting profession to perform its tasks diligently and responsibly. In short, auditors are the first line of defense. (p. 2)

He also noted (1999b):

> [There] are indicators that financial fraud is still occurring at too great a pace. . . . National Economic Research Associates (NERA) issued a report on recent trends in securities litigation. NERA found that a whopping 55 percent of all securities claims actions in the first half of 1999 were based on claims of fraudulent accounting. (p. 2)

Although he did not say so directly, Walker implied that the instances of fraudulent financial reporting should have been detected by the relevant company's auditors.

Turner (1999), former Chief Accountant of the SEC, was more direct in his criticism of auditors for failing to detect fraud – in particular, fraudulent financial reporting:

> You only have to look as far as the March 1999 report sponsored by the Committee of Sponsoring Organizations of the Treadway Committee (COSO) on

fraudulent financial reporting to understand the problems with today's audits. One startling fact in that report, which summarizes fraud cases from 1987–1998, is that over 80% of the fraud cases involved the highest levels of management ... the very group responsible for ensuring the adequacy of the control environment. The irony of today's audit processes is that significant audit assurance is derived from internal controls; however, the very group ... charged with ensuring the effectiveness of internal controls is responsible for committing fraud. (p. 4)

In Turner's (2000) view, auditors should be required to perform additional forensic-type procedures during their audits, specifically designed to detect fraudulent activities by management.

Since the 1980s, in response to the criticism levelled against it, the auditing profession (led principally by the AICPA) has progressively acknowledged greater responsibility for detecting corporate fraud. In 1988, the AICPA issued Statement on Auditing Standards (SAS) no. 53, *The auditor's responsibility to detect and report errors and irregularities*. This adopted a new positive approach towards defining auditors' duties with respect to fraud. In place of the former defensive tone and insistence that audits cannot be relied on to disclose irregularities, SAS no. 53 stated:

Because of the characteristics of irregularities, particularly those involving forgery and collusion, a properly designed and executed audit may not detect a material irregularity. [However], the auditor should exercise (a) due care in planning, performing and evaluating the results of audit procedures, and (b) the proper degree of professional skepticism to achieve reasonable assurance that material errors or irregularities will be detected. (paras 7–8)

Auditors' role in detecting fraud was strengthened in SAS no. 82: *Consideration of fraud in a financial statement audit* (published by the AICPA in 1997). Unlike its predecessor (SAS no. 53), which embraced both errors and irregularities (i.e., fraud), SAS no. 82 dealt only with fraud in financial statement audits. Further, SAS no. 82 (unlike SAS no. 53) went beyond requiring auditors to plan and perform their audits to obtain reasonable assurance that the financial statements are free of material misstatement: it required them to actively consider the likelihood of fraud occurring. The Standard required auditors to assess, specifically, the risk of material misstatement in the financial statements resulting from fraud and to consider that assessment when planning and performing the audit. In making their assessment, auditors were required:

(i)   to consider whether risk factors that might indicate the existence of fraud are present; and

(ii) to make enquiries of management to obtain management's understanding and assessment of the likelihood of fraud occurring within the entity.

To assist auditors with their fraud risk assessment, SAS no. 82 provided an extensive list of fraud risk factors[5] to consider when making this assessment. SAS no. 82 also explicitly required auditors to respond appropriately to the risk factors they identified, and to document:

(i) the performance of their fraud risk assessment;

(ii) the specific risk factors they identified; and

(iii) their response to those factors.

At the conclusion of their audits, auditors were required to reassess, in the light of all the evidence gathered during the audit, the risk of material misstatement in the financial statements due to fraud.

In 2002, SAS no. 82 was superseded by SAS no. 99: *Consideration of fraud in a financial statement audit*. Although it has the same name as its predecessor, the new standard represents a major shift in the level of responsibility acknowledged by the auditing profession to detect fraud. As Ramos (2003) explains:

> [SAS no. 99 requires auditors to] enter a much expanded arena of procedures to detect fraud. . . . [They] will gather and consider much more information to assess fraud risks than . . . in the past. . . . It has the potential to be a watershed for how auditors think about and perform an audit. (pp. 1, 10)

The key elements of SAS no. 99 include: its emphasis on the importance of auditors exercising professional scepticism, its introduction of a requirement for audit team members to discuss how and where the financial statements might be susceptible to material misstatement as a result of fraud, and its extension of auditors' responsibilities in respect of:

(a) gathering information needed to identify risks of material misstatement due to fraud;

(b) identifying risks (from the information gathered) that may result in material misstatement due to fraud;

(c) assessing the identified risks, after taking into account an evaluation of the client's programmes and controls that address the identified risks;

(d) responding to the results of the assessment.

The standard also highlights the need for auditors' assessment of the risks of material misstatement due to fraud to be ongoing throughout the audit, describes requirements relating to the documentation of auditors' consideration of fraud, and provides guidance regarding communicating possible fraud to management, the audit committee and others.

In the international arena, ISA 240: *Fraud and error* (as revised, 2001) closely resembled the AICPA's SAS no. 82; the major point of difference was that ISA

---

[5] Fraud risk factors are "events or conditions that indicate an incentive or pressure to commit fraud or provide an opportunity to commit fraud" [ISA 240, 2006, para 11].

240 covered both fraud and error in financial statement audits rather than being confined (like SAS no. 82) to auditors' responsibilities with respect to fraud. Similarly, ISA 240: *The auditor's responsibility to consider fraud in an audit of financial statements* (2004; Redrafted 2006)[6] is very similar to SAS no. 99. We will discuss the requirements of ISA 240 (Redrafted) after we have considered developments relating to auditors' responsibility to detect and report fraud in the UK prior to the UK's adoption of ISA 240 (2004).

In the UK, as far as detecting fraud is concerned, SAS 110: *Fraud and error* [published in 1995 – thus pre-dating SAS no. 82 (1997) and ISA 240 (2001)] required auditors to "plan, perform and evaluate their audit work in order to have a reasonable expectation of detecting material misstatements arising from error and fraud" (para 18). Thus, its requirements, like those of the AICPA's SAS no. 53 (published in 1988), were relatively inexplicit and undemanding. Unlike SAS no. 82, it did not require auditors to make a formal fraud risk assessment or to respond, specifically, when planning or performing their audits, to fraud risk factors that had been identified.

However, with respect to auditors reporting actual or suspected fraud encountered during an audit, SAS 110 (1995) went beyond the requirements of both SAS no. 82 (1997) and ISA 240 (2001). SAS 110 required auditors in the UK:
- if they suspected or discovered fraud, to communicate their findings as soon as practicable to the appropriate level of management, the board of directors or the audit committee. Even if the potential effect of a fraud or suspected fraud was immaterial to the financial statements, the auditor should still report it to the appropriate level of management (para 41);
- to qualify their audit report when they formed the opinion that, as a result of fraud, the financial statements did not give a true and fair view.[7] Similarly, they were required to qualify the audit report if they disagreed with the accounting treatment, or with the extent or lack of disclosure, of the fraud or its consequences (para 45).

Thus far, the reporting requirements of SAS 110 were very similar to those of SAS no. 82 and ISA 240 (2001). However, SAS 110 went further: it also recognised that there may be circumstances in which auditors should go beyond their reporting duty as outlined above and report suspected or actual instances of fraud to an appropriate external authority. More specifically, it required auditors who encountered a suspected or actual fraud during an audit to

---

[6] As explained in the Important Note following the Preface to this book, the IAASB has redrafted the ISAs (including ISA 240) as part of its 'clarity project'.

[7] Different types of audit report are discussed in Chapter 14.

consider whether the matter ought to be reported "to a proper authority in the public interest" (para 50). In normal circumstances, the auditor's duty of confidentiality to the client[8] is paramount and SAS 110 acknowledged this by noting: "confidentiality is an implied term of the auditor's contract". Nevertheless, it went on to state: "In certain exceptional circumstances auditors are not bound by their duty of confidentiality and have the right or duty to report matters to a proper authority in the public interest" (para 53). In particular:

> When a suspected or actual instance of fraud casts doubt on the integrity of the directors, auditors should make a report direct to a proper authority in the public interest without delay and without informing the directors in advance. (para 52)

SAS 110 explained that, providing auditors report a suspected or actual fraud encountered during an audit to a proper authority in the public interest, and the disclosure is not motivated by malice, they are protected from the risk of liability for breach of their duty of confidentiality or defamation (para 55).

When deciding whether disclosure of a suspected or actual fraud to a proper authority in the public interest is justified, the auditor was required to consider factors such as (para 56):

- the extent to which the fraud is likely to affect members of the public;
- whether the directors are taking corrective action or are likely to do so;
- the extent to which non-disclosure of the fraud is likely to enable it to recur with impunity;
- the gravity of the matter;
- the weight of evidence and degree of suspicion that fraud has occurred.

Acceptance of a duty to report to a proper authority when it is in the public interest to do so represents a significant extension to the responsibility to report fraud previously acknowledged by auditors. Prior to the issuance of SAS 110, auditing standards in the UK interpreted public interest reporting as a right rather than a duty, and the reporting of fraud to anyone outside the entity was generally considered by auditors as likely to be perceived as a breach of their duty of confidentiality.

After publication of SAS 110, the issue of auditors' responsibility for detecting and reporting fraud remained high on the APB's list of priorities. In 1998 it published a Consultation Paper: *Fraud and Audit: Choices for Society*, in which it reported that research it had undertaken had shown that most material frauds involve management; more than half of frauds involve misstated financial reporting (i.e., fraudulent financial reporting) but do not involve diversion of funds from the company (i.e., theft of company assets); and management fraud is unlikely to be detected in a financial statement audit. (These

---

[8] We discuss auditors' duty of confidentiality to their clients in section 6.5.

findings support those reported by Turner in the USA, and by Ernst and Young and Yirrell in the UK, noted earlier.)

The APB also reported that "a review of the effectiveness of new Auditing Standards on fraud [that is, SAS 110] indicates that auditors have increased the emphasis they place on fraud in the course of their work" (APB, 1998, p. 5). However, the APB further noted that, despite the steps taken by both the APB and audit firms to improve performance in this regard, there was a continuing gap between society's expectations of auditors and auditors' performance. It reported that although society expects auditors to find fraud, "particularly when a fraud involves factors that threaten the entity's ability to continue in business . . . , auditors cannot ensure that they will discover management fraud" (p. 15). It cited factors that hamper auditors in detecting fraud; these include:

- the nature of evidence available to auditors[9] which results in them rarely having sufficient evidence to resolve suspicions that fraud may have occurred;
- the ability of directors and senior managers to override internal controls;
- the focus of external financial statements – and the audit thereof – on the provision of a "true and fair view" rather than on the incidence of fraud. Company law does not require directors or auditors to report on fraud discovered within an auditee;
- the ability of auditees to impose time constraints by specifying the date when the audited financial statements are due to be published to discourage auditors from seeking evidence to resolve suspicions of fraud.

Notwithstanding these and other difficulties, the APB suggested ways in which auditors' performance in detecting corporate fraud might be better aligned with society's expectations. More specifically it suggested:

(i)   Auditing Standards might be changed, for example:
  - to increase the emphasis given to professional scepticism; and
  - to introduce more specific requirements for particular types of evidence to be gathered or procedures to be performed;

(ii) the auditor's role in detecting fraud within an entity might be extended by, for example:
  - requiring auditors to report to boards of directors and audit committees on the adequacy of controls within the entity to prevent and detect fraud;

---

[8] The concept of audit evidence is discussed in Chapter 3, section 3.4.1.

- encouraging the use of forensic fraud reviews based on an assessment of the risks of fraud that are inherent in an auditee;
- considering whether it would be beneficial to extend auditors' responsibility for reporting fraud – including suspected fraud. In this regard the APB explains:

> Auditors of regulated entities are normally required to report frauds. Current Auditing Standards require auditors of other entities who suspect fraud to report to an appropriate authority if they consider it necessary in the public interest. There may be benefit in reviewing these arrangements to determine whether auditors should report suspicions in a wider range of circumstances ... (p. 27)

6.2.4 Auditors' responsibilities to detect and report fraud under ISA 240 (Redrafted)[10]

It is interesting to observe that many of the APB's suggestions have been incorporated in ISA 240: *The auditor's responsibilities relating to fraud in an audit of financial statements* (2004; Redrafted 2006). As noted earlier, this Standard closely resembles SAS no. 99 (AICPA, 2002) and, like SAS no. 99, its key elements include:

(i)   noting the limitation of audits to detect fraud;
(ii)   identifying the conditions conducive to fraud;
(iii) emphasising the importance of professional scepticism;
(iv)   requiring a discussion of audit engagement team members about the susceptibility of the financial statements to material misstatement due to fraud;
(v)   specifying the requirements of auditors in respect of identifying, assessing and responding to the risk of material misstatement due to fraud;
(vi)   detailing auditors' responsibilities to communicate detected or suspected fraud to management (i.e., executives), the board of directors (or audit committee) and regulatory authorities;
(vii) detailing the documentation required of matters relating to detecting and reporting fraud.

We discuss each of these elements below.

(i)   Limitation of audits to detect fraud

Reminiscent of auditing standards in previous decades, ISA 240 states that primary responsibility for the prevention and detection of fraud rests with management. It notes that, although an auditor is responsible for obtaining

---

[10] Unless indicated otherwise, all references to ISA 240 in this section refer to ISA 240: *The auditor's responsibilities relating to fraud in an audit of financial statements* (2004; Redrafted 2006).

reasonable assurance that the audited financial statements are free from material misstatement, whether caused by fraud or error, because of the inherent limitations of an audit [such as those identified by the APB (1998) noted above], there is an unavoidable risk that some material misstatements may not be detected even though the audit is properly planned and performed in accordance with the ISAs (paras 4–5). The Standard explains:

> The risk of not detecting a material misstatement resulting from fraud is higher than the risk of not detecting one resulting from error. This is because fraud may involve sophisticated and carefully organized schemes designed to conceal it, such as forgery, deliberate failure to record transactions, or intentional misrepresentations being made to the auditor. . . . Collusion may cause the auditor to believe that audit evidence is persuasive when it is, in fact, false. The auditor's ability to detect fraud depends on factors such as the skillfulness of the perpetrator, the frequency and extent of manipulation, the degree of collusion involved, the relative size of individual amounts manipulated, and the seniority of those individuals involved. . . . [T]he risk of the auditor not detecting a material misstatement resulting from management fraud is greater than for employee fraud, because management is frequently in a position to directly or indirectly manipulate accounting records, present fraudulent financial information or override control procedures designed to prevent similar frauds by other employees. (paras 6–7)

Having cautioned that a properly planned and conducted audit may not detect material misstatement due to fraud, ISA 240 provides some exacting requirements for auditors designed to ensure that, if a significant fraud has been committed within the auditee, unless it has been cleverly concealed, there is a reasonable likelihood that the auditor will detect it.

(ii)   Conditions conducive to fraud

ISA 240 identifies three conditions which are conducive to fraud, namely: incentive or pressure, opportunity, and rationalisation or attitude. These three conditions are frequently referred to as 'the fraud triangle'. The Standard explains them as follows:

- Incentive or pressure to commit fraudulent financial reporting may exist when management is under pressure, from sources outside or inside the entity, to achieve an expected . . . earnings target or financial outcome. . . . Similarly, individuals may have an incentive to misappropriate assets, for example, because the individuals are living beyond their means.
- A perceived opportunity to commit fraud may exist when an individual believes internal control can be overridden, for example, because the individual is in a position of trust or has knowledge of specific deficiencies in internal control.
- Individuals may be able to rationalize committing a fraudulent act. Some individuals possess an attitude, character or set of ethical values that allow them knowingly and intentionally to commit a dishonest act. However, even

otherwise honest individuals can commit fraud in an environment that imposes sufficient pressure on them. (para A1)

(iii) Importance of professional scepticism[11]

A key theme permeating ISA 240 is the importance of auditors maintaining an attitude of professional scepticism at every stage of the audit. The Standard explains that this requires auditors to conduct their audits with a questioning mind and critical assessment of audit evidence. They must not be swayed by past experience of honesty and integrity of clients' managements and they must continually question whether information and other audit evidence indicate that a material misstatement due to fraud may have occurred. If they have cause to believe that records or other documents are not genuine or have been wrongfully modified, or if responses from management to their enquiries are inconsistent, they are required to investigate further to resolve their concerns (paras 12–14, A7–A8).

(iv) Discussion of audit engagement team members

A significant feature of ISA 240 is its requirement for audit engagement team members to have a discussion regarding how and where the auditee's financial statements may be susceptible to material misstatement due to fraud, and how it might occur. During their discussion they are to "[set] aside beliefs ... that management and those charged with governance are honest and have integrity" (para 15).

Among the matters ISA 240 (para A11) suggests might be discussed are the following:
- how and where the entity's financial statements may be susceptible to material misstatement due to fraud, how management could perpetrate and conceal fraudulent financial reporting, and how assets of the entity could be misappropriated;
- the circumstances that might indicate earnings management and the practices management might adopt to manage earnings that could lead to fraudulent financial reporting;
- how external and internal factors affecting the entity may create an incentive or pressure for management or others to commit fraud, provide the opportunity for fraud to be perpetrated, and indicate a culture or environment that enables management or others to rationalise committing fraud;
- management's involvement in overseeing employees with access to cash or other assets susceptible to theft;

---

[11] The concept of professional scepticism is discussed in Chapter 3, section 3.4.5.

- any unusual or unexplained changes in behaviour or lifestyle of management or employees which have come to the attention of engagement team members.

Unlike ISA 240, SAS no. 99 (AICPA, 2002) refers to this discussion as "brainstorming", which, according to Ramos (2003, p. 2) "is a new concept in auditing literature". Ramos (2003) suggests that the discussion provides an opportunity "to set the proper tone at the top for conducting the engagement". He notes that it should be conducted with an attitude that "includes a questioning mind" and that it should "model the proper degree of professional skepticism and set the culture for the engagement" (p. 2). He also observes:

> The mere fact that the engagement team has a serious discussion about the entity's susceptibility to fraud also serves to remind auditors that the possibility does exist in every engagement – in spite of any history or perceived biases about management's honesty and integrity. (p. 2)

(v) Identifying, assessing and responding to the risk of material misstatement due to fraud

In order to gather the information needed to identify risks of material misstatement due to fraud, ISA 240 requires auditors to:

- make enquiries of management, those charged with governance of the entity (i.e., the directors), the internal audit function (if the entity has one) and other appropriate individuals within the entity [for example, operating personnel not directly involved in the financial reporting process, employees with different levels of authority, in-house legal counsel, and the person(s) responsible for dealing with allegations of fraud]. Such enquiries enable auditors to determine whether those questioned have knowledge of any actual, suspected or alleged fraud affecting the auditee and, in the case of internal auditors, to ascertain their views on the risks of fraud affecting the entity;
- gain an understanding of how the directors oversee the executives' processes for identifying and responding to risks of fraud, and the internal controls management has established to mitigate those risks;
- evaluate whether any unusual or unexpected relationships have been identified through analytical procedures[12] or other evidence gathered during the audit that may indicate risks of material misstatement due to fraud;
- evaluate whether information obtained from other fraud risk assessment procedures and related activities indicates that one or more fraud risk factors are present. (These factors are discussed below.)

---

[12] Analytical procedures are explained in Chapter 7, section 7.4.2.

Among these information gathering procedures, making enquiries of management (i.e., the entity's executives) is particularly important. ISA 240 (para 17) requires the enquiries to include management's:

- assessment of the risk that the financial statements may be materially misstated due to fraud and the nature, extent and frequency of its assessments;
- process for identifying and responding to the risk of fraud in the entity;
- communication, if any, to the board of directors regarding its (management's, i.e., the executives') processes for identifying and responding to the risk of fraud in the entity;
- communication, if any, to employees regarding its views on business practices and ethical behaviour.

Notwithstanding the importance of these enquires ISA 240 also advises:

Management is often in the best position to perpetrate fraud. Accordingly, when evaluating management's responses to inquiries with an attitude of professional skepticism, the auditor may judge it necessary to corroborate responses to inquiries with other information. (para A17)

Fraud, especially management fraud, may be difficult to detect as it is usually carefully concealed; however, events or conditions may indicate an incentive or pressure, or an opportunity, to commit fraud. Such events or conditions are known as 'fraud risk factors'. Just because such factors are present does not necessarily mean that fraud exists but they are often warning signs where it does. To help auditors consider whether fraud risks are present, ISA 240 (Redrafted), like its predecessor ISA 240 (2001), provides an extensive list of fraud risk factors in Appendix 1. However, unlike ISA 240 (2001), these are arranged in two sets – one for fraudulent financial reporting, the other for misappropriation of assets – and in each set the factors are grouped under the subheadings 'Incentives/Pressure', 'Opportunities and 'Attitudes/Rationalisation'.

Once auditors have gathered information to assist them identify the risks of material misstatement due to fraud, they are required to identify and assess the risks at both the financial statement level and at the assertion level for classes of transactions, account balances and disclosures.[13] In this context, an interesting requirement of ISA 240 (as in SAS no. 99) relates to revenue recognition. According to Ramos (2003, pp. 6–7): "The vast majority of fraudulent financial reporting schemes involved improper revenue recognition." Given this situation, it is not surprising that ISA 240 specifically requires

---

[13] Assertions for classes of transactions, account balances and disclosures are discussed in Chapter 10.

auditors, when identifying and assessing the risks of material misstatement due to fraud, to evaluate which types of revenue and revenue transactions and/or assertions give rise to such risks, based on a presumption that there are risks of fraud in revenue recognition. Further, if auditors conclude that this presumption is not applicable in the particular circumstances of the audit (i.e., they do not identify improper revenue recognition as a risk of material misstatement due to fraud), they are to document the reasons supporting their conclusion (paras 26, 47).

When auditors identify risks of material misstatement due to fraud, they are required to treat them as significant risks and, as a consequence, they must obtain a good understanding of the internal controls relevant to those risks. It is possible that the controls mitigate the identified risks to an extent that enables the auditor to conclude that the risks have not resulted in material misstatement in the financial statements and, therefore, make it unnecessary to conduct procedures that would otherwise be required.

Having identified and assessed the risks of material misstatement due to fraud, auditors need to respond to them. ISA 240 requires them to provide overall responses at the financial statement level and also to provide responses at the assertion level and in respect of management's ability to override internal controls.

ISA 240 explains that auditors' overall responses to assessed risks of material misstatement due to fraud generally include considering how the performance of the audit can reflect increased professional scepticism. This may be achieved through, for example:
- increased sensitivity in selecting for examination documentation that supports material transactions; and
- increased recognition of the need to corroborate management's explanations regarding material matters.

Additionally, the audit engagement partner is required to:
- take account of (a) individuals' knowledge, skill and ability to be given significant engagement responsibilities, and (b) his/her (i.e., the partner's) assessment of the risk of material misstatement due to fraud, when assigning audit work to, and supervising, engagement team members;
- evaluate whether the selection and application of accounting policies, particularly those relating to subjective measurements and complex transactions, may indicate fraudulent financial reporting resulting from management's efforts to manage the entity's reported earnings;

 – incorporate an element of unpredictability in the nature, timing and extent of audit procedures[14] performed during the audit so that entity personnel cannot 'second guess' what the engagement team will examine – or when.

For assessed risks at the assertion level, auditors are required to design and perform audit procedures whose nature, timing and extent are responsive to the assessed risks. ISA 240 provides extensive illustrative examples (in paras A37–A39 and Appendix 2) of ways in which the nature, timing and extent of audit procedures may be modified, and additional procedures that may be performed, in order to address, specifically, the assessed risks of material misstatement due to fraud in classes of transactions, account balances and/or financial statement disclosures.

In respect of responding to the risk of fraud arising from management's ability to override internal controls, ISA 240 (para 31) states:

> Management is in a unique position to perpetrate fraud because of management's ability to manipulate accounting records and prepare fraudulent financial statements by overriding controls that otherwise appear to be operating effectively. ... Due to the unpredictable way in which such override could occur, it is a risk of material misstatement due to fraud and thus a significant risk.

Following from this stance, irrespective of their assessment of the likelihood of management overriding the entity's internal controls, auditors are required to design and perform audit procedures to test, *inter alia*, journal entries, accounting estimates and significant transactions that appear unusual given the auditee's business. The significance of each of these factors is discussed below.

Journal entries are particularly prone to manipulation and, according to ISA 240 (para A41), material misstatement of financial statements due to fraud often involves the recording of inappropriate or unauthorised journal entries. As a consequence, auditors are required to design and perform audit procedures to test the appropriateness of journal entries and other adjustments made during the preparation of the financial statements. In designing these procedures auditors are, among other things, required to enquire of individuals involved in the financial reporting process about inappropriate or unusual activity relating to the processing of journal entries and other adjustments.

During the preparation of financial statements, management is responsible for making a number of judgments or assumptions that affect significant accounting estimates and for monitoring, on an ongoing basis, the reasonableness of

---

[14] The nature, timing and extent of audit procedures are discussed in Chapter 7, section 7.4.4.

such estimates. However, estimates are just that – and therefore prone to bias and error. A motivated manager could use the subjective nature of accounting estimates to bias the financial statements in order to achieve, for example, a 'desired' level of earnings. As ISA 240 points out: "[f]raudulent financial reporting is often accomplished through intentional misstatement of accounting estimates" (para A45). In order to uncover such actions, auditors are required to review accounting estimates for bias, and also the reasonableness of management's judgments and assumptions that underlie the estimates. If auditors find evidence of bias they are required to evaluate whether the circumstances surrounding the bias are such as to result in a risk of material misstatement due to fraud.

Significant transactions outside the normal course of an auditee's business may, like manipulated journal entries and biased accounting estimates, signal an intent to commit fraud. For any significant transaction that appears unusual (given the auditor's understanding of the entity, its environment, and other information obtained during the course of the audit), the auditor is required to evaluate whether the business reasons (or absence thereof) for the transaction suggests that it may have been entered into in order to facilitate fraudulent financial reporting or to conceal misappropriation of assets. Examples of signals of possible ill intent include:
- the form of the transaction appears to be unnecessarily complex;
- the entity's executives have not discussed the nature of, or accounting for, the transaction with the non-executive directors (or audit committee);
- documentation supporting the transaction is inadequate;
- executives place greater emphasis on the adoption of a particular accounting treatment for the transaction than on its underlying substance.

In addition to responding (as outlined above) to identified risks of material misstatement due to fraud, auditors are required to evaluate analytical procedures performed during the 'completion and review stage' of the audit[15] to ascertain whether they indicate a previously unidentified risk of material misstatement due to fraud. If they identify a misstatement and establish that it may indicate fraud, recognising that an instance of fraud is unlikely to be an isolated event, they are required to evaluate the implications of the misstatement for other aspects of the audit, especially the reliability of management representations. Further, irrespective of the materiality of the misstatement, if auditors believe that management (in particular, senior executives) are

---

[15] The completion and review stage of an audit is the subject of Chapter 13. Analytical procedures are performed during this stage of the audit, among other things, to assist auditors form an overall conclusion as to whether the financial statements are consistent with their understanding of the entity and its environment.

involved, they are required to re-evaluate their assessment of the risks of material misstatement due to fraud and its resulting impact on the nature, timing and extent of audit procedures performed in response to the assessed risks. Additionally, when reconsidering the reliability of evidence previously obtained, they are required to "consider whether circumstances or conditions indicate possible collusion involving employees, management or third parties" (ISA 240, para 36).

During the completion and review stage of the audit, auditors routinely obtain a 'written representations' from management in which management confirms, in writing, significant representations made to the auditor.[16] However, ISA 240 (para 39) specifically requires auditors to obtain written representations from management that confirm that it (i.e., management):

(a) acknowledges its responsibility for designing, implementing and main-taining internal controls to prevent and detect fraud;

(b) has disclosed to the auditor:
- the results of its assessment of the risk that the financial statements may be materially misstated as a result of fraud;
- its knowledge of fraud or suspected fraud affecting the entity involving:
  - management,
  - employees who have significant roles in internal control, or
  - others where the fraud could have a material effect on the financial statements;
- its knowledge of any allegations of fraud, or suspected fraud, affecting the entity's financial statements communicated by employees, former employees, analysts, regulators or others.

(vi) Communicating detected or suspected fraud

If an auditor believes that an auditee's financial statements are materially misstated as a result of fraud and, on having the matter drawn to their attention, the directors refuse to correct the misstatement(s), the auditor must report to the company's shareholders accordingly. Similarly, if the auditor is prevented by the entity, or by circumstances beyond the entity's control, from obtaining sufficient appropriate evidence to establish whether or not fraud which may be material to the financial statements has occurred, (s)he is required to reflect the position in the audit report.[17] However (as indicated in section 6.2.3 above) auditors' reporting duties go beyond this.

---

[16] Written representations are discussed in Chapter 13, section 13.5.

[17] Auditors' duty to report to shareholders is discussed in Chapter 14.

If auditors detect fraud, or have reason to believe that fraud may have occurred within an auditee, they are required to report the matter to the appropriate level of management as soon as practicable.[18] ISA 240 explains that auditors should perform this duty: "even if the matter might be considered inconsequential (for example, a minor defalcation by an employee at a low level in the entity's organization)" (para A59). What constitutes an 'appropriate level of management' is a matter for the auditor's professional judgment but, ordinarily, it is at least one level above those who appear to be involved in the detected or suspected fraud.

In cases where a detected or suspected fraud involves (i) management (i.e., company executives), (ii) employees who have a significant role in relation to the auditee's internal controls, or (iii) other employees (or even external parties) if the fraud has resulted in material misstatement in the financial statements, auditors have a duty to report the matter, on a timely basis, orally or in writing, to the board of directors (or audit committee).[19] In some circumstances, auditors may consider it appropriate to report fraud involving 'other employees' to the directors (or audit committee) even if the fraud (or suspected fraud) has not resulted in a material misstatement in the financial statements. In the audits of some entities, the directors or audit committee may indicate to the auditor that they wish all matters involving detected or suspected fraud to be reported to them. However, ISA 240 (para A61) points out that, for all audits, it is helpful if an auditee's directors and auditor clarify, at an early stage of the audit, the nature and extent of matters relating to fraud that the directors wish the auditor to communicate to the full board or its audit committee.

If auditors believe that management (i.e., one or more executive) is involved in a detected or suspected fraud, they are not only required to report the matter to the directors (or audit committee); they are also required to "discuss with them [i.e., the directors] the nature, timing and extent of audit procedures necessary to complete the audit" (ISA 240, para 41). This is because, if fraud involving management is detected or suspected, the auditor will need to reassess the audit evidence already gathered – in particular, the reliability of

---

[18] It should be recalled from Chapter 5 (section 5.3) that Moffit J, when ruling on the *Pacific Acceptance* case, established that auditors have a duty to make prompt and frank disclosure, to the appropriate level of management, of material matters discovered during the course of an audit. This includes a duty to report promptly to the company's directors if suspicious circumstances are encountered.

[19] ISA 260: *Communication of audit matters with those charged with governance* is discussed in Chapter 14, section 14.8.

management's responses to the auditor's enquiries – and additional audit procedures are likely to be needed. This has time and cost implications for the audit – and thus for the audit fee.

Even if fraud or suspected fraud has not been encountered, ISA 240 explains that auditors should discuss with the directors (or audit committee) concerns they have relating to fraud. These may include, for example:

- Concerns about the nature, extent and frequency of management's [i.e., executives'] assessments of the controls in place to prevent and detect fraud and of the risk that the financial statements may be misstated.
- A failure by management to appropriately address identified material weaknesses in internal control, or to appropriately respond to an identified fraud.
- The auditor's evaluation of the entity's control environment,[20] including questions regarding the competence and integrity of management.
- Actions by management that may be indicative of fraudulent financial reporting, such as management's selection and application of accounting policies that may be indicative of management's effort to manage earnings in order to deceive financial statement users. . . .
- Concerns about the adequacy and completeness of the authorization of transactions that appear to be outside the normal course of business. (para A63)

In addition to their duty to report detected or suspected fraud to the appropriate level of management (executives or directors, as appropriate), notwithstanding their duty of confidentiality to their clients,[21] auditors may have an obligation to report detected or suspected fraud to a party outside the auditee such as a regulatory authority. ISA 240 explains:

> The auditor's professional duty to maintain the confidentiality of client information may preclude reporting fraud to a party outside the client entity. However, . . . in certain circumstances, the duty of confidentiality may be overridden by statute, the law or courts of law.[22] In some countries [for example, the UK], the auditor of a financial institution has a statutory duty to report the occurrence of fraud to supervisory authorities. . . . (para A64)

The Standard adds:

> The auditor may consider it appropriate to obtain legal advice to determine the appropriate course of action in the circumstances, the purpose of which is to

---

[20] The term 'control environment' is explained in Chapter 10, section 10.3.1.

[21] This duty is discussed in section 6.5.

[22] ISA (UK and Ireland) 240 states:

In the UK and Ireland, the money laundering legislation . . . imposes a duty on auditors to report all suspicions that a criminal offence giving rise to any direct or indirect benefit from criminal conduct has been committed regardless of whether that offence has been committed by a client or a third party. Suspicions relating to fraud are likely to be required to be reported under this legislation. (footnote 3a)

ascertain the steps necessary in considering the public interest aspects of the identified fraud. (para A65)

Under ISA 240 (Redrafted) auditors' duty to report fraud is not dissimilar from that embodied in earlier Standards such as ISA 240 (2001). However, it is interesting to observe that, as regards reporting to external parties, ISA 240 (Redrafted) seems less demanding of auditors than SAS 110 (effective in the UK from 1995 to 2004), which it has superseded. It may be recalled (from section 6.2.3) that SAS 110 (APB, 1995) stated:

> In certain exceptional circumstances auditors are not bound by their duty of confidentiality and have the right or duty to report matters to a proper authority in the public interest.... When a suspected or actual instance of fraud casts doubt on the integrity of the directors, auditors should make a report direct to a proper authority in the public interest without delay and without informing the directors in advance. (paras 52–53)[23]

(vii) Required documentation relating to detecting and reporting fraud

One of the characteristic features of the post-2002 regulatory auditing environment is a significant increase in the documentation required of auditors. It is, therefore, no surprise that ISA 240 significantly extends the requirements of previous Standards in respect of documenting audit procedures performed to detect fraud, and steps taken to report detected and/or suspected fraud. The matters auditors are required to document include:

- significant decisions reached during the audit team's discussion about the susceptibility of the entity's financial statements to material misstatement due to fraud;
- identified and assessed risks of material misstatement due to fraud at both the financial statement and assertion level;
- overall responses to assessed risks at the financial statement level and the nature, timing and extent of audit procedures performed in response to assessed risks at the assertion level – and the relationship between those procedures and the overall responses;
- the results of audit procedures performed, including those designed to address the risk of management override of controls;
- if the auditor concludes that improper revenue recognition does not present a risk of material misstatement due to fraud in the particular circumstances of the audit, the reasons supporting that conclusion;

---

[23] As will be seen in section 6.4.4, auditors' duty to report to parties external to the entity under ISA (UK and Ireland) 250: *Section A – Consideration of laws and regulations in an audit of financial statements* is very similar to that set out in SAS 110. As perpetrating fraud constitutes non-compliance with law (i.e., an illegal act), the reporting provisions of ISA (UK and Ireland) 250 apply to auditors in the UK and Ireland reporting detected or suspected fraud.

- the nature, timing and extent of communications about fraud to the entity's executives, directors (and/or the audit committee) and others.

Thus, in essence, auditors are required to document their compliance with all of the key provisions of ISA 240.

6.2.5 Possible withdrawal from an audit engagement

In certain exceptional circumstances, such as when an auditor detects or suspects fraud has been perpetrated by the auditee's executives and/or (more particularly) its directors, the auditor may have such serious doubts about the integrity and honesty of the entity's management that (s)he doubts his/her ability to continue with the engagement. In such circumstances, ISA 240 (para 38) requires auditors:

- to consider whether it is appropriate to withdraw from the engagement;
- if withdrawal is considered appropriate to:
    (a) discuss the intended withdrawal with the appropriate level of management (in the UK, the directors or audit committee), and the reasons for the withdrawal; and
    (b) determine whether there is a professional or legal requirement to report the withdrawal to those who appointed the auditor (in the UK, this is the shareholders) or, in some cases, to regulatory authorities,[24] and to explain the reasons for the withdrawal.

ISA 240 (para A62) notes that, before proceeding to withdraw from an engagement, the auditor may consider it appropriate to obtain legal advice to assist in determining the appropriate course of action.

6.3 AGGRESSIVE EARNINGS MANAGEMENT

In 2001, the APB issued a Consultation Paper entitled *Aggressive Earnings Management*. This seems to be closely linked to the research finding the APB reported in its earlier Consultation Paper: *Fraud and Audit: Choices for Society* (1998), namely: "more than half of frauds involved misstated financial

---

[24] As we noted in Chapter 5 (section 5.2.4), auditors in the UK are required to notify the 'appropriate audit authority' when they cease to hold office as the auditor of a company (whatever the reason therefor), and to send with their notice, a 'statement of circumstances' setting out matters that need to be drawn to the attention of shareholders or creditors in relation to their ceasing to hold office and/or the reasons for them ceasing to hold office.

reporting ... "[25] (APB, 1998, p. 5) and that of research conducted in the USA by, for example, National Economic Research Associates (NERA), which reported: "55 percent of all securities claims actions in the first half of 1999 were based on claims of fraudulent accounting" [see quotation from Walker (1999b) in section 6.2.3 above].

The APB (2001) defines aggressive earnings management as follows:

[A]ccounting practices including the selection of inappropriate accounting policies and/or unduly stretching judgments as to what is acceptable when forming accounting estimates. These practices, while presenting the financial performance of the companies in a favourable light, [do] not necessarily reflect the underlying reality. (paras 4–5)

The APB explains that as a result of, and in response to, commercial pressures (for example, to report earnings in line with the market's expectations, or to conform with financial thresholds or ratios requirements specified by law or regulations), a company may begin in a small legitimate way to ensure that it reports the 'desired results'. However, over time, manipulation of the financial statements may increase until it "crosses the border of acceptability" (APB, 2001, p. 7). Thus 'aggressive earnings management' may be seen as a rung on the ladder leading to fraudulent financial reporting. An example of how aggressive earnings management can develop into 'unacceptable financial reporting' is presented in Figure 6.1.

In its Consultation Paper, the APB asserted that it wished auditors to be alert, and responsive, to the risk of aggressive earnings management. It also reported that it would consider whether Auditing Standards needed to be enhanced in order to ensure that auditors:

- better understand the pressures on directors and management to report a specific level of earnings;
- act with greater scepticism when circumstances are encountered that may be indicative of aggressive earnings management;
- take a more robust attitude with directors when seeking adjustments for misstatements identified by the audit;
- communicate openly and frankly with the entity's directors – and, more particularly, with its audit committee (if it has one).

---

[25] The APB explains:

Misstatements include (1) errors, (2) other inaccuracies (whether intentional or not), and (3) with regard to estimates and amounts dependent upon an exercise of judgment, unreasonable differences between (a) the amount intended to be included in the financial statements [by the directors] and (b) the auditors' assessment of what that amount should be based on the available audit evidence. (APB, 2001, p. 9)

Figure 6.1: Example to demonstrate how legitimate business practices can develop into unacceptable financial reporting

Year ended 31 December XXX1

A listed manufacturing company has thrived in an economic expansion and announced a series of record-breaking results. Analysts believe earnings will continue their strong upward trend and have forecast the results for the year and the earnings per share to the penny. Shareholders see increased earnings producing an ever-higher share price.

Management perceives a slow-down in its business and is very concerned about the impact on the share price if the analysts' forecasts are not met. Departmental heads are told to pull out all the stops; targets are set; management will see missing the target as a failure. The pressure is on.

Being a manufacturing company, earnings are based on completed items shipped and invoiced. In this instance, for the earnings target to be met, overtime is authorised and worked to accelerate completions so that the necessary shipments are made, an invoices raised before the year-end.

Year ended 31 December XXX2

The analysts, seeing their forecast met by the company at December XXX1, project a further increase in the company's earnings in line with its record-breaking past. Management, believing, or hoping, that the slow-down will be temporary, issues departments with new targets to enable it to meet the analysts' forecast for the next year-end.

Unfortunately, the business slow-down turns out not to be temporary. Not only have completions and shipments failed to increase to meet the new forecast but some method has to be found to make up in this year for the sales and profit which were accelerated into the previous year. The pressure is now greater than at the previous year-end.

Overtime is again authorised to increase shipments but will not be enough to meet the target. To further stimulate sales the company announces a price discount that will apply to sales and shipments made in December. In addition to the continued efforts to accelerate shipments for completed goods, the provisions for bad debts, returns and warranty costs are also reduced. While individually each provision can be justified, each has been calculated on the basis of the most optimistic view of the ranges of possible outcomes. No disclosures are given in the financial statements, nor in the other information published with the financial statements, of the actions taken to stimulate sales or the fact that each provision is determined on the most optimistic basis.

Year ended 31 December XXX3

A year later the position has escalated out of control and many employees are now involved. In addition to all the actions taken in XXX2, goods are now being shipped on sale or return (without a provision for returns) and fictitious shipments are made close to the year end on the basis of false documentation, both being designed to deceive the auditors.

At some point the 'balloon goes up', the police are called in and, inevitably, the cry goes up 'what were the directors doing and where were the auditors?'

Source: APB, 2001

By tackling 'aggressive earnings management' as soon as they suspect an auditee may be engaging in it, auditors may well prevent their client from sliding down the slippery slope to cross the boundary from 'undesirable practices' into fraudulent financial reporting.

As we have seen in this chapter, the provisions of ISA 240 incorporate the steps needed to counter aggressive earnings management identified by the APB (2001).

6.4 AUDITORS' RESPONSIBILITY TO DETECT AND REPORT NON-COMPLIANCE WITH LAWS AND REGULATIONS[26]

6.4.1 Definition of non-compliance

Before we can examine auditors' responsibilities with respect to auditees' non-compliance with laws and regulations, we need to know what we mean by 'non-compliance'. ISA 250: *consideration of laws and regulations in an audit of financial statements*[27] defines it as follows:

> Acts of omission or commission by the entity being audited, either intentional or unintentional, which are contrary to the prevailing laws or regulations. Such acts include transactions entered into by, or in the name of, the entity, or on its behalf, by those charged with governance, management or employees. (para 11)

6.4.2 Nature of non-compliance with laws and regulations

As we saw in Chapter 5, many laws and regulations (including the Companies Act 2006 and Accounting Standards) govern the form and content of companies' financial statements and certain other disclosures in their annual reports. Other laws and regulations, such as those governing entities' operations (including, for example, obtaining a licence to conduct business within an industry and health and safety regulations), may seem far removed from the financial statements. However, non-compliance with *any* laws and regulations that apply to an entity may result in adverse financial consequences, such as fines or litigation – consequences that impact on financial statements.

Clearly, a company's executives (i.e., managers) and directors (and not the auditor) are responsible for ensuring their company complies with all applicable laws and regulations, and that controls are in place to prevent non-compliance from occurring – or, if it does, to detect it in a timely manner. Nevertheless, auditors also have a role to play: they are responsible for ensuring their audits are conducted so as to obtain reasonable assurance that their auditees' financial statements are not materially misstated as a result of, *inter alia*, non-compliance with applicable laws and regulations. Notwithstanding

---

[26] It should be noted that ISA (UK and Ireland) 250 contains two sections:
- Section A – Consideration of Laws and Regulations in an Audit of Financial Statements;
- Section B – The Auditor's Right and Duty to Report to Regulators in the Financial Sector.

As it is outside the scope of this book to discuss auditing requirements that are specific to any particular sector, we do not refer to the provisions in Section B of ISA (UK and Ireland) 250.

[27] Unless indicated otherwise, all references to ISA 250 in this section refer to ISA 250: *consideration of laws and regulations in an audit of financial statements* (2004; Redrafted 2008).

this responsibility, as ISA 250 points out: "there is an unavoidable risk that some material misstatements in the financial statements may not be detected, even though the audit is properly planned and performed in accordance with the ISAs" (para 5). In the case of material misstatements resulting from non-compliance with laws and regulations (like those due to fraud), the risk of non-detection may be particularly high because, amongst other things:

- non-compliance may involve efforts to conceal it – for example, by collusion, forgery, deliberate failure to record transactions, management override of controls or intentionally giving erroneous responses to the auditor's enquiries;
- many laws and regulations relate principally to the operating aspects of the entity and, typically, are not captured by the accounting system or reflected in the financial statements.

6.4.3 Detection of non-compliance with laws and regulations

As for detecting fraud, key requirements of auditors in respect of detecting non-compliance with applicable laws and regulations include:

(i) maintaining an attitude of professional scepticism throughout the audit; and

(ii) being alert to the possibility that procedures performed at any time, and for any purpose, during the audit may indicate possible non-compliance with applicable laws and regulations.

In addition to these overarching requirements, auditors need to perform specific procedures directed towards detecting non-compliance with laws and regulations that apply to their auditees. As we will see in Chapter 7, one of the earliest, and possibly the most important, step in the audit process is gaining a thorough understanding of the client, its business, its industry, its key personnel, and so on. As an element of gaining this general understanding of the client, auditors need to obtain an understanding of:

(a) the legal and regulatory framework, and the industry or business sector, within which the client operates;

(b) how the entity complies with that framework, and with relevant industry or business sector requirements.

In order to gain this understanding, auditors may, amongst other things, make enquiries of management (and/or, if it has one, the auditee's in-house lawyer) about, for example:

- the laws and regulations likely to have a significant effect on the operations of the entity and its financial statements;
- the entity's policies and procedures which are designed:

- to ensure the entity, and entity personnel, comply with applicable laws and regulations, and
- to detect any non-compliance with applicable laws and regulations;
- the entity's policies and procedures for identifying, evaluating and accounting for litigation claims.

Auditors may need to be particularly alert to the possibility of non-compliance with laws and regulations that may have a fundamental effect on the operations of the business – non-compliance that may result in the entity having to cease its operations (such as failing to obtain a required licence to operate in the industry) or call into question its ability to continue as a going concern (for example, a breach of tax or environmental laws which is likely to result in crippling fines or other penalties).

Once auditors have gained a sound understanding of their auditees' general legal and regulatory environment, they are required by ISA 250 (paras 13, 14) to perform procedures in relation to two different sets of laws and regulations. These are as follows:

(i) For laws and regulations that are generally recognised by auditors as having a direct effect on material amounts and other disclosures in the financial statements (for example, income tax and pension laws and regulations), auditors are to obtain sufficient appropriate evidence so as to be reasonably assured about their auditees' compliance with these laws and regulations (i.e., auditors seek evidence of compliance).

(ii) For other laws and regulations that do not, in general, have a direct effect on the amounts and other disclosures in the financial statements, but compliance with which may be fundamental to auditees' ability to continue in business or avoid material penalties (for example, the terms of an operating licence or environmental requirements), auditors are to perform procedures designed to identify instances of non-compliance (i.e., auditors seek evidence of non-compliance).

To help them detect instances of non-compliance, auditors should, *inter alia*:
- enquire of management (and/or the directors) whether the entity is in compliance with all applicable laws and regulations; and
- inspect any correspondence between the entity and relevant regulatory authorities (ISA 250, para 14).

They may also be alerted to possible non-compliance with laws and regulations by signals such as:
- an investigation by regulatory authorities into the entity's affairs;
- payment of fines or penalties;

- payments for unspecified services or loans to consultants, related parties or employees;
- purchasing goods, services or assets at prices significantly above or below market price;
- payments for goods or services made to a country other than that from which the goods or services originated;
- the failure of an information system, deliberately or accidentally, which results in an inadequate audit trail or insufficient evidence;
- unauthorised or improperly recorded transactions.

Auditors are also required to request auditees' managements to provide written representations to the effect that all known actual, or possible, instances of non-compliance with laws and regulations, whose effects should be considered when the financial statements, have been disclosed to the auditor (ISA 250, para 16).[28]

Once possible non-compliance with laws and/or regulations has been detected, auditors need to obtain:

(i) an understanding of the nature of the non-compliance and the reasons why it has occurred; and

(ii) information to enable them to evaluate the possible effect of the non-compliance on the financial statements – in particular:
- the potential financial consequences of the non-compliance (for example, fines, penalties or litigation),
- whether they require disclosure in the financial statements, or
- whether they are so serious as to render the financial statements misleading (for example, where the consequences of the non-compliance threaten the ability of the auditee to continue as a going concern).

Armed with the necessary understanding and information about the detected or suspected non-compliance, the auditor should discuss the matter with the auditee's senior executives and/or its directors with a view to obtaining evidence that the entity is, in fact, in compliance with all applicable laws and regulations. If the executives, or directors, fail to provide such evidence, the auditor needs to consider:

---

[28] In the UK and Ireland, management's written representations should include, where applicable, the actual or contingent consequences which might arise from identified instances of non-compliance [ISA (UK and Ireland) 250, para 23-1].

(i) the effect of the lack of evidence on the audit opinion;[29] and

(ii) the implications for other aspects of the audit, including the auditor's risk assessment[30] and the reliability of written representations from management.

If the auditor considers the effect of the detected or suspected non-compliance is material to the financial statements, (s)he is required to assess the need to obtain legal advice concerning the possible non-compliance. ISA 250 explains:

> [T]he auditor may consider it appropriate whether to consult with the entity's in-house legal counsel or external legal counsel about the application of the laws and regulations to the circumstances, including the possibility of fraud, and the possible effects on the financial statements.... [Alternatively] the auditor may consider it appropriate to consult [his/her] own legal counsel as to whether a contravention of a law or regulation is involved, the possible legal consequences, including the possibility of fraud, and what further action, if any, the auditor should take. (para A16)

6.4.4   Reporting non-compliance with laws and regulations

Auditors' duty to report instances of detected or suspected non-compliance with laws and regulations parallels their duty to report detected or suspected fraud. If auditors believe that non-compliance with laws and/or regulations is material to, but not properly reflected in, the financial statements, they are required to express a qualified or adverse audit opinion.[31] Similarly, if auditors are prevented by an auditee, or by circumstances beyond the auditee's control, from obtaining sufficient appropriate evidence to establish whether or not non-compliance with applicable laws and/or regulations, which may be material to the financial statements, has occurred, they are required to reflect the position in their audit report. However, as for fraud, auditors' reporting duties in respect of non-compliance with laws and regulations goes beyond reporting to shareholders and other users of audited financial statements.

If auditors encounter or suspect non-compliance with laws and/or regulations, they should report the matter promptly to the next level of authority within the entity above that at which the non-compliance appears to have occurred. If they believe that executives are involved, the matter should be reported to the audit committee or full board of directors. Additionally, unless auditors have already discussed instances of non-compliance they have detected or suspect with the auditee's directors, they should communicate to the directors:

---

[29] Different types of audit opinion, and the circumstances in which each should be expressed, are discussed in Chapter 14.

[30] Auditors' risk assessment is discussed in Chapter 8, section 8.4.

[31] These forms of audit opinion are explained in Chapter 14.

(i) any significant matter(s) involving non-compliance with laws and regulations that have a material effect on the financial statements; and

(ii) any other (non-inconsequential) matter(s) involving non-compliance that have come to their attention.

If auditors believe the entity's directors are involved in the detected or suspected non-compliance with applicable laws and/or regulations, or they believe the directors will not act on their (the auditors') communication about non-compliance, they are required to consider the need to obtain legal advice (ISA 250, para 24).

In addition to their duty to report detected or suspected non-compliance with laws and regulations to shareholders and to the appropriate level of management, as for reporting fraud, notwithstanding their duty of confidentiality to their clients, auditors may have an obligation to report detected or suspected non-compliance with laws and/or regulations to an external party such as a regulatory authority. ISA 250 explains:

> The auditor's professional duty to maintain the confidentiality of client information may preclude reporting identified or suspected non-compliance with laws and regulations to a party outside the entity. However, ... in certain circumstances, the duty of confidentiality may be overridden by statute, the law or courts of law. (para A19)

In the UK and Ireland, a distinction is made between auditors reporting to an appropriate authority when they have a statutory duty to do so and when it is in the public interest to do so. A statutory duty "to report matters that are likely to be of material significance to the regulator" may arise, for example, in the audits of financial service entities, pension schemes and charities [ISA (UK and Ireland) 250, footnote 28]. In such cases, if auditors detect or suspect non-compliance with laws and regulations, subject to compliance with legislation on 'tipping off',[32] they are required to report the matter to the appropriate authority without undue delay.

Even if there is no statutory duty to report, auditors may encounter circumstances in which they consider detected or suspected non-compliance with laws and/or regulations should be reported to a proper authority[33] in the public

---

[32] ISA (UK and Ireland) 250, footnote 21, explains:
    In the UK, "tipping off" is an offence under section 333 of the Proceeds of Crime Act 2002. It arises when an individual discloses matters where:
    (a) There is knowledge or suspicion that a report has already been made, and
    (b) That disclosure is likely to prejudice any investigation which might be conducted following the report.

[33] In the UK, 'proper authorities' could include the Serious Fraud Office, the Crown Prosecution Service, the police, the Financial Services Authority, HM Revenue & Customs, the Department for Business, Enterprise & Regulatory Reform (formerly the Department of Trade and Industry) and the Health and Safety Executive [ISA (UK and Ireland) 250, footnote 29].

interest. When deciding whether or not disclosure is justified in the public interest, auditors should consider factors such as the following:

- the extent to which the suspected or actual non-compliance with laws or regulations is likely to affect members of the public;
- whether the entity's directors are taking effective corrective action or are likely to do so;
- the extent to which non-disclosure is likely to enable non-compliance with laws and/or regulations to recur with impunity;
- the gravity of the matter;
- whether there is a general ethos within the entity of disregarding laws and regulations.

Having decided that the detected or suspected non-compliance with laws and/or regulations justifies reporting to a proper authority in the public interest, unless the circumstances are such that the auditor has lost confidence in the integrity of the company's directors,[34] (s)he should first discuss the non-compliance with the audit committee and/or board of directors. If, after considering the audit committee's/directors' response, and any legal advice (s)he has obtained, the auditor concludes the matter should be reported to a proper authority in the public interest, (s)he should notify the directors in writing of this conclusion. If the directors do not voluntarily do so themselves, or are unable to provide evidence that the matter has been reported, the auditor should report it.

Auditors may be concerned that, by reporting to a party external to the entity, they may be liable for breaching their duty of confidentiality to the client, or for defamation. However, ISA (UK and Ireland) 250 explains that auditors are protected from the risk of exposure to such liability providing:

(i) the disclosure is made in the auditor's capacity as auditor of the entity;

(ii) it is made in the public interest to an appropriate authority; and

(iii) there is no malice motivating the disclosure.

ISA (UK and Ireland) 250 further explains:

> An auditor who can demonstrate having acted reasonably and in good faith in informing an authority of a breach of law or regulations which the auditor thinks has been committed would not be held by the court to be in breach of a duty to

---

[34] Such loss of confidence may occur, for example, where the auditor suspects, or has evidence of, the directors' involvement in possible non-compliance with laws or regulations which could have a material effect on the financial statements, or where the auditor knows the directors are aware of such non-compliance and, contrary to regulatory requirements or the public interest, have not reported the matter to a proper authority within a reasonable period.

the client even if, an investigation or prosecution having occurred, it was found that there had been no offence. (para 38-10)

6.4.5 Documentation of non-compliance with laws and regulations

As for all other aspects of an audit, auditors are required to document fully matters relating to an auditee's actual or suspected non-compliance with applicable laws and regulations. Such documentation includes detailing the instances of non-compliance detected or suspected, audit procedures performed to confirm compliance or non-compliance, copies of relevant records or documents, minutes of meetings held with executives, the board of directors (and/or audit committee) and, in applicable cases, parties external to the entity, and the results of such meetings.

6.5 AUDITORS' DUTY OF CONFIDENTIALITY TO CLIENTS

During the course of an audit, members of the audit team become very knowledgeable about the client's business, its operations, and its financial affairs, and it is imperative that they respect the confidential nature of this knowledge – that is, adhere to their duty of confidentiality to their clients. IFAC, in its *Code of Ethics for Professional Accountants* (2006), section 140: *Confidentiality*,[35] explains this duty in the following terms:

> The principle of confidentiality imposes an obligation on professional accountants [including auditors] to refrain from:
> (a) Disclosing outside the firm or employing organization confidential information acquired as a result of professional and business relationships without proper and specific authority or unless there is a legal or professional right or duty to disclose; and
> (b) Using confidential information acquired as a result of professional and business relationships to their personal advantage or the advantage of third parties.
> A professional accountant ... should be alert to the possibility of inadvertent disclosure, particularly in circumstances involving long association with a business associate or a close or immediate family member. (paras 140.1–140.2)

Although this duty of confidentiality is paramount, as we have noted earlier in this chapter, there are circumstances in which auditors may (or are required to) override the duty and disclose information which would otherwise remain confidential. Such circumstances include those where the auditor has:

---

[35] The Codes of Ethics of each of the professional bodies in the UK and Ireland are based on IFAC's *Code of Ethics for Professional Accountants* (2006). The section on Confidentiality in each of the UK and Ireland professional bodies' Codes is very similar to that in the IFAC Code.

- the client's consent to disclose information;
- a legal duty to disclose information, for example, to enable documents to be located or to give evidence in legal proceedings;
- a legal duty to disclose information to appropriate authorities, for example, to regulators such as the Financial Services Authority and, in appropriate cases, issuing a 'statement of circumstances'[36] when the auditor ceases to hold office;
- a professional duty to disclose information in compliance with, for example:
  - ethical requirements (for example, disclosing information to a successor auditor),
  - auditing standards [for example, reporting when it is in the public interest to do so under ISA (UK and Ireland) 240 and ISA (UK and Ireland) 250],
  - quality review (or inspection) requirements of a professional accounting or regulatory body,
  - in response to an enquiry from a professional accounting or regulatory body.

In order to ensure that auditors adhere to their duty of confidentiality to the extent possible, and do not disclose information when it is inappropriate to do so, IFAC's *Code of Ethics* (para 140.8) requires auditors, before disclosing otherwise confidential information, to consider three factors, namely:
  (i)   whether the interests of all parties, including third parties whose interests may be affected, could be harmed if the client consents to the auditor disclosing the information;
  (ii) whether all the relevant information is known and substantiated, to the extent it is practicable; if this is not the case, the auditor should use professional judgment to determine the disclosure to be made, if any;
  (iii) the type of communication expected, and to whom it should be addressed; auditors should be satisfied that the communication is addressed to the appropriate recipient(s).

Prior to 1990, when the Auditing Practices Committee (predecessor of the APB) issued an Auditing Guideline: *The auditor's responsibility in relation to fraud, other irregularities and errors*[37] the circumstances in which auditors could go beyond their duty of confidentiality and disclose matters of concern to parties outside the auditee were extremely limited. In essence, they could only disclose otherwise confidential information when:

---

[36] 'Statements of circumstances' are explained in Chapter 5, section 5.2.5.

[37] As noted in the following paragraph, the APB carried forward the relevant provisions from the Guideline into SAS 110: *Fraud and error* and SAS 120: *Consideration of law and regulations* and, subsequently, into ISA (UK and Ireland) 240 and ISA (UK and Ireland) 250.

- they had their client's permission to do so;
- in response to a subpoena (summons from a court of law).

However, during the 1980s, as increasing numbers of cases of corporate fraud and other illegal acts by company directors or senior executives came to light – primarily during investigations of significant companies which collapsed unexpectedly – politicians, the courts, financial journalists and the public questioned why the auditors had not discovered such acts and reported them to an appropriate authority. In response, the auditing profession pointed out that, in the absence of a legal requirement to do so, auditors' duty of confidentiality to their clients precluded them from reporting matters of concern discovered during an audit to third parties – including authorities such as the Serious Fraud Office, the police, or the Department of Trade and Industry.[38]

It was largely in response to public and political pressure that the APB included provisions in SAS 110: *Fraud and error* and SAS 120: *Consideration of law and regulations* and, subsequently, in their replacements, ISA (UK and Ireland) 240 and ISA (UK and Ireland) 250, whereby auditors are required to override their duty of confidentiality and to report, *inter alia*, suspected or actual instances of fraud or non-compliance with other applicable laws and regulations discovered during an audit to a proper authority when they have a statutory duty, or it is in the public interest, to do so.

Clearly, today, the application of auditors' duty of confidentiality is a far cry from that pertaining in the 1980s, and it seems to be better aligned to society's expectations of auditors. In brief, in the absence of particular circumstances, auditors are required to adhere to their duty of confidentiality but when a statutory or regulatory duty exists, or it is in the public interest to do so, they are required to subordinate this duty and disclose matters of concern to an appropriate authority. This position is reflected in the second portion of the fundamental principle of external auditing – *Integrity*:

> Confidential information obtained in the course of an audit is disclosed only when required in the public interest, or by operation of law. (Auditing Practices Board, 2008, Appendix 2)

6.6 SUMMARY

In this chapter we have examined auditors' responsibilities in relation to corporate fraud and auditees' non-compliance with laws and/or regulations. We have noted that auditors today acknowledge significantly greater responsibility to detect fraud than they did 40 years ago, and that the requirements

---

[38] In 2007, this Department was replaced by the Department of Business, Enterprise & Regulatory Reform.

of auditors in this regard are now very exacting. We have also observed that auditors' responsibilities in respect of auditees' non-compliance with laws and regulations depend on whether the laws and regulations:

- have a direct effect on the financial statements – for these laws and regulations auditors seek evidence of auditees' compliance; or
- are related to auditees' operations but non-compliance may have consequences which impact on the financial statements – for these laws and regulations auditors seek evidence of auditees' non-compliance.

If auditors detect or suspect fraud or non-compliance with applicable laws and/or regulations, they are required to report it to an appropriate level of management within the entity. Further, if the fraud or non-compliance with laws and/or regulations is material to the financial statements, and is not properly dealt with in those financial statements, auditors are required to reflect this in their report to the company's shareholders. Additionally, when auditors have a statutory duty, or it is in the public interest to do so, they are required to report the detected or suspected fraud, or non-compliance with laws and/or regulations, to an appropriate authority.

In the concluding section of the chapter, we have highlighted the confidential nature of knowledge gained by audit team members and the importance of audit staff respecting their duty of confidentiality to the client. However, we have also observed that, corresponding with the reporting duty noted above, auditors may have an overriding duty to report to third parties (such as regulatory authorities) when there is a statutory duty to so report or when it is in the public interest to do so.

SELF-REVIEW QUESTIONS

6.1 Distinguish briefly between two types of corporate fraud that are particularly relevant to auditors.

6.2 The importance of detecting fraud as an audit objective has changed markedly over the period from 1844 to the present time. State the significance of fraud detection as an audit objective in each of the following periods:
   (i)   1844–1920s,
   (ii) 1920s–1960s,
   (iii) 1960s–1990s,
   (iv) 1990s–present.
List reasons to explain the change in the importance of fraud detection as an audit objective during each of these periods.

6.3 Describe briefly the changes to auditors' responsibilities in respect of detecting fraud introduced in ISA 240: *The auditor's responsibilities relating to fraud in an audit of financial statements* (2004, Redrafted 2006).

6.4 Explain the factors that constitute 'the fraud triangle'.

6.5 Explain what is meant by 'a fraud risk factor' and the role of such factors in auditors' detection of fraud.

6.6 Explain briefly why a company's non-compliance with laws and regulations that govern the entity's operations (and seem far removed from the financial statements) are of concern to the company's auditor.

6.7 Describe briefly the procedures auditors may perform to detect non-compliance with laws and regulations.

6.8 Outline auditors' responsibility to report detected or suspected instances of non-compliance with laws and/or regulations to:
   (i) shareholders,
   (ii) the auditee's directors,
   (iii) parties external to the auditee.

6.9 Explain the meaning of the phrase 'auditors' duty of confidentiality to their clients'.

6.10 Describe briefly the circumstances in which auditors' duty of confidentiality to their clients should be overridden and matters of concern encountered during the audit reported to an appropriate authority.

REFERENCES

American Institute of Certified Public Accountants (AICPA). (1951). *Codification of Statements on Auditing Procedure*. New York: AICPA.

American Institute of Certified Public Accountants (AICPA). (1988). Statement on Auditing Standards (SAS) no. 53, *The Auditor's Responsibility to Detect and Report Errors and Irregularities*. New York: AICPA.

American Institute of Certified Public Accountants (AICPA). (1997). Statement on Auditing Standards (SAS) no. 82: *Consideration of Fraud in a Financial Statement Audit*. New York: AICPA.

American Institute of Certified Public Accountants (AICPA). (2002). Statement on Auditing Standards (SAS) no. 99: *Consideration of Fraud in a Financial Statement Audit*. New York: AICPA.

Auditing Practices Board (APB). (1995). Statement of Auditing Standards (SAS) 110: *Fraud and Error*. London: APB.

Auditing Practices Board (APB). (1998). *Fraud and Audit: Choices for Society*. Consultation Paper. London: APB.

Auditing Practices Board (APB). (2001). *Aggressive Earnings Management*. Consultation Paper. London: APB.

Auditing Practices Board (APB). (2008). *The Auditing Practices Board – Scope and Authority of Pronouncements*. London: Financial Reporting Council.

Carty, J. (1985, September). Fraud and other irregularities. *Certified Accountant*, p. 30.

Commission on Auditors' Responsibilities (CAR). (1978). *Report, Conclusions and Recommendations* (The Cohen Commission). New York: AICPA.

Ernst and Young. (2000). *Fraud The Unmanaged Risk: An International Survey of the Effect of Fraud on Business*. London: Ernst and Young.

International Auditing and Assurance Standards Board (IAASB). (2007). *Glossary of Terms*. New York: IFAC.

International Federation of Accountants (IFAC). (2001). *International Standard on Auditing (ISA) 240: Fraud and Error*. New York: IFAC.

KPMG. (1997, 28 April). *Fraud still costs the UK dear, despite lowest figures for seven years*. News Release.

KPMG. (2001, 12 February). *Fraud case values decreased by two thirds during 2000, says KPMG's Fraud Barometer*. News Release.

KPMG. (2006, 30 January). *Massive surge in fraud in 2005*, www.kpmg.co.uk/news/detail.

Porter, B.A. (1997). Auditors' responsibilities with respect to corporate fraud: A controversial issue. In Sherer, M., & Turley, S. (eds), *Current Issues in Auditing* (3rd edn.). Chapter 2. London: Paul Chapman Publishing.

Ramos, M. (2003, January). Auditors' responsibility for fraud detection. *Journal of Accountancy*. Online Issues, pp. 1–11.

Smith, T. (1985, 22 August). Expectation gap trips up frauds fight's 'front line'. *Accountancy Age*, p. 10.

Turner, L.E. (1999, 7 October). *Remarks to the Panel on Audit Effectiveness*, New York.

Turner, L.E. (2000, 10 July). *Remarks to the Panel on Audit Effectiveness*, New York.

Walker, R.H. (1999a, 7 December). *Behind the Numbers of the SEC's Recent Financial Fraud Cases*. Speech, 27th National AICPA Conference on Current SEC Developments.

Walker, R.H. (1999b, 9 October). *Remarks to the Panel on Audit Effectiveness*, New York.

Woolf, E. (1978). Profession in peril – Time running out for auditors. *Accountancy* **89**(1014), 58–65.

Yirrell, S. (2007, 30 January). Fraud explodes in 2006, *Accountancy Age*, www. accountancyage.com/2173741.

ADDITIONAL READING

BDO Stoy Hayward. (2007). *BDO Fraud Track research shows that crime does pay if you are a fraudster*, www.bdo.co.uk/80265D750056C45B.

Carlello, J.V., and Nagy, A.L. (2004). Audit firm tenure and fraudulent financial reporting. *Auditing: A Journal of Practice & Theory* **23**(2), 55–69.

Carpenter, T.D. (2007) Audit team brainstorming, fraud risk identification, and fraud risk assessment: Implications of SAS No. 99. *The Accounting Review* **82**(5), 1119–1141.

Collier, J. (2004). *Aggressive Earnings Management – Is it still a significant threat?* London: Institute of Chartered Accountants in England and Wales (ICAEW).

Cullinan, C., and Sutton, S.G. (2002). Defrauding the public interest: a critical examination of reengineered audit processes and the likelihood of detecting fraud. *Critical Perspectives on Accounting* **13**(3), 297–310.

Fédération des Experts Comptables Européens (FEE). (2005). *Good Practice in Tackling Fraud*. Brussels: FEE.

Fraser, I.A.M., and Lin, K.Z. (2004). Auditors' perceptions of responsibilities to detect and report client illegal acts in Canada and the UK: A comparative experiment. *International Journal of Auditing* **8**(2), 165–184.

Gillett, P.R., and Uddin, N. (2005). CFO intentions of fraudulent financial reporting. *Auditing: A Journal of Practice & Theory* **24**(1), 55–75.

Institute of Chartered Accountants in England and Wales (ICAEW, Audit and Assurance Faculty). (2003). *Fraud: Meeting the Challenge through External Audit*. London: ICAEW.

Institute of Chartered Accountants in England and Wales (ICAEW, Audit and Assurance Faculty). (2004). *Aggressive Earnings Management. Is it still a significant threat?* London: ICAEW.

Mock, T.J., and Turner, J.L. (2005). Auditor identification of fraud risk factors and their impact on audit programs. *International Journal of Auditing* **9**(1), 59–77.

Shelton, S.W., Whittington, O.R., and Landsitter, D. (2001). Auditing firms' fraud risk assessment practises. *Accounting Horizons* **15**(1), 19–33.

7 Overview of the Audit Process, Audit Evidence, Staffing and Documenting an Audit

LEARNING OBJECTIVES

After studying the material in this chapter you should be able to:
- outline the steps in the audit process from 'Appointment' to 'Reporting';
- list and describe audit procedures which are used to gather evidence;
- discuss the different sources of audit evidence;
- explain the factors which should be considered when deciding which audit evidence to seek;
- discuss the requirements with respect to auditors' capabilities and competence;
- explain the importance of auditors directing, supervising and reviewing the work of audit staff;
- explain auditors' responsibilities when part of an audit is performed by experts or 'component auditors';
- discuss the purpose and importance of audit working papers;
- explain the importance of working paper review;
- describe auditors' responsibilities with respect to assembling and retaining the final audit file.

The following publications are particularly relevant to this chapter:
- International Standard on Quality Control (ISQC) 1 (Redrafted): *Quality Control for Firms that Perform Audits and Reviews of Financial Statements, and Other Assurance and Related Services Engagements* (IFAC, June 2008)**[1]
- International Standard on Auditing (ISA) 200 (Redrafted): *Overall Objectives of the Independent Auditor and the Conduct of an Audit in Accordance with International Standards on Auditing* (IFAC, June 2008)**
- International Standard on Auditing (ISA) 220 (Redrafted): *Quality Control for an Audit of Financial Statements* (IFAC, June 2008)**
- International Standard on Auditing (ISA) 230 (Redrafted): *Audit Documentation* (IFAC, 2007)
- International Standard on Auditing (ISA) 500 (Redrafted): *Audit Evidence* (IFAC, June 2008)**
- International Standard on Auditing (ISA) 600 (Redrafted): *Special Considerations – Audits of Group Financial Statements (Including the Work of Component Auditors)* (IFAC, 2007)
- International Standard on Auditing (ISA) 620 (Redrafted): *Using the Work of an Auditor's Expert* (IFAC, June 2008)**

---

[1] The status of the ISAs referred to in this chapter is explained in the Important Note following the Preface to this book.

7.1 INTRODUCTION

In Chapter 5 we observed that the primary responsibility of auditors in the United Kingdom (UK) is to form and express an opinion on whether or not their audit clients' financial statements provide a true and fair view of their entity's financial position and performance, and are properly prepared in accordance with International Accounting Standards (IASs) or UK Generally Accepted Accounting Practice (GAAP).[2] In order to form this opinion, auditors must gather and evaluate sufficient appropriate audit evidence – evidence which is collected through the audit process. Although the audit process is very similar in all audits, audit clients differ markedly in size, nature and complexity. In order to ensure that audits are conducted effectively and efficiently they must be carefully planned and controlled. This involves, *inter alia*, ensuring they are properly staffed and documented.[3]

In the next seven chapters of this book we describe and discuss the various stages of the audit process. In this chapter we 'set the scene' by providing a general overview of the process and discussing important administrative aspects of an audit. In particular, we examine the capabilities and competence auditors need to possess, the importance of engagement partners (and other senior members of the audit team) directing, supervising and reviewing work delegated to audit staff, and engagement partners' responsibilities when part of an audit is performed by experts or other auditors. Before concluding the chapter we consider the importance, purpose, content and preparation of audit working papers and discuss the process of (i) working paper review and (ii) assembling the final audit file.

7.2 OVERVIEW OF THE AUDIT PROCESS

As may be seen from Figure 7.1, the audit process comprises a series of logical, well-defined steps; each step has a specific objective or purpose and is performed using appropriate audit procedures. However, the steps are not as distinct as Figure 7.1 might imply: instead, each complements the others as auditors gradually accumulate evidence to enable them to form an opinion about, *inter alia*, the truth and fairness of their auditees' financial statements. In order to illustrate the relationship between the audit steps, their objectives and the procedures used to achieve those objectives, we will refer to step 4 of the

---

[2] See Chapter 5, section 5.2.6.

[3] As noted in Chapter 3, an important aspect of ensuring that audits are conducted effectively and efficiently is the implementation and operation of proper quality control policies and procedures. This issue is discussed further in Chapter 16.

Figure 7.1: Summary of the audit process

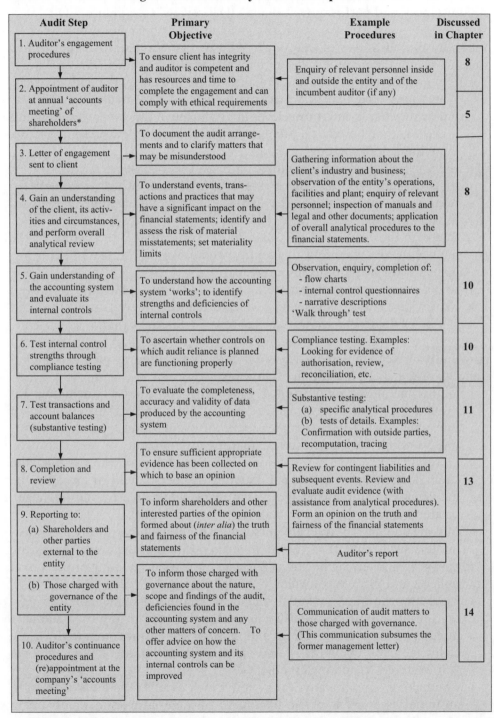

audit process, that is: 'Gain an understanding of the client, its activities and its circumstances, and perform overall analytical review' (see Figure 7.1).

What are the objectives of this step?. Why is it performed?. It is performed so as to ensure the auditor gains an understanding:

   (i)   of events, transactions and practices of (or affecting) the auditee which may have a significant impact on its financial statements; and

   (ii) how the events and transactions are reflected in the financial statements and whether, based on a preliminary analysis of the financial statements, anything 'looks wrong'.

The auditor needs this understanding, amongst other reasons:

- to ascertain whether there are circumstances which increase (or reduce) the likelihood of the financial statements containing material misstatements;
- to assess the likelihood that material misstatements are present in the financial statements and to identify where, within the statements, they appear most likely to have occurred;
- to determine appropriate materiality levels for the audit; and
- to provide a background against which evidence gathered during the audit can be evaluated to see if it 'makes sense' and 'looks right'.

How is this objective achieved?. Audit procedures used to gain this understanding of the client include the following:

- Gathering information from a wide range of sources (including, for example, the Internet, relevant trade magazines, and making enquiries of relevant knowledgeable people) about the client's industry and its operating, economic, legislative and regulatory environment.
- Observing the client's operations, facilities and plant; i.e., visiting the client, touring the premises and meeting key personnel (for example, the managing director, financial director, marketing manager, sales manager, production manager, and human resources manager).
- Making enquiries of relevant personnel; i.e., discussing with key personnel matters such as the trading and financial position of the entity during the past year, and any significant changes in business, accounting or personnel policies and procedures which occurred during the year.
- Inspecting the entity's manuals and legal and other documents; i.e., reviewing the organisation's legal documents, policy and procedures manuals, minutes of directors' meetings and those of significant committees (especially the audit committee), and any important commercial agreements (for example, franchise agreements).
- Conducting overall analytical review which enables the auditor to form an initial assessment of the likelihood of material misstatements being present in the financial statements.

This audit step is supported, in particular, by audit step 5, that is, 'gaining an understanding of the accounting system and its internal controls' – the audit step that is focused on gaining a thorough understanding of the auditee's financial reporting process. Audit step 5 helps the auditor gain an in-depth understanding of the client; at the same time, audit step 4 (gaining an understanding of the client and overall analytical review) assists the auditor accomplish audit step 5. The steps are complementary and mutually supportive. As auditors proceed through the audit process, they seek confirmatory – or contradictory – evidence that supports – or brings into question – the opinion they are gradually forming about their auditee's financial statements (and other matters on which they are required to express an opinion: see Chapter 5, section 5.2.6.).

It should be noted that the summary of the audit process presented in Figure 7.1 is designed to give a general overview of the process. It is intended to provide a contextual setting for the detailed discussion of the individual steps in the process which are the subject of Chapters 8 to 14 of this book. The chapter in which each audit step is discussed is indicated in the extreme right column of Figure 7.1. However, before moving on to discuss the collection of audit evidence, we need to clarify the meaning of some troublesome jargon.

7.3 CLARIFICATION OF SOME JARGON

Considerable confusion appears to exist in relation to the terms 'audit objectives' and 'audit procedures'. This seems to stem from three main causes, namely:
  (i)   failure to distinguish between audit objectives and audit procedures;
  (ii) use of different terms to mean the same thing;
  (iii) use of the single term 'audit objective' when separate levels of objectives exist.

(i)   *Failure to distinguish between audit objectives and audit procedures*: The term 'compliance tests' or 'compliance procedures' provides an example of this cause of misunderstanding. The term refers to audit procedures which are used to meet the objective of ascertaining whether audit client personnel have complied with identified internal controls. The audit procedures adopted (such as enquiry) are not restricted to compliance testing: they are also used to meet other audit objectives. Thus the term 'compliance testing' does not denote a particular set of audit procedures; rather, it indicates the objective or purpose for which the procedures are employed.

(ii) *Use of different terms to mean the same thing*: This cause of confusion may be illustrated by reference to the use of the terms 'audit procedures', 'audit tests' and 'audit techniques', to convey essentially the same meaning, that is, methods used to gather audit evidence. Indeed, the terms are frequently used interchangeably.

(iii) Use of the single term 'audit objective' when separate levels of objectives exist: Notwithstanding use of the term 'audit objective', as shown in Figure 7.2, three distinct levels of audit objectives may be distinguished: the overall audit objective, general audit objectives and specific audit objectives.

Figure 7.2: Hierarchy of audit objectives

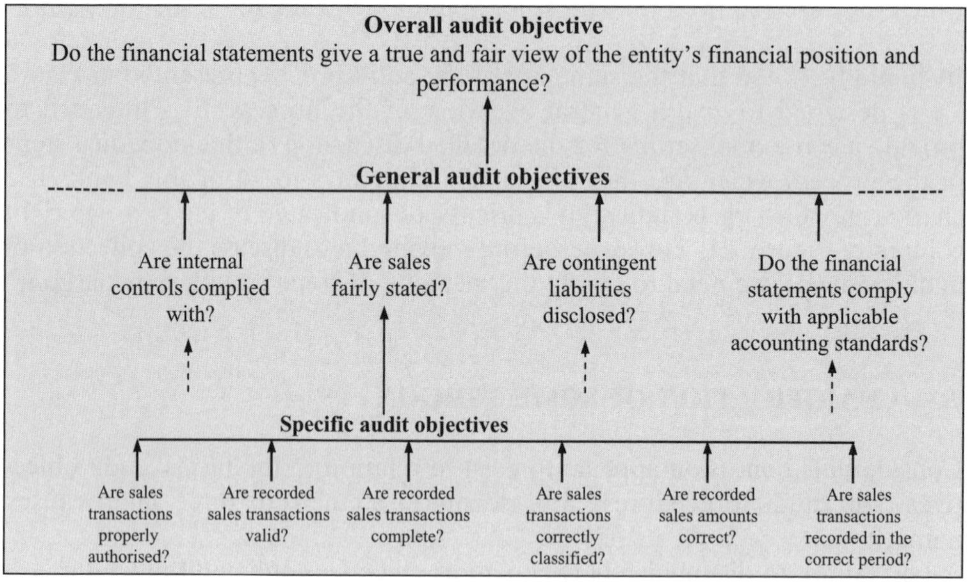

An audit objective is the object of the auditor's investigation: it is what the auditor is trying to find out and the purpose for which audit procedures are performed. It is often helpful to express an audit objective in the form of a question. From Figure 7.2 it can be seen that at the highest level is the overall audit objective. This is reflected in the question: Do the financial statements give a true and fair view of the entity's state of affairs and its profit or loss?

In order to answer this question, and thus accomplish the overall audit objective, further, more detailed, questions need to be asked. For example, do the financial statements comply with accounting standards? Have the entity's internal controls operated effectively throughout the reporting period? Is the amount shown in the financial statements for, say, sales or trade debtors fairly stated? Questions of this general nature reflect general audit objectives.

To accomplish these general objectives, even more specific questions need to be asked. These are expressions of the specific audit objectives (or assertions).[4] For example, to accomplish the general objective of ascertaining whether sales are fairly stated in the financial statements, the auditor needs to determine whether:

- sales transactions have been properly authorised;
- recorded sales transactions are valid;
- all valid sales transactions have been recorded;
- sales transactions have been correctly classified;
- sales transactions have been recorded at their correct amount;
- sales transactions have been recorded in their proper accounting period.

Each of these factors constitutes a specific audit objective or assertion.

7.4 AUDIT EVIDENCE

7.4.1 General requirement

As auditors proceed through the audit process, they accumulate audit evidence to meet specific audit objectives and thereby form conclusions about the related general audit objectives. Eventually, they will have sufficient appropriate audit evidence to support their opinion as to whether or not the financial statements:

- provide a true and fair view of the entity's financial position and performance; and
- comply with the applicable financial reporting framework (i.e., IAS or UK GAAP).

The importance of auditors accumulating sufficient appropriate audit evidence is explained in International Standard on Auditing (ISA) 200: *Overall objectives of the independent auditor and the conduct of an audit in accordance with international standards on auditing*. It states that an overall objective of the auditor is:

> [t]o obtain reasonable assurance about whether the financial statements as a whole are free from material misstatement ... Reasonable assurance ... is obtained when the auditor has obtained sufficient appropriate audit evidence to reduce audit risk (i.e., the risk that the auditor expresses an inappropriate opinion when the financial statements are materially misstated) to an acceptably low level. (paras 5, 11)

In Chapter 3 (section 3.4.1) we noted that 'sufficiency' refers to the quantity of evidence, and 'appropriateness' refers to its relevance and reliability.

---

[4] In its *Glossary of terms*, the IAASB (2007) defines 'assertions' to mean: "Representations by management, explicit or otherwise, that are embodied in the financial statements". We discuss financial statement assertions in Chapter 11.

7.4.2 Audit procedures

Audit procedures are the methods used to gather audit evidence. As we observed in section 7.3, the terms 'audit tests' and 'audit techniques' are frequently used in place of, or interchangeably with, 'audit procedures'.

ISA 500: *Audit evidence* identifies seven audit procedures and explains them as follows:

Inspection
  Inspection involves examining records or documents, whether internal or external, in paper form, electronic form, or other media, or a physical examination of an asset. Inspection of records and documents provides audit evidence of varying degrees of reliability, depending on their nature and source and, in the case of internal records and documents, on the effectiveness of the controls over their production. An example of inspection used as a test of controls is inspection of records for evidence of authorization. (para A14)

  Some documents represent direct evidence of the existence of an asset, for example, a document constituting a financial instrument such as a stock [i.e., shares] or bond. Inspection of such documents may not necessarily provide audit evidence about ownership or value. (para A15)

  Inspection of tangible assets may provide reliable audit evidence with respect to their existence, but not necessarily about the entity's rights and obligations or the valuation of the assets. Inspection of individual inventory [i.e., stock] items may accompany the observation of inventory counting. (para A16)

Observation
  Observation consists of looking at a process or procedure being performed by others, for example, the auditor's observation of inventory counting by the entity's personnel, or of the performance of control activities. Observation provides audit evidence about the performance of a process or procedure, but is limited to the point in time at which the observation takes place, and by the fact that the act of being observed may affect how the process or procedure is performed. (para A17)

External Confirmation
  An external confirmation represents audit evidence obtained by the auditor as a direct written response to the auditor from a third party (the confirming party), in paper form, or by electronic or other medium. External confirmation procedures frequently are used in relation to account balances and their constituent parts. For example, the auditor may seek direct confirmation of receivables [debtors] by communication with debtors. However, external confirmations need not be restricted to these items. For example, the auditor may request confirmation of the terms of agreements or transactions an entity has with third parties; the confirmation request is designed to ask if any modifications have been made to the agreement and, if so, what the relevant details are. External confirmation procedures are also used to obtain audit evidence

about the absence of certain conditions, for example, the absence of a "side agreement"[5] that may influence revenue recognition. (para A18)

Recalculation

Recalculation consists of checking the mathematical accuracy of documents or records. Recalculation can be performed manually or electronically. (para A19)

Reperformance

Reperformance involves the auditor's independent execution of procedures or controls that were originally performed as part of the entity's internal control. (para A20)

Analytical procedures

Analytical procedures consist of evaluations of financial information made by a study of plausible relationships among both financial and non-financial data. Analytical procedures also encompass the investigation of identified fluctuations and relationships that are inconsistent with other relevant information or deviate significantly from predicted amounts. (para A21)

Inquiry

Inquiry consists of seeking information of knowledgeable persons, both financial and non-financial, within the entity or outside the entity. Inquiry is used extensively throughout the audit in addition to other audit procedures. Inquiries may range from formal written inquiries to informal oral inquiries. Evaluating responses to inquiries is an integral part of the inquiry process. (para A22)

Responses to inquiries may provide the auditor with information not previously possessed or with corroborative audit evidence. Alternatively, responses might provide information that differs significantly from other information that the auditor has obtained, for example, information regarding the possibility of management override of controls. In some cases, responses to inquiries provide a basis for the auditor to modify or perform additional audit procedures. (para A23)

7.4.3 Further clarification of the jargon

Those first encountering auditing jargon frequently find the distinction and relationship between (a) compliance and substantive procedures and (b) tests of details, tests of transactions and tests of balances far from clear. The relationship between these terms and some specific audit procedures, is depicted in Figure 7.3.

(a) Compliance vs substantive procedures

In order to form an opinion, *inter alia*, on whether or not the auditee's financial statements give a true and fair view of its financial position and performance,

---

[5] A 'side agreement' is an agreement between the audited entity and a customer which enables the entity to inflate revenue. For example, the entity may enter into a side agreement with a customer whereby a significant item is 'sold' to the customer but the entity agrees to repurchase it (at a profit to the 'customer') if the customer is unable to sell the item within a specified period.

Figure 7.3: Relationship between compliance and substantive procedures, tests of details, tests of transactions and tests of balances

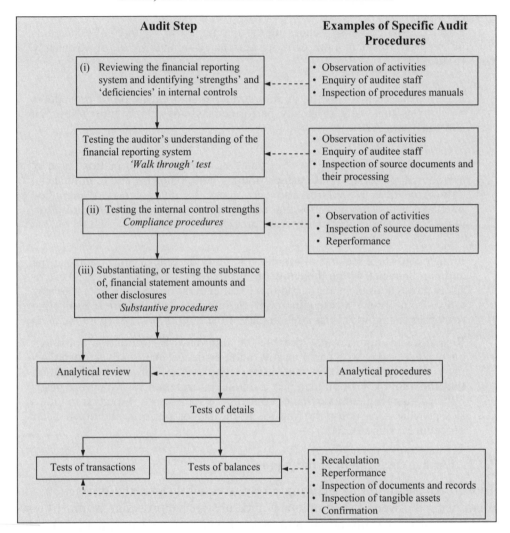

and comply with the applicable financial reporting framework, the auditor needs to establish, amongst other things, whether each financial statement amount and disclosure is fairly stated (i.e., not materially misstated).

Auditors can reduce their work in determining whether the financial statement amounts and disclosures are fairly stated if they can assure themselves that the auditee's financial reporting system incorporates effective controls which can be relied upon to prevent or detect errors and irregularities in the accounting data. If such controls are in place and working effectively, the auditor can feel reasonably assured that the accounting data passing through the system and presented in the financial statements is reliable and does not contain material misstatements.

Thus, an audit includes the following three distinct steps:

(i) *A review of the financial reporting system* [see Figure 7.3(i)]: This review is undertaken for two main purposes, namely:
- to enable the auditor to understand how the financial reporting system captures and processes the accounting data, and how it converts the data into the information which is presented in the entity's financial statements;
- to identify the system's 'strengths' and 'deficiencies', that is, internal controls which, if operating properly, can be relied upon to prevent or detect errors and irregularities in the accounting data (strengths), and internal controls which are needed, but which are absent or ineffective (deficiencies).

In order to ensure the auditor has a proper understanding of the financial reporting system and its controls, a 'walk through' test is conducted. This test consists of following a small number of transactions through the entire financial reporting system – from their initial recording on source documents to their final inclusion in the financial statements.

(ii) *Testing internal control 'strengths'* [see Figure 7.3(ii)]: As noted above, during the initial review of the financial reporting system, the auditor identifies internal control 'strengths'. These controls, if operating properly, will help to ensure that the data which pass through the system are complete, valid, and accurate as to amount, account classification and reporting period. However, before the auditor can rely on these controls to protect the integrity of the accounting data, they must be tested to establish that they are, in fact, operating effectively and that they have been so operating throughout the reporting period. Such tests are referred to as compliance procedures (or tests of control): they are tests or procedures which are performed in order to ascertain whether the controls on which the auditor plans to rely to prevent or, failing this, to detect errors or irregularities in the accounting data have been complied with by personnel within the reporting entity.[6]

(iii) *Testing the financial statement amounts and other disclosures* [see Figure 7.3(iii)]: The auditor is required to form and express an opinion on the truth and fairness of the financial statements rather than on the entity's internal controls. Further, as we will see in Chapter 10 (section 10.3.6), all systems of internal control have inherent limitations, including, for example, the possibility of human error and the ability of management to

---

[6] Compliance procedures are discussed in detail in Chapter 10, section 10.6.

override the controls. Therefore, compliance procedures will never constitute sufficient appropriate audit evidence on their own and, irrespective of how effective an entity's internal controls may appear to be, tests must always be performed to substantiate, or to test the substance of, the information presented in the financial statements. Such tests are referred to as substantive procedures.[7]

(b) Tests of detail, tests of transactions and tests of balances

Substantive procedures fall into two broad categories:
(i) analytical procedures;
(ii) tests of details.

(i) *Analytical procedures*: As indicated in section 7.4.2 above, analytical procedures analyse meaningful relationships between accounting data, and between financial and non-financial data.[8] As a substantive procedure, they are primarily used to establish the reasonableness of financial statement amounts. For example, the relationship between average debt and average interest rates may provide an estimate of an entity's interest expense. If, based on this estimate, the interest expense looks 'reasonable' (i.e., not materially misstated), this may be the extent of the audit tests conducted to substantiate this balance. If, however, there is a marked discrepancy between the estimated amount and the amount shown in the entity's draft financial statements, this discrepancy will need to be investigated. For other account balances, such as debtors or inventory (stock), analytical procedures may be used to establish whether or not the balance looks 'reasonable' or materially misstated. The results of the analytical procedures are likely to affect the nature, timing and extent of other audit procedures used to substantiate these balances.

(ii) *Tests of details*: Two subsets of tests of details may be distinguished, namely, tests of transactions and tests of balances.

- *Tests of transactions* are audit tests or procedures which are applied to transactions or, more correctly, to the source documents which provide evidence of the transactions. Transaction testing is normally used to substantiate revenue and expense account balances in the profit and loss

---

[7] Substantive procedures are discussed in detail in Chapter 11.

[8] Analytical procedures are used at three stages of the audit:
    (i)   to assess the likelihood of material misstatement in the financial statements during the initial stages of the audit;
    (ii) as a substantive procedure;
    (iii) during the 'completion and review' stage.
These different uses of analytical procedures are discussed in Chapters 9, 11 and 13, respectively.

account (income statement); however, it may also be used to substantiate (indirectly) balance sheet account balances. This is because, if the opening balance of a particular balance sheet account is correct (substantiated by the previous year's audit) and all of the transactions affecting that account during the reporting period are complete, accurate as to amount, account classification and reporting period and valid, then logically the balance shown in the closing balance sheet must also be correct.

- *Tests of balances* are audit tests or procedures which, rather than testing the transactions which constitute particular financial statement balances, directly test the completeness, accuracy and validity of the balances themselves. Such tests of balances are frequently used to substantiate balance sheet account balances. An example is debtors' confirmation, where the auditor writes to an entity's debtors requesting them to confirm their outstanding account balance with the audit client.[9]

In relation to tests of transactions, it is important to note that source documents used to substantiate the completeness, accuracy and validity of transactions may also be used for compliance tests. For example, a customer order and a despatch note may be used to substantiate the validity of a sale (a substantive test). The same source documents might also be examined for evidence indicating that an internal control, designed to ensure that despatches are only made against customer orders, has been complied with (that is, for compliance testing).

7.4.4 Different sources and types of audit evidence

It was noted in Chapter 3 that auditors generally examine only part of the evidence available to them. They may select evidence from different sources and of different types. Which evidence they decide to collect depends on a number of factors, in particular, its relevance, reliability, availability, timeliness and cost.

- *Relevance* of evidence refers to how closely the evidence relates to the particular objective the auditor is trying to accomplish. For example, observation is a useful procedure for verifying the existence, but not the ownership, of tangible assets. To establish ownership, relevant purchase (or similar) documents need to be scrutinised.

- *Reliability* of evidence refers to how confident the auditor is that the evidence reflects the facts of the matter being investigated. For example, the auditor can have greater confidence in bank reconciliations (s)he has performed personally than in assurances from client personnel that the

---

[9] Confirmation of debtors' balances is explained in Chapter 11.

entity's bank statements and bank balances have been reconciled. In general, audit evidence is more reliable when:

- it is obtained directly by the auditor (for example, the auditor personally observing the operation of an internal control provides more reliable audit evidence than enquiring of entity personnel about the operation of the control);
- it is obtained from independent sources outside, rather than from inside, the entity;
- it exists in documentary form, whether paper, electronic, or other medium (for example, written minutes of a meeting are more reliable than a subsequent oral report of the matters discussed);[10]
- it is derived from original documents rather than from photocopies or facsimiles;
- for internally generated evidence, if related internal controls are (and have been) operating effectively.

- *Availability* of evidence refers to how readily the auditor can acquire the evidence. For example, the auditor has ready access to the client's accounting records – including the balances of individual trade debtors (accounts receivable). Evidence of the validity of these balances, obtained by confirming them with the individual debtors concerned, is less readily available.

- *Timeliness* of evidence refers to how quickly the evidence can be obtained. For example, the auditor may be aware that the amount of a contingent liability arising from disputed tax payable to (or receivable from) HM Revenue & Customs will be clarified when the case is heard by the relevant taxation authority. However, if the case is to be deferred for some months, the auditor may decide to forgo that evidence and rely on an estimated amount. If audited financial statements are to be useful to external parties interested in the reporting entity, they must be made available – and hence the audit must be completed – on a timely basis.[11]

- *Cost* of evidence. The auditor generally has a choice of evidence which may be used to establish, for example, whether internal controls have been complied with or financial statement amounts are fairly stated. Therefore, the cost of obtaining particular evidence should be weighed against its benefits, that is, the contribution the evidence may make towards the auditor forming an opinion about the degree of compliance with an

---

[10] However, we might observe that minutes of meetings do not always portray accurately what was said during the meeting. A request can be (and often is) made for certain observations and/or remarks not to be minuted!

[11] Further, as we saw in Chapter 5, section 5.2.2, companies must file their audited financial statements with the Registrar of Companies within six or nine months (for public and private companies, respectively) of the end of their financial year.

internal control, or the truth and fairness of a financial statement amount, under investigation.

Reviewing the above factors it may be seen that, with the exception of relevance, they are all affected by the source from which the evidence is derived. As shown in Figure 7.4, audit evidence may be obtained from three sources:
- (i)   direct personal knowledge;
- (ii) sources external to the client;
- (iii) sources internal to the client.

Evidence obtained by direct personal knowledge is the most reliable, is generally readily available on a timely basis, but is very costly to acquire. At the other extreme, evidence obtained from sources internal to the client is the least reliable, but is generally readily available on a timely basis and is the least costly evidence to obtain. Evidence derived from sources external to the client has an intermediate placing in terms of reliability and cost, but is frequently less readily available, and is less timely to acquire, than evidence obtained from the other two sources (see Figure 7.4).

Figure 7.4:   Sources of evidence and accompanying characteristics

	Sources of evidence		
	Direct personal knowledge	**External to the client**	**Internal to the client**
Examples **Characteristics of evidence**	• *Observation* • *Re-performance*	• *Confirmation from third parties* • *Documents (e.g., invoices) from third parties*	• *Accounting records* • *Responses to enquiries by auditee personnel*
Reliability	High level of reliability	High to medium level of reliability	Low level of reliability
Availability	Readily available	Less readily available	Readily available
Timeliness	Available on a timely basis	May not be available on a timely basis	Available on a timely basis
Cost	High cost	High to medium cost	Low cost

As we noted in section 7.4.1 above, auditors are required to obtain sufficient appropriate audit evidence to be reasonably assured that the financial statements do not contain an unidentified material misstatement. However, what amounts to sufficient appropriate evidence varies with the circumstances of each audit client and each audit engagement. It depends on a wide range of factors, including, for example:
- – the auditor's assessment of the risk of material misstatement at the overall financial statement level, and at the assertion level for classes of transactions, account balances and other financial statement disclosures;

- the auditor's assessment of the effectiveness of the entity's financial reporting system and its internal controls;
- the materiality (importance) of the internal control, or financial statement amount or disclosure, being examined;
- the findings of audit procedures already performed, including any indication that fraud or non-compliance with other laws or regulations may have occurred;
- the source and reliability of the evidence obtained.

Factors such as those outlined above also affect the nature, timing and extent of audit procedures performed during an audit. These terms are explained as follows:

- *The nature of audit procedures* refers to the type of audit procedures to be performed. Whether, for example, emphasis should be placed on compliance or substantive tests and, in either case, which procedures from those set out in section 7.4.2 above are the most appropriate to meet the particular audit objective.

- *The timing of audit procedures* refers to when the selected procedures are to be performed. Should they, for example, be performed prior to the entity's year-end in an 'interim audit', or should they be performed at, or shortly after, the end of the entity's financial year. For example, if, in previous audits, an audit client was found to have an effective system of internal control, and an initial review of the controls indicates that the system has continued to operate effectively throughout the current financial year, some audit procedures (particularly compliance tests) may be performed during an interim audit, two or three months before the auditee's year-end.

- *The extent of audit procedures* refers to how extensive audit testing needs to be to achieve an audit objective, that is, how many different audit procedures should be performed and the extensiveness of each. For example, in order to test the compliance of entity personnel with an internal control, should observation and/or enquiry and/or inspection of records or documents be used?. To what extent should the relevant personnel be observed or questioned?. How large should the sample of records inspected be?

Notwithstanding that the factors indicated above (and other similar factors) affect what qualifies as 'sufficient appropriate evidence' in particular cases, for any given set of circumstances there is a trade-off between the quantity of evidence that is required (its sufficiency) and its relevance and reliability (its quality or appropriateness). The greater the relevance and reliability of evidence, the less that is needed to enable the auditor to form an opinion about the truth and fairness of the financial statements. This trade-off is depicted in Figure 7.5. All points on the curve represent combinations of quantity and quality of evidence which meet the 'sufficient appropriate' requirement. The particular combination the auditor selects will be affected by consideration of factors such as availability, timeliness and cost of the evidence. The auditor will seek the combination which will provide a sufficient amount of reliable evidence, relevant to the objective under investigation, within a reasonable time – at the lowest possible total cost.

Figure 7.5:   Sufficient appropriate evidence trade-off

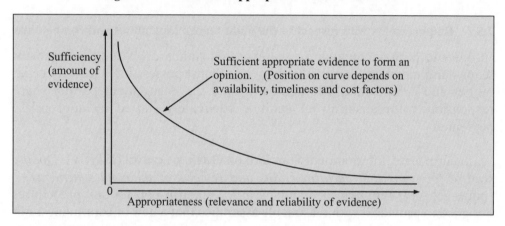

7.5   STAFFING AN AUDIT

7.5.1   Audit team personnel

Having discussed the meaning and some important aspects of audit evidence, we need to consider who actually collects this evidence. Although the audit engagement partner has responsibility for the audit, an audit engagement team (varying from two or three to about 20 or more people – depending on the size, complexity and specific circumstances of the audit) – is usually involved in collecting the audit evidence.

When considering audit teams we need to distinguish between three categories of audit personnel, namely:
* *the audit engagement partner* – the person who is responsible for the audit and its performance, and who signs the audit report;
* *audit staff* – the professional staff members employed by the audit firm who assist with the audit. They range from new entrants to the firm (train-ees) to highly experienced audit managers;

- *other auditors and experts* – auditors and experts from outside the audit firm who, for a variety of reasons, may be employed by the audit engagement partner to perform some part(s) of the audit.

In order for an audit to be performed effectively and efficiently, it is essential that:
- it is adequately staffed by personnel who possess the capabilities and competence required for the tasks to be performed; and
- any work assigned to audit staff is properly directed, supervised and reviewed.

We examine these two requirements below.

7.5.2 Requirements with respect to the audit team's capabilities and competence

In order to perform an audit to the expected standard, an audit engagement team – and members comprising the team – must possess the necessary capabilities and competence. The audit firm and the engagement partner share responsibility for ensuring an audit is adequately staffed by appropriate personnel.

At the firm level, International Standard on Quality Control (ISQC) 1: *Quality control for firms that perform audits and reviews of financial statements...* (paras 25, A17) requires each audit firm to establish policies and procedures designed to provide it with reasonable assurance that a new or continuing audit engagement will only be accepted if the firm has the capabilities, competence, time and resources to undertake the engagement. In particular, the firm is to consider whether:
- firm personnel have knowledge of the client's industry (or industries), and have experience with relevant regulatory and reporting requirements, or the ability to gain the necessary knowledge and skills;
- the firm has sufficient personnel with the necessary capabilities and competence;
- experts are available, if needed;
- the firm is able to complete the engagement within the reporting deadline.

The firm is also responsible for assigning responsibility for each audit engagement to an engagement partner. In so doing, the firm should ensure:
- the identity and role of the engagement partner are communicated to key members of the audit client's management (senior executives and directors);
- the engagement partner has the appropriate capabilities, competence, authority and time to perform the role; and

- the engagement partner's responsibilities are clearly defined and communicated to the partner concerned.

Additionally, the firm should ensure that staff assigned to an engagement have the necessary capabilities, competence and time to perform the audit in accordance with professional standards and regulatory and legal requirements, and to enable the firm or engagement partner to issue appropriate audit reports (ISQC 1, paras 31, 32).

Once appointed to an audit engagement, the engagement partner is primarily responsible for ensuring that the audit team is appropriately constituted. This is reflected, for example, in the Auditing Practices Board's (APB) Ethical Standard (ES) 4: *Fees, remuneration and evaluation policies, litigation, gifts and hospitality*, which requires an audit engagement partner:

> [to] be satisfied and able to demonstrate that the audit engagement has assigned to it sufficient partners and staff with appropriate time and skill to perform the audit in accordance with all applicable Auditing and Ethical Standards, irrespective of the audit fee to be charged. (APB, 2008, para 5)

Along similar lines, ISA 220: *Quality control for an audit of financial statements* (para 13) requires the audit engagement partner to be satisfied that the engagement team, and any external experts, collectively have the appropriate capabilities, competence and time to perform the audit engagement in accordance with professional standards and regulatory and legal requirements, and to enable an appropriate auditor's report to be issued.[12] According to ISA 220 (para A10), the capabilities and competence expected of the engagement team as a whole include the following:

- an understanding of, and practical experience with, audit engagements of a similar nature and complexity through appropriate training and participation;
- an understanding of professional standards and legal and regulatory requirements;
- appropriate technical knowledge and expertise, including knowledge of relevant information technology;
- knowledge of relevant industries in which the client operates;
- ability to apply professional judgment;
- an understanding of the firm's quality control policies and procedures.

It should be noted that not all audit team members are required to possess all of the capabilities and competencies required for a particular audit; they need

---

[12] The engagement partner must also be satisfied that engagement team members comply with the ethical requirements of integrity, objectivity, professional competence and due care, confidentiality and professional behaviour; (s)he must also remain alert to any evidence of non-compliance with these requirements (ISA 220, paras 8, A3, A4). These ethical principles are discussed in Chapter 3.

to be possessed by the team as a whole. For most audits, the engagement partner and other senior audit team members are expected to possess the capabilities and competencies outlined above, but trainees and other junior team members are unlikely to do so. Nevertheless, for some audits, particularly those of a highly specialised or technical nature, even senior and experienced members of the audit team may not possess the required skills. In such circumstances, the engagement partner (and audit firm) should ensure that the required expertise is available, and secured, at the appropriate time. If, for example, the audit firm lacks the competence needed to perform specialised aspects of an audit, technical advice may be sought from experts such as lawyers, actuaries, engineers and valuers. External experts would probably be required to assist in the audit of, say, a company specialising in jewellery manufacture. If the audit firm lacks the competence to evaluate the company's valuation of, say, its inventory (i.e., stock) of diamonds, the auditor may (indeed, should!) seek assistance from a jewellery valuation expert. If the firm does not possess, and cannot acquire, the necessary skills and/or competence to perform or complete a particular audit engagement to the required standard within a reasonable timeframe, the engagement should be declined or discontinued (as applicable).

It is pertinent to note that, if an engagement partner seeks advice or assistance from an expert, the partner remains responsible for all aspects of the audit, including the work performed by the expert. It is, therefore, important that the engagement partner is satisfied that the expert possesses the capabilities and competence needed to perform the task in question, and to obtain reasonable assurance that the work is performed to the appropriate standard. More specifically, ISA 620: *Using the work of an auditor's expert* requires the auditor:
   (a) to evaluate whether the expert has the necessary competence, capabilities and objectivity for the purposes of the audit. This may be achieved by considering, *inter alia*, information derived from sources such as:
     • personal experience of previous work performed by the expert;
     • discussions with the expert;
     • discussions with other auditors and others who are familiar with the expert's work;
     • knowledge of the expert's qualifications, membership of a professional body or industry association, licence to practice or other forms of external recognition;
     • published papers or books by the expert (paras 9, A10);
   (b) to be satisfied that no relationship exists between the expert and the client that may create a threat to the expert's objectivity that cannot be reduced to an acceptable level by the application of available safeguards (paras 9, A16);
   (c) to obtain an understanding of the field of expertise of the expert including, for example:

- whether any professional or other standards and regulatory or legal requirements apply;
- the assumptions made and methods, including models where applicable, used by the expert, and whether these are generally accepted within the expert's field and are appropriate for financial reporting purposes; and
- the nature of internal and external data and information used by the expert.

The auditor's understanding should be sufficient to enable him or her to:

- determine the nature, scope and objectives of the expert's work for the purposes of the audit; and
- evaluate the adequacy of that work (para 10, A19);

(d) to agree, usually in writing, with the expert:

- the nature, scope and objectives of the expert's work;
- the respective roles of the auditor and the expert; for example, whether:
  - the auditor or the expert will perform detailed testing of source data,
  - the expert consents to the auditor discussing the expert's findings with the entity and other third parties and to including details of the findings in a modified audit report,[13] if necessary,
  - the auditor and expert will have access to each other's working papers;
- the nature, timing and extent of communication between the auditor and the expert. Effective two-way communication helps to facilitate the proper integration of the nature, timing and extent of work done by the expert with other audit work;
- the form of any report to be provided by the expert (paras 11, A23–A25);

(e) to evaluate the appropriateness of the expert's work for the purposes of the audit, including:

- the relevance and reasonableness of the expert's findings, and their consistency with other audit evidence;
- if significant to the auditor's use of the expert's work:
  - the relevance and reasonableness of the expert's assumptions and methods including models where applicable; and
  - the relevance, accuracy and completeness of source data used by the expert.

In order to evaluate the appropriateness of the expert's work for the purposes of the audit, the auditor may perform procedures such as:

---

[13] Anything other than a 'clean' audit report is termed a 'modified' audit report. Modified audit reports are discussed in Chapter 14.

- enquiries of the expert;
- reviewing the expert's working papers;
- observing the expert's work;
- examining documentary evidence the expert provides;
- examining published data, such as statistical reports from reputable, authoritative sources;
- reviewing how inconsistencies in evidence examined were resolved;
- discussing with another expert with relevant expertise the findings of the expert when these are not consistent with other audit evidence;
- discussing the expert's report with the audit client's management (paras 12, A27).

If the engagement partner concludes that the expert's work is not adequate for the purposes of the audit, ISA 620, para 13, requires him or her to:
- (a) agree with the expert on the nature and extent of further work to be performed by the expert; or
- (b) perform further audit procedures appropriate to the circumstances.

Similar conditions apply when an auditor relies on the work of another auditor. This may arise, for example, when a branch, division or subsidiary (i.e., 'a component') of the audit client is located at a distant geographical location and the auditor relies on another auditor (the 'component auditor') to gather evidence in relation to that component. ISA 600: *Special considerations – audits of group financial statements (including the work of component auditors)* requires an engagement partner in this sort of position, *inter alia*:
- (a) to ascertain whether the 'component auditor' understands, and will comply with, the ethical requirements that are relevant to the audit and, in particular, meets the independence requirements (para 19a);
- (b) to be satisfied that the 'component auditor' possesses the necessary professional competence to perform the assignment to the required standard (para 19b, A38);
- (c) to determine whether the engagement team and the component auditor:
  - adopt similar audit methodologies,
  - have common quality control policies and procedures,
  - are subject to similar external professional oversight, disciplinary procedures and quality assurance mechanisms (such as monitoring or inspections) (para A33);
- (d) to perform procedures to obtain sufficient appropriate audit evidence that the work of the component auditor is adequate for the purposes of the audit as a whole.[14] Such procedures may include:

---

[14] For significant components, the group audit team is required to be involved in the component auditor's risk assessment in order to identify significant risks of material misstatement of the group financial statements. As a minimum this 'involvement' is to include performing the procedures identified under (d).

- discussing with the component auditor (or management) the component's business activities that are significant to the group,
- discussing with the component auditor the susceptibility of the component's financial information to material misstatement due to fraud or error,
- reviewing the component auditor's overall audit strategy and audit plan (or audit programme),
- participating in the closing and other key meetings between the component management and component auditor,
- reviewing the component auditor's documentation (paras 30, A55);

(e) to request the component auditor to communicate matters such as:
- whether (s)he has complied with relevant ethical requirements,
- identification of the financial information of the component on which the component auditor is reporting,
- uncorrected misstatements in the component's financial information,
- any indications of management bias in the component's financial information,
- any significant deficiencies identified in the component's internal financial controls,
- other significant matters the component auditor has, or expects to communicate to the component's management, including fraud or suspected fraud involving the component's management, employees who have significant roles in the component's internal control system, or others where the fraud resulted in a material misstatement of the component's financial information,
- the component auditor's overall findings, conclusions and opinion (para 41).

7.5.3 Directing, supervising and reviewing the work of audit staff

In section 7.5.2 above, we noted that ISQC 1 (para 32) requires audit firms to ensure that staff who are assigned to an audit engagement have the necessary capabilities, competence and time to perform the engagement in accordance with professional standards and regulatory and legal requirements. However, it is clear that trainees and other junior audit team members, in particular, require 'on-the-job' training in order for them to develop their capabilities and competence. Further, the audit engagement partner needs to ensure that the audit is conducted to a high standard. Reflecting these factors, ISA 220: *Quality control for an audit of financial statements*, requires engagement partners to "take responsibility for the direction, supervision and performance of the audit engagement in compliance with professional standards and regulatory and legal requirements" (para 14).

'Direction' means more than merely informing audit staff of their responsibilities and the tasks they are to perform. It also involves:

- ensuring they understand the need to comply with relevant ethical requirements and to plan and perform the audit with an attitude of professional scepticism; and
- providing them with background information about both the client and the audit so they can understand the importance and context of the audit procedures they are asked to perform.

Audit staff should, for example, be provided with information about the nature of the entity's business, risk-related issues, accounting or auditing problems that may arise, and the detailed approach to the performance of the audit. ISA 220 makes particular reference to the importance of audit team members understanding the objectives of the work they are to perform, and notes:

> Appropriate teamwork and training assist less experienced members of the engagement team to clearly understand the objectives of the assigned work.... Discussion among members of the engagement team allows less experienced team members to raise questions with more experienced team members so that appropriate communication can occur within the engagement team. (paras A12, A13)

Free and frank communication between audit team members is vitally important for both the performance of a high-quality audit and the personal development of audit staff: it facilitates audit team members clarifying matters when they have incomplete understanding, and seeking advice or guidance, when needed, on appropriate action(s) in particular circumstances. It also helps to ensure that all members of the audit team remain informed of significant matters, including unexpected results of audit procedures or other findings, relating to the auditee and the audit engagement *per se*.

Assigning audit work to engagement team members is not the end of the story – the work needs to be properly supervised and reviewed to ensure that it has been conducted appropriately. According to ISA 220, supervision of audit work includes:

- Tracking [monitoring] the progress of the audit engagement.
- Considering the capabilities and competence of individual members of the audit team, whether they have sufficient time to carry out their work, whether they understand their instructions, and whether the work is being carried out in accordance with the planned approach to the audit engagement.
- Addressing significant issues arising during the audit engagement, considering their significance and modifying the planned approach appropriately.
- Identifying matters for consultation[15] or consideration by more experienced engagement team members during the audit engagement. (para A14)

The requirement to review audit work involves more experienced team members, including the engagement partner, reviewing the work of less

---

[15] The meaning and importance of 'consultation' are explained in Chapter 16, section 16.2.2.

experienced members. The reviewers should consider, amongst other things, whether:

- the work has been performed in accordance with professional standards and regulatory and legal requirements;
- the work performed supports the conclusions reached;
- significant matters have been raised for further consideration and, where necessary, appropriate consultation has taken place and the resulting conclusions have been documented and implemented;
- based on the results of audit procedures performed, there is a need to revise the planned nature, timing and/or extent of audit procedures;
- the objectives of audit procedures have been met, and the evidence obtained is sufficient and appropriate to support the opinion expressed in the audit report;
- the audit work performed, results obtained and conclusions reached are adequately documented (ISA 220, para A15).

The review of audit work by more senior members of the audit team is not a remote and post-event process. Rather, those who perform the work discuss it upon completion directly with the more senior audit team member. This enables the reviewer to question the more junior staff member about the work performed and results obtained – and this, in turn, enables any audit issues to be identified and followed up on a timely basis. It also facilitates developing the capabilities and competence of, and providing training for, the more junior staff member.

The provisions of ISQC 1 and ISA 220 relating to staffing an audit are clearly very important. If an audit is to be conducted effectively, efficiently and with due professional care, but much (most) of the work is to be performed by audit staff, it is essential that care is taken to ensure that work delegated to audit staff members:

- is within their capabilities and competence to perform; and
- is carefully directed, supervised and reviewed.

If these responsibilities are not discharged properly, the audit is in danger of being performed inadequately and the door may be opened to allegations of negligence.

7.6 DOCUMENTING AN AUDIT

7.6.1 Definition, purpose and importance of audit working papers

It was noted in section 7.5.3 above that among the matters reviewers of audit work are to consider is whether audit work performed, results obtained and conclusions reached, and also the conclusions resulting from consultation, are adequately documented. It is essential that audit work is fully and properly

documented in audit working papers. As ISA 230: *Audit documentation* (para 2) indicates, such documentation provides evidence:
- of the basis for the opinion expressed in the audit report; and
- that the audit was performed in accordance with ISAs and applicable legal and regulatory requirements.

The Standard also explains that "[a]udit documentation may be recorded on paper or on electronic or other media" (para A3) and it cites as examples of documentation: audit programmes, analyses, issues memoranda, summaries of significant matters, letters of confirmation and representation, checklists, and correspondence (including e-mail) concerning significant matters. It further notes: "The auditor may include abstracts or copies of the entity's records (for example, significant and specific contracts and agreements) as part of audit documentation" (para A3).

The primary purpose of audit working papers is to provide evidence that work performed during the audit, the results obtained and the conclusions reached all accord with ISAs and legal and regulatory requirements, and that evidence resulting from audit work is sufficient and appropriate to support the opinion expressed in the audit report. However, they also serve other more specific purposes. For example, they provide:

(i) *a basis for planning the audit*: Records of preliminary discussions with the client, notes relating to the assessment of audit risk and the setting of materiality limits, and other similar documentation, provide a basis for planning the nature, timing and extent of audit procedures to be performed;

(ii) *a basis for performing the audit*: The audit plan (or programme;[16] an important working paper) provides directions on the audit procedures to be performed. Other documents provide evidence of procedures already completed and conclusions reached based on the results of those procedures. Additionally, the audit working papers include notes on any particular matters audit staff need to consider or accommodate when performing certain procedures detailed in the audit plan;

(iii) *a basis for reviewing work done and evaluating evidence gathered and conclusions reached*: The audit working papers provide a record of work done by audit staff in relation to particular audit objectives. They therefore provide a means for the engagement partner and other members of the audit team to assess the adequacy of the work performed, the quality of the results obtained, and the validity of the conclusions reached;

---

[16] In recently issued ISAs, the term 'audit plan' is used in place of 'audit programme'.

(iv) *a means of supervising more junior members of the audit team*: This purpose of audit working papers is closely related to that outlined in (iii) above. Because audit working papers record audit procedures to be performed and audit work completed, they enable personnel responsible for directing and supervising the work of more junior members of the audit team to monitor and assess the work performed by their subordinates;

(v) *an aid to planning subsequent audits*: The findings of previous audits and other matters of continuing significance to future audits, as recorded in the audit working papers, provide a good basis from which to begin the initial planning of a subsequent audit;

(vi) *enabling subsequent reviews by the engagement quality control reviewer and external audit monitors [or inspectors]*: ISA 220: *Quality control for an audit of financial statements* (para 18) requires a quality control reviewer to be appointed for each audit engagement of listed companies; his or her primary function is to determine whether the opinion the audit engagement partner plans to express in the audit report is appropriate and is adequately supported by the audit procedures performed, evidence gathered, results obtained and conclusions reached, as documented in the audit working papers. In addition, all registered auditors in the UK are subject to monitoring by the Recognised Supervisory Body with which they are registered and/or inspections by the Audit Inspection Unit of the Financial Reporting Council's Public Oversight Board.[17] The audit working papers provide important evidence for the monitors/inspectors of the quality of audits performed.

7.6.2 Form and content of audit working papers

ISA 230: *Audit documentation* specifies that audit documentation must be:
sufficient to enable an experienced auditor, having no previous connection with the audit, to understand:
(a) The nature, timing, and extent of the audit procedures performed to comply with ISAs and applicable legal and regulatory requirements;
(b) The results of the audit procedures performed, and the audit evidence obtained; and
(c) Significant matters arising during the audit, the conclusions reached thereon, and significant professional judgments made in reaching those conclusions. (para 8)

(We will expand on these requirements when discussing the content of the current audit file below.)

---

[17] In Chapter 5 (section 5.2.3 and footnote 70, respectively) we refer to monitoring of auditors by the Recognised Supervisory Body with which they are registered and inspections by the Audit Inspection Unit. We discuss audit engagement quality reviews and monitoring/inspections of registered auditors in detail in Chapter 16, section 16.2.4.

Although this general standard applies to the documentation of all audits, the form, content and extent of working papers vary from audit to audit, reflecting such things as:
- the size, nature and complexity of the client, its organisational structure and its activities;
- the nature and quality of the client's record keeping, accounting system and internal controls;
- the nature of the audit procedures performed;
- the identified risks of material misstatement in the financial statements;
- the extent of judgment required in performing audit procedures and evaluating the results;
- the significance of the evidence obtained;
- the nature and extent of exceptions found in evidence gathered.

Although all matters of audit significance must be documented so that the requirements of the general standard for audit documentation (noted above) are met, ISA 230 observes: "it is neither necessary nor practicable for the auditor to document every matter considered, or professional judgment made, in an audit" (para A7).

Notwithstanding differences in audit working papers resulting from factors such as those mentioned above, certain documents (in paper or electronic form) are present in virtually every audit, and these are arranged logically in either the permanent or the current audit file.

(i) The permanent audit file

As Figure 7.6 indicates, the permanent audit file contains documents of a 'permanent' nature which are required in every audit of the client. Typical permanent audit file documents include the following:

(a) *Legal documents* – extracts or copies of documents such as the entity's Memorandum and Articles of Association, contracts (including, for example, pension plans and leases), agreements (such as loan agreements), and debenture deeds. A copy of the audit engagement letter[18] is also frequently kept in this section of the audit file.

(b) *General information about the client's industry, business and operations* – information relating to the auditee's industry; its business, economic, legislative and regulatory environment; its historical development; and its present organisational and operational structure. This information includes details of the company's board of directors and board committees (for example, remuneration and audit committee), details of any subsidiaries, divisions or departments (their geographical location, size,

---

[18] Engagement letters are explained in Chapter 8, section 8.3.

Figure 7.6: Form and content of audit working papers

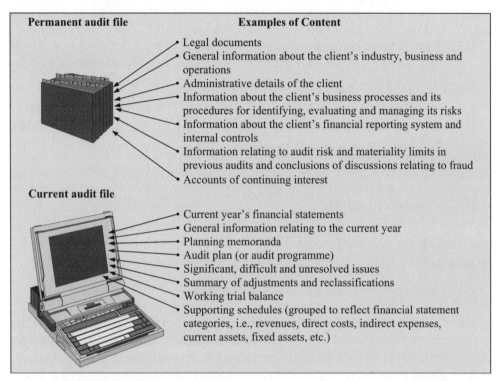

Permanent audit file	Examples of Content
	Legal documents
	General information about the client's industry, business and operations
	Administrative details of the client
	Information about the client's business processes and its procedures for identifying, evaluating and managing its risks
	Information about the client's financial reporting system and internal controls
	Information relating to audit risk and materiality limits in previous audits and conclusions of discussions relating to fraud
	Accounts of continuing interest

Current audit file

- Current year's financial statements
- General information relating to the current year
- Planning memoranda
- Audit plan (or audit programme)
- Significant, difficult and unresolved issues
- Summary of adjustments and reclassifications
- Working trial balance
- Supporting schedules (grouped to reflect financial statement categories, i.e., revenues, direct costs, indirect expenses, current assets, fixed assets, etc.)

principal products, etc.), and details of key suppliers, customers, competitors, bankers, solicitors, etc.

(c) *Administrative details of the client* – documents reflecting the client's administrative structure, for example, its organisation chart, chart of accounts, policies and procedures manuals and job descriptions.

(d) *Business processes and risks* – information gathered during previous audits about the auditee's business processes and its procedures for identifying, evaluating and managing its business, financial, operational and other risks.

(e) *Financial reporting system and internal controls* – information relating to the client's financial reporting system and internal controls, including flowcharts, internal control evaluations and narrative descriptions, completed during previous audits. Also, notes made in previous audits about strengths and deficiencies identified in the internal controls, and copies of communications to the client's directors, audit committee and/or senior executives.[19]

---

[19] Internal controls, and audit documents relating thereto, are discussed in Chapter 10. Communication of audit matters to the entity's directors, audit committee and executives is discussed in Chapter 14, section 14.8.

(f) *Information on audit risk and materiality limits* – the results of analytical review and other information relating to the assessment of audit risk and setting of materiality limits in previous audits. Also, the conclusions of audit team discussions in previous audits about the susceptibility of the client's financial statements to material misstatement due to fraudulent financial reporting or misappropriation of assets;[20]

(g) *Accounts of continuing interest* – analyses from previous audits of accounts that are of continuing importance to the auditor. These include shareholders' equity accounts, long-term liabilities, tangible and intangible fixed assets.

(ii)   The current audit file

As may be seen from Figure 7.6, the current audit file (which is usually in electronic form, accessible to all members of the audit team) contains information pertaining to the current year's audit. It includes records such as:

(a) *The financial statements under examination.*

(b) *General information* – information of a general nature relating to the current year's audit. This includes, for example, notes on discussions with the client about business, financial, operational and other matters which have occurred during the reporting period; abstracts or copies of directors' (and similar) meetings; abstracts or copies of contracts or agreements not included in the permanent file; and comments on the current year's evaluation of the auditee's internal controls and risk management procedures.

(c) *Planning memoranda relating to the current audit* – records of audit team planning meetings where matters such as relevant features of the audit client (its industry, business, operations, and organisation), the audit strategy, matters of particular audit interest or concern, and the planned nature, timing and extent of audit tests are discussed.[21] A record of the audit team's discussion about the susceptibility of the current year's financial statements to material misstatement due to fraud, and management's assessment of the risk of the financial statements being materially misstated, may also be retained in this section of the audit file.

(d) *The audit plan (or audit programme)* – a list of the audit procedures to be performed. As the audit progresses, each staff member performing

---

[20] These discussions are explained in Chapter 6, section 6.2.4.

[21] Planning the audit (and planning memoranda) are discussed in Chapter 9.

a procedure initials and dates the audit programme to indicate the procedure has been completed.

(e) *Significant issues arising during the audit* – for example, comments arising from the review of working papers and conclusions reached in relation to various segments of the audit and, more particularly, notes on:
   (i) difficult issues which have arisen during the audit and how they have been resolved; and
   (ii) issues remaining to be resolved prior to completion of the audit.

The documentation of significant matters arising during the audit must be sufficient "to enable an experienced auditor, having no previous connection with the audit, to understand ... the procedures performed, ... significant matters arising during the audit, the conclusions reached thereon, and significant professional judgments made in reaching those conclusions" (ISA 230, para 8). The standard observes (para A8) that significant matters include:
   – matters that give rise to significant risks (i.e., risks of material misstatement in the financial statements that require special audit consideration);
   – the results of audit procedures that indicate the financial statements could be materially misstated and/or the need to revise the auditor's previous assessment of the risk of the financial statements being materially misstated, and the auditor's responses to those risks;
   – circumstances that cause the auditor significant difficulty in applying necessary audit procedures;
   – findings that could result in a modification to the auditor's opinion or the inclusion of an Emphasis of Matter paragraph in the audit report.[22]

ISA 230 places particular emphasis on the need to document significant professional judgments, noting that such documentation "serves to explain the auditor's conclusions and to reinforce the quality of the judgment" (para A9). The standard also requires documentation of discussions of significant matters with management and others (for example, the directors, other entity personnel, or external parties such as those providing professional advice to the entity). The nature of the significant matters discussed, and when and with whom the discussions took place, are all to be recorded. Similarly, if, having reached a conclusion about a significant matter, the auditor encounters information that

---

[22] Modifications to the auditor's opinion and Emphasis of Matter paragraphs are discussed in Chapter 14.

is inconsistent with that conclusion, (s)he is required to document how the inconsistency was resolved (paras 10, 11).

(f) *Summary of adjusting and reclassification entries* – as the audit proceeds, audit team members almost invariably encounter accounting entries which require correction as to amount or classification – for example, a direct payment into the client's bank account by a credit customer on balance sheet date may not have been recorded as a receipt in the current period, or office equipment purchased during the year may have been recorded as 'repairs and maintenance' instead of 'office equipment'. All errors discovered during the audit which require adjustment or reclassification are recorded on a summary schedule. Such a summary enables the engagement partner (or another senior member of the audit team) to assess at a glance the significance of individual errors, and the cumulative effect of errors, in relation to the financial statements as a whole and the affected components thereof, such as net or gross profit, current assets, long-term liabilities, etc.

Although the audit team will find and note errors as the audit progresses, no adjustments to the client's ledger accounts or financial statements can be made without the consent of the client's directors. As noted in Chapter 5, maintaining the accounting records and preparing the financial statements are the responsibility of the directors. The auditor will request the directors to effect adjusting entries to correct errors discovered during the audit. In many cases no difficulty is encountered and the directors approve the changes. If the directors refuse to correct what the auditor considers to be a material error (or a number of non-material errors which, in aggregate, constitute a material error), the auditor will have little choice but to express a modified audit opinion in the audit report.

(g) *Working trial balance*: Usually, as soon as possible after balance sheet date, the auditor obtains or prepares a list of general ledger accounts and their year-end balances. This is known as a working trial balance.

Frequently, the working trial balance is in the form of a list of balances which appear in the financial statements. Each line of the trial balance is supported by a lead schedule. This lists the general ledger accounts (and their balances) which constitute the relevant financial statement balance. (For example, the 'Cash' balance in the financial statements may comprise petty cash and a number of current and deposit account balances held at a number of banks – possibly in different currencies in different countries.). Each significant account shown in the lead schedule is, in turn, supported by detailed working papers. These show the audit work performed in relation to the account in question, the results obtained, and the conclusion reached regarding the validity (or otherwise) of the account balance.

The relationship between the financial statements, the working trial balance, the lead schedule and supporting schedules is shown in simplified form in Figure 7.7. This shows that the cash balance presented in the financial statements for 20×8 and recorded in the working trial balance is £254,790. The composition of this balance is detailed in the 'Lead Schedule: Cash'. Audit work has revealed that a receipt from a customer of £320 has not been recorded in the correct period and, as a consequence, an adjusting entry is required.

(h) *Supporting schedules*: The supporting schedules which provide details of audit work performed in relation to individual financial statement balances constitute the major portion of the current audit file. Frequently, they are grouped in the file in sections which reflect financial statement categories. There may, for example, be sections for revenues, direct costs, indirect expenses, current assets, tangible fixed assets, investments, intangible fixed assets, current liabilities, long-term liabilities and shareholders' funds. Each of these sections may be subdivided into groups of related accounts. The amount of subdivision largely depends on the size and complexity of the particular audit client.

Each group of accounts has a lead schedule which is cross-referenced to the working trial balance, relevant 'working accounts' and supporting schedules (see, respectively, C-1, B-1 and C-2 to C-4 in Figure 7.7, and Figure 7.8). Each supporting schedule presents, in relation to an individual account balance, details of:
- the objective(s) of audit procedures performed;[23]
- the procedures performed;
- the results of the procedures;
- relevant comments;
- the conclusion reached with respect to the account balance investigated.

These features are reflected in Figure 7.8.

As noted earlier, ISA 230, para 8, requires documentation of the nature, timing and extent of audit procedures to be such that an experienced auditor, having no previous connection with the audit, is able to

---

[23] The objectives of audit procedures, and the procedure to be performed, may be specified in the audit plan rather than in the relevant supporting schedule.

Figure 7.7: Simplified representation of the relationship between the financial statements and audit working papers

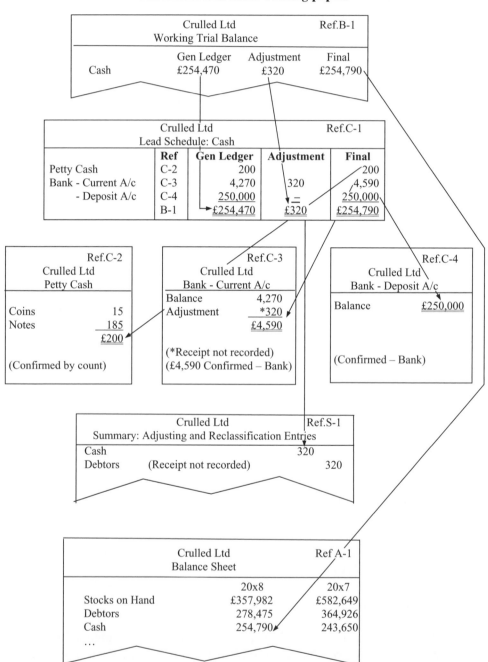

Figure 7.8: Example of a supporting schedule

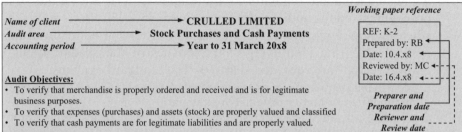

Name of client ————————► **CRULLED LIMITED**
Audit area ——————————► **Stock Purchases and Cash Payments**
Accounting period ——————► **Year to 31 March 20x8**

Working paper reference

REF: K-2
Prepared by: RB ◄
Date: 10.4.x8 ◄
Reviewed by: MC ◄
Date: 16.4.x8 ◄

*Preparer and
Preparation date
Reviewer and
Review date*

Audit Objectives:
• To verify that merchandise is properly ordered and received and is for legitimate business purposes.
• To verify that expenses (purchases) and assets (stock) are properly valued and classified
• To verify that cash payments are for legitimate liabilities and are properly valued.

Audit Procedures:
\# Traced payment to purchase invoice. Agreed invoice with amount of cheque and payment date. Each payment is 5% less than invoice amount as cash discount received. Recalculated all discounts. (A-6) ←*Audit programme reference*
< Compared invoice prices with master price list. All agreed except those marked*. (A-7)
Ø Examined purchase invoices for evidence that company employee verified prices, extensions and footings. Markings or initials present in all cases. (A-8)
> Verified arithmetical accuracy of extensions and totals of invoices. (A-9)
v Examined cancelled cheques for amounts, dates, signatures, and payee. (A-10)
t Examined receiving report for agreement with purchase invoice as to description and quantity. All reports were properly signed by Backhouse (Receiving Officer). (A-11)
@ Examined purchase order with receiving report and invoice. Verified account code. All orders agreed with receiving report and were properly approved except those marked + and ❷. (A-12)

Sample selection: [24]
Population: All purchases were from Yumslip Products, Western Corporation and Capers Ltd.
Sample: Judgmental. Selected 12 payments for merchandise from Cash Payments Journal for period 1.7.x7 to 31.3.x8 beginning with cheque 1690.

Results of Procedures:

Date	Payee	Cheque No.	Amount	1	2	3	4	5	6	7
10.4.x7	Western Corporation	1690	£1,432.67	#	<	Ø	>	v	t	@
9.5.x7	Yumslip Products	1725	£2,568.91	#	<*	Ø	>	v	t	@+
15.6.x7	Western Corporation	1744	£1,021.05	#	<	Ø	>	v	t	@
6.7.x7	Yumslip Products	1769	£456.26	#	<	Ø	>	v	t	@❷
10.8.x7	Capers Ltd	1780	£461.34	#	<	Ø	>	v	t	@❷
8.9.x7	Yumslip Products	1795	£1,263.76	#	<*	Ø	>	v	t	@
14.10.x7	Western Corporation	1841	£1,246.34	#	<	Ø	>	v	t	@
17.11.x7	Yumslip Products	1860	£319.38	#	<	Ø	>	v	t	@❷
9.12.x7	Capers Ltd	1887	£248.21	#	<	Ø	>	v	t	@❷
15.1.x8	Yumslip Products	1898	£1,219.47	#	<	Ø	>	v	t	@
13.2.x8	Western Corporation	1924	£2,639.31	#	<	Ø	>	v	t	@
15.3.x8	Yumslip Products	1953	£1,632.19	#	<	Ø	>	v	t	@

NOTE: Symbols used are shown alongside relevant audit procedure.

Comments:
* Prices on purchases of 9.5.x7 and 8.9.x7 do not agree with master price list by £56.00 and £124.34, respectively. According to Smithson (Purchasing Officer) the differences represent special prices available in May and September which differed from price list. (Confirmed with Yumslip.)
+ Purchase order does not agree with receiving report for one item. Smithson indicated that replacement (similar) item was supplied as a result of a stock-out. (Confirmed replacement item ordered.)
❷ Four orders were approved by Thomas (Chief Accountant) instead of Mates (Finance Director). According to Smithson only orders in excess of £1,000 need be approved by Mates. (Confirmed with Mates.)
 NOTE: Need to alter flow chart to reflect this. (MC 16.4.x8) ◄——— *Follow-up by audit staff member*

Conclusions:
(1) The purchases are properly ordered and received and are for legitimate purposes.
(2) Purchases are properly valued and classified.
(3) Payments are properly valued and are for legitimate liabilities.
(4) Purchases and payments transactions are fairly stated in the accounts. (K-1)◄——— *Lead schedule reference*

Review: Review and discussion of results of audit procedures and conclusions; MC 16.4.x8. Follow up on flow chart amendment actioned: MC 17.4.x8.

_____

[24] Sample sizes and selection are discussed in Chapter 12.

understand (a) that the procedures performed comply with ISAs[25] and applicable legal and regulatory requirements and (b) the results of the procedures and the audit evidence obtained. ISA 230 also requires that, when documenting the nature, timing and extent of audit procedures performed: "[t]he identifying characteristics of the specific items or matters tested" are recorded (para 9). The Standard explains:

> Identifying characteristics will vary with the nature of the audit procedure and the item or matter tested. For example:
> - For a detailed test of entity-generated purchase orders, the auditor may identify the documents selected for testing by their dates and unique purchase order numbers.
> - For a procedure requiring selection or review of all items over a specific amount from a given population, the auditor may record the scope of the procedure and identify the population (for example, all journal entries over a specified amount from the journal register).
> - For a procedure requiring systematic sampling from a population of documents, the auditor may identify the documents selected by recording their source, the starting point and the sampling interval (for example, a systematic sample of shipping reports selected from the shipping log for the period from April 1 to September 30, starting with report number 12345 and selecting every 125th report).[26]
> - For a procedure requiring inquiries of specific entity personnel, the auditor may record the dates of the inquiries and the names and job designations of the entity personnel.
> - For an observation procedure, the auditor may record the process or matter being observed, the relevant individuals, their respective responsibilities, and where and when the observation was carried out. (para A12)

The identifying characteristics of the cheques selected for examination in the audit of Crulled Limited are shown in Figure 7.8.

7.6.3 Preparation of audit working papers

We noted in section 7.6.1 above that the primary objective of audit working papers is to provide evidence (a) of the basis for the opinion expressed in the audit report and (b) that the audit was conducted in accordance with ISAs and applicable legal and regulatory requirements. In order to meet these objectives, it is essential that audit working papers are properly prepared.

Although the details of working papers vary according to the nature of the schedule concerned and the specific audit objectives being met, audit working papers should always contain certain features. These are discussed below and illustrated in Figure 7.8.

---

[25] ISA 230, para 12, states: "If, in exceptional circumstances, the auditor judges it necessary to depart from a relevant requirement in an ISA, the auditor shall document how the alternative audit procedures performed achieve the aim of that requirement, and the reasons for the departure."

[26] We discuss sampling procedures in Chapter 12.

(i) Each working paper should be clearly headed to indicate:
- the name of the client;
- the audit area (or account) to which the working paper (schedule) relates;
- the relevant accounting period.

(ii) Each working paper should have a unique reference number and be cross-referenced to the relevant lead schedule, working trial balance and/or other related working papers.

(iii) Completed working papers must show:
- the initials (or name) of the person who performed the audit work and the date the work was completed;
- the initials (or name) of the person who reviewed the audit work performed and the date and extent of the review.

(iv) Audit working papers also need to show:
- the audit objectives of the procedures performed;
- the audit procedures performed (these should be cross-referenced to the audit plan);
- the results of the audit procedures (these frequently involve the use of tick marks or symbols and all such notation must be clearly explained);
- the conclusion(s) reached in terms of the audit objectives, based on the results of the audit procedures performed.

(v) Where sampling is used, the relevant working paper should indicate the population from which the sample was drawn, the size of the sample and the means by which the sample was selected.

(vi) Where any deviation from the expected result of an audit procedure is encountered, such deviation, and an explanation thereof, should be clearly recorded in the relevant working paper. In cases where some follow-up is required, the person undertaking the follow-up should initial and date the relevant working paper entry to indicate that the follow-up has been performed.

7.6.4 Working paper review

In Chapter 3 we noted that a characteristic feature of all audits (and all stages of an audit) is the importance of, and necessity for, the exercise of professional judgment – a fact that will become increasingly evident as we study the steps in the audit process in more detail. This characteristic, combined with the fact that members of audit teams are human (and therefore prone to make mistakes and faulty judgments), means that reliance cannot be placed on audit staff correctly identifying audit objectives, performing appropriate audit procedures, making optimal judgments, and drawing correct conclusions, on *every* occasion. Clearly, if an effective audit is to be conducted, it is essential that the work of each audit team member is reviewed by a more senior member of the audit team. This is reflected in the requirement of ISA 220: *Quality control for an audit of financial statements* (para 15) for the work of audit team members to be reviewed. Such review should ensure, *inter alia*, that audit objectives have been met; audit procedures performed, significant judgments made, and results obtained have been properly documented; and conclusions reached are consistent with the results obtained and support the opinion expressed in the audit report.[27]

Working paper review is usually effected in the following manner.

(i) As each section of the audit is completed, the working papers of the relevant audit staff member are discussed with, and reviewed by, a more senior member of the audit team. The audit procedures performed are compared with those set down in the audit plan (or audit programme) and the results obtained and conclusions reached (based on those results) are evaluated by the reviewer and discussed with the staff member. The working papers are also reviewed for completeness, orderly presentation and cross-referencing to other relevant working papers. Any matters requiring follow-up are noted and either actioned by the staff member or reviewer, or referred to the appropriate member of the audit team for actioning.

(ii) *The reviewer* (the more senior audit team member) prepares summary notes on each segment of the audit for which (s)he is responsible, regarding:
   (a) the evidence gathered and conclusions reached;
   (b) any problems encountered and how they were dealt with;
   (c) the scope of, and conclusions resulting from, any consultations on difficult or contentious issues (matters consulted on, and the resulting conclusions, must be documented and agreed by the party consulted: ISA 220, para 17);
   (d) matters requiring the attention of the audit manager (usually the most senior member of the audit team other than the engagement partner) or the engagement partner;
   (e) matters to be considered for inclusion in the communication of audit matters to the client's directors (and/or audit committee).

(iii) *The audit manager* (or another senior member of the audit team) reviews the summary notes prepared by the reviewer of the audit work performed. (S)he also reviews the detailed working papers prepared by the audit staff

---

[27] Further details of matters reviewers should consider are provided in section 7.5.3.

member(s) who undertook the work to ensure they contain evidence indicating they have been reviewed, and to evaluate the reviewer's findings. The manager discusses with the audit staff members who performed and/or reviewed the audit work any matters which require clarification, any difficult or contentious issues, whether consultation occurred and how the issues were resolved, and any issues remaining to be resolved.

(iv) The audit manager prepares summary notes on each major segment of the audit and on the audit as a whole. (S)he comments on:
    (a) the sufficiency and appropriateness of the audit evidence gathered;
    (b) conclusions reached, based on that evidence;
    (c) problems encountered and how they were resolved;
    (d) the scope of, and conclusions resulting from, any consultations on difficult or contentious issues;
    (d) any outstanding unresolved issues.

The audit manager also prepares the formal communication (i.e., letter) of audit matters to the client's directors (and/or audit committee). (This frequently amounts to approving or amending a draft communication prepared by a senior audit staff member.)

The audit manager will be particularly concerned to see that:
    (a) all audit problems have been adequately dealt with;
    (b) any unresolved issues are either resolved or highlighted, by way of an audit working paper note, for the audit engagement partner;
    (c) sufficient appropriate evidence has been obtained in each audit segment and for the audit as a whole to support the audit opinion;
    (d) the conclusions reached are supported by the evidence gathered;
    (e) all significant audit matters (including all significant judgments made) are fully and properly documented.

(v) *The audit engagement partner* considers, in detail, the final draft of the financial statements, the summary notes, and the formal communication of audit matters to the client's directors prepared by the audit manager. The engagement partner also:
    (i) reviews the audit working papers for completeness, orderliness, adequacy, cross-referencing and evidence of review. (S)he will pay particular attention to working papers that relate to:
        – critical areas of judgment, especially any relating to difficult or contentious matters identified during the audit,
        – identified areas or matters of significant audit risk,
        – any other areas which the audit engagement partner considers important;

> (ii) discusses with the audit manager and/or relevant audit staff members any matters that require clarification, and/or difficult or unresolved audit issues.

Although the audit partner reviews the audit working papers at the conclusion of the audit as outlined above, this is not the only time (s)he reviews the audit documentation. As ISA 220 observes: "[t]imely reviews of [the working papers] by the engagement partner at appropriate stages during the engagement allow significant matters to be resolved on a timely basis to the engagement partner's satisfaction before the auditor's report is issued" (para A16).

The key concerns of the engagement partner are to ensure:

> (a) an appropriate opinion on the financial statements under examination can be formed based on the evidence recorded in the audit working papers, assessed against a background of his or her knowledge of the client, its operations and its financial affairs;
> (b) if the adequacy of the audit engagement is challenged in a court of law, the working papers will:
> - stand up to the scrutiny of the court;
> - clearly show:
>   - the audit was conducted in accordance with ISAs and applicable legal and regulatory requirements, and
>   - the opinion expressed in the audit report is supported by audit evidence that is both sufficient and appropriate.

For all but small audits, in order to ensure that objectives (a) and (b) above are met, most audit firms require the audit working papers to be reviewed by a second audit partner who has not had any involvement in the audit in question. Indeed, ISQC 1 (para 36) requires an engagement quality control review to be conducted for the audits for all listed companies and for other audits which meet criteria specified by the audit firm. ISQC 1 (para A40) explains that the criteria a firm considers when determining which audit engagements should be subject to an engagement quality control review include:

- The nature of the engagement, including the extent to which it involves a matter of public interest.
- The identification of unusual circumstances or risks in an engagement or class of engagements.
- Whether laws or regulations require an engagement quality control review.

Before considering what an engagement quality control review entails, we need to know what it is and who qualifies as a reviewer. In its *Glossary of terms*, the IAASB (2007) defines the terms as follows:

Engagement quality control review – A process designed to provide an objective evaluation, before the [audit] report is issued, of the significant judgments the engagement team made and the conclusions they reached in formulating the report.

Engagement quality control reviewer – A partner, other person in the firm, suitably qualified external person, or a team made up of such individuals, with sufficient and appropriate experience and authority to objectively evaluate, before the [audit] report is issued, the significant judgments the engagement team made and the conclusions they reached in formulating the report.

ISA 220, para 18, expands on the requirements of ISQC 1, noting that the engagement partner is responsible for:
  (a) determining that an engagement quality control reviewer has been appointed;
  (b) discussing with the engagement quality control reviewer significant issues arising during the audit (including those identified during the quality control review);
  (c) not issuing the audit report until the engagement quality control review has been completed.
The Standard also notes (para A22) that the engagement partner remains responsible for the audit engagement and its performance notwithstanding the involvement of the engagement quality control reviewer.

Regarding what an engagement quality control review entails, ISA 220 explains that it involves:
  discussion with the engagement partner, a review of the financial statements and the proposed auditor's report, and consideration of whether the proposed auditor's report is appropriate. It shall also involve a review of selected working papers relating to the significant judgments the engagement team made and the conclusions they reached. (para 20)
More specifically, for the audits of listed entities, the quality control review is to include consideration of the following factors:
  (a) The engagement team's evaluation of the firm's independence in relation to the audit engagement;
  (b) Whether appropriate consultation has taken place on matters involving differences of opinion or other difficult or contentious matters, and the conclusions arising from those consultations; and
  (c) Whether audit documentation selected for review reflects the work performed in relation to the significant judgments and supports the conclusions reached. (ISA 220, para 21)[28]

As for all other aspects of the audit, the engagement quality control review is to be documented. More specifically, the quality control reviewer is required to document, for the engagement reviewed, that:

---

[28] Engagement quality control reviews are discussed further in Chapters 13 (section 13.6.1) and 16 (section 16.2.3).

(a) The procedures required by the firm's policies on engagement quality control review have been performed;
(b) The engagement quality control review has been completed before the auditor's report is issued; and
(c) The reviewer is not aware of any unresolved matters that would cause the reviewer to believe that the significant judgments the engagement team made and the conclusions they reached were not appropriate. (ISA 220, para 25)

7.6.5 Assembly and retention of the final audit file

One of the causes of the demise of Arthur Andersen in 2002 (as part of the fallout from the Enron debacle) was the shredding of audit working papers by Andersen staff. It is, therefore, not surprising that ISA 230: *Audit documentation* includes a section relating to assembling and retaining the final audit file. This Standard requires auditors to:

> complete the administrative process of assembling the final audit file on a timely basis after the date of the auditor's report.... An appropriate time limit within which to complete the assembly of the final audit file is ordinarily not more than 60 days after the date of the auditor's report (paras 14, A21).

Assembling the final audit file is an administrative process that does not involve any additional audit procedures. It involves making sure the audit documentation is complete and in good order. It includes, for example:
– deleting or discarding documentation which has been superseded;
– sorting, collating and cross-referencing working papers;
– signing off on completion checklists relating to the final assembly of the file;
– documenting audit evidence (not yet recorded) that the auditor obtained, discussed and agreed with relevant members of the audit team, before the date of the auditor's report.

After the final audit file has been assembled, the auditor is not permitted to delete or discard audit documentation of any nature before the end of the applicable retention period (ISA 230, para 15). In the UK, registered auditors are required to keep all audit working papers for a period of at least six years from the end of the accounting period to which the papers relate [ISA (UK and Ireland) 230, footnote 3a].

If auditors find it necessary to modify, or add to, existing audit documentation after assembly of the final audit file has been completed, irrespective of the nature of the modifications or additions, they are required (by ISA 230, para 16) to document:
– the specific reasons for making the modifications or additions; and
– when, and by whom, the modifications or additions were made and reviewed.

7.6.6 Ownership of audit working papers

Working papers prepared in relation to an audit engagement, including those prepared by the client at the request of the auditor, are the property of the auditor (that is, the audit firm). As we observed in Chapter 6 (section 6.5), the occasions on which anyone else has a legal right to examine audit documentation are extremely limited. However ISQC 1 makes it clear that, auditors may, if they wish, make parts of, or extracts from, their audit working papers available to audit clients, "provided such disclosure does not undermine the validity of the work performed, or ... the independence of the firm or its personnel" (para A61).

Not only are audit files normally to be kept confidential; they must also be kept secure. ISQC 1 requires audit firms to "establish policies and procedures designed to maintain the confidentiality, safe custody, integrity, accessibility and retrievability of engagement documentation" (para 47). The Standard also points out:

> Whether engagement documentation is in paper, electronic or other media, the integrity, accessibility or retrievability of the underlying data may be compromised if the documentation could be altered, added to or deleted without the firm's knowledge, or if it could be permanently lost or damaged. (para A55)

Accordingly, audit firms need to establish controls that will:

(i) enable determination of when, and by whom, audit working papers were created, changed and reviewed;

(ii) protect the integrity of the audit documentation at all stages of the engagement, especially when information is shared between audit team members or transmitted to other parties via the Internet; and

(iii) prevent unauthorised changes to the documentation (ISCQ 1, para A55).

7.7 SUMMARY

In this chapter we have reviewed the audit process, discussed the meaning and nature of audit evidence, and examined some important administrative aspects of auditing – in particular, staffing and documenting an audit. We have seen that the audit process comprises a series of well-defined steps through which auditors proceed, gradually gathering evidence to enable them to form an opinion on (amongst other things) whether the financial statements under examination provide a true and fair view of the entity's financial position and performance, and comply with IAS or UK GAAP (as applicable) and the Companies Act 2006.

We have also drawn a distinction between audit objectives (the purpose for which audit evidence is obtained) and audit procedures (the methods by which the evidence is gathered). Additionally, we have identified three levels of audit objectives (overall, general and specific objectives), outlined some common audit procedures, and explained terms such as compliance and substantive procedures, and tests of transactions and tests of balances. We have also examined some characteristics of evidence obtained from different sources and explored factors affecting auditors' choice of evidence, namely, reliability, relevance, availability, timeliness and cost. We have observed that there is a trade-off between the quantity of evidence an auditor needs to gather (sufficiency) and the relevance and reliability (appropriateness or quality) of the evidence.

In relation to staffing an audit we have considered the capabilities and competence required of auditors, auditors' responsibilities in cases where they rely on experts or 'component auditors' to perform part of an audit, and the need for audit engagement partners to carefully assign, direct, supervise and review work delegated to audit staff. As regards documenting an audit, we have discussed the purpose and importance of audit working papers and their form, content and preparation. We have also explained working paper review, and the requirements with respect to assembling and retaining the final audit file and ownership of audit documentation.

From our examination of these topics it is evident that, in order for an audit to be conducted effectively, efficiently and with due professional care, it must be adequately staffed by personnel who possess the personal qualities of integrity, objectivity and independence, and who also have the capabilities, competence and time required to perform the tasks assigned to them. Additionally, work assigned to audit staff must be carefully directed and supervised and all audit work must be fully and properly documented, and carefully reviewed. Proper documentation is also required to provide evidence that sufficient appropriate audit evidence was gathered during the audit and that the conclusions reached accord with that evidence and support the opinion expressed in the audit report.

SELF-REVIEW QUESTIONS

7.1   Identify the major steps in the audit process.

7.2   Briefly explain the objective of:
      (i)   compliance procedures, and
      (ii) substantive procedures.
    For each of these objectives give one example of an audit procedure which is designed to meet that objective.

7.3 State whether you agree or disagree with the following statement. Briefly explain your answer.

> Gathering evidence in accordance with ISAs requires the auditor to obtain the strongest possible evidence for each item in the financial statements regardless of cost or difficulties that may be encountered.

7.4 Outline the requirements of audit engagement partners with respect to:
  (i) directing,
  (ii) supervising, and
  (iii) reviewing
the work of audit staff.

7.5 Briefly explain the responsibilities of the audit engagement partner when (s)he relies on the work of experts to perform part of an audit.

7.6 (a) Define 'audit working papers'; and
  (b) List five specific purposes of audit working papers.

7.7 (a) Distinguish between information contained in:
  (i) the permanent audit file,
  (ii) the current audit file.
  (b) Provide two examples of the information contained in each of the above files.

7.8 Briefly explain:
  (a) the purpose and importance of audit working paper review;
  (b) when, and by whom, working paper review is conducted.

7.9 (a) Define. the term: 'engagement quality control review';
  (b) List the criteria to qualify as an engagement quality control reviewer;
  (c) Briefly explain the purpose and importance of an engagement quality control review.

7.10 Outline the requirements of ISA 230: *Documentation* with respect to:
  (i) assembling the final audit file and subsequent modifications or additions; and
  (ii) retention, ownership and custody of audit working papers.

REFERENCES

Auditing Practices Board (APB). (2006). International Standard on Auditing (ISA) (UK and Ireland) 230: *Audit documentation*. London: Financial Reporting Council.

Auditing Practices Board (APB). (2008). Ethical Standard (ES) 4: *Fees, remuneration and evaluation policies, litigation, gifts and hospitality*. London: Financial Reporting Council.

International Auditing and Assurance Standards Board (IAASB). (2007). *Glossary of Terms*. New York: International Federation of Accountants.

ADDITIONAL READING

Harding, N., and Trotman, K.T. (1999). Hierarchical differences in audit working paper review performance. *Contemporary Accounting Research* **16**(4), 671–684.

Institute of Chartered Accountants in England and Wales (ICAEW). (2000*). Towards Better Auditing*. London: ICAEW, Audit Faculty.

Institute of Chartered Accountants of Scotland (ICAS). (2007). *Appraising your Auditors: A Guide to the Assessment and Appointment of Auditors* (2nd edn.). Edinburgh: ICAS.

Rudolph, H.R., and Welker, R.B. (1998). The effects of organizational structure on communication within audit teams. *Auditing: A Journal of Practice & Theory* **17**(2), 1–14.

Shankar, P.G., and Tan, H-T. (2006). Determinants of audit preparers' workpaper justifications. *The Accounting Review* **81**(2), 473–496.

Shelton, S.W. (1999). The effect of experience on the use of irrelevant evidence in auditor judgment. *The Accounting Review* **74**(2), 217–224.

Tan H-T., and Jamal, K. (2001). Do auditors objectively evaluate their subordinates' work? *The Accounting Review* **76**(1), 99–110.

Tan, H-T., and Trotman, K.T. (2003). Reviewers' responses to anticipated stylization attempts by preparers of audit workpapers. *The Accounting Review* **78**(2), 581–606.

8 Commencing an Audit: Engagement Procedures, Understanding the Client and Identifying Risks

LEARNING OBJECTIVES

After studying the material in this chapter you should be able to:

- outline the reasons for, and the process of, pre-engagement investigations;
- discuss the purpose and content of audit engagement letters;
- explain the importance of gaining a thorough understanding of the client, its business (including its processes, operations and risks), and its industry;
- identify and discuss external and internal environmental factors which impact on an entity and its external audit;
- outline the audit procedures used to gain an understanding of the client and its business and to identify and assess risks of material misstatement in the financial statements;
- discuss the importance of analytical procedures for identifying and assessing audit risk.

The following publications are particularly relevant to this chapter:

- International Standard on Quality Control (ISQC) 1 (Redrafted): *Quality Control for Firms that Perform Audits and Reviews of Financial Statements, and Other Assurance and Related Services Engagements* (IFAC, June 2008)**[1]
- International Standard on Auditing (ISA) 210 (Redrafted): *Agreeing the Terms of Audit Engagements* (IFAC, 2008)*
- International Standard on Auditing (ISA) 315 (Redrafted): *Identifying and Assessing the Risks of Material Misstatement through Understanding the Entity and its Environment* (IFAC, 2006)
- International Standard on Auditing (ISA) 510 (Redrafted): *Initial Audit Engagements – Opening Balances* (IFAC, 2008)
- International Standard on Auditing (ISA) 520 (Redrafted): *Analytical Procedures* (IFAC, 2007)*
- *Code of Ethics for Professional Accountants* (IFAC, 2006), Section 290 (IFAC, 2006)[2,3]

---

[1] The status of the ISAs referred to in this chapter is explained in the Important Note following the Preface to this book.

[2] The IFAC *Code of Ethics* was revised in July 2006 but an Exposure Draft (ED) of section 290 (Independence – Audit and Review Engagements) was issued in December 2006. A further ED of some paragraphs of section 290 was issued in July 2007. In this chapter, IFAC (2006*) is used to refer to the ED of section 290 and IFAC (2006) is used to denote the revised *Code of Ethics*.

[3] The Institutes of Chartered Accountants in England and Wales, of Scotland and in Ireland, and the Association of Chartered Certified Accountants has each issued a *Code of Ethics* which applies to their respective members. These *Codes* are based on, and very similar to, the IFAC (2006) *Code of Ethics*.

8.1 INTRODUCTION

In this chapter we begin our journey through the audit process. We assume that an auditor (an individual or an audit firm) has been approached by a company to accept appointment as its auditor. We discuss the steps the auditor should take before accepting the engagement and the audit engagement letter (s)he should prepare. We also explore the all-important audit step of the auditor gaining a thorough understanding of the client, its business (including its processes, operations and risks) and its industry and, through this, identifying and assessing risks of material misstatement in the financial statements.[4] This provides the foundation for planning the audit which is the subject of Chapter 9.

8.2 PRE-ENGAGEMENT INVESTIGATION

8.2.1 The need for a pre-engagement investigation

In a competitive environment it is not always easy to obtain and retain audit clients. Nevertheless, when auditors are offered a new or continuing audit engagement they should consider carefully whether it is prudent to accept the offer. It is, for example, generally unwise to accept (or continue with) an audit client whose management lacks integrity or constantly argues about the proper conduct of the audit and/or the audit fee. Equally, it is important that an audit engagement is not accepted if the audit cannot be adequately staffed with personnel possessing the necessary levels of independence, capabilities and competence. These matters are covered by International Standard on Quality Control (ISQC) 1: *Quality control for firms that perform audits and reviews of financial statements* . . . (para 25), which specifies that each audit firm:

> shall establish policies and procedures for the acceptance and continuance of client relationships and specific [audit] engagements, designed to provide the firm with reasonable assurance that it will only undertake or continue relationships and engagements where the firm:
> (a) Is competent to perform the engagement and has the capabilities, time and resources to do so;
> (b) Can comply with ethical requirements; and
> (c) Has considered the integrity of the client, and does not have information that would lead it to conclude that the client lacks integrity.

International Standard on Auditing (ISA) 220: *Quality control for an audit of financial information* (para 11) adds to this by requiring the engagement

---

[4] It should be noted that gaining a preliminary understanding of the client's control environment and other internal control components is an element of 'Gaining an understanding of the client'. However, we do not address the topic in this chapter: internal control is the subject of Chapter 10.

partner to be satisfied that appropriate acceptance or continuance procedures have been followed and that the conclusions reached in this regard are appropriate.

In the light of the requirements of ISQC 1 cited above, it is convenient to discuss the elements of a pre-engagement investigation under the following headings:
- assessing the auditor's competence to perform the audit;
- complying with ethical requirements, including those relating to communicating with a predecessor auditor;
- evaluating the integrity of the client's owners, directors and senior managers.

8.2.2 Assessing the auditor's competence to perform the audit

In Chapters 3 and 7 we consider the importance of auditors possessing (or, in the case of specialised skills and knowledge, having available) the capabilities and competence, and also the time and resources, required to complete the audit.

Our earlier discussions of these matters highlighted the need for an audit firm, before accepting a new or continuing audit engagement, to consider carefully the specific requirements of the engagement and whether it (or, more pertinently, the audit engagement partner):
- possesses the required levels of training, experience and competence to perform the audit satisfactorily.[5] This includes possessing:
  - technical skills and experience in auditing,
  - adequate knowledge of the (potential) client's industry (or industries),
  - adequate knowledge of the relevant regulatory and reporting requirements;
- has available, at the appropriate time, adequate audit staff who possess the required capabilities, competence and time necessary to perform the work to be assigned to them;
- is able to direct, supervise and review the work of audit staff;
- has available, at the appropriate time, assistance from experts and/or other auditors if they are to perform part of the audit;

---

[5] The importance of auditors possessing required capabilities and competence to conduct an audit was highlighted in July 2007 when the Securities and Exchange Commission (SEC) in the United States of America (USA) censured Ernst & Young in Dublin for failing to assign auditors with sufficient expertise to examine the financial statements of a software company, SkillSoft plc (a company based in New Hampshire which, at the time of the offence, was known as SmartForce). Ernst & Young in Dublin agreed to pay $725,000 (approximately £362,500) as settlement for its failure (Accountancy Age, 2007).

- if the audit is to be subject to an engagement quality control review (for example, if the potential client is a listed company), has available, at the appropriate time, an engagement quality control reviewer;
- is able to complete the audit within the reporting timeframe.

Additionally, before accepting a new audit client, an audit firm needs to consider the impact of the engagement on its audit portfolio. In particular, the firm should consider whether acceptance of the client would give rise to any conflict of interest with existing clients and/or whether it would adversely affect its ability to service existing clients properly.

8.2.3 Complying with ethical standards including communicating with a predecessor auditor

In Chapters 3 and 4 we examine in some detail the importance of auditors (engagement partners and audit staff) being independent of their audit clients and their clients' managements. We identify several threats that may endanger auditors' independence – in appearance if not in fact,[6] and various requirements the law, the APB's Ethical Standards and the profession's Codes of Ethics[7] have imposed on auditors in order to protect and/or strengthen their independence. In section 8.2.2 above we noted the importance of auditors ensuring they have the necessary capabilities, competence, time and resources to perform a particular audit before accepting the engagement. However, the International Federation of Accountants' (IFAC) *Code of ethics for professional accountants* (2006, para 210.1) requires more than this: before accepting a particular engagement, all professional accountants (including auditors) are to consider whether acceptance would create any threats not just to their independence and competence but to their compliance with *any* of the fundamental ethical principles – integrity, objectivity, professional competence and due care, confidentiality and professional behaviour.[8]

The *Code of ethics* (IFAC, 2006, para 210.3) requires auditors to evaluate the significance of any identified threats and, unless they are insignificant, to apply safeguards to eliminate or reduce them to an acceptable level. The Code explains (para 210.8):

Such safeguards may include:
- Acquiring an appropriate understanding of the nature of the client's business, the complexity of its operations, the specific requirements of the engagement and the purpose, nature and scope of the work to be performed.

---

[6] In Chapter 3 we note that, in the United Kingdom, the Auditing Practices Board adopts the term 'independence' for independence in appearance and 'objectivity' for independence in fact (or mind). See Chapter 3, section 3.3.1b.

[7] See footnote 3.

[8] Each of these concepts is discussed in Chapter 3.

- Acquiring knowledge of relevant industries or subject matters.
- Possessing or obtaining experience with relevant regulatory or reporting requirements.
- Assigning sufficient staff with the necessary competencies.
- Using experts where necessary.
- Agreeing on a realistic time frame for the performance of the engagement.
- Complying with quality control policies and procedures designed to provide reasonable assurance that specific engagements are accepted only when they can be performed competently.

If auditors are unable to apply safeguards that can eliminate or reduce the identified threats to an acceptable level, the engagement should be declined.

In situations where audit firms are invited to accept nomination, or to tender, for appointment as auditor for a potential client, and the audit engagement is currently held by another audit firm, in addition to evaluating the firm's ability to comply with all of the ethical principles, the *Code of ethics* requires the prospective auditor to ascertain whether there are any professional or other reasons for not accepting the appointment. It is important that the prospective audit firm establishes all the facts and circumstances surrounding the proposed change of auditor so that it can make an informed decision about whether or not to accept nomination, or to tender, for appointment as auditor.

Ascertaining the facts and circumstances surrounding a change of auditor usually involves direct communication with the incumbent auditor. However, the incumbent is bound by his or her duty of confidentiality to the client. Therefore, prospective auditors, when first invited by a client to accept nomination, or to submit a tender, for appointment as auditor, should explain to the potential client that they have a professional duty to communicate with the existing auditor.[9] They should also request the potential client to inform the existing auditor of the proposed change and to give the existing auditor written authority to discuss the client's affairs with the prospective auditor. If the client fails or refuses to grant the existing auditor permission to discuss its affairs with the prospective auditor, the *Code of ethics* suggests that the prospective auditor "should try to obtain information about possible threats [to adherence to the fundamental principles] by other means such as through inquiries of third parties or background investigations on senior management or those charged with governance of the client" (IFAC, 2006, para 210.16).[10] If the prospective

---

[9] ISA 300 (Redrafted): *Planning an audit of financial statements* (IAASB, 2006) includes as an activity auditors are required to undertake prior to starting an initial engagement: "Communicating with the predecessor auditor, where there has been a change of auditors, in compliance with ethical standards" (para 12). As explained in Chapter 5, ISAs have the status of regulations in the UK and, therefore, for auditors in the UK, communicating with the existing auditor is also a regulatory duty.

[10] However, a client's refusal to give the existing auditor permission to discuss its affairs with the proposed auditor may also raise questions for the latter about the wisdom of accepting nomination, or tendering, for appointment as auditor for the client.

auditor is unable to ascertain the necessary facts to make an informed decision as to whether or not to accept nomination, or to tender, for the engagement, (s)he should decline to accept nomination or to submit a tender.

Once an existing auditor receives permission from the client to disclose information to a prospective auditor, the existing auditor should provide to the prospective auditor:

> honestly and unambiguously ... known information on any facts or circumstances that, in the existing [auditor's] opinion, the proposed [auditor] should be aware of before deciding whether to accept the engagement. (IFAC, 2006, paras 210.15, 210.16)

Normally the communication between the existing and proposed auditor is a matter of routine and nothing of significance needs to be reported by the former to the latter. However, occasionally circumstances arise which are likely to affect the proposed auditor's decision to accept or reject the nomination or invitation to submit a tender. These are the matters the incumbent auditor should communicate to the proposed auditor.[11] For example:

(i) reasons for the change of auditor advanced by the client, of which the existing auditor is aware, are not in accordance with the facts (as understood by the latter);

(ii) in the opinion of the existing auditor, the proposal to replace him or her has resulted from the auditor conducting the audit in accordance with Auditing Standards in the face of opposition or evasions which have given rise to important differences of opinion with the client;

(iii) the existing auditor has serious doubts regarding the integrity of the directors and/or senior managers of the client;

(iv) the client, its directors, or employees have deliberately withheld information required by the existing auditor for the performance of his or her duties or have limited, or attempted to limit, the scope of audit work;

(v) the existing auditor proposes to bring to the attention of shareholders or creditors of the company circumstances surrounding the proposed

---

[11] However, the Institute of Charted Accountants of Scotland's (ICAS) *Code of ethics* (2006) warns:

> care must be taken when communicating all relevant facts to a [prospective auditor] in situations where the existing [auditor] knows or suspects that their client is involved in money laundering or a terrorist activity. Under the Money Laundering Regulations 2003 and the Terrorism Act 2000, it is a criminal offence to "tip off" a money launderer or terrorist. Accordingly:
>
> • The prospective [auditor] should not specifically enquire whether the existing [auditor] has reported suspicions of money laundering or terrorism. Such questions place the existing [auditor] in a difficult position and are likely not to be answered ... ;
>
> • Disclosure of money laundering or terrorism suspicion reporting by the existing [auditor] to the potential successor should be avoided because this information may be discussed with the client or former client. (para 210.12)
>
> The *Codes of Ethics* of the other UK professional bodies contain similar warnings.

change of auditor (i.e., file a 'statement of circumstances' in accordance with the Companies Act 2006, s. 519; see Chapter 5, section 5.2.5).

From the above, it is evident that the communication between the proposed and existing auditor serves two main purposes, namely:
  (i) it reduces the likelihood of the prospective auditor accepting an invitation to be nominated, or to tender, for an audit engagement in circumstances where all of the pertinent facts are not known; and
  (ii) it protects the interests of the existing auditor when the proposed change arises from, or is an attempt to interfere with, the conscientious exercise of the existing auditor's duty to act as an independent professional.

It is frequently contended that an audit firm should not continue as auditor for a client that owes a significant amount of fees. While noting that, in general, the audit report for a subsequent year should not be issued before the fees for the previous year's audit have been paid, the *Code of ethics* (IFAC, 2006*, para 290.215) states that, where fees are owed:

> the significance of the threat [to independence] should be evaluated. If the threat is not clearly insignificant, safeguards should be considered and applied when necessary to eliminate the threat or reduce it to an acceptable level. Such safeguards might include having an additional professional accountant who did not take part in the audit engagement, provide advice, or review the work performed. The firm should also consider whether the overdue fees might be regarded as being equivalent to a loan to the client and whether, because of the significance of the overdue fees, it is appropriate for the firm to be re-appointed.[12]

A further matter relating to a change of auditors concerns the incoming auditor substantiating the balances presented in the financial statements for the period preceding that in which (s)he is appointed. In this regard, ISA 510: *Initial audit engagements – opening balances* requires auditors to:

> obtain sufficient appropriate evidence about whether the opening balances contain misstatements that materially affect the current period's financial statements by:
> (a) Determining whether the prior period's closing balances have been correctly brought forward to the current period or, when appropriate, have been restated;
> (b) Determining whether the opening balances reflect the application of appropriate accounting policies; and
> (c) Performing one or more of the following:
>   (i) Where the prior year financial statements were audited, reviewing the predecessor auditor's working papers;
>   (ii) Evaluating of whether audit procedures performed in the current period provide evidence relevant to the opening balances; or

---

[12] We should note that, if a potential client owes fees to the predecessor (or incumbent) auditor, this is not of itself a reason for a prospective auditor to decline appointment as auditor.

(iii) Performing audit procedures to obtain evidence regarding the opening balances. (para 6)

If the prior period's financial statements were audited by a predecessor auditor, the current auditor may be able to obtain sufficient appropriate audit evidence regarding the opening balances by reviewing the predecessor auditor's working papers. Whether such a review provides sufficient appropriate audit evidence is influenced by the professional competence and independence of the predecessor auditor. (para A4)

If the auditor finds evidence to suggest the opening balances may contain misstatements which could materially affect the current period's financial statements, what should (s)he do? According to ISA 510, para 7, the auditor should perform additional audit procedures to determine whether or not such misstatements are present in the opening balances. If (s)he concludes the misstatements exist, the auditor is required to inform the appropriate level of management, the directors and, subject to authorisation from the client's management, the predecessor auditor.

ISA 510, para 8, also requires auditors to obtain sufficient appropriate audit evidence to determine whether:
(i) the accounting policies reflected in the opening balances have been consistently applied in the current period's financial statements; and
(ii) any changes in the accounting policies have been properly accounted for and adequately presented and disclosed.

8.2.4 Evaluating the integrity of the client's owners, directors and management

It has been noted in earlier chapters that an auditor is required, *inter alia*, to examine financial statements prepared by an audit client's directors for parties external to the entity, and to form and express an opinion on whether or not these financial statements present a true and fair view of the entity's financial position and performance, and comply with the applicable financial reporting framework.[13]

Over the past 30 to 40 years, deliberate manipulation of financial statement information has become a problem in many parts of the world. Indeed, the problem was so serious in the United States of America (USA) in the mid-1980s that, in 1986, the National Commission on Fraudulent Financial

---

[13] In the United Kingdom, an applicable financial reporting framework means International Accounting (or Financial Reporting) Standards (IAS) or United Kingdom Generally Accepted Accounting Practice (UK GAAP): see Chapter 5, section 5.2.2. ISA (UK and Ireland) 200: *Objectives and general principles governing an audit of financial statements* (APB, 2004) notes: "The 'applicable financial reporting framework' comprises those requirements of accounting standards, law [including the Companies Act 2006] and regulations applicable to the entity that determine the form and content of its financial statements" (para 2-1).

Reporting (the Treadway Commission, 1987) was established to investigate it. In some cases, entity managements[14] have manipulated financial statement information in order to cover up a fraud (as, for example, in the infamous *Equity Funding* and *Parmalat* cases); in other cases, management has been motivated by a desire to portray the entity's financial position and performance in a more favourable light than is warranted by the underlying facts. This has arisen from management's wish to avoid events such as a decline in the value of the company's shares, or public criticism of its performance; or its desire to secure outcomes such as personal bonuses which are linked to reported profits, or raising new debt or equity capital in financial markets on favourable terms.

In the United Kingdom (UK) (as elsewhere in the world), deliberate but legal manipulation of financial statements (somewhat flatteringly entitled 'creative accounting') has received considerable attention. The International and UK Accounting Standards Boards have sought to eliminate so-called 'creative practices' by issuing more tightly prescribed accounting standards. However, in recent years aggressive earnings management, a variant of creative account-ing, has emerged as a significant problem and, as noted in Chapter 6, the UK's APB is keen for auditors to be alert to, and respond to, the risk of clients engaging in this activity – an activity which, unless checked, may progress into fraudulent financial reporting.

If an entity's management lacks integrity, there is a fairly high probability that some manipulation of financial statement information will occur whenever the management perceives it advantageous so to do. Additionally, such a man-agement is likely to be at pains to deceive the auditor to the extent necessary to ensure that the auditor does not discover the underlying situation. In this regard it is pertinent to observe that, in many of the court cases where auditors have faced charges of negligence as a result of failing to uncover management fraud, it has been revealed that the senior executives and/or directors who were respon-sible for the fraud had a past history of such deeds. Arens and Loebbecke (1980), amongst others, have drawn attention to this phenomenon. They state:

> An analysis of recent court cases involving management fraud shows that in most instances the individuals responsible for the fraud had also been previously involved in illegal or unethical business practices. (p. 176)

A specific example of such a case is afforded by de Angelis, instigator of the massive salad oil fraud in the 1960s at the Allied Crude Vegetable Oil Refining Corporation of New Jersey. During the court hearing it was revealed that de

---

[14] Readers are reminded that in the Preface to this book we note the term 'management' is defined to mean a company's executive directors, non-executive directors, and non-director executives (that is, all execu-tives and directors).

Angelis had a string of previous convictions for fraud and other illegal acts committed whilst acting as a company director.

The importance of auditors evaluating the integrity of a potential client's management was emphasised by Pratt and Dilton-Hill (1982). They suggested that management integrity is probably the single most important factor in the potential for (intentional) material misstatements in financial statements. They also drew attention to the extent to which an auditor relies on information and responses provided by the auditee's management. The nature of an audit is such that auditors make many decisions based on discussions with management. If an auditee's management lacks integrity, information and responses given to the auditor may be untrustworthy and, as a result, erroneous audit decisions may be made. Examples of cases in the UK where auditors have found themselves in court for alleged negligence, in which the integrity of the directors is highly questionable, include Maxwell Communications, Polly Peck and the Bank of Credit and Commerce International (BCCI).

ISQC 1 (para A18) explains that, in ascertaining the integrity of a potential client, the audit firm should consider matters such as:
- The nature of the client's operations, including its business practices.
- Information concerning the attitude of the client's principal owners, key management and those charged with its governance towards such matters as aggressive interpretation of accounting standards and the internal control environment.
- Whether the client is aggressively concerned with maintaining the [audit] firm's fees as low as possible.
- Indications of an inappropriate limitation in the scope of [audit] work.
- Indications that the client might be involved in money laundering or other criminal activities.
- The reasons for the proposed appointment of the [audit] firm and non-reappointment of the previous firm.
- The identity and business reputation of related parties.

For a continuing audit engagement, the auditor should evaluate the integrity of the client's management by reviewing his or her past experience with that management. However, if significant changes have occurred amongst the client's senior executives and/or directors, further investigation may be necessary, similar to that undertaken for a new audit engagement.

In the case of a new engagement, if the potential client has been audited previously, information pertaining to the integrity of its management can usually be obtained from the predecessor auditor. As we explained in section 8.2.3 above, before a proposed auditor can accept an audit engagement, (s)he is required by the profession's Code of Ethics to communicate with the predecessor auditor. One of the matters to be communicated by the incumbent (or outgoing) auditor to the proposed auditor is doubts the former auditor has regarding the integrity of the auditee's directors and/or senior managers.

As noted above, among the matters ISQC 1 suggests audit firms should investigate when approached to accept a new audit engagement is the reason for the proposed appointment and the non-reappointment of the incumbent auditor. ISQC 1, para A19, also suggests the firm should seek information about the integrity of the client's owners, directors and management from third parties such as the prospective client's bankers, legal counsel and others in the financial or business community, or in the same industrial sector, who may have relevant knowledge about the prospective client. Additionally, the firm should conduct background searches of relevant databases for references to the potential client or any of its directors, senior executives or influential shareholders during the past three to five years, to ascertain whether there is any information in the public domain which indicates that they may have been associated with anything untoward (in particular, with any unethical or illegal activities).

In the USA, some auditors and audit firms consider the integrity of a potential client's management is so important that they hire professional investigators to obtain information about the reputation and background of key members of its management. In the UK, it is not usual to go to such lengths but, faced by the spate of unexpected company failures and allegations of corporate fraud which have occurred in recent years, audit firms in the UK have become more diligent than formerly about investigating the integrity of senior executives and directors of potential audit clients, and more willing to refuse to accept nomination to act as auditors for companies where that integrity is in doubt.[15]

8.3 AUDIT ENGAGEMENT LETTERS

Once the pre-engagement investigation is complete and the auditor has decided to accept the engagement, an engagement letter is prepared. This is required by ISA 210: *Agreeing the terms of audit engagements*, which states: "The auditor shall agree terms of the audit engagement with [the directors] . . . [T]he agreed terms of the audit engagement shall be recorded in an engagement letter or other form of written agreement" (paras 7, 9). The purpose of the letter (or other form of written agreement) is to document and confirm the auditor's acceptance of the appointment and to ensure there is no misunderstanding between the auditor and the client about the auditor's and directors' respective

---

[15] Since the turn of the 21st century, most audit firms in the UK have introduced stringent acceptance and continuance audit engagement procedures; these include considering an extensive list of factors (including a set of factors addressing the integrity of the potential client's management) that are listed in engagement acceptance or continuance checklists.

responsibilities, the scope of the audit engagement, and the form of the reports the auditor is to provide at the conclusion of the audit.

Although the details of engagement letters vary according to the circumstances of the particular audit, certain items are almost invariably included. They usually include, for example, statements referring to the following matters:
- the objective of the audit of financial statements;
- the directors' responsibility for preparing financial statements that give a true and fair view of the entity's state of affairs (financial position) and profit or loss (financial performance), and comply with an appropriate financial reporting framework,[16] and that this responsibility includes the design, implementation and maintenance of internal controls relevant to the preparation and presentation of financial statements that are free from material misstatement, whether due to fraud or error;[17]
- identification of the applicable financial reporting framework;
- the directors' responsibility for ensuring that all of the company's records and documents, and any other information requested in connection with the audit, are made available to the auditors. Similarly, that the auditor will have unrestricted access to those within the entity from whom the auditor determines it is necessary to obtain audit evidence;
- the auditor's responsibility to form and express an opinion on the financial statements and to report, in the audit report, if the financial statements do not comply in any material respects with the applicable financial reporting framework, unless the auditor considers that non-compliance is justified in the circumstances;
- other matters the auditor must consider and may need to refer to in the audit report – for example, whether adequate accounting records have been kept by the entity, whether information given in the directors' report is consistent with the financial statements, and whether the financial statements give the details of the directors' remuneration required by the Companies Act 2006;
- the scope (extent) of the audit and the fact that the audit will be conducted in accordance with applicable legislation, regulations, International Standards on Auditing and ethical or other professional requirements. Reference is also made to any additional work the auditor is to do beyond that required for a statutory audit;

---

[16] See footnote 13.

[17] ISA 210, para A11, points out that the directors' assumption of this responsibility is a premise that is "fundamental to the conduct of an effective independent audit. To avoid misunderstanding, agreement is reached with [the directors] that they acknowledge and understand their responsibilities, as part of agreeing and recording the terms of the audit engagement". As we explain in Chapter 13, during the completion and review stage of the audit, the auditee's directors are requested to provide the auditor with written representations, *inter alia*, confirming they have fulfilled their responsibilities for the financial statements and financial reporting process.

- how the auditor plans to approach and perform the audit;
- in appropriate cases, the involvement of other auditors or experts in certain aspects of the audit; similarly, any planned involvement of the client's internal auditors or other personnel;
- the fact that the audit is not designed to detect significant deficiencies in the company's accounting, internal control or risk management systems but that any such deficiencies which come to light during the audit will be reported to the directors;
- the fact that, because of the test nature and other inherent limitations of an audit, together with the inherent limitations of internal control, there is an unavoidable risk that even some material misstatements in the financial statements may remain undiscovered;
- the expectation that the directors will provide written confirmation of certain oral representations expressed by them to the auditor during the course of the audit. In this regard, attention is drawn to the legislative provision under which it is an offence for any person to withhold information from, or to provide information or explanations which are misleading, false or deceptive, to the auditor which relate to any matter that is material to the audit (i.e., Companies Act 2006, s. 501);
- the auditor will request sight of all documents or statements (such as the directors' remuneration report governance statement and business review) to be published in the entity's annual report along with the audited financial statements;
- the fact that safeguarding the entity's assets and preventing and detecting fraud, error, and non-compliance with applicable law or regulations is the responsibility of the directors and senior executives; nevertheless, the audit will be planned so as to provide a reasonable expectation of detecting material misstatements in the financial statements – including those resulting from fraud, error, or non-compliance with legal requirements;
- the auditor's responsibility for the financial statements for the year in question ceases once the audit report has been issued; however, the auditor should be informed of any material event occurring between the issue of the audit report and the general meeting of the company's shareholders at which the financial statements are presented (the 'accounts meeting'; see Chapter 5, section 5.2.4);
- the form of any reports or other communications that are to be provided by the auditor in relation to the audit;
- the basis on which fees are to be computed and billed;
- any limitation of the auditor's liability that may apply.

An example of an audit engagement letter is provided in Figure 8.1. The auditor prepares two copies of the letter. They are both sent to the client for signing: one is retained by the client; the other is returned to the auditor for inclusion in the audit file.

Figure 8.1:   Example of audit engagement letter for use in the UK
(This specimen letter is modified to meet the needs of specific circumstances)

To the directors of Foolproof plc

The objective of the audit

You have requested that we audit the financial statements of Foolproof plc, which comprise the balance sheet as at 31 March 20X2, and the income statement, statement of changes in equity and cash flow statement for the year then ended, and a summary of significant accounting policies and other explanatory notes.   We are pleased to confirm our acceptance and our understanding of this audit engagement by means of this letter. Our audit will be conducted with the objective of our expressing an opinion on the financial statements.

Responsibilities of the auditor

We have a statutory responsibility to report to the members of the company whether in our opinion the financial statements give a true and fair view and whether they have been properly prepared in accordance with the Companies Act 2006.   In arriving at our opinion, we are required to consider the following matters, and to report on any in respect of which we are not satisfied:

(a) Whether adequate accounting records have been kept by the company and proper returns adequate for our audit have been received from branches not visited by us;

(b) Whether the company's balance sheet and profit and loss account are in agreement with the accounting records and returns;

(c) Whether we have obtained all the information and explanations which we consider necessary for the purposes of our audit; and

(d) Whether the information given in the directors' report is consistent with the financial statements.

In addition, there are certain other matters which, according to the circumstances, may need to be dealt with in our report.   For example, where the financial statements do not give details of directors' remuneration or of their transactions with the company, the Companies Act 2006 requires us to disclose such matters in our report.

We have a responsibility to report if the financial statements do not comply in any material respect with applicable financial reporting standards, unless in our opinion the non-compliance is justified in the circumstances.   In determining whether or not the departure is justified we consider:

(a) Whether the departure is required in order for the financial statements to give a true and fair view;   and

(b) Whether adequate disclosure has been made concerning the departure.

Our responsibilities also include:

• Including in our report a description of the directors' responsibilities for the financial statements; and

• Considering whether other information in documents containing audited financial statements is consistent with those financial statements.

Once we have issued our report we have no further direct responsibility in relation to the financial statements for that financial year.   However, we expect that you will inform us of any material event occurring between the date of our report and that of the members' Accounts Meeting which may affect the financial statements.

Scope of the audit

We will conduct our audit in accordance with International Standards on Auditing.   Those Standards require that we comply with ethical requirements and plan and perform the audit to obtain reasonable assurance whether the financial statements are free from material misstatement.   An audit involves performing procedures to obtain audit evidence about the amounts and disclosures in the financial statements.   The procedures selected depend on the auditor's judgment, including the assessment of the risks of material misstatement of the financial statements, whether due to fraud or error.   An audit also includes evaluating the appropriateness of accounting policies used and the reasonableness of accounting estimates made by the directors, as well as evaluating the overall presentation of the financial statements.

Because of the test nature and other inherent limitations of an audit, together with the inherent limitations of any accounting and internal control system, there is an unavoidable risk that even some material misstatements may remain undiscovered.

In making our risk assessments, we consider internal control relevant to the entity's preparation and presentation of financial statements that give a true and fair view in order to design audit procedures that are appropriate in the circumstances, but not for the purpose of expressing an opinion on the effectiveness of the entity's internal control.   However, we will communicate to you in writing concerning any significant deficiencies in internal control relevant to the audit of the financial statements that we have identified during the audit.

Figure 8.1: *Continued*

The responsibility for safeguarding the assets of the company and for the prevention and detection of fraud, error and non-compliance with law or regulations rests with yourselves. However, we shall endeavour to plan our audit so that we have a reasonable expectation of detecting material misstatements in the financial statements or accounting records (including those resulting from fraud, error or non-compliance with law or regulations), but our examination should not be relied upon to disclose all such material misstatements or frauds, errors or instances of non-compliance as may exist.

Our audit will be conducted on the basis that the directors acknowledge and understand their responsibility:

(a) For the preparation and presentation of financial statements that give a true and fair view in accordance with International Financial Reporting Standards; this includes the design, implementation and maintenance of internal control relevant to the preparation and fair presentation of financial statements that are free from material misstatement, whether due to fraud or error.

(b) To provide us with:

    (i) All information, such as records and documentation, and other matters that are relevant to the preparation and presentation of the financial statements;

    (ii) Any additional information that the auditor may request from the company's directors or executives; and

    (iii) Unrestricted access to those within the entity from whom we determine it necessary to obtain audit evidence.

As part of our audit process, we will request you to provide written confirmation of representations made to us in connection with the audit.

We look forward to full co-operation from your staff during our audit.

Fees

Our fees, which will be billed as work progresses, are based on the time required by the individuals assigned to the engagement plus out-of-pocket expenses. Individual hourly rates vary according to the degree of responsibility involved and the experience and skill required.

Agreement of terms

This letter will be effective for future years unless it is terminated, amended or superseded.

Please sign and return the attached copy of this letter to indicate that it is in accordance with your understanding of the arrangements for our audit of the financial statements.

Yours faithfully

Robinson & Crusoe
(Registered Auditors)

We agree to the terms of this letter

--   --

Signed for and on behalf of Foolproof plc   *Date*

Source: Adapted from ISA 210 (IAASB) and ISA (UK and Ireland) 210: *Terms of audit engagements*, Appendices

In cases where an auditor of a parent entity is also the auditor of a subsidiary, branch or division (i.e., a component) thereof, ISA 210 (para A21) notes that whether or not a separate engagement letter is sent to the component depends on factors such as:

- who appoints the auditor of the component;
- whether a separate audit report is to be issued on the component's financial statements;
- relevant legal and regulatory requirements;

- the extent of any work performed by other auditors;
- the degree of ownership by the parent entity;
- the degree of independence of the component's management from the parent entity.

ISA (UK and Ireland) 210: *Terms of audit engagements* (para 9-1) further specifies that, if auditors send one letter relating to the entity and its components (i.e., the group) as a whole, they should identify the components for which they are appointed as auditor. They are to request the directors of the parent entity (to whom the letter is sent) to forward the letter to the directors of the components concerned and to request each board of directors to confirm acceptance of the terms of the engagement.

In the case of a continuing audit engagement (or, as ISA 210 terms it, a 'recurring audit'), the auditor may decide that an engagement letter is not needed. However, as part of the annual planning process, the auditor should consider whether a new engagement letter is required. ISA 210 (para A24) notes:

the following factors may make it appropriate to revise the terms of the audit engagement or to remind the entity of existing terms:
- Any indication that the entity misunderstands the objective and scope of the audit.
- Any revised or special terms of the audit engagement.
- A recent change of senior management or those charged with governance [i.e., the directors].
- A significant change in ownership.
- A significant change in nature or size of the entity's business.
- A change in legal or regulatory requirements.
- A change in the financial reporting framework adopted in the preparation and presentation of the financial statements.[18]
- A change in other reporting requirements.

Before leaving the subject of audit engagement letters, we should note that these letters do not absolve the auditor from any duties in relation to the audit. Their principal purpose is to clarify the objective and scope of the audit and to ensure that the client's directors/management are aware of the nature of the audit engagement and of their own responsibilities with respect to the financial statements and other matters mentioned in the engagement letter.[19]

---

[18] A change in the financial reporting framework adopted will occur rarely: see Chapter 5, footnote 13.

[19] We should also note that the Companies Act 2006 provides for the Secretary of State to develop regulations that require the terms on which a company's auditor is appointed to be disclosed in the company's annual report.

The regulations may require disclosure of –
   (i) a copy of any terms that are in writing, and
   (ii) a written memorandum setting out any terms that are not in writing. (s. 493)

Although in June 2008 there was no indication that such regulations are on the horizon, should they be developed, it seems likely that they will have a significant impact on the form and content of audit engagement letters.

8.4 UNDERSTANDING THE CLIENT, ITS BUSINESS AND ITS INDUSTRY AND IDENTIFYING AND ASSESSING RISKS

8.4.1 Importance of gaining an understanding of the client and its business

In order to perform an effective and efficient audit it is essential that the auditor obtains a thorough understanding of the client – its organisation, structure and key personnel; its business, business operations and processes; its operational, financial and compliance risks; its economic, commercial and competitive environment; and its industry. ISA 315: *Identifying and assessing the risks of material misstatement through understanding the entity and its environment* (para A1) explains:

> Obtaining an understanding of the entity and its environment, including the entity's internal control ... is a continuous, dynamic process of gathering, updating and analyzing information throughout the audit. The understanding establishes a frame of reference within which the auditor plans the audit and exercises professional judgment throughout the audit, for example, when:
> • Assessing risks of material misstatement of the financial statements;
> • Establishing materiality and evaluating whether the judgment about materiality remains appropriate as the audit progresses;
> • Considering the appropriateness of the selection and application of accounting policies, and the adequacy of financial statement disclosures;
> • Identifying areas where special audit consideration may be necessary, for example, related party transactions, the appropriateness of management's use of the going concern assumption, or considering the business purpose of transactions;
> • Developing expectations for use when performing analytical procedures;
> • Responding to the assessed risks of material misstatement, including designing and performing further audit procedures to obtain sufficient appropriate audit evidence; and
> • Evaluating the sufficiency and appropriateness of audit evidence obtained, such as the appropriateness of assumptions and of management's oral and written representations.

It should be noted that gaining an understanding of the client is a "continuous, dynamic process" – one which continues throughout the audit; it therefore overlaps the other audit steps we identified in Chapter 7 (see Figure 7.1). Nevertheless, before the auditor can plan the audit (s)he must have a sound understanding of the client and its environment. It is only with such an understanding that the auditor can:

• understand the classes of transactions, account balances and disclosures expected to be present in the financial statements; and
• identify factors that may give rise to the risk of material misstatement in the financial statements (whether through fraud or error) and to assess the likelihood of such misstatement occurring.[20]

---

[20] It may be recalled from Chapter 2, section 2.2.6, that an in-depth and wide-ranging knowledge of the client underlies the business risk approach to auditing.

Indeed, identifying and assessing the risks that may threaten the integrity of the financial statements is a key objective of this step in the audit process – a topic we discuss further in section 8.4.3 below. Once the risks have been identified and assessed, appropriate responses to those risks (i.e., the nature, timing and extent of further audit procedures) may be determined. This takes us into the realm of planning the audit, which is the subject of Chapter 9.

A thorough understanding of the client entity and its internal and external environment is not only necessary for planning the audit and exercising appropriate judgment throughout its progress; the auditor also needs to be thoroughly familiar with all aspects of the client in order to understand 'how the client ticks' and to obtain a background (or context) against which the credibility of evidence gathered during the audit, and responses given by the client's management and employees to the auditor's enquiries, can be evaluated: in the light of his or her knowledge of the business, its circumstances, and its internal and external environment, does the evidence gathered and responses given 'make sense' and 'ring true'?

8.4.2 Factors affecting the client and its business

In order to gain an understanding of the client, its business and its industry – and to identify factors that may give rise to risks of material misstatement in its financial statements – the auditor must obtain knowledge of the external and internal factors which affect it.

(i) External environmental factors

External factors that affect all business entities are very wide ranging. Some are generic to the economy as a whole or to the industry in which an entity operates; others are more entity specific. Those affecting an auditee may include:

- economy-wide factors such as general economic conditions, interest rates, the availability of financing, inflation and foreign currency exchange rates;
- the general economic and competitive conditions of the industry within which the client operates, and the industry's vulnerability to changing economic and political factors;
- government policies affecting the entity's industry or business such as monetary (including financial exchange) controls, financial or tax incentives, and tariffs and trade restrictions;

- governmental or other regulatory requirements which affect the client and its industry (such as the need to obtain a licence, or be registered, to carry on business within the industry; and relevant consumer protection and employment laws and regulations);
- environmental requirements affecting the industry and/or the client's business;
- the presence or absence of characteristics such as changes in product or process technology, cyclical or seasonal activity, business risk (for example, products prone to consumer fads or rapid obsolescence or deterioration) and rapidly declining or expanding markets, that may typify the client's industry or its strategy;
- environmental considerations such as energy and/or water supply and cost, and supplier and customer relations, that affect the industry in general and/or the client in particular;
- major policies and practices of the industry, and industry specific accounting policies and practices (if any) (for example, loans and investments for banks, and research and development for pharmaceutical businesses);
- the client's reporting obligations to external parties such as shareholders, debenture holders, regulators (in the case of clients in regulated industries), HM Revenue & Customs, the Department of Business, Enterprise & Regulatory Reform, and the Companies Registrar.

(ii) Internal environmental factors

In addition to external factors, a wide range of internal factors affect, *inter alia*, the client's business, its risk exposures and its financial statements. Internal environmental factors affecting an auditee include:

- the ownership interests and relationships of the entity;
- its organisational structure, and management and governance characteristics;
- the relationship between the client's owners, directors and non-director executives, and the influence of stakeholders other than shareholders;
- the client's geographical dispersion and industry segmentation;
- the location of production facilities, warehouses and inventories;
- the client's objectives and strategies and related business risks;[21]

---

[21] ISA 315 explains:

> An understanding of the business risks facing the entity increases the likelihood of identifying risks of material misstatement, since most business risks will eventually have financial consequences and, therefore, an effect on the financial statements.... Usually, management identifies business risks and develops approaches to address them. Such a risk assessment process is part of internal control ... (para A27, A30)

We discuss assessment of management's risk assessment process in Chapter 10, section 10.4.

- its financial characteristics – in particular, its financial structure and solvency, and asset structure and investment activities;
- its operating characteristics including its revenue sources, outputs, markets (including involvement in electronic commerce), stages and methods of production, and activities exposed to environmental risks;
- employment arrangements, including pensions and incentive payment arrangements;
- the ethical tone within the entity;
- the effectiveness of the client's control environment and internal controls;[22]
- the directors' objectives, philosophy, and general approach (for example, entrepreneurial or conservative, planned or haphazard, management).

In addition to obtaining an understanding of the environmental factors that affect an auditee, the auditor needs to gain an understanding of both its financial and non-financial performance measures – in particular:
- the measurement and review of its financial performance;
- its selection and application of accounting policies – and why and how changes to the policies are effected. The auditor needs to consider in particular: "whether the entity's accounting policies are appropriate for its business and consistent with the applicable financial reporting framework and accounting policies used in the relevant industry" (ISA 315, para 11c);
- its key performance indicators (financial and non-financial) and key ratios, trends and operating statistics;
- the preparation and use of budgets, variance analyses, and segmental, divisional and departmental information;
- the entity's performance compared with that of its competitors and industry norms.

8.4.3 Identifying and assessing risks of material misstatement in the financial statements

As indicated in section 8.4.1 above, at the same time as the auditor gains an understanding of the client, its external and internal environment, and its financial and non-financial performance measures, the auditor assesses the various items in terms of their likelihood of giving rise to, or helping to identify, the risk of material misstatement in the financial statements. For example, obtaining knowledge about new products may help identify potential product liability and/or inventories (stock) with values lower than cost; and knowledge

---

[22] See footnote 4.

of current and prospective financing arrangements may indicate a risk of loss of financing which may raise questions about the auditee's ability to continue as a going concern.

ISA 315 (para 24) requires auditors to perform audit procedures (termed 'risk assessment procedures') that are designed to identify and assess the risk of material misstatement, whether due to fraud or error, at both:

    (a) the financial statement level; and

    (b) the assertion level[23] for classes of transactions, account balances and disclosures.

ISA 315 explains the relevance of these two levels of risk to auditors as follows:

> Risks of material misstatement at the financial statement level refer to risks that relate pervasively to the financial statements as a whole ... Risks of this nature are not necessarily risks identifiable with specific assertions at the class of transactions, account balance, or disclosure level. Rather, they represent circumstances that may increase the risks of material misstatement at the assertion level, for example, through management override of internal control. Financial statement level risks may be especially relevant to the auditor's consideration of the risks of material misstatement arising from fraud. (para A98)

> Risks of material misstatement at the assertion level for classes of transactions, account balances, and disclosures need to be considered because such consideration directly assists in determining the nature, timing, and extent of further audit procedures at the assertion level necessary to obtain sufficient appropriate audit evidence.[24] (para A102)

In addition to identifying and assessing the risks of material misstatement at the financial statement and assertion level, auditors are required to identify and assess any significant risks, that is, risks of material misstatement that, in the auditor's judgment, require special audit attention. Such risks frequently relate to transactions that:

    • are unusual because of their size, nature, infrequency of occurrence, are outside the normal course of the entity's business, or relate to recent significant economic, accounting or other developments and, through lack of established practice, are prone to error;

---

[23] Assertions are defined in ISA 315, para 4, to mean: "Representations by management, explicit or otherwise, that are embodied in the financial statements, as used by the auditor to consider the different types of potential misstatements that may occur." The specific audit objectives referred to in Chapter 7, section 7.3, and shown in Figure 7.2, are assertions about sales transactions: i.e., by presenting 'sales' (or revenue) in the financial statements, management is implicitly asserting that recorded sales transactions are authorised, valid, complete, and accurate as to amount, account classification and accounting period. We discuss assertions, and audit procedures designed to test them, in Chapter 11.

[24] Expressed alternatively, identification of these risks is necessary for the development of the audit plan which we discuss in Chapter 9.

- involve significant judgment, such as estimates, for which there is a wide range of measurement uncertainty;
- are particularly complex; or
- involve significant transactions with related parties.

Other identified areas of significant risk may relate to, for example, the possibility of fraud, non-compliance with applicable laws and regulations, or doubt about the ability of the entity to continue as a going concern.

8.4.4 Obtaining an understanding of the client and its business

Having established that auditors need to obtain a thorough understanding of their auditees and, through this understanding, to identify and assess the risks of material misstatement at the financial statement and assertion level, as well as those that require special audit attention (i.e., significant risks), we need to consider how they go about achieving these objectives.

A variety of procedures (known as 'risk assessment procedures') are available to assist auditors in this task. They include:
- (i)   visiting the client and touring the premises;
- (ii)   having discussions with key personnel inside and outside the entity;
- (iii) inspecting the client's documentation;
- (iv) reviewing industry and business data and publications;
- (v)   reviewing previous years' audit working papers and, if relevant, drawing on previous experience with the client;
- (vi) discussion among engagement team members;
- (vii) performing analytical procedures (or analytical review).

We discuss below (i) to (vi) of the procedures listed above; analytical procedures are explained in section 8.5.

(i)   Visiting the client and touring the premises

By visiting the client, touring its premises and meeting key personnel (such as the chief executive officer, finance director, marketing, production and human resources department managers, and the chief internal auditor), the auditor can become familiar with the client's layout, organisation and operations.

A tour of the premises enables the auditor to obtain knowledge about the client's production or service provision processes, its storage facilities and its dispatching procedures. It also enables him or her to gain insight (by observation and enquiry) into the security (or otherwise) of inventories (stock), supplies and fixed assets, and the quantity and quality of inventories and fixed assets. Additionally, it enables the auditor to obtain information (by observation and inspection of records) about the client's accounting records, information technology, and the expertise and work habits of its accounting and other personnel. Further, it provides the opportunity to gauge (by observation of activities) the general attitude of client personnel to the control environment and the care with which they discharge their responsibilities.

(ii) Having discussions with key personnel inside and outside the entity

By having discussions with key client personnel (for example, the directors and/or audit committee members, chief executive officer, finance director, sales and production managers, and chief internal auditor), the auditor is able to learn about the environment in which the entity's financial statements are prepared. (S)he is also able to determine its operational and human resources policies and procedures and any changes to these which have occurred during the reporting period or are expected to occur in the current or future periods. Such discussions additionally enable the auditor to ascertain the views of key personnel about the entity's financial position and performance during the past year, and any changes in its operations, organisation, financial structure or personnel which are planned or expected in the near to medium-term future. Discussions with these key personnel should embrace topics such as likely changes in premises or plant facilities, divisions or departments; expected developments in technology, products or services, markets, or production and distribution methods; and any planned changes to the client's accounting system, information technology, management information systems and internal controls. The discussions also afford the opportunity for the auditor to gauge the objectives, philosophy, strategic plans and general approach/attitudes of key executives within the entity.

ISA 315 (para A6) explains that enquiries directed to specific entity personnel may be particularly valuable. For example:
- Inquiries directed toward internal audit personnel may provide information about internal audit procedures performed during the year relating to the design and effectiveness of the entity's internal control and whether management has satisfactorily responded to findings from those procedures.
- Inquiries of employees involved in initiating, processing or recording complex or unusual transactions may help the auditor to evaluate the appropriateness of the selection and application of certain accounting policies.
- Inquiries directed toward in-house legal counsel may provide information about such matters as litigation, compliance with laws and regulations, knowledge of fraud or suspected fraud affecting the entity, warranties, . . . and the meaning of contract terms.
- Inquiries directed towards marketing or sales personnel may provide information about changes in the entity's marketing strategies, sales trends, or contractual arrangements with its customers.

Discussions with significant people outside the client, such as economists and industry regulators, as well as other auditors, legal, financial (including valuation experts) and other advisors who have provided services to the client or within the industry, enable the auditor to obtain some understanding of the external factors affecting the client – and may also provide some insight into how other external parties view the client, its directors and its senior executives.

(iii) Inspecting the client's documentation

The auditor may gain considerable knowledge about internal aspects of the client by inspecting its documentation. Such documentation includes its legal documents (for example, Memorandum and Articles of Association, and any debenture trust deeds or other loan agreements); significant commercial agreements; its organisation chart, policies and procedures manuals, and job descriptions; its code of corporate conduct and compliance procedures; minutes of directors' and other (especially board committee) meetings; reports to shareholders and to regulatory agencies (such as HM Revenue & Customs); promotional material (in hard copy and electronic form); internal financial management reports, budgets, and chart of accounts; marketing, sales and production strategies and plans; and internal audit reports.

(iv) Reviewing industry and business data and publications

A review of industry and business data, reading reports by analysts and rating agencies, trade journals and magazines, and similar publications relating to the client or its industry, and also visiting relevant Internet sites, provides the auditor with information which is helpful in understanding the general economic, political, commercial and competitive factors and processes which are likely to affect the client's operational and financial well-being – and, hence, its financial statements.

(v) Reviewing previous years' audit working papers and past experience with the client

Reviewing previous years' audit working papers may highlight problems encountered during previous audits which need to be followed up, or watched for, during the current audit. It may also reveal planned or expected developments which are of significance to the present year's audit – for example, plans disclosed during the previous year to expand or change production and sales, to amend distribution policies, to develop new products, processes and/or markets, or to alter the accounting system, are likely to have an impact on this year's audit.

Along similar lines, the auditor may glean information, helpful for identifying risks of material misstatements in the current year's financial statements, from the engagement acceptance (or continuance) process and/or from previous audits of the client in which the engagement partner or other senior members of the audit team were involved. Such information may be useful, for example, in enhancing the auditor's understanding of the entity, and its external and internal (including its control) environment, and in identifying significant changes the entity or its operations have undergone since the previous audit which may have ramifications for the current year's audit. However, before using information from the past (recorded in previous years' working papers, engagement procedures or prior experience with the client), the auditor should perform audit procedures designed to identify any significant changes which have affected the client, its business or its industry since the last audit, and to determine whether the subsequent changes have affected the relevance of that information for the current audit.

(vi) Discussion among engagement team members

It is important that knowledge of the client, its business, its business processes and risks, and its industry are not the prerogative of the audit engagement partner and senior members of the audit team. It is essential that all members of the audit team have sufficient relevant knowledge to enable them to perform effectively audit work assigned to them. It is also important to harness the observations, expertise and thoughts of all members of the audit team in identifying risks of material misstatement in the financial statements. Hence, a key risk assessment procedure is a discussion of audit team members regarding the susceptibility of the client's financial statements to material misstatement.[25] ISA 315 (para A12) notes that this discussion, among other things:

- Allows the engagement team members to exchange information about the business risks to which the entity is subject and about how and where the financial statements might be susceptible to material misstatement due to fraud or error.
- Assists the engagement team members to gain a better understanding of the potential for material misstatement of the financial statements in the specific areas assigned to them, and to understand how the results of the audit procedures that they perform may affect other aspects of the audit including the decisions about the nature, timing, and extent of further audit procedures.
- Provides a basis upon which engagement team members communicate and share new information obtained throughout the audit that may affect the assessment of risks of material misstatement or the audit procedures performed to address these risks.

---

[25] This meeting is discussed in Chapter 6, section 6.2.4, in connection with identifying risks of misstatement resulting from fraud.

ISA 315 (para A13) points out that, for practical reasons, this discussion may not include all members of the audit team (for example, it may be a multi-location and/or large audit, with widely dispersed and/or many members in the audit team). Further, it may not be necessary for all members of the engagement team to be informed about all of the matters discussed or decisions reached during the discussion. In some cases, the engagement partner may hold the discussion with key members of the engagement team, including, if considered appropriate, specialists and those responsible for the audits of components (i.e., subsidiaries or divisions of the client entity), and delegate responsibility for communicating with others in the audit team to one or more key people involved in the original discussion. Where this responsibility is delegated, the engagement partner should determine the extent of the information to be provided to, and discussed with, other members of the engagement team.

It should be noted that (as highlighted in ISA 315, para A1, cited in section 8.4.1 above) acquiring knowledge and understanding of a client, its business and its industry is not a one-off event which is completed at the commencement of an audit. Rather, it is a continuous and cumulative process which proceeds as the audit progresses. Although information is gathered and assessed during the initial stage of an audit as a basis for planning the rest of the audit, it is usually refined and added to as the engagement partner and other members of the audit team learn more about the client and its business. However, both the discussion among audit team members (outlined above) and analytical procedures (discussed below) are generally specific risk assessment procedures which are performed during the initial phase of the audit.

8.5 ANALYTICAL PROCEDURES

8.5.1 Meaning of analytical procedures

Analytical procedures are the means by which meaningful relationships and trends in both financial and non-financial data may be analysed, actual data may be compared with budget or forecast data, and the data of an entity may be compared with that of similar entities and industry averages. By this means, any unusual or unexpected characteristics in the audit client's data may be identified. ISA 520: *Analytical Procedures* (paras 2, 3) explains:

> Analytical procedures include the consideration of comparisons of the entity's financial information with, for example:
> * Comparable information for prior periods.
> * Anticipated results of the entity, such as budgets or forecasts, or expectations of the auditor, such as an estimation of depreciation.

- Similar industry information, such as a comparison of the entity's ratio of sales to accounts receivable [trade debtors] with industry averages or with other entities of comparable size in the same industry.

Analytical procedures also include consideration of relationships, for example:

- Among elements of financial information that would be expected to conform to a predictable pattern based on the entity's experience, such as gross margin percentages.
- Between financial information and relevant non-financial information, such as payroll costs to number of employees.

Analytical procedures primarily consist of ratio, percentage, trend and comparative analyses although they also include more sophisticated statistical techniques such as regression analysis. In financial accounting the term 'interpretation and analysis' is used to mean essentially the same thing as 'analytical procedures' in auditing. As the ratios, percentages, trends and comparisons used by financial statement users for interpreting the financial statements are essentially the same as those used by auditors in analytical procedures, it follows that analytical procedures prompt consideration of the size of errors which would be material to financial statement users.[26] For example, the auditor would seek an explanation for a gross profit percentage which moved from, say, 18 to 20 per cent if such a change would cause financial analysts to change their assessment of the entity's financial performance. It follows that any error in the sales and/or cost of sales account(s) which caused such a shift in the gross profit percentage would be material.

8.5.2 Importance of analytical procedures

Analytical procedures are generally regarded as highly efficient and effective audit procedures; however, it must be borne in mind that their effectiveness is always dependent on the quality of the underlying data. As indicated above, these procedures provide a useful means of establishing whether financial statement amounts display unexpected characteristics, that is, whether they deviate from the auditor's expectations, given his or her understanding of the client, its business, its industry, and detailed knowledge of events which have affected the client's financial position and/or performance over the reporting period.

As shown in Figure 8.2, analytical procedures are used at three different stages during an audit to achieve three different objectives.

1. *During the risk identification and assessment stage* they are used to help:
   - obtain an understanding of the client's business;

---

[26] Materiality, and the link between the auditor's determination of what is material and financial statement users, is discussed in Chapter 3, section 3.4.2 and Chapter 9, section 9.3.

- assess the likelihood of material misstatements in the financial statements as a whole and in specific classes of transactions, account balances and/or disclosures;
- determine appropriate levels of materiality; and
- plan the nature, timing and extent of further audit procedures.

2. *During the substantive testing stage* they are used to obtain audit evidence in relation to individual classes of transactions, account balances and other disclosures to help establish whether or not they are materially misstated.

3. *During the final review stage* they are used to help confirm (or challenge) conclusions reached by the auditor regarding the truth and fairness of the financial statements.

Figure 8.2: The use of analytical review procedures in an audit

Stage in the Audit	Objective	Nature of Procedures Used
Risk identification and assessment	• To understand the client's business • To assess the likelihood of material misstatements in the financial statements • To identify high-risk audit areas (i.e., significant risks) • To set materiality limits • To plan the nature, timing and extent of further audit procedures	• Trend analysis • Ratio analysis of entity data • Comparative analysis of entity data with that of other similar entities and industry averages • Relationship between financial and non-financial data (Focus is on the entity's overall financial position and performance)
Substantive procedures	To obtain evidence to help confirm (or refute) the truth and fairness of individual classes of transactions, account balances and other disclosures	Ratio analysis based on direct relationships amongst individual accounts (Focus is on the reasonableness of individual account balances)
Final review	To confirm (or question) conclusions reached with respect to the truth and fairness of: – profit and loss statement amounts – balance sheet amounts – cash flow statement amounts – financial statement note disclosures	• Trend and percentage analysis of individual accounts • Ratio analysis of financial statement data (Focus is on the truth and fairness of the financial statements as a whole in portraying the entity's financial position, performance and cash flows)

The use of analytical procedures as substantive tests and in the final review of the financial statements is discussed in Chapters 11 and 13, respectively.

8.5.3 Analytical procedures as risk assessment procedures

ISA 315: *Identifying and assessing the risks of material misstatement . . .*, para 6, requires analytical procedures to be performed as risk assessment procedures. The Standard explains (para A7):[27]

---

[27] Para A7 was inserted into ISA 315 as a conforming amendment resulting from the issue of ISA 520: *Analytical Procedures*. Previously, the paragraph was para 8 in ISA 520. (In June 2008, ISA 520 (Redrafted) remained a proposed rather than a promulgated Standard.)

Analytical procedures performed during risk assessment of the entity may indicate aspects of the entity of which the auditor was unaware and will assist in assessing the risks of material misstatement in order to determine the nature, timing and extent of further audit procedures.

Analytical procedures performed as risk assessment procedures use both financial and non-financial information; for example, the relationship between sales and square footage of selling space, or between sales and quantity of goods sold; however, their focus is primarily on the overall financial position and performance of the entity, in particular, its liquidity, solvency (or capital adequacy) and profitability. Analytical procedures performed at this stage of the audit frequently use highly aggregated data. As a consequence, they provide only an initial indication of whether the financial statements may be materially misstated and their results need to be interpreted in the light of information the auditor has obtained through the performance of other procedures designed to provide an understanding of the entity and its financial affairs.

On the basis of his or her general understanding of the client entity and its business, and knowledge of events and significant transactions which have affected the client's financial position and performance during the reporting period, the auditor will have certain expectations regarding the results of the analytical procedures performed as risk assessment procedures. Where the results differ from the auditor's expectations, they raise questions about the accuracy of the financial and/or non-financial data used in the analysis (and, hence, about the accuracy of the entity's information systems as well as its financial statements), and/or about information previously obtained by the auditor on which his or her understanding of the entity and its financial affairs is based. Thus, analytical procedures performed during the initial phase of an audit are useful for confirming or challenging the auditor's understanding of the entity's business, and its financial position and performance, as well as for ascertaining whether it is likely that the financial statements are materially misstated in one or more respects, and for identifying the classes of transactions, account balances or disclosures in which material error appears most likely to be present. Once the likelihood of errors being present in the financial statements has been established, and areas requiring particular audit consideration (i.e., significant risks) have been identified, the auditor can determine the audit segments where audit effort is to be concentrated and plan the nature, timing and extent of audit procedures to be performed.

8.6 SUMMARY

In this chapter we have discussed the first steps in the audit process. We have considered why an auditor should conduct an investigation before accepting an audit engagement and pointed out that this investigation involves

(i) assessing the auditor's competence to perform the audit, (ii) complying with ethical requirements, including communicating with the predecessor auditor and (iii) evaluating the integrity of the (potential) client's management.

We have also discussed the purpose and content of audit engagement letters, and examined the importance of the auditor gaining a thorough understanding of the client, its business and its industry. We have emphasised, in particular, the importance of this understanding for identifying and assessing risks of mis-statement in the financial statements, and therefore for planning the audit, and also for providing a background (or context) against which the credibility of audit evidence may be evaluated.

For a new audit engagement, the auditor (or, more specifically, the audit engage-ment partner and senior members of the audit team) needs to expend consid-erable time and effort in establishing a sound understanding of the client, its business and its industry. For continuing engagements, less time and effort may be devoted to this audit step, but it should not be skipped altogether. The auditor needs to update and re-evaluate information gathered during previous audits to determine whether it remains valid and relevant.

In the latter part of the chapter, we have considered various means by which the auditor gains an understanding of the client and identifies the risk of material misstatement in the financial statements (i.e., risk assessment procedures). We have paid particular attention to the meaning and importance of analytical procedures and noted that these are used as substantive and final review procedures as well as risk assessment procedures during the initial phase of the audit.

SELF-REVIEW QUESTIONS

8.1   List three elements of the auditor's pre-engagement investigation.

8.2   Explain briefly the factors auditors should consider before concluding that they are competent to accept a particular audit engagement.

8.3   Explain briefly the purpose of a proposed auditor communicating with the existing or predecessor auditor, and list three pieces of information the proposed auditor should seek.

8.4   Explain briefly why it is advisable for an auditor to investigate the integ-rity of a (prospective) client's management before accepting an audit engagement.

8.5   Explain briefly the purpose and content of audit engagement letters.

8.6   Explain briefly the importance of an auditor gaining a thorough under-standing of the client, its business, business processes and risks, and its industry.

8.7   List five external environmental factors and five internal environmental factors which are likely to affect an entity and its external audit.

8.8   Explain briefly the importance of each of the following risk assessment procedures:
   (i)   touring the client's premises;
   (ii)   reading trade journals and magazines;
   (iii) reviewing the client's documentation;
   (iv)   reviewing prior years' audit working papers and drawing on past experience with the client;
   (v)   discussion among engagement team members.

8.9   Briefly explain the meaning of the term 'analytical procedures' and outline three ways in which these procedures are used during an audit.

8.10   List four ways in which analytical procedures can assist the auditor during the risk assessment stage of an audit.

REFERENCES

Accountancy Age. (2007, 20 July). Google man settles accounting claim at SkillSoft. *Accountancy Age*, www.accountancyage.com/articles/print/2194623.

Arens, A.A., and Loebbecke, J.K. (1980). *Auditing: An Integrated Approach* (2nd edn.). Englewood Cliffs, NJ: Prentice-Hall.

Auditing Practices Board (APB). (2004). International Standard on Auditing (ISA) (UK and Ireland) 200: *Objectives and General Principles Governing an Audit of Financial Statements*. London: Financial Reporting Council.

Auditing Practices Board (APB). (2004). International Standard on Auditing (ISA) (UK and Ireland) 210: *Terms of audit engagements*. London: Financial Reporting Council.

Institute of Chartered Accountants of Scotland (ICAS). (2006). *Code of Ethics*. Edinburgh: ICAS.

International Auditing and Assurance Standards Board (IAASB). (2006). International Standard on Auditing (ISA) 300 (Redrafted): *Planning an audit of Financial Statements*. New York: International Federation of Accountants.

International Auditing and Assurance Standards Board (IAASB). (2008, June)**.[28] International Standard on Auditing (ISA) 220 (Redrafted): *Quality Control for an Audit of Financial Statements*. New York: International Federation of Accountants.

National Commission on Fraudulent Financial Reporting. (1987). *Report of the National Commission on Fraudulent Financial Reporting* (Treadway Commission). New York: American Institute of Certified Public Accountants.

Pratt, M.J., and Dilton-Hill, K. (1982). The elements of audit risk. *The South African Chartered Accountant* **18**(4), 137–141.

ADDITIONAL READING

Asare, S.K., and Wright, A. (1997). Hypothesis revision strategies in conducting analytical procedures. *Accounting, Organizations and Society* **22**(8), 737–755.

Audit Quality Forum. (2005). *Shareholder Involvement – Auditor Engagement: Disclosure of Contractual Terms.* London: Institute of Chartered Accountants in England and Wales.

Canadian Institute of Chartered Accountants (CICA). (2000). *Audit Enquiry: Seeking more Reliable Evidence from Audit Enquiry*. Toronto: CICA.

Epps, K.K., and Messier Jr., W.F. (2007). Engagement quality reviews: A comparison of audit firm practices. *Auditing: A Journal of Practice & Theory* **26**(2), 167–181.

Gendron, Y. (2001). The difficult client-acceptance decision in Canadian audit firms: a field investigation. *Contemporary Accounting Research* **18**(2), 283–310.

Gendron, Y. (2002). On the role of the organization in auditors' client-acceptance decisions. *Accounting, Organizations and Society* **27**(7), 659–684.

Glover, S.M., Jiambalvo, J., and Kennedy, J. (2000). Analytical procedures and audit-planning decisions. *Auditing: A Journal of Practice & Theory* **19**(2), 27–45.

Helliar, C., Monk, E., Stevenson, L., and Allison, C. (2007). *The Development of an Audit Learning Package: Scam.* Edinburgh: Institute of Chartered Accountants of Scotland. (The Scam learning package is available at www.scam-plc.co.uk.)

Moroney, R. (2007). Does industry expertise improve the efficiency of audit judgment? *Auditing: A Journal of Practice & Theory* **26**(2), 69–94.

Pollins, M. (2007). Engaging behaviour. *Accountancy* **140**(1372), 50–51.

---

[28] The status of ISAs referred to in this chapter is explained in the Important Note following the Preface to this book.

9 Planning the Audit: Materiality and Audit Risk

LEARNING OBJECTIVES

After studying the material in this chapter you should be able to:
- differentiate between the two phases of planning an audit;
- distinguish between planning materiality, tolerable error and performance materiality;
- describe the documentation auditors are required to prepare in relation to planning an audit and materiality limits;
- explain what is meant by the auditor's desired level of assurance (or desired level of audit risk) and factors which affect this;
- discuss the relationship between the auditor's desired level of audit risk, inherent risk, internal control risk and detection risk;
- explain the relationship between materiality, audit risk and audit planning.

The following publications are particularly relevant to this chapter:

- International Standard on Auditing (ISA) 200 (Redrafted): *Overall Objectives of the Independent Auditor and the Conduct of an Audit in accordance with International Standards on Auditing* (IFAC, June 2008)**[1]
- International Standard on Auditing (ISA) 300 (Redrafted): *Planning an Audit of Financial Statements* (IFAC, 2006)
- International Standard on Auditing (ISA) 320 (Redrafted): *Materiality in Planning and Performing an Audit* (IFAC, June 2008)**

---

[1] The status of the ISAs referred to in this chapter is explained in the Important Note following the Preface to this book.

9.1 INTRODUCTION

If a task is to be accomplished effectively and efficiently it must be carefully planned. This is no less true for an audit than it is for a social event such as a party. The auditor needs to plan what evidence to collect in order to be able to express an opinion, amongst other things, on whether or not the financial statements give a true and fair view of the state of affairs and profit or loss of the reporting entity, and how and when to collect this evidence.

Planning an audit has two phases – establishing the overall audit strategy and developing the audit plan (or audit programme).[2] We outline each of these phases in this chapter but, as we discuss developing the audit plan in Chapter 10, we do not consider it in detail here. In this chapter we focus on developing the audit strategy. More specifically, we explain the importance to the audit strategy of materiality limits, the auditor's desired level of assurance (or desired level of audit risk), and the auditor's assessment of inherent and internal control risk. We also discuss the distinction between planning materiality, tolerable error and performance materiality, factors which affect the auditor's desired level of assurance (or desired level of audit risk), and the relationship between inherent and internal control risk on the one hand and detection risk on the other. Before concluding the chapter we explore the interrelationship between materiality, audit risk and audit planning.

9.2 PHASES OF PLANNING AN AUDIT

9.2.1 Benefits and characteristics of audit planning

International Standard on Auditing (ISA) 300: *Planning an audit of financial statements* states:

> The objective of the auditor is to plan the audit so that it will be performed in an effective manner. The engagement partner and other key members of the engagement team shall be involved in planning the audit . . . (paras 3, 4)

Adequate planning provides a number of benefits for an audit. They include ensuring that:
- engagement team members with the required capabilities and competence are selected for the audit and assigned appropriately to segments of the audit;

---

[2] Recent ISAs adopt the term 'audit plan' for what has traditionally been referred to as the 'audit programme'. Similarly, recent ISAs refer to 'overall audit strategy' in place of the formerly used term 'overall audit plan'.

- the work to be done by experts and/or other auditors is properly integrated with the audit as a whole;
- potential problems are identified on a timely basis;
- engagement team members are adequately directed and supervised, and their work is properly reviewed in a timely manner;
- appropriate attention is given to the different segments of the audit;
- the work is completed in an efficient and timely manner.

ISA 300 (paras 6, 8) notes that planning an audit entails two distinct phases, namely:

(i) establishing an overall audit strategy which defines the scope, timing and approach of the audit, and guides the development of the audit plan;

(ii) developing an audit plan which sets out, in detail, the expected nature, timing and extent of audit procedures to be performed.

The Standard also emphasises that planning is not a 'one-off' event at the start of the audit but continues throughout an audit. It states:

> Planning is not a discrete phase of an audit, but rather a continual and iterative process that often begins shortly after (or in connection with) the completion of the previous audit and continues until the completion of the current audit engagement ... As a result of unexpected events, changes in conditions, or the audit evidence obtained from the results of audit procedures, the auditor may need to modify the overall audit strategy and audit plan and thereby the resulting planned nature, timing and extent of further audit procedures ... The auditor shall update and change the overall audit strategy and the audit plan as necessary during the course of the audit. (paras 9, A3, A14)

9.2.2 The overall audit strategy (overall audit plan)

Once the auditor has gained a thorough understanding of the client and its business (as outlined in Chapter 8) – or, more accurately, during the phase of the audit when that understanding is being obtained and the risks of material misstatement in the financial statements are being identified and assessed – the overall audit strategy is developed. That is, the scope and approach of the audit is determined; more specifically, high-level (i.e., broad) plans are made regarding:

- how much and what evidence to gather;
- how, when and by whom this should be done.

Establishing the overall audit strategy depends on a wide range of factors, such as the following:[3]

---

[3] The Appendix to ISA 300 provides a comprehensive list of matters the auditor should consider when establishing the overall audit strategy.

- the general economic factors and industry conditions affecting the entity's business and important characteristics of the entity including its organisational structure, business operations, financial position and performance, and statutory, regulatory and reporting requirements. (These factors coincide with those identified in Chapter 8 in relation to 'Understanding the client, its business and its industry');
- the limits beyond which misstatements in the financial statements as a whole, and in individual financial statement amounts or disclosures, are to be regarded as 'material'. (This factor is discussed in section 9.3 below);
- the level of assurance (or level of confidence) the auditor wishes to gain regarding the appropriateness of the opinion expressed in the audit report (or, alternatively, the level of risk (s)he is prepared to accept that the opinion expressed in the audit report may be inappropriate). (This factor is discussed in section 9.4 below);
- the likelihood of material errors being present in the (pre-audited) financial statements as a whole, and in sections thereof (that is, the level of inherent risk and internal control risk). (This factor is discussed in section 9.5 below);
- the appropriate segments into which the audit should be divided to facilitate the conduct of audit work. (This factor is discussed in Chapter 10);
- the availability of audit evidence from different sources and of different types. (This factor is discussed in Chapter 7);
- the likely impact of the use of information technology by (i) the entity and (ii) the auditor. (This factor is discussed in Chapter 12);
- the availability of audit staff with the appropriate level of capabilities and competence and, where applicable, other (outside) auditors and experts. (This factor is discussed in Chapter 7.)

Taking into consideration factors such as those outlined above, the overall audit strategy sets out in broad terms, *inter alia*:

(i) the resources (number and experience level of audit team members and hours) expected to be allocated to specific audit segments – for example, the use of appropriately experienced team members for high-risk areas (i.e., significant risks),[4] the involvement of experts on complex and specialised matters, and the number of team members expected to be required to observe the inventory (stock) count at various locations;

(ii) the nature of audit procedures to be performed – in particular, the expected emphasis to be placed on, respectively, testing compliance with internal controls and substantive testing of transactions and account balances;[5]

---

[4] Significant risks are explained in Chapter 8, section 8.4.3.

[5] Compliance testing is discussed in Chapter 10; substantive testing in Chapter 11.

(iii) the timing of audit procedures – the procedures expected to be performed during the interim audit (part of the audit generally performed two or three months before the client's year-end) and the final audit (performed at and/or shortly after the client's year-end);[6]

(iv) the extent of audit procedures – the amount of audit evidence expected to be collected in relation to each audit segment;

(v) how audit team members are to be directed and supervised, when team briefing and debriefing meetings are expected to be held, and how audit working paper reviews are expected to take place (for example, on-site or off-site; face-to-face or electronically).

9.2.3 The audit plan (or audit programme)

The audit plan, in effect, operationalises the overall audit strategy. It sets out in detail the audit procedures to be performed in each segment of the audit, indicating those to be performed during the interim audit and those to be performed during the final audit. It frequently also includes details of such things as the size of samples to be tested and how the samples are to be selected.

As noted in Chapter 7, the audit plan often lists audit procedures in the form of instructions audit staff can follow. As the procedures are performed, they are signed off by the staff member concerned and cross-referenced to relevant audit working papers. (Developing the audit plan is discussed in Chapter 10.)

9.2.4 Audit planning documentation

In addition to developing the overall audit strategy and audit plan, auditors are required to prepare related documentation. More specifically, ISA 300 (paras 11, A17–A19) requires auditors to document:

(a) the overall audit strategy: this is to record the key decisions considered necessary to properly plan the audit and to communicate significant matters to the audit team. The audit strategy may be summarised in the form of a memorandum that contains key decisions regarding the overall scope, timing and conduct of the audit;

(b) the audit plan: this is to record the planned nature, timing and extent of audit procedures. Standard audit programmes or audit checklists may be used, tailored appropriately to reflect the particular circumstances of the audit engagement;

---

[6] In general, the interim audit focuses on understanding the entity's accounting system and testing compliance with internal controls; the final audit focuses more particularly on substantive testing.

(c) any significant changes made during the audit engagement to the overall audit strategy or audit plan, and resulting changes to the planned nature, timing and extent of audit procedures – and the reasons for the changes. This documentation is to provide a record of, and reflect the audit team's responses to, significant changes that occurred during the audit.

9.3 IMPACT OF MATERIALITY ON PLANNING AN AUDIT

9.3.1 Planning materiality and tolerable error

It was noted in Chapter 3 (section 3.4.2) that auditors are required to express an opinion "on whether the financial statements are prepared, in all *material* respects, in accordance with an applicable financial reporting framework"[7] (ISA 200: *Overall objectives of the independent auditor and the conduct of an audit* . . . , para 4; emphasis added). It was also noted that:

- Misstatements, including omissions, are considered to be material if they . . . could reasonably be expected to influence the economic decisions of users taken on the basis of the financial statements.
- Judgments about materiality are made in the light of the surrounding circumstances, and are affected by the size or nature of a misstatement or a combination of both. (ISA 320: *Materiality in planning and performing an audit*, para 2)

From these quotations it is evident that, when planning their audits, auditors need to form a judgment as to what is 'material' in the context of a particular audit. In Chapter 3 we explain that auditors need to consider materiality at both (i) the financial statement level and (ii) at an individual account or disclosure level. The distinction between financial statement and account level materiality is of particular significance in planning an audit.

(i) Planning materiality at the financial statement level

This refers to the amount of error the auditor is prepared to accept in the financial statements as a whole while still concluding that they provide a true and fair view of the state of affairs and profit or loss of the reporting entity. The auditor needs to estimate this level of error, or materiality level, prior to commencing the audit, based on his or her understanding of the client, its

---

[7] International Accounting (or Financial Reporting) Standards (IAS) or United Kingdom Generally Accepted Accounting Practice (UK GAAP; see Chapter 5, section 5.2.2). ISA (UK and Ireland) 200: *Objectives and general principles governing an audit of financial statements* (APB, 2004) notes: "The 'applicable financial reporting framework' comprises those requirements of accounting standards, law [including the Companies Act 2006] and regulations applicable to the entity that determine the form and content of its financial statements" (para 2-1).

business and its industry, and on his or her assessment of the decision needs of users of the auditee's financial statements. It is often referred to as 'planning materiality' and it provides a basis for planning the nature, timing and extent of procedures to be performed during the audit. The lower the level of this planning materiality (the smaller the amount of error in the financial statements as a whole which qualifies as 'material'), the greater the amount and/or the more appropriate the evidence[8] that needs to be collected in order to establish that the combined errors in the financial statements do not exceed it.

There are essentially three steps in determining planning materiality, namely:
- (a) selecting one or more appropriate benchmark(s);
- (b) identifying appropriate financial data for the selected benchmark(s);
- (c) determining a percentage to be applied to the selected benchmark(s).

(a) *Selecting appropriate benchmarks*: ISA 320 (para A3) identifies a number of factors that may affect the selection of an appropriate benchmark. These include:
  - The elements of the financial statements (for example, assets, liabilities, equity, income, expenses);
  - Whether there are items on which the attention of the users of the particular entity's financial statements tends to be focused (for example, for the purpose of evaluating financial performance users may tend to focus on profit, revenue or net assets);
  - The nature of the entity, where the entity is in its life cycle,[9] and the industry and economic environment in which the entity operates;
  - The entity's ownership structure and the way it is financed (for example, if an entity is financed solely by debt rather than equity, users may put more emphasis on assets, and claims on them, than on the entity's earnings); and
  - The relative volatility of the benchmark.[10]

  The standard cites as examples of benchmarks that may be appropriate:
  categories of reported income such as profit before tax, total revenue, gross profit and total expenses, total equity or net asset value. Profit before tax from continuing operations is often used for profit-oriented entities ... [but if this] is volatile, other benchmarks may be more appropriate, such as gross profit or total revenues. (para A4)

(b) *Identifying financial data*: Once appropriate benchmarks have been selected, financial data for the benchmark(s) need to be identified. This is

---

[8] The relationship between the sufficiency and appropriateness of evidence is discussed in Chapter 7.

[9] During their initial years of existence, for instance, companies and other businesses may (and frequently do) trade at a loss.

[10] For example, profit before tax may be more variable than sales (or *vice versa*).

not quite as straightforward as it might appear, because, as we noted above, materiality limits provide the basis for planning the nature, timing and extent of audit procedures to be performed during the audit and, for most audits, the materiality limits are determined, and the audit is planned, prior to the end of the client's reporting period. As a consequence the end-of-year financial statement figures are not usually available. Thus, alternative financial data need to be used for the selected benchmark(s). ISA 320 explains that such data:

> ordinarily includes prior periods' financial results and financial positions, the period-to-date financial results and financial position, and budgets or forecasts for the current period, adjusted for significant changes in the circumstances of the entity (for example, a significant business acquisition) and relevant changes of conditions in the industry or economic environment in which the entity operates. (para A5)

(c) Determining the percentage to apply: In this regard, ISA 320 (para A7) notes:

> Determining a percentage to be applied to a chosen benchmark requires the exercise of professional judgment. There is a relationship between the percentage and the chosen benchmark, such that a percentage applied to profit before tax from continuing operations will normally be higher than a percentage applied to total revenue.... [T]he auditor may consider five percent of profit before tax from continuing operations to be appropriate for a profit-oriented entity in a manufacturing industry ... Higher or lower percentages, however, may be deemed appropriate in the circumstances.

Notwithstanding the guidance provided by ISA 320, planning materiality is not a fixed monetary amount which, if exceeded even by a small margin, will necessarily cause the auditor to conclude that the financial statements are materially misstated but which, if not exceeded, will lead to the contrary conclusion. When forming an opinion on a set of financial statements, the auditor considers a myriad of factors – including the size and direction of the difference between the actual error estimated to exist in the financial statements (as estimated at the conclusion of the audit) and the auditor's planning materiality; that is, the amount of error the auditor planned to accept while still concluding the financial statements are 'true and fair'. Planning materiality provides a starting point for the auditor's conclusion.

To emphasise the imprecise nature of planning materiality, auditors frequently express it as a range of monetary amounts, rather than as a single figure. Surveys in the United States of America (USA), New Zealand (NZ) and elsewhere have shown that auditors use a variety of bases for this purpose. A survey conducted in the USA by Read, Mitchell and Akresh (1987), for example, found that the 97 auditors surveyed used nine different benchmarks to establish planning materiality. The most popular benchmark was pre-tax operating income (used by 45 per cent of respondents), followed by total revenue (used by 15 per cent), and after-tax operating income (used by 10 per cent). Other benchmarks used include total assets, current assets, current liabilities and long-term liabilities. Interestingly, 12 per cent of the auditors surveyed did not use a financial statement amount to arrive at a figure (or range of figures) for planning materiality but relied instead on judgment (or 'instinct').[11] The study also showed that even where different auditors adopted the same benchmark to estimate their planning materiality (such as pre-tax operating income), they applied a variety of percentages to the benchmark.

Similarly, a survey conducted in NZ by Pratt and Cuthbertson in 1988 (reported in Pratt, 1990) found that all of the 'Big 7' international firms then represented in NZ[12] used either net profit before or after tax (five and two firms, respectively) as a planning materiality benchmark, five firms also used total revenue, and five firms used total assets. Other benchmarks used were total equity, gross profit and working capital. One firm derived planning materiality from the results of applying percentages to six different benchmarks, another used four, and two others used three benchmarks. Only one firm relied on just one benchmark. Further, the percentages applied to the various benchmarks differed widely. For example, two firms applied five per cent, and two applied 10 per cent, to net profit before tax; similarly, two firms applied 0.5 per cent to total assets, two others applied one per cent, and one firm applied 'one to two per cent' to this benchmark (i.e., total assets).

A survey conducted in NZ in 2007[13] found that the 'Big 4' international accounting firms and three middle-tier firms (all represented internationally) determined their planning materiality based on the benchmarks and percentages shown in Figure 9.1. From Figure 9.1, we can see that, as in the earlier studies, audit firms in NZ in 2007 used a variety of benchmarks and applied different percentages to the same benchmark. However, all of the respondents emphasised that the results derived from applying percentages to benchmarks provide only an initial guide to planning materiality. They stressed that determining planning materiality involves considerable judgment and that a wide range of factors are taken into consideration. They observed, for example, that the size and complexity of the entity, in addition to the factors identified in ISA 320,

---

[11] Given the requirements of ISA 300: *Planning an audit of financial statements*, it seems unlikely that such a finding would be obtained today. Nevertheless, as shown by the results of a survey conducted in NZ in 2007 (presented in Figure 9.1), key benchmarks used by auditors in 1987 remain important benchmarks adopted by auditors in the current audit arena.

[12] Arthur Young, Coopers & Lybrand, Deloitte Haskins & Sells, Ernst & Whinney, KPMG Peat Marwick, Price Waterhouse, and Touche Ross.

[13] The survey was conducted by one of the authors for the purposes of this chapter. The results are not reported elsewhere.

para A3 (cited above), may affect the selection of appropriate benchmarks. Similarly, according to the respondents, the percentage applied to a particular benchmark is affected by factors such as the expectations of users of the entity's financial statements, the measure of planning materiality adopted in prior years, the entity's concept of materiality, and the risk of the engagement – in particular, the potential for fraud, and the industry in which the entity operates.

Figure 9.1: Planning materiality guidelines used in New Zealand in 2007 by the 'Big Four' and three middle-tier firms for profit-oriented companies

Criteria	Accounting Firms						
	1	2	3	4	5	6	7
Net profit – before tax	5–10%		5–10%	-	5–10%‡	5%	5%
– after tax		5–10%*					
Sales (or Turnover)	0.5%–1%	0.5–3%	0.5%	1%	0.5–1%	0.5%††	0.5%
Gross Profit	-	-	1–2% (rarely used)	-	-	-	-
Total assets	1.5%	-	0.25–0.5%	2%†	0.5–1%	-	-
Current assets	-	2%	-	-	-	-	-
Net assets	-	-	-	-	0.5–1%	-	0.5%
Shareholders' funds	5–10%	2%	1–5%	1–5%	1–2%	-	-

Notes: * 5–10% of net profit after tax is used for public companies. All five benchmarks are used for non-public companies.
† Used for financial institutions.
‡ 5% of pre-tax profit is used for public companies; 5–10% for non-public companies.
†† The most appropriate of these two benchmarks are used when net profit before tax is not the most suitable benchmark for setting planning materiality.

(ii) Planning materiality at the account level (Tolerable error)

The monetary amount or range established for planning materiality at the financial statement level defines the amount of error the auditor is prepared to accept in the financial statements as a whole before concluding they are materially misstated and, therefore, not 'true and fair'. It also provides the basis for establishing the maximum amount of error the auditor will accept in an individual class of transactions, account balance or other disclosure before concluding that the relevant balance or disclosure is materially misstated. Similarly, while planning materiality at the financial statement level helps to determine the amount of audit effort required for the audit as a whole, materiality at the account level helps to determine the nature, timing and extent of audit procedures to be performed in relation to classes of transactions, account balances and other disclosures. Use of the term 'tolerable error' for materiality at the account or disclosure level is a useful means of distinguishing between this level of materiality and materiality at the financial statement level (i.e., planning materiality). We therefore adopt this term for use in this book.

However, it should be noted that auditors are not required to determine a tolerable error for every class of transactions, account balance or other disclosure. Rather, ISA 320 states:

> If, in the specific circumstances of the entity, there are particular classes of trans-
> actions, account balances or disclosures for which misstatements of lesser amounts
> than materiality for the financial statements as a whole[14] could reasonably be
> expected to influence the economic decisions of users taken on the basis of the
> financial statements, the auditor shall also determine the materiality level or
> levels to be applied to those particular classes of transactions, account balances
> or disclosures. (para 10)

In most cases, audit firms set a tolerable error for significant individual classes of transactions, account balances and other disclosures. However, as for setting planning materiality, the task involves considerable professional judgment and different audit firms approach it in different ways. Nevertheless, in general, as a starting point, tolerable error for each class of transactions, account balance or other disclosure for which a tolerable error is to be determined is set at a selected level of planning materiality (for example, it may be set at 75 or 50 per cent of planning materiality, or somewhere between these limits[15]). Factors that influence the auditor's decision as to whether tolerable error should be set closer to 75 or 50 per cent of planning materiality include the following:

(a) past history with the client's audits and, more especially, whether or not audit adjustments have usually been required. If this is the case, tolerable error will be set closer to 50 per cent of planning materiality; if not, it is likely to be set closer to 75 per cent;

(b) the level of risk attaching to the audit engagement, that is, whether the likelihood of the auditor failing to detect a material misstatement is higher or lower than the average. The risk is higher, for example, where the industry in which the client operates is characterised by volatile revenues and/or profits, or where it is a first-time audit and the auditor is not familiar with the client. The riskier the audit engagement, the closer tolerable error will be to 50 per cent of planning materiality.

The monetary amount initially established as the tolerable error for classes of transactions, account balances and disclosures may then be adjusted upwards

---

[14] If planning materiality is the maximum amount of error the auditor will accept in the financial statements as a whole while still concluding that they give a true and fair view of the financial position and performance of the reporting entity, it is evident that the tolerable error (the maximum amount of error the auditor will tolerate in a class of transactions, account balance or disclosure while concluding that the relevant balance or disclosure is true and fair) cannot exceed the monetary amount of planning materiality.

[15] These percentages reflect the basis for setting tolerable error used by firms included in the materiality survey conducted in NZ in 2007.

or downwards for factors which are specific to the particular class of transactions, account balance or disclosure in question. Such factors include:

- the significance of the account balance to the decisions of users of the financial statements. The cash balance, for instance, with its implications for company liquidity and flexibility may be more material to financial statement users than, say, prepaid expenses. The more important a particular financial statement account balance is to users, the more important that it is stated accurately – hence, the smaller the tolerable error. In the case of cash, it may even be set at, or close to, zero;
- the size of the account balance. For example, if the debtors balance is £1,500,000 and the inventory (or stock) balance is £4,700,000, the tolerable error for the debtors account (in monetary terms) is likely to be set at a lower level than for the stock account;
- the auditability of the account. Certain accounts such as cash and loans are capable of more accurate verification than others, such as debtors and depreciation, where provisions (or allowances) need to be estimated. This variation should be reflected in the expectations of financial statement users with respect to the accuracy of account balances. The greater the expected accuracy of an account balance, the smaller the tolerable error;
- the sensitivity of the account or disclosure and/or its susceptibility to fraud (whether in the form of misappropriation of assets, such as inventory, or fraudulent financial reporting, such as estimates). For example, a disclosure relating to loan covenants or directors' remuneration is likely to be highly sensitive and as a consequence the tolerable error is likely to be reduced significantly. In the case of disclosures about directors' remuneration that are required by law, tolerable error will be, or be very close to, zero;
- the relative significance of understatement and overstatement of an account balance. In general, overstatements of assets and understatements of liabilities are more likely to be material to financial statement users than their counterparts (understatements of assets and overstatements of liabilities), and this can be reflected in the materiality limits. Tolerable error may, therefore, be set at different levels for understatements and overstatements in certain classes of transactions, account balances or other disclosures.

Some of the ideas presented above in relation to planning materiality and tolerable error may, perhaps, be best understood if they are illustrated by an example. Let us assume that, from calculations based on net profit before tax, sales, total assets and shareholders' funds, planning materiality for a particular set of financial statements is estimated at £100,000. Let us also assume that, given the particular circumstances of the audit, the auditor considers it appropriate to set tolerable error initially at 70 per cent of planning materiality (£70,000). If the account being considered is, say, inventory (or stock), the auditor will be aware of, amongst other things, the difficulty of auditing this account as a consequence of, for example, assessing the condition of the inventories, possible obsolescence, etc. Given such factors, the initial estimate of tolerable error may be adjusted downwards by a relatively small amount, to, say, £65,000. On the other hand, if the account being considered is cash, the significance of this account balance for users of the financial statements and their likely expectation that the balance will be stated fairly accurately is likely to result in the initial estimate of tolerable error being adjusted downwards by a significant amount – to, say, £5,000. In this case, if, after appropriate audit procedures have been applied, the inventory or cash balance is estimated to be misstated by an amount in the region of £65,000 or £5,000, respectively, the auditor is likely to require the auditee's directors to adjust the errant account balance before an unqualified (or 'clean') audit report will be issued.

It should be noticed that we have referred to the inventory and cash account balances causing concern for the auditor when they are estimated to be misstated by an amount *in the region of* £65,000 or £5,000, respectively. This underscores the point that tolerable error (like planning materiality) is an estimate, not a 'magic number', which, if exceeded by even a minuscule amount, will cause the auditor to require the account balance to be adjusted but which, if not exceeded, prompts no action. Indeed, all errors which are detected, irrespective of their size, need to be investigated to establish their cause and the likely implications for the estimated total error in the account (i.e., errors found and those estimated to exist in the portions of the populations not included in the samples examined by the auditor).

As for determining planning materiality, determining the tolerable error for individual classes of transactions, account balances or other disclosures is an important step in planning the audit; the magnitude of the tolerable error in each account or disclosure has a direct impact on what qualifies as 'sufficient appropriate audit evidence' (see Chapter 7) that must be gathered. The smaller the tolerable error, the more relevant and reliable and/or the greater the amount of evidence the auditor must collect in order to be assured that error in the account in question does not exceed the pre-determined limit.

9.3.2 Performance materiality

It should be recalled that planning materiality and tolerable error limits are defined to mean the estimated amounts of error in the financial statements as a whole, or class of transactions, account balance or disclosure, respectively, at which the decisions or actions of users of the financial statements might reasonably be expected to be affected. It follows that these limits should include all detected errors (whether they are material or immaterial[16]) and also an allowance for undetected errors, that is, errors that might be expected to exist (based on the detected errors) in the portions of populations not included in the samples examined by the auditor. Following from this, ISA 320 (para 9) requires auditors to determine what the Standard refers to as 'performance materiality'. It defines this term as follows:

> [P]erformance materiality means the amount or amounts set by the auditor at less than materiality for the financial statements as a whole to reduce to an appropriately low level the probability that the total of uncorrected and undetected misstatements exceeds materiality for the financial statements as a whole. ...[P]erformance materiality also refers to the amount or amounts set by the auditor at less than the materiality level or levels for particular classes of transactions, account balances or disclosures [i.e., tolerable error].

The Standard explains:

> Planning the audit solely to detect individually material misstatements overlooks the fact that the aggregate of individually immaterial misstatements may cause the financial statements to be materially misstated, and leaves no margin for possible undetected misstatements. Performance materiality is set to reduce to an appropriately low level the probability that the total of uncorrected and undetected misstatements in the financial statements exceeds materiality for the financial statements as a whole. The determination of performance materiality is not a simple mechanical calculation and involves the exercise of professional judgement. It is affected by the auditor's understanding of the entity, updated during the performance of the risk assessment procedures;[17] and the nature and extent of misstatements identified in previous audits and thereby the auditor's expectations in relation to misstatements in current period. (para A12)

Thus, auditors are required to determine an amount which, if equalled or exceeded by detected errors (singly or in aggregate in the financial statements as a whole, or in a class of transactions, account balance or disclosure), highlights the risk that the financial statements as a whole, or an account balance or disclosure, may be materially misstated (i.e., the risk that total error in the financial statements, or in a class of transactions, account balance or disclosure, exceeds planning materiality or tolerable error, respectively). The auditor will then need to conduct further audit procedures to determine whether or not the financial statements (or the class of transactions, account balance or disclose in question) is materially misstated. For example, based on past experience, an auditor may set performance materiality at 10 per cent of planning

---

[16] Auditors will require the auditee's directors to correct errors (misstatements) they adjudge to be 'material' (i.e., errors that exceed their planning materiality or tolerable error) before they will issue a 'clean' audit report. However, they may not require immaterial misstatements to be corrected before they will issue a 'clean' report. Such errors are termed 'uncorrected' or 'unadjusted' errors (or misstatements).

[17] We describe risk assessment procedures in Chapter 8.

materiality or tolerable error.[18] If errors, singly or in aggregate, are detected which equal or exceed this amount, further audit procedures will need to be conducted in order to estimate the total error (or misstatement) in the population (including an allowance for errors which are not detected as they lie outside the auditor's samples). The total estimated error can then be compared with planning materiality or tolerable error, as applicable.

9.3.3 Amending materiality estimates

When considering materiality in the auditing context it is important to remember that planning materiality and tolerable error are set by the auditor during the planning phase of the audit and reflect his or her judgment as to the level of misstatement in the financial statements as a whole, and in individual classes of transactions, account balances or disclosures, at which the decisions or actions of users of the financial statements could reasonably be expected to be affected. Although the quantitative limits of planning materiality and tolerable error are determined as objectively as possible, this does not mean they should be regarded as fixed and immutable. As explained in Chapter 3 (section 3.4.2), qualitative characteristics of financial statement items are also important and, when the materiality (or otherwise) of a misstatement is evaluated, as much attention should be given to the nature of the misstatement as to its size.

Further, as the audit progresses, the auditor may find that the level of planning materiality and/or tolerable error in one or more class of transactions, account balance or disclosure needs to be changed. This may occur, for instance, because a benchmark used to establish planning materiality is amended (for example, sales or pre-tax profits) and/or because new information comes to light which causes the auditor to conclude that planning materiality or tolerable error was established at a level that is too high or too low. As ISA 320 explains:

> Materiality for the financial statements as a whole (and, if applicable, the materiality level or levels for particular classes of transactions, account balances or disclosures) may need to be revised as a result of a change in circumstances that occurred during the audit (for example, a decision to dispose of a major past of the entity's business), new information, or a change in the auditor's understanding of the entity and its operations as a result of performing further audit procedures. (para A13)

If the changed circumstances or new information are such that, had the auditor known the facts initially, different planning materiality and/or tolerable error limits would have been determined, the auditor should revise the materiality levels accordingly (ISA 320, para 12). Additionally, the implications of the revised materiality levels for the planned audit procedures – their nature,

---

[18] A firm included in the materiality survey conducted in NZ in 2007 specified that performance materiality is set at 10 per cent of planning materiality or tolerable error (as applicable) in that firm.

timing and extent – need to be considered and any necessary modifications made to the audit plan (i.e., audit programme).

In general, auditors find it easier to adjust materiality estimates upwards. They tend to be less willing to adjust them downwards or to maintain those which are found to have been exceeded. This asymmetry arises because, the lower the level of materiality:

- the greater the amount and/or the more appropriate (relevant and/or reliable) the audit evidence that needs to be collected to make sure the limit has not been exceeded. (The lower the materiality limit, the smaller the margin of error within which the auditor must work – and, thus, the more 'careful' the auditor must be to establish, through the collection of evidence, that the limit has not been exceeded); and
- the more likely it is that misstatements which are discovered will exceed the limit and thus qualify as 'material'. Such (material) errors, if not adjusted by the reporting entity, should give rise to a modified audit report.[19]

The auditor will not relish having to increase the extent, or amend the nature, of planned audit procedures, largely because such an extension or amendment is likely to have an adverse impact on audit time and cost.[20] Similarly, the auditor will not welcome having to put pressure on the reporting entity's management (if this becomes necessary) to correct misstatements in the financial statements which are judged by the auditor to be material and, in the event of the auditee's directors not making the required amendments, issuing a modified audit report. Such eventualities almost invariably cause a strain in the relations between the auditor and the entity's management.

Thus, when factors are encountered during an audit which raise questions about the propriety of planning materiality and/or tolerable error established during the planning phase of the audit, justification for amending those estimates must be considered carefully. Upward adjustments should only be made, and downward adjustments should not be resisted, when examination of the benchmarks on which planning materiality and tolerable error limits were determined reveals that the initial materiality estimates were inappropriate. In particular, if the auditor finds that misstatements in individual account balances, or in the financial statements as a whole, exceed the pre-set materiality limits, (s)he must avoid any temptation to adopt spurious arguments to justify adjusting the relevant materiality level(s) upwards (and thus avoid additional audit work).

---

[19] The various types of audit report are discussed in Chapter 14.

[20] An increase in audit time may create difficulties for scheduling the work of audit team members. If they remain on the current audit for longer than planned, they will not be available to commence work, as scheduled, on their next audit. Additionally, an increase in audit time will result in an increase in audit cost and, thus, in the audit fee charged to the client and/or a reduction in the income and profits of the audit firm.

9.3.4 Documenting materiality

As for other steps in the audit process, ISA 320 (para 14) is precise in its requirements regarding documentation of materiality levels. It requires auditors to document:

(a) the materiality level for the financial statements as a whole (i.e., planning materiality);

(b) the materiality level or levels for particular classes of transactions, account balances or disclosures, if applicable (i.e., tolerable error);

(c) the amount(s) determined for the purpose of assessing risks of material misstatement and designing further audit procedures (i.e., performance materiality); and

(d) changes made to any of the above as the audit progressed.

They are also required to document the factors they considered when determining planning materiality, tolerable error and performance materiality.

9.4 DESIRED LEVEL OF ASSURANCE (DESIRED LEVEL OF AUDIT RISK)

9.4.1 Meaning of desired level of assurance (desired level of audit risk)

The Companies Act 2006 requires auditors to state in their audit reports, amongst other things, whether, *in their opinion*, the audited financial statements give a true and fair view of the state of affairs of the company (and, in relevant cases, of the group) and its (or the group's) profit or loss, and have been properly prepared in accordance with the relevant financial reporting framework (emphasis added.)

It should be noted that auditors are required to *express an opinion*, not *to certify* that the financial statements give a true and fair view and comply with the relevant financial reporting framework. Thus it seems that, in passing the legislation, Parliament did not expect auditors to reach a state of certainty with respect to the matters on which they are required to express their opinion in the audit report. The position is reflected in ISA 200: *Overall objectives of the independent auditor and the conduct of an audit . . .* , which explains:

> As the basis for the auditors' opinion, ISAs require the auditor to obtain *reasonable assurance* about whether the financial statements as a whole are free from material misstatement, whether due to fraud or error. (para 5, emphasis added)

The term 'reasonable assurance' is clearly of critical importance, but what does it mean? The International Auditing and Assurance Standards Board's (IAASB) *Glossary of terms* (2007) defines it as: "a high, but not absolute, level of assurance". This does not seem to shed much light on the matter; however, ISA 200 (para A4) is more helpful. It explains:

The auditor is not expected to, and cannot ... obtain absolute assurance [i.e., certainty] that the financial statements are free from material misstatement due to fraud or error. This is because there are inherent limitations of an audit, which result in most of the audit evidence on which the auditor draws conclusions and basis, the auditor's opinion being persuasive rather than conclusive. The inherent limitations of an audit arise from:
- The nature of financial reporting;
- The nature of audit procedures; and
- The need for the audit to be conducted within a reasonable period of time and at a reasonable cost.

Expanding on these three sources of an audit's inherent limitations, ISA 200 notes:

The preparation of financial statements involves judgment by management in applying the requirements of the entity's applicable financial reporting framework to the facts and circumstances of the entity. In addition, many financial statement items involve subjective decisions or assessments or a degree of uncertainty; and there may be a range of acceptable interpretations or judgments that may be made. Consequently, some financial statement items are subject to an inherent level of variability which cannot be eliminated by the application of additional auditing procedures. For example, this is often the case with respect to certain accounting estimates ... (para A45)

There are legal and practical limitations on the auditor's ability to obtain audit evidence. For example:
- There is the possibility that management or others may not provide, intentionally or unintentionally, the complete information that is relevant to the preparation and presentation of the financial statements or that has been requested by the auditor. Accordingly, the auditor cannot be certain of the completeness of information, even though the auditor has performed audit procedures to obtain assurance that all relevant information has been obtained.
- Fraud may involve sophisticated and carefully organized schemes designed to conceal it. Therefore, audit procedures used to gather audit evidence may be ineffective for detecting an intentional misstatement that involves, for example, collusion to falsify documentation which may cause the auditor to believe that audit evidence is valid when it is not ... (para A46)

[T]he relevance of information, and thereby its value, tends to diminish over time, and there is a balance to be struck between the reliability of information and its cost. ... [T]here is an expectation by users of financial statements that the auditor will form an opinion on the financial statements within a reasonable period of time and at a reasonable cost, recognizing that it is impracticable to address all information that may exist or to pursue every matter exhaustively on the assumption that information is in error or fraudulent until proved otherwise. ... Consequently, it is necessary for the auditor to:
- Plan the audit so that it will be performed in an effective manner;
- Direct audit effort to areas most expected to contain risks of material misstatement, whether due to fraud or error, with correspondingly less effort directed at other areas; and

- Use testing, including sampling, and other means of examining populations for misstatements. (paras A47, A48)

From the above extracts from ISA 200, it is clear that auditors are not expected to be – indeed, cannot be – *certain* that financial statements, which they report as giving a true and fair view of the entity's financial position and performance, and as complying with the relevant financial reporting framework, are not, in fact, materially misstated. However, they clearly want to be reasonably confident that the opinion they express is appropriate. The level of confidence they wish to attain about the 'correctness' of the opinion they express on the financial statements is known as their desired level of assurance. Arens and Loebbecke (1980) define the concept as follows:

> The *desired level of assurance* is the subjectively determined level of confidence that the auditor wants to have about the fair presentation of the financial statements after the audit is completed. The higher the level of assurance attained, the more confident the auditor is that the financial statements [on which a 'clean' opinion is expressed] contain no material misstatements or omissions. (p. 142)

The auditor's desired level of assurance is the complement of his or her desired level of audit risk. It is noted in Chapter 3 (section 3.4.3) that the IAASB's *Glossary of terms* (2007) defines audit risk as: "the risk that the auditor may give an inappropriate audit opinion when the financial statements are materially misstated". It follows that if, for example, the auditor wishes to be 95 per cent assured (or confident) that the financial statements on which (s)he expresses a 'clean' audit opinion are free of material misstatements, this means (s)he is prepared to accept a five per cent risk that the financial statements on which a 'clean' opinion is expressed contain such errors. ISA 200 conveys succinctly the link between the concepts of reasonable assurance and audit risk by stating:

> To obtain reasonable assurance, the auditor shall obtain sufficient appropriate audit evidence to reduce audit risk to an acceptably low level and thereby enable the auditor to draw reasonable conclusions on which to base the auditor's opinion. (para A17)

This also reflects the fact that the more assured the auditor wishes to be about the appropriateness of the opinion expressed in the audit report [the more (s)he wishes to reduce the risk of expressing the 'wrong' opinion], the more the audit evidence (in terms of quantity and/or relevance and reliability) that needs to be collected and evaluated.

9.4.2 Factors affecting the auditor's desired level of assurance (desired level of audit risk)

An auditor's desired level of assurance will always be high (i.e., his or her desired level of audit risk will always be low). It is sometimes expressed in quantitative terms (a 95 per cent level of assurance or five per cent level of audit risk is often quoted as a rule of thumb), but it is clearly difficult to pinpoint when a particular numeric level of assurance has been reached. As a result, in practice, auditors often adopt a qualitative approach and think in terms of a 'high' or 'medium' level of assurance (or 'low' or 'medium' level of risk) rather than in precise percentage terms.

In certain circumstances auditors wish to attain a particularly high level of assurance (a particularly low level of audit risk). This applies, for example, in cases where a large number of users are likely to rely on the financial statements and/or where there is doubt about the client's ability to continue as a going concern. In each of these cases, if the auditor signifies that the financial statements give a true and fair view of the entity's financial position and performance when they contain a material error or omission, serious consequences may ensue for both the financial statement user(s) and for the auditor.

Generally speaking, the larger the entity (in terms of total revenues or total assets), and the more widely disbursed its ownership and its debts, the greater the number of users of its audited financial statements. A large listed public company, such as BP, GlaxoSmithKline, HSBC or Vodafone, which has extensive economic resources and numerous shareholders, debtholders and creditors, is likely to have its audited financial statements used far more widely than are companies with few shareholders and/or few debtholders and other creditors. Private companies, wholly owned subsidiaries and companies whose directors hold a large proportion of the company's equity and debt (as applies in some smaller companies) are likely to have relatively few financial statement users who are remote from the company. As Arens, Elder and Beasley (2005) point out:

> When the [financial] statements are heavily relied on, a great social harm could result if a significant error were to remain undetected. . . . The cost of additional evidence [that is, raising the auditor's level of assurance] can be more easily justified when the loss to users from material errors is [likely to be] substantial. (p. 244)

Additionally, where audited financial statements have a large number of users, each of whom may suffer loss if the auditor fails to detect a material error or omission, and inappropriately issues a 'clean' audit report thereon, the auditor may have a wide exposure to potential liability for negligence.[21] Thus, where

---

[21] In the UK, the *Caparo* case has limited the parties to whom auditors owe a duty of care and thus their exposure to potential liability. This is discussed in detail in Chapter 15. Other recent developments in limiting auditors' liability are discussed in Chapter 16.

a large number of users rely on financial statements, it is in the auditor's own interest to seek a particularly high level of assurance (low level of audit risk). The same is true (in countries where the *Caparo* decision does not apply), where one or more users are likely to rely on the audited financial statements when making a major investment decision (such as in a takeover situation). If the potential investor(s) decide to make the investment and the audited financial statements on which they rely subsequently prove to be materially misstated, they are likely to suffer serious financial loss. As a result, they are likely to seek redress from the auditors for the loss they sustain.[22]

Another situation in which the auditor may desire a particularly low level of audit risk is where there is some doubt about the entity's status as a going concern. This is because, if a client is forced into liquidation shortly after receiving a 'clean' audit report and the financial statements are subsequently found to contain one or more material error(s) and/or omission(s), the auditor may be exposed to litigation, brought by the company's liquidator or by those who suffer loss as a result of the entity's collapse. If, in such circumstances, the auditor reduces his or her desired level of audit risk, (s)he will gather more evidence than would otherwise be the case, and will be particularly concerned to see that the nature of the going concern problem is adequately disclosed in the notes to the financial statements. As a result of these actions, the auditor is more likely to detect material errors and/or omissions in the financial statements (if they exist) and, failing this, will be better placed to defend the quality of the audit should a challenge arise.[23]

---

[22] It should be noted that regulators may also bring actions against auditors. For example, the Securities and Exchange Commission (SEC) in the USA has brought actions against auditors when financial statements on which a 'clean' audit report was issued were subsequently found to be materially misstated. An example is the SEC's action against KPMG LLP, two former KPMG partners and a current partner and senior manager:

> for engaging in improper professional conduct as auditors for Gemstar-TV Guide International, Inc. ... [F]rom September 1999 through March 2002, the respondents' conduct resulted in repeated audit failures in connection with KPMG's audits of Gemstar's financial statements ... the respondents reasonably should have known that Gemstar improperly recognized and reported ... material amounts of licensing and advertising revenue. ... Stephen M. Cutler, the SEC's Director of Enforcement, said, "... The sanctions in this case should reinforce the message that accounting firms must assume responsibility for ensuring individual auditors properly discharge their special and critical gatekeeping responsibilities". Randall, R. Lee, Regional Director of the SEC's Pacific Regional Office, said, "... KPMG's auditors repeatedly relied on Gemstar management's representations even when those representations were contradicted by their audit work. The auditors thus failed to abide by one of the core principles of public accounting – to exercise professional skepticism and care".

KPMG agreed to a settlement that included censure and payment of $10 million to Gemstar's shareholders – the largest payment ever made by an accounting firm in an SEC action (SEC, 2004).

[23] Auditors' responsibilities in relation to assessing their audit clients' going concern status are discussed in Chapter 13.

9.5 IMPACT OF AUDIT RISK ON PLANNING THE AUDIT

9.5.1 Risk-based approach to auditing

We noted in section 9.4 above that audit risk (the risk of the auditor expressing an inappropriate opinion on a set of financial statements)[24] is the complement of the auditor's level of assurance (the auditor's level of confidence that the opinion expressed is 'correct'). Ultimately, to the auditor, audit risk amounts to exposure to legal liability if, as a result of issuing a 'clean' audit report on financial statements which are materially misstated, a user of the financial statements is misled and suffers a loss as a consequence. However, as noted in section 9.4, an auditor is required to *express an opinion* on the financial statements, not *to certify* their truth and fairness. As a result, some degree of audit risk (expressing an inappropriate opinion) is unavoidable, and legal action against an auditor should succeed only if the auditor wittingly or negligently accepts an unreasonably high level of audit risk (i.e., forms an opinion based on evidence (s)he knows, or ought to know, to be inadequate or does not care whether or not it is adequate).

In today's highly competitive audit environment, audit firms have focused their attention on conducting efficient, cost-effective audits. This has led to them adopting a risk-based approach to auditing; that is, identifying and assessing the risk of the financial statements being materially misstated and planning the nature, timing and extent of their audit procedures accordingly.

Like establishing materiality limits, the risk of errors (or omissions) occurring in the pre-audited financial statements (which we refer to as pre-audit risk) is considered at two levels, namely, the overall (financial statement) level and at the level of individual classes of transactions, account balances or disclosures.

- *Pre-audit risk at the overall level* refers to the risk of material misstatement being present in the financial statements as a whole (that is, the likelihood of planning materiality being exceeded) and, based on this, determining the total amount of effort (or work) required for the audit as a whole. (The higher the likelihood of material misstatements being present, the greater the amount, and/or the more relevant and reliable, the audit evidence that needs to be collected).
- *Pre-audit risk at class of transactions, account balance or disclosure level* refers to identifying high audit risk areas; that is, identifying specific classes

---

[24] As explained in Chapter 3 (section 3.4.3), because the likelihood of the auditor expressing a modified audit opinion on financial statements which are, in fact, not materially misstated is so small, the term audit risk is usually taken to mean the risk of an auditor expressing an unqualified (i.e., 'clean') audit opinion on financial statements that are materially misstated.

of transactions, account balances or disclosures where material misstatement seems most likely to occur (or, alternatively stated, tolerable error is most likely to be exceeded). Once these areas have been identified, total audit effort may be allocated so as to ensure that audit work is concentrated primarily in the high-risk areas.

The objective of risk-based auditing is to achieve maximum effectiveness and efficiency (that is, to arrive at the appropriate audit opinion whilst incurring least cost). It is designed to ensure that neither the financial statements as a whole, nor any segment thereof, are under- or over-audited; that is, that neither too little nor too much audit evidence is gathered to achieve the auditor's desired level of audit risk (or desired level of assurance). Too little audit evidence leaves the auditor with greater exposure to audit risk than (s)he wishes to accept; too much evidence means the auditor's exposure to risk is reduced to beyond the level (s)he is prepared to accept and, as a result, represents unnecessary expenditure of audit time and cost.

The auditor assesses the overall risk of material misstatement being present in the financial statements, and identifies high audit risk areas, primarily through:
- gaining a thorough understanding of the client, its business, its industry and its key personnel (as discussed in Chapter 8, section 8.4);
- performing analytical procedures (as discussed in Chapter 8, section 8.5); and
- evaluating the client's system of internal control (discussed in Chapter 10).

9.5.2 Relationship between inherent risk, internal control risk and detection risk

In Chapter 3 (section 3.4.3) we note that audit risk comprises two main components:
(i) the risk that the pre-audited financial statements are materially misstated in one or more respects. (This is a function of inherent risk and internal control risk); and
(ii) the risk that the auditor fails to detect a material misstatement which is present. (This is a function of sampling and quality control risk, collectively referred to as detection risk.)[25]

The relationship between audit risk and its components may be presented (in simplified form) as an equation as follows:

---

[25] Inherent risk, internal control risk, sampling risk and quality control risk are discussed in detail in Chapter 3, section 3.4.3.

Risk of the auditor expressing a 'clean' opinion on materially misstated financial statements	=	Risk of material misstatement being present in the pre-audited financial statements	+	Risk of the auditor failing to detect material misstatement
Audit risk	=	Inherent risk + internal control risk	+	Detection risk

At this point it may be helpful to recall (from Chapter 7) that audit procedures are basically of two kinds: compliance procedures and substantive procedures.

- *Compliance procedures* are designed to ascertain whether the entity's internal controls are operating effectively (that is, are being complied with) and have been so operating throughout the reporting period. In the context of the audit risk equation, compliance procedures are particularly relevant to the evaluation of internal control risk.

- *Substantive procedures* are designed to substantiate, or to evaluate the substance (validity, completeness and accuracy) of, financial statement balances. They fall into two broad categories, namely:
  - specific analytical procedures,
  - tests of details. These tests are of two types: tests of transactions and direct tests of account balances.

Substantive procedures have a direct bearing on detection risk. In general, the lower the level of inherent risk and internal control risk (that is, the lower the risk of material misstatement being present in the pre-audited financial statements), the less extensive the substantive procedures which are required to confirm that the financial statements are, in fact, free of material misstatements. Expressed differently, where the auditor believes there is little likelihood of material misstatements occurring in the pre-audited financial statements (inherent and internal control risk are low), the greater the risk (s)he is prepared to accept that a material error, if present, will not be detected (i.e., the auditor is prepared to accept a high detection risk). As a consequence, less extensive substantive procedures will be conducted. Alternatively, if the auditor considers there is a high likelihood that the pre-audited financial statements contain material misstatement(s). (i.e., inherent + internal control risk is high), then (s)he will want to be fairly sure that, should material misstatement(s) be present, they will be detected (i.e., the auditor will seek low detection risk). As a result, extensive substantive tests will be performed.

When considering the relationship between the components of audit risk, we need to bear in mind the following four separate sets of factors.

(i) Inherent risk is the risk of material misstatements being present in the pre-audited financial statements in the absence of internal controls. Thus, conceptually, the auditor determines the likelihood of misstatements occurring in the financial statements in two stages:

- first, inherent risk is assessed, then
- the extent to which the entity's internal controls can be relied upon to reduce the likelihood of misstatements occurring in the financial statements is evaluated.

(ii) Gaining an understanding of the client (and its internal and external environment) and performing analytical procedures are particularly important for assessing inherent risk; evaluating the effectiveness of the client's internal control system and performing compliance procedures are the primary means of determining internal control risk.

(iii) Inherent risk and internal control risk are beyond the direct control of the auditor. As a consequence, the auditor must adjust detection risk (primarily by increasing or reducing the extent and/or appropriateness of substantive procedures) in order to achieve his or her desired level of audit risk (or, alternatively stated, his or her desired level of assurance).

(iv) Inherent risk and internal control risk may both be assessed as high, may both be assessed as low or one may be assessed as high and the other as low. However, whatever their combined level of risk may be, this directly impacts the nature, timing and extent of the substantive procedures the auditor must conduct in order to achieve his or her desired level of audit risk.

The conceptual aspects of the relationships indicated above may be illustrated (in simplified form) by reference to numerical examples.

Example 1: Assume the following facts:
- The auditor's desired level of audit risk is five per cent (equivalently, the auditor's desired level of assurance is 95 per cent).
- After assessing inherent risk the auditor believes there is a 60 per cent risk of material misstatement being present in the pre-audited financial statements.
- After evaluating the entity's internal controls, the auditor reduces his or her assessment of the risk of material misstatement occurring in the pre-audited financial statements to 20 per cent (a reduction of 40 percentage points).

Given the facts outlined above, it is evident that in order to achieve a desired level of audit risk of five per cent the auditor must reduce his or her assessment of audit risk by a further 15 percentage points through the performance of substantive procedures.

Desired level of audit risk		Assessment of inherent risk		Risk reduction through internal control assessment		Risk reduction through substantive audit procedures
5%	=	60%	–	40%	–	15%

Example 2: Assume the following facts:
- The auditor's desired level of audit risk is five per cent (equivalently, the auditor's desired level of assurance is 95 per cent).
- After assessing inherent risk, the auditor believes there is an 85 per cent risk of material misstatement being present in the pre-audited financial statements.
- After assessing the effectiveness of the entity's internal controls, the auditor assesses the risk of material misstatement occurring in the pre-audited financial statements as 75 per cent (a reduction of 10 percentage points).

Given the above facts, it is evident that in order to achieve a desired level of audit risk of five per cent, the auditor must reduce audit risk by a further 70 percentage points through the performance of substantive procedures.

Desired level of audit risk		Assessment of inherent risk		Risk reduction through internal control assessment		Risk reduction through substantive audit procedures
5%	=	85%	–	10%	–	70%

In the first example the auditor plans to use substantive procedures to reduce overall audit risk by 15 percentage points, whereas in the second case such procedures need to reduce audit risk by 70 percentage points. It follows that, in the second case, substantive procedures need to be significantly more extensive (and/or more relevant and reliable) than in the first.

The above examples illustrate how, conceptually, inherent risk (the risk or likelihood of errors being present in the financial data in the absence of internal controls) is reduced to the auditor's desired level of audit risk in two stages:
- (i) assessing (by performing compliance procedures) the likelihood of misstatements that are present in the financial data not being detected and corrected by internal controls and thus occurring in the pre-audited financial statements; and
- (ii) performing substantive procedures to reduce the likelihood of undetected misstatements remaining in the financial statements on which the auditor expresses a 'clean' audit opinion.

Although we have represented this risk reduction process conceptually as two sequential subtractions from inherent risk, a simple probability multiplication rule is more appropriate (and is adopted as guidance by some firms) to determine the level of detection risk which should be planned for in order to reduce audit risk to the desired level. In statistics, the probability of two events (A and B) both happening is the multiple of the probability of $A[p(A)]$ and the probability of $B[p(B)]$. Thus the multiple of the risk (or probability) of a material misstatement occurring in the pre-audited financial statements, and the risk (or probability) of the substantive tests failing to detect it, gives the risk of the auditor expressing a 'clean' opinion on materially misstated financial statements (that is, audit risk). This reasoning underlies what is commonly referred to as the 'audit risk model', which may be represented as follows:[26]

Desired level of audit risk	=	Risk of material misstatement occurring in the pre-audited financial statements	×	Risk of failing to detect material misstatement
Audit risk	=	Inherent risk × Control risk	×	Detection risk
AR	=	IR × CR	×	DR

Applying this to the figures given in the examples set out above:

Example 1:

Desired level of audit risk	=	Risk of material misstatement occurring in the pre-audited financial statements	×	Risk of failing to detect material misstatement
Audit risk	=	Inherent risk × Control risk	×	Detection risk
AR	=	IR × CR[27]	×	DR
5%	=	60% × 34%	×	DR

Rearranging the equation to find detection risk:

$$DR = \frac{5\%}{60\% \times 34\%} = 25\%$$

Example 2:

Desired level of audit risk	=	Risk of material misstatement occurring in the pre-audited financial statements	×	Risk of failing to detect material misstatement
Audit risk	=	Inherent risk × Control risk	×	Detection risk
AR	=	IR × CR[28]	×	DR
5%	=	85% × 88%	×	DR

Rearranging the equation to find detection risk:

---

[26] The audit risk model is widely cited in auditing literature as a useful audit planning tool. However, it is not without its critics. As indicated above, the model is grounded in probability theory and, in order for it to be valid, the probability of the events IR, CR and DR must be independent of each other. A number of commentators have raised doubt about the independence of IR, CR and DR and thus about the validity of the audit risk model. Nevertheless, the model provides useful insights into the relationship between inherent risk, internal control risk, detection risk and the auditor's desired level of audit risk.

[27] [IR = 60% × CR = 34%] = Risk of error occurring in pre-audited financial statements = 20% (as in previous Example 1).

[28] [IR = 85% × CR = 88%] = Risk of error occurring in pre-audited financial statements = 75% (as in previous Example 2).

$$DR = \frac{5\%}{85\% \times 88\%} = 6.7\%$$

It may be seen that in Example 1, in order to achieve a desired level of audit risk of five per cent, the auditor can accept a 25 per cent risk of failing to detect material error, whereas in Example 2 the auditor can accept a detection risk of only 6.7 per cent.

From Examples 1 and 2 it is evident that, the greater the likelihood of material misstatement occurring in the pre-audited financial statements (the higher the combined level of inherent and internal control risk), the lower the risk the auditor can take of not detecting material misstatement which is present. The lower the detection risk the auditor can accept, the more extensive the substantive audit procedures (s)he must perform.

We can use a town's water supply (as in Figure 9.2) to illustrate the inverse relationships between:
  (a) inherent risk and internal control risk on the one hand and detection risk on the other;
  (b) detection risk and the extent of substantive testing.

For the purpose of illustration, assume that:
  • the population of Jolleytown derives its water supply from Smillie Reservoir;
  • three rivers flow into Smillie Reservoir; and
  • the water from the rivers passes through a purification filter before flowing into the reservoir.

Figure 9.2: Jolleytown's water supply

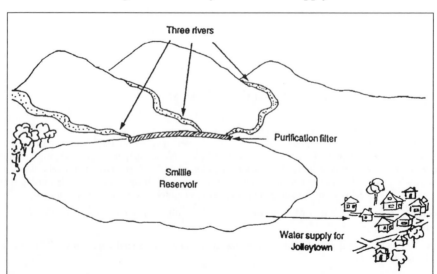

Figure 9.2: *Continued*

Jolleytown's water supply	*Parallel in audit risk terms*
Situation 1	
1. The rivers (mountain streams) flowing down towards the purification filter are crystal clear.	1. Management integrity appears to be high, there are no apparent pressures likely to motivate management to manipulate the financial statement information, and business risk is low. (Inherent risk is low.)
2. The purification filter is in excellent order and can be relied upon to filter out impurities in the river water.	2. Internal controls appear to be effective in preventing and detecting errors in the financial data. (Internal control risk is low.)
3. In order for the authorities to be assured that the water in Smillie Reservoir is safe for the population of Jolleytown to drink, relatively little testing will be required.	3. The auditor, having assessed inherent risk and internal control risk, will be fairly confident that the financial statements are not materially misstated. Thus (s)he will conduct relatively little substantive testing to confirm that material error is not present.
Because the authorities believe the reservoir water is 'pure', they will not test it extensively. They thus run the risk of failing to detect impurities which may, in fact, have 'slipped through' the system	By conducting relatively little substantive testing, the auditor runs the risk of not detecting material misstatement which may, in fact, have 'slipped through' the system. Thus detection risk is high.
Situation 2	
1. The three rivers flowing down from the hills towards the purification filter are muddy and carry lots of impurities such as rocks, stones and vegetation.	1. Management integrity appears to be fairly low and business risk is high. The risk of material misstatement occurring in the pre-audited financial statements in the absence of internal controls (i.e., inherent risk) is high.
2. The purification filter is not in a good state of repair. A number of holes have developed and the filter is in need of replacement.	2. Internal controls do not appear to be effective: they seem unlikely to prevent or detect errors which are present in the financial data. (Internal control risk is high.)
3. Before the water in the reservoir can be accepted as safe for Jolleytown residents to drink, extensive testing will be required. (A large number of water samples will need to be taken from various parts of the reservoir.)	3. Before the financial statements can be adjudged 'true and fair', account balances and disclosures will need to be tested extensively.
As a result of the extensive testing, the failure to detect impurities in the water (if they are present) will be fairly low.	As a result of the extensive (substantive) testing, the chance of failing to detect material error in the financial statements is fairly low (i.e., low detection risk).

9.5.3 Audit risk at the overall and individual account (or audit segment) level

The discussion set out in section 9.5.2 above focuses on assessing inherent risk and internal control risk at the overall (financial statement) level and considers the extent of the substantive procedures required to reduce detection risk, and thus audit risk, to the desired level for the audit as a whole. However, as we noted in section 9.5.1, audit risk is also considered at the level of individual classes of transactions, account balances and disclosures. The principles explained in relation to overall audit risk apply equally to audit risk at the more detailed level. Indeed, in practice, the audit risk equation and determination of the substantive procedures required to reduce detection risk to the desired level has greater application at the classes of transactions, account balances and disclosures level than at the overall (financial statement) level.

9.5.4   Relationship between materiality, audit risk and audit planning

It follows from our discussion of audit risk that the relationship among the audit risk components has a significant impact on audit planning. Audits must be planned so as to ensure that:
*   inherent risk is properly assessed [which largely depends on gaining an adequate knowledge of the client (and its internal and external environment) and analytical procedures];
*   internal control risk is properly evaluated (which includes planning, performing and evaluating compliance procedures); and
*   sufficient appropriate substantive procedures are performed so that detection risk – and thus audit risk – is reduced to the level desired by the auditor.

Hence, in order to reduce audit risk to the desired level, the auditor must carefully plan the nature, timing and extent of audit procedures.

Like audit risk, the level at which materiality limits (planning materiality and tolerable error) are set affects the planning of audit procedures – their nature, timing and extent. In section 9.3 we noted that a misstatement, omission or inadequate disclosure in the financial statements is material if it is likely to affect the decisions or actions of a reasonable user of those financial statements. We also noted that the level at which the auditor sets the limits for planning materiality and tolerable error affects the amount and/or appropriateness of the audit evidence the auditor needs to gather: the lower the materiality limits, the more (and/or more relevant and reliable) the evidence the auditor must collect in order to ensure those limits are not exceeded.

Linking materiality to audit risk and the extent of audit procedures, we can say that, the lower the materiality limits, the more readily misstatements (or omissions) that exist in the pre-audited financial statements will exceed those limits and thus qualify as material misstatements. It follows that, the lower the materiality limits, all other things remaining constant, the higher the auditor's assessment of inherent and control risk and, consequently, the more extensive the audit procedures that need to be performed in order to reduce audit risk to a low level. Additionally, the lower the materiality limits, the more careful the auditor needs to be in determining whether or not those limits are exceeded. Thus, the auditor will wish to reduce detection risk to a level lower than would otherwise be the case – and, accordingly, plan to perform more extensive substantive procedures.

Following the reasoning set out above, we can see there is an inverse relationship between materiality and audit risk and thus between materiality and the extent of substantive procedures. This relationship is depicted in Figure 9.3.

Figure 9.3:   The effect of setting materiality limits at different levels on audit risk and planned audit procedures

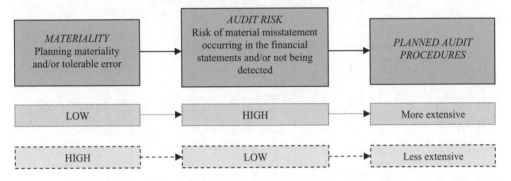

9.6   SUMMARY

In this chapter we have identified the two phases involved in planning an audit – developing the overall audit strategy and designing the audit plan (or audit programme) – and we have discussed various aspects of developing the overall audit strategy. More specifically, we have discussed the distinction between planning materiality, tolerable error and performance materiality, the setting of materiality limits and the auditor's desired level of assurance (desired level of audit risk). We have also examined the relationship between inherent risk, internal control risk, and detection risk and noted that, in order to achieve their desired level of audit risk, auditors need to assess inherent risk and internal control risk (over which they have no direct control) and then to plan the nature, timing and extent of audit procedures so as to ensure that detection risk, and hence audit risk, is reduced to the desired level. We have additionally noted the inverse relationship between materiality and audit risk – and the relationship between these factors and the extent of substantive testing.

A summary of the main ideas discussed in this chapter (and some of the notions considered in Chapters 3 and 7) is presented in Figure 9.4.

Figure 9.4: **Relationship between steps in the audit process,**[29] **planning the audit, establishing materiality limits, and assessing audit risk**

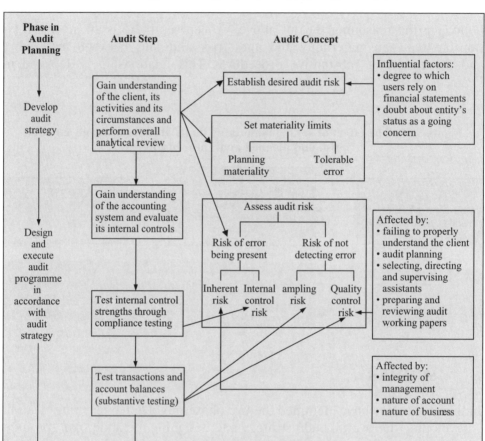

SELF-REVIEW QUESTIONS

9.1 State the two main phases in planning an audit and outline the main objective of each.

9.2 Define 'materiality' and explain briefly the distinction between:
(i) planning materiality, and
(ii) tolerable error.

9.3 Explain briefly what is meant by 'performance materiality'.

---

[29] As shown in Figure 7.1.

9.4 Describe briefly the three stages in determining planning materiality.

9.5 Explain briefly how setting materiality limits at different levels affects planned audit procedures.

9.6 Explain briefly what is meant by 'the auditor's desired level of assurance' and how it relates to the auditor's 'desired level of audit risk'.

9.7 Explain briefly the circumstances in which the auditor's desired level of audit risk is likely to be particularly low.

9.8 Explain briefly how the auditor's assessment of inherent risk and internal control risk affects his or her planning of substantive procedures.

9.9 Explain briefly the relationship between materiality limits, audit risk and audit planning.

9.10 When planning an audit, the auditor must consider:
- the extent of audit procedures,
- the timing of audit procedures,
- the nature of audit procedures.
(a) Briefly explain the meaning of each of these terms.
(b) Give one example for each term to illustrate its effect on planning an audit.

REFERENCES

Arens, A.A., Elder, R.J., and Beasley, M.S. (2005). *Auditing and Assurance services: An Integrated Approach*. 11th edn. Upper Saddle River, NJ: Prentice-Hall.

Arens, A.A., and Loebbecke, J.K. (1980). *Auditing: An Integrated Approach* (2nd edn.). Englewood Cliffs, NJ: Prentice-Hall.

Auditing Practice Board (APB). (2004). International Standard on Auditing (ISA) (UK and Ireland) 200: *Objectives and General Principles Governing an Audit of Financial Statements*. London: Financial Reporting Council.

International Auditing and Assurance Standards Board (IAASB). (2007). *Glossary of Terms*. New York: International Federation of Accountants.

Pratt, M.J. (1990). *External Auditing: Theory and Practice in New Zealand*. New Zealand: Longman Paul.

Read, J.W., Mitchell, J.E., and Akresh, A.D. (1987). Planning materiality and SAS No. 47. *Journal of Accountancy* **164**(12), 72–79.

Securities and Exchange Commission (SEC). (2004, 20 October). *KPMG LLP and four auditors sanctioned for improper professional conduct in connection with Gemstar-TV Guide International, Inc. audits*. New York: SEC, Press Release.

ADDITIONAL READING

Bedard, J.C., Graham, L., and Jackson, C. (2005). Information systems risk and audit planning. *International Journal of Auditing* **9**(2), 147–163.

Bierstaker, J.L., and Wright, A. (2004). Does the adoption of a business risk audit approach change internal control documentation and testing practices. *International Journal of Auditing* **8**(1), 67–78.

Blokdijk, H., Drieenhuizen, F. Simunic, D.A., and Stein, M.T. (2003). Factors affecting auditors' assessments of planning materiality. *Auditing: A Journal of Practice & Theory* **22**(2), 297–307.

Cohen, J.R., Krishnamoorthy, G., and Wright, A.M. (2007). The impact of roles of the board on auditors' risk assessments and program planning decisions. *Auditing: A Journal of Practice & Theory* **26**(1), 91–112.

DeZoort, T., Harrison, P., and Taylor, M. (2006). Accountability and auditors' materiality judgments: the effects of differential pressure strength on conservatism, variability, and effort. *Accounting, Organizations and Society* **31**(4–5), 373–390.

Fédération des Experts Comptables Européens (FEE). (2005). *Risk Management and Control in the EU.* Brussels: FEE.

Kizirian, T.G., Mayhew, B.W., and Sneathen Jr., L.D. (2005). The impact of management integrity on audit planning and evidence. *Auditing: A Journal of Practice & Theory* **24**(2), 49–67.

Lloyd, P., and Goldschmidt, P. (2003). Modelling audit risk assessments: exploration of an alternative to the use of knowledge-based systems. *International Journal of Auditing* **7**(1), 21–35.

Messier Jr., W.F., Martinov-Bennie, N., and Eilifsen, A. (2005). A review and integration of empirical research on materiality: two decades later. *Auditing: A Journal of Practice & Theory* **24**(2), 153–187.

O'Donnell, E., and Schultz Jr., J.J. (2005). The halo effect in business risk audits: Can strategic risk assessment bias auditor judgment about accounting details? *The Accounting Review* **80**(3), 921–940.

Page, M., and Spira, L. (2004). *The Turnbull Report, Internal Control and Risk Management: The Developing Role of Internal Audit.* Edinburgh: Institute of Chartered Accountants of Scotland.

Taylor, M.H. (2000). The effects of industry specialization on auditors' inherent risk assessments and confidence judgements. *Contemporary Accounting Research* **17**(4), 693–712.

10 Internal Control and the Auditor

LEARNING OBJECTIVES

After studying the material in this chapter you should be able to:
- explain what is meant by 'an accounting system';
- explain why the accounting system is divided into sub-systems for audit purposes and the basis on which this is done;
- define 'internal control' and describe its five components;
- describe the elements of a good system of internal control relevant to financial reporting;
- describe the objectives of internal accounting controls;
- discuss the inherent limitations of all systems of internal control;
- describe the techniques for reviewing and documenting the accounting sub-systems and their related internal controls;
- explain what is meant by 'a walk through test' and why it is conducted;
- explain how an audit plan (or audit programme) is developed;
- discuss the importance of auditors identifying the strengths and deficiencies of an audit client's system of internal control;
- explain the meaning of the term 'compliance testing';
- describe the audit procedures used for compliance testing;
- discuss the factors auditors need to consider when planning to rely on the results of compliance tests performed during an interim audit or in a prior year.

The following publications are particularly relevant to this chapter:

- International Standard on Auditing (ISA) 265: *Communicating Deficiencies in Internal Control* (IFAC, 2007)*[1]
- International Standard on Auditing (ISA) 300 (Redrafted): *Planning an Audit of Financial Statements* (IFAC, 2006)
- International Standard on Auditing (ISA) 315 (Redrafted): *Identifying and Assessing the Risks of Material Misstatement through Understanding the Entity and its Environment* (IFAC, 2006)
- International Standard on Auditing (ISA) 330 (Redrafted): *The Auditor's Responses to Assessed Risks* (IFAC, 2006)

---

[1] The status of ISAs referred to in this chapter is explained in the Important Note following the Preface to this book.

10.1 INTRODUCTION

As the auditor has journeyed through the audit process to reach the present stage, (s)he has performed engagement procedures; gained an understanding of the client, its internal and external environment and its activities; identified and assessed risks of material misstatement in the financial statements as a whole and at the assertion level[2] for classes of transactions, account balances and disclosures; defined materiality limits; and established a desired level of audit risk (see Chapter 7, Figure 7.1, Audit Steps 1–4).

The auditor will now wish to obtain a detailed knowledge of the client's accounting system and evaluate the effectiveness of its internal controls. Once the auditor has assessed the level of reliance (s)he can place on the entity's internal controls to eliminate errors and/or irregularities from the accounting data, the audit plan (or audit programme) can be designed; that is, the nature, timing and extent of audit procedures to be performed during the rest of the audit can be planned in detail.

In this chapter we examine what is meant by an accounting system and how the system is segmented for audit purposes. We explore some conceptual aspects of internal control, and discuss how auditors obtain knowledge of their clients' accounting system and evaluate its related internal controls. We also investigate how auditors develop an audit plan (or audit programme). Before concluding the chapter we consider the tests auditors conduct in order to determine whether the internal controls on which they plan to rely (in order to reduce their substantive tests) are operating as effectively as their preliminary evaluation suggests and the factors they need to consider when planning to rely on the results of compliance tests performed during an interim audit or an audit conducted in a prior year.

10.2 THE ACCOUNTING SYSTEM

Like all systems, the accounting system has an input, a processing and an output stage. As Figure 10.1 indicates:
- *the input stage* involves capturing a mass of accounting data from either:
  - source documents, which are completed manually or electronically when transactions take place, or
  - memoranda generated by the entity's accountant. These generally record non-transactions data, for example, writing off bad debts and period end adjustments;

---

[2] Assertions are explained in Chapter 11.

- *the processing stage* involves converting the mass of raw data into useful information. This may be achieved using manual or, as in most cases today, electronic data processing methods but, in each case, it is accomplished through recording, classifying and summarising the data;
- *the output stage* involves preparing the accounting information in a form useful to those who wish to use it; that is, appropriately classifying, grouping and titling information in a meaningful manner.

Figure 10.1: The accounting system

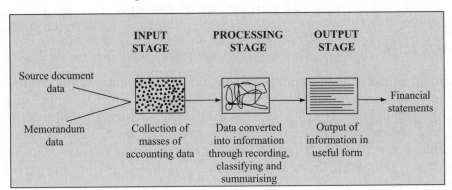

In order to ensure that all, but only, relevant data are captured as input to the accounting system, and to ensure that the data are properly and correctly processed during their conversion into output in the form of financial statements, special checking mechanisms or internal controls are built into the system. The elements, characteristics and objectives of internal control systems are discussed in section 10.3 below.

The auditor is required, *inter alia*, to form and express an opinion on whether or not the entity's financial statements give a true and fair view of its financial position and performance. In order to reach this opinion, the auditor needs to understand the system which generates the financial statements. If the auditor tried to gain this understanding by approaching the entity's accounting system as a single unit, (s)he would find it cumbersome, inefficient and, in many cases, somewhat overwhelming. In order to facilitate the audit (or to put it on to a more practical footing), the auditor (conceptually) dissects the accounting system into sub-systems, or audit segments.

The audit segments recognised for any audit vary according to the nature, size and complexity of the audit client and its activities; however, they are almost invariably based on either classes of transaction (such as sales, purchases, administration expenses, long-term loans, etc.) or (more commonly) accounting cycles. When they are based on accounting cycles, groups of closely related accounts and associated transactions are audited as a single unit. As an example of audit segments based on accounting cycles in an audit of a wholesale or retail business the following segments may be recognised:

- Sales-debtors-receipts cycle;
- Purchases-creditors-payments cycle;
- Inventory (stock)-warehousing cycle;
- Payroll and personnel cycle;
- Financing and investing cycle.

These audit segments are depicted in Figure 10.2. To illustrate related accounts which constitute audit segments, the accounts comprising the sales-debtors-receipts cycle are shown in Figure 10.3.

It should be noted that, until audit segments are identified during the review of the entity's accounting system, the audit is generally approached holistically. As is shown in Figure 10.2, the auditor gains an understanding of the client, its external and internal environment and its activities, identifies and assesses the likelihood of material misstatements being present in the financial statements, determines materiality limits, and establishes a desired level of audit risk, based

Figure 10.2:   Steps in the audit process conducted on entity-wide and audit segment basis

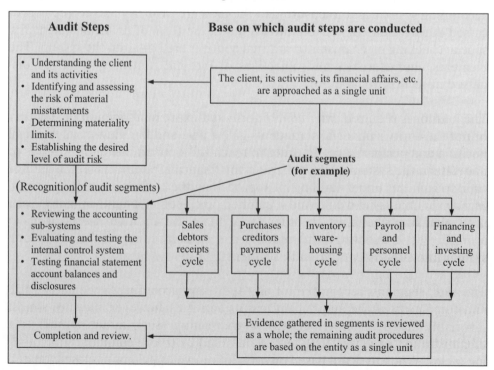

Figure 10.3: Accounts comprising the sales-debtors-receipts cycle

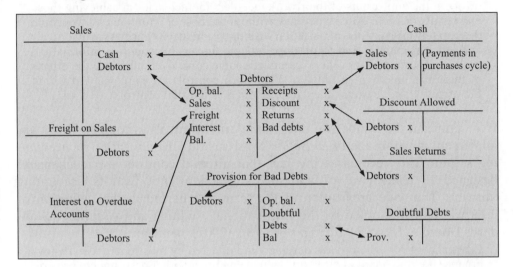

on the client as a whole.[3] Once audit segments have been recognised, obtaining detailed knowledge of the accounting system, evaluating and testing its internal controls, and assessing the accuracy, validity and completeness of financial statement balances and other disclosures, revolve around particular audit segments. When the detailed segment-based work is complete, the auditor reviews as a whole the evidence gathered in the segments, and conducts the remaining audit procedures on an entity-wide basis. These final steps of the audit constitute the review and completion stage, which is discussed in Chapter 13.

10.3 CONCEPTUAL ASPECTS OF INTERNAL CONTROL

10.3.1 Meaning and importance of internal control

When an entity is small, its owner or manager can personally perform, or directly oversee, all of the entity's functions. However, as the entity grows larger it becomes necessary to delegate functional responsibilities to employees. Once this occurs, mechanisms need to be established which enable the performance of the employees to be checked, to ensure they are fulfilling their responsibilities as intended. As Anderson (1977) explains:

---

[3] However, we should note that, when auditors assess the risk of material misstatements in the financial statements, they identify the audit segments (or classes of transactions, account balances or disclosures) where material misstatements appear most likely to occur. Similarly, as we note in Chapter 9, materiality limits are set for both the financial statements as a whole (planning materiality) and for classes of transactions, account balances and disclosures (tolerable error).

With the best of intentions, most people make mistakes. The mistakes may be errors in the end results of their work, needless inefficiencies in achieving those end results, or both. And sometimes, without the best of intentions, a few people deliberately falsify. Any organisation wishing to conduct its business in an orderly and efficient manner and to produce reliable financial accounting information, both for its own and for others' use, needs some controls to minimise the effects of these endemic human failings. When such controls are implemented within the organisation's systems they are described as internal controls ... (p. 143)

It is significant that Anderson refers to internal controls as controls which are implemented within the *organisation's* systems rather than within its *accounting* system. This recognises the fact that internal controls are mechanisms designed to control *all* of an entity's functions, not just its accounting function. The wide application of the term is reflected in the definition of internal control adopted by the International Auditing and Assurance Standards Board's (IAASB) *Glossary of terms* (2007), namely:

Internal control – The process designed and effected by those charged with governance [i.e., the board of directors], management and other personnel to provide reasonable assurance about the achievement of the entity's objectives with regard to reliability of financial reporting, effectiveness and efficiency of operations and compliance with applicable laws and regulations.[4] Internal control consists of the following components:
(a) The control environment;
(b) The entity's risk assessment process;
(c) The information system, including the related business processes, relevant to financial reporting, and communication;
(d) Control activities; and
(e) Monitoring of controls.

We discuss these components of internal control, which we collectively refer to as 'an internal control system', in section 10.3.2 below.

Over the past couple of decades, the issue of internal control has gained prominence in the United Kingdom (UK), largely as a result of recognition of its importance in Codes of Corporate Governance, starting with that of the Committee on the Financial Aspects of Corporate Governance (Cadbury Committee; 1992) to the most recent – the Financial Reporting Council's (FRC) *Combined Code on Corporate Governance* (2006),[5] and the adoption

---

[4] This definition is derived from, and is almost identical to, that proposed by the Committee of Sponsoring Organisations of the Treadway Commission (COSO, 1992).

[5] This Code essentially consolidates the recommendations of earlier reports, especially those of the Committee on the Financial Aspects of Corporate Governance (Cadbury Committee; 1992), the Committee on Corporate Governance (Hampel Committee; 1998a), the Study Group on Directors' Remuneration (Greenbury Committee; 1995), Higgs on non-executive directors (2003) and Smith on audit committees (2003). It also supersedes the FRC's 2003 *Combined Code on Corporate Governance* (FRC, 2003) which, in turn, replaced the *Combined Code* of the Committee on Corporate Governance (1998b).

of the Codes' requirements by the UK Listing Authority (UKLA). In respect of internal control the FRC's 2006 Code states:

Principle C.2: The board [of directors] should maintain a sound system of internal control to safeguard shareholders' investment and the company's assets.

Provision C.2.1: The board should, at least annually, conduct a review of the effectiveness of the group's system of internal controls [i.e., that of the parent company and its subsidiaries] and should report to shareholders that they have done so. The review should cover all material controls, including financial, operational and compliance controls and risk management.

As we note in Chapter 5 (section 5.5), under the UKLA's rules, companies listed on the London Stock Exchange are required to include in their annual report a governance statement explaining how they have applied the Code's principles (including Principle C.2, cited above) and stating whether or not they have complied with the Code's provisions throughout the reporting period – and, if not, the respects in which they have not done so and the reasons therefor. Additionally, auditors are required to review the company's governance statement insofar as it relates to nine of the Combined Code's provisions – including Provision C.2.1 (cited above).

It should be noted that the Combined Code (FRC, 2006) requires the directors of listed companies to review the effectiveness of their company's internal controls and to report to shareholders that they have done so. Similarly, auditors are required to review the directors' statement. Neither party is required to report on the effectiveness of the controls *per se*. Managements[6] and auditors of companies subject to the provisions of the Sarbanes-Oxley Act of 2002 (SOX) must go further. SOX, s. 404, requires the managements of all public companies registered with the Securities and Exchange Commission (SEC) or listed on a stock exchange in the United States of America (USA), and any subsidiary of such a company (irrespective of where in the world such company or subsidiary is located), to include in their annual report:

(i) a statement to the effect that management is responsible for establishing and maintaining an adequate internal control structure and procedures for financial reporting; and

(ii) an assessment, as of the end of the most recent reporting period, of the effectiveness of the company's internal control structure and procedures for financial reporting.

---

[6] Readers are reminded that in the Preface to this book we note the term 'management' is defined to mean a company's executive directors, non-executive directors, and non-director executives (that is, all executives and directors).

Additionally, the auditor of the company's financial statements is required to "attest to, and report on, the [internal control] assessment made by the management of the [company]". Thus, auditors subject to this provision are required to evaluate and report on the effectiveness of their audit clients' internal controls related to financial reporting.

10.3.2 Internal control components

We noted in section 10.3.1 above that IAASB (2007) identifies five internal control components, namely:

(a) *The control environment* – the environment created by the entity's directors and executives, through their attitudes, awareness and actions, regarding the entity's internal controls and their importance in the entity;

(b) *The entity's risk assessment process* – the process adopted by the entity for identifying business risks relevant to financial reporting, deciding how to respond to those risks and the results of those responses;

(c) *The information system, including the related business processes, relevant to financial reporting, and communication* – the financial reporting system and its procedures and records for initiating, recording, processing and reporting entity transactions, events and conditions, and accounting for related assets, liabilities and equity; also the means by which the entity communicates financial roles and responsibilities and significant matters relating to financial reporting;

(d) *Control activities* – policies and procedures designed to ensure that responsibilities delegated by management are fulfilled and performed in the intended manner. This internal control component includes control activities that relate to information technology (IT) environments. These are explained below;

(e) *Monitoring of controls* – a process designed to assess the effectiveness of internal control performance over time. It includes assessing the design and operation of controls on a timely basis, taking corrective action when required and modifying the controls, as appropriate, for changed conditions.

These components are shown in Figure 10.4.

In an IT environment two types of controls are generally recognised, namely, general IT-controls and application controls.

(i) General IT-controls

General controls are policies and procedures designed to control the IT environment (including the development and maintenance of computer

Figure 10.4: Relationship between the components of an internal control system

Internal control system

Process designed, implemented and maintained by management to provide reasonable assurance about achieving the entity's objectives in respect of reliable financial reporting, effective and efficient operations and compliance with applicable laws and regulations.

Control environment

Sets the tone of the entity: the attitudes, awareness and actions of directors and managers regarding internal controls and their importance to the entity.
Examples:
• Management philosophy and operating style;
• Organisational structure and methods of assigning authority and responsibility.

Entity's risk assessment process

Process designed to identify business risks relevant to financial reporting objectives, responses to those risks and the results thereof.

Information system, including financial reporting system

Procedures and records to initiate, record, process and report transactions, events and conditions and to maintain accountability for assets, liabilities and equity. Also the means of communicating financial roles and responsibilities.

Control activities

Policies and procedures established to help ensure responsibilities delegated by management are fulfilled as intended.
Examples:
• Approval and control of documents;
• Restricting direct access to assets and records;
• Procedures for authorising transactions;
• Segregation of duties.

Monitoring of controls

Process to assess the effectiveness of internal controls over time. Assesses the design and operation of controls, effects corrective action and implements changes when needed.
Examples:
• Review of documents;
• Supervision of subordinates;
• Internal audit;
• Reviewing customer complaints.

Use of IT affects control activities

General (computer environment) controls

Policies and procedures that support the effective functioning of application controls and maintain the integrity and security of data.
Examples:
• Restricting access to computers, programs, data and files to authorised personnel;
• Ensuring there are adequate back-up facilities for both hardware and software;
• Ensuring all computer applications are fully documented;
• Acquiring, developing and changing system and application software.

Application controls

Procedures that apply to the processing of individual applications that are designed to ensure the integrity of the accounting records and financial data. Controls over the input, processing and output of accounting applications.
Examples:
• Controls to ensure that:
  – all transactions input to the system are properly authorised,
  – output is checked against input data,
  – transactions are properly and accurately recorded and processed,
  – data files are properly maintained and protected.

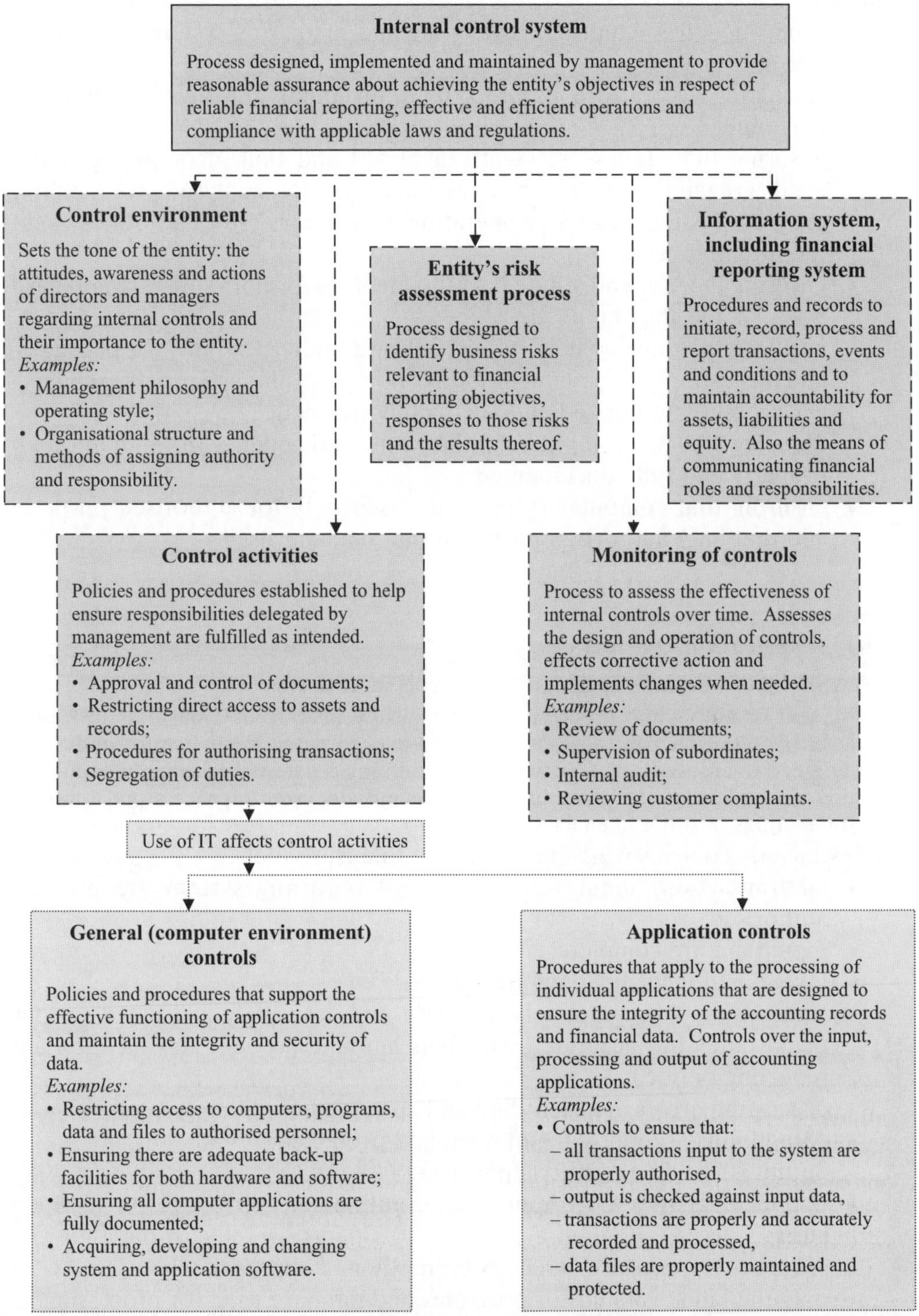

systems) and support the effective functioning of application controls. They include:

- procedures for acquiring, developing and modifying system and application software;
- restricting access to computers, data, programs and files to authorised personnel;
- ensuring that duties are clearly assigned and that incompatible duties are segregated; for example, assigning systems analysis, programming, program testing, computer operation, and library (storage) duties to different employees;
- ensuring there are adequate back-up facilities for both software and hardware, should they be needed;
- ensuring the development or acquisition of new programs (or packages), and the testing and implementation of new programs and program changes, are properly authorised and adequately planned;
- ensuring that all computer applications, and modifications thereof, are properly and fully documented;
- ensuring that computer systems are used only for authorised purposes, and that only authorised programs and data are used.

(ii) Application controls

IAASB (2007) defines application controls as follows:

> Manual or automated procedures that typically operate at a business process level. Application controls can be preventive or detective in nature and are designed to ensure the integrity of the accounting records. Accordingly, application controls relate to procedures used to initiate, record, process and report transactions or other financial data.

They include controls which are designed to ensure that:

- all transactions input to the financial reporting system are properly authorised;
- input data are complete;
- invalid and incorrect data are rejected;
- transactions are completely, properly and accurately processed (in particular, they are accurate as to their amount, account classification and reporting period);
- processing errors are identified and corrected on a timely basis;
- data files are properly maintained and protected;
- output is checked against input data;
- output is provided to appropriate, authorised personnel on a timely basis;
- exception reports are acted on promptly and appropriately;
- only the latest versions of programs and data are used for processing.

Although the control environment is identified as one of five internal control components, it should be noted that, if the control environment is weak or defective, it is likely that the other control components will not function properly and the internal control system as a whole will not be effective in providing reasonable assurance that the entity's objectives, regarding reliable financial reporting, effective and efficient operations, and compliance with applicable laws and regulations, will be met. Similarly, if the general IT-controls are weak or defective, it is likely that the application controls will not be applied properly. Deficiencies in the control environment or general IT-controls cannot be adequately compensated for by other control components, or application controls, which are 'foolproof'. By the same token, the existence of a strong control environment and 'excellent' general IT-controls does not, of itself, mean that the other control components and application controls are unnecessary. Each element is essential for an effective internal control system. The control environment and general IT-controls set the culture and context within which the more specifically targeted control components and application controls operate: each component of the internal control system complements the other components.

Where entities have internal auditors, these auditors are generally responsible for implementing, monitoring and maintaining all aspects of the internal control system. External auditors need to be familiar with the internal control system and they need to evaluate the quality of the control environment. However, as we explain in section 10.4 below, external auditors are primarily concerned with the internal control components that relate to the accounting function – in particular, those relating to safeguarding the entity's assets and accounting records, and ensuring the provision of reliable financial information: they are less concerned with the entity's operational and compliance controls.

10.3.3 Preliminary understanding of internal control components

In Chapter 8 (footnote 4) we note that a part of auditors gaining an understanding of the client – its external and internal environments, structure, operations, risks, key personnel, etc. – involves gaining a preliminary understanding of the entity's internal control system. We now examine the requirements of auditors as regards gaining an understanding of the five components of internal control. We discuss the characteristics of a good internal control system relevant to financial reporting in section 10.3.4 below.

(a) Control environment

In relation to gaining an understanding of the control environment, International Standard on Auditing (ISA) 315: *Identifying and assessing the risks of material misstatement* . . . (para 14) requires auditors to evaluate whether:

- management has created and maintained a culture of honesty and ethical behaviour; and
- the control environment supports the other components of internal control.

The Standard explains (para A66) that elements of the control environment which may be relevant to the auditor's understanding include the following:

(i)   the manner in which the principles of integrity and ethical values are communicated and enforced within the entity. These attributes have a major impact on the effectiveness of the design, implementation and monitoring of internal controls;

(ii)   management's consideration of the competence levels required for particular jobs and how these translate into requisite skills and knowledge;

(iii)   attributes of the board of directors – in particular, the directors' independence from executives, their experience and stature, the extent of their involvement in the entity, the information they receive, their scrutiny of the company's activities, the degree to which they raise and pursue difficult questions with executives, and their interaction with the entity's internal and external auditors;

(iv)   the philosophy and operating style of senior executives, in particular, their approach to taking and managing business risks, and their attitudes towards the accounting function, information processing and financial reporting;

(v)   the organisational structure within which the entity plans, and seeks to achieve, control and review, its objectives;

(vi)   how authority and responsibility for operating activities are assigned, and how reporting relationships and authorisation hierarchies are established;

(vii)   human resource policies and practices relating to, for example, recruitment, orientation, training, evaluation, counselling, promotion, compensation, and remedial actions.

(b)   Entity's risk assessment process

ISA 315 (paras 15, 16) requires auditors to determine whether their auditees have established a process for identifying business risks relevant to financial reporting objectives, estimating the significance and the likelihood of occurrence of those risks, and effecting actions to address those risks – and, if so, to gain an understanding of that process. If auditees have such a process and auditors identify risks of material misstatement in the financial statements that management failed to identify, they need to determine whether there is an underlying risk that they would have expected the entity's risk assessment process to identify. If this is the case, auditors are required to

obtain an understanding of why the process failed to identify the risk, and evaluate whether:
- the process is appropriate to the entity's circumstances; or
- a significant deficiency exists in the entity's risk assessment process.

In cases where audit clients have not established a formal risk assessment process, auditors are required to discuss with management whether business risks relevant to financial reporting objectives have been identified and, if so, how they have been addressed. They are also required to evaluate whether the absence of a documented risk assessment process is:
- appropriate in the entity's circumstances; or
- represents a significant deficiency in the entity's internal control (ISA 315, para 17).

(c) Information system and related business processes relevant to financial reporting

ISA 315 (para 18) requires auditors to obtain an understanding of the entity's information system, and the related business processes, that are relevant to financial reporting. The Standard explains (para A80):

> An entity's business processes are the activities designed to:
> - Develop, purchase, produce, sell and distribute an entity's products and services;
> - Ensure compliance with laws and regulations; and
> - Record information, including accounting and financial reporting information.
>
> Business processes result in the transactions that are recorded, processed and reported by the information system. Obtaining an understanding of the entity's business processes, which include how transactions are originated, assists the auditor obtain an understanding of the entity's information system relevant to financial reporting in a manner that is appropriate to the entity's circumstances.

The particular aspects of the information system auditors are required to understand include the following:
- (i) the classes of transactions which are significant to the entity's financial statements;
- (ii) the procedures (in both electronic and manual systems) by which those transactions are initiated, recorded, processed, corrected as necessary, transferred to the general ledger and reported in the financial statements;
- (iii) the accounting records, supporting information and specific accounts in the financial statements that are used to initiate, record, process and report transactions;

(iv) how the information system captures events and conditions, other than transactions, that are significant to the financial statements (for example, depreciation and amortisation of assets and changes in the recoverability of accounts receivable);

(v) the financial reporting process used to prepare the entity's financial statements (including the determination of significant accounting estimates and disclosures);

(vi) controls over journal entries, in particular controls over non-standard journal entries which record non-recurring, unusual transactions or adjustments (ISA 315, para 18).

In addition to gaining an understanding of the information system relevant to financial reporting (which we refer to as 'the accounting system'), auditors are required to gain an understanding of how financial reporting roles and responsibilities, and significant matters relating to financial reporting, are communicated within the entity. This includes understanding matters such as:

- the extent to which entity personnel understand:
  - how their activities within the financial reporting information system relate to the work of others, and
  - the means of reporting exceptions to an appropriate higher level within the organisation;
- how the entity's executives and directors communicate about financial reporting and related matters;
- how the entity communicates with external parties such as regulatory authorities.

Communication of the financial reporting roles and responsibilities may be through policy and financial reporting manuals or by other means (ISA 315, paras 19, A82).

(d) Control activities

In respect of control activities, auditors are required to gain an understanding of the control activities they judge "it necessary to understand in order to assess the risks of material misstatement at the assertion level[7] and design further audit procedures responsive to assessed risks" (ISA 315, para 20). These control activities, which we discuss in section 10.3.5 below, primarily relate to controls within the accounting system. We refer to these control activities as 'internal accounting controls'.

---

[7] Assertions relate to classes of transactions, account balances and disclosures; they are discussed in Chapter 11.

(e) Monitoring of controls

Auditors need to gain an understanding of the activities their clients use to monitor the internal controls over their financial reporting process, and the manner in which they effect corrective action. Gaining this understanding includes understanding the sources of the information used for the monitoring activities, and the basis upon which management considers the information to be sufficiently reliable for this purpose. As ISA 315 explains (paras A94, A95, A97):

> Management accomplishes monitoring of controls through ongoing activities, separate evaluations, or a combination of the two. Ongoing monitoring activities are often built into the normal recurring activities of an entity and include regular management and supervisory activities. ... [They] may also include using information from communications from external parties such as customer complaints and regulator comments that may indicate problems or highlight areas in need of improvement.... Much of the information used in monitoring may be produced by the entity's information system. If management assumes that data used for monitoring are accurate without having a basis for that assumption, errors may exist in the information ... Accordingly, [auditors need to gain] an understanding of:
> • The sources of the information related to the entity's monitoring activities; and
> • The basis upon which management considers the information to be sufficiently reliable for the purpose.

10.3.4 Characteristics of a good internal control system relevant to financial reporting

If an entity's control environment relevant to financial reporting possesses certain characteristics, it is likely that the entity's assets will be adequately safeguarded and its accounting data (and thus its financial statements) will be reliable. These internal control characteristics are as follows:
(i)   competent, reliable personnel who possess integrity;
(ii)   clearly defined areas of authority and responsibility;
(iii)   proper authorisation procedures;
(iv)   adequate records;
(v)   segregation of incompatible duties;
(vi)   independent checks on performance;
(vii)   physical safeguarding of assets and records.

(i) Competent, reliable personnel who possess integrity

The most important factor in safeguarding an entity's assets and records, and in securing reliable financial data, is the quality of the entity's personnel. If the entity's directors, executives and other employees are competent, they are able to fulfil their responsibilities efficiently and effectively; if they are also reliable and possess integrity, they will fulfil their responsibilities carefully and honestly. Indeed, if this control characteristic is satisfied, it is probable that the entity's assets will remain safe and its financial data will be free of material misstatements, even if the other elements are weak.

(ii) Clearly defined areas of authority and responsibility

Irrespective of how competent and reliable an entity's personnel may be, in order to ensure that all necessary tasks are performed – and performed in an efficient, timely manner – it is important that the authority and responsibility of each employee is clearly defined. This not only ensures that employees know what is expected of them; it also facilitates pinpointing responsibility in cases where tasks are not performed properly. Such identification of responsibility motivates employees to work carefully and also enables management to ascertain where corrective action is required.

(iii) Proper authorisation procedures

In order to safeguard its physical assets and protect the integrity of its records, an entity requires proper authorisation procedures. For example, procedures need to be established to ensure that all transactions are initiated or approved by a person who has the requisite authority. An entity may, for instance, establish procedures for approving credit sales whereby:
- all credit sales have to be authorised in writing by the credit manager before the goods are sold;
- the credit manager has discretion to extend credit to individual customers up to a maximum of, say, £8,000;
- if the £8,000 limit is to be exceeded, written authority must be obtained from the managing director.

Similarly, a purchases manager may be granted authority to purchase inventory and/or supplies up to the value of a specified amount, or a departmental manager may be authorised to purchase capital equipment for his or her department up to a specified value. If the purchases or departmental manager wish to exceed their authorised limit, they must seek approval to do so from a higher authority, such as a divisional manager, managing director or the Board of Directors (depending on the procedures established in the entity).

Procedures are also required to ensure that the acquisition or development of all new computer programs or packages, and their testing and implementation, are properly authorised. The same applies to all program changes. Even small errors in computer programs can cause considerable harm to an organisation. They can result in erroneous data (and hence in faulty decisions based on that data) and cause much wasted organisational effort in locating and correcting the errors and in rectifying the damage they have done. This may extend to faulty documents being sent to third parties and, thereby, damage to the entity's reputation.

(iv) Adequate records

If an entity is to secure reliable financial data and to safeguard its assets, it is essential that it maintains adequate records. This includes ensuring that:
- the entity's records (such as order forms, receiving reports, sales invoices, receipts, and payments vouchers – whether in paper or electronic form) are numbered consecutively and are designed so that they may be completed easily and fully at the time the transaction takes place;
- every transaction is supported by a source document in paper or electronic form;
- all accounting entries are supported by a source document (for transactions) or a memorandum generated by the entity's accountant (for non-transactions such as period-end adjustments and writing off bad debts);
- authorisations are supported by appropriate and adequate evidence;
- an adequate chart of accounts is maintained to facilitate recording transactions in the correct accounts;
- adequate procedures manuals and job descriptions are maintained to ensure that employees:
    - know (or can find out) the procedures to follow when undertaking organisational activities, and
    - are aware of the requirements of their own position in the entity and how this relates to the duties attaching to associated positions;
- in the IT area, the specifications and authorised application of computer programs (and any modifications thereof) are properly and fully documented.

(v) Segregation of incompatible duties

When defining areas of responsibility and assigning tasks to employees, it is essential that incompatible duties are vested in different people. In particular:
- no one person should have custody of assets and also maintain the records of those assets. For example, the cashier (who handles money) should not record cash received or paid. If the same person performs these duties (s)he is able to steal cash and cover his or her traces by making appropriate adjustments in the cash records;

- no one person should have custody of assets and also authorise transactions relating to those assets. For example, the stores manager should not be given authority to authorise purchases or sales of items under his or her control. If these tasks are vested in the same person, it enables that person to obtain assets for their own benefit by authorising fictitious transactions;
- no one person should be given responsibility for both:
  - software design and computer programming,
  - computer programming and computer operations,
  - computer programming and software testing.

  In each of these cases, if the responsibilities are assigned to one person, it enables him or her to manipulate computer programs to their own advantage; it also allows unintentional errors to remain undetected;
- no one person should have responsibility for all of the entries in the accounting records. Careful allocation of accounting duties enables the work of different employees to be organised so that the work of one automatically cross-checks the work of another. This facilitates the detection of unintentional errors.

(vi) Independent checks on performance

Even if personnel are competent, reliable and trustworthy, and their responsibilities are clearly defined and carefully assigned so that no one person performs incompatible duties, there remains the possibility that errors will occur. All employees are humans, not robots, and humans are prone to make mistakes. Unintentional errors may occur, for example, as a result of tiredness, boredom or failure to concentrate fully on the task in hand. On occasions, employees may become careless in following defined procedures or may deliberately fail to do so, either because they perceive an 'easier' way to accomplish the task or because they wish to defraud the entity. In any event, if financial data are to be reliable, and the entity's assets and records are to be safeguarded, it is important that there are independent checks on employees' performance.

One means of achieving these checks is to assign accounting duties so that the work of one employee automatically cross-checks the work of another – a process known as 'internal check'. For example, one accounts clerk may maintain the Debtors Subsidiary Ledger and another clerk, the Debtors Control account in the General Ledger. Similarly, before preparing a cheque, the payments clerk may be required to match the supplier's invoice with a copy of the relevant order form (from the purchases department) and receiving note (from the receiving department), to check for authorised signatures on the order form and receiving note, and to verify and reconcile the items, quantities and monetary amounts shown on the documents. In computerised systems, the computer can be programmed so that a cheque is prepared (electronically) once the purchase order, receiving report and supplier's invoice (all in electronic form) have been properly authorised and 'matched' by the computer. In other situations, two employees may be involved in a single task, so that each provides a check on the performance of the other; for example, two employees may be involved in opening the mail when it is expected to contain remittances from debtors.

A further means of checking employees' performance is for supervisors to review the work of subordinates; for example, the financial controller may review journal and ledger entries and completed bank reconciliations.

(vii) Physical safeguarding of assets and records

As noted above, one of the objectives of an internal control system is to safeguard the entity's assets and records. The most effective way to achieve this objective is to provide physical protection for assets and records, combined with restricted access. For example, inventory (stock) and supplies may be stored in a locked storeroom with access restricted to a limited number of authorised personnel; cash, cheques, marketable securities and similar items may be kept in a fireproof safe, with few personnel having access to the safe keys or being privy to the combination lock number; the entity's land and buildings may be protected by such things as fences, locked entry doors, closed-circuit television, burglar and fire alarms, smoke detectors, water sprinklers and similar devices.

An entity's legal, accounting and other documents are important components of its assets and should be protected in the same way as its other assets; that is, secure facilities should be provided for their safekeeping and access should be strictly limited to authorised personnel. The same applies to computer hardware, programs, data and files. Additionally, back-up copies should be kept (preferably at a secure, off-site location) of information generated or stored in computers, and emergency use of computer facilities should be arranged in case the entity's system should fail.

It was noted in section 10.3.1 above that internal controls become necessary when an entity grows beyond the size at which the owner or manager can personally perform or oversee all of the entity's functions, and functional responsibilities have to be delegated to employees. It follows that the extent of an internal control system and its degree of formalisation are likely to vary according to the size and complexity of the entity and its operations. However, once functional responsibilities are delegated to employees, it is necessary to institute control procedures and, irrespective of the entity's size and complexity, if the internal control system possesses the seven characteristics outlined above, then it is likely that the entity's assets and records will be adequately safeguarded and its financial data (and hence its financial statements) will be reliable.

10.3.5 Objectives of internal accounting controls

As explained in section 10.2 above, an entity's accounting system is designed to capture accounting data and to convert and output this data as useful financial information. In order for financial information to be useful, it must be reliable. Thus, the underlying accounting data must be valid, complete and accurate. To generate data which meets these criteria, control activities are built into the accounting system. These control activities, which we refer to as 'internal accounting controls', are designed, in particular, to ensure that transactions which give rise to the accounting data are:

(i) properly recorded; that is, all relevant details of transactions are recorded at the time the transactions take place;

(ii) properly authorised; that is, all transactions are authorised by a person with the requisite authority;

(iii) valid; that is, transactions recorded in the accounting system represent genuine exchanges with *bona fide* parties;

(iv) complete; that is, all genuine transactions are input to the accounting system; none is omitted;

(v) properly valued; that is, transactions are recorded at their correct exchange value;

(vi) properly classified; that is, transactions are recorded in the correct accounts;

(vii) recorded in the correct accounting period.

As practically all entities' accounting systems are now largely or wholly electronic, these internal accounting controls are, in essence, application controls. If the objectives of the internal accounting controls (outlined above) are met, it is probable that the information presented in the financial statements will be reliable. If the seven characteristics of a good internal control system relevant to financial reporting are present (as outlined in section 10.3.4), then it is likely that the internal accounting control objectives will be met.

In addition to control activities which are designed to ensure that all transactions are properly recorded (i.e., all data input to the accounting system are valid, complete and accurate as to amount, account and accounting period), controls are needed to ensure that the transactions (or input data) are properly processed. Thus, application controls are required to ensure, for example, that:

- invalid and incorrect data are rejected;
- processing errors are identified and corrected on a timely basis;
- data files are properly maintained and protected;
- exception reports are acted on promptly and appropriately;
- only the latest versions of programs and data are used for processing.

10.3.6 Inherent limitations of systems of internal accounting controls

Irrespective of how well designed a system of internal accounting controls may be, and how effectively it operates, it will always possess inherent limitations. These may be illustrated by the following examples:

(i) The extent of an entity's internal accounting control procedures depends on their cost-effectiveness. Beyond some point, the cost of instituting additional control activities will exceed the benefits to be gained from more accurate financial data or increased safeguarding of assets. For example, there is little point in installing a £50,000 surveillance system to prevent the theft of, say, one 20p biro each week!

(ii) Internal accounting controls are designed to prevent and detect errors and irregularities in normal, frequently recurring transactions. However, errors are more likely to occur in recording and/or processing of infrequent, unusual transactions – for the very reason that they are unusual.

(iii) The potential for error is always present because accounting personnel are human and therefore prone to make mistakes. Similarly, there may be an error in the design of a control activity or a person responsible for performing a particular control function (for example, reviewing exception reports) may not fully understand the purpose of the function and fails to take appropriate action. Thus, internal accounting controls may not always operate as intended.

(iv) There is the possibility that management will override the controls, or two or more employees will collude so as to circumvent controls, or a computer operator may override or disable checks within a software program. For example, a computer operator may override or disable edit checks designed to identify and report transactions that exceed a specified amount.

(v) Internal accounting control procedures may become inadequate or inappropriate as a result of changes in the entity's internal and/or external environment and, as a consequence, compliance with the controls may deteriorate.[8]

Because of the inherent limitations of all systems of internal accounting controls, irrespective of how 'perfect' a system may appear to be, an auditor can

---

[8] Inherent limitations of internal controls are detailed in ISA 315, paras A42–A44.

never rely on the system to prevent, or detect and correct, *all* material errors and irregularities in the accounting data. An auditor will always have to evaluate, at least to some extent, the accuracy, validity and completeness of the information presented in the financial statements; that is, some substantive audit procedures will always be necessary.

10.3.7 Significance of internal control to the external auditor

External auditors are not responsible for establishing or maintaining an entity's internal control system – that is the responsibility of the entity's management. Nevertheless, the quality of internal control can, and usually does, have a significant impact on the audit. Indeed, as ISA 315 (para A38) explains:

> An understanding of internal control assists the auditor in identifying types of potential misstatements [in the financial statements] and factors that affect the risks of material misstatement, and in designing the nature, timing and extent of further audit procedures.

If the client's internal control system is well designed (if it contains the seven characteristics of a good internal control system outlined in section 10.3.4), and if the related control activities operate effectively so as to meet the seven internal accounting control objectives set out in section 10.3.5, then the auditor will be reasonably assured that any material errors or irregularities in the accounting data will be prevented, or detected and corrected, as the data passes through the accounting system. Thus, the auditor will feel fairly confident that the financial statements are free of material misstatement. Expressed in terms of audit risk, where an entity has a well-designed and effective internal control system, the risk of material misstatements in the accounting data not being eliminated (that is, internal control risk) will be fairly low. However, before the auditor can rely on internal controls to eliminate material misstatements from the financial statements, (s)he must conduct compliance tests[9] to confirm the controls are operating as his or her preliminary assessment suggests. Further, as a consequence of the inherent limitations of all systems of internal accounting controls, internal control risk can never be reduced to zero. As explained in Chapter 9 (section 9.5), when inherent risk and internal control risk are low, the likelihood of material misstatements being present in the (pre-audited) financial statements is considered to be low and, as a result, substantive procedures need not be extensive. Thus, in audits that are characterised by effective internal controls, the auditor is likely to place greater emphasis on compliance testing (which may largely be conducted during an interim audit) than on substantive testing conducted at, or shortly after, the end of the client's financial year.

---

[9] Compliance tests are discussed in section 10.6.

By the same token, if an entity's internal control system is poorly designed and/or is ineffective in meeting the internal accounting control objectives, the auditor will gain little assurance that the financial statements are free of material misstatement (that is, internal control risk will be assessed as high). As a consequence, before a 'clean' audit report can be issued, the auditor will need to conduct extensive substantive testing in order to gain sufficient assurance that the financial statements are, in fact, free of material misstatement. Thus, in audits characterised by poorly designed and/or ineffective internal controls, the auditor is likely to place greater emphasis on substantive testing and will conduct little compliance testing.

10.4 REVIEWING THE ACCOUNTING SYSTEM AND EVALUATING ITS RELATED CONTROLS

10.4.1 Gaining an understanding of the accounting sub-systems and related controls

In section 10.2 we pointed out that, in order to facilitate the audit, auditors (conceptually) divide their auditees' accounting system into sub-systems, or audit segments. They then conduct their detailed audit examination based on these audit segments.

As the starting point of the detailed examination, auditors seek to understand, and to document, the entity's accounting sub-systems,[10] and to conduct a preliminary evaluation of the related controls. We examined the requirements of auditors with respect to gaining an understanding of the components of internal control in section 10.3.3. We now need to consider how they obtain this understanding and, more particularly, how they gain an understanding of the accounting sub-systems and related internal accounting controls. They obtain their understanding primarily through the following audit procedures.

(i) *Enquiries of client personnel*: Auditors ask questions of relevant personnel from management, supervisory and staff levels of the audit client about various aspects of the accounting sub-systems. For example, they enquire how data are captured and input to the accounting sub-system, and how the data are recorded, classified and summarised. Auditors also make enquiries as to which employees are responsible for what duties, how employees know what to do, how much guidance is provided by procedures manuals and similar documents, and what reviews of employees' work take place.

---

[10] Expressed in ISA 315 terminology, sub-systems within the information system, and related business processes, relevant to financial reporting.

(ii) *Inspection of client documents*: Auditors gain significant insight into the structure and operation of a client's accounting sub-systems by consulting its documents. They examine, for example, the auditee's organisation chart, its chart of accounts and the guidance given on account classification of transactions, and its policies and procedures manuals insofar as they relate to each accounting sub-system. Auditors also inspect more detailed documents such as source documents, journals, ledgers and trial balances, and discuss the various documents with client personnel to ascertain how well they are used and understood.

(iii) *Observation of client personnel*: In addition to asking client personnel about their various duties, and inspecting documents which specify the duties which should be performed, auditors observe personnel at various levels of the organisation carrying out their normal accounting and review functions.

10.4.2 Documenting the accounting sub-systems

Once auditors have gained a preliminary understanding of a particular accounting sub-system, they document that understanding (or, more usually, obtain relevant documents from the audit client and check their understanding against those documents). Two primary forms of documentation are used, namely:
  (a) narrative descriptions; and
  (b) flowcharts.

(a) Narrative descriptions

A narrative description is a detailed description of accounting routines which take place within an accounting sub-system. An example of part of a narrative description from the purchases-creditors-payments cycle is provided in Figure 10.5.

A narrative description should include details of:

  (a) *all of the documents (whether in paper or electronic form) which are used in the accounting routine*: For example, in a purchases routine the narrative description should refer to order forms, receiving reports, suppliers' invoices and credit notes, payments vouchers, etc. The description should detail how each document is initiated, the steps through which it passes between initiation and filing, where and how it is filed (for example, the name of the relevant file and whether it is arranged alphabetically, by document number or by date), and who is responsible for preparing, reviewing, using and filing the document;

  (b) *all of the processes which take place within the routine*: For example, what triggers goods to be ordered, how a supplier is selected, how quantities

Figure 10.5: Narrative description of part of a purchases-creditors-payments cycle

When the issue of a regular item of stock results in the re-order point for that stock item being reached, the staff member in the Stores Department responsible for that stock item prepares a requisition. The requisition is sent electronically to the manager or assistant manager of the Stores Department. He authorises the requisition and sends a copy to the Purchasing Department. A copy is also filed (by requisition number) in the Approved Requisitions (Pending) file. The filed copy is subsequently matched by the Stores Department with a copy of the purchases order and receiving report and moved to a Goods Received file. Discrepancies between goods requested, ordered and received are reported (by means of a computer-generated exception report) to the Stores Department, Purchasing Department, Receiving Department and Creditors Ledger clerk and filed with the relevant (matched) documents.

On receiving a copy of the approved requisition, the Purchasing Department prepares a purchase order. Copies are sent electronically to the supplier, the Stores Department (see above), the Receiving Department, and the Creditors Ledger clerk. A copy is also filed in the Purchase Orders (Pending) file according to the purchase order number.

The Receiving Department files the purchase order (by number) pending the arrival of the goods. On arrival, the goods are inspected and counted and compared with the purchase order. A receiving report is prepared and copies are sent (electronically) to the Purchasing Department, Creditors Ledger clerk and Stores Department (see above). A copy is also filed, by receiving report number, together with purchase order, in a Goods Received file ...

to be ordered are determined, how price is ascertained, how goods received are checked against goods ordered, how discrepancies between goods ordered and received are handled and so on;

(c) *internal control procedure*: The narrative should refer to controls such as the segregation of incompatible duties, authorisation procedures, independent checks on performance, and safeguards for assets and records (for example, the use of locked storerooms and fireproof safes, and access being restricted to authorised personnel, etc.).

As a means of documenting the entity's accounting sub-systems, compared to flowcharts, narrative descriptions are generally less time-consuming and less technically demanding to prepare. However, they do not convey the sequence of processes or document flows as clearly as flowcharts, they are time-consuming to read, they may be difficult to comprehend and key points may not be readily apparent.

Narrative descriptions are appropriate for describing simple accounting routines or sub-systems but their use requires a careful balance between giving sufficient detail to provide an adequate description, and giving too much detail which mitigates clarity and ease of comprehension. Narrative descriptions are frequently used, and are useful, as supplements to flowcharts, to expand on elements of a flowchart where additional detail or explanation is considered necessary.

(b) Flowcharts

A flowchart is a diagrammatic representation of the flow of documents or information through an accounting sub-system and the processes which take place within the system. An example of a flowchart of part of a purchases-creditors-payments cycle is presented in Figure 10.6.[11,12]

The primary advantages of a flowchart are the clear overview of the accounting sub-system it provides and the ease with which internal control strengths and deficiencies can be identified. Compared with a narrative description, a flowchart is easier to read and understand and, when changes are made to the accounting sub-system, it is easier to update. However, on the downside, a flowchart is time-consuming and technically demanding to prepare and its preparation is, therefore, costly. It is largely for these reasons (together with the inefficiency of duplicating effort) that external auditors generally obtain and use (at least as a starting point) flowcharts of the accounting sub-systems prepared by their audit clients (or usually, if they have one, their internal audit function) for their own internal use.

10.4.3 Walk through test

Once auditors have documented (or checked, using the auditee's documentation) their understanding of each accounting sub-system, they will test this understanding against the system itself. They achieve this by means of a 'walk through test' (also known as a 'cradle to the grave test'). One or two transactions of each major class (for example, credit sales, credit purchases, cash received, cash paid) are traced through the entire accounting system, from their initial recording at source to their final destination as components of account balances in the financial statements.

It should be noted that a walk through test is not an audit procedure designed to evaluate compliance with internal accounting controls or to test financial statement balances: instead, it is a procedure designed to confirm (or correct) the auditor's understanding of the flow of transactions data through the client's accounting system and the accuracy of their (or their clients') documents (narrative description and/or flowcharts) recording the system.

---

[11] The narrative description in Figure 10.5 describes part of the system depicted in Figure 10.6. This is for illustrative purposes only. In practice one or other method would be adopted to represent the system. However, this is not to say that one form may not be used to supplement the other. For example, a narrative description may be used to clarify an element of a flowchart. Similarly, a flowchart component may be used to clarify a point in a narrative description.

[12] Although Figure 10.6 depicts the flow of paper documents through part of the purchases-creditors-payments cycle, it could equally depict the flow of information in electronic form from one department to another. The basic principles remain unchanged.

Figure 10.6: Flowchart of part of a purchases-creditors-payments cycle

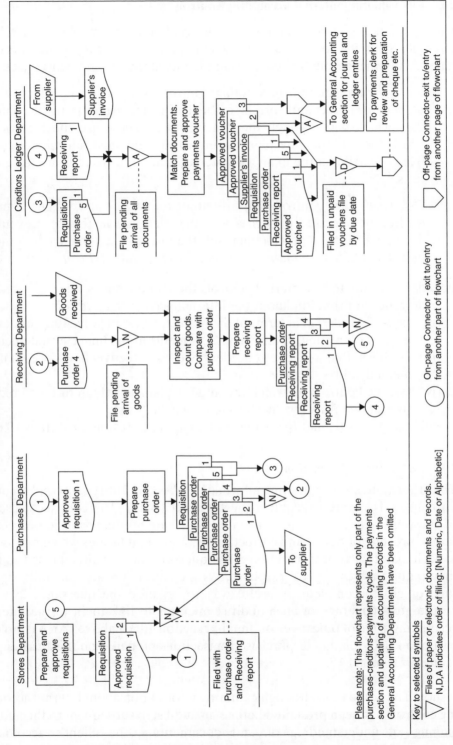

10.4.4 Evaluating internal accounting controls

Having gained an understanding of the accounting sub-systems and related internal accounting controls, and documented that understanding, auditors evaluate the internal accounting controls to identify strengths and deficiencies.

- *Strengths* are internal accounting controls which operate effectively to prevent, or detect and correct, errors and irregularities in the accounting data which pass through the control point. These are the controls on which the auditor may plan to rely to prevent material misstatements from occurring in the financial statements and thus to reduce substantive tests.

- *Deficiencies* are controls that are either missing or are designed, implemented or operated in such a way that they are unable to prevent, or detect and correct, misstatements in the financial statements on a timely basis (ISA 265: *Communicating deficiencies in internal control*, para 6).

In order to evaluate the internal controls the auditor needs to:
  (i)   gather information about the internal accounting controls;
  (ii)   assess their design in terms of their effectiveness in preventing, or detecting and correcting, potential misstatements in the financial statements;
  (iii) establish that the controls identified as effective have been implemented; and
  (iv)   test the controls on which the auditor plans to rely in order to reduce substantive tests (i.e., perform compliance tests).
We discuss points (i) and (ii) below and compliance testing in section 10.6.

(i)   Gathering information

The primary means of gathering information about an entity's internal accounting controls is an internal control questionnaire (ICQ). This consists of a series of questions relating to control activities which are normally considered necessary to prevent, or detect and correct, errors and irregularities which may occur in each major class of transactions. The questions are usually phrased so that they require a 'yes' or 'no' response. As a result, ICQs are generally simple (and quick) to complete. A useful way to organise the questions, so as to ensure good coverage of each audit segment, is to link them to the internal accounting control objectives outlined in section 10.3.5 above. An example of part of an ICQ relating to purchase transactions prepared on this basis is presented in Figure 10.7.

It should be noted that, although gathering information about internal accounting controls has been presented here as an audit step subsequent to the auditor gaining an understanding of, and documenting, the client's accounting

Figure 10.7:   Part of an ICQ relating to the purchases-creditors-payments cycle

Internal Control Questionnaire Purchases				Ref: C-4
Client: Jasper Limited Period: Year to 31 March 2008		Prepared by: RB Date: 12/12/07 Reviewed by: MC Date: 15/12/07		
Control Procedure	**Yes**	**No**	**N/A**	**Remarks**
1. Are sequentially numbered requisitions used to initiate purchase orders?	✓			
2. Are all numbered requisitions accounted for?	✓			Copies are filed numerically. Cancelled requisitions also filed (marked to indicate cancellation)
3. Are requisitions approved by a responsible official?	✓			Manager or Assistant Manager of Stores Department
4. Is initiation of requisitions limited to authorised personnel?		✓		All Stores Department employees have access
5. Can purchase orders be prepared without a requisition?		✓		
6. Are purchase orders sequentially numbered?	✓			
7. Are all numbers accounted for?	✓			Copies are filed numerically (including cancelled order forms)
8. Are purchase orders prepared by a responsible official?	✓			Manager or Assistant Manager of Purchasing Department
9. Is initiation of purchase orders restricted to authorised personnel?	✓			

10. Do all purchase orders show:
    (a) Quantities ordered?
    (b) Prices of goods ordered?
    (c) Special terms of the order?
    (d) Initials of preparer?
    (e) Date of preparation?
	
	✓
	✓
	✓
	✓
	✓			

11. Is there a limit to the value of goods that may be ordered?	✓			Maximum order size £5,000

12. Is a copy of the purchase order sent to:
    (a) Stores Department?
    (b) Receiving Department?
    (c) Creditors Ledger Clerk?
	
	✓
	✓
	✓			

sub-systems, ICQs are commonly completed during the 'understanding and documenting' stage.

(ii)   Assessing the design and implementation of internal accounting controls

Once information about the client's internal accounting controls has been gathered, the auditor needs to evaluate the design of the controls in terms of their effectiveness in preventing, or detecting and correcting, errors in the accounting data. In performing this evaluation the auditor will consider, in particular:

- the errors and irregularities that could occur in each audit segment;
- whether controls that have been implemented are effective in preventing, or detecting and correcting, such errors and irregularities;
- where effective controls appear to be absent, whether there are compensating controls which overcome the apparent internal control deficiency.

Once the auditor has identified internal accounting controls which appear to be effective in preventing material misstatements from occurring in the financial statements, (s)he must decide whether or not (s)he wishes to rely on any of these procedures to reduce substantive testing. This decision affects the nature, timing and extent of audit tests.

10.4.5 Internal control assessment and audit planning

Irrespective of how effective internal accounting controls may appear to be in preventing material misstatements from occurring in the financial statements, before auditors can rely on them to reduce related substantive tests, they must test them in order to obtain audit evidence which demonstrates the controls are working as effectively as the auditors' assessment of their design and implementation suggests, and that they have been so working throughout the reporting period. As ISA 330: *The auditor's responses to assessed risks* explains:

> The auditor shall design and perform tests of controls to obtain sufficient appropriate audit evidence as to the operating effectiveness of relevant controls when:
> (a) The auditor's assessment of risks of material misstatement at the assertion level includes an expectation that the controls are operating effectively (i.e., the auditor intends to rely on the operating effectiveness of controls in determining the nature, timing and extent of substantive procedures); or
> (b) Substantive procedures alone cannot provide sufficient appropriate audit evidence at the assertion level. (para 8)

The greater the reliance the auditor plans to place on internal accounting controls to eliminate material misstatements from the financial statements (and thus reduce substantive tests), the more extensive the tests of those controls (i.e., compliance tests) need to be. According to ISA 330, para A24, extensive compliance testing is also required in situations where it is not possible:

> to design effective substantive procedures that by themselves provide sufficient appropriate audit evidence at the assertion level. This may occur when an entity conducts its business using IT and no documentation of transactions is produced or maintained, other than through the IT system.

Further, when the auditor believes that internal accounting controls can be relied upon, a significant proportion of the audit procedures (especially compliance tests) may be performed during an interim audit two or three months prior to the end of the client's financial year. This enables the audit to be completed in a timely manner following the end of the financial year. It also facilitates efficient scheduling of audit work (and thus audit staff) over the calendar year and avoids 'bottlenecks' occurring when the year-ends of a number of audit clients coincide.

It can be seen that, when auditors consider a client's internal accounting controls can be relied upon to prevent misstatements from occurring in the financial statements, compliance procedures will be given greater emphasis, substantive testing will be less extensive[13] and more audit procedures will be conducted during an interim (rather than year-end) audit than would otherwise be the case. Thus, auditors' assessment of their auditees' internal control systems has a direct impact on audit planning and, once the assessment is complete, the auditor proceeds to develop the audit plan (or audit programme).

When considering the audit procedures to be included in the audit plan, the following points need to be borne in mind:

(i) Irrespective of how effective a client's internal accounting controls may appear to be, auditors may not rely upon them to reduce substantive procedures until they have been tested and found to be operating effectively – and operating in this manner throughout the reporting period. This may appear to preclude the planning of substantive procedures until compliance testing is complete. However, such a delay would introduce inefficiencies into the audit process. As a consequence, auditors proceed to develop their audit plan on the assumption that the internal accounting controls on which they plan to rely operate as indicated by the auditors' assessment of their design and implementation, and that the controls have functioned effectively throughout the reporting period. Nevertheless, auditors must remain alert to the possibility that compliance tests may reveal that internal accounting controls are not as effective as they first thought, and adjustments to the audit plan may be required as a result.

(ii) Although particular internal accounting controls may appear to be operating effectively, auditors may decide not to rely on them to reduce substantive procedures because they consider that the audit effort required to test compliance with the controls is likely to exceed the reduction in effort (in terms of reduced substantive testing) that would be achieved through reliance upon the controls. In this case, no testing of the relevant controls is undertaken and internal control risk is assumed to be high.

---

[13] As explained in Chapter 9, low internal control risk (combined with low inherent risk) results in the auditor's desired level of audit risk being attained with less substantive testing than is needed when internal control risk (and/or inherent risk) is assessed as high.

10.5 DEVELOPING THE AUDIT PLAN (AUDIT PROGRAMME)

The audit plan includes a set of detailed audit procedures designed to meet the specific audit objectives of each audit segment (or, expressed alternatively, audit procedures designed to test the assertions related to with classes of transactions, account balances and disclosures associated with the audit segment). According to ISA 300: *Planning an audit of financial statements*, audit plans are to describe:

(a) The nature, timing and extent of planned risk assessment procedures . . . ;
(b) The nature, timing and extent of further audit procedures at the assertion level . . . ;
(c) Other planned audit procedures that are required to be carried out so that the engagement complies with ISAs. (para 8)

Although audit plans are required to describe the nature, timing and extent of risk assessment procedures (procedures performed when gaining an understanding of the client and its risks as discussed in Chapter 8), it is not until these procedures have been performed, and risks of material misstatements in the various audit segments have been identified and assessed, that detailed planning of compliance and substantive tests can be undertaken.

The audit plan is usually prepared (at least conceptually) in the following two stages:

(i) planning format;
(ii) performance format.

(i) Planning format

In this stage, the audit objectives (or assertions) for each class of transactions, account balance or other financial statement disclosure within each audit segment are identified. For example, audit objectives for purchase transactions might be ascertaining whether:

- purchase transactions are recorded;
- purchase transactions are authorised;
- recorded purchase transactions are valid;
- recorded purchase transactions are complete;
- purchase transactions are properly classified (i.e., recorded in the correct accounts);
- purchase transactions are stated at their correct amount;
- purchase transactions are recorded in their correct accounting period.

Based on the auditor's understanding of the client, the results of overall analytical review procedures, and his or her assessment of the design and implementation of the client's internal accounting controls, the auditor determines how each audit objective (or assertion) is best met through compliance and/or substantive procedures, and identifies the specific procedure(s) to be performed. Certain procedures may be identified as appropriate for meeting more than one objective.

This process is repeated systematically for each audit segment.

(ii) Performance format

Once the lists of audit procedures to be performed have been compiled, the procedures are arranged in a logical sequence and any overlapping procedures are eliminated. This results in a list of audit procedures which are set out in a manner suitable for their performance. This is the audit plan.

Although we can identify (and describe) two stages in preparing the audit plan, where audit plans are generated electronically (which is normally the case) the two stages may occur concurrently (that is, the planning format procedures are concurrently arranged in their performance format).

We should also note that, although we describe as a sequential process, the auditor's:
(i)   risk assessment procedures;
(ii)   assessment of the design and implementation of internal accounting controls;
(iii) tests of the operating effectiveness of the controls on which (s)he plans to rely (i.e., compliance tests); and
(iv)   substantive tests of classes of transactions, account balances and other disclosures,
in practice more than one audit step may be performed concurrently.

The overlapping nature of various audit procedures is described in ISA 330: The auditor's responses to assessed risks, as follows:

> Testing the operating effectiveness of controls is different from obtaining an understanding of and evaluating the design and implementation of controls. However, the same types of audit procedures are used. The auditor may, therefore, decide it is efficient to test the operating effectiveness of controls at the same time as evaluating their design and determining that they have been implemented. (para A21)

> Further, although some risk assessment procedures may not have been specifically designed as tests of controls, they may nevertheless provide audit evidence about the operating effectiveness of the controls and, consequently, serve as tests of controls. For example, the auditor's risk assessment procedures may have included:

- Inquiring about management's use of budgets.
- Observing management's comparison of monthly budgeted and actual expenses.
- Inspecting reports pertaining to the investigation of variances between budgeted and actual amounts.

These audit procedures provide knowledge about the design of the entity's budgeting policies and whether they have been implemented, but may also provide audit evidence about the effectiveness of the operation of budgeting policies in preventing or detecting material misstatements in the classification of expenses. (para A22)

In addition, the auditor may design a test of controls [i.e., a compliance test] to be performed concurrently with a test details [i.e., a substantive test] on the same transaction.... For example, the auditor may design, and evaluate the results of, a test to examine an invoice to determine whether it has been approved [a compliance test] and to provide substantive audit evidence of a transaction [its occurrence, amount, accounting period, etc.]. (para A23)

Notwithstanding factors such as those described above, this stage of the auditor's planning process results in an audit plan (in paper or electronic form) in performance format which specifies for each audit segment:

- the audit objectives to be met;
- the compliance and substantive procedures to be performed to meet the stated objectives;
- the timing of the procedures, that is, whether they are to be performed during the interim or final (year-end) audit.

An example of part of an audit plan relating to purchase transactions is presented in Figure 10.8.

Review of the audit plan

The audit plan is not a document which is prepared near the commencement of an audit and then followed slavishly. Rather, it is kept under continuous review. Its adequacy and appropriateness are re-evaluated as evidence is gathered, and it is revised as and when this is found to be necessary. ISA 300: *Planning an audit of financial statements*, para 9, specifies that auditors are to update and change the audit plan as necessary during the course of the audit. The Standard expands on this, stating:

As a result of unexpected events, changes in conditions, or the audit evidence obtained from the results of audit procedures, the auditor may need to modify the overall audit strategy and audit plan and thereby the resulting planned nature, timing and extent of further audit procedures, based on the revised consideration of assessed risks. This may be the case when information comes to the auditor's attention that differs significantly from the information available when the auditor planned the audit procedures. For example, audit evidence obtained through the

Figure 10.8: Part of an audit plan for purchase transactions

	Procedure	Completed by	Date	Workpaper Ref
1	*Test sequence of purchase orders.* Randomly select five purchase orders from total. Test number sequence – five forwards and five backwards.			
2	*Test purchase order approval.* (See 3(i) below)			
3	*Test adherence to authority limits and compatibility with nature of client's business.* Randomly select 25 purchase orders: (i) Vouch for initials of purchasing officer. (ii) Compare value of order with authorised limit. (iii)Evaluate compatibility of goods ordered with nature of client's business.			
4	*Test sequence of receiving reports.* Randomly select five receiving reports from total. Test number sequence – five forwards and five backwards.			
5	*Test for matching of purchase orders with receiving reports.* Randomly select 25 receiving reports: (i) Check for matching with purchase orders. (ii) Vouch for independent check of items and quantities ordered and received.			
6	*Test sequence of purchase returns records.* Randomly select three purchases returns records. Test number sequence – five forwards and five backwards.			
7	*Test for matching of purchases returns records and suppliers' credit notes.* Randomly select 15 purchases returns records: (i) Check for matching with credit notes. (ii) Vouch for independent check of items and quantities returned and credited.			

8	*Test suppliers' invoices and payments vouchers.*
	Randomly select 25 payments vouchers:
	(i) Check for matching with
	  – supplier's invoice
	  – purchase order
	  – receiving report
	  – purchase returns report
	  – supplier's credit note.
	(ii) Vouch supplier's invoice for evidence of independent check of:
	  – items, quantities and prices of goods ordered and received
	  – extensions and footings.
	(iii) Vouch payments vouchers for:
	  – account classification shown
	  – evidence of independent check of:
	    • amount of payment
	    • account codes.
	(iv) Test accuracy of amounts and account classifications:
	  – recalculate extensions and footings on supplier's invoices and credit notes
	  – recalculate VAT on invoices and credit notes
	  – check propriety of account codes.			

9	*Review all outstanding pu rchase orders at year-end.*
	Check for goods in transit at year end.
	    •
	    •
	    •			

performance of substantive procedures may contradict the audit evidence obtained through tests of controls. (para A14)

10.6 COMPLIANCE TESTING

10.6.1 Purpose of compliance procedures

We noted in section 10.4.4 above that as auditors assess the design and implementation of their clients' internal accounting controls they identify internal control strengths, that is, control activities which appear to be operating effectively to meet certain audit objectives. Two examples are presented in Figure 10.9.

Figure 10.9: Examples of control activities meeting audit objectives

Audit objective	Control activities meeting the audit objective
1. Sales transactions are properly authorised.	The credit manager approves all credit sales before goods leave the premises and initials the sales invoice to indicate approval.
2. Sales transactions are properly valued.	All sales invoices are checked (prices are checked against price lists, and extensions and additions are checked) by an independent person prior to a copy of the invoice being sent to the customer. The 'checker' initials the invoice to indicate that it has been checked.

However, we noted in section 10.4.5 that, irrespective of how effective internal accounting controls may appear to be, before auditors can rely on them to eliminate errors and irregularities from the accounting data, their operating effectiveness must be tested through compliance procedures. In this regard ISA 330 observes that "inquiry alone is not sufficient" (para A26). Instead, auditors are required to:
  (a) Perform other audit procedures in combination with inquiry to obtain audit evidence about the operating effectiveness of the controls, including:
    (i)   How the controls were applied at relevant times during the period under audit.
    (ii) The consistency with which they were applied.
    (iii) By whom or by what means they were applied.
  (b) Determine whether the controls to be tested depend upon other controls (indirect controls), and if so, whether it is necessary to obtain audit evidence supporting the effective operation of those indirect controls. (para 10)

To explain the meaning of 'indirect controls', ISA 330 provides the following example:

[W]hen the auditor decides to test the effectiveness of a user review [i.e., review by entity personnel] of exception reports detailing sales in excess of authorized credit limits, the user review and related follow up is the control that is directly of relevance to the auditor. Controls over the accuracy of the information in the reports (for example, the general IT-controls) are described as 'indirect' controls. (para A30)

10.6.2 Types of compliance procedures

Compliance procedures fall into two main categories:
   (i) those performed where the control activities leave no audit trail;
   (ii) those performed where the control activities leave an audit trail.

(i) Procedures where the control activities leave no audit trail

The primary compliance procedures performed where the client's control activities do not leave an audit trail are enquiry, observation and – for certain computer applications – reperformance. For example, in order to ascertain whether controls which are designed to ensure the segregation of incompatible duties are being complied with, the auditor will enquire and observe which personnel perform what duties, and when and how these duties are performed. In order to determine whether controls designed to protect assets and records are being complied with, the auditor will observe if access to restricted areas is limited to authorised personnel. Additionally, tests may be performed on specific computer applications or on the general control environment; for example, the auditor can check whether access is restricted to computer hardware, files and data, and to the implementation of program changes, by trying to gain access thereto.

(ii) Procedures where the control activities leave an audit trail

Where an audit trail is available (that is, where there is tangible evidence that a control procedure has or has not been performed), the primary audit tests are enquiry and observation (as for cases where no audit trail is left), and also inspection of source documents and, accounting records and documents, and reperformance. For example, in addition to enquiring and observing who performs what duties, and how and when the duties are performed, source documents are inspected for evidence of compliance with authorisation procedures and independent verification of prices, quantities, extensions and additions (such as the initials of the person performing the control procedure). Similarly, other documents, such as reconciliations, journals and ledgers, are inspected for evidence indicating that independent reviews have been performed. Along similar lines, automated logs may be inspected to ascertain whether controls restricting access to elements of the IT system (hardware, programs, files, data, etc.) have been effective. Reperformance of control activities may take the form of, for example, reperforming bank reconciliations to ascertain whether they have been performed correctly, and trying to gain unauthorised access to computer hardware, programs, files and data.

10.6.3 Using audit evidence from an interim audit or audits conducted in prior years

We noted in section 10.4.5 that, when the auditor's assessment of the design and implementation of a client's internal control system indicates that the internal accounting controls can be relied upon to prevent, or detect and correct, errors and irregularities in the accounting data, a significant portion of the compliance testing is likely to be performed during an interim audit. In cases where auditors test the operating effectiveness of controls in an interim audit, they need to assure themselves that the controls they found to be operating effectively continued to do so between the interim audit and the end of the reporting period. More specifically, they need to establish if any significant changes have been made to those controls since they were tested, and determine what additional audit evidence needs to be obtained regarding the continued effective operation of the controls.

When deciding what additional evidence needs to be obtained, auditors consider factors such as the following:
- the significance of the assessed risks of material misstatement at the assertion level for classes of transactions, account balances and disclosures;
- the significance of changes to the controls that were tested during the interim audit, including changes within the accounting system and in relevant personnel;
- the length of the period between the interim audit and the client's year-end;
- the extent to which substantive procedures are to be reduced based on reliance of the effective operation of the controls;
- the strength of the client's control environment.

The additional audit evidence may be obtained by performing further compliance tests and/or testing the effectiveness of the client's monitoring of controls and responses thereto.

Along similar lines, auditors may wish to use audit evidence about the operating effectiveness of internal accounting controls obtained during audits conducted in prior years. However, before relying on such evidence, ISA 330, para 13, requires auditors to consider:

(a) The effectiveness of other elements of internal control, including the control environment, the entity's monitoring of controls, and the entity's risk assessment process;

(b) The risks arising from the characteristics of the control, including whether it is manual or automated;[14]

(c) The effectiveness of general IT-controls;

(d) The effectiveness of the control and its application by the entity, including the nature and extent of deviations in the application of the control noted in previous audits, and whether there have been personnel changes that significantly affect the application of the control;

(e) Whether the lack of a change in a particular control poses a risk due to changing circumstances; and

(f) The risks of material misstatements and the extent of reliance on the control.

In addition to considering the factors outlined above, auditors are required to establish whether changes to the controls on which they plan to rely have rendered evidence obtained in previous years' audits irrelevant. In this case, the controls in question are to be tested during the current period (ISA 330, para 14). Illustrating changes to controls that do, and do not, affect the relevance of evidence obtained during previous years' audits, ISA 330, para A36, observes:

[C]hanges in a system that enable an entity to receive a new report from the system probably do not affect the relevance of audit evidence from a previous audit; however, a change that causes data to be accumulated or calculated differently does affect it.

ISA 330 further specifies that, irrespective of the relevance of evidence obtained during previous years' audits, controls on which auditors plan to rely to reduce substantive tests must be tested at least once every three years. Additionally, auditors are to:

test some controls each audit to avoid the possibility of testing all the controls on which the auditor intends to rely in a single audit period with no testing of controls in the subsequent two audit periods. (para 14)

In some cases, controls may be tested more frequently than every third year. Shorter intervals between re-testing are appropriate, for example, in circumstances where:

- the client's control environment, general IT-controls, and/or monitoring of controls is weak;

---

[14] In relation to automated controls, ISA 330, para A29, notes:

An automated control can be expected to function consistently unless the program (including the tables, files, or other permanent data used by the program) is changed. Once the auditor determines that an automated control is functioning as intended … the auditor may consider performing tests to determine that the control continues to function effectively. Such tests might include determining that:

- Changes to the program are not made without being subject to the appropriate program change controls,
- The authorized version of the program is used for processing transactions, and
- Other relevant general controls are effective.

- the relevant controls include a significant manual element and are, therefore, prone to human error or manipulation (factors that do not characterise automated controls);
- personnel changes have occurred that may significantly affect the application of the control; and
- changed circumstances indicate a need for changes in the control.

10.6.4 Evaluating the operating effectiveness of controls

ISA 330 explains:

> The concept of effectiveness of the operation of controls recognizes that some deviations in the way controls are applied by the entity may occur. Deviations from prescribed controls may be caused by such factors as changes in key personnel, significant seasonal fluctuations in volume of transactions and human error. The detected rate of deviation, in particular in comparison with the expected rate, may indicate that the control cannot be relied on to reduce risk at the assertion level to that assessed by the auditor. (para A41)

Thus, even if some deviations are discovered by the auditor's compliance procedures, the auditor may still judge the relevant control to be operating effectively and able to be relied upon to reduce substantive testing. Nevertheless, if any deviations are found, the auditor needs to understand why they occurred and their potential consequences. More particularly, the auditor is required to determine whether:

(a) The tests of controls that have been performed provide an appropriate basis for reliance on the controls;
(b) Additional tests of controls are necessary; or
(c) The potential risks of misstatement need to be addressed using substantive procedures. (ISA 330, para 17)

If deviations discovered by compliance procedures are numerous (especially if they exceed the error rate expected by the auditor), or are significant in terms of their potential consequences, the auditor is likely to conclude that the control(s) in question is (are) not operating effectively and, therefore, cannot be relied upon to reduce substantive testing. The same applies if misstatements the auditor would have expected to be prevented by internal accounting controls are detected by substantive procedures. In either case, the auditor will need to re-assess his or her conclusion about the operating effectiveness of the control(s) in question and to adjust the planned nature, timing and extent of further audit procedures (and thus the audit plan).

It should be noted that ISA 330 makes particular reference to the possibility that deviations from the controls may occur as a result of personnel changes in key control functions (for example, a change of credit manager). Such personnel changes may be permanent or temporary; they may occur, for example, during the holiday period. It is important that the auditor's compliance procedures cover any such periods of change in relevant personnel.

10.7 REPORTING INTERNAL CONTROL DEFICIENCIES TO MANAGEMENT

Deficiencies identified in the internal accounting controls (that is, points in the accounting system where errors and irregularities could arise and/or be present but not detected) are not compliance tested by the auditor. The controls are absent or ineffective and therefore they cannot be relied upon to meet audit objectives. However, the auditor does not ignore them. Deficiencies in the design, implementation or operating effectiveness of controls identified by the auditor (unless they are clearly trivial) are reported to managers at an appropriate level of responsibility and to the board of directors (or more usually, if the entity has one, to the audit committee). Such reporting should occur at the earliest opportunity, preferably in writing, so that appropriate corrective action may be taken on a timely basis. Similarly, deficiencies in internal controls discovered during compliance testing, and errors in the financial statements (indicating internal control deficiencies) discovered during substantive testing, are reported to an appropriate level of management and/or the audit committee. Suitable action to correct internal control deficiencies is usually suggested by the auditor at the same time as the deficiencies are reported.

At the conclusion of the audit significant deficiencies in internal control identified by the auditor, together with other audit matters, are communicated to the directors or audit committee. (This communication is discussed in Chapter 14, section 14.8.)

10.8 SUMMARY

In this chapter we have discussed what is meant by an accounting system and considered why and how a client's system is divided into sub-systems (or audit segments) for audit purposes. We have also examined the process by which an auditor gains a detailed understanding of each audit segment and documents and tests this understanding.

Additionally, we have explored the topic of internal control. We have noted that the internal control system comprises five elements, namely: (i) the control environment, (ii) the entity's risk assessment process, (iii) the information system relevant to financial reporting, (iv) the entity's control activities and (v) the entity's monitoring of controls. We have also observed that the control activities include both general IT-controls and application controls.

An entity's management frequently delegates responsibility for establishing and maintaining the organisation's internal control system to the internal audit function (if the entity has one). However, the external auditor is particularly interested in those controls which are designed to safeguard the entity's assets and to ensure that its accounting data are free of material errors and irregularities. (We have referred to the latter set of controls as 'internal accounting controls'.) We have discussed the seven characteristics of a good internal control system relevant to financial reporting, identified the seven objectives of internal accounting controls and observed that, irrespective of how effective a system of internal control may appear to be, it will always possess certain inherent limitations.

We have also examined why and how the auditor conducts a preliminary evaluation of the internal accounting controls in each audit segment. Once the auditor has identified internal control strengths (controls which are effective in preventing or detecting errors in the accounting data) and deficiencies (controls which are required to prevent or detect errors but which are either absent or ineffective), the auditor is in a position to develop the audit plan (or audit programme). This is accomplished (at least on a conceptual level) in two stages, a planning and a performance stage, and the final document comprises a list of audit procedures set out in a format which audit staff can follow.

We have emphasised throughout the chapter that, although certain internal accounting controls may appear to be operating effectively, the auditor may not rely on them to prevent material misstatements from occurring in the financial statements until their operating effectiveness has been tested. We have discussed compliance procedures; that is, procedures designed to test whether the internal controls on which the auditor plans to rely are operating as effectively as his or her preliminary evaluation suggests, and whether they have been so operating throughout the reporting period. If the compliance procedures confirm that internal controls are operating effectively, this will result in reduced substantive testing – the topic of the next chapter.

SELF-REVIEW QUESTIONS

10.1   Explain briefly what is meant by 'an accounting system'.

10.2   Explain briefly why a client's accounting system is divided into sub-systems (or audit segments) for audit purposes. State two bases on which this sub-division may be based.

10.3 Explain briefly the meaning of each of the following terms:
    (i)   internal control system,
    (ii)   control environment,
    (iii) the entity's risk assessment process,
    (iv) control activities,
    (v)   monitoring of controls,
    (vi) general IT-controls,
    (vii) application controls.

10.4 Outline the seven characteristics of a good system of internal control relevant to financial reporting.

10.5 Describe briefly two procedures which are used to document auditees' accounting sub-systems.

10.6 Explain briefly the purpose of a 'walk through test' and how it is conducted.

10.7 Define in relation to internal controls:
    (i)   a strength,
    (ii) a deficiency.

10.8 List five examples of inherent limitations of internal control systems.

10.9 (a) Explain briefly the purpose of 'compliance procedures'.
    (b) Give two examples of compliance procedures and link each to the audit objective it is designed to test.

10.10 Describe briefly what is meant by 'an audit plan' and how it is prepared.

REFERENCES

Anderson, R.J. (1977). *The External Audit*. Toronto: Cropp Clark Pitman.

Committee on Corporate Governance. (1998a). *Final Report of the Committee on Corporate Governance* (Hampel Committee). London: The London Stock Exchange.

Committee on Corporate Governance. (1998b). *The Combined Code*. London: The London Stock Exchange.

Committee on the Financial Aspects of Corporate Governance. (1992). *Report of the Committee on the Financial Aspects of Corporate Governance* (Cadbury Committee). London: Gee.

Committee of Sponsoring Organisations of the Treadway Commission (COSO). (1992). *Integrated Control – Integrated Framework, Executive Summary*. Jersey City, NJ: COSO.

Financial Reporting Council (FRC). (2003). *The Combined Code on Corporate Governance*. London: FRC.

Financial Reporting Council (FRC). (2006). *The Combined Code on Corporate Governance*. London: FRC.

Higgs, D. (2003). *Review of the role and effectiveness of non-executive directors*. London: Department of Trade and Industry.

International Auditing and Assurance Standards Board (IAASB). (2007). *Glossary of Terms*. New York: International Federation of Accountants.

Smith, Sir Robert. (2003). *Audit Committees: Combined Guidance. A report and proposed guidance by an FRC-appointed group chaired by Sir Robert Smith*. London: Financial Reporting Council.

Study Group on Directors' Remuneration. (1995). *Report of the Study Group on Directors' Remuneration* (Greenbury Committee). London: Gee.

ADDITIONAL READING

Auditing Practices Board (APB). (2001). *Providing Assurance on the Effectiveness of Internal Control*. London: Financial Reporting Council.

Hermanson, H.M. (2000). An analysis of the demand for reporting on internal control. *Accounting Horizons* **14**(3), 325–341.

Institute of Internal Auditors UK and Ireland (IIA) & PricewaterhouseCoopers (PWC). (2007). *IT Risk – Closing the Gap*. London: IIA & PWC.

Godfrey, A. (2007). Internal control: is compliance dead? *Accountancy* **140**(1368), 43–44.

Jensen, K.L., and Payne, J.L. (2003). Management trade-offs of internal control and external auditor expertise. *Auditing: A Journal of Practice & Theory* **22**(2), 99–119.

Kopp, L.S., and O'Donnell, E. (2005). The influence of a business-process focus on category knowledge and internal control evaluation. *Accounting, Organizations and Society* **30**(5), 423–434.

Krishnan, G.V., and Visvanathan, G. (2007). Reporting internal control deficiencies in the Post-Sarbanes-Oxley era: the role of auditors and corporate governance. *International Journal of Auditing* **11**(2), 73–90.

Patterson, E.R., and Smith, R.J. (2007). The effects of Sarbanes-Oxley on auditing and internal control strength. *The Accounting Review* **82**(2), 427–456.

Spira, L.F., and Page, M. (2003). Risk management: the reinvention of internal control and the changing role of internal audit. *Accounting, Auditing & Accountability Journal* **16**(4), 640–661.

11 Testing Financial Statement Assertions: Substantive Testing

LEARNING OBJECTIVES

After studying the material in this chapter you should be able to:

- explain the significance of substantive testing in the audit process;
- explain the terms 'misstatement' and 'financial statement assertions';
- state the audit objectives of substantive procedures;
- discuss the purpose and importance of analytical procedures as substantive tests (substantive analytical procedures);
- explain what is meant by 'testing the details' of financial statement balances;
- distinguish between the two approaches to testing the details – testing transactions generating account balances and directly testing account balances;
- describe common audit procedures used to test the details of financial statement balances;
- explain the actions auditors are required to take in respect of misstatements identified during the audit;
- discuss the importance of, and procedures used for, confirming the existence, ownership and value of inventory (stock);
- discuss the importance and performance of confirmations as a substantive test of debtors;
- explain the factors the auditor should consider when assessing the adequacy of the client's allowance for bad debts.

The following publications are particularly relevant to this chapter:

- International Standard on Auditing (ISA) 315 (Redrafted): *Identifying and Assessing the Risks of Material Misstatement through Understanding the Entity and its Environment* (IFAC, 2006)[1]
- International Standard on Auditing (ISA) 330 (Redrafted): *The Auditor's Responses to Assessed Risks* (IFAC, 2006)
- International Standard on Auditing (ISA) 450 (Redrafted): *Evaluation of Misstatements Identified during the Audit* (IFAC, June 2008)**
- International Standards on Auditing (ISA) 501 (Redrafted): *Audit Evidence Regarding Specific Financial Statement Account Balances and Disclosures* (IFAC, 2007)*
- International Standard on Auditing (ISA) 505 (Redrafted): *External Confirmations* (IFAC, June 2008)**
- International Standard on Auditing (ISA) 520 (Redrafted): *Analytical Procedures* (IFAC, 2007)*

---

[1] The status of ISAs referred to in this chapter is explained in the Important Note following the Preface to this book.

11.1 INTRODUCTION

A company's (or group's) financial statements comprise a set of statements by the entity's directors which, taken together, provide a picture of the entity's financial position, the results of its operations, and (in applicable cases) its cash flows. These statements are presented as account balances (appropriately grouped and classified in the balance sheet, profit and loss account and, in applicable cases, statement of cash flow), a statement of accounting policies and notes to the financial statements. The accounting policies and notes explain, amongst other things, the bases on which the financial statements have been prepared. In presenting the financial statement balances (and accompanying notes), the entity's directors are making implicit assertions about the balances and the items they represent. More particularly, they are implicitly asserting that the balances are valid, complete and accurate.

The auditor is required, *inter alia*, to form and express an opinion as to whether or not the financial statements give a true and fair view of the entity's state of affairs and its profit or loss. To accomplish this, the auditor conducts substantive tests – tests which examine the substance of (or, more correctly, assertions embodied in) the financial statement balances.

In this chapter we examine the significance of substantive testing in the audit process and discuss the objectives of substantive procedures. We also explore the different approaches which may be taken to test the financial statement balances and explain the audit procedures commonly adopted for each approach. More particularly, we discuss substantive analytical procedures and procedures used for testing the details of the financial statement balances – whether this be through testing the transactions which generate the balances or testing the balances directly. We also explain the actions auditors are required to take in respect of misstatements they identify during the audit. After studying the principles of substantive testing, we examine in more detail the application of substantive procedures in auditing the balances of the inventory (stock) and debtors accounts.

11.2 SIGNIFICANCE OF SUBSTANTIVE TESTING IN THE AUDIT PROCESS

When considering the significance of substantive testing in the audit process, it is important to appreciate the integrative character of an audit. The nature, timing and extent of substantive procedures are essentially determined by the preceding audit steps, more particularly:

- understanding the client, its industry, its business, its activities and its risks;
- identifying and assessing the likelihood of material misstatements in the financial statements whether due to fraud or error;
- setting materiality limits (planning materiality, tolerable error and performance materiality);
- establishing the desired level of audit risk (or desired level of assurance);
- assessing inherent risk; that is, assessing the likelihood of material misstatements being present in each audit segment (or, more particularly, class of transactions, account balance or disclosure) in the absence of internal controls;
- understanding and documenting the client's internal control system, and evaluating its effectiveness, at both the client and audit segment level;
- testing the controls on which the auditor plans to rely to prevent material misstatement from occurring in each audit segment (or, more particularly, class of transactions, account balance or disclosure) and, thereby, to reduce substantive testing.

From Figure 11.1 it may be seen that both the auditor's assessment of the effectiveness of the client's internal control system and the results of testing

Figure 11.1:   Impact of internal control evaluation and testing on substantive testing

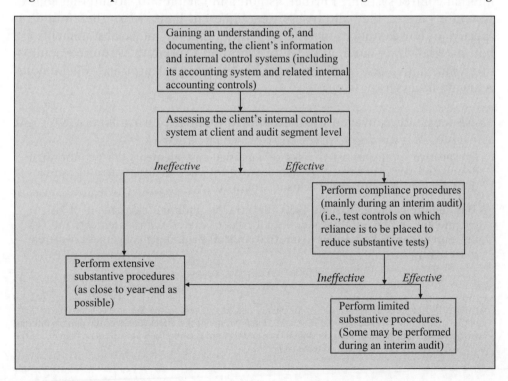

the controls on which (s)he plans to rely have a significant impact on the nature, timing and extent of substantive testing.

If, based on his or her assessment of the client's internal control system, the auditor concludes that the controls are not effective in preventing material misstatements from occurring in the financial statements or, alternatively, having initially concluded that the controls appear to be effective but the results of compliance tests prove this not to be the case, the auditor will need to perform extensive substantive procedures before attaining his or her desired level of assurance that the financial statements are not materially misstated. Further, this testing will need to take place as close as possible to the end of the accounting period.

Conversely, if the auditor's assessment of the client's internal control system indicates that it is effective and this belief is supported by the results of compliance tests, (s)he will feel reasonably confident that the information contained in the financial statements is valid, complete and accurate. As a result, the auditor will perform more limited substantive testing than would otherwise be the case. However, substantive tests may not be omitted altogether. The auditor is required to form and express an opinion about the truth and fairness of the financial statements *per se* – not about the effectiveness of the client's internal control system.[2] Further, as noted in Chapter 10, no internal control system is perfect; they all possess some inherent limitations. Therefore, irrespective of how confident the auditor may be that the financial statements are not materially misstated, in order to form and express the required opinion, some substantive testing of the financial statement balances and related notes is always necessary.

These ideas are conveyed in International Standard on Auditing (ISA) 330: *The auditor's responses to assessed risks*, which states:

> Irrespective of the assessed risks of material misstatement, the auditor shall design and perform substantive procedures for each material class of transactions, account balance, and disclosure. (para 20)

> This requirement reflects the facts that: (i) the auditor's assessment of risk is judgmental and so may not identify all risks of material misstatement; and (ii) there are inherent limitations to internal control, including management override. (para A42)

---

[2] As noted in Chapter 10, section 10.3.1, for clients that are subject to the Sarbanes-Oxley Act of 2002, auditors are required to attest to the directors' statement about the effectiveness of the entity's internal controls. These, like all other financial statements, auditors are also required to express an opinion on the truth and fairness of the financial statements *per se*.

11.3 OBJECTIVES OF, AND APPROACHES TO, SUBSTANTIVE TESTING

11.3.1 Objectives of substantive procedures

The overall objective of substantive testing is to verify the validity, completeness and accuracy of the financial statement balances and note disclosures. Alternatively stated, it is to ascertain whether or not the financial statements are materially misstated. As ISA 450: *Evaluation of misstatements identified during the audit* explains, misstatements can take a variety of forms. The Standard defines a misstatement as follows:

> Misstatement – A difference between the amount, classification, presentation, or disclosure of a reported financial statement item and the amount, classification, presentation, or disclosure that is required for the item to be in accordance with the applicable financial reporting framework. Misstatements can arise from error or fraud. Misstatements may result from:
> (a) An inaccuracy in gathering or processing data from which the financial statements are prepared;
> (b) An omission of an amount or disclosure;
> (c) An incorrect accounting estimate arising from overlooking, or clear misinterpretation of, facts; and
> (d) Judgments of management concerning accounting estimates that the auditor considers unreasonable or the selection and application of accounting policies that the auditor considers inappropriate. (ISA 450, para 4, A1)

Each financial statement amount or disclosure embodies a number of assertions and, if any of the assertions are erroneous, then the amount or disclosure will be misstated. ISA 315: *Identifying and assessing the risks of material misstatement through understanding the entity and its environment* (para 4) defines "assertions" to mean: "Representations by management, explicit or otherwise, that are embodied in the financial statements, as used by the auditor to consider the different types of potential misstatements that may occur." The Standard (para A104) distinguishes three categories of assertions as follows:

(a) Assertions about classes of transactions and events for the period under audit:
    (i) Occurrence – transactions and events that have been recorded have occurred and pertain to the entity.
    (ii) Completeness – all transactions and events that should have been recorded have been recorded.
    (iii) Accuracy – amounts and other data relating to recorded transactions and events have been recorded appropriately.
    (iv) Cut-off – transactions and events have been recorded in the correct accounting period.
    (v) Classification – transactions and events have been recorded in the proper accounts.

(b) Assertions about account balances at the period end:
  (i) Existence – assets, liabilities and equity interests exist.
  (ii) Rights and obligations – the entity holds or controls the right to assets, and liabilities are the obligations of the entity.
  (iii) Completeness – all assets, liabilities and equity interests that should have been recorded have been recorded.
  (iv) Valuation and allocation – assets, liabilities, and equity interests are included in the financial statements at appropriate amounts and any resulting valuation or allocation adjustments are appropriately recorded.

(c) Assertions about presentation and disclosure:
  (i) Occurrence and rights and obligations – disclosed events, transactions, and other matters have occurred and pertain to the entity.
  (ii) Completeness – all disclosures that should have been included in the financial statements have been included.
  (iii) Classification and understandability – financial information is appropriately presented and described, and disclosures are clearly expressed.
  (iv) Accuracy and valuation – financial and other information are disclosed fairly and at appropriate amounts.

These assertions may conveniently be summarised as representations by the entity's directors about the validity, completeness and accuracy (as to amount, account and accounting period) of classes of transactions, account balances and disclosures.

Verifying each assertion relating to a class of transactions, account balance or disclosure constitutes a specific audit objective.[3] If the specific audit objectives are met, the overall objective of confirming the validity, completeness and accuracy of the financial statement balances and disclosures will also be met.

11.3.2 Alternative approaches to substantive testing

Although all substantive testing has as its objective, determining the validity, completeness and accuracy of financial statement balances and disclosures, two basic approaches may be adopted, namely:
  (i) substantive analytical procedures;
  (ii) tests of details.

(i) *Substantive analytical procedures*: Where this approach is adopted, meaningful relationships between account balances, or between financial and

---

[3] Readers may find it helpful to refer to Chapter 7, section 7.3 (and Figure 7.2), where we introduce the notion of specific audit objectives.

non-financial information, are examined to ascertain the reasonableness (or otherwise) of the relevant financial statement amounts.

(ii) *Tests of details*: This approach may take one of two forms:
      (a) testing the transactions which give rise to the account balances;
      (b) testing the closing account balances directly.

(a) Where the transactions approach is adopted, attention is focused on the opening balance of the account in question and the transactions which affect the account during the reporting period. If the opening balance and the transactions are recorded and added correctly, the closing balance must, of necessity, be correct.[4]

(b) Where closing account balances are tested directly, components of the balance are usually tested. For example, individual debtors' account balances are tested as a means of substantiating the debtors account balance in the balance sheet.

Regarding the selection of the appropriate approach to substantive testing, ISA 330: *The auditor's responses to assessed risks* explains:

Depending on the circumstances, the auditor may determine that:
- Performing only substantive analytical procedures will be sufficient to reduce audit risk to an acceptably low level. . . .
- Only tests of details are appropriate.
- A combination of substantive analytical procedures and tests of details are most responsive to the assessed risks. (para A43)

ISA 520: *Analytical procedures* adds to this by noting:

The decision about which audit procedures to use is based on the auditor's judgment about the expected effectiveness and efficiency of the available audit procedures to reduce audit risk at the assertion level to an acceptably low level. (para A1)

Although different approaches to substantive testing may be adopted, auditors frequently use a combination of substantive analytical procedures and tests of details, and the two approaches interlock in a mutually supportive manner. This may be illustrated by reference to the sales-debtors-receipts cycle, as shown in Figure 11.2.

Substantive analytical procedures may be used to ascertain the reasonableness of the debtors closing balance. If it appears to be reasonable, the extent of further detailed testing may be reduced. Conversely, if substantive analytical procedures indicate that the balance may be materially misstated, more extensive testing will be required to identify the nature and extent of any

---

[4] In the case of balance sheet accounts, the opening balance is established from the audited closing balances of the previous period; for profit and loss statement accounts, the opening balance is, of course, zero.

Figure 11.2: Substantive testing of debtors and related accounts

Verified by	Debtors				Verified by
Previous year's audit ——→	Opening bal.	x	Receipts Discount	x ← x	Testing cash receipts transactions
Testing sales transactions ——→	Sales	x			
Substantive analytical ——→ procedures or testing transactions (depending on materiality)	Freight Interest	x x	Returns Bad debts	x ← x	Substantive analytical procedures or testing transactions (depending on materiality)
		=		=	
Substantive analytical ——→ procedures (for reasonableness) and direct tests of balance	Closing bal.	x			
NB: Verification of complementary account balances (such as sales) simultaneously helps to confirm the debtors account balance. Verification of the debtors account balance (through direct testing) simultaneously helps to confirm the balances of related accounts (such as sales).					

misstatement(s). Substantive analytical procedures may also be used to substantiate less material account balances such as 'interest on overdue accounts' and 'freight charged to credit customers'. (Substantive analytical procedures are discussed in section 11.4 below.)

In order to determine the validity, completeness and accuracy of the sales account balance, the period's sales transactions are tested. Similarly, cash receipts, discount received and sales returns transactions may be tested to substantiate their respective account balances. It should be noted that testing these transactions serves two purposes: it confirms the relevant account balance in the profit and loss statement and simultaneously provides support for an element of the debtors account. If the balance of the debtors account is also confirmed through direct testing this, by implication, provides support for the accuracy of the related accounts (such as sales). By obtaining mutually supportive evidence in this manner, the auditor can feel confident that all of the accounts constituting the sales-debtors-receipts cycle are fairly stated.

We should emphasise that substantive testing is concerned with verifying the validity, completeness and accuracy of information presented in the financial statements. Its objective is very different from that of compliance testing. Compliance testing is concerned with confirming that the internal controls on which the auditor plans to rely to prevent material misstatements from occurring in the financial statements are operating effectively, and have been so operating throughout the reporting period. Thus, compliance procedures conducted in relation to, for example, sales transactions, seek evidence which indicates, *inter alia*, that credit sales transactions have been authorised, and that extensions, additions, and account codes shown on sales invoices have been independently checked. By contrast, substantive procedures are concerned with examining the monetary amounts and the correctness with which transactions are recorded in terms of their amount, account classification and reporting period.

Confusion between the two types of procedures frequently arises in relation to testing transactions. This is because the source documents recording transactions are used for both types of tests. For example, copies of sales invoices may be inspected to see if initials are present which indicate that extensions, additions and account classifications have been checked by an independent person. In this case, evidence of compliance with an internal control procedure is sought. The same document may be used for substantive testing; that is, for the auditor to check for him- or herself that the extensions and additions are arithmetically correct, and that the transaction has been correctly classified. The same source document (and transaction) is used for two entirely different purposes.[5]

11.4   SUBSTANTIVE AUDIT PROCEDURES

11.4.1   Overview of substantive audit procedures

We noted above that there are two broad categories of substantive tests – substantive analytical procedures and tests of details. We also noted that tests of details may be either tests of transactions or direct tests of account balances. The relationship between these types of substantive tests, and the procedures used for each, are depicted in Figure 11.3.

During the initial stages of an audit, analytical procedures are used as risk assessment procedures – more specifically, as procedures to assist the auditor:
- understand the client's financial and non-financial information;
- identify unusual transactions or events;
- assess the likelihood of material misstatements being present in the (pre-audited) financial statements; and
- identify areas or items of significant audit risk.[6]

At this stage, broad entity-wide measures are important, such as the current ratio, debt to equity ratio, gross profit percentage, return on assets, and return on shareholders' funds. During the substantive testing stage, auditors focus on individual classes of transactions, account balances and disclosures. To

---

[5] We referred to the overlapping nature of audit procedures in Chapter 10, section 10.5, when discussing the performance format of audit plans.

[6] The use of analytical procedures as risk assessment procedures is explained in Chapter 8, and a general discussion of analytical procedures is provided in section 8.5.

Figure 11.3: Overview of substantive audit procedures

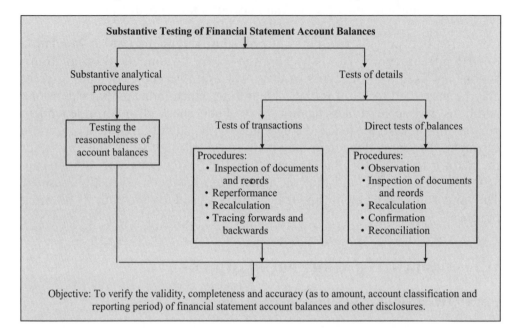

distinguish between the two uses of analytical procedures, the term 'overall analytical procedures' is frequently applied to the broad risk assessment procedures and 'substantive analytical procedures' to the account-focused substantive tests.

11.4.2 Requirements for substantive analytical procedures

ISA 520: *Analytical procedures* explains:

> The application of analytical procedures is based on the expectation that relationships among data exist and continue in the absence of known conditions to the contrary. The presence of these relationships provides audit evidence as to the completeness, accuracy and occurrence of transactions captured in the information produced by the entity's information system relevant to financial reporting. However, the suitability of a particular analytical procedure will depend upon the auditor's assessment of how effective it will be in detecting a misstatement that, when aggregated with other misstatements, may cause the financial statements to be materially misstated. (para A3)

Before auditors apply substantive analytical procedures they need to be assured that:

(i)   the expected results of the analytical procedures can be predicted with reasonable accuracy; and

(ii) the information required to perform the procedures is (a) available and (b) reliable.

(i) Predictability of the results of substantive audit procedures

As indicated by ISA 520, para A3 (cited above), substantive analytical procedures are only appropriate where there is a known relationship between the data examined and where, in the absence of any evidence to the contrary, this relationship can be expected to continue. For example, unless the auditor has information that suggests otherwise, the gross profit percentage and the relationship between sales and debtors and sales and inventory (stock) can be expected to be similar from one period to the next. By contrast, the relationship between sales and advertising, and between sales and research expense, is less likely to be consistent between reporting periods.

(ii) Availability and reliability of required information

Regarding the availability and reliability of required information, ISA 520 observes:

> The auditor may inquire of management as to the availability and reliability of information needed to apply analytical procedures as substantive procedures, and the results of any such procedures performed by the entity. It may be efficient to use analytical data prepared by management, provided the auditor is satisfied that such data is properly prepared. (para A2)

In order to perform substantive analytical procedures, auditors generally require (in addition to the financial statement data) financial information, such as budgets or forecasts, and non-financial information, such as the number of units produced and/or sold. They also need to consider the degree to which the information can be disaggregated, for example, whether information is available for individual components of a diversified entity. Further, if auditors plan to use budgeted information, they need to establish whether the budgets have been prepared based on expected results or as goals (or targets) to be achieved.

However, having required information available is not sufficient for auditors to perform substantive analytical procedures; they must also satisfy themselves that the information is reliable. Where information is obtained from independent sources outside the entity it is generally considered to be reliable. However, for internally generated information, auditors will seek evidence that controls over the preparation of the relevant data are effective. ISA 520 (para A10) observes:

> When such controls are effective, the auditor generally has greater confidence in the reliability of the information and, therefore, in the results of analytical procedures. The operating effectiveness of controls over non-financial information may often be tested in conjunction with other tests of controls. For example, in establishing controls over the processing of sales invoices, an entity may include controls over the recording of unit sales. In these circumstances, the

auditor could test the operating effectiveness of controls over the recording of unit sales in conjunction with tests of the operating effectiveness of controls over the processing of sales invoices.

11.4.3 Application of substantive analytical procedures

During the substantive testing phase of an audit, analytical procedures are usually used in two different ways, namely:
  (i) as preliminary tests for assertions relating to classes of transactions, account balances and disclosures which are also to be tested through tests of details; and
  (ii) as complete tests for assertions for which tests of details are not planned.

(i) Substantive analytical procedures as preliminary tests

For material classes of transactions, accounts or disclosures which are to be subjected to tests of details (for example, assertions relating to debtors and inventory), substantive analytical procedures are frequently used as preliminary tests – to test the reasonableness of the account balance in question as a basis for deciding the extent to which tests of details are required. If an account balance appears to be reasonable (i.e., close to that expected by the auditor based on his or her understanding of the client's business, overall analytical procedures, and other relevant audit evidence) material misstatement may be considered unlikely and, as a result, less extensive tests of details are needed to confirm the absence of material misstatements than in situations where material misstatement seems more likely. Substantive analytical procedures may also be used in combination with tests of details. For example, when auditing the collectability of amounts owed by debtors, the auditor may apply substantive analytical procedures to an ageing of customers' accounts in addition to performing tests of details on subsequent cash receipts. Use of substantive analytical procedures as a preliminary test in auditing inventory (stock) is illustrated in section 11.7 below.

(ii) Specific analytical procedures as complete tests

For less significant classes of transactions, account balances and disclosures for which less substantive testing is usually required (as frequently applies in the case of, for example, prepaid expenses and interest paid), substantive analytical procedures are commonly used to test the reasonableness of their balances. If they appear to be reasonable, no further testing is undertaken. However, if misstatement appears likely, then the relevant class of transactions, account balance or disclosure is subjected to detailed testing.

The following two examples illustrate ways in which substantive analytical procedures may constitute complete substantive tests.

1. Historically, a fairly stable relationship may exist between sales returns and sales. Therefore, assuming that nothing has come to the auditor's attention which suggests that the relationship may not hold in the current year, if the sales returns account balance is calculated as a percentage of sales, the result should be similar to that for previous years. If it is, the account balance will probably be considered reasonable and accepted as 'true and fair'.

2. The balance of the interest paid account may be estimated by using a known relationship between debt and interest rates. More specifically, the average debt and the average interest rate for the reporting period may be ascertained, and the average interest rate then applied to the average debt to provide an estimate of the interest paid account balance. In the absence of exceptional circumstances known to the auditor, if the interest paid account balance is close to the estimated amount, it will probably be judged to be reasonable and accepted as 'true and fair'.

11.4.4 Tests of details

As noted in section 11.3 above, substantive tests of details may involve testing the transactions which give rise to an account balance or directly testing the balance itself. The approach adopted is generally that which provides the most efficient means of determining the validity, completeness and accuracy of the account balance in question.

(i) Testing transactions

Profit and loss statement accounts (i.e., revenue and expense accounts) commence the accounting period with a zero balance and the transactions comprising the account are generally of a similar type. For example, entries in sales and purchases accounts are usually confined to cash and credit sales and purchases, respectively. The similarity of the transactions facilitates selecting and testing representative samples of transactions and, as a result, testing the transactions that constitute the relevant account balance is generally more efficient than directly testing the account balance.

For some balance sheet accounts (such as fixed assets), where the number of transactions affecting the account during the reporting period is small relative to the size of the account balance, it may be more efficient to test the transactions generating the account balance than to directly test the account's closing balance. An example is afforded by the motor vehicle account in entities which have large fleets of vehicles but relatively few additions and disposals during any one financial year (such as British Telecom). The opening balance of balance sheet accounts was verified during the previous year's audit and, if the opening balance and the transactions affecting the account are recorded and added correctly, the closing balance must be correct.

As shown in Figure 11.2, the primary procedures for testing the accuracy, validity and completeness of transactions are inspection of documents and records, reperformance, recalculation, and tracing forwards and backwards. All of these procedures, other than tracing, are directed towards examining the accuracy of financial statement account balances – their accuracy as to amount, account and reporting period. These audit procedures may be illustrated as follows:

- *Inspection of documents and records*: Source documents may be inspected to determine whether transactions are *bona fide* and have been recorded in the correct account and period. The auditor checks the account codes used for recording the transactions and, particularly for transactions near year-end, examines the dates and terms of the transactions to ascertain the accounting period to which they relate. Other documents, such as price lists, may also be inspected to check that correct prices have been applied to goods and services bought and sold.
- *Reperformance*: The auditor may, for example, match purchase orders with receiving reports, suppliers' invoices and payments vouchers to ensure that the quantities and prices of goods ordered and received, invoiced and paid for are in agreement. Similarly, source document totals may be matched with journal entries, and journal entries with ledger records.
- *Recalculation*: The auditor may recalculate extensions and additions on source documents in order to check that transactions have been recorded at their correct amount.

Tracing backwards and forwards are substantive procedures designed to test the validity and completeness, respectively, of recorded transactions, rather than their accuracy.

- *Tracing backwards* involves tracing selected entries back through the accounting records, from the financial statements, through the ledgers and journals, to the source documents. This procedure is designed to check that the amounts recorded in the financial statements represent valid transactions and that financial statement account balances are not overstated. Because of the (usual) desirability of having more rather than less assets and revenue, there may be an incentive to inflate asset and revenue accounts. Tracing backwards has particular application in ensuring that asset and revenue transactions are valid and the account balances not overstated.
- *Tracing forwards* involves tracing selected transactions forwards through the accounting records, from source documents, through the journals and ledgers, to the financial statements. This procedure is designed to check that financial statement account balances include all relevant transactions

and that they are not understated. Because of the desirability of having less rather than more liabilities and expenses, there may be an incentive to understate liability and expense accounts. Tracing forwards has particular application for testing the completeness of liability and expense transactions and ensuring that the accounts are not understated.

(ii)   Direct tests of balances

For some accounts it is more efficient to audit the closing balance directly rather than examine the transactions that generate the balance. This applies, for example, to many balance sheet accounts such as cash, inventory, debtors, investments and loans.

The primary audit procedures used to examine the validity, completeness and accuracy of account balances are observation, inspection of documents and records, recalculation, confirmation and reperformance. These may be illustrated as follows:

- *Observation*: The auditor will, for example, observe the existence, quantity and quality of inventory (stock) and of fixed assets such as plant, equipment and motor vehicles. In some cases, observation extends to observing identification numbers of fixed assets, for example, the engine and chassis numbers of motor vehicles.
- *Inspection of documents and records*: Documents such as marketable securities and loan, lease and hire-purchase contracts are inspected to confirm the existence of the items concerned and to ascertain their terms and conditions.
- *Recalculation*: Accounts such as depreciation and accumulated depreciation, doubtful debts and allowance for bad debts are usually recalculated to confirm the arithmetical accuracy of their balances.
- *Confirmation*: The auditor will confirm certain information with parties outside the audit client. For example, the auditor is likely to confirm the balance of debtors and bank accounts, and items such as contingent liabilities and commitments, by communicating with the client's debtors, bank(s) and legal counsel, respectively. (Confirmation of debtors is discussed in detail in section 11.8 below and confirmation of contingent liabilities and commitments is considered in Chapter 13.)
- *Reperformance*: The auditor will, for example, compare the general ledger bank account balance with the confirmation letter received from the bank, and the subsidiary ledger totals with the relevant general ledger control account to ensure they are in agreement.

With reference to their clients' year-end closing process (when misstatements relating to recording transactions in the correct accounting period are most likely), ISA 330: *The auditor's responses to assessed risks* requires auditors to perform substantive procedures that include:

    (a) Agreeing or reconciling the financial statements with the underlying accounting records; and

    (b) Examining material journal entries and other adjustments made during the course of preparing the financial statements. (para 21)

The nature, and also the extent, of the auditor's examination of journal entries and other adjustments depends on the nature and complexity of the entity's financial reporting process and the related risks of material misstatement. (para A48)

11.4.5 Substantive procedures performed during an interim audit

In certain circumstances, auditors may perform some substantive procedures during an interim audit.[7] However, if they do so, ISA 330, para 23, requires them to perform, for the period between the interim audit and period end:

    (i) substantive procedures, combined with tests of controls; or

    (ii) if they have decided it is sufficient, further substantive procedures only.

In either case, auditors are to obtain sufficient appropriate audit evidence to provide a reasonable basis for extending the audit conclusions reached during the interim audit to the period end. More particularly, ISA 330 requires auditors:

> to compare and reconcile information concerning the balance at the period end with the comparable information at the interim date to:
>
> (a) Identify amounts that appear unusual,
>
> (b) Investigate any such amounts, and
>
> (c) Perform substantive analytical procedures or tests of details to test the intervening period. (para A51)

When deciding whether or not it is effective to perform substantive procedures during an interim audit, auditors need to consider factors such as the following:

- the effectiveness of the control environment and other relevant controls (the more effective the internal controls, the more likely it is that it will be effective to perform substantive tests during an interim audit);
- the availability and reliability of information required to perform substantive tests at the period end compared with its availability at an interim date;
- the assessed risk of material misstatement in the relevant classes of transactions, account balances or disclosures (the greater the risk, the less likely it is that it will be effective to perform substantive procedures during an interim audit);
- the ability to perform appropriate substantive procedures, or substantive procedures combined with tests of control, for the period between the interim audit and period end, that will reduce to an acceptably low level

---

[7] We note in Chapter 10 that compliance procedures are frequently performed during an interim audit; in certain circumstances, some substantive procedures may be performed at the same time.

the risk of failing to detect misstatements that exist in the relevant classes of transactions or account balances at the period end.

When auditors perform substantive procedures for the period between an interim audit and the period end, they need to decide whether or not it is effective to perform substantive analytical procedures – alone, in combination with tests of details, or not at all. ISA 330, para A53, explains that, when making this decision, auditors consider factors such as the following:

- Whether the period end balances of the particular classes of transactions or account balances are reasonably predictable with respect to amount, relative significance, and composition.
- Whether the entity's procedures for analyzing and adjusting such classes of transactions or account balances at interim dates and for establishing proper accounting cutoffs[8] are appropriate.
- Whether the information system relevant to financial reporting will provide information concerning the balances at the period end and the transactions in the remaining period [i.e., period between the interim audit and year-end] that is sufficient to permit investigation of:
  (a) Significant unusual transactions or entries (including those at or near the period end),
  (b) Other causes of significant fluctuations, or expected fluctuations that did not occur, and
  (c) Changes in the composition of the classes of transactions or account balances.

When auditors conduct substantive tests during an interim audit and they encounter misstatements that, based on their assessment of the risks of material misstatement, they did not expect, they are required to evaluate whether their (i) related assessment of risk and (ii) planned nature, timing and extent of substantive procedures covering the period between the interim audit and period end need to be modified. Such modification may include extending, or repeating at the period end, procedures performed during the interim audit (ISA 330, paras 24, A54).

11.5 REQUIREMENTS OF AUDITORS WITH RESPECT TO IDENTIFIED MISSTATEMENTS

As the audit proceeds, but particularly during the substantive testing process, auditors invariably identify misstatements in various account balances and other financial statement disclosures. Having discovered them, what are they required to do about them? As we explain below, the misstatements must be:

---

[8] 'Cutoff' refers to the date which ends the accounting period and thus defines the transactions and events (or parts thereof) that should be recorded in the accounting periods before and after that date.

  (i)   accumulated;
  (ii) evaluated to determine whether the audit strategy and audit plan require revision; and
  (iii) communicated to management.

(i) Accumulation of misstatements

ISA 450: *Evaluation of misstatements identified during the audit*, para 4, specifies that auditors are to accumulate misstatements identified during the audit, other than those that are clearly trivial. It explains that the term "clearly trivial":

> is not another expression for "not material". Matters that are clearly trivial will be of a wholly different (smaller) order of magnitude than materiality [used in planning and performing the audit], ... and will be matters that are clearly inconsequential, whether taken individually or in aggregate and whether judged by any criteria of size, nature or circumstances. When there is any uncertainty about whether one or more items are clearly trivial, the matter is considered not to be clearly trivial. (para A2)[9]

ISA 450 (para A3) also notes that when evaluating the effect on the financial statements of misstatements accumulated during the audit, and communicating them to management, auditors may find it useful to distinguish between:
  • factual misstatements, that is, misstatements about which there is no doubt;
  • judgmental misstatements, that is, differences arising from management's judgments concerning accounting estimates that the auditor considers to be unreasonable, or the selection or application of accounting policies that the auditor considers to be inappropriate; and
  • projected misstatements, that is, the auditor's best estimate of misstatements in populations determined by projecting (or extrapolating) misstatements identified in samples to the populations from which the samples were drawn[10] (paras 4, 5).

(ii) Evaluation to determine whether the audit strategy and audit plan require revision

As misstatements are accumulated, auditors are required to consider whether their magnitude and/or nature are such that the overall audit strategy and audit plan need to be revised. This applies particularly in situations where:
  • the nature of misstatements, and the circumstances of their occurrence, indicate that other misstatements may exist that, when aggregated with

---

[9] For one of the firms included in the materiality survey reported in Chapter 9, the 'clearly trivial' threshold is two per cent of planning materiality.

[10] Audit sampling is discussed in Chapter 12.

the misstatements accumulated during the audit, could be material. This may be the case, for example, if a misstatement arose from a breakdown in internal control or from inappropriate assumptions or valuations that have been applied widely by the entity; or

- the aggregate of the accumulated misstatements approaches planning materiality or tolerable error.[11] In this event, as a result of sampling risk and quality control risk,[12] if auditors do not revise the overall audit strategy and audit plan, they run the risk of unknowingly exceeding their planning materiality and/or tolerable error and thus expressing an inappropriate audit opinion on the financial statements (ISA 450, paras 6, A4, A5).

(iii) Communication with management

ISA 450, para 8, requires auditors to "communicate on a timely basis all misstatements accumulated during the audit to the appropriate level of management. . . . The auditor shall request management to correct them" (para 9). The Standard explains the importance of such communication as follows:

> Timely communication of misstatements to the appropriate level of management is important as it enables management to evaluate whether the items are misstatements, inform the auditor if it disagrees, and take action as necessary. Ordinarily, the appropriate level of management is the one that has responsibility and authority to evaluate the misstatements and to take the necessary action. (para A7)

In some circumstances (such as when the auditor thinks it desirable based on his or her projections of misstatements in a population based on the audit sample examined), the auditor may request management (that is, a senior executive such as the finance director, or equivalent) to examine a class of transactions, account balance or disclosure so that management can ascertain the cause of the misstatement identified by the auditor, determine the extent of the actual misstatement in the class of transactions, account balance or disclosure, and make appropriate adjustments to the financial statements (ISA 450, para A6).

If, in response to a request from the auditor, management examines a class of transactions, account balance or disclosure and corrects identified misstatements, the auditor is required to perform additional audit procedures to determine whether misstatements remain (ISA 450, para A7).

If the senior executives (for example, the finance director and chief executive) refuse to correct some or all of the misstatements, the auditor is required to obtain an understanding of their reasons for so doing and to consider that

---

[11] Planning materiality and tolerable error are discussed in Chapter 9, section 9.3.

[12] Sampling risk and quality control risk are explained in Chapter 3, section 3.4.3.

understanding when evaluating whether the financial statements as a whole are free from material misstatement. If the executives refuse to correct identified misstatements on the grounds that their effect on the financial statements is immaterial, the auditor is to obtain written representations from the executives stating that they believe the effects of the uncorrected misstatements are immaterial, individually and in aggregate, to the financial statements as a whole. A summary of such items is to be included in, or attached to, the written representations.[13]

11.6 INTRODUCTION TO SUBSTANTIVE TESTING OF INVENTORY AND DEBTORS

To illustrate the application of substantive procedures, some aspects of auditing inventory (stock) and debtors account balances are discussed in sections 11.7 and 11.8, respectively. These accounts frequently constitute the largest proportion of a company's current assets[14] and represent its primary sources of short-term cash. They are also accounts which are prone to misstatement. In the case of inventory this arises, in particular, from its possible over-valuation resulting from obsolescence and/or some of the recorded inventory not being owned by the client. For debtors, it results primarily from the subjectivity involved in estimating the allowance for bad debts. As a consequence of these factors, the inventory and debtors account balances almost invariably attract considerable audit attention. Particular interest in these accounts initially arose as a result of the infamous *McKesson & Robbins* case in the United States of America (USA) in the 1930s, which involved many millions of dollars' worth of fictitious inventory and debtors. Subsequent to this case, in all audits where these items are material (which, as noted above, is usually the case), auditors have generally attended their clients' year-end stocktaking and confirmed their debtors' balances.

11.7 SIGNIFICANT ASPECTS OF AUDITING INVENTORY (STOCK)

11.7.1 Overview of auditing inventory

When auditing inventory, the auditor is particularly concerned to confirm its existence, ownership and value. As shown in Figure 11.4, each of these audit objectives requires a different set of audit procedures.

---

[13] We discuss written representations, and further actions required of auditors in respect of uncorrected misstatements, in Chapter 13 (sections 13.5 and 13.6.1, respectively) and we also explain auditors' responsibility to report uncorrected misstatements to the directors in Chapter 14, section 14.8.

[14] In companies (or groups) that sell services rather than goods, inventory is frequently immaterial. However, in these, as in companies selling goods, debtors almost always constitute a material financial statement amount.

Figure 11.4: Procedures for auditing inventory

Assertion/Audit Objective	Audit Procedures
Existence – Does inventory exist?	Observation (attendance at stocktaking)
Ownership – Is inventory owned?	Inspection of source documents and other documents for dates and terms of 'purchase' of inventory
Valuation – Is inventory correctly valued?	• Observation of the quality of inventory and degree of completion of work-in-progress • Inspection of source documents and price lists for the cost of inventory • Recalculation of inventory valuation

Before testing the details of the inventory account balance, in order to ascertain whether misstatement seems likely, substantive analytical procedures may be performed. For example, the ratio of inventory to cost of goods sold (COGS) may be calculated for each significant type of inventory, at each material location. The trend for the current and past years may then be plotted and the resultant 'picture' evaluated in the light of the auditor's understanding of the client's business and its operations. Some possible scenarios (where no change in the ratio was expected) are presented in Figure 11.5.

When assessing the results of substantive analytical procedures it is essential that they are not viewed in isolation. The auditor must evaluate the results within the context of his or her understanding of the client and its operations, and must give due consideration to all of the relevant external and internal environmental factors that affect the entity. Additionally, graphs such as those presented in Figure 11.5 need to be assessed on the basis of the inventory item(s) and/or location(s) to which they relate and how they compare with the graphs of other inventory items and/or locations. Consideration must be given to pertinent policy decisions of management, such as planned changes in product mix, changes in target market(s), and/or changes in purchases and sales policies. Similarly, due allowance needs to be given to local and national economic, competitive and other factors which may have a bearing on sales and, therefore, on inventory levels.

It is important that substantive analytical procedures be regarded, not as a source of answers, but as a means of identifying questions which need to be asked.

11.7.2 Ascertaining the existence of inventory

The primary means by which an auditor ascertains that inventory exists is attending the client's inventory count (or stocktake).[15] ISA 501: *Audit evidence*

---

[15] It should be noted that this applies whether the client employs a periodic or a perpetual system for recording inventory. However, where a perpetual recording system is used, the auditor may attend inventory counts one or more times during the year.

Figure 11.5: Scenarios of the ratio between inventory and COGS over time

Inventory/COGS vs Years	(1) A steady relationship between inventory and COGS is indicated suggesting that significant misstatement is unlikely.
Inventory/COGS vs Years	(2) A steady increase in inventory levels is indicated suggesting the possibility of overstocking. This may indicate that inventory obsolescence is a problem and that some write-down in value may be necessary.
Inventory/COGS vs Years	(3) A steady decrease in inventory levels is indicated suggesting the possibility of stockouts. This may indicate that future sales and profits are threatened. The reduction in inventory may signal liquidity problems.
Inventory/COGS vs Years	(4) A marked decline in inventory in the current year is indicated. This raises the possibility of theft, a material error in the accounts, or a reduction in inventory in anticipation of a decline in sales.
Inventory/COGS vs Years	(5) A marked increase in inventory in the current year is indicated. This raises the possibility of manipulation of the accounts by senior management, a material error in the accounts, or an increase in inventory in anticipation of an increase in sales or, possibly, an anticipated increase in purchase prices.

regarding specific financial statement account balances and disclosures recognises the importance of this audit procedure. It states:

> When inventory is material to the financial statements, the auditor shall obtain sufficient appropriate audit evidence regarding its existence and condition by, unless impracticable, attendance at the entity's physical inventory count (or counts) and:
> (a) Evaluating management's instructions and procedures for recording and controlling the results of the entity's physical inventory count;
> (b) Observing management's count procedures, inspecting the inventory, and performing test counts; and
> (c) Performing audit procedures over the entity's final inventory records to determine whether they accurately reflect actual inventory count results. (para 4)

If the auditor is unable to attend the entity's physical inventory count on the date planned due to unforeseen circumstances, the auditor shall make or observe some physical counts on an alternative date and perform audit procedures on intervening transactions. (para 6)

In some cases, attendance at the entity's physical inventory count may be impracticable ... due to factors such as the nature and location of the inventory, for example, where inventory is held in a location that may pose threats to the safety or well-being of the auditor. ... In some cases ... alternative audit procedures, for example, inspection of documentation of the subsequent sale of specific inventory items acquired or purchased prior to the physical inventory count, may provide sufficient appropriate audit evidence of the existence and condition of inventory. In other cases, however, it may not be possible to obtain sufficient appropriate audit evidence regarding the existence and condition of inventory by performing alternative audit procedures. In such cases [the auditor is required] to modify the opinion in the auditor's report as a result of the scope limitation.[16] (paras A11–A13)

Audit procedures relating to stocktaking (physical inventory count) fall into three main groups:
   (i)   those conducted prior to the commencement of stocktaking;
  (ii) those conducted during stocktaking; and
 (iii) those conducted when stocktaking is completed.

(i)   *Procedures conducted prior to stocktaking*

Before attending their clients' inventory counts, auditors need to consider factors that are likely to affect their planned attendance and procedures at the counts. For example:
- the assessed risks of material misstatement relating to inventory;
- the effectiveness of internal controls relating to the safeguarding and recording of inventory;
- whether adequate procedures are expected to be established, and proper instructions given to client staff, for the physical counting of inventory;
- the locations at which inventory is held;
- whether the specialised nature of the stock is such that an expert's assistance is required.

Before the inventory count is due to begin, auditors should review their clients' inventory counting procedures to ensure they are adequate. They need to establish, *inter alia*:
- when the inventory count is to take place and whether sufficient time has been allowed to enable the task to be completed satisfactorily;

---

[16] This form of audit opinion is explained in Chapter 14.

- which personnel are to be involved in the count, their seniority and experience, and whether they are to work in pairs;
- how the count is to be performed (whether, for example, stocksheets are to be used);
- whether the instructions given to the stocktaking teams are clear, easily understood and complete;
- whether management's control procedures are adequate (whether, for example, appropriate procedures have been established to facilitate accounting for used and unused stocksheets, for counting and recounting inventory, and to prevent inventory from being counted twice, or omitted from the count);
- whether management has established adequate procedures for identifying the stage of completion of work-in-progress, obsolete or damaged items, and/or inventory owned by a third party (such as goods held on consignment);
- whether appropriate arrangements have been made for counting inventory moved between locations (or within one location) just prior to, during or shortly after the inventory count, and the despatch and receipt of inventory before and after the cutoff date.[17]

If, having reviewed their clients' stocktaking procedures, auditors are of the opinion that they are inadequate, they should discuss their concerns with management so the deficiencies can be rectified before the inventory count begins.

Where inventory is held at several locations, auditors need to decide at which locations audit attendance is appropriate. In making this decision, they should consider (amongst other things) the materiality of the inventory held, and the assessment of inherent and internal control risk at each location. Audit staff should attend the inventory count at each location where the inventory held is material and/or inherent risk and internal control risk are assessed as high.

(ii) Procedures conducted during stocktaking

During the inventory count auditors should observe whether their clients' employees adhere to the procedures prescribed by management and they should also perform test counts. ISA 501 explains:

> Observing management's count procedures assists the auditor in obtaining audit evidence that management's instructions and count procedures, for example,

---

[17] 'Cutoff' date is the end of the accounting period. It defines (or 'cuts off') the inventory (and other assets and liabilities) owned – and those not owned – by the entity at the balance sheet date. Only (but all) inventory owned by the entity at the end of the accounting period should be included in the inventory count.

those relating to the control over the movement of inventory before, during and after the count, are adequately designed and implemented. (para A5)

When performing test counts, audit evidence about the completeness and the accuracy of management's physical count records may be obtained by tracing items selected from those count records to the physical inventory, and tracing items selected from the physical inventory to management's count records. (para A7)

When attending the entity's physical inventory count ... the auditor may obtain copies of management's completed physical inventory count records to assist the auditor in performing subsequent audit procedures to determine whether the entity's final inventory records accurately reflect actual inventory count results. (para A8)

Many inventory counts are conducted with the aid of stocksheets. In an effective stocksheet system:
- all stocksheets are pre-numbered sequentially and a record is kept of the stocksheets issued to identified members of the stocktaking team;
- all items of stock at a location are identified and listed on the stocksheets;
- working in pairs, one team of stocktakers counts the inventory and records the quantity on the stocksheets;
- a second team of stocktakers (also working in pairs) recounts the inventory and records the quantity on duplicate stocksheets;
- the completed (and unused) stocksheets are returned to the stocktaking clerk who checks off the returned stocksheet numbers and compares the inventory counts recorded by the two teams of stocktakers;
- any significant discrepancies in the counts recorded by the two teams are investigated and the affected inventory items are recounted to establish the correct quantity.[18]

(iii)   Procedures following completion of stocktaking

When stocktaking is complete, a master inventory list is prepared. Auditors should determine whether this list accurately reflects the inventory counts. Where perpetual inventory records are maintained, auditors should also compare the quantities listed on the master list with the perpetual inventory records. Discrepancies between the physical count and perpetual records should be noted and investigated. Additionally, the accounting and perpetual inventory records should be inspected to ascertain whether they have been adjusted appropriately.

---

[18] The stocktaking procedures we describe are highly effective but they are demanding in terms of human resources. Some entities adopt a less effective system (with just one, rather than two, teams of stocktakers). However, this is likely to result in less reliable results and the need for closer examination of the stocktaking figures by the auditors.

Because the balance of the inventory account in the financial statements reflects the value of inventory owned by the entity at the balance sheet date, stocktaking is usually undertaken at, or as close as possible to, the end of the accounting period. However, ISA 501 recognises that this is not always practical. It observes:

> For practical reasons, the entity's physical inventory count may be conducted at a date, or dates, other than the date of the financial statements. This may be done irrespective of whether management determines inventory quantities by an annual physical inventory count or maintains a perpetual inventory system. In either case, the effectiveness of the design, implementation and maintenance of controls over changes in inventory determines whether the conduct of a physical inventory count at a date other than the date of the financial statements is appropriate for audit purposes. (para A9)

If the auditor concludes that the controls over changes in inventory are adequate for an inventory count performed at a date other than that of the financial statements to be appropriate for audit purposes, ISA 501 (para 5) requires the auditor to perform procedures to establish that changes in inventory between the date of the count and that of the financial statements are properly recorded.

11.7.3 Ascertaining ownership of inventory

Inventory recorded as a current asset in the financial statements should reflect the value of inventory owned by the entity at balance sheet date. It should not include inventory which is not owned by the entity: neither should it exclude inventory which is owned. Therefore, as part of the audit of inventory, the auditor inspects source documents and other relevant documents in order to determine inventory ownership. The two following situations are of particular concern to the auditor:

(i) The ownership of goods bought and sold near year-end

The auditor needs to determine whether legal title to (i.e., ownership of) goods purchased, but in transit on balance sheet date, had passed to the client by that date. [This usually depends on whether the terms of the contract are f.o.b. (free on board) at shipping point or destination]. The auditor must also ascertain whether the goods in question have been properly included in, or excluded from, the client's inventory list at balance sheet date.

Similarly, the auditor needs to ensure that where goods have been sold (and legal title has passed to the customer) but are still on the client's premises awaiting delivery on balance sheet date, these goods have not been recorded as part of the client's inventory.

(ii) Goods on consignment

The auditor needs to ascertain whether any inventory included in the client's master inventory list is held on consignment, or under a franchise agreement, whereby title to the goods does not pass to the client until a specified condition is met, for example, the goods are sold to a third party. Such goods are not owned by the client and, therefore, do not form part of the client's inventory.

By the same token, the auditor needs to ensure that inventory owned by the client which is held on consignment, or under a franchise agreement, by a third party is included as part of the client's inventory. ISA 501 explains auditors' responsibilities in this situation. It states:

> When inventory under the custody and control of a third party is material to the financial statements, the auditor shall either:
> (a) Request confirmation from the third party as to the quantities and condition of inventory held on behalf of the entity; or
> (b) Perform inspection or other audit procedures appropriate in the circumstances to obtain sufficient appropriate audit evidence regarding the existence and condition of that inventory. (para 8)

> Depending on the circumstances, for example, where information is obtained that raises doubt about the integrity and independence of the third party, the auditor may consider it appropriate to perform other audit procedures instead of, or in addition to, confirmation with the third party, for example:
> • Attending, or arranging for another auditor to attend, the third party's physical count of inventory, if practicable.
> • Obtaining another auditor's report . . . on the adequacy of the third party's internal control for ensuring that inventory is properly counted and adequately safeguarded.
> • Inspecting documentation regarding inventory held by third parties, for example, warehouse receipts.
> • Requesting confirmation from other parties when inventory has been pledged as collateral. (para A15)

11.7.4 Ascertaining that stock is correctly valued

In addition to establishing the quantity and ownership of inventory, auditors must verify that it is correctly valued. To accomplish this audit objective, they perform procedures such as the following:

- determining the valuation method adopted by the client and confirming that this method:
  - is in accordance with International Accounting Standard (IAS) 2: *Inventories* (IASB, 2006),
  - has been applied consistently across all inventory items,
  - is consistent with previous years';

- inspecting suppliers' invoices, price lists and other relevant documents to determine the cost of items held as inventory;
- recalculating the value of inventory based on its quantity (from the master list), cost information, and the valuation method adopted;
- establishing that the degree of completion of work-in-progress has been determined appropriately, and that raw materials, work-in-progress and finished goods inventory are properly classified;
- assessing the quality, condition and possible obsolescence of inventory items, and determining whether the net realisable value of inventory is lower than its cost;
- determine whether 'the lower of cost or market' rule has been applied correctly.

In relation to assessing the value of inventory, it is important that the auditor evaluates his or her competence to estimate its value and, if necessary, seeks assistance from an appropriate expert. A commonly cited example to illustrate this point is the auditor's inability, in general, to distinguish between diamonds and glass. The following case, reported in a BBC news broadcast in 1983, also provides a pertinent example. In this case the problem was an inability to distinguish between brass and gold.

> A North Wales jeweller committed suicide when it was discovered that his company's stock of gold was really brass. The Chester coroner was told that the jeweller had instructed his staff not to use the stock of what he said was gold wire, but when the bank sent investigators around, he admitted to a friend that the stock had been over-valued by £1 million. He then drove to a hotel where he drank a solution of cyanide poison. (BBC, *News about Britain*, August 1983)

11.8 SIGNIFICANT ASPECTS OF AUDITING DEBTORS

11.8.1 Overview of auditing debtors

The debtors account balance is frequently audited as an element of the sales-debtors-receipts cycle. Auditing this cycle involves, *inter alia*:
- performing substantive analytical procedures to test the reasonableness of relevant profit and loss statement and balance sheet accounts (for example, sales, sales returns, doubtful debts, allowance for bad debts, and debtors);
- verifying the validity, completeness and accuracy of sales and cash receipts transactions;
- directly testing the debtors account balance.

In this section, our focus of attention is the debtors account balance. When auditing this balance the auditor is concerned, in particular, to verify the existence, ownership and value of debtors. As for auditing inventory, each of these audit objectives (or assertions) requires a different set of audit procedures. These are shown in Figure 11.6.

Figure 11.6: Procedures for auditing debtors

Assertion/Audit Objective	Audit Procedures
Existence – Do debtors exist?	Confirmation
Ownership – Are debtors owned?	Enquiry and inspection of documents for possible factoring of debtors
Valuation – Are debtors correctly valued?	• Confirmation • Recalculation of allowance for bad debts

11.8.2 Confirmation of debtors

As noted in section 11.6 above, confirmation of debtors became a standard audit procedure as a result of the *McKesson & Robbins* case in the USA in the 1930s. ISA 505: *External confirmations* defines external confirmation as follows:

> External confirmation – Audit evidence obtained as a direct written response to the auditor from a third party (the confirming party), in paper form, or by electronic or other medium. (para 6)

We note in Chapter 7 (section 7.4.4) that audit evidence obtained directly by the auditor from external independent sources and in documentary form (whether paper, electronic or other medium) is generally regarded as reliable. Hence, in general, external confirmations received directly by the auditor are considered to provide reliable audit evidence.

However, ISA 505 notes that external confirmations may not provide evidence that is relevant to certain assertions: "[f]or example, external confirmations provide less relevant evidence relating to the recoverability of accounts receivable [i.e., debtors] balances, than they do of their existence" (para A3). The Standard also indicates that auditors should not confirm debtors' balances as a matter of course but should determine "whether external confirmation procedures are an appropriate response to an assessed risk of misstatement" (para A5). This will depend, among other things, on:

- the confirming party's knowledge of the subject matter; a confirmation request should be addressed to a person who is knowledgeable about the information being confirmed;
- the ability or willingness of the intended confirming party to respond; the confirming party may, for instance, be disinclined to respond if doing so is costly or time-consuming;
- the objectivity of the intended confirming party; if the confirming party is not independent of the client entity, his or her response to a confirmation request may not be reliable.

Notwithstanding the caveats noted above, it should be appreciated that external confirmations constitute the most widely used, and most reliable, audit procedure available for verifying the existence and accuracy of debtors. However, as will become evident as we explore the steps involved in the debtors' confirmation process, the extent of auditors' reliance on confirmations as a procedure for auditing the debtors account balance is affected by the characteristics of the environment in which the audit client operates and the practice of potential respondents in dealing with requests for direct confirmation. Hence, it varies from audit to audit.

Seven steps may be identified in the process of confirming debtors' balances. These are as follows:
   (i)   designing the confirmation request;
   (ii)   deciding on the timing of confirmations;
   (iii) selecting the sample of debtors;
   (iv)   preparing and despatching the confirmations;
   (v)   following up non-responses;
   (vi)   analysing discrepancies;
   (vii) drawing conclusions with respect to the accuracy of the debtors account balance.

(i)   Designing the confirmation request

As ISA 505 explains:

> The design of a confirmation request may directly affect the confirmation response rate, and the reliability and the nature of the audit evidence obtained from responses. (para A8)

> Factors to consider when designing confirmation requests include:
> • The assertions [or specific audit objectives] being addressed.
> • Specific identified risks of material misstatement, including fraud risks.
> • The layout and presentation of the confirmation request.
> • Prior experience on the audit or similar engagements.
> • The method of communication (for example, in paper form, or by electronic or other medium).
> • Management's authorization or encouragement to the confirming parties to respond to the auditor. ...
> • The ability of the intended confirming party to confirm or provide the requested information (for example, individual invoice amount versus total balance). (para A9)

Confirmations may be of two types: positive and negative.

   • A *positive confirmation* requests the respondent to reply to the auditor signifying agreement or disagreement with the information provided (for example, on a given date the respondent owed the client a specified amount) or to provide requested information (for example, how much the respondent owed the client on a given date).

- A *negative confirmation* requests the respondent to reply to the auditor only if (s)he disagrees with the information provided.

Positive confirmations are generally considered to provide more reliable evidence as the debtor is requested to respond whether the amount stated in the confirmation request is correct or incorrect. This enables the auditor to perform follow-up procedures in cases where responses are not received. However, the auditor also needs to bear in mind the possibility that a respondent may reply to a confirmation request without actually verifying that the information is correct. Where the auditor considers this is likely, instead of stating an amount in the confirmation request, the respondent may be asked to fill in the relevant amount. The problem with this type of 'blank' confirmation request is that it may result in a reduced response rate because more is required of the respondents.

Where negative confirmations are used, debtors are asked to respond only if the amount stated in the confirmation request is incorrect. Thus, all non-responses are treated as if the amount stated in the confirmation request is correct – even though the debtor may have merely ignored the request. However, negative confirmations are less expensive than positive confirmations (because there are no follow-up procedures for non-responses) and, therefore, for a given total cost, more negative than positive confirmation requests may be sent. Nevertheless, because negative confirmations provide less reliable evidence than positive confirmations, the auditor needs to consider whether other substantive procedures are required to supplement the negative confirmations.

Determining which type of confirmation to use in any given audit is a matter of judgment. Nevertheless, it is generally accepted that positive confirmations are appropriate when the following circumstances apply:
- A small number of large accounts represent a significant proportion of the total debtors account balance.
- The auditor has reason to believe that there may be disputed or inaccurate accounts (for example, when internal controls are weak).
- The auditor has good reason to expect that recipients of confirmation requests will not give them reasonable consideration. (For example, low response rates have been experienced in previous years. In this circumstance negative confirmations are not appropriate.)

By way of contrast, it is generally accepted that negative confirmations are appropriate in the following circumstances:
- The auditor considers that internal controls are reliable and that, as a result, material misstatement in debtors' accounts is unlikely.

- The auditor has no reason to believe that recipients will disregard the confirmation request or fail to treat it seriously.
- A large number of small account balances is involved.

It is pertinent to note that in some audits a combination of positive and negative confirmations is used. For example, where the total debtors account balance comprises a small number of large balances and a large number of small balances, positive confirmations may be used for all or a sample of large balances and negative confirmations for a sample of small balances.

A further factor auditors should consider when designing confirmation requests is the type of information respondents will be able to confirm readily. For example, certain respondents' accounting systems may facilitate the confirmation of single transactions rather than account balances. Where this is the case, the confirmation request should contain details of one or more transactions rather than the total account balance. If information is sought in confirmations that is not readily available to the respondent, this is likely to result in a reduced response rate.

(ii) Deciding on the timing of confirmations

There is little doubt that the most reliable evidence is obtained from confirmations when requests are sent close to the end of the client's reporting period. When this occurs, the debtors' account balances are tested directly, without any inferences having to be made about transactions which take place between the confirmation date and the period end. However, in order to complete the audit on a timely basis, and to facilitate scheduling of audit staff workloads, it is often convenient to confirm debtors at an interim date (generally, two or three months prior to the period end). This timing of confirmations is acceptable providing the client's internal controls over debtors' accounts are evaluated as effective and the auditor can be reasonably assured that sales, sales returns and cash receipts transactions are properly recorded between the confirmation date and the period end.

(iii) Selecting the sample of debtors

In order to select the sample of debtors to be confirmed, two separate decisions need to be made, namely:
- (a) how large the sample is to be;
- (b) how the sample is to be selected.[19]

The auditor also needs to consider characteristics of the intended respondents.

---

[19] Determining sample size and selecting samples are discussed in detail in Chapter 12.

(a) *The size of the sample* will depend on a number of factors, including the following:
- the materiality of the total debtors account balance. (The more material the balance, the larger the sample size);
- the number of accounts which constitute the total debtors balance;
- the size distribution of individual debtors' account balances;
- the results of substantive analytical procedures and internal control evaluation which indicate the likelihood (or otherwise) of the total debtors account balance being materially misstated;
- the results of confirmations in previous years;
- the type of confirmation being used.

(b) *The sample selection* usually involves some stratification of the total population of debtors. In most audits where confirmation is adopted as an audit procedure, the population is stratified based on size and age of outstanding balances. Emphasis is given to testing large and old accounts as these accounts are the most likely to contain a material error. (Old accounts may indicate a dispute between the company and debtor about the amount or even the existence of the debt, or may raise other questions about its collectability.) However, it is important that the auditor's sample includes some items from every material stratum of the population.

In most cases, the auditor confirms all balances which exceed some designated monetary amount and all accounts beyond a specified age limit (for example, 90 days) and selects a random sample from the remainder.

(c) *Characteristics of respondents*: Responses to confirmation requests are more likely to provide relevant and reliable audit evidence if the confirmation requests are sent to debtors who are:
- knowledgeable about the information to be confirmed;
- able and willing to respond to the request; and
- independent of the client entity.

Thus, the auditor needs to take these factors into account when deciding whether to rely on confirmation procedures to verify the debtors account balance and, more particularly, when selecting debtors to whom confirmation requests are to be sent.

(iv) Preparing and despatching the confirmations

Once the auditor has decided on the type of confirmation to be used and selected the sample of debtors to be confirmed, the confirmation requests are prepared.

A confirmation request is usually in the form of a letter (in paper or electronic form) which is sent to a selection of the client's customers. It generally sets out the amount owed by the customer to the client as shown in the client's accounts on a specified date (confirmation date). As noted earlier, if a positive confirmation is used, the debtor is usually requested to confirm that the amount stated in the letter is correct or indicate that it is not. If the auditor considers that the debtor may not verify the amount stated in the confirmation request before confirming it, instead of stating an amount, the debtor may be asked to fill in the amount owed on confirmation date. If a negative confirmation is used, the debtor is asked to respond only if the amount stated is not correct. In either case, if the amount is incorrect, the debtor is asked to state what (s)he believes the correct amount to be. The letter is frequently prepared on the client's letterhead but, in any event, it should include an authorisation from the client to the debtor to disclose the requested information to the auditor.

Notwithstanding the use of the client's letterhead, it is essential that all aspects of the confirmation process remain completely under the control of the auditor. This includes preparing the confirmation requests, placing them in envelopes and stamping and mailing the envelopes. A stamped addressed envelope should be enclosed with the confirmation request, with the envelope addressed to the audit firm. Additionally, the audit firm's address should be shown as the return address on the outside of the envelope addressed to the debtor. This is to ensure that any undelivered requests are returned to the audit firm.

When a confirmation request is returned as undelivered mail, the reason for the non-delivery needs to be carefully evaluated. In most cases it represents a customer who has moved away without settling his or her account, but there is always the possibility that it represents a fictitious account. Further, even if the debtor is valid, a large number of undelivered confirmation requests could signal errors in the client's debtors' address records and a consequential collectability problem. This will need to be reflected in the allowance for bad debts.

(v) Following up non-responses

As noted above, when negative confirmations are used it is assumed that amounts stated in confirmations which are not returned are correct. Non-responses are not followed up. However, when positive confirmations are used, no assumption is made as to the correctness or otherwise of amounts stated in confirmations which receive no response. Instead, second, and in some cases even third, confirmation requests are sent.

If a debtor still fails to respond, the auditor has to rely on alternative audit procedures to confirm the amounts in question. (S)he will, for example, examine the cash receipts records to ascertain whether the debtor paid an amount subsequent to the date of the confirmation. However, receipt of cash from the debtor does not necessarily establish that the amount being investigated was owed at confirmation date; it could relate to a subsequent sale. Therefore, in addition to examining the cash receipts records, the auditor needs to examine copies of:

- sales invoices – to confirm that the customer was billed for the relevant goods or services;
- despatch records – to confirm that the goods were despatched to the customer;
- sales returns records – to confirm that the goods were not returned by the customer.

In each case, careful attention must be paid to the dates and details of the records to ensure they all relate to the same transaction(s).

Inspection of correspondence in a disputed accounts file may also provide evidence that a debtor who failed to respond to a confirmation request owed the amount in question at the confirmation date.

The nature and extent of alternative audit procedures performed as follow-ups to non-responses largely depend upon the materiality of the non-responses, the types of errors discovered in the confirmed responses, subsequent cash receipts from non-respondents and the auditor's evaluation of the quality of the client's internal controls over debtors' accounts. However, in order for valid conclusions to be drawn about the population of debtors from the sample of accounts examined, all of the unconfirmed balances (following positive confirmation requests) should be investigated using alternative procedures, even if the amounts involved are small.

Although not a 'non-response' in the usually understood meaning of the term, ISA 505, para A18, observes:

> An oral response to a confirmation request does not meet the definition of an external confirmation because it is not a direct written response to the auditor. However, upon obtaining an oral response to a confirmation request, the auditor may, depending on the circumstances, request the confirming party to respond in writing directly to the auditor, or seek other audit evidence to support the information in the oral response.

Notwithstanding that external confirmations are usually considered to provide reliable audit evidence, ISA 505, para A16, points out that:

circumstances may exist that affect [a confirmation's] reliability. No response is without some risks of interception, alteration or fraud. . . . Factors that may indicate doubts about the reliability of a response include that it:
- Was received by the auditor indirectly;
- Appeared not to come from the originally intended confirming party; and
- Was received by a means that does not provide sufficient evidence as to the identity of the originating party. (para A16)

If the auditor concludes that a response to a confirmation request is not reliable, (s)he is required to evaluate the implications for, and if appropriate amend:
- the assessment of the relevant risks of misstatement, including the risk of fraud, and
- the nature, timing and extent of other audit procedures (ISA 505, para 12).

(vi)   Analysing discrepancies

When confirmations are returned to the auditor by debtors, any disagreements with amounts stated in the confirmation requests must be analysed carefully. In many cases these will result from timing differences between the customer's and the client's records (for example, a payment by a debtor may not have been recorded in the client's records by the confirmation date). However, in other cases, disagreements may signal errors in the client's accounts. These may arise, for example, from incorrect recording of amounts (that is, clerical errors), or from failure to record certain transactions, such as goods returned by the customer. Alternatively, they may reflect disputed amounts where the customer claims, for instance, that the wrong price has been charged, incorrect quantities or items were received, or the goods arrived in a damaged condition.

All disagreements with amounts in confirmation requests should be investigated to determine whether the client's records are in error and, if this is the case, by how much. Generally, the auditor asks the client to perform the necessary reconciliation but, if necessary, will communicate with the customer to settle discrepancies which have come to light.

(vii)   Drawing conclusions with respect to the debtors account balance

When all discrepancies found in the sample of debtors have been explained, including those discovered as a result of procedures performed as follow-ups to non-responses, the auditor needs to:
- re-evaluate the client's system of internal control and determine whether detected errors are consistent with the auditor's original assessment of the controls;

- generalise from the sample of debtors examined to the total population of debtors;
- draw conclusions as to whether sufficient appropriate evidence has been gathered regarding the assertions being tested (i.e., the existence and accuracy of debtors' balances recorded in the client's accounts).

If the auditor concludes that the confirmation process and any alternative or additional procedures have not provided sufficient appropriate audit evidence regarding the assertions tested, additional procedures will need to be performed.

11.8.3 Adjusting debtors for doubtful debts

Based on evidence gathered by the confirmation process and any additional procedures the auditor considered necessary, the auditor may conclude that the debtors' balances shown in the client's records are fairly stated. However, before concluding that the value of debtors is presented fairly in the financial statements, the auditor must assess the adequacy of the client's allowance for bad debts. To make this assessment, the auditor [if (s)he has not already done so] usually prepares or, more commonly, obtains from the client an 'aged debtors' schedule'; that is, a listing of all of the debtors' account balances classified according to the length of time they have been outstanding. Frequently they are grouped into account balances that have been outstanding for less than 30 days, 31 to 60 days, 61 to 90 days and more than 90 days. Based on the premise that the longer debtors' balances are outstanding the greater the probability that they will never be paid, it is usually appropriate to apply a sliding scale of percentages to each group of debtors' balances to establish an allowance for doubtful debts. When assessing the propriety of the percentages applied to the debtors' balances by the client in determining the allowance for doubtful debts, the auditor will also consider whether, compared with previous years, there has been any change in factors such as the following:

- the client's credit policy;
- the client's credit approval procedures;
- the level of compliance by employees with the credit approval procedures;
- the volume of credit sales;
- general economic conditions which are likely to affect debtors' ability to meet their financial obligations.

The auditor will also recalculate for the allowance for bad debts to determine whether management's estimate is reasonable.

11.8.4 Ownership of debtors

In most cases ownership of debtors does not give rise to problems; the amounts owed by debtors are owed to the client. However, particularly where there is evidence that the client has cash flow problems, the auditor must remain alert to the possibility that all or part of the client's debtors may have been factored, that is, sold to a financial institution at a discount. When this occurs, customers are frequently not aware of the change in the ownership of their debt because they continue to make payments to the client. As a consequence, factoring does not, in general, come to light through the confirmation process. The most common means by which the auditor discovers that factoring has occurred is through discussions with management and inspection of documents such as minutes of directors' meetings and correspondence.

11.9 SUMMARY

In this chapter we have discussed substantive testing, that is, testing the substance of (or, more correctly, the assertions embodied in) the financial statement account balances and other disclosures. It is these balances and disclosures about which the auditor is required to form and express an opinion and, irrespective of how 'perfect' a client's internal control system may appear to be, some substantive testing is always necessary.

We have noted that substantive testing may take one of two basic forms – substantive analytical procedures or tests of details – and that tests of details may involve testing the transactions which give rise to a financial statement account balance or testing the balance directly. However, whichever form of substantive testing is used, the objective is always the same, namely, to test the validity, completeness and accuracy of the financial statement disclosures.

In addition to discussing the general principles of substantive testing, we have discussed the application of commonly used substantive audit procedures (for example, observation, inspection, recalculation, tracing, confirmation and reperformance) and examined in some detail significant aspects of auditing the inventory and debtors accounts.

SELF-REVIEW QUESTIONS

11.1 Explain briefly the significance of substantive testing in the audit process.

11.2 State the overall audit objective of substantive testing.

11.3 Explain the meaning of the term 'assertion' and list four assertions about classes of transactions and four relating to account balances.

11.4   Explain briefly what is meant by 'tests of details'.

11.5   Explain briefly the two ways in which substantive analytical procedures are used as substantive tests.

11.6   (a) Describe briefly how the following audit procedures are performed:
       (i)   tracing forwards,
       (ii) tracing backwards.
       (b) Using a specific example to illustrate your answer, explain the purpose of each of the above audit procedures.

11.7   Describe briefly the 'stocksheet system' which may be used for a client's stocktaking (or physical inventory count).

11.8   Explain briefly two special factors the auditor must consider when testing the audit objective: Is inventory owned by the client?

11.9   In relation to auditing debtors, distinguish between a positive confirmation and a negative confirmation.

11.10 (a) List five elements of the process of confirming debtors which must remain under the auditor's control.
       (b) Explain briefly why it is important that audit-client personnel are not permitted to assist the auditor in the process of confirming debtors.

REFERENCES

International Accounting Standards Board (IASB). (2006). International Accounting Standard (IAS) 2: *Inventories*. London: IASB.

ADDITIONAL READING

Auditing Practices Board (APB). (2007). *Practice Note 16: Bank Reports for Audit Purposes in the United Kingdom*. London: Financial Reporting Council.

Canadian Institute of Chartered Accountants (CICA). (2000). *Use of Specialists in Assurance Engagements*. Toronto: CICA.

Canadian Institute of Chartered Accountants (CICA). (2003). *Electronic Audit Evidence*. Toronto: CICA.

Green, W.J., and Trotman, K.T. (2003). An examination of different performance outcomes in an analytical procedures task. *Auditing: A Journal of Practice & Theory* **22**(2), 219–235.

Hoffman, V.B., Joe, J.R., and Moser, D.V. (2003). The effect of constrained processing on auditors' judgments. *Accounting, Organizations and Society* **28**(7–8), 699–714.

Hoitash, R., Kogan, A., and Vasarhelyi, M.A. (2006). Peer-based approach for analytical procedures. *Auditing: A Journal of Practice & Theory* **25**(2), 53–84.

Krogstad, J.K., and Romney, H.B. (1980). Accounts receivable confirmation – an alternative auditing approach. *The Journal of Accountancy* **149**(2), 68–74.

Lin, K.Z., Fraser I.A.M., and Hatherly, D.J. (2003). Auditor analytical review judgement: a performance evaluation. *The British Accounting Review* **35**(1), 19–34.

McDaniel, L.S., and Simmons, L.E. (2007). Auditors' assessment and incorporation of expectation precision in evidential analytical procedures. *Auditing: A Journal of Practice & Theory* **26**(1), 1–18.

12 Audit Sampling and Computer-assisted Auditing Techniques (CAATs)

LEARNING OBJECTIVES

After studying the material in this chapter you should be able to:

- explain what is meant by 'sampling' and why this technique is important in auditing;
- explain the meaning of the basic terminology used in sampling;
- distinguish between judgmental and statistical sampling and explain the advantages and disadvantages of each;
- describe the methods commonly used for selecting samples;
- distinguish between attributes sampling and variables sampling;
- explain the process of attributes sampling;
- explain the basic principles of sampling with probability proportional to size (monetary unit sampling);
- discuss how auditors follow up the results obtained from testing samples of items;
- explain what is meant by 'computer-assisted auditing techniques' (CAATs);
- distinguish between 'test data' and 'audit software' and explain how each technique may be used in audit testing;
- discuss the use and control of CAATs in auditing.

The following publication is particularly relevant to this chapter:

- International Standard on Auditing (ISA) 530 (Redrafted): *Audit Sampling* (IFAC, June 2008)**[1]

---

[1] The status of ISAs referred to in this chapter is explained in the Important Note following the Preface to this book.

12.1   INTRODUCTION

In this chapter we consider two audit techniques that traverse both compliance and substantive testing, namely, audit sampling and computer-assisted auditing techniques (CAATs). We explain the meaning and importance of sampling in auditing, the meaning of basic terminology relating to sampling, and the differences between, and advantages and disadvantages of, judgmental and statistical sampling. We also discuss factors affecting the size of samples and describe some commonly used methods of selecting samples. Additionally, we examine in more detail some aspects of statistical sampling. More particularly, we discuss the difference between attributes and variables sampling and describe the application of attributes sampling to compliance testing, and sampling with probability proportioned to size (PPS, or monetary unit sampling) to substantive tests. Before concluding this part of the chapter we discuss the ways in which the auditor follows up the results obtained from testing samples of items.

In the second part of the chapter we explain what is meant by CAATs and discuss the meaning and use of 'test data' and 'audit software' in relation to audit procedures. We also examine the use and control of CAATs during an audit.

12.2   MEANING AND IMPORTANCE OF SAMPLING IN AUDITING

International Standard on Auditing (ISA) 530: *Audit sampling* defines audit sampling as: "The application of audit procedures to less than 100% of items within a population of audit relevance such that all sampling units have a chance of selection" (para 5a). The Standard also explains:

> The objective of the auditor when using audit sampling is to provide an appropriate basis for the auditor to draw conclusions about the population from which the sample is selected. (para 4)

Expressed in more general terms, sampling is the examination of a few items (or sampling units) drawn from a defined mass of data (or population), with a view to inferring characteristics about the mass of data as a whole. This may be illustrated by reference to a simple example.

Example: Assume that a client has 200,000 suppliers' invoices and that the auditor wishes to ascertain:
  (i)   whether, before payment, the invoices were:
    • matched with purchase orders and receiving reports;
    • checked for correct extensions and additions;
    • checked for correct account classifications; and

    (ii) whether:
- the extensions and additions are arithmetically correct;
- the transactions have been coded to the correct accounts;
- the correct amounts have been recorded in the accounts;
- the transactions have been recorded in the correct accounting period.

Reviewing these audit objectives, it should be noted that the first group relates to the client's internal control procedures. In order to test the level of compliance with these control procedures, the auditor will perform compliance tests. The second group of objectives relates to the accuracy of the recorded amounts, account classifications, and accounting periods of the transactions. To test these, the auditor will perform substantive tests (or, more precisely, tests of details).

Clearly, it is not economically feasible for the auditor to apply the seven tests to all 200,000 invoices. Instead, a sample of, say, 40 invoices, will be selected and the seven tests will be applied to these. Based on the results of the tests, the auditor will draw conclusions about the population of suppliers' invoices with respect to each of the characteristics tested. (That is, for each characteristic tested, the results obtained from testing 40 invoices will be inferred for the population as a whole.)

Sampling has been an accepted auditing technique since the early part of the 20th century and today is recognised as an essential feature of most audits. Three main reasons account for its importance, namely:
- in the modern business environment it is not economically feasible to examine the details of every transaction and account balance;
- testing a sample of transactions is faster and less costly than testing the whole population;
- auditors are required to form an opinion about the truth and fairness of the financial statements. They are not required to reach a position of certainty or to be concerned about the statements' absolute accuracy. The task can usually be accomplished by testing samples of evidence; there is no need to test the whole.

Notwithstanding its undoubted advantages, reliance on audit sampling introduces a concern for auditors. It exposes them to sampling risk, that is, the risk of reaching a conclusion about the population based on the sample of items examined that may differ from that which would have been reached had the entire population been subjected to the same audit procedure. Expressed in different terms, it is the risk that auditors will draw an inappropriate conclusion about the population because the sample examined is not representative of the population.

ISA 530 notes that sampling risk can lead to two types of erroneous conclusion, namely:

(i) In the case of a test of controls, that controls are more effective than they actually are, or in the case of a test of details, that a material misstatement does not exist when in fact it does. The auditor is primarily concerned with this type of erroneous conclusion because it affects audit effectiveness and is more likely to lead to an inappropriate audit opinion.

(ii) In the case of a test of controls, that controls are less effective than they actually are, or in the case of a test of details, that a material misstatement exists when in fact it does not. This type of erroneous conclusion affects audit efficiency as it would usually lead to additional work to establish that initial conclusions were incorrect. (para 5c)

If sampling procedures are used, sampling risk cannot be avoided altogether; however, it can be reduced by increasing the size of the sample and by selecting sample units at random (see section 12.5.3 below). Additionally, sampling risk may be quantified and controlled through the use of statistical sampling techniques.

12.3 BASIC TERMINOLOGY RELATING TO SAMPLING

In order to understand the fundamental principles of audit sampling, it is necessary to have a good grasp of a few terms which are commonly used. These include the following:

- *Population*: This refers to all of the items within an account balance or class of transactions which display a particular characteristic about which the auditor wishes to draw a conclusion.

- *Frame*: This is the physical representation of the population. For example, if the auditor is interested in the initials of the credit manager on duplicates of sales invoices as evidence of compliance with authorisation procedures, the sales invoices are the frame. If the auditor is interested in the accuracy of debtors' account balances, subsidiary debtors' ledger records may be the frame.

- *Sampling unit*: A sampling unit is a unit selected from the population which is included in the sample to be examined.

- *Characteristic of interest*: This term refers to the characteristic the auditor wishes to test. There are two basic characteristics of interest, namely, an attribute and a variable.
  - *An attribute* is a characteristic of the population which is either present or absent. Attributes sampling measures how frequently the

characteristic is present (or absent); for example, how frequently the credit manager's initials, signalling approval of the credit sale, is present (or absent) on duplicates of sales invoices.

– A *variable* is a measurement which is possessed by every member of the population but which can take any one of a wide range of values. An example of a variable is the monetary amount of a transaction or account balance. In variables sampling the auditor is concerned with estimating a monetary value; for example, the auditor may wish to estimate the balance of the debtors account, or estimate the amount by which this balance may be in error.

- *Stratification*: This refers to dividing a single population into sub-populations, or strata, of sampling units with a similar characteristic. It is undertaken to improve audit efficiency and effectiveness. As ISA 530 explains:

  1. Audit efficiency may be improved if the auditor stratifies a population by dividing it into discrete sub-populations which have an identifying characteristic. The objective of stratification is to reduce the variability of items within each stratum and therefore allow sample size to be reduced without increasing sampling risk.
  2. When performing tests of details, the population is often stratified by monetary value. This allows greater audit effort to be directed to the larger value items, as these items may contain the greatest potential misstatement in terms of overstatement. Similarly, a population may be stratified according to a particular characteristic that indicates a higher risk of misstatement, for example, when testing the allowance for doubtful accounts in the valuation of accounts receivable [i.e., debtors], balances may be stratified by age. (Appendix 1)

Debtors' account balances are frequently stratified according to size and/ or age. Balances exceeding some monetary amount and balances beyond some age limit (say, 90 days) may be subjected to 100 per cent testing (that is, no sample will be selected and the entire population will be tested). The remaining balances will be treated as a homogeneous population from which a sample may be selected and tested.

An important advantage of stratification is that it permits allowance to be made for variations in the risk attaching to identifiable components of the population. In the debtors example cited above, the risk of material misstatement being present is higher for large and old account balances than it is for balances which are smaller and those which have been outstanding for a shorter period.

- *Precision limits*: This term refers to how closely the results obtained from the sample of items examined match the results that would have been obtained had the entire population been tested. For example, in attributes sampling, if the sample shows that a particular characteristic occurs in two per cent of cases, how closely this reflects the rate of occurrence which would have been found had every item in the population been checked. Alternatively, in variables sampling, if, based on testing a sample of items, the auditor estimates the balance of the inventory (stock) account is £1,250,000, how close this is to the amount that would have been arrived at had the value of every individual item of inventory been ascertained and added.

- *Level of assurance (or confidence) (or level of sampling risk)*: This term refers to how confident the auditor wishes to be that the sample units examined will produce a result for the population with the desired precision. For example, if the auditor wishes to estimate the balance of the inventory account and specifies a precision limit of £10,000 with a 95 per cent level of confidence, this means that the auditor wishes his or her estimate of the balance of the inventory account to be within £10,000 of the actual value of the account balance at least 95 times out of every 100. By inference, it also means that the auditor is prepared to accept that, on five occasions out of 100, his or her estimate of the inventory account balance (based on the sample units examined) may differ from its actual value by more than £10,000. This five per cent risk of the results derived from the sample falling outside the specified precision limits is known as sampling risk. Expressed alternatively, there is a five per cent risk that the sample selected will not be representative of the population from which it is selected.

- ISA 530 defines two further terms related to precision limits and assurance levels. These are as follows:
  - Tolerable misstatement – A monetary amount set by the auditor in respect of which the auditor seeks to obtain an appropriate level of assurance that ... [it] is not exceeded by the actual misstatement in the population. (para 5i)
  - Tolerable rate of deviation – A rate of deviation from prescribed internal control procedures set by the auditor in respect of which the auditor seeks to obtain an appropriate level of assurance that ... [it] is not exceeded by the actual rate of deviation in the population. (para 5j)

12.4   JUDGMENTAL SAMPLING vs STATISTICAL SAMPLING

When discussing audit sampling, it is important to distinguish between judgmental and statistical sampling.

(i)   Judgmental sampling

Judgmental sampling refers to the use of sampling techniques in circumstances where the auditor relies on his or her own judgment to decide:

- how large the sample should be;
- which items from the population should be selected;
- whether to accept or not accept the population as reliable based on the results obtained from the sample units examined.

This sampling method has advantages over statistical sampling in that it is generally faster, and therefore less costly, to apply. Additionally, it enables the auditor to incorporate in the sampling procedures allowance for factors of which (s)he is aware as a result of earlier audit steps such as gaining an understanding of the client and its business, and evaluating its internal control system; for example, the size of samples can be increased for areas identified as high risk (i.e., prone to misstatement). However, unlike statistical sampling, the method provides no measure of sampling risk and, should the auditor's judgment be challenged (particularly in a court of law), the conclusions reached with respect to the sample may be difficult to defend. Further, when using judgmental sampling it is difficult not to introduce bias – whether it be in relation to sample size, the items selected or the conclusions reached with respect to the population.

(ii) Statistical sampling

Statistical sampling refers to the use of sampling techniques which rely on probability theory to help determine:

- how large the sample should be;
- whether to accept or not accept the population as reliable based on the results obtained from the sample units examined.

We should note that, when statistical sampling is used, sample units *must* be selected at random. (Random sample selection is discussed in section 12.5.3 below.)

This sampling method has three important advantages over judgmental sampling:

- it is unbiased;
- should aspects of the sampling be challenged, because it is based on probability theory and, therefore, considered to be objective (rather than based on the auditor's subjective judgment), it is readily defensible;
- it permits quantification of sampling risk. For example, if a sample is selected on the basis of a five per cent sampling risk, there is a five per cent chance that the sample is not representative of the population and, as a result, an inappropriate conclusion may be reached about the population.

However, statistical sampling has the disadvantage of being more complex and costly to apply than judgmental sampling. Further, in general, small and many medium-sized entities do not have populations which are sufficiently large and homogeneous for full application of statistical sampling methods. As a consequence, in the audits of small and medium-sized clients where statistical sampling is applied, it tends to be applied in a modified form.

In relation to statistical sampling it is pertinent to note that, notwithstanding the distinction between statistical and judgmental sampling, significant elements of judgment are involved in the application of statistical sampling techniques. This will be evident from our discussion of attributes and probability proportional to size (PPS) sampling procedures in section 12.7 below.

12.5 DESIGNING AND SELECTING SAMPLES

12.5.1 Designing a sample

When designing a sample the auditor must consider:
- the audit objective(s) to be met by testing a sample of items; and
- the attributes (or characteristics) of the population from which the sample is to be selected.

As we have observed in previous chapters, the audit objective largely determines the audit procedure(s) to be applied. In applying the audit procedure(s), the auditor needs to define what constitutes an error, and this, in turn, affects the population to be used for sampling. For example, if the objective of a compliance test relating to credit sales is to ascertain whether credit sales are properly authorised, and the client's control procedures include requiring the credit manager to initial sales invoices to signify approval of the sales, an appropriate audit procedure is to inspect a sample of duplicates of sales invoices[2] for the credit manager's initials. In this case, the absence of the credit manager's initials constitutes an error, and the population comprises the duplicates of all sales invoices (or, more correctly, the credit manager's initials that are, or should be, present on those invoices) issued during the accounting period. If, however, the objective of a test of details is to ascertain whether sales invoices have been properly extended (price per item multiplied by the quantity sold) and totalled, an appropriate audit test is to recalculate the extensions and additions on a sample of duplicates of sales invoices. In this case, an error is an arithmetical error in an extension or in the total of a sales invoice and the population is, once again, the duplicates of all the sales invoices (or, more correctly, all the extensions and totals on those invoices) issued during the accounting period.

---

[2] The original of a sales invoice is given to the customer; a duplicate is retained by the company.

12.5.2 Sample size

Once the auditor has decided to apply a certain audit procedure to a sample of items in a population, (s)he must decide how many sampling units to include in the sample. This decision is affected by: (i) sampling risk, (ii) tolerable misstatement or tolerable rate of deviation and (iii) the misstatement or rate of deviation in the population expected by the auditor.[3]

(i)   *Sampling risk*: The size of a sample is affected by the level of sampling risk the auditor is willing to accept. The smaller the risk the auditor wishes to accept that a conclusion about a population, based on testing a sample of items, will differ from that which (s)he would have reached had all the items in the population been examined, the larger the sample will need to be (and vice versa).

(ii) *Tolerable error*: Sample size is also affected by the maximum misstatement or rate of deviation (for a test of details or a test of controls, respectively) in the population the auditor is willing to accept (or tolerate), while still concluding the audit objective has been reached.[4] The smaller the tolerable error, the larger the sample the auditor needs to select.

(iii) *Expected misstatement or rate of deviation in the population*: The size of samples is also affected by the misstatement, or rate of deviation, the auditor expects to find in the population.[5] If misstatements or deviations are expected, a larger sample of items will need to be examined (than if no misstatements or deviations are expected) to enable the auditor to conclude that the actual misstatement or rate of deviation in the population does not exceed his or her tolerable error. When no misstatements or deviations (as applicable) are expected in the population, sample sizes may be smaller.

As is shown in section 12.7 below, when statistical sampling methods are used, sampling risk, tolerable error, and expected misstatement or rate of deviation (i.e., performance materiality) in the population are incorporated in the sampling method. However, when judgmental sampling methods are used, the auditor needs to take into consideration the factors outlined above when determining sample size.

---

[3] These and other factors influencing sample size for tests of controls and tests of details are explained in detail in ISA 530, Appendix 2 and 3, respectively.

[4] As noted in Chapter 9, section 9.3.1, tolerable error is the auditor's judgment of what is material to users of the relevant client's financial statements in respect of a particular class of transactions, account balance or disclosure.

[5] This corresponds to the performance materiality in Chapter 9, section 9.3.2.

12.5.3 Sample selection

Once the auditor has determined the size of the sample to be selected, (s)he needs to decide how the items are to be selected. ISA 530 specifies:

> The auditor shall select items for the sample in such a way that each sampling unit in the population has a chance of selection....With statistical sampling sample items are selected so that each sampling unit has a known probability of being selected. With non-statistical sampling, judgment is used to select the sample items. Because the purpose of sampling is to draw conclusions about the entire populations, it is important that the auditor selects a representative sample by choosing sample items, which have characteristics typical of the population. (paras 8, A12)

There are many methods of selecting audit samples but the most commonly used fall into two groups. These are shown in Figure 12.1 and discussed below.

Figure 12.1:   Methods of selecting audit samples

Broad groups of sample selection methods	Sub-groups of sample selection methods
(a) Random selection	• Unrestricted random selection
	• Systematic sampling – Cluster selection (a variation of systematic sampling)
	• Selection with probability proportional to size
(b) Non-random selection	• Haphazard selection
	• Judgmental selection

(a)   Random selection

The key feature of random sample selection is that each item in the population has an equal chance of selection. Whilst maintaining this characteristic, three variations of random selection may be recognised, namely:

(i)   unrestricted random selection;
(ii)   systematic selection;
(iii) selection with probability proportional to size.

(i)   Unrestricted random selection

This method of selection treats the total population as a homogeneous mass of data, and random number tables or computer-generated random numbers are used to identify the sampling units to be selected.

(ii)   Systematic selection

For systematic selection, a sampling interval is first determined by dividing the population to be tested by the required sample size. For example, if the population comprises 2,625 sales invoices and the sample size is 125, the selection interval is: 2,625/125 = 21.

A number between 0 and 21 is selected at random (i.e., haphazardly) by the auditor or (preferably, if the sample is to be truly random) by means of a random-number table or computer-generated random number, and this gives the starting point. Every 21st item in the population is then selected, beginning with that point.

Systematic selection is simple to use, and is generally quicker, and therefore less costly, than unrestricted random selection. However, it has the disadvantage that it can introduce bias into the sample if the characteristic of interest is not randomly distributed through the population. For example, the use of systematic selection to select a sample of duplicates of sales invoices to test for authorisation of credit sales will not generally cause any problem. However, if every 25th person on the payroll is fictitious, systematic selection using a sampling interval of 25 could result in a sample consisting entirely of fictitious employees. Alternatively, by selecting a different starting point and using a sampling interval of 25, the sample may fail to include any of the fictitious employees (a situation which is potentially more serious for the auditor).

Cluster selection: As noted in Figure 12.1, cluster selection is a variant of systematic selection. This method of sample selection involves selecting clusters of items in the population (or groups of contiguous items or records) rather than individual items. For example, if a sample of 125 units is required, 25 clusters of five units may be selected. If the first unit in each cluster is selected using a random-number table or computer-generated random number, then the sample is regarded as a random sample.

This method of selection provides a straightforward and relatively quick means of selecting a sample. However, in some circumstances it may be less efficient than selecting samples comprising individually selected items as it may result in a larger sample size. For example, if a sample of duplicates of sales invoices is to be checked for authorisation (for example, the credit manager's initials signalling authorisation), a sample of 125 units selected individually may provide good coverage of invoices issued during the accounting period. However, 25 clusters of five units may not give adequate coverage of invoices issued during the accounting period and the number of clusters may need to be increased. In other cases, cluster selection may be particularly appropriate, for example, in testing for completeness of records. If the auditor wishes to check that all sales invoices, purchase orders, stocktaking sheets and similar documents are accounted for (that is, documents which are numbered sequentially), it may be more effective to check the number sequence of 125 documents in 25 clusters of five than to check 125 documents selected in one block.

(iii)   Selection with probability proportional to size (PPS selection)

When PPS selection is used, each individual monetary unit (that is, each individual £1) in a population is regarded as a separate unit within the population and each has an equal chance of selection. This method may be explained by reference to the following simple example.

Example: Assume that the debtors account balance in a client's balance sheet comprises 10 individual debtors' accounts and that the balances of these accounts at the end of the accounting period are as presented in Figure 12.2. Also assume that a sample of six units is required for testing.

Figure 12.2:   PPS selection: population of debtors' pounds

Account	Recorded balance	Cumulative total (pounds units)	Location of sample units
	£	£	
1	276	276	√
2	1,194	1,470	√
3	683	2,153	√
4	25	2,178	
5	1,221	3,399	√
6	94	3,493	
7	76	3,569	
8	684	4,253	√√
9	135	4,388	
10	302	4,690	

The accounts are recorded in the order in which they appear in the subsidiary ledger and the cumulative pounds (£s) in the accounts are calculated (see Figure 12.2, column 3). These cumulative pounds constitute the population of 4,690 individual pounds. Pounds 1 to 276 are contained in account 1, pounds 277 to 1,470 in account 2, and so on. Unrestricted random sampling or systematic sampling is used to select the required number of sample units, that is, individual identified pounds.

With reference to Figure 12.2, assume that unrestricted random sampling generated the random numbers: 2,997, 3,595, 3,762, 2,003, 0023, 0444. These random numbers correspond to individual pounds in the cumulative total and result in accounts 5, 8, 8, 3, 1 and 2 being selected for examination. Account 8 is a 'double hit' but is, of course, only examined once.

The advantage of PPS selection is that larger account balances have a greater chance of selection and it is these balances which, because of their size, are more likely to contain a misstatement which is material. However, the method also has the disadvantage that small balances have a low probability of being included in the sample, yet a small balance may be small because it is significantly understated; additionally, a series of errors in small balances may together constitute a material misstatement. These concerns may be overcome by stratifying the population and treating balances which are smaller than a specified limit as a separate population. A sample may then be selected from this (sub)population of small balances using, for example, unrestricted random sampling.

Another problem of PPS selection is the inability to include negative balances, for example, debtors' accounts with credit balances. A possible approach to this difficulty is to treat negative balances as if they were positive, and to include them in the cumulative total on that basis.

(b)   Non-random selection[6]

As shown in Figure 12.1, there are two main methods of non-random sample selection, namely:
  (i)   haphazard selection;
  (ii) judgmental selection.

(i)   Haphazard selection

When using haphazard selection, the auditor attempts to replicate random sample selection but without using random number tables or computer-generated random numbers. The auditor selects items from the population haphazardly, without regard to the size, source, date, or any other distinguishing feature of the items constituting the population.

This method of sample selection is simple and quick but has the disadvantage that unintended bias may be introduced into the sample. Certain items in the population tend to have a greater chance of selection than others; for example, the auditor may have a propensity to select (or avoid) items at the top, bottom or middle of a page; known (or unknown) persons; names which attract attention for some reason; and so on.

(ii) Judgmental selection

When using judgmental selection, the auditor deliberately tries to select a sample which is representative of the population and/or includes those items which (s)he considers require close attention.

---

[6] It should be remembered that non-random sample selection is not appropriate when using statistical sampling methods.

When attempting to select a representative sample, the auditor will be particularly concerned to include, for example:
- a selection of items representing transactions occurring in each month (or even in each week) of the accounting period, and for each employee who has been involved in handling the transactions during the period;
- a selection of account balances or transactions which are representative of those in the population. Thus, the proportion of large and small account balances included in the sample will reflect the proportion of these balances in the population.

When the auditor wishes to select a sample which emphasises high-risk areas (or significant risks),[7] care will be taken to include:
- a high proportion of large transactions or account balances, as a misstatement in a large transaction or balance is more likely to be material;
- items representative of period(s) when internal control procedures may have been functioning less effectively than normal; for example, when the key control person (such as the credit manager, or supervisor responsible for reviewing bank reconciliations and journal entries) was on holiday or absent through illness.

The major advantage of judgmental sample selection is that it enables the auditor to tailor his or her sample to the unique circumstances of the client. However, it also has the significant disadvantage (which it shares with haphazard sampling) that, should the sample be challenged (for example, in a court of law), it may be more difficult to defend than random sample selection.

12.5.4 Documentation of sample selection

Before leaving the subject of sample selection, we should note that all aspects of selecting a sample should be clearly and fully documented in the audit working papers. The documentation should include details of:
- the size of the sample selected – and how this was determined;
- the method of sample selection.

When random sampling is used, the source of random numbers (for example, the random number table or computer program) should be noted. When a population is stratified, the basis of, and rationale for, the stratification should be noted. Similarly, when judgmental sample selection is used, factors the auditor took into account when exercising his or her judgment should be recorded.

---

[7] Significant risks are explained in Chapter 8, section 8.4.3.

12.6 JUDGMENTAL SAMPLING

As noted in section 12.2 above, sampling is used to facilitate the performance of a compliance procedure or test of details. Instead of applying the audit procedure to all of the items constituting the population, it is applied to a sample of the items. The results obtained by applying the procedure to the sample of items are then inferred into (or extrapolated to) the population as a whole.

When judgmental sampling is adopted, the sampling process rests on the exercise of the auditor's judgment. The steps in the process are as follows:
(i)   the sample size is determined judgmentally;
(ii) the sample is selected using a random or a non-random sample selection method;
(iii) the sample is examined for the characteristic being tested; that is, compliance with a specific internal control procedure, or the validity, completeness and/or accuracy of the monetary amount of a class of transactions or account balance;
(iv) the sample results are extrapolated to the population and, based on these results, the population is accepted – or not accepted – as 'satisfactory'; that is, exercising judgment, the auditor concludes that the control being tested has (or has not) been adequately complied with, or the class of transactions or account balance is (or is not) free of material misstatement (or, more correctly, misstatements in the population do not exceed the tolerable rate of deviation or misstatement determined by the auditor).

As will be seen in the next section, when statistical sampling techniques are used, steps (i) and (iv) above are determined by applying probability theory, and step (ii) must be performed using random selection methods.

12.7 INTRODUCTION TO STATISTICAL SAMPLING

12.7.1 Sampling plans

Statistical sampling is undertaken by means of sampling plans (or methods). The most common fall into two main categories, namely, attributes sampling plans and variables sampling plans. Banks (1979, p. 113) provides a clear explanation of the difference between the two. He says:

> From a practical audit point of view, generally the extrapolation of the sample results to arrive at a population conclusion is limited to the following two techniques:
> (a) sampling for Attributes (how many);
> (b) sampling for Variables (how much).

In the case of attribute sampling the type of conclusion one would reach might read as follows:

> "I am 95 per cent confident, based upon the results of the bias-free [i.e., random] sample selected, that the population error rate will not exceed five per cent in respect of those attributes being tested."

With the variable sampling techniques the type of conclusion one might reach would read as follows:

> "I am 95 per cent confident, based upon the sample selected without bias, that the total monetary value of the entire population will be within the range of (say) $293,789 and $316,323."

As may be seen from Figure 12.3, although the sampling plans used in auditing fall into two broad categories, different variations of attributes and variables sampling are recognised.

Figure 12.3: Relationship between sampling methods

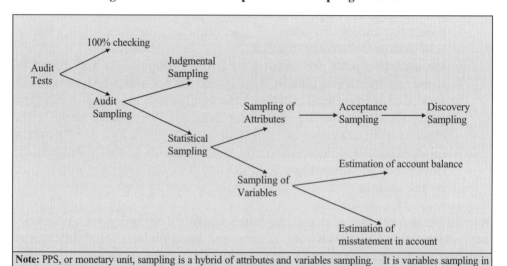

Note: PPS, or monetary unit, sampling is a hybrid of attributes and variables sampling. It is variables sampling in the sense that it measures monetary amounts but attributes sampling techniques are employed to determine sample size and evaluate the sample results.

Source: Adapted from McRae (1971, p. 376)

12.7.2 Attributes sampling plans

As noted above, attributes sampling is concerned with ascertaining whether a characteristic of interest is present or absent. Because evidence of compliance with internal control procedures (such as the credit manager's initials on duplicates of sales invoices signifying authorisation of credit sales) is generally either present or absent, attributes sampling has particular application in compliance testing.

Two variations of attributes sampling are often used in auditing, namely, acceptance sampling and discovery sampling. Each of these is discussed below.

- *Acceptance sampling*: As a pre-requisite to using acceptance sampling, the auditor needs to specify:
  1. the tolerable rate of deviation in the population (i.e., the rate of deviation in the population the auditor will accept whilst still concluding the control activity is effective and can be relied upon);
  2. the expected rate of deviation in the population (i.e., the rate of deviation the auditor expects to exist in the population, given his or her assessment of inherent audit risk and preliminary evaluation of the client's internal control system); and
  3. the desired level of sampling risk (i.e., the level of risk the auditor is prepared to accept that the conclusion reached about the deviation rate in the population, based on the results of examining a sample of items, is not valid). Alternatively stated, the level of confidence the auditor wishes to achieve that the conclusion reached about the deviation rate in the population, based on the sample results, is valid.

As shown in the detailed example of attributes sampling provided below, using this information, the auditor can use statistical sampling tables to determine the appropriate size of the sample of items to be tested.

The sample is then selected using a random selection method and examined for the characteristic being tested. Based on the presence (or more usually the absence) of the characteristic in the sample, statistical sampling tables are used to determine the estimated maximum rate of deviation in the population. This sampling method gives rise to a statement such as: 'There is a five per cent risk that the rate of sales invoices not carrying the credit manager's initials exceeds two per cent.' (Alternatively stated: 'I am 95 per cent confident that the rate of sales invoices not carrying the credit manager's initials does not exceed two per cent.')

The estimated maximum rate of deviation in the population is compared with the tolerable rate of deviation, and if the former does not exceed the latter, the auditor will probably accept the population as reliable (that is, the auditor will conclude that the internal control procedure is effective and can be relied upon).

- *Discovery sampling*: This is a subset of acceptance sampling where the expected rate of deviation in the population is set at zero. This gives the smallest sample size possible under acceptance sampling but, if a single deviation is found in the sample of items examined, then the tolerable rate of deviation will be exceeded and the population cannot be accepted (or the relevant internal control procedure cannot be relied upon) without further investigation.

As the discovery of a single deviation in a sample of items examined results in the population not being accepted by the auditor (at least, not without further investigation), discovery sampling reduces the number of populations which are accepted on the basis of the sample examined. However, discovery sampling is useful to the auditor as it involves small samples, and deviations which are discovered in the sample examined provide guidance as to the nature and cause of deviations in the population: discovery sampling is thus useful in directing the auditor's attention to areas which require more detailed investigation.

12.7.3 Detailed illustration of attributes sampling

To provide an overview of attributes sampling, the procedure for acceptance sampling is presented in Figure 12.4. For purposes of illustration, it is assumed that the audit client has 20,000 sales invoices and that the auditor wishes to establish whether or not the control procedure for authorising credit sales is effective.

Figure 12.4:   Steps involved in acceptance sampling

Steps in acceptance sampling	Illustration
1. Define the objective of the audit procedure.	To ascertain whether credit sales are properly authorised.
2. Define the attribute of interest.	Initials of credit manager on duplicates of sales invoices signalling approval of credit sales.
3. Define the population (or, more correctly, the frame).	Sales invoices issued during the accounting period. These are numbered from 24,494 to 44,501.
4. Specify the tolerable rate of deviation in the population.	A 4% tolerable rate of deviation. The auditor will tolerate up to 4% of duplicates of sales invoices not showing the credit manager's initials and still conclude the control can be relied upon.
5. Specify the desired level of sampling risk (or, alternatively, the desired level of confidence).	A 5% sampling risk is required. The auditor is prepared to accept a 5% risk that the deviation rate in the population may, in fact, exceed 4% and thus, based on the sample, (s)he may incorrectly conclude that the control procedure can be relied upon. [This is equivalent to the auditor wishing to be 95% confident that, if, based on the results of the sample, (s)he concludes the rate of deviation in the population does not exceed 4%, this conclusion is valid.]

Figure 12.4: *Continued*

6. Estimate the rate of deviation in the population. (This is an estimation of the deviation rate based on the auditor's preliminary evaluation of the client's compliance with control procedures.)	It is estimated that 1% of duplicates of sales invoices in the population do not contain the credit manager's initials.
7. Use the relevant table to determine the required sample size.	See Figure 12.5 for table entitled *Sample size for attributes sampling*. [A different table exists for each desired level of sampling risk. The lower the level of sampling risk (or the higher the desired level of confidence), other things being held constant, the larger the sample size.]
8. Using the table and the parameters established by judgment noted above, ascertain the sample size.	Tolerable rate of deviation is 4% (see step 4 above). This identifies the relevant column in the table. The estimated population deviation rate is 1% (see step 6 above). This identifies the relevant row in the table. The required sample size is located at the intercept of the relevant column and row. It is seen to be 156.
9. Randomly select a sample of the required size.	Using computer-generated random numbers, identify and select a sample of 156 duplicates of sales invoices.
10. Perform the relevant audit procedure and record deviations.	Inspect the 156 duplicates of sales invoices and record all those which do not show the credit manager's initials. Assume one such sales invoice is found.
11. Generalise from the sample to the population using the relevant table for evaluating attributes sampling results.	See Figure 12.6 for table entitled *Evaluating attributes sampling results*. (A different table exists for each desired level of sampling risk/desired level of confidence.) The actual number of deviations found identifies the relevant column in the table. (In our example, one deviation is assumed: see step 10.) The sample size identifies the relevant row in the table. (In our example 150; this is the closest to 156: see step 8.) From the table it is seen that (given our assumptions) the estimated maximum rate of deviation in the population (% of sales invoices without the sales manager's initials) is 3.1%. (This is not the most likely deviation rate but the 'worst case', or upper limit, of the deviation rate.)
12. Analyse detected deviations to ascertain whether they result from 'one-off' situations or are indicative of a more widespread problem, for example, the control procedure failing to function effectively when the key control person is absent.	Investigate the cause of the deviation detected. Assume this is found to be an isolated incident of control failure. [For example, two sales invoices were presented to the credit manager at one time for approval. (S)he reviewed both, but only initialled one invoice.]
13. Apply the decision rule for acceptance sampling. If the estimated maximum rate of deviation in the population (as shown in the sample results evaluation table) exceeds the tolerable rate of deviation, conclude that the control procedure may not be reliable. If the estimated maximum rate of deviation in the population is less than the tolerable rate, subject to analysis of detected deviations (see step 12), conclude the control procedure can be relied upon.	The projected maximum rate of deviation in the population is 3.1%. This is less than the 4% tolerable rate of deviation specified as acceptable by the auditor (see step 4). Additionally, the deviation detected has been found to be an isolated incident of control failure (see step 12). As a consequence of these findings, the auditor concludes that the control procedure may be relied upon.

Figure 12.5: Sample size for attributes sampling

	5% Sampling Risk (95% Confidence Level)										
Expected Population Deviation Rate (in percentage)	Tolerable Deviation Rate (in percentage)										
	2	3	4	5	6	7	8	9	10	11	12
0.00	149	99	74	59	49	42	36	32	29	19	14
0.25	236	157	117	93	78	66	58	51	46	30	22
0.50	*	157	117	93	78	66	58	51	46	30	22
0.75	*	208	117	93	78	66	58	51	46	30	22
1.00	*	*	156	93	78	66	58	51	46	30	22
1.25	*	*	156	124	78	66	58	51	46	30	22
1.50	*	*	192	124	103	66	58	51	46	30	22
1.75	*	*	227	153	103	88	77	51	46	30	22
2.00	*	*	*	181	127	88	77	68	46	30	22
2.25	*	*	*	208	127	88	77	68	61	30	22
2.50	*	*	*	*	150	109	77	68	61	30	22
2.75	*	*	*	*	173	109	95	68	61	30	22
3.00	*	*	*	*	195	129	95	84	61	30	22
3.25	*	*	*	*	*	148	112	84	61	30	22
3.50	*	*	*	*	*	167	112	84	76	40	22
3.75	*	*	*	*	*	185	129	100	76	40	22
4.00	*	*	*	*	*	*	146	100	89	40	22
5.00	*	*	*	*	*	*	*	158	116	40	30
6.00	*	*	*	*	*	*	*	*	179	50	30
7.00	*	*	*	*	*	*	*	*	*	68	37

Figure 12.6: Evaluating attributes sampling results

	95% Confidence Level (5% sampling risk)										
Sample Size	Actual Number of Deviations Found										
	0	1	2	3	4	5	6	7	8	9	10
25	11.3	17.6	*	*	*	*	*	*	*	*	*
30	9.5	14.9	19.5	*	*	*	*	*	*	*	*
35	8.2	12.9	16.9	*	*	*	*	*	*	*	*
40	7.2	11.3	14.9	18.3	*	*	*	*	*	*	*
45	6.4	10.1	13.3	16.3	19.2	*	*	*	*	*	*
50	5.8	9.1	12.1	14.8	17.4	19.9	*	*	*	*	*
55	5.3	8.3	11.0	13.5	15.9	18.1	*	*	*	*	*
60	4.9	7.7	10.1	12.4	14.6	16.7	18.8	*	*	*	*
65	4.5	7.1	9.4	11.5	13.5	15.5	17.4	19.3	*	*	*
70	4.2	6.6	8.7	10.7	12.6	14.4	16.2	18.0	19.7	*	*
75	3.9	6.2	8.2	10.0	11.8	13.5	15.2	16.9	18.4	20.0	*
80	3.7	5.8	7.7	9.4	11.1	12.7	14.3	15.8	17.3	18.8	*
90	3.3	5.2	6.8	8.4	9.9	11.3	12.7	14.1	15.5	16.8	18.1
100	3.0	4.6	6.2	7.6	8.9	10.2	11.5	12.7	14.0	15.2	16.4
125	2.4	3.7	4.9	6.1	7.2	8.2	9.3	10.3	11.3	12.2	13.2
150	2.0	3.1	4.1	5.1	6.0	6.9	7.7	8.6	9.4	10.2	11.0
200	1.5	2.3	3.1	3.8	4.5	5.2	5.8	6.5	7.1	7.7	8.3

12.7.4 Variables sampling plans

As noted earlier, variables sampling is concerned with estimating the monetary value of an account balance or the amount by which it might be misstated.

Because it focuses on monetary amounts, variables sampling has particular application in tests of details.

As may be seen from Figure 12.3, variables sampling includes estimation sampling which may take the form of estimating an account balance or estimating the maximum misstatement of an account balance.

- *Estimating an account balance*: In this form of variables sampling, the auditor selects a sample of items (that is, a sample of transactions or components of an account balance, such as items of inventory) and, based on this sample, estimates the range of values (between upper and lower limits) within which the financial statement account balance should fall. This form of estimation sampling might give rise to a statement such as: 'From the items of inventory examined, there is a five per cent risk that the value of the inventory account balance exceeds £765,000 or is less than £683,000.' (Alternatively stated: 'I am 95 per cent confident that the value of the inventory account balance lies between an upper limit of £765,000 and a lower limit of £683,000.')

- *Estimating the maximum error in an account balance*: In this case, rather than estimating the value of an account balance, the auditor estimates the maximum amount of error which may exist in the balance. It might give rise to a statement such as: 'From the items of inventory examined, there is a five per cent risk that the amount of error in the inventory account balance is greater than £50,000.' (Alternatively stated: 'I am 95 per cent confident that the amount of error in the inventory account balance does not exceed £50,000.')

Although variables sampling is a useful auditing technique, for many populations the application of variables sampling procedures results in a sample size which is impractically large. As a result, PPS (or monetary unit) sampling is often preferred to variables sampling.

12.7.5 Probability proportional to size (PPS, or monetary unit) sampling

As noted in Figure 12.3, PPS (or monetary unit) sampling is a hybrid of attributes and variables sampling. It is a technique which is based on monetary values in a population and therefore possesses elements of variables sampling; however, attributes sampling techniques are employed in determining the sample size and evaluating the sample results.

To provide an overview of monetary unit sampling, the procedure followed is presented in Figure 12.7. For purposes of illustration, it is assumed that the client's pre-audited balance sheet shows total debtors at an amount of £3,198,426. The auditor wishes to confirm that this balance is not materially misstated.

Figure 12.7: Steps involved in PPS (monetary unit) sampling

Steps involved in PPS sampling	Illustration
1. Define the objective of the audit procedure.	To reach a conclusion as to whether the debtors balance of £3,198,426 is materially misstated.
2. Define the population (or, more correctly, the frame).	3,198,426 individual £1 monetary units. (Each pound in the population is treated as equivalent to a physical unit in attributes sampling.)
3. Specify the tolerable deviation rate in the population.	Assume a tolerable deviation rate of 4%, i.e., an upper and lower materiality limit of £128,000 (4% of £3,198,426).
4. Specify the desired level of sampling risk (or, alternatively, the desired level of confidence).	Assume a sampling risk of 5% is required (or a confidence level of 95%).
5. Estimate the expected deviation rate in the population. This is an estimate of the deviation rate in pounds (based on prior audit work). It is equivalent to the expected population deviation rate in attributes sampling.	Assume the expected deviation rate in the population is 1%; i.e., the auditor expects the population to contain a misstatement of £32,000 (1% of £3,198,426) above or below the stated balance of £3,198,426.
6. Use the relevant table to determine the required sample size.	See Figure 12.5 for table entitled *Sample size for attributes sampling*.
7. Using the table and the parameters established by judgment noted above, ascertain the sample size.	Tolerable deviation rate is 4% (see step 3 above). This identifies the relevant column in the table. The estimated population deviation rate is 1% (see step 5 above). This identifies the relevant row in the table. The required sample size is located at the intercept of the relevant column and row. It is seen to be 156.
8. Randomly select a sample of the required size.	Using PPS selection, select a sample of 156 pounds and identify the individual debtors' account balances in which they are contained (see section 12.5.3).
9. Perform the relevant audit procedure and record deviations.	Confirm the debtors' balances containing the 156 sample pounds using confirmations or alternative procedures in the normal way. Assume that one debtor's account balance recorded as £20,000 should be £10,000 and that no other errors are found.
10. Generalise from the sample to the population using the relevant table for evaluating attributes sampling results.	See Figure 12.6 for table entitled *Evaluating attributes sampling results*. The actual number of deviations found identifies the relevant column in the table. (In our example, one deviation is assumed. Although the debtor's total balance of £20,000 is checked, only one of these 20,000 pounds was included in the sample. It is this one pound which is in error.) (See step 9.) The sample size identifies the relevant row in the table (in our example, 150; this is the closest to 156: see step 7). From the table it is seen that (given our assumptions) the estimated maximum rate of deviation in the population (percentage of pounds misstated) is 3.1%.

Figure 12.7: *Continued*

11. Analyse detected deviations to ascertain whether they result from 'one-off' situations or are indicative of a more widespread problem, for example, a control failing to function properly when the key control person is absent.	Investigate the cause of the deviation detected. Assume this is found to be an isolated incident of control failure. (For example, two sales invoices of £10,000 were paid but only one was recorded as paid in the debtors ledger.)
12. Apply the decision rule for acceptance sampling. If the estimated maximum deviation rate in the population (as shown in the sample results evaluation table) exceeds the tolerable deviation rate, conclude that the account may be misstated. If the estimated maximum deviation rate in the population is less than the tolerable deviation rate, subject to analysis of the detected errors (see step 11), conclude the account is not materially misstated.	The estimated maximum deviation rate in the population of 3.1% is less than the 4% tolerable deviation rate specified as acceptable by the auditor (see step 3). Additionally, the deviation detected has been found to be an isolated incident of control failure (see step 11). As a consequence of these findings, the auditor concludes that the debtors balance of £3,198,426 is not materially misstated.

Two points need to be made in respect of this illustration, namely:

1. It was noted in section 12.5.3 that PPS selection gives small balances a low probability of being included in the sample. It might therefore be necessary to supplement the sample of 156 account balances with a selection of small account balances to investigate the possibility of small balances being significantly understated.

2. The deviation found in the illustration was a debtor's balance recorded as £20,000 instead of £10,000. This was treated as one deviation, being one debtor's pound included in the sample which was in error (step 10). Thus, to ascertain the estimated maximum deviation rate in the population, the relevant column in Figure 12.6 is that for one deviation actually found. In reality the debtor's balance is not entirely misstated; it is misstated by 50 per cent since the £20,000 recorded should not be zero but £10,000. This is known as a partial error. For a misstatement of 50 per cent (or a misstatement of 0.5) it is possible to interpolate between the columns in Figure 12.6 for zero errors and for one error, giving an estimated maximum deviation rate in the population of 2.55 per cent [that is, half way between the estimated deviation rate for zero errors (two per cent) and for one deviation (3.1 per cent)]. Such a refinement in respect of partial errors can reduce the projected maximum population error rate (from 3.1 per cent to 2.55 per cent in our

example). This can affect the auditor's conclusion with respect to the acceptability of the population.

12.8   FOLLOWING UP SAMPLE RESULTS

Irrespective of whether judgmental or statistical sampling techniques are used, the auditor does not slavishly follow the sampling method's accept/not accept rule. For example, if the estimated maximum deviation rate in the population in acceptance sampling is less than the specified tolerable deviation rate, this does not mean the auditor will automatically accept the control activity as functioning effectively throughout the reporting period. Similarly, if the estimated value of an account balance falls within the auditor's specified range of tolerable misstatement, this does not automatically result in the conclusion that it is fairly stated. Instead, the auditor remains alert to the possibility that the control procedure under investigation may not have functioned effectively throughout the reporting period, or the account balance being examined may be materially misstated. As indicated in sections 12.7.3 and 12.7.5 above, *all* deviations detected during the examination of sample units in acceptance and monetary unit sampling are analysed to ascertain their cause, irrespective of whether the auditor's tolerable deviation rate is, or is not, exceeded.

However, assuming that nothing has come to the auditor's attention to cause him or her to conclude otherwise, if the examination of a sample of items produces results which accord with the sampling method's 'accept' rule, the auditor will generally conclude that the internal control procedure on which (s)he plans to rely to prevent material misstatements from occurring in the financial statements is functioning effectively, or that the account balance examined is not materially misstated. Nevertheless, the auditor remains aware of his or her exposure to sampling risk and continues to watch for evidence which suggests that the conclusion reached about the internal control procedure or account balance may be invalid.

Where the results of an examination of a sample of items indicate that an internal control procedure cannot be relied upon, or an account balance may be materially misstated, this finding must be followed up by alternative auditing techniques. In the case of a control procedure which is found not to be operating effectively, other control procedures might be found and tested to see if reliance can be placed on them to detect or prevent the relevant (potential) misstatement, or substantive tests may be extended. If examination of the sample of items indicates that an account balance might be materially misstated, alternative techniques must be employed to ascertain whether this is, or is not, the case.

12.9 COMPUTER-ASSISTED AUDIT TECHNIQUES

12.9.1 Meaning and types of Computer-assisted Audit Techniques (CAATs)

Like audit sampling, CAATs are audit techniques that apply to both compliance and substantive procedures. In brief, they are audit procedures which use computer facilities to investigate the reliability (or otherwise) of the client's accounting system and the information it generates. The two best-known CAATs are:

(i)   test data (or test decks or test packs); and
(ii) audit software.

(i)   Test data

The test data technique is principally designed to test the effectiveness of internal controls which are incorporated in the client's computer programs. Thus, it is essentially a compliance procedure.

The technique involves entering data (such as a sample of transactions) into, and having the data processed by, the client's accounting system, and comparing the output with pre-determined results. The data may be used to test the effectiveness of general IT-controls,[8] such as online passwords which are designed to restrict access to specified data and programs to authorised personnel. Alternatively, the data may comprise a set of transactions representing all types of transactions normally processed by the client's programs, and incorporating a variety of errors. These transactions (and errors) are designed to ascertain whether programmed controls (application controls) are operating effectively, for example, whether exception reports are generated in appropriate cases, and whether transaction dates and amounts lying outside specified parameters are rejected.

Use of the test data technique is generally straightforward and does not require the auditor to possess a sophisticated knowledge of computer processes. Further, the tests are usually fairly quick to perform and generally cause little or no disruption to the client's normal processing schedules. However, a major disadvantage of the technique is that the test data are usually processed separately from the client's normal processing runs. Although the auditor can establish whether the controls are, or are not, operating effectively at the time the audit procedure is performed, (s)he does not know whether the controls operate effectively at other times.

---

[8] General IT-controls and application controls are discussed in Chapter 10, section 10.3.2.

In order to overcome this disadvantage, the test data technique can be extended to an integrated test facility (ITF). This involves establishing a dummy department, employee, or other unit appropriate for audit testing. Transactions affecting the dummy unit are interspersed among, and processed with, the client's ordinary transactions. The resultant output, relating to the dummy unit, is compared with pre-determined results.

When the ITF technique is used, the auditor must be alert to the danger of contaminating the client's files and care must be taken to reverse out all of the audit test transactions.

(ii) Audit software

In contrast to the test data technique, which requires the auditor to input test data to be processed by the client's computer programs, the audit software technique involves the auditor using audit software to process the client's accounting data. Audit software is of three main types. These are as follows:

(a) *Utility programs and existing programs used by the entity*: In this case, general (non-audit-specific) application programs, or enquiry facilities available within a software package, are used to perform common data-processing functions, such as the sorting, retrieving and printing of computer files. These programs may assist the auditor perform a variety of audit procedures but they are not specifically designed for audit purposes and, in general, their audit application is limited. They are used principally to extend or to speed up procedures which would otherwise be performed manually (for example, accessing and printing all or part of the debtors account balances or items comprising the inventory account balance).

(b) *General audit software*: This software consists of generally available computer packages which have been specially designed to perform a variety of functions for audit purposes. These include reading computer files, selecting and retrieving desired information and/or samples, performing various calculations, making comparisons and printing required reports.

(c) *Specialised audit software*: This software comprises specially developed programs which are designed to perform audit tests in specific circumstances – usually those pertaining to a particular entity or, possibly, to an industry. These programs may be prepared by the auditor (or auditor's firm), by an outside programmer engaged by the auditor, or (less desirably because of independence considerations) the entity's computer (IT) personnel.

Although the development of specialised audit software may be appropriate for certain clients (for example, clients in specialised industries such as banking or mining), and may be a desired ideal in other cases, developing such software is extremely expensive and is often beyond the expertise of the auditor. Nevertheless, whenever specialised audit software is to be developed for use in certain audits, it is essential that the auditor is actively involved in designing and testing the program(s). This is necessary to ensure that the auditor fully understands the operation (and limitations) of the software and also to ensure that it meets the requirements of the audit.

During recent years, the availability of general audit software has increased significantly and these packages are now used extensively to assist auditors perform a wide range of audit procedures. They are used, for example, for performing analytical procedures, for selecting and testing a sample of transactions or account balances, and for performing statistical sampling techniques such as monetary unit sampling.

In the current auditing environment, audit software is invaluable as computers are used to process accounting data in virtually all audit clients. However, its use may be resisted by an audit client's management or IT personnel because running additional programs for audit purposes may interrupt and cause delays to the auditee's normal processing. Be that as it may, where an entity's accounting system involves extensive use of computer processing (as is normally the case), manual audit procedures may be rendered inappropriate and application of audit software may be the only means by which a satisfactory audit can be conducted. In such circumstances, if the client's management restricts the use of audit software, this could amount to a limitation on the scope of the audit and give rise to a modified audit report.[9]

12.9.2 Use and control of CAATs

CAATs may be used to assist the auditor with a variety of audit procedures. They may, for example, assist the auditor perform:
- compliance tests of general IT-controls – for example, to analyse processing or access logs, or to review the effectiveness of library (or other storage facility) access procedures;
- compliance tests of application controls – for example, using test data to test the effectiveness of programmed controls such as the rejection of data outside specified parameters;

---

[9] Limitation on the scope of an audit, and its impact on the audit report, is discussed in Chapter 14, section 14.5.

- analytical procedures – for example, using audit software to calculate specified financial statement ratios and to identify unusual fluctuations or items;
- detailed tests of transactions and balances – for example, using audit software to test all (or a sample of) transactions in a computer file, or to perform statistical sampling routines to estimate account balances or the maximum misstatement in account balances or classes of transactions.

CAATs are generally user-friendly, so auditors do not require specialised computer knowledge in order to apply them. Although this is clearly an advantage to many auditors, it also carries the danger that auditors may be lulled into a false sense of security. This danger is particularly high when, in order to use CAATs, auditors require the co-operation of client computer (IT) personnel (who have an extensive and detailed knowledge of the client's system). The same applies where auditors use their clients' own enquiry facilities. Such an enquiry facility could, for example, be programmed by client staff not to reveal certain records when accessed by means of the auditor's password.

Before using test data or audit software, the auditor must ensure that (s)he understands the process by which the computer performs the relevant audit procedures and the limitations of, or pitfalls related to, the process. If the auditor has limited computer knowledge, (s)he should obtain assistance from, or have ready access to, assistants within the audit firm who have computer expertise, or suitable experts from outside the firm. The auditor should guard against the temptation to rely upon the client's IT personnel for explanations in circumstances which render it inappropriate to do so. As for all audit procedures, the auditor must ensure that the performance of CAATs remains under his or her control and that client personnel are not able to influence improperly the results obtained therefrom.

When planning an audit in which CAATs are to be used, the auditor must be cognisant of the fact that certain computer files, such as transaction files, may be retained by the client for only a short period of time. In such cases, the auditor may need to make special arrangements for certain data to be retained, or to alter the timing of audit work, in order to facilitate the testing of data while they are still available.

An interesting sideline to the advent of CAATs is that, for some audit tests, they are once again making possible an examination of *all* accounting data, instead of just samples thereof.[10] This, as in the 19th and early 20th centuries,

---

[10] This can happen whenever the audit procedure does not require reference to information held outside the computer system. For example, a CAAT can check calculations on the value of all inventory items but it cannot check on the condition or ownership of the inventory.

when detailed checking of all transactions was the norm, may increase the likelihood of detecting certain types of corporate fraud (although not necessarily computer fraud). Further, this is occurring at a time when, as we observed in Chapter 6, auditors are (and in recent years have been) subject to pressure from the courts, politicians, the media and the public to assume greater responsibility for detecting fraud, and ISA 240: *The auditor's responsibilities relating to fraud in an audit of financial statements* (IAASB, 2006), has imposed more stringent requirements on auditors in this regard. However, these changes are also occurring at a time when increased sophistication of computer networks is opening up new possibilities for computer fraud. This seems likely to present new challenges – and difficulties – for auditors.

We note in Chapter 2 that history reveals that changes in the audit environment, changes in audit techniques and changes in audit objectives go hand in hand. It seems possible that this is being demonstrated at the present time in relation to corporate fraud and that, in the not-too-distant future, fraud detection will re-emerge as an important (if not a primary) audit objective.

12.10 SUMMARY

This chapter has provided an introduction to audit sampling and computer-assisted auditing techniques – two somewhat specialised techniques that traverse both compliance and substantive procedures. The first part of the chapter focused on audit sampling. We explained the meaning and importance of sampling and the meaning of terms associated with this technique. We also considered the distinction between judgmental and statistical sampling, and the advantages and disadvantages of each. Additionally, we identified factors affecting the size of audit samples and described some of the commonly used methods of selecting samples (randomly and non-randomly). Further, we provided an overview of the application of attributes sampling to compliance testing and of PPS (monetary unit) sampling to tests of details, and discussed the auditor's follow-up to sample results.

In the second part of the chapter we turned our attention to CAATs. We briefly explored the meaning and use of CAATs and explained that these techniques are of two main types – test data and audit software. We also noted that CAATs are equally applicable in compliance testing and substantive testing and mentioned some of the ways in which CAATs can assist auditors. In the concluding section of the chapter we discussed the importance of auditors fully understanding the application of CAATs and the dangers of relying on clients' IT personnel for assistance.

SELF-REVIEW QUESTIONS

12.1 Explain briefly what is meant by 'audit sampling'.

12.2 In relation to audit sampling, explain briefly what is meant by:
(i)   precision limits;
(ii) sampling risk (and levels of assurance);
(iii) tolerable error;
(iv) stratification.

12.3 Distinguish between judgmental sampling and statistical sampling and list two advantages and two disadvantages of each approach.

12.4 State the characteristic feature of random sample selection and list three methods (or variations) of random sample selection.

12.5 Distinguish between:
(i)   haphazard sample selection; and
(ii) judgmental sample selection.

12.6 Explain briefly the essential difference between attributes sampling and variables sampling.

12.7 (a) Define a sampling plan.
(b) Explain briefly the key features of three sampling plans.

12.8 Explain briefly why probability proportional to size (PPS, or monetary unit) sampling can be referred to as a hybrid of attributes and variables sampling.

12.9 With reference to CAATs, explain briefly:
(i)   the test data technique;
(ii) three types of audit software.

12.10 List five ways in which CAATs may assist the auditor during an audit.

REFERENCES

Banks, A. (1979). Current status of statistical sampling. *Accountants' Journal* **58**(3), 113.

International Auditing and Assurance Standards Board (IAASB). (2006). International Standard on Auditing (ISA) 240 (Redrafted): *The Auditor's Responsibilities Relating to Fraud in an Audit of Financial Statements*. New York: International Federation of Accountants.

McRae, T.W. (1971). Applying statistical sampling in auditing: Some practical problems. *The Accountant's Magazine* **LXXV**(781), 369–377.

ADDITIONAL READING

Elder, R.J., and Allen, R.D. (2003). A longitudinal field investigation of auditor risk assessments and sample size decisions. *The Accounting Review* **78**(4), 983–1003.

Fischer, M.J. (1996). "Real-izing" the benefits of new technologies as a source of audit evidence: an interpretive field study. *Accounting, Organizations and Society* **21**(2/3), 219–242.

Kriel, E.J. (Principal author). (2007). *Application of computer-assisted audit techniques* (2nd edn.). Toronto: Canadian Institute of Chartered Accountants.

Lymer, A., and Debreceny, R. (2003). The auditor and corporate reporting on the internet: challenges and institutional responses. *International Journal of Auditing* **7**(2), 103–120.

Messier Jr., W.F., Eilifsen, A., and Austen, L.A. (2004). Auditor detected misstatements and the effect of information technology. *International Journal of Auditing* **8**(3), 223–235.

Nelson, M.K. (1995). Strategies of auditors: evaluation of sample results. *Auditing: A Journal of Practice & Theory* **14**(1), 34–49.

Ponemon, L.A., and Wendell, J.P. (1995). Judgment versus random sampling in auditing: an experimental investigation. *Auditing: A Journal of Practice & Theory* **14**(2), 17–34.

13 Completion and Review

> **LEARNING OBJECTIVES**
>
> After studying the material in this chapter you should be able to:
> - explain the position and importance of completion and review procedures within the audit process;
> - discuss the importance of, and procedures used for, the review for contingent liabilities and commitments and the review for subsequent events;
> - distinguish between subsequent events which necessitate adjustments to the financial statements and those which require only note disclosure;
> - discuss the actions auditors should take if events come to light after the audit report is signed;
> - explain the importance of re-assessing, during the completion stage of the audit, the validity of basing the financial statements on the going concern assumption;
> - explain the nature and importance of written representations;
> - discuss the nature and importance of the final review of audit working papers;
> - explain what is meant by an 'engagement quality control review', when it is required and what it involves;
> - explain the significance of dating the audit report.

The following publications and fundamental principle of external auditing are particularly relevant to this chapter:

Publications:
- International Standard on Auditing (ISA) 450 (Redrafted): *Evaluation of Misstatements Identified during the Audit* (IFAC, June 2008)**[1]
- International Standard on Auditing (ISA) 501 (Redrafted): *Audit Evidence Regarding Specific Financial Statement Account Balances and Disclosures* (IFAC, 2007)*
- International Standard on Auditing (ISA) 520 (Redrafted): *Analytical Procedures* (IFAC, 2007)*
- International Standard on Auditing (ISA) 560 (Redrafted): *Subsequent Events* (IFAC, 2008)*
- International Standard on Auditing (ISA) 570 (Redrafted): *Going Concern* (IFAC, 2008)
- International Standard on Auditing (ISA) 580 (Redrafted): *Written Representations* (IFAC, 2008)
- International Standard on Auditing (ISA) 720 (Redrafted): *The Auditor's Responsibility in Relation to Other Information in Documents Containing Audited Financial Statements* (IFAC, 2007)

Fundamental principle of external auditing included in *The Auditors' Code*:[2] Association

---

[1] The status of ISAs refered to in this chapter is explained in the Important Note following the Preface to this book.

[2] The fundamental principles of external auditing are reproduced on the inside of the front cover of this book.

13.1 INTRODUCTION

As explained in Chapter 10, in order to conduct the detailed work of evaluating and testing the effectiveness of the client's internal control system and verifying the validity, completeness and accuracy of classes of transactions, account balances and disclosures, the auditor divides the client's accounting system into sub-systems, or audit segments. Once the detailed audit work is complete, the auditor approaches the audit holistically (as is the case for the early part of the audit), and the completion and review stage is conducted on an entity-wide basis.

As shown in Figure 13.1, the completion and review phase of an audit comprises five main steps, namely:
(i)   review for contingent liabilities and commitments;
(ii) review for subsequent events before and after the audit report is signed;
(iii) re-assessment of the validity of preparing the financial statements based on the going concern assumption;
(iv) obtaining written representations from management;
(v)   final review of the financial statements, evaluation of the audit evidence and working papers, and formation of the audit opinion.

Figure 13.1:   Place of completion and review in the audit process

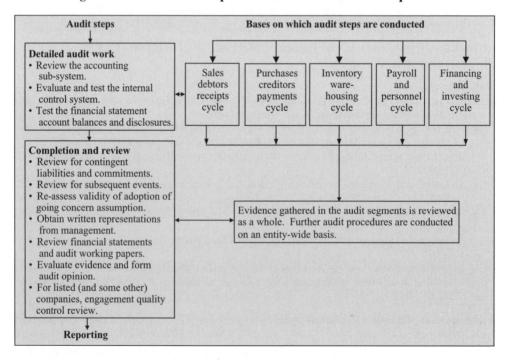

For the audits of listed (and some other) companies, there is an additional step – a review of the audit and audit working papers by the engagement quality control reviewer.[3]

In this chapter we discuss each of these important audit steps.

13.2 REVIEW FOR CONTINGENT LIABILITIES AND COMMITMENTS

Before considering the importance of the auditor's review for contingent liabilities and commitments, we need to clarify the meaning of these terms.

- *Contingent liabilities* are possible obligations that arise from past events but which, at the date of the financial statements, are uncertain as to their existence and/or amount. Their existence and/or amount are contingent upon the occurrence or non-occurrence of some uncertain future event not wholly within the entity's control. Examples include taxation in dispute, and pending litigation for infringement of, for instance, product safety, product description, or environmental regulations.[4]

- *Commitments* are contractual undertakings. Examples include bonus and profit-sharing schemes, and agreements to purchase raw materials or other inventory (stock) at a fixed price on a particular date in the future, or to lease or buy fixed assets, or to sell a certain quantity of goods at an agreed price on a specified future date.

The auditor faces two major problems in relation to the review for contingent liabilities and commitments, namely:
  (i) management may not feel disposed to disclose them in the financial statements;
  (ii) they do not involve transactions which are recorded in the accounting system. It is generally more difficult for the auditor to discover events and agreements which lie outside the accounting records.

Nevertheless, the existence of contingent liabilities and commitments may have a significant impact on the assessment of a reporting entity's financial position and performance by a user of its financial statements. Therefore, in order to provide a true and fair view of the entity's financial affairs, its financial statements must disclose any material contingent liabilities and commitments. As

---

[3] We explain engagement quality control reviews in Chapter 7, section 7.6.4.

[4] A full definition of contingent liabilities may be found in International Accounting Standard (IAS) 37: *Provisions, Contingent Liabilities and Contingent Assets* (International Accounting Standards Board, 2005).

a consequence, when forming an opinion on the financial statements, the auditor has an obligation to determine the client's position with respect to these items.

The procedures most commonly adopted by auditors to ascertain the existence (or otherwise) of contingent liabilities and commitments include the following:
- enquiries of management;
- reviewing the minutes of directors' meetings;
- reviewing correspondence files (in particular, correspondence between the client and its lawyers);
- reviewing the current and previous years' tax returns;
- reviewing the current year's audit working papers for any information that may indicate a potential contingent liability;
- obtaining confirmation from the client's external legal counsel (i.e., lawyers)[5] regarding any known existing, pending or expected contingent liabilities (especially arising from litigation) and commitments.

With respect to the last procedure noted above, International Standard on Auditing (ISA) 501: *Audit evidence regarding specific financial statement account balances and disclosures* states:

> When the auditor assesses a risk of material misstatement regarding litigation or claims that have been identified, or when the auditor believes that other litigation or claims may exist, the auditor shall . . . :
> (a) Seek direct communication with the entity's external legal counsel through a letter of general inquiry or specific inquiry, prepared by management and sent by the auditor, requesting the entity's legal counsel to communicate directly with the auditor; and
> (b) When considered necessary, meet with the entity's external legal counsel to discuss the likely outcome of the litigation or claims. (para 10)

The Standard explains:

> Direct communication with the entity's external legal counsel assists the auditor in obtaining sufficient appropriate audit evidence as to whether potentially material litigation and claims are known and management's estimates of the financial implications, including costs, are reasonable. (para A19)

In a letter of general enquiry, the client's lawyers are requested to inform the auditor of any litigation and claims of which they are aware, their likely outcome, and the expected financial implications for the client. If the auditor considers the lawyers are unlikely to respond appropriately to a letter of general enquiry, (s)he will send a letter of specific inquiry. ISA 501 explains that such a letter includes:

---

[5] Some (especially larger) companies have 'in-house' as well as external lawyers to advise them. When seeking to establish the position regarding actual or potential litigation and claims against the client, it is appropriate for the auditor to seek confirmation from the entity's external (i.e., independent) lawyers.

(a) A list of litigation and claims;
(b) Management's assessment of the outcome of each of the identified litigation and claims and its estimate of the financial implications, including costs involved; and
(c) A request that the entity's legal counsel confirm the reasonableness of management's assessments and provide the auditor with further information if the list is considered . . . to be incomplete or incorrect. (para A21)

In some circumstances (for example, where the auditor believes the matter is a significant risk[6] or the client's management and lawyers are in disagreement), the auditor may decide it is necessary to meet with the client's external lawyers to discuss the likely outcome of litigation and claims. Ordinarily, the auditor will seek management's permission to engage in such a meeting and a management representative will be in attendance (ISA 501, para A22).

13.3 REVIEW FOR SUBSEQUENT EVENTS

13.3.1 Events between the date of the balance sheet and the date of the audit report

The auditor has a responsibility to form and express an opinion as to whether or not the auditee's financial statements give a true and fair view of its financial position and performance as at the date of its period end balance sheet. As a result, the auditor has an obligation to consider events which occur between the balance sheet date and the date on which the audit report is signed which might affect a financial statement user's assessment of the entity's financial position and/or performance as at the date of its financial statements.

The auditor's responsibility to review events which occur subsequent to the balance sheet date is normally limited to the period between the balance sheet date and the date of the audit report. The review usually takes place during the final two to three weeks before the audit report is signed. The timing of the subsequent events review is depicted in Figure 13.2.

Subsequent events may be of two types, namely:
  (i) adjusting events;
  (ii) non-adjusting events.

(i) Adjusting events

Adjusting events are events that clarify conditions which existed at the balance sheet date and/or which permit more accurate valuation of account balances

---

[6] 'Significant risks' are explained in Chapter 8, section 8.4.3.

Figure 13.2:   Timing of the subsequent events review

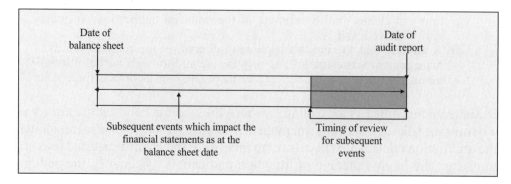

or other disclosures in the financial statements at that date. These events require the financial statements to be adjusted so that they reflect, as accurately as possible, the entity's financial position and performance as at the end of its reporting period.

Examples of adjusting events include:
 (a) the resolution of tax disputes and litigation which existed at the balance sheet date but the amount involved was then uncertain; and
 (b) the unexpected collapse of a material debtor which was regarded as 'good' at the end of the reporting period. This is an adjusting event if the conditions which caused the customer's collapse existed at the date of the financial statements.[7] If the conditions causing the customer's collapse arose after the balance sheet date, the event is a 'non-adjusting event'.

(ii)   Non-adjusting events

Non-adjusting events are events that occur subsequent to the balance sheet date. They result in changes to the auditee's situation as it existed at the end of its reporting period and, therefore, should not be incorporated in the financial statements as adjustments to account balances or other disclosures. However, if these events are considered to be material to financial statement users (i.e., they are likely to affect users' evaluation of the entity's financial position and/or future prospects), the events should be disclosed by way of a note to the financial statements.

---

[7] It should be noted that, as the customer's collapse arose subsequent to the balance sheet date, the debt was not 'bad', and therefore the account should not be written off, at year-end. However, if the relevant conditions causing the collapse existed at the balance sheet date, the debt was under threat at that time and an adjustment should be made to the allowance for bad debts.

Examples of non-adjusting events include:
  (a) a major fire or flood that affects the auditee subsequent to the balance sheet date where the resultant loss is not covered by insurance; and
  (b) the entry of the entity into a significant transaction subsequent to the balance sheet date (such as the purchase or divestment of a subsidiary) which has a material impact on the entity's resources.

In order to identify all of the events that occur between the date of the financial statements and the date of the auditor's report that require adjustment of, or disclosure in, the financial statements, ISA 560: *Subsequent events* requires auditors to perform audit procedures that include the following:
  (a) Obtaining an understanding of the procedures management has established to ensure that subsequent events are identified.
  (b) Inquiring of management and, where appropriate, those charged with governance [i.e., the board of directors] as to whether any subsequent events have occurred which might affect the financial statements.
  (c) Reading minutes, if any, of the meetings, of the entity's owners [i.e., shareholders], management and those charged with governance, that have been held after the date of the financial statements and inquiring about matters discussed at any such meetings for which minutes are not yet available.
  (d) Reading the entity's latest subsequent interim external financial statements, if any. (para 7)

In inquiring of management, and where appropriate, those charged with governance, ... the auditor may inquire as to the current status of items that were accounted for on the basis of preliminary or inconclusive data and may make specific inquiries about the following matters:
  • Whether new commitments, borrowings or guarantees have been entered into.
  • Whether sales or acquisitions of assets have occurred or are planned.
  • Whether there have been increases in capital or issuance of debt instruments, such as the issue of new shares or debentures, or an agreement to merge or liquidate has been made or is planned.
  • Whether any assets have been appropriated by government or destroyed, for example, by fire or flood.
  • Whether there have been any developments regarding contingencies.
  • Whether any unusual accounting adjustments have been made or are contemplated.
  • Whether any events have occurred or are likely to occur that will bring into question the appropriateness of accounting policies used in the financial statements, as would be the case, for example, if such events call into question the validity of the going concern assumption.
  • Whether any events have occurred that are relevant to the measurement of estimates or provisions made in the financial statements.

- Whether any events have occurred that are relevant to the recoverability of assets. (para A9)

[T]he auditor may [also] consider it necessary and appropriate to:
- Read the entity's latest available budgets, cash flow forecasts and other related management reports for periods after the date of the financial statements;
- Inquire, or extend previous oral or written inquiries, of the entity's legal counsel concerning litigation and claims; or
- Consider whether written representations covering particular subsequent events may be necessary to support other audit evidence and thereby obtain sufficient appropriate audit evidence. (para A8)

As we explain in section 13.5 below, when auditors need to rely on management's responses to enquiries (because alternative audit evidence is not available), they seek to have any significant responses (or representations) confirmed in writing. However, whenever possible, they endeavour to substantiate significant responses from management by seeking information from alternative sources.

13.3.2 Events subsequent to the date of the audit report

(i) Prior to issuance of the financial statements to the entity's shareholders

The auditor has an obligation to seek out events which occur between the date of the financial statements and the date of the audit report which might necessitate adjustment to, or disclosure in, the financial statements. However, the auditor does not have a responsibility to perform procedures to identify events after the audit report has been signed. Nevertheless, events may come to the auditor's attention after signing the audit report, but before the financial statements are issued to the entity's shareholders, which (s)he considers should be reflected in the financial statements. In this circumstance, the auditor should discuss with the auditee's directors whether the financial statements require amendment and, if so, how they intend to effect this. If the financial statements are amended, the subsequent period is, in effect, extended to a later date. Appropriate subsequent events procedures should be performed relative to this extended period and a new audit report issued on the amended financial statements (ISA 560, paras 10, 11).

If management refuses to amend the financial statements, the auditor's future action depends on whether the audit report has been released to the client.

(a) If the audit report has not been released to the client, and the auditor considers the circumstances warrant a modified audit opinion, such an opinion should be expressed.[8]

(b) If the audit report has been released to the client but the financial statements have not been issued to the entity's shareholders, the auditor is required to:

> notify management and ... those charged with governance [i.e., the directors], not to issue the financial statements to third parties before the necessary amendments have been made. If the financial statements are nevertheless subsequently issued without the necessary amendments, the auditor shall take appropriate action, to seek to prevent reliance on the auditor's report. (ISA 560, para 13)

(ii) Subsequent to the issue of the financial statements to the entity's shareholders

Occasionally, a matter may come to the auditor's attention after the financial statements have been issued to the entity's shareholders which materially affects the truth and fairness of those financial statements. If this occurs, the auditor is required to discuss the situation with the client's directors, determine whether the financial statements need to be amended, and consider the implications for the audit report. If the financial statements have been issued but the shareholders' 'accounts meeting'[9] has not yet been held, the auditor may request the directors to make an appropriate statement at the accounts meeting and/or to make a statement him- or herself. Alternatively, or additionally, the directors may decide to issue a revised set of financial statements. If this course of action is followed, auditors need to take the following steps:

- carry out the audit procedures necessary in the circumstances; such procedures may be limited to the amendment to the financial statements but, if a new audit report is issued, the subsequent event procedures (outlined in section 13.3.1 above) need to be extended to the date of the new audit report;
- review the steps taken by the directors to ensure that anyone in receipt of the previously issued financial statements together with the auditor's report thereon is informed of the situation;
- if warranted by the circumstances, amend the auditor's report on the previously issued financial statements to cover the amendment, or issue a new report on the revised financial statements;

---

[8] Modified audit opinions are discussed in Chapter 14, section 14.5.

[9] Annual meeting of shareholders at which the audited financial statements are presented. (This meeting is explained in Chapter 5, section 5.2.2.)

- for listed companies, consider whether Stock Exchange regulations require the revision of the financial statements to be publicised;
- for businesses authorised under the Financial Services Act 1986 or other regulated businesses, consider whether there is any requirement to communicate with the relevant regulator.

When a new audit report is issued on revised financial statements, auditors are required to:

(a) include an Emphasis of Matter paragraph[10] in their report which refers to a note to the financial statements which more extensively discusses the reason for the revision of the previously issued financial statements, or to provide such reason in their report;

(b) refer to the earlier report issued by them on the financial statements; and

(c) date their new report no earlier than the date the revised financial statements are approved by the entity's directors.

If the auditee's directors do not take adequate steps to ensure that those in receipt of the (original) financial statements are notified that the information in those statements has been superseded (whether by issuing revised financial statements, or otherwise), the auditor should notify the directors that (s)he will take action to seek to prevent future reliance on the auditor's report and then take such action (ISA 560, para 17).

The 2000 financial statements of Wiggins Group plc provide an example of revised financial statements accompanied by a revised audit report. These financial statements are the last in a series of revisions which commenced with the 1995 financial statements. As the Wiggins Group Chairman explains:

> The Financial Reporting Review Panel ("the Panel") opened an enquiry following the publication in August 2000 of our accounts for the year ended March 2000. The Panel had previously opened an enquiry into our accounts for the year ended March 1999 and had, by a letter of 27 June 2000, extended its enquiry in respect of the treatment of revenue from contracts for the sale of land to our accounts for the years ended March 1996 to 1998. ... The Company announced on 22 December 2000 that it had decided to accept the Panel's position with respect to all the matters in dispute and that it was going to issue restated accounts for the years 1996 to 2000. On March 6 2001, the Company issued restated accounts for the years 1996 to 2000. The Company also issued restated accounts for the year ended March 1995 as it was appropriate to reclassify a particular transaction originally recorded in that year.

---

[10] An 'Emphasis of Matter paragraph' is explained in Chapter 14, section 14.6.

In respect of the revised accounts for the year to 31 March 2000, the Wiggins Group directors, in an explanatory note,[11] provide details of a number of issues to which the Panel took exception. They explain the company's reasons for its treatment of the items in the original accounts, the grounds for the Panel's objection, and the remedial action taken by the company in the revised accounts. They also explain, in the following words, the manner in which they have revised the Group's 2000 financial statements and the effect of the revisions on profit:

> The directors are, by this [supplementary] note, revising the directors' report and accounts in accordance with Statutory Instrument 2570 Companies (Revision of Defective Accounts and Report) Regulations 1990, which permits revision by way of supplementary note. . . . As a result of the revisions, the profit on ordinary activities before taxation originally stated of £25,077,000 (1999: £12,113,000) is changed to a loss of £9,898,000 (1999: revised loss of £5,127,000). The original tax charge of £2,066,000 (1999: £3,295,000) has been revised to a credit of £24,000.

The directors presented a set of revised financial statements and amended a paragraph in the Directors' Report headed 'Review of the business and future trading prospects'. The auditors (HLB Kidsons) issued a revised audit report that complies with the requirements of ISA 560. This is reproduced in Figure 13.3.

13.4 (RE)ASSESSMENT OF THE GOING CONCERN ASSUMPTION

An important audit step performed during the completion and review stage of the audit is that of assessing the propriety of the auditee preparing its financial statements based on the going concern assumption. ISA 570: *Going concern* explains:

> Under the going concern assumption, an entity is viewed as continuing in business for the foreseeable future. General purpose financial statements are prepared on a going concern basis, unless management either intends to liquidate the entity or to cease operations, or has no realistic alternative but to do so. . . . When the use of the going concern assumption is appropriate, assets and liabilities are recorded on the basis that the entity will be able to realize its assets and discharge its liabilities in the normal course of business. (ISA 570, para 2)

The amounts at which assets can reasonably be expected to realise, and liabilities to be discharged, in the ordinary course of business may differ quite

---

[11] The explanatory note precedes the formal 'Supplementary note' to the 2000 financial statements. The latter supplements the original 2000 financial statements and comprises the revised 2000 financial statements (including the related notes) and an amended paragraph of the Directors' Report.

Figure 13.3:   Auditors' report on Wiggins Group plc's 2000 revised financial statements

Report of the auditors to the shareholders of Wiggins Group plc

We have audited the revised accounts of Wiggins Group plc for the year to 31 March 2000 which have been prepared under the historical cost convention and accounting policies set out on pages 38 to 40 in the original accounts and on page 10 of these revised accounts. The revised accounts replace the original accounts approved by the directors on 26 July 2000 and consist of the attached supplementary note together with the original accounts, which were dated 26 July 2000.

Respective responsibilities of directors and auditors
The directors are responsible for preparing the Annual Report, including, as described on page 27 of the original accounts, the accounts. Our responsibilities, as independent auditors, are established by statute, the Auditing Practices Board, the Listing Rules of the Financial Services Authority, and by our profession's ethical guidance.

We report to you our opinion as to whether the accounts give a true and fair view and are properly prepared in accordance with the Companies Act. We also report to you if, in our opinion, the directors' report is not consistent with the accounts, if the Company has not kept proper accounting records, if we have not received all the information and explanations we require for our audit, or if information specified by law or the Listing Rules regarding directors' remuneration and transactions with the Group and the Company is not disclosed. We are also required to report whether in our opinion the original accounts failed to comply with the requirements of the Companies Act in the respects identified by the directors.

We review whether the corporate governance statement on pages 24 to 26 of the original accounts reflects the Company's compliance with those provisions of the Combined Code specified for our review by the Financial Services Authority, and we report if it does not. We are not required to consider whether the Board's statements on internal control cover all the risks and controls, or form an opinion on the effectiveness of the Company's corporate governance procedures or its risk and control procedures.

We read the other information contained in the annual report, including the corporate governance statement, and consider whether it is consistent with the audited accounts. We consider the implications for our report if we become aware of any apparent misstatements or material inconsistencies with the accounts.

Basis of opinion
We conducted our audit in accordance with Auditing Standards issued by the Auditing Practices Board. An audit includes examination, on a test basis, of evidence relevant to the amounts and disclosures in the accounts. It also includes an assessment of the significant estimates and judgements made by the directors in the preparation of the accounts, and of whether the accounting policies are appropriate to the Group's and the Company's circumstances, consistently applied and adequately disclosed. The audit of the revised accounts includes the performance of additional procedures to assess whether the revisions made by the directors are appropriate and have been properly made.

We planned and performed our audit so as to obtain all the information and explanations which we considered necessary in order to provide us with sufficient evidence to give reasonable assurance that the revised accounts are free from material misstatement, whether caused by fraud or other irregularity or error. In forming our opinion we also evaluated the overall presentation of information in the revised accounts.

Opinion
In our opinion the revised accounts give a true and fair view, seen as at 26 July 2000, the date the original accounts were approved, of the state of the Group's and the Company's affairs as at 31 March 2000 and of the Group's loss and cash flows for the year then ended and have been properly prepared in accordance with the provisions of the Companies Act 1985 as they have effect under The Companies (Revision of Defective Accounts and Report) Regulations 1990.

In our opinion the original accounts for the year ended 31 March 2000 failed to comply with the requirements of the Companies Act 1985 for the reasons identified by the directors on pages 1 to 4 of the supplementary note.

Ocean House	HLB Kidsons
Waterloo Lane	Registered Auditors
Chelmsford	Chartered Accountants
Essex CM1 1BD	
Date: 6 March 2001	

significantly from those that would apply in the event of the entity's liquidation. Thus, when forming an opinion about the truth and fairness (or otherwise) of the entity's financial statements, the auditor must consider whether adherence to the going concern assumption is justified.

In the United Kingdom (UK), until the Auditing Practices Board (APB) issued Statement of Auditing Standards (SAS) 130: *The going concern basis in financial statements* in 1995,[12] auditors were merely required, during the planning and evidence gathering stages of an audit, to remain alert to the possibility that the going concern assumption may not be valid. In the absence of anything which raised doubt in auditors' minds regarding the going concern status of their clients, formal evaluation of the propriety of their clients adopting the going concern basis for the preparation of its financial statements was left until the completion and review stage of the audit. However, if, during the course of the audit or through the completion and review procedures, something came to light which raised doubt in their minds about the ability of an auditee to continue in operation, they were required to perform specific audit procedures to resolve those doubts. If, after conducting those procedures and evaluating management's plans for future action, auditors still had doubts about an auditee's ability to continue as a going concern, they were required to express those doubts in their audit report. This duty was unequivocal. However, during the 1980s and early 1990s (particularly following the Stockmarket Crash in October 1987), auditors in the UK, United States of America (USA) and elsewhere were severely criticised for not fulfilling this duty adequately, that is, for not expressing doubts about the ability of auditees to continue in business – auditees that received "a clean bill of health one day and collapse[d] just one day later" (Congressman Dingell, 1985, p. 22)].[13]

Responding to the criticism, the auditing profession has developed new – more stringent and explicit – going concern auditing standards. Instead of requiring auditors merely to remain alert to the possibility that the going concern assumption may be subject to question, auditors are now required to be proactive – to assess the propriety of their auditees adhering to the going concern assumption when preparing their financial statements by performing audit procedures at various stages of the audit. These are shown in Figure 13.4. However, as ISA 570: *Going concern* explains, primary responsibility for

---

[12] In 2004, the APB's Statements of Auditing Standards were replaced by the APB's International Standards on Auditing (UK and Ireland).

[13] Research investigating the audit expectation–performance gap in New Zealand in 1989 found that auditors were more severely criticised for not performing adequately their responsibility to report doubts (or doubts they should have had) about the going concern status of auditees than in respect of any other of their responsibilities. Even the auditor survey group was highly critical of auditors in this regard (see Porter, 1993).

assessing the appropriateness of preparing the entity's financial statements based on the going concern assumption lies with management.[14,15] The auditor's responsibility is to evaluate the validity of management's conclusion in this regard. ISA 570 states:

> [S]ince the going concern assumption is a fundamental principle in the preparation of financial statements ... management's responsibility for the preparation and presentation of the financial statements includes a responsibility to assess the entity's ability to continue as a going concern ... [This] involves making a judgment, at a particular point in time, about inherently uncertain future outcomes of events or conditions. The following factors are relevant to that judgment:
> - The degree of uncertainty associated with the outcome of an event or condition increases significantly the further into the future an event or condition or the outcome occurs. ...
> - The size and complexity of the entity, the nature and condition of its business and the degree to which it is affected by external factors affect the judgment regarding the outcome of events or conditions.
> - Any judgment about the future is based on information available at the time at which the judgment is made. Subsequent events may result in outcomes that are inconsistent with judgments that were reasonable at the time they were made. (paras 4, 5)
>
> The auditor's responsibility is to obtain sufficient appropriate audit evidence about the appropriateness of management's use of the going concern assumption in the preparation and presentation of the financial statements and to conclude whether there is a material uncertainty about the entity's ability to continue as a going concern. (para 6)

As shown in Figure 13.4, auditors perform procedures to assess the appropriateness of the auditee adopting the going concern assumption during (i) the initial phase of the audit, (ii) the evidence gathering phase and (iii) the completion and review phase of the audit. They must also consider the issue during (iv) the reporting phase.

(i) Initial phase of the audit

It may be recalled from Chapter 8 that, once the audit engagement procedures are complete, the auditor embarks on gaining a thorough understanding of the client, its internal and external environments, operations, key personnel, etc. During this phase of the audit, the auditor seeks to identify and assess the risks of material misstatement in the financial statements. One of those risks is that the entity may be unable to continue as a going concern and, as a

---

[14] Readers are reminded that in the Preface to this book we note that we use the term 'management' to embrace directors (executive and non-executive) and senior executives (directors and non-directors).

[15] It is pertinent to note that the United Kingdom Listing Authority's listing rules require the directors of all companies listed on the London Stock Exchange to comply with provisions of *The Combined Code on Corporate Governance* (Financial Reporting Council, 2006) or disclose that they have not done so and the reasons therefor. Provision C.1.2 of the Code states: "The directors should report that the business is a going concern, with supporting assumptions or qualifications as necessary". Thus the directors of listed companies need to assess the going concern status of their company.

Figure 13.4: Assessment of propriety of entity's adoption of the going concern assumption

Audit Steps		Audit Phase
Preliminary assessment of the risk that the client may be unable to continue as a going concern based on understanding the client's business, assessing risk factors, discussions with the directors and senior executives, and establishing how the directors plan to support their adoption of the going concern assumption.		(i) Initial phase of the audit
Perform specific procedures to evaluate the directors'/senior executives' assessment of the client's going concern status and to identify signals of going concern difficulties	Perform other routine audit procedures.	(ii) Evidence gathering phase
Decide on the need for a meeting with, or confirmation from, the client's bankers.		
Consider and, if necessary, revise the preliminary going concern assessment. Determine and document the extent of concern (if any).		(iii) Completion and review phase
Decide on the need for formal representations from the client's directors.		
Assess the need for, and adequacy of, disclosures relating to the client's going concern status.		
Express the appropriate opinion in the audit report, if necessary making relevant disclosures about going concern uncertainties.		(iv) Reporting phase

consequence, preparation of its financial statements based on the going concern assumption is inappropriate. In order to make a preliminary assessment of the auditee's going concern status, ISA 570, para 10, requires the auditor to:

(a) ascertain whether the directors or senior executives have performed an assessment of the entity's ability to continue as a going concern and, if so, whether they have identified events or conditions that, individually or collectively, may cast significant doubt on the entity's status as a going concern and their plans to address them;

(b) if such an assessment has not been performed, ascertain the basis for the directors' adoption of the going concern assumption for the preparation of the entity's financial statements;

(c)   enquire of the directors and senior executives whether events or conditions exist that, individually or collectively, may cast significant doubt on the entity's ability to continue as a going concern.

ISA 570, para A2, provides a list of examples of events or conditions that, individually or collectively, may cast significant doubt about the appropriateness of the auditee adopting the going concern assumption. Grouped under three headings: Financial, Operating and Other, they include the following:

Financial
• Net liability or net current liability position.
• Fixed-term borrowings approaching maturity without realistic prospects of renewal or repayment; or excessive reliance on short-term borrowings to finance long-term assets.
• Adverse key financial ratios.
• Substantial operating losses or significant deterioration in the value of assets used to generate cash flows.
• Inability to pay creditors on due dates.

Operating
• Loss of key management without replacement.
• Loss of a major market, key customer(s), franchise, licence, or principal supplier.
• Labour difficulties.
• Shortages of important supplies.
• Emergence of a highly successful competitor.

Other
• Non-compliance with capital or other statutory requirements.
• Pending legal or regulatory proceedings against the entity that may, if successful, result in claims that the entity is unlikely to be able to satisfy.
• Changes in law or regulation or government policy expected to adversely affect the entity.

ISA 570 notes that the auditor's assessment of the auditee's status as a going concern during the initial risk assessment process allows: "for more timely discussions with management, including a discussion of management's plans and resolution of any identified going concern issues" (para A3). If the auditor initially concludes that the auditee does not have going concern difficulties, (s)he is nevertheless required to: "remain alert throughout the audit for audit evidence of events or conditions that may cast significant doubt on the entity's ability to continue as a going concern" (para 11).

(ii)   Evidence gathering phase

During the evidence gathering phase of the audit, the auditor is primarily concerned with evaluating the directors'/senior executives' assessment of the entity's ability to continue as a going concern. ISA 570 explains auditors' responsibilities as follows:

[W]hen there is a history of profitable operations and a ready access to financial resources, management may make its assessment without detailed analysis. In this case, the auditor's evaluation of the appropriateness of management's assessment may be made without performing detailed evaluation procedures if the auditor's other procedures are sufficient to enable the auditor to conclude whether management's use of the going concern assumption . . . is appropriate in the circumstances. (para A8)

In other circumstances, evaluating management's assessment of the entity's ability to continue as a going concern . . . may include an evaluation of the process management followed to make its assessment, the assumptions on which the assessment is based and management's plans for future action and whether management's plans are feasible in the circumstances. (para A9)

ISA (UK and Ireland) 570 (APB, 2004) spells out auditors' responsibilities in the latter case in some detail. It states (para 17-1):

The auditor should assess the adequacy of the means by which those charged with governance [i.e., the directors] have satisfied themselves that:
(a) It is appropriate for them to adopt the going concern basis in preparing the financial statements; and
(b) The financial statements include such disclosures, if any, relating to going concern as are necessary for them to give a true and fair view.
For this purpose:
(i) The auditor should make enquiries of those charged with governance and examine appropriate available financial information; and
(ii) Having regard to the future period to which those charged with governance have paid particular attention in assessing going concern[16] . . . the auditor should plan and perform procedures specifically designed to identify any material matters which could indicate concern about the entity's ability to continue as a going concern.

ISA (UK and Ireland) 570, para 20-1, further notes that the auditor may need to consider some or all of the following matters:
• whether the period to which the directors have paid particular attention in assessing going concern is reasonable in the entity's circumstances;
• the systems the entity has in place for identifying, in a timely manner, warnings of future risks and uncertainties the entity might face;
• budget and/or forecast information, and cash flow information in particular, produced by the entity;
• whether key assumptions underlying the budgets and/or forecasts appear appropriate in the circumstances;
• the sensitivity of budgets and/or forecasts to variable factors both within and outside the control of the directors;

---

[16] This should be a period of at least 12 months and, according to ISA 570 (IFAC, 2008), para 13:
If management's assessment of the entity's ability to continue as a going concern covers less than twelve months from the date of the financial statements . . ., the auditor shall request management to extend its assessment period to at least twelve months from that date.

- any obligations, undertakings or guarantees arranged with other entities (in particular, lenders, suppliers and companies within the group) for giving or receiving financial support;
- the existence, adequacy and terms of borrowing facilities, and supplier credit;
- the directors' plans for resolving any matters giving rise to doubts, if any, about the appropriateness of adopting the going concern assumption.

In relation to the last matter, the Standard observes:

> [T]he auditor may need to consider whether the plans are realistic, whether there is a reasonable expectation that the plans are likely to resolve any problems foreseen and whether those charged with governance are likely to put the plans into practice effectively. (para 20-1)

In respect of borrowing facilities available to the client, ISA (UK and Ireland) 570 encourages auditors to make their own assessment of the intentions of the entity's bankers about extending borrowing facilities to the client and the terms thereof. More particularly, auditors should examine written evidence, or make notes of their discussions with the directors or, if appropriate, with the directors and bankers, regarding bank lending facilities. In making their assessment of the intentions of the entity's bankers, auditors should ascertain, usually through enquiring of the directors, whether the bankers are aware of the matters that have prompted the auditors to decide that such an assessment is necessary. In some circumstances, auditors may seek written confirmation from their clients' bankers about the existence and terms of borrowing facilities available to the client and the bank's intentions. This is particularly likely when:

- financial resources available to the audit client are limited;
- the auditee is dependent on borrowing facilities shortly due for renewal;
- correspondence between the bankers and the entity shows that the last renewal of facilities was agreed with difficulty;
- a significant deterioration in cash flow is expected;
- the value of assets granted as security is declining;
- the auditee has breached the terms of borrowing covenants or there are indications of potential breaches [ISA (UK and Ireland) 570, paras 21-1, 21-2].

Thus far we have been concerned with auditors evaluating directors'/senior executives' assessments of their entity's ability to remain in business as a going concern, and we have also noted that ISA 570 (IFAC, 2008) requires auditors to remain alert, throughout the audit, for events or conditions that cast doubt on the going concern status of their auditees. But, supposing auditors identify such events or conditions – what then? ISA 570, para 16, requires them to perform procedures that include the following:

(a) If management has not performed an assessment of the entity's ability to continue as a going concern, to request management to perform such an assessment.

(b) Evaluate management's plans for future actions in relation to its going concern assessment, whether the outcome of these plans is likely to improve the situation, and whether management's plans are feasible in the circumstances.

(c) When the entity has prepared a cash flow forecast, and analysis of the forecast is a significant factor in considering the future outcome of events or conditions:

(i) evaluate the reliability of the data underlying the cash flow forecast; and

(ii) determine whether there is adequate support for the assumptions underlying the forecast.

(d) Consider whether any additional facts or information have become available since the date on which management made its going concern assessment.

(e) Request written representations from management regarding its plans for future action and the feasibility of these plans.

Audit procedures appropriate for evaluating management's plans for future actions generally include some or all of the following:

- analysing cash flow, profit and other relevant forecasts, and discussing these forecasts with management;
- analysing the entity's latest available interim financial statements and discussing these with management;
- reading the terms of debentures and loan agreements, and determining whether any of these have been breached;
- reading the minutes of shareholders' and directors' meetings, and those of other relevant committees (such as the audit committee), for any reference to financing difficulties;
- enquiring of the entity's lawyers about the existence of litigation and claims against the client and the reasonableness of management's assessments of their outcome and estimate of their financial implications;
- confirming the existence, legality and enforceability of arrangements to provide financial support to, or receive financial support from, related and third parties, and assessing the financial position of these parties;
- evaluating the entity's plans in respect of unfilled customer orders;
- evaluating subsequent events to identify those that affect the entity's ability to continue as a going concern.

(iii) Completion and review phase

During the completion and review phase of the audit, auditors need to reconsider, and if necessary revise, their preliminary assessment of the entity's status as a going concern. They should determine and document the extent of their concern, if any, about the entity's ability to continue as a going concern and decide whether to obtain formal written representations from the client's directors confirming their considered view that the entity is a going concern, together with supporting assumptions or qualifications, as necessary. This generally applies when auditors consider there are significant uncertainties regarding their auditees' ability to remain in existence.

However, this is not the end of the story for auditors. They must also decide whether financial statement disclosure is required about uncertainties regarding the entity's continued existence. As expressed in ISA 570:

> Based on the audit evidence obtained, the auditor shall conclude whether, in the auditor's judgment, a material uncertainty exists related to events or conditions that, individually or collectively, may cast significant doubt on the entity's ability to continue as a going concern. A material uncertainty exists when the magnitude of its potential impact and likelihood of occurence is such that, in the auditor's judgment, appropriate disclosure of the nature and implications of the uncertainty is necessary for ... the fair presentation of the financial statements ... (para 17)

(iv) Reporting phase

When the auditor believes there is material uncertainty about the entity's ability to continue as a going concern, (s)he needs to determine whether the relevant matter(s) is adequately disclosed in the financial statements. More specifically, the auditor is required to conclude whether the financial statements:

(a) adequately describe the principal events or conditions that raise significant doubt about the entity's ability to continue as a going concern and management's plans to deal with these events or conditions; and

(b) disclose clearly that there is a material uncertainty relating to events or conditions that may cast significant doubt on the entity's ability to continue as a going concern and, therefore, it may be unable to realise its assets and discharge its liabilities in the normal course of business (ISA 570, para 18).

The various reporting options available to the auditor in relation to a going concern uncertainty are depicted in Figure 13.5. As may be seen from Figure 13.5, when the auditor considers the uncertainty is adequately disclosed, an unqualified audit opinion is appropriate. However, the auditor is required to highlight in an Emphasis of Matter paragraph[17] in the audit report:

(a) the existence of a material uncertainty relating to the event or condition that gives rise to significant doubt about the entity's ability to continue as a going concern; and

(b) the note in the financial statements that discloses the relevant matters.

---

[17] The various types of audit report, and Emphasis of Matter paragraphs, are discussed in Chapter 14.

Figure 13.5: Auditors' reporting options in relation to a going concern uncertainty

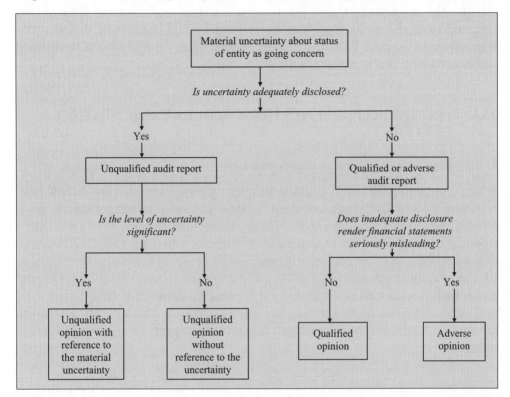

Should the auditor consider that the going concern uncertainties are not adequately disclosed in the financial statements, in most cases, a qualified opinion should be expressed in the audit report and specific reference should be made to the fact that there is a material uncertainty which gives rise to significant doubt about the entity's ability to continue as a going concern.

In circumstances where auditors conclude that financial statement disclosures regarding material uncertainty about the entity's status as a going concern are seriously misleading, they are required to express an adverse opinion. They are similarly required to express an adverse opinion if the financial statements have been prepared on a going concern basis and the auditors consider that adoption of this basis is inappropriate. However, we should note that the latter situation arises only in extreme circumstances, such as impending liquidation.

From the above discussion it is evident that auditors' responsibilities in relation to assessing auditees' ability to continue as going concerns are fairly exacting. However, by helping to ensure that uncertainties about the propriety of an entity adopting the going concern assumption are identified, evaluated and adequately disclosed in the financial statements and, where appropriate, referred to in the audit report, auditors help to enable users of the financial statements to assess for themselves the impact of any major uncertainties and the consequent risk to the viability of the entity.

13.5 WRITTEN REPRESENTATIONS AND REPRESENTATION LETTERS

13.5.1 Importance of written representations

When conducting an audit, auditors frequently have cause to rely on information given to them by management – especially when audit evidence from alternative sources is not available. Examples include management's responses to auditors' enquiries about instances of fraud or other illegal acts known to management, and management's intentions with respect to holding or disposing of a long-term investment. As part of the completion and review stage of the audit, auditors seek to have significant representations made by management and other relevant parties within the auditee recorded in writing. These are known as 'written representations' and are documented in 'representation letters'.

Technically, these letters are written by the client's directors (with input from other relevant parties) to the auditor but, in practice, they are normally prepared by the auditor and signed by the directors. They have two primary purposes, namely:

- to obtain evidence that the client's directors acknowledge their responsibility for the entity's financial statements, and for making available complete information to the auditor;[18] and
- to place on record management's (and other relevant parties') responses to enquiries by the auditor that relate to specific assertions about classes

---

[18] We note in Chapter 5 (sections 5.2.2 and 5.2.7) that the Companies Act 2006 (CA 2006) requires the directors of companies to:
  (i) provide complete information and explanations to the auditor as and when they are requested to do so (s. 499); and
  (ii) to state in their directors' report that, as far as each director is aware:
      – there is no relevant information of which the company's auditor is unaware, and
      – (s)he has taken all necessary steps to become aware of any relevant audit information, and establish that the auditor is aware of that information (s. 418).
Additionally, under the CA 2006, s. 501, if any person knowingly or recklessly makes a written or oral statement to the auditor that is misleading, false or deceptive in a material particular, they are guilty of an offence which can result in imprisonment for up to two years or a fine up to an unlimited maximum. Therefore, under the provisions of CA 2006, company directors are legally bound to provide complete and truthful information to the company's auditor.

of transactions, account balances or other disclosures in the financial statements. These written representations ensure there is no misunderstanding between management and the auditor as to what was said – and provide management with an opportunity to correct any response the auditor has misinterpreted. They also ensure that management assumes responsibility for representations made to the auditor.

ISA 580: *Written representations* explains the importance of auditors obtaining written representations as follows:

> Written representations are necessary information that the auditor requires in connection with the audit of the entity's financial statements. Accordingly, similar to responses to inquiries, written representations are audit evidence. [However,] ... they do not provide sufficient appropriate audit evidence on their own about any of the matters with which they deal. ... [Nevertheless,] if management modifies or does not provide the requested written representations, it may alert the auditor to the possibility that one or more significant issues may exist. Further, a request for written, rather than oral, representations in many cases may prompt management to consider such matters more rigorously, thereby enhancing the quality of the representations. (paras 3, 4, A1)

13.5.2   From whom, and about what, should written representations be requested?

In order for written representations to have value for the auditor, they must be requested from an appropriate party. Accordingly, ISA 580 requires auditors to "request written representations from management with appropriate responsibilities for the financial statements and knowledge of the matters concerned" (para 8). In practice, the directors (or, more correctly, if the company has one, members of its audit committee) generally sign representation letters but they usually seek input (or information) from senior executives or other employees who are particularly knowledgeable about the preparation of the financial statements and the assertions therein, and individuals who have specialised knowledge about matters for which written representations are requested. ISA 580, para A6, explains:

> Such individuals may include:
> - An actuary responsible for actuarially determined accounting measurements.
> - Staff engineers who may have responsibility for and specialized knowledge about environmental liability measurements.
> - Internal counsel [i.e., in-house lawyers] who may provide information essential to provisions for legal claims.

While some matters addressed in representation letters are unique to the particular client and audit engagement, others, such as the following, are required by Auditing Standards and are, therefore, invariably included. In accordance with ISAs, auditors request the auditee's directors to provide written representations confirming:

- they have fulfilled their responsibility for preparing and presenting the financial statements as set out in the audit engagement letter[19] and, more particularly, that the financial statements are prepared and presented in accordance with the applicable financial reporting framework[20] (ISA 580, para 10);
- all transactions have been recorded and are reflected in the financial statements (ISA 580, para 11);
- they have provided the auditor with all relevant information as agreed in the audit engagement letter and required by the Companies Act 2006 (ISA 580, para 11);
- they are responsible for the design, implementation and maintenance of internal control to prevent and detect fraud, and they have disclosed to the auditor:
    - the results of their assessment of the risk that the financial statements may be materially misstated as a result of fraud;
    - any known fraud, or suspected fraud, affecting the entity that involves executives, employees who have significant roles in internal control, or others where the fraud could have a material effect on the financial statements;
    - any known allegations of fraud, or suspected fraud, affecting the entity's financial statements communicated by employees, former employees, analysts, regulators or others (ISA 240: *The auditor's responsibilities relating to fraud*, para 39; IAASB, 2006a); and
    - all known actual, or possible, instances of non-compliance with laws and regulations whose effects should be considered when preparing the financial statements (ISA 250: *Consideration of laws and regulations*, para 16; IAASB, 2008b);
- their belief that:
    - the effects of misstatements identified by the auditor which the directors have refused to correct (as set out in, or attached to, the written representations) are immaterial, individually and in aggregate, to the financial statements as a whole (ISA 450: *Evaluation of misstatements identified during the audit*, para 14);[21]

---

[19] These letters are discussed in Chapter 8, section 8.3. The directors' responsibilities should be described in the representation letter in the same manner as they are described in the audit engagement letter (ISA 580: *Written representations*, para 12).

[20] International Accounting (or Financial Reporting) Standards or UK Generally Accepted Accounting Practice (as applicable; see Chapter 5, section 5.2.2).

[21] As we explain in Chapter 14, section 14.8, as an element of the auditor's governance communication to the directors, the auditor reports misstatements identified during the audit which the senior executives have refused to correct. The directors have responsibility for the financial statements so it is their prerogative to decide which, if any, of the uncorrected misstatements are to be corrected. The written representations the auditor obtains from the directors confirms their belief that any misstatements that remain uncorrected are immaterial to the financial statements.

- significant assumptions underlying significant estimates included in the financial statements are reasonable (ISA 540: *Auditing acounting estimates . . .* , para 22; IAASB, 2008c);
- all events subsequent to the date of the financial statements, for which the applicable financial reporting framework requires adjustment or disclosure, have been adjusted or disclosed (ISA 560: *Subsequent events,* para 9);
- in respect of related party relationships and transactions:
    - the information provided to the auditor is complete; that is, the identity of the entity's related parties, and all of the related party relationships and transactions of which the directors are aware, have been disclosed to the auditor, and
    - the accounting for, and disclosure of, related party relationships and transactions is in accordance with the requirements of the applicable financial reporting framework (ISA 550: *Related parties*, para 26; IAASB 2008d).

ISA 580: *Written representations*, para A12, notes that auditors may also consider it necessary to request written representations from the directors confirming that:
- the selection and application of accounting policies are appropriate;
- the following matters, where relevant, have been recognised, measured and/or disclosed in accordance with the applicable financial reporting framework:
    - plans or intentions that may affect the carrying value or classification of assets and liabilities;
    - liabilities, both actual and contingent;
    - title to or control over assets, liens or encumbrances on assets, and assets pledged as collateral; and
    - aspects of laws, regulations and contractual agreements that may affect the financial statements, including non-compliance therewith.

Additionally, in some circumstances auditors may consider it necessary to obtain written representations about specific financial statement assertions in order to corroborate other audit evidence. This applies, in particular, in cases where auditors need to be assured that information is complete or the directors' judgment or intent is involved. For example: "if the intent of management is important to the valuation basis for investments, it may not be possible to obtain sufficient appropriate audit evidence without a written representation from management about its intentions" (ISA 580, para A15).

Despite the acknowledged need for auditors to obtain written representations from management, it is important to note that auditors cannot just accept these representations without question. Written representations do not, by themselves, provide sufficient appropriate audit evidence about the truth and fairness of the financial statements or specific assertions about classes of transactions, account balances or other disclosures. They serve to corroborate, not provide a substitute for, evidence the auditor should obtain through other audit procedures.[22] For example, a written response to a specific inquiry about the cost of an asset is not a substitute for audit evidence relating to the cost of the asset the auditor would ordinarily be expected to obtain by other means. In other cases, auditors may obtain audit evidence that is inconsistent with written representations provided by management. They cannot merely accept the written representation as 'correct'; as we explain below, they must perform alternative procedures to resolve the inconsistency.

13.5.3 Problematic, or the non-provision of, written representations

If a written representation from management appears to be inconsistent with other audit evidence, auditors need to perform additional audit procedures to determine the reasons for the inconsistency. If, after performing those procedures, they have reason to doubt the reliability of management's written representation, ISA 580 requires them to reconsider their assessment of the integrity of management, and determine the effect this may have on the reliability of other representations (oral and written), audit evidence in general, and their assessment of the risk of material misstatements in the financial statements. If the reconsideration of their risk assessment results in its revision, additional audit procedures will need to be planned and performed in response to the newly assessed risk (ISA 580, paras 17, A25).

In some cases, unreliable written representations from management, or management's failure to provide requested written representations, may cause the auditor to question management's commitment to, and enforcement of, expected standards of competence, communication, integrity, ethical values, and diligence. In such cases, the auditor is required to:
  (a) Discuss the matter with management [or, more pertinently, the directors or audit committee];
  (b) Reevaluate the integrity of management and evaluate the effect this may have on the reliability of representations (oral or written) and audit evidence in general; and
  (c) Take appropriate actions, including determining the possible effect on the opinion in the auditor's report.... (ISA 580, para 19)

---

[22] This corresponds to one of the principles enunciated by Moffit J in the *Pacific Acceptance* case discussed in Chapter 5, section 5.3, namely: An auditor has a paramount duty to check material matters for him- or herself. However, reliance may be placed on enquiries from others where it is reasonable to do so. Nevertheless, reliance on others is to be regarded as an aid to, and not a substitute for, the auditor's own procedures.

The auditor may also consider withdrawing from the engagement unless the directors implement appropriate corrective measures. However, as ISA 580 observes, even if such measures are implemented: "[they] may not be sufficient to enable the auditor to issue an unmodified [i.e., clean] audit opinion" (para A26).

In the event that management fails to provide written representations confirming that:
  (i)   they have fulfilled their responsibilities for preparing and presenting financial statements that give a true and fair view of the entity's financial position and performance and comply with the applicable financial reporting framework; and
  (ii) they have provided the auditor with all relevant information; and
  (iii) all of the entity's transactions have been recorded and are reflected in the financial statements,
or the auditor concludes that the written representations provided are unreliable, ISA 580, para 20, specifies that the auditor should take the extreme step of disclaiming an opinion on the financial statements. [23]

13.5.4   Form and content of representation letters

Figure 13.6 presents an example of a representation letter appropriate for use in the audit of a company where neither the company's going concern status nor the completeness and reliability of the written representations is in question. It should be noted that the letter is prepared on the auditee's letterhead, is addressed to the auditor and is dated. The date should be the same as, or "as near as practicable to, but not after," (ISA 580, para 14) that of the audit report as that date signals the end of the period during which the auditor has considered subsequent events and other audit evidence.

13.6   FINAL REVIEW OF AUDIT EVIDENCE, CONCLUSION AND CONFERENCE

13.6.1   Final review of the financial statements and audit working papers

Towards the end of the completion and review phase of the audit, auditors:
  (i)   perform analytical procedures;
  (ii) evaluate the effect of uncorrected misstatements;
  (iii) conduct an overall review of the financial statements; and
  (iv) evaluate the audit evidence gathered during the audit and conclusions reached thereon.
We discuss each of these audit steps below.

---

[23] Disclaimers of audit opinion are explained in Chapter 14, section 14.5.

Figure 13.6:   Example of a representation letter

(Company letterhead)

(To Auditor)   (Date)

This representation letter is provided in connection with your audit of the financial statements of ABC Company for the year ended 31 December 20X9 for the purpose of expressing an opinion as to whether the financial statements give a true and fair view in accordance with International Financial Reporting Standards.

We confirm, to the best of our knowledge and belief, having made such enquiries as we considered necessary for the purpose of appropriately informing ourselves:

Financial Statements
- We have fulfilled our responsibilities for the preparation and presentation of the financial statements as set out in the terms of the audit engagement dated 30 September 20X8 and, in particular, the financial statements give a true and fair view in accordance with International Financial Reporting Standards.
- Significant assumptions used by us in making accounting estimates, including those measured at fair value, are reasonable.
- Related party relationships and transactions have been appropriately accounted for and disclosed in accordance with the requirements of International Financial Reporting Standards.
- All events subsequent to the date of the financial statements and for which International Financial Reporting Standards require adjustment or disclosure have been adjusted or disclosed.
- The effects of uncorrected misstatements are immaterial, both individually and in the aggregate, to the financial statements as a whole. A list of the uncorrected misstatements is attached to the representation letter.
- We confirm that:
  - Our selection and application of accounting policies is appropriate.
  - All plans or intentions that may materially alter the carrying value or classification of assets and liabilities in the financial statements have been accounted for or disclosed in accordance with International Financial Reporting Standards.
  - All liabilities, both actual and contingent, have been recorded and, where appropriate, disclosed in accordance with International Financial Reporting Standards.
  - The entity has satisfactory title to, or control over, all assets disclosed in the financial statements and, where appropriate, all liens or encumbrances on these assets have been disclosed in accordance with International Financial Reporting Standards.
  - We have complied with the aspects of contractual agreements that could have a material effect on the financial statements and instances of non-compliance have been disclosed in accordance with International Financial Reporting Standards.

Information provided
- We have provided you with:
  - All information that is relevant to the preparation and presentation of the financial statements, such as records, documentation, and other matters that support the financial statements;
  - Additional information that you have requested from us; and
  - Unrestricted access to those within the entity.
- All transactions have been recorded in the accounting records and are reflected in the financial statements.
- We have disclosed to you the results of our assessment of the risk that the financial statements may be materially misstated as a result of fraud.
- We have disclosed to you all information in relation to fraud or suspected fraud that we are aware of and that affects the entity and involves:
  - Management;
  - Employees who have significant roles in internal control; or
  - Others where the fraud could have a material effect on the financial statements.
- We have disclosed to you all information in relation to allegations of fraud, or suspected fraud, affecting the entity's financial statements communicated by employees, former employees, analysts, regulators or others.
- We have disclosed to you all known actual or possible non-compliance with laws and regulations whose effects should be considered when preparing financial statements.
- We have disclosed to you the identity of the entity's related parties and all the related party relationships and transactions of which we are aware.

Director   Director

Source: Adapted from ISA 580: *Written representations*, Appendix 2

(i) Analytical procedures

We note in Chapter 8, section 8.5, that analytical procedures are used in three stages of the audit – as risk assessment procedures, substantive tests, and in the final review of the financial statements.[24] During the final review stage, analytical procedures are used to corroborate (or challenge) conclusions drawn from the results of tests performed on the classes of transactions, account balances and disclosures in the audit segments and, thereby, to assist the auditor form a conclusion about the absence (or otherwise) of material misstatement in the financial statements as a whole. Analytical procedures performed for the overall review of the financial statements may reveal unusual fluctuations and/or unexpected results or relationships that are inconsistent with other audit evidence. In this event, the auditor is required to make enquiries of management about the findings and to evaluate management's responses in the light of the auditor's understanding of the entity and its environment and audit evidence gathered during the audit. If management is unable to provide an adequate explanation of the findings, the auditor is required to perform additional audit procedures to resolve the matter (ISA 520: *Analytical procedures*, paras 10, A18, A19).

(ii) Evaluation of uncorrected misstatements

In Chapter 11, section 11.5, we note that, as the audit progresses, the auditor is required to accumulate all identified misstatements ["other than those that are clearly trivial" (ISA 450: *Evaluation of misstatements identified during the audit*, para 5)], distinguishing between those that are factual, judgmental and projected. We also note that the auditor is required to communicate the accumulated misstatements to the appropriate level of management (i.e., senior executives) on a timely basis and to request them to correct them. In the event that the senior executives refuse to correct some or all of the misstatements, the auditor is required to obtain an understanding of their reasons for so doing and to consider that understanding when evaluating whether the financial statements as a whole are free from material misstatement (ISA 450, paras 8, 9).

As we observe in section 13.5 (footnote 21) above, the auditee's directors are responsible for the entity's financial statements; therefore, it is their prerogative to decide which, if any, of the misstatements the senior executives have refused to correct are to be corrected. However, in cases where the directors partially or fully support their executives' stance, and misstatements identified by the auditor remain uncorrected, the auditor is required to obtain written representations from the auditee's directors stating that they believe the uncorrected misstatements are immaterial to the financial statements. However, the

---

[24] A summary of the use, objective and nature of analytical procedures is provided in Figure 8.2.

auditor cannot leave the matter there. Although the directors may consider that uncorrected misstatements are immaterial to the financial statements, it is the task of the auditor to decide whether this is, or is not, the case.

Before evaluating the effect of uncorrected misstatements on the financial statements, ISA 450, para 10, requires the auditor to re-assess planning materiality and tolerable error thresholds to determine whether they remain appropriate in the context of the entity's actual financial results.[25] Once the appropriate levels of planning materiality and tolerable error have been determined, the auditor is required to evaluate whether the uncorrected misstatements are material, individually or in aggregate, to the financial statements. Each misstatement is to be considered separately in order to evaluate its effect on relevant classes of transactions, account balances or disclosures. This includes ascertaining whether the tolerable error of the particular class of transactions, account balance or disclosure, if any, has been exceeded. In evaluating the effect of the misstatements on the financial statements, the auditor is to consider their size and their nature, in relation both to particular classes of transactions, account balances and disclosures and to the financial statements as a whole, and also the circumstances of their occurrence.

In respect of evaluating the effect of individual misstatements, ISA 450 explains:

> If an individual misstatement is judged to be material, it is unlikely that it can be offset by other misstatements. For example, if revenue has been materially overstated, the financial statements as a whole will be materially misstated, even if the effect of the misstatement on earnings is completely offset by an equivalent overstatement of expenses. It may be appropriate to offset misstatements within the same account balance or class of transactions; however, the risk that further undetected misstatements may exist is [to be] considered before concluding that offsetting even immaterial misstatements is appropriate. (para A14)

Some uncorrected misstatements may involve incorrect classification rather than incorrect amounts. When determining whether or not a classification misstatement is material the auditor needs to consider qualitative characteristics

---

[25] In Chapter 9, section 9.3.1, we explain that, during the planning stage of the audit, planning materiality and tolerable error are frequently determined on the basis of estimates of the entity's financial performance and position because the entity's actual financial results are not then known. As the audit progresses, the auditor is required to revise planning materiality and/or tolerable error levels for classes of transactions, account balances or disclosures if audit evidence gathered indicates that such revision is appropriate. Therefore, any significant revision of planning materiality and tolerable error levels is likely to have been made before evaluating the effect of uncorrected misstatements on the financial statements. Nevertheless, when evaluating the effect of uncorrected misstatements, the auditor may consider it appropriate in the circumstances and findings of the audit to lower the level(s) of planning materiality and/or tolerable error for certain classes of transactions, account balances or disclosures and, in this event, further audit procedures may need to be performed to ensure that sufficient appropriate audit evidence is obtained on which to base the audit opinion.

relating to the misclassification, such as its effect on debt or other contractual covenants, the effect on individual line items or subtotals, and the effect on key ratios. In some circumstances, the auditor may conclude that a classification misstatement is not material in the context of the financial statements as a whole even though it may exceed the materiality levels applied in evaluating other misstatements. For example, a misstatement between balance sheet line items may not be considered material in the context of the financial statements as a whole when the effect of the misclassification is small in relation to the size of the related balance sheet line items, and the misclassification does not affect the income statement or any key ratios (ISA 450, para A15).

In some circumstances, the auditor may judge misstatements that fall below the levels of planning materiality or tolerable error for a particular class of transactions, account balance or disclosure, to be material, individually or when considered together with other misstatements. ISA 450, para A16, explains that such circumstances include the extent to which the misstatement:

- affects compliance with regulatory requirements, debt covenants or other contractual requirements; or
- relates to the incorrect selection or application of an accounting policy that has an immaterial effect on the current period's financial statements but is likely to have a material effect on future periods' financial statements;
- masks a change in earnings or other trends, especially in the context of general economic and industry conditions;
- affects ratios used to evaluate the entity's financial position, results of operations or cash flows;
- has the effect of increasing management compensation, for example, by ensuring that the requirements for the award of bonuses or other incentives are satisfied;
- is significant having regard to the auditor's understanding of known previous communications to the financial statements' users, for example, in relation to earnings forecasts;
- is an omission of information not specifically required by the applicable financial reporting framework but which, in the auditor's judgment, is important to the financial statement users' understanding of the financial position, financial performance or cash flows of the entity;
- affects other information that will be communicated in documents containing the audited financial statements (such as the annual report) that may reasonably be expected to influence the economic decisions of users of the financial statements.

The cumulative effect of immaterial uncorrected misstatements in prior periods may have a material effect on the current period's financial statements. As a result, auditors' consideration of uncorrected misstatements is not limited to the current period. As indicated above, they must also be conscious of the effect of uncorrected errors in the current year affecting a future period; similarly, they are required to consider the effect of uncorrected misstatements in prior periods on relevant classes of transactions, account balances or disclosures, and the financial statements as a whole, in the current period (ISA 450, paras 11, A18).

(iii)   Review of the overall presentation of the financial statements

During the completion and review stage of the audit, auditors are required to evaluate the overall presentation of the financial statements and their conformity (or otherwise) with the applicable financial reporting framework. This involves, *inter alia*, evaluating whether the information presented in the individual financial statements and the notes thereto is properly classified and described, and whether the form, arrangement and content of the financial statements are appropriate. The evaluation includes consideration of the terminology used, the amount of detail provided and the clarity with which the measurement bases are disclosed (ISA 330: *The auditor's responses to assessed risks*, paras 25, A55; IAASB, 2006b).

(iv)   Evaluation of the audit evidence gathered

Before reaching a final opinion on the audited financial statements, auditors are required to determine:
  (a) whether their assessment of the risks of material misstatement at the assertion level remains appropriate; and
  (b) whether sufficient appropriate audit evidence has been gathered in relation to each assertion in each class of transactions, account balance and disclosure in the various audit segments (ISA 330, paras 26, 27; IAASB, 2006b).
Let us examine the reasons for these requirements a little more closely.

(a)   Re-evaluation of risk assessment

Auditors need to re-evaluate their assessment of the risks of material misstatement at the assertion level at this stage of the audit (i.e., after the completion of audit testing) because the results of audit procedures used to test the assertions in each class of transactions, account balance and disclosure, and/or the analytical procedures performed for the overall review of the financial statements [as in *(i)* above] may indicate the existence of a previously unidentified internal control deficiency or material misstatement. If this is the case, the auditor's risk assessment may need to be amended, and additional audit procedures planned and performed to address the newly assessed risk (ISA 330, para A56; IAASB, 2006b).

(b) Sufficient appropriate audit evidence

Before concluding the audit, the auditor (i.e., the audit engagement partner) is required to "be satisfied that sufficient appropriate audit evidence has been obtained to support the conclusions reached and for the auditor's report to be issued" (ISA 220: *Quality control for an audit of financial statements*, para 16; IAASB, 2008a). This means the engagement partner needs to establish whether sufficient appropriate audit evidence has been gathered to form a conclusion about the assertions in each class of transactions, account balance and disclosure in the various audit statements and for the financial statements as a whole. ISA 330, para A58 (IAASB, 2006b), explains that the auditor's judgment as to what constitutes sufficient appropriate audit evidence will be affected by a number of factors, including the following:

- the auditor's understanding of the auditee and its environment (including the effectiveness of its internal controls);
- the effectiveness of management's responses, and controls, to address identified risks;
- the significance of potential misstatements in an assertion and its likelihood individually, or collectively with other misstatements, of having a material effect on the financial statements;
- the source and reliability (and hence the persuasiveness) of the audit evidence gathered;
- experience gained in previous audits with respect to similar potential misstatements.

In order to determine that sufficient appropriate audit evidence has been obtained, the engagement partner reviews the work conducted during the audit, as documented in the audit working papers, and holds discussions with audit team members as (s)he thinks appropriate. The review of the audit documentation is designed to achieve a number of objectives. These include ensuring that:

- sufficient appropriate audit evidence has been collected in each audit segment, and for the audit as a whole, on which to base an audit opinion;
- all audit work has been properly performed, documented and reviewed;
- conclusions reached in relation to specific audit objectives are consistent with the results obtained from the audit procedures performed;
- all questions and difficulties arising during the course of the audit have been resolved;
- the information presented in the financial statements complies with statutory and regulatory requirements;
- the accounting policies adopted are in accordance with the financial reporting framework adopted by the entity, and are appropriate to the entity, properly disclosed and consistently applied;

- the financial statements as a whole, and the assertions contained therein, are consistent with the auditor's knowledge of the entity's business and the results of audit procedures performed;
- the presentation of the financial statements (including their form, content and manner of disclosure) is appropriate.

Audit engagement partners frequently use checklists to ensure that all aspects of the financial statements are properly covered.

On the basis of the review of the audit working papers, together with knowledge gained as the audit has progressed, the audit engagement partner forms an opinion as to whether or not the financial statements give a true and fair view of the reporting entity's state of affairs (financial position) and financial performance and comply with the applicable financial reporting framework. However, for all but small audits, in order to ensure:

- the opinion formed is consistent with the audit evidence collected (as documented in the working papers);
- sufficient appropriate audit evidence has been gathered; and
- the working papers provide evidence that the audit has been carried out in accordance with International Standards on Auditing,

a second audit partner, who has not been involved in the audit, usually reviews the audit working papers. Indeed, as we note in Chapter 7, section 7.6.4, for all listed companies and other companies that meet the audit firm's criteria for an engagement quality control review, ISA 220 (IAASB, 2008a) requires an engagement quality control review to be performed.

ISA 220 (IAASB, 2008a) explains that an engagement quality control review:

- includes an objective evaluation of the significant judgments made by the audit engagement team, and the conclusions reached in formulating the opinion expressed in the auditor's report; and
- involves:
  - discussion with the audit engagement partner, a review of the financial statements and the proposed auditor's report, and consideration of whether the proposed auditor's report is appropriate, and
  - a review of selected working papers relating to the significant judgments the audit team made and the conclusions they reached (paras 19, 20).

The Standard also explains (para A20) that matters of significant judgment include:

- Significant risks identified during the engagement ... and the responses to those risks ..., including the engagement team's assessment of, and response to, the risk of fraud.

- Judgments made, particularly with respect to materiality and significant risks.
- The significance and disposition of corrected and uncorrected misstatements identified during the audit.
- The matters to be communicated to [the directors] and, where applicable, other parties such as regulatory bodies.[26,27]

13.6.2 Review of unaudited information

Even if everything is found to be in order, before the auditor can prepare the appropriate audit report a further audit procedure needs to be performed. ISA 720: *The auditor's responsibility in relation to other information in documents containing audited financial statements* requires auditors to review the portions of their auditees' annual reports or other documents containing the audited financial statements that are not subject to audit (i.e., 'other information') to determine whether they contain information which is materially inconsistent with the financial statements and, in so doing, identify any statement in the other information which is factually incorrect (paras 6, 14). This accords with the fundamental principle of external auditing – *Association*, which states:

> Auditors allow their reports to be included in documents containing other information only if they consider that the additional information is not in conflict with the matters covered by their report and they have no cause to believe it to be misleading. [Auditing Practices Board (APB), 2008, Appendix 2]

We can see from the above that ISA 720 addresses two types of problem:
(a) misstatements of fact in the other information; and
(b) inconsistencies between the financial statements and the other information.

The Standard defines other information, inconsistency and misstatement of fact as follows:

> Other information – Financial and non-financial information (other than the financial statements and the auditor's report thereon) which is included, either by law, regulation or custom, in a document containing audited financial statements and the auditor's report thereon. (para 5a)

> Inconsistency – Other information that contradicts information contained in the audited financial statements. A material inconsistency may raise doubt about the audit conclusions drawn from audit evidence previously obtained and, possibly, about the basis for the auditors' opinion on the financial statements. (para 5b)

---

[26] Further details about engagement quality control reviews are provided in Chapter 7, section 7.6.4.

[27] Auditors' communication with their auditees' directors and parties external to the entity are discussed in Chapter 14.

Misstatement of fact – Other information, that is unrelated to matters appearing in the audited financial statements that is incorrectly stated or presented. A material misstatement of fact may undermine the credibility of the document containing the audited financial statements. (para 5c)

(a) Misstatements of fact in other information

If the auditor discovers an apparent misstatement of fact in the other information, (s)he is required to discuss the matter with the entity's directors (or audit committee) and/or senior executives. ISA 720 (para A10) observes that the auditor may not be in a position to evaluate the validity of some of the statements in the other information or the directors'/senior executives' responses to his or her enquiries. In such a case, the auditor may conclude that the matter in question reflects a valid difference of judgment or opinion rather than a misstatement of fact. However, if, after discussing the matter with the directors/senior executives, the auditor stills considers there is a misstatement of fact, (s)he is required to request the directors to consult with a qualified third party, such as the entity's lawyer(s), and the auditor is to consider the advice received. In the event that the directors continue to refuse to effect a correction in the other information that the auditor considers necessary, "the auditor shall notify [the directors] of the auditor's concern regarding the other information and take any further appropriate action.... [This] may include obtaining advice from the auditor's legal counsel" (ISA 720, paras 13, A9). As we observe below, in extreme cases, it may also extend to the auditor resigning from the engagement.

A special situation arises if the auditee is a company listed on the London Stock Exchange and the misstatement the directors refuse to correct relates to a required disclosure in respect of the company's compliance (or otherwise) with the provisions of *The Combined Code on Corporate Governance* (FRC, 2006), and the disclosure is subject to the auditor's review.[28] In this case, the auditor is required to describe the matter in a separate paragraph in the audit report. The paragraph is to be headed 'Other Matter(s)' and is to be located after the Opinion paragraph and, if applicable, an Emphasis of Matter paragraph (APB, 2006a, paras 20, 55).[29]

(b) Material inconsistency

If auditors discover a material inconsistency between the other information and the financial statements, they need to determine whether it is the financial statements or the other information which requires amendment. However, in

---

[28] Auditors' duties in respect of the Listing Rules of the United Kingdom Listing Authority (a division of the Financial Services Authority) are discussed in Chapter 5, section 5.5.

[29] Different forms of audit report are discussed in Chapter 14.

either case, they should seek to resolve the matter through discussion with the directors (or audit committee). If the financial statements are in error and the directors refuse to make the necessary adjustments, the auditor is required to express a modified opinion in the audit report (ISA 720, para 9). However, if it is the other information which requires amendment and the directors refuse to make the amendment requested by the auditor, ISA 720, para 10, provides the auditor with three options, namely:

- to describe the material inconsistency in an Other Matter(s) paragraph in the audit report;
- to withhold the audit report; or
- to withdraw from the engagement. (We expand on this option below.)

Two other options may apply to auditors in the UK under the Companies Act (CA) 2006.

1. If the auditee is a limited company (which applies to most companies) and the directors' report is inconsistent with the financial statements, the auditor has a statutory responsibility to refer to the inconsistency in the audit report (CA 2006, s. 496). ISA (UK and Ireland) 720 explains that inconsistencies include:

   - Differences between amounts or narrative appearing in the financial statements and the directors' report.
   - Differences between the bases of preparation of related items appearing in the financial statements and the directors' report, where the figures themselves are not directly comparable and the different bases are not disclosed.
   - Contradictions between figures contained in the financial statements and narrative explanations of those figures in the directors' report. (APB, 2006b, para 8)

2. The CA 2006, s. 502, provides auditors with the right to be heard at any general meeting of the company's shareholders on matters that concern them as auditors. Thus, they have an opportunity to highlight any material inconsistency between the other information in the company's annual report and the audited financial statements. Similarly, they can use this opportunity to draw members' attention to a misstatement of fact in the other information.

The CA 2006, s. 519, requires auditors of companies who cease to hold office as auditor to provide a written statement of any circumstances (s)he considers should be brought to the attention of the company's shareholders or creditors (or a statement that there are no such circumstances), and to send a copy of this statement to the Registrar of Companies. Hence, if, in extreme circumstances, the auditor of a company withdraws from an audit engagement as a consequence of a misstatement of fact in the other information or a material inconsistency between the other information and the audited financial statements, (s)he is required to provide a 'statement of circumstances' or of 'no circumstances'. It seems likely that, if the refusal by the auditee's directors to correct a material inconsistency or a misstatement of fact in the other information is sufficiently serious to prompt the auditor's resignation, then it is sufficiently serious to qualify as a circumstance that should be drawn to the attention of the company's shareholders. The CA 2006, s. 522, also requires auditors of companies who vacate office for any reason to notify the 'appropriate audit authority' and to send with their notice, the 'statement of circumstances' or of 'no circumstances': in the latter case, the auditor is required to provide a statement setting out the reasons for ceasing to hold office.[30]

13.6.3 Final conference

Once all audit matters have been resolved and the audit engagement partner (in consultation with senior audit team members and, in applicable cases, the engagement quality control reviewer) has reached a conclusion on the financial statements and prepared the audit report, a final conference is held between the client's directors (or its audit committee), the audit engagement partner and (usually) the audit manager. The conduct and findings of the audit are discussed, the financial statements are signed by one or more director[31] (if this has not already been done at a previous directors' meeting) and, finally, the audit report is signed and dated by the audit engagement partner.[32] It is important that the engagement partner does not sign the audit report prior to the directors signing the financial statements. By signing the financial statements, the directors signal their responsibility for, and acceptance of, the statements as presented. The auditor's report expresses an opinion on the financial statements prepared, presented and approved by the directors.[33]

The date of the audit report is of the utmost importance because it signifies the end of the period considered by the auditor when expressing an opinion on the financial statements. It marks the end of the 'subsequent period' in

---

[30] We discuss the requirements of auditors who cease to hold office and 'statements of circumstances' (or of 'no circumstances') in Chapter 5, section 5.2.5.

[31] The statutory requirement for one or more directors to sign the auditee's balance sheet is referred to in Chapter 5, section 5.2.2.

[32] As noted in Chapter 5 (sections 5.2.2 and 5.2.6), CA 2006, s. 505, requires the audit report to state the name of the auditor and, where the auditor is a firm, the name of the person who signed it as senior statutory auditor (in effect, the audit engagement partner).

[33] Cuthbert (1982) reports some salutary tales about what can happen if the auditor signs the audit report before the directors sign the financial statements.

which events may have occurred that impact on the truth and fairness of the financial statements as at the balance sheet date.

13.7 SUMMARY

In this chapter we have discussed the steps which constitute the completion and review phase of the audit. More specifically, we have examined the importance of, and procedures used for, the review for contingent liabilities and commitments, and the review for events (adjusting and non-adjusting) occurring subsequent to the balance sheet date. We have also discussed the auditor's duty with respect to the going concern assumption and the meaning and significance of written representations. Additionally, we have reviewed the steps involved in the final review of evidence gathered during the audit and the forming of an opinion with respect to the truth and fairness of the financial statements and their compliance with the applicable financial reporting framework. In the concluding sections of the chapter, we have drawn attention to the need for the auditor to review unaudited information in the client's annual report (or other documents containing the audited financial statements), and explained the significance of the date of the audit report and the importance of auditors signing their audit reports after the directors have signed the financial statements.

SELF-REVIEW QUESTIONS

13.1 Define (a) contingent liabilities and (b) commitments and explain briefly why contingent liabilities and commitments may present problems for the auditor.

13.2 List five procedures auditors commonly use during their review for contingent liabilities and commitments.

13.3 (a) Briefly distinguish between (i) adjusting and (ii) non-adjusting subsequent events.
(b) Give one specific example to illustrate each of these types of subsequent events.

13.4 (a) State the period which is subject to the auditor's review for subsequent events.
(b) List three procedures auditors commonly use during their review for subsequent events.

13.5 Explain briefly what is meant by the going concern assumption.

13.6 Explain briefly the auditor's responsibility for assessing the propriety of the auditee adopting the going concern assumption during:
   (a) the initial phase of the audit;
   (b) the evidence gathering phase of the audit;
   (c) the completion and review phase of the audit.

13.7 Explain briefly what is meant by written representations and outline three matters for which auditors are required to obtain such representations.

13.8 List four objectives of the audit engagement partner's final review of audit working papers.

13.9 Explain briefly the objectives of an engagement quality control review and how it is conducted.

13.10 Explain briefly the significance of dating the audit report.

REFERENCES

Auditing Practices Board (APB). (1995). Statement of Auditing Standards (SAS) 130: *The Going Concern Basis in Financial Statements*. London: APB.

Auditing Practices Board (APB). (2004). International Standard on Auditing (ISA) (UK and Ireland) 570: *Going Concern*. London: Financial Reporting Council.

Auditing Practices Board (APB). (2006a). *The Combined Code on Corporate Governance: Requirements of Auditors under the Listing Rules of the Financial Services Authority and Irish Stock Exchange*. Bulletin 2006/5. London: Financial Reporting Council.

Auditing Practices Board (APB). (2006b). International Standard on Auditing (ISA) (UK and Ireland) 720: *Other Information in Documents Containing Audited Financial Statements Section B – The Auditor's Statutory Reporting Responsibility in Relation to Directors' Reports*. London: Financial Reporting Council.

Auditing Practices Board (APB). (2008). *The Auditing Practices Board – Scope and Authority of Pronouncements (Revised)*. London: Financial Reporting Council.

Cuthbert, S. (1982). How easy to hoodwink the auditor! *Accountancy* **93**(1063), 136.

Dingell, J. (1985). Accountants must clean up their act. *Management Accounting* **66**(1), 21–23, 53–56.

Financial Reporting Council (FRC). (2006). *The Combined Code on Corporate Governance*. London: FRC.

International Accounting Standards Board (IASB). (2005). International Accounting Standard (IAS) 37: *Provisions, Contingent Liabilities and Contingent Assets*. London: IASB.

International Auditing and Assurance Standards Board (IAASB). (2006a).[34] International Standard on Auditing (ISA) 240 (Redrafted): *The Auditor's Responsibilities Relating to Fraud in an Audit of Financial Statements.* New York: International Federation of Accountants.

International Auditing and Assurance Standards Board (IAASB). (2006b). International Standard on Auditing (ISA) 330 (Redrafted): *The Auditor's Responses to Assessed Risks.* New York: International Federation of Accountants.

International Auditing and Assurance Standards Board (IAASB). (2008a, June**). International Standard on Auditing (ISA) 220 (Redrafted): *Quality Control for an Audit of Financial Statements.* New York: International Federation of Accountants.

International Auditing and Assurance Standards Board (IAASB). (2008b). International Standard on Auditing (ISA) 250 (Redrafted): *Consideration of Laws and Regulations in an Audit of Financial Statements.* New York: International Federation of Accountants.

International Auditing and Assurance Standards Board (IAASB). (2008c). International Standard on Auditing (ISA) 540 (Redrafted): *Auditing Accounting Estimates, Including Fair Value Accounting Estimates, and Related Disclosures.* New York: International Federation of Accountants.

International Auditing and Assurance Standards Board (IAASB). (2008d). International Standard on Auditing (ISA) 550 (Redrafted): *Related Parties.* New York: International Federation of Accountants.

Porter, B.A. (1993). An empirical study of the audit expectation-performance gap. *Accounting and Business Research*, **24**(93), 49–68.

ADDITIONAL READING

Bame-Aldred, C.W., and Kida, T. (2007). A comparison of auditor and client initial negotiation positions and tactics. *Accounting, Organizations and Society* **32**(6), 497–511.

Beattie, V., Fearnley, S., and Brandt, R. (2004). A grounded theory model of auditor-client negotiations. *International Journal of Auditing* **8**(1), 1–19.

Behn, B.K., Kaplan, S.E., and Krumwiede, K.R. (2001). Further evidence on the auditor's going-concern report: the influence of management plans. *Auditing: A Journal of Practice & Theory* **20**(1), 13–28.

Billing, K. (2007). Written representations. *Accountancy* **139**(1365), 84–85.

Carey, P.J., and Clarke, B. (2001). An investigation of Australian auditors' use of the management representation letter. *The British Accounting Review* **33**(1), 1–21.

Fargher, N.L., Mayorga, D., and Trotman, K.T. (2005). A field-based analysis of audit workpaper review. *Auditing: A Journal of Practice & Theory* **24**(2), 85–110.

---

[34] The status of ISAs referred to in this chapter is explained in the Important Note following the Preface to this book.

Knechel, W.R., and Vanstraelen, A. (2007). The relationship between auditor tenure and audit quality implied by going concern opinions. *Auditing: A Journal of Practice & Theory* **26**(1), 113–131.

Rau, S.E., and Moser, D.V. (1999). Does performing other audit tasks affect going-concern judgments? *The Accounting Review* **74**(4), 493–508.

Sanchez, M.H., Agoglia, C.P., and Hatfield, R.C. (2007). The effect of auditors' use of a reciprocity-based strategy on auditor-client negotiations. *The Accounting Review* **82**(1), 241–264.

Wilks, T.J. (2002). Predecisional distortion of evidence as a consequence of real-time audit review. *The Accounting Review* **77**(1), 51–68.

14 Auditors' Reports to Users of Financial Statements and to Management

LEARNING OBJECTIVES

After studying the material in this chapter you should be able to:
- state the auditor's statutory reporting obligation in respect of companies;
- explain what is required in order for financial statements to provide a true and fair view;
- explain what is meant by 'adequate accounting records';
- describe the format of the standard audit report used for companies in the United Kingdom;
- explain the various types of audit opinion expressed in audit reports and the circumstances in which each is appropriate;
- describe significant differences between the standard 'expanded' audit report and the former 'short form' report;
- discuss the advantages and disadvantages of (i) the 'expanded' audit report and (ii) the 'short form' report;
- discuss the advantages and disadvantages of (i) a standard form of audit report and (ii) a 'free form' report;
- explain the requirement for, and purpose and content of, auditors' communication of audit matters to those charged with the governance of companies.

The following publications and fundamental principles of auditing are particularly relevant to this chapter:

Publications:
- Companies Act 2006
- International Standard on Auditing (ISA) 260 (Redrafted): *Communication with those Charged with Governance* (IFAC, 2007)[1]
- International Standard on Auditing (ISA) 265 (Redrafted): *Communicating Deficiencies in Internal Control* (IFAC, 2007)*
- International Standard on Auditing (ISA) 700 (Redrafted): *Forming on Opinion and Reporting on Financial Statements* (IFAC, June 2008)**
- International Standard on Auditing (ISA) 705 (Redrafted): *Modifications to the Opinion in the Independent Auditor's Report* (IFAC, June 2008)**
- International Standard on Auditing (ISA) 706 (Redrafted): *Emphasis of Matter Paragraphs and Other Matter(s) Paragraphs in the Independent Auditor's Report* (IFAC, June 2008)**

Fundamental principles of external auditing included in *The Auditors' Code*:[2]
- Clear communication
- Providing value

---

[1] The status of ISAs referred to in this chapter is explained in the Important Note following the Preface to this book.

[2] The fundamental principles of external auditing are reproduced on the inside of the front cover of this book.

14.1 INTRODUCTION

For companies, the audit process culminates in the auditor's statutory report to shareholders. This report is the end product of the audit examination and communicates to shareholders, and other users of the company's financial statements, the auditor's conclusions about, amongst other things, the truth and fairness with which the statements portray the entity's financial position and performance and their compliance (or otherwise) with the relevant financial reporting framework and the Companies Act 2006. The auditor is also required to communicate with those charged with the company's governance (i.e., the board of directors). This usually covers various aspects of the audit and the entity's financial affairs but also highlights any significant deficiencies in the entity's internal control system discovered during the audit, and recommends ways in which these might be overcome. This communication is frequently referred to as a 'management letter' but is broader in scope than the (former) traditional management letter (which focused almost exclusively on internal control deficiencies and how they might be rectified). However, like the traditional management letter, the auditor's communication with the directors is a private communication and its contents are generally not revealed to shareholders or other third parties.[3]

In this chapter we discuss the statutory and professional reporting obligations of auditors of companies. We explore the issue of what is required for financial statements to be adjudged 'true and fair' and what is meant by 'adequate accounting records'. We also examine the format of standard audit reports and consider the various types of audit opinion the auditor may express and the circumstances in which each is appropriate. We observe that the audit report is frequently the auditor's only opportunity to communicate with users of the audited financial statements and we discuss the differences between, and the advantages and disadvantages of, the 'expanded' audit report currently in use and the former 'short form' report. We also consider the advantages and disadvantages of using a standard, rather than a 'free form' of audit report. Before concluding the chapter we address the topic of auditors' communications to those charged with the entity's governance, focusing in particular on their purpose and content.

---

[3] Nevertheless, there is an argument that, as company auditors are appointed by the shareholders (although they frequently delegate this responsibility to the directors; see Chapter 5, section 5.2.4) and audits are conducted primarily for the benefit of the shareholders, the 'management letter' should be made available to the shareholders.

14.2 AUDITORS' REPORTING OBLIGATIONS UNDER THE COMPANIES ACT 2006

As we note in Chapter 5, the Companies Act 2006 (CA 2006) places a major responsibility on auditors. First, it specifies that the directors of every company must prepare financial statements comprising a balance sheet and profit or loss account for each financial year (and, in the case of companies with subsidiaries, group financial statements).[4] These financial statements are required to:
- give a true and fair view of the company's (or group's) state of affairs as at the end of the financial year and of its profit or loss for the financial year;
- comply with the relevant financial reporting framework;[5]
- be properly prepared in accordance with CA 2006; and
- for the consolidated financial statements of groups whose securities are traded on the regulated market of any EU Member State, comply with EU Regulation (EC) No. 1606/2002 *on the application of International Accounting Standards* (EU, 2002).

The preparation of financial statements which meet the statutory requirements outlined above is a responsibility which belongs exclusively to the entity's directors. However, except in the case of exempt companies,[6] the Act places on auditors the responsibility of examining the financial statements and forming and expressing an opinion as to whether or not they meet the statutory requirements. Auditors are also required to form an opinion on whether:
- adequate accounting records have been kept by the company;
- proper returns have been received from branches not visited by the auditors;
- the financial statements are in agreement with the underlying accounting records;
- they have received all the information and explanations they required for the purposes of their audit;
- the information given in the directors' report is consistent with the financial statements.

In cases where auditors are of the opinion that any of these requirements have not been met, they are required to report that fact in their audit report. Additionally, for quoted companies, auditors are required to report on the auditable part of the directors' remuneration report stating whether, in their opinion, that

---

[4] See Chapter 5, footnote 12.

[5] International Financial Reporting Standards (IFRS; 'IAS accounts') or United Kingdom Generally Accepted Accounting Practice (UK GAAP; 'Companies Act accounts'). The requirements relating to these financial reporting frameworks are explained in Chapter 5, section 5.2.2 and footnote 13.

[6] See Chapter 5, section 5.2.2, for an explanation of companies exempted from an audit.

part of the directors' remuneration report has been properly prepared in accordance with CA 2006.[7]

Two of the matters about which the auditors must form an opinion require some explanation, namely:
  (i) adequate accounting records;
  (ii) a true and fair view.

(i) Adequate accounting records

CA 2006 (s. 386) requires all companies to maintain adequate accounting records. The Act explains that such records must be sufficient to show and explain the company's transactions and, amongst other things:

- disclose the company's financial position, with reasonable accuracy, at any time;
- enable the directors to prepare a balance sheet and profit and loss account which comply with the relevant reporting framework;
- record the day-to-day details of all receipts and payments of cash;
- provide details of the company's assets and liabilities.

Additionally for companies dealing in goods:

- provide details of stock (inventory) held by the company at the end of each financial year and the related stocktaking records;
- provide details of trading goods bought and sold (other than goods sold by way of ordinary retail trade). The records must be in sufficient detail to enable the goods, and the buyers and the sellers, to be identified.

It can be seen from these requirements that the Act is both specific and strict as regards the criteria to be met in order for a company's accounting records to be considered adequate. It does not, however, lay down any detailed requirements for particular procedures or controls to be implemented.

It is important to appreciate that, in *every* audit, auditors must form an opinion on whether or not adequate accounting records have been kept by the auditee. However, their opinion is only stated in the audit report in cases where they consider that adequate accounting records have *not* been kept.

(ii) A true and fair view

Although the directors of companies are required to prepare financial statements which give a true and fair view of their company's financial position and

---

[7] The 'auditable part of the directors' remuneration report' is specified in regulations to be issued by the Secretary of State pursuant to CA 2006, s. 421. Until such regulations are issued, those contained in Statutory Instrument 2002 No. 1986: *The Directors' Remuneration Report Regulations 2002* apply.

performance, neither legislation nor the courts have explained what is meant by a 'true and fair view'. This has led to conflicting interpretations. As Johnston, Edgar and Hays (1982) observed:

> It is clear that the interpretation applied by most accountants is that the words 'true and fair' have a technical meaning. It is also clear that many lawyers (as well as investors) are of the opinion that these words have a popular meaning which should be followed by those responsible for their application. (p. 259)

The following quotations serve to illustrate the opposing viewpoints of lawyers and accountants. First the lawyers:

> [I]t is probably not an exaggeration to assert that company accounts remain almost unintelligible to the general public, including shareholders and intending investors, and that practices continue which are difficult to reconcile with the statutory obligations that balance sheets give a true and fair view of the company's affairs and that the auditors certify that the accounts give a true and fair view of the company's affairs ... Essentially, the question is: are the accounts where there has been an undervaluation of assets[8] 'true'? ... 'True and fair' are unambiguous words. Practice needs to conform to the legal obligation. (Northey, 1965, pp. 41–42)

Although this view may have intuitive appeal, it does not give guidance as to how it may be operationalised. It does not recognise, for example, that a range of possible 'true values' exist – historical cost, net realisable value, current replacement cost, deprival value, and net present value. Which should be used to give a true and fair view of asset values?

Recognising such difficulties, accountants assert that criteria are needed to provide benchmarks against which the 'true and fair' requirement can be judged. This has resulted in accountants giving the phrase a technical interpretation. The Inflation Accounting Committee (Sandilands Committee; 1975) explained this as follows:

> Accounts drawn up in accordance with generally accepted accounting principles, consistently applied, are in practice regarded as showing a 'true and fair view'.... The [Companies] Acts ... give only limited guidance to the accountancy profession in interpreting the phrase 'true and fair' and it has been traditionally left to the profession to develop accounting practices which are regarded as leading to a 'true and fair view' being shown. (paras 50 and 52)

From the above quotation, it appears that the Sandilands Committee was of the opinion that financial statements prepared in accordance with accounting

---

[8] As a result of adherence to historical cost principles. The introduction of 'fair value accounting' in International Financial Reporting Standards (IFRS) has, to some extent, overcome Northey's difficulty of undervaluation of assets. However, the fact that a number of values may be identified as 'true' remains valid.

standards will provide a true and fair view. This stance was supported by legal counsel, whose opinion on the matter was sought by the Accounting Standards Board. Counsel stated:

> Accounts which meet the true and fair requirement will in general follow rather than depart from standards and [any] departure is sufficiently abnormal to require to be justified. . . . [It is likely] that the Courts will hold that in general compliance with accounting standards is necessary to meet the true and fair requirement. (Arden, 1993, para 7)

However, Counsel went on to observe:

> [T]rue and fair is a dynamic concept. Thus what is required to show a true and fair view is subject to continuous rebirth. (Arden, 1993, para 14)

It is interesting to note that some commentators have expressed the view that the legislature deliberately delegated to the accountancy profession the task of defining what qualifies as 'true and fair' financial statements at any point of time. For example, Ryan (1974) (Commissioner for Corporate Affairs in New South Wales) observed that, if a court were called upon to determine whether a particular set of financial statements presented a true and fair view, the fact that they had or had not been drawn up in accordance with the principles embodied in professional pronouncements would be very persuasive. He continued:

> I have come to the conclusion . . . that in selecting the phrase 'true and fair view' as the standard by which the profit or loss of a company and the state of its affairs are to be judged, the Legislature in effect conferred a legislative function on the accountancy profession. It is a legislative function of an ambulatory nature: what is 'true and fair' at any particular point of time will correspond with what professional accountants as a body conceive to be proper accounting principles. The evolution, development and general acceptance of those principles will cause the concept of what is 'true and fair' to shift accordingly. (p. 14)

Although accountants have applied a technical interpretation to the phrase 'true and fair', they nevertheless acknowledge that financial statements drawn up in strict conformity with accounting standards may not, in all circumstances, provide the required true and fair view. This point was emphasised by Flint (1980) when he observed:

> [P]rescription by legislation and professional standards and guidance statements . . . [is] necessary in the interests of good order and effective communication. . . . But giving a 'true and fair view' must always be a standard of a higher order. Whatever may be the extent of prescription, an overriding requirement to give a 'true and fair view' is, at the lowest level of its utility, a safety valve protecting users from bias, inadequacy or deficiency in the rules; a fail-safe device for the unavoidable shortcomings of prescription. More positively, its real utility is in establishing an enduring conceptual standard for disclosure in accounting and reporting to ensure that there is always relevant disclosure – where necessary beyond the prescription – based on an independent professional judgement. (p. 9)

Similarly, as we note in Chapter 5 (section 5.2.2), CA 2006 acknowledges that compliance with the relevant financial reporting framework may not always result in the provision of a true and fair view. In respect of 'Companies Act accounts',[9] the Act provides that, if compliance with United Kingdom Generally Accepted Accounting Practice (UK GAAP) results in financial statements that are "not sufficient to give a true and fair view", additional information is to be provided [CA 2006, s. 396(4)]. The Act also provides that where compliance with the reporting framework would result in financial statements not giving a true and fair view, accounting standards should be departed from to the extent necessary to give a true and fair view. In this situation, the departure, the reasons therefor, and its effect, are to be disclosed in a note to the financial statements [CA 2006, s. 396(5)]. Similar departures from International Financial Reporting Standards (IFRS) are permitted in order for 'IAS accounts' to present a true and fair view.[10]

Given the recognition that compliance with the relevant financial reporting framework does not always result in a true and fair view, we suggest that the most appropriate interpretation of the phrase lies somewhere between the literal and the technical viewpoints. This interpretation was explained by Porter (1990) when she drew a parallel with a good landscape painting. Such a painting portrays the landscape so 'truly and fairly' that anyone seeing the picture will gain an impression of the scene depicted, similar to the one they would have gained had they been present when the picture was painted. In similar vein, in order to meet the 'true and fair' requirement, financial statements must portray the financial affairs of the reporting entity in such a way that anyone reading the statements can gain an impression of the entity's financial position and performance similar to the one they would have obtained had they personally monitored the recording of the entity's transactions.

Many of the items presented in financial statements are subject to judgment.[11] As a consequence, in order to provide a good reproduction of the entity's financial picture (and to avoid the impressionist artist's creativity) some conventions or rules are needed to guide and direct the exercise of that judgment. Such 'rules' are embodied in accounting standards (or, more correctly in the

---

[9] See footnote 5.

[10] Departures are permitted under IAS 1: *Presentation of Financial Statements*, paras 13 and 17. It should be noted that IAS 1 refers to 'fair presentation' rather than true and fair view but the Companies Act 1985, s. 262(2) made it clear that the terms are synonymous. Further, as noted in chapter 5, footnote 17, in a legal Opinion, Martin Moore QC has "confirmed the centrality of the true and fair requirement to the preparation of financial statements in the UK, whether they are prepared is accordance with international or UK accounting standards" (Financial Reporting Council, 2008)

[11] For example, what allowance should be made for debts which might prove to be 'bad'? For how many accounting periods are long-term assets likely to generate income?

UK context, UK GAAP and IFRSs). For financial statements to meet the required standard, they must be presented in such a way as to create the 'correct' impression of the entity's financial affairs (Porter, 1990). In most circumstances this will be achieved through judgmental application of UK GAAP or IFRS, as applicable, to the particular circumstances of the entity.

Similar ideas were expressed by Tweedie (1983) when he provided the following test for evaluating whether or not a set of financial statements presents a true and fair view:

> While the detailed requirements necessary to show a true and fair view will continually evolve as social attitudes and technical skills change, the basic question to be posed by both director and auditor will remain. "If", they should ask, "if I were on 'the outside' and did not have the detailed knowledge of the company's trading performance and ultimate financial position that I have as I look at these accounts, would I be able to obtain a *clear and unambiguous* picture of that reality from these accounts?" If the picture is poorly painted, or worse, fails to represent reality, then the directors have failed to meet the paramount principle of financial reporting – to show a true and fair view. (p. 449)

14.3 FORMAT OF AUDIT REPORTS

14.3.1 Audit reports complying with the Companies Act 2006 and ISA 700

The content of standard audit reports is prescribed by CA 2006 and International Standard on Auditing (ISA) 700 (Revised): *Forming an opinion and reporting on financial statements.*[12] An example of an unqualified audit report that complies with CA 2006 and ISA 700 (Revised) is presented in Figure 14.1.[13]

14.3.2 Companies Act 2006 requirements regarding the content of audit reports

The CA 2006 (ss. 495–497) specifies certain items the auditor's report is to include, namely:

---

[12] It is pertinent to note that the Auditing Practices Board (APB) has not adopted for use in the UK the revised version of ISA 700 which became effective for audit reports dated on or after 31 December 2006 [ISA 700 (Revised); IAASB, 2006b]. Further, it is not clear whether the European Commission will adopt ISA 700 (Revised) or exercise its right under Article 28 of the EU's 8th Directive *on statutory audits of annual accounts and consolidated accounts* (Directive 2006/43/EC) to require all Member States to adopt a common standard audit report instead of that prescribed by ISA 700. In this chapter we have reported the requirements of ISA 700 (Revised and Redrafted), as reported in the agenda papers of the International Auditing and Assurance Standards Board (IAASB) in June 2008, on the assumption that the European Union will adopt this standard for use in all Member States. We also discuss, in section 14.7, the standard audit report which complies with the pre-revised version of ISA 700: *The independent auditor's report on general purpose financial statements*, that was adopted by the APB for use in the UK in 2004.

[13] We are not able to provide an example of an actual unqualified audit report which complies with CA 2006 and ISA 700 as, at the time of writing, auditors were not required to prepare their reports in accordance with these requirements, and as noted in footnote 12, the APB had not adopted ISA 700 (Revised) for use in the UK. Auditors are required to prepare audit reports in accordance with CA 2006 for periods beginning on or after 6 April 2008.

Figure 14.1: Example unqualified audit report that complies with the Companies Act 2006 and ISA 700 (Revised)

INDEPENDENT AUDITOR'S REPORT TO THE MEMBERS OF BSH PLC

Report on the financial statements

We have audited the group and parent company financial statements (the 'financial statements') of BSH plc for the year ended 31 December 20X1 which comprise the Group and Parent Income Statements, the Group and Parent Balance Sheets, the Group and Parent Cash Flow Statements, the Group and Parent Statements of Changes in Equity, and the related notes. These financial statements have been prepared under the accounting policies set out therein.

Directors' responsibilities for the financial statements

The directors are responsible for the preparation of these financial statements in accordance with applicable law and International Financial Reporting Standards (IFRSs) as adopted by the European Union and for being satisfied that they give a true and fair view. This responsibility includes the design, implementation and maintenance of internal control relevant to the preparation and fair presentation of financial statements that are free from material misstatement, whether due to fraud or error.

Auditor's responsibility

Our responsibility is to express an opinion on these financial statements based on our audit, having regard to the directors' duty to ensure that they give a true and fair view. We conducted our audit in accordance with International Standards on Auditing (UK and Ireland). Those standards require that we comply with ethical requirements and plan and perform the audit to obtain reasonable assurance as to whether the financial statements are free from material misstatement.

An audit involves performing procedures to obtain audit evidence about the amounts and disclosures in the financial statements. The procedures selected depend on the auditor's judgment, including assessment of the risks of material misstatement of the financial statements, whether due to fraud or error. In making those risk assessments, the auditor considers internal control relevant to the preparation and fair presentation of the financial statements in order to design audit procedures that are appropriate in the circumstances, but not for the purpose of expressing an opinion on the effectiveness of internal control. An audit also includes evaluating the appropriateness of accounting policies used and the reasonableness of accounting estimates made by the directors, as well as evaluating the overall presentation of the financial statements. We believe the audit evidence we have obtained is sufficient and appropriate to provide a basis for our audit opinion.

Opinion

In our opinion the financial statements:
- give a true and fair view of the state of the group's and the parent company's affairs as at 31 December 20X1 and of the group's and the parent company's profit and cash flows for the year then ended;
- have been properly prepared in accordance with IFRSs as adopted by the European Union; and
- have been prepared in accordance with the requirements of the Companies Act 2006 and, as regards the group financial statements, Article 4 of the IAS Regulation.

Report on other legal and regulatory requirements

Auditor's responsibilities

In addition to reporting on the financial statements, United Kingdom law and regulations require us to:
(a) Audit the information in the Directors' Remuneration Report that is described as having been audited.[14]
(b) State in our report whether, in our opinion, the information given in the Directors' Report is consistent with the financial statements.
(c) Report to you if, in our opinion:
   - Adequate accounting records have not been kept, or that returns adequate for our audit have not been received from branches not visited by us.
   - The parent company's financial statements are not in agreement with the accounting records and returns.
   - The part of the Directors' Remuneration Report to be audited is not in agreement with the accounting records and returns.
   - We have not received all the information and explanations we require for our audit.
(d) Include in our report a statement giving the required particulars where disclosures of directors' benefits, remuneration, pensions and compensation for loss of office specified by law have not been made.

---

[14] This applies only to quoted companies (see Chapter 5, section 5.2.6).

Figure 14.1: *Continued*

(e) Review whether the Corporate Governance Statement reflects the company's compliance with the nine provisions of the 2006 Combined Code specified for our review by the Listing Rules of the Financial Services Authority and report if it does not. We are not required to consider whether the board's statement on internal control covers all risks and controls, or form an opinion on the effectiveness of the company's corporate governance procedures or its risk and control procedures.

Opinion
In our opinion:
- the part of the Directors' Remuneration Report to be audited has been properly prepared in accordance with the Companies Act 2006; and
- the information given in the Directors' Report is consistent with the financial statements.

Jenkins, Walls & Thompson LLP	London
Registered auditor	United Kingdom
Jeremy Walls	
Senior Statutory Auditor	10 March 20X2

Source: Adapted from *The Auditor's Report: A Time for Change* (APB, 2007a, Example 1)

(i) an introduction identifying the financial statements that are the subject of the audit and the financial reporting framework that has been applied in their preparation;

(ii) a description of the scope of the audit identifying the auditing standards in accordance with which the audit was conducted;

(iii) the auditor's opinion as to whether:

(a) the financial statements:
- give a true and fair view of the company's (and, in applicable cases, the group's[15]) state of affairs and its profit or loss,
- have been properly prepared in accordance with the relevant financial reporting framework,
- have been prepared in accordance with CA 2006 and, in applicable cases, the European Union's IAS regulation;[16]

(b) the information given in the directors' report is consistent with the financial statements;

(c) for a quoted company, that part of the directors' remuneration report which is subject to audit has been prepared in accordance with CA 2006.[17]

The Act further requires that the auditor's report:

---

[15] As we note in Chapter 5, footnote 13, in general, in accordance with CA 2006, s. 399, the parent company in a group is required to produce annual financial statements for both the parent company and the group.

[16] See section 14.2 above. It may be seen that, under CA 2006, auditors are required to express an opinion on three distinct matters. As a consequence, it has come to be termed a 'three part opinion' (APB, 2007a, para 3.6).

[17] See footnote 7.

- be qualified or unqualified; and
- include a reference to any matters to which the auditor wishes to draw attention by way of emphasis without qualifying the report [CA 2006, s. 495(4)].

14.3.3   ISA 700 (Revised) requirements regarding the content of audit reports

ISA 700 (Revised) expands on CA 2006's requirements regarding the content of the auditor's report but, unlike CA 2006, also details its format. In essence, an auditor's report prepared in accordance with ISA 700 (Revised) has two parts – the first reporting on the auditee's financial statements and the second reporting on matters, other than the financial statements, that are required by law or regulation to be commented upon in the auditor's report. In terms of content, ISA 700 (Revised) requires the auditor's report to include:

- a title that clearly indicates it is the report of an independent auditor;
- the addressee of the report. (For the audits of companies' financial statements, the auditor's report is addressed to the company's members or shareholders);
- if the report also contains a section on other legal and regulatory requirements (see below), a sub-heading 'Report on the financial statements';
- an introductory paragraph that:
  - identifies the entity whose financial statements have been audited,
  - states that the financial statements have been audited,
  - identifies the title and date of, or period covered by, each statement that comprises the financial statements,
  - refers to the summary of significant accounting policies and other explanatory notes;
- a statement of the directors' responsibilities for the financial statements;
- a statement explaining the auditor's responsibility for the financial statements;
- the auditor's opinion on the financial statements;
- other matters on which the law or regulations require auditors to comment upon, or the auditor considers it appropriate to do so;
- where relevant, a sub-heading 'Report on other legal and regulatory requirements';
- a description and, if appropriate, the auditor's opinion on the other legal or regulatory reporting responsibilities of auditors;
- the auditor's signature;
- the date of the auditor's report;
- the auditor's address.

We explain some of these elements of the auditor's report below, but we discuss the auditor's opinion on the financial statements in section 14.4.

(i) Responsibilities of the directors

ISA 700 (Revised; paras 24–27) requires the auditor's report to include a section headed 'Directors responsibilities for the financial statements'. This section is to explain that the directors are responsible for the preparation and presentation of financial statements that comply with the applicable financial reporting framework and give a true and fair view. It is also to explain that this responsibility includes the design, implementation and maintenance of internal controls relevant to the preparation and presentation of financial statements that are free from material misstatement, whether due to fraud or error.[18]

(ii) Auditor's responsibility

ISA 700 (Revised; paras 28–33) specifies that this section of the auditor's report is to be headed 'Auditor's responsibility' and is to include the following information. It is to state that:

- the auditor's responsibility is to express an opinion on the financial statements based on the audit;
- the audit was conducted in accordance with International Standards on Auditing. The report is to explain that those standards require the auditor to comply with ethical requirements and to plan and perform the audit so as to obtain reasonable assurance whether or not the financial statements are free from material misstatement;
- an audit involves:
  - performing procedures to obtain audit evidence about the amounts and disclosures in the financial statements. The procedures selected depend on the auditor's judgment, including his or her assessment of

---

[18] CA 2006, s. 416(4) empowers the Secretary of State to "make provision by regulation as to other matters that must be disclosed in a directors' report", and it is possible that the directors' responsibilities for the financial statements could constitute an "other matter". However, at the time of writing, there is no evidence that the Secretary of State plans to make such a regulation. Nevertheless, companies whose transferable securities are admitted to trading, and whose home country [as defined in the EU's *Transparency Directive* (EU, 2004, Article 2)] is the UK, are required by the *Transparency Directive*, Article 4, and the United Kingdom's Listing Authority's (UKLA; see Chapter 5, footnote 46) listing rules, to include in their annual report a 'responsibility statement'. This is to state:
  (i) the name and function of any person making the responsibility statement;
  (ii) that to the best of his or her knowledge:
    (a) the financial statements, prepared in accordance with the applicable financial reporting framework, give a true and fair view of the assets, liabilities, financial position and profit or loss of the company (and, in applicable cases, of the group), and
    (b) the directors' report includes a fair review of the development and performance of the business and the position of the company (and, in applicable cases, of the group), together with a description of the principal risks and uncertainties it faces.
As ISA 700 (Revised) does not provide for cross-referencing to other sections of an entity's annual report, the requirements of ISA 700, combined with the EU (2004) and UKLA requirements, mean that the annual reports of all companies listed on the London Stock Exchange (or, indeed, the stock exchange of any EU Member State) will include two statements of directors' responsibilities – one within the auditor's report and another elsewhere in the annual report (APB, 2007a, para 4.12).

the risks of material misstatement in the financial statements, whether due to fraud or error. In making those risk assessments, the auditor considers internal control relevant to the entity's preparation and presentation of the financial statements in order to design audit procedures that are appropriate in the circumstances but not for the purpose of expressing an opinion on the effectiveness of the entity's internal control;[19]

- evaluating the appropriateness of the accounting policies adopted by the entity and the reasonableness of accounting estimates made by the directors, as well as the overall presentation of the financial statements;

• whether the auditor believes the audit evidence obtained is sufficient and appropriate to provide a basis for the auditor's opinion.[20]

(iii) 'Emphasis of Matter' and 'Other Matter(s)' paragraphs

In some circumstances, the auditor may wish to elaborate on some aspects of matters that are:

• presented or disclosed in the financial statements; such explanations are placed in an 'Emphasis of Matter' paragraph immediately following the Opinion paragraph;
• presented or disclosed other than in the financial statements but are relevant to readers' understanding of the financial statements; such matters are explained in an 'Other Matter(s)' paragraph immediately following an Emphasis of Matter paragraph (if there is one; otherwise, it follows the Opinion paragraph).[21]

(iv) Other legal or regulatory reporting responsibilities

In this section of the audit report, the auditor is to report on statutory or regulatory responsibilities that are additional, or supplementary, to expressing an opinion on the financial statements. ISA 700 (Revised) explains:

> [T]he auditor may be asked to report certain matters if they come to the auditor's attention during the course of the audit of the financial statements. Alternatively, the auditor may be asked to perform and report on additional specified procedures, or to express an opinion on specific matters, such as the adequacy of accounting books and records. (para A39)

---

[19] For companies that are subject to the Sarbanes-Oxley Act of 2002, auditors are to omit reference to their consideration of internal control not being for the purpose of expressing an opinion on the effectiveness of internal control.

[20] We should note that the provisions of CA 2006, s. 493, may render the disclosure of the auditor's responsibilities in companies' audit reports redundant in the UK. Section 493 empowers the Secretary of State to "make . . . regulations for securing the disclosure of the terms on which a company's auditor is appointed, remunerated or performs his duties". However, we should also note that, in December 2007, "the Secretary of State [had] neither made, nor proposed, any such regulations" (APB, 2007a, para 4.16).

[21] 'Emphasis of Matter' and 'Other Matter(s)' paragraphs are explained in section 14.6.

As may be seen from Figure 14.1, in this section of the audit report, auditors in the UK disclose the duties they are required to perform by CA 2006 and also, for listed companies, by the Listing Rules of the Financial Services Authority (FSA)[22] that are additional to expressing an opinion on the auditee's financial statements. In applicable cases, the auditor's opinion on other legal and regulatory responsibilities is expressed in a sub-section following the description of those responsibilities.

(v) Auditor's signature

As we note in Chapter 5 (section 5.2.6), CA 2006, s. 503, requires the auditor's report to state the name of, and be signed by, the auditor. Where the auditor is an individual, it is to be signed by him or her; where the auditor is a firm, it is to be signed by the senior statutory auditor in his or her own name, for and on behalf of the audit firm.[23]

(vi) Dating the audit report

In Chapter 13 (section 13.6.3) we emphasise the significance of the date of the audit report: it signifies the end of the period following the end of the auditee's financial year during which events occurring, or information coming to light, may result in adjustments to the financial statements or require note disclosure. The auditor expresses an opinion on the truth and fairness of the entity's financial statements as presented on the date of the auditor's report. ISA 700 (Revised), para 42, expands on this, stating:

> The auditor's report shall be dated no earlier than the date on which the auditor has obtained sufficient appropriate audit evidence on which to base the auditor's opinion on the financial statements, including evidence that:
> (a) All the statements that comprise the financial statements, including the related notes, have been prepared; and
> (b) Those with the recognized authority have taken responsibility for those financial statements [i.e., the directors have signed the financial statements].

The Standard further explains:

> The date of the auditor's report informs the user of the auditor's report that the auditor has considered the effect of events and transactions of which the auditor became aware and that occurred up to that date.... Since the auditor's opinion is provided on the financial statements and the financial statements are the responsibility of [the directors], the auditor is not in a position to conclude

---

[22] More precisely, the United Kingdom Listing Authority (UKLA) – in effect, a subsidiary of the FSA.

[23] The senior statutory auditor is, in effect, the audit engagement partner – the partner (or other person) in the firm who is responsible for the audit engagement and its performance, and also for the audit report that is issued on behalf of the firm.

that sufficient appropriate audit evidence has been obtained until evidence is obtained that all the statements that comprise the financial statements, including the related notes, have been prepared and [the directors have] accepted responsibility for them. (paras A43, A44)

Referring to Figure 14.1, it should be noted that, in accordance with ISA 700 (Revised), the report has a title indicating that it is the report of an independent auditor, it identifies the persons to whom it is addressed (the members of BSH plc) and the financial statements on which the auditor's opinion is expressed. The report also contains separate, suitably headed, sections dealing with the respective responsibilities of the directors and auditors, the auditor's opinion on the financial statements, and a description of the auditor's other legal and regulatory responsibilities and the auditor's opinion thereon. The report additionally includes the auditors' signature (the firm and the senior statutory auditor) and address, and the report is dated (10 March 20X2).

14.4 TYPES OF AUDIT REPORT

14.4.1 Overview of types of audit report

There are basically two types of audit report:
- an unmodified (or unqualified) report (that is, a 'clean' report); and
- a modified report.[24]

However, there are three types of modified report, namely, those containing:
- a qualified (or an 'except for') opinion;
- an adverse opinion;
- a disclaimer of opinion.

We explain below the circumstances in which each type of report is appropriate.

Irrespective of the type of audit report issued, the auditor should provide a clear expression of opinion on the financial statements and on any other matter(s) on which (s)he is required by statute, regulations or the particular engagement to express an opinion. The fundamental principle of external auditing in *The Auditors' Code – Clear Communication* also observes that the audit report should contain sufficient information for a reader to gain a proper understanding of the auditor's opinion. In the words of the principle:

---

[24] While CA 2006, s. 495, requires auditors' reports to be 'unqualified' or 'qualified', ISA 700 refers to the reports as being 'unmodified' or 'modified'. Traditionally, qualified reports have been identified as containing 'except for', adverse or disclaimers of opinion; however, ISA 700 refers to modified reports as expressing qualified, adverse or disclaimers of opinion. Thus, ISA 700 uses the term 'qualified' as synonymous with 'except for'. In this chapter we adopt the terminology of ISA 700.

Auditors' reports contain clear expressions of opinion and set out information necessary for a proper understanding of that opinion. (APB, 2008)

14.4.2 Unmodified (unqualified) audit reports

In order to express an unmodified (or unqualified) audit opinion, the auditor must have gathered and evaluated sufficient appropriate audit evidence on which to base a conclusion as to whether the auditee's financial statements:

- give a true and fair view of the company's (and, in applicable cases, the group's) state of affairs as at the end of the financial year and its profit or loss and cash flow for the financial year;[25]
- comply with the relevant financial reporting framework;
- are properly prepared in accordance with CA 2006;
- in applicable cases, comply with EU Regulation (EC) No. 1606/2002 *on the application of international accounting standards* (EU, 2002);
- are consistent with the information provided in the directors' report;
- are consistent with unaudited financial information in the annual report containing the audited financial statements and, as far as the auditor is aware, unaudited information in the annual report is not materially misleading.[26]

In reaching a conclusion about the truth and fairness of the financial statements, the auditor is required to consider, *inter alia*, whether:

- the financial statements have been prepared using appropriate accounting policies which have been consistently applied;
- estimated amounts in the financial statements are reasonable;
- the amounts and disclosures in the financial statements are presented so as to enable users to gain a proper understanding of the entity's financial position, profit or loss, and cash flow.

Figure 14.1 provides an example of an unqualified audit report that complies with the requirements of CA 2006 and ISA 700 (Revised).[26]

14.4.3 Modified audit reports

ISA 705: *Modifications to the opinion in the independent auditor's report* (para 8) explains that a modified audit opinion is expressed when the auditor:

---

[25] As noted in Chapter 5, footnote 38, IFRS and UK GAAP require all but small companies to produce a cash flow statement for each financial year, in addition to the profit and loss account and balance sheet.

[26] These last requirements are explained in Chapter 13, section 13.6.2.

[27] As noted in footnote 12, at the time of writing, the APB had not adopted ISA 700 (Revised) for use in the UK.

    (i) concludes that the financial statements as a whole are not free from material misstatement; or

    (ii) is unable to obtain sufficient appropriate audit evidence to conclude that the financial statements as a whole are free from material misstatement.

Although each of these circumstances will give rise to a modified audit report, as reflected in Figure 14.2, which of the three forms of modification is appropriate (qualified, adverse or disclaimer) depends on the pervasiveness of the effects, or possible effects, on the financial statements of the matter(s) in question.

Figure 14.2: Circumstances giving rise to different types of modified audit reports

Nature of matter giving rise to the modification	Auditor's judgment about the pervasiveness of the effect, or possible effect, on the financial statements	
	Material but not pervasive	Material and pervasive
Financial statements are materially misstated.	Qualified (or 'Except for') opinion	Adverse opinion
Inability to obtain sufficient appropriate audit evidence (limitation on the scope of the audit)	Qualified (or 'Except for') opinion	Disclaimer of opinion

Source: Adapted from ISA 705: *Modifications to the opinion in the independent auditor's report*, para A1

A misstatement or an inability to obtain sufficient appropriate audit evidence is considered to be pervasive if the effects, or possible effects, of the matter:

    (a) are not confined to specific elements, accounts or items of the financial statements, or,

    (b) if so confined, represent or could represent a substantial proportion of the financial statements or are fundamental to users' understanding of the financial statements. (ISA 705, para 7)

14.5 DIFFERENT FORMS OF MODIFIED AUDIT REPORT

14.5.1 Modifications resulting from material misstatement

ISA 705, para A3, explains that material misstatement of the financial statements may arise in relation to:

    (a) The appropriateness of the selected accounting policies;

    (b) The application of the selected accounting policies; or

    (c) The adequacy of disclosures in the financial statements.

The standard expands on the circumstances in which each of the above factors may result in material misstatement of the financial statements:

    (a) In relation to the appropriateness of the selected accounting policies, ISA 705, para A4, notes that the selected accounting policies may not:

- be consistent with the applicable financial reporting framework;
- result in the financial statements, including the related explanatory notes, not representing the underlying transactions and events in a manner that achieves fair presentation.

(b) In relation to the application of the selected accounting policies, ISA 705, para A6, observes that material misstatement may result from:
- the accounting policies not being applied consistently to similar transactions and events, and/or in different accounting periods;
- an error in the application of an accounting policy (such as may occur unintentionally).

(c) In relation to the adequacy of disclosures, ISA 705, para A7, states that material misstatement may arise when the financial statements:
- do not include all of the disclosures required by, or the disclosures are not presented in accordance with, the applicable financial reporting framework;
- do not provide the disclosures necessary to achieve fair presentation.

If, in the auditor's opinion, any of the situations outlined above are material to the financial statements,[28] they will give rise to a modified audit opinion. However, as indicated in section 14.4.3 above, the type of modification depends on the pervasiveness of the effect(s), or possible effect(s), of the misstatement on the financial statements. If, in the auditor's opinion the effects, or possible effects of the misstatements, individually or in aggregate, are:
- material to the financial statements but are not pervasive, a qualified (or 'except for') opinion is expressed. (That is, the auditor states that, in his or her opinion, the financial statements give a true and fair view of the reporting entity's state of affairs and profit or loss except for the matter(s) specified in the audit report);
- material and pervasive and, as a consequence, the financial statements are seriously misleading, an adverse opinion is expressed. (That is, the auditor states that, in his or her opinion, the financial statements do not give a true and fair view.)

14.5.2 Inability to obtain sufficient appropriate audit evidence

ISA 705, para A8, explains that the auditor may not be able to obtain sufficient appropriate audit evidence (or, alternatively expressed, the scope of the audit is limited) as a result of:

---

[28] The concept of materiality is explained in Chapter 3, section 3.4.2.

(a) Circumstances beyond the control of the entity;
(b) Circumstances relating to the nature or timing of the auditor's work; or
(c) Limitations imposed by management.

The Standard illustrates each of the above situations by means of examples.

(a) Examples of circumstances beyond the control of the entity include:
- the destruction of the entity's accounting records (for example, through fire or flood);
- the indefinite seizing by governmental agencies of the accounting records of a significant component of the reporting entity (para A10).

(b) Examples of circumstances relating to the nature or timing of the auditor's work include:
- the auditor's inability to obtain sufficient appropriate audit evidence about an associated entity's financial affairs to evaluate whether the entity (which is required to use the equity method accounting for an associated entity) has applied the method appropriately;
- the timing of the auditor's appointment precludes observing the counting of the physical inventories;
- the auditor determines that performing substantive procedures alone is not sufficient but the entity's controls are not effective (para A11).

(c) Examples of a limitation on the scope of the audit imposed by management include management preventing the auditor from:
- observing the counting of the physical inventory; or
- requesting external confirmation of specific account balances.
The auditor's actions in cases where management limits the scope of the audit are explained further in section 14.5.4 below.

When any of the above matters are material, the auditor issues a modified audit report. However, as for modifications arising from misstatements and as shown in Figure 14.2, the type of modification depends on the pervasiveness of the effect(s), or possible effect(s), of the limitation on the scope of the audit. If, in the auditor's opinion the effects, or possible effects, of the limitation on the scope of the audit, individually, or in aggregate are:
- material to the financial statements but are not pervasive, a qualified (or 'except for') opinion is expressed. (That is, the auditor states that, in his or her opinion, the financial statements give a true and fair view of the reporting entity's state of affairs and profit or loss except for the matter(s) specified in the audit report);
- material and pervasive and, as a consequence, the auditor is unable to form an opinion on the financial statements, the auditor disclaims an opinion. (That is, the auditor states that (s)he is unable to form an opinion on the financial statements.)

14.5.3 Format of modified audit reports

Whenever a material misstatement of the financial statements results in a qualified or adverse opinion, or the auditor's inability to obtain sufficient appropriate audit evidence results in a qualified or disclaimer of opinion, ISA 705 requires the following changes to be made to the standard unqualified audit report:

(i) The description of the auditor's responsibility is to be amended.
  - When a qualified or adverse opinion is expressed, it is to state that the auditor believes the audit evidence obtained is sufficient and appropriate to provide a basis for the auditor's qualified or adverse opinion (para 28).
  - When a disclaimer of opinion is expressed, the paragraph is to be limited to stating:

    > Our responsibility is to express an opinion on the financial state-ments based on conducting the audit in accordance with Interna-tional Standards on Auditing (UK and Ireland). Because of the matter(s) described in the Basis for Disclaimer of Opinion para-graph, however, we were not able to obtain sufficient appropriate audit evidence to provide a basis for an audit opinion. (para 29)

(ii) A paragraph, headed 'Basis for qualified opinion', 'Basis for adverse opinion' or 'Basis for disclaimer of opinion', as applicable, is to be included in the audit report immediately before the Opinion paragraph. The paragraph is to provide a description of the matter giving rise to the modified audit report.
  - If a material misstatement relates to specific amounts in the finan-cial statements (including quantitative note disclosures), unless it is impracticable to do so, the auditor is to describe and quantify the financial effects of the misstatement (for example, the effect on income tax, income before taxes, net profit and equity of an over-statement of inventory). If it is impracticable to quantify the effects of the misstatement, the auditor is to state that this is the case (paras 18, 19, A19).
  - If a material misstatement relates to narrative disclosures, the auditor is to provide an explanation of how the disclosures are misstated. If information required to be disclosed has been omitted, the auditor is required to describe the nature of the omitted information and, providing it is practicable to do so and sufficient appropriate audit evidence about the omitted information has been obtained, include the omitted infor-mation (paras 20, 21). ISA 705, para A23, explains that it would not be practicable for the auditor to include the omitted information if:

- the disclosures have not been prepared by management or are otherwize not readily available to the auditor; or
- in the auditor's opinion, the disclosures would be voluminous in comparison to the auditor's report.

- If the auditor is unable to obtain sufficient appropriate audit evidence, (s)he is to explain the reasons for this inability (ISA 705, para 22).

We should note that, if the auditor expresses an adverse or disclaimer of opinion, (s)he is still required to provide a description of any other matter(s) that would have given rise to a qualified audit report (in the absence of the adverse, or disclaimer of, opinion) and the financial effects of the matter(s) in question. This would apply, for example, if the financial statements contained a material misstatement arising from the recognition, measurement or disclosure of specific assets and/or liabilities (such as the existence of inventory) (ISA 705, paras 23, A21).

(iii) The Opinion paragraph is to be headed 'Qualified opinion', 'Adverse opinion' or 'Disclaimer of Opinion', as applicable, and state that, in the auditor's opinion:
- in the case of a qualified opinion:

  except for the effects of the matter(s) described in the Basis for Qualified Opinion paragraph, the financial statements give a true and fair view in accordance with the applicable financial reporting framework (ISA 705, para 25);[29]
- in the case of an adverse opinion:

  because of the significance of the matter(s) described in the Basis for Adverse Opinion paragraph, the financial statements do not give a true and fair view in accordance with the applicable financial reporting framework (para 26);
- in the case of a disclaimer of opinion:

  (a) because of the significance of the matter(s) described in the Basis for Disclaimer of Opinion paragraph, the auditor has not been able to obtain sufficient appropriate audit evidence to provide a basis for an audit opinion; and
  (b) accordingly, the auditor does not express an opinion on the financial statements. (para 27)

Examples of modified audit reports that comply with CA 2006 and ISA 705 are presented in Figures 14.3, 14.4, 14.5 and 14.6.[30] We have reproduced a full

---

[29] If the qualified opinion arises from the auditor's inability to obtain sufficient appropriate audit evidence, the statement is to begin with: "except for the possible effects ...".

[30] We are not able to provide examples of actual modified audit reports which comply with CA 2006, ISA 700 (Revised), and ISA 705 as, at the time of writing, auditors were not required to prepare their reports in accordance with the requirements of CA 2006 and, as noted in footnote 12, the APB had not adopted ISA 700 (Revised). Auditors in the UK are required to prepare audit reports in accordance with CA 2006 for periods beginning on or after 6 April 2008.

Figure 14.3:   A qualified opinion arising from a material misstatement of inventory

---

INDEPENDENT AUDITOR'S REPORT TO THE MEMBERS OF ALS PLC

Report on the financial statements
We have audited the group and parent company financial statements (the 'financial statements') of ALS plc for the year ended 31 March 20X1, which comprise the Group and Parent Income Statements, the Group and Parent Balance Sheets, the Group and Parent Cash Flow Statements, the Group and Parent Statements of Changes in Equity, and the related notes. These financial statements have been prepared under the accounting policies set out therein.

Directors' responsibilities for the financial statements
The directors are responsible for the preparation of these financial statements in accordance with applicable law and International Financial Reporting Standards (IFRSs) as adopted by the European Union and for ensuring that they give a true and fair view. This responsibility includes the design, implementation and maintenance of internal control relevant to the preparation and fair presentation of financial statements that are free from material misstatement, whether due to fraud or error.

Auditor's responsibilities
Our responsibility is to express an opinion on these financial statements based on our audit, having regard to the directors' duty to ensure that they give a true and fair view. We conducted our audit in accordance with International Standards on Auditing (UK and Ireland). Those standards require that we comply with ethical requirements and plan and perform the audit to obtain reasonable assurance as to whether the financial statements are free from material misstatement.

An audit involves performing procedures to obtain audit evidence about the amounts and disclosures in the financial statements. The procedures selected depend on the auditor's judgment, including assessment of the risks of material misstatement of the financial statements, whether due to fraud or error. In making those risk assessments, the auditor considers internal control relevant to the preparation and presentation of financial statements that give a true and fair view in order to design audit procedures that are appropriate in the circumstances, but not for the purpose of expressing an opinion on the effectiveness of internal control. An audit also includes evaluating the appropriateness of accounting policies used and the reasonableness of accounting estimates made by the directors, as well as evaluating the overall presentation of the financial statements. We believe the audit evidence we have obtained is sufficient and appropriate to provide a basis for our qualified audit opinion.

Basis for Qualified Opinion
The company's inventories are carried in the balance sheet at £10,579,000. The inventories are carried at cost rather than at the lower of cost and net realisable value, which constitutes a departure from IFRS as adopted by the European Union. Had the directors stated the inventories at the lower of cost and net realisable value, they would have been written down by £995,600. Accordingly, cost of sales would have been increased by £995,600, and income tax, net income and shareholders equity would have been reduced by £298,680, £696,920 and £696,920, respectively.

Qualified Opinion
In our opinion, except for the effects of the matter described in the Basis for Qualified Opinion paragraph, the financial statements:
• give a true and fair view of the state of the group's and the parent company's affairs as at 31 March 20X1 and of the group's and the parent company's profit for the year then ended;
• have been properly prepared in accordance with IFRSs as adopted by the European Union; and
• have been prepared in accordance with the requirements of the Companies Act 2006 and, as regards the group financial statements, Article 4 of the IAS Regulation.

Report on other legal and regulatory requirements

Auditor's responsibilities
In addition to reporting on the financial statements, United Kingdom law and regulations require us to:
(a) Audit the information in the Directors' Remuneration Report that is described as having been audited.[31]
(b) State in our report whether, in our opinion, the information given in the Directors' Report is consistent with the financial statements.
(c) Report to you if, in our opinion:
    • Adequate accounting records have not been kept, or that returns adequate for our audit have not been received from branches not visited by us.
    • The parent company's financial statements are not in agreement with the accounting records and returns.
    • The part of the Directors' Remuneration Report to be audited is not in agreement with the accounting records and returns.
    • We have not received all the information and explanations we require for our audit.
(d) Review whether the Corporate Governance Statement reflects the company's compliance with the nine provisions of the 2006 Combined Code specified for our review by the Listing Rules of the Financial Services Authority and report if it does not. We are not required to consider whether the board's statement on internal control covers all risks and controls, or form an opinion on the effectiveness of the company's corporate governance procedures or its risk and control procedures.

Opinion
In our opinion:
• the part of the Directors' Remuneration Report to be audited has been properly prepared in accordance with the Companies Act 2006; and
• the information given in the Directors' Report is consistent with the financial statements.

King & Young   York
Registered auditor   United Kingdom

Francis King
Senior Statutory Auditor   12 June 20X1

Source: Adapted from ISA 705 and APB (2007) Example 1, Appendix, Illustration 1

---

[31] This is applicable to quoted companies only (see Chapter 5, section 5.2.6).

Figure 14.4: An adverse opinion arising from a pervasive material misstatement: non-consolidation of a subsidiary

INDEPENDENT AUDITOR'S REPORT TO THE MEMBERS OF MMP PLC

Report on the financial statements

As for the audit report in Figures 14.1 and 14.3

Directors' responsibilities for the financial statements

As for the audit report in Figures 14.1 and 14.3

Auditor's responsibilities

Our responsibility is to express an opinion on these financial statements based on our audit, having regard to the directors' duty to ensure that they give a true and fair view. We conducted our audit in accordance with International Standards on Auditing (UK and Ireland). Those standards require that we comply with ethical requirements and plan and perform the audit to obtain reasonable assurance as to whether the financial statements are free from material misstatement.

An audit involves performing procedures to obtain audit evidence about the amounts and disclosures in the financial statements. The procedures selected depend on the auditor's judgment, including assessment of the risks of material misstatement of the financial statements, whether due to fraud or error. In making those risk assessments, the auditor considers internal control relevant to the preparation and presentation of financial statements that give a true and fair view in order to design audit procedures that are appropriate in the circumstances, but not for the purpose of expressing an opinion on the effectiveness of internal control. An audit also includes evaluating the appropriateness of accounting policies used and the reasonableness of accounting estimates made by the directors, as well as evaluating the overall presentation of the financial statements. We believe the audit evidence we have obtained is sufficient and appropriate to provide a basis for our adverse audit opinion.

Basis for Adverse Opinion

As explained in Note 2, the company has not consolidated the financial statements of subsidiary Trade Secrets Ltd it acquired during 20X0 because it has not yet been able to ascertain the fair values of certain of the subsidiary's material assets and liabilities at the acquisition date. This investment is therefore accounted for on a cost basis. Under International Financial Reporting Standards, the subsidiary should have been consolidated because it is controlled by the company. Had Trade Secrets Ltd been consolidated, many elements in the accompanying financial statements would have been materially affected. In the absence of further information about the accounting for the acquisition, however, it is not possible to quantify those effects.

Adverse Opinion

In our opinion, because of the significance of the matter discussed in the Basis for Adverse Opinion paragraph, the financial statements:

- do not give a true and fair view of the state of the group's and the parent company's affairs as at 31 March 20X1 and of the group's and the parent company's profit for the year then ended;
- have not been properly prepared in accordance with IFRSs as adopted by the European Union; and
- have not been prepared in accordance with the requirements of the Companies Act 2006 and, as regards the group financial statements, Article 4 of the IAS Regulation.

Report on other legal and regulatory requirements

Auditor's responsibilities

As for the audit report in Figures 14.1 and 14.3

Opinion

In our opinion:

- the part of the Directors' Remuneration Report to be audited has been properly prepared in accordance with the Companies Act 2006; and
- the information given in the Directors' Report is consistent with the financial statements.
- in respect solely of the limitation on our work relating to the fair values of Trade Secrets Ltd:
  - we have not obtained all the information and explanations that we considered necessary for the purpose of our audit; and
  - adequate accounting records have not been maintained.

Mason & Jarvis   Manchester
Registered auditor   United Kingdom

Rebecca Mason
Senior Statutory Auditor   24 May 20X1

Source: Adapted from ISA 705: *Modifications to the opinion in the independent auditor's report*, Appendix, Illustration 2

Figure 14.5:   A qualified opinion arising from the auditor's inability to obtain sufficient appropriate audit evidence about an investment in a foreign affiliate

---

INDEPENDENT AUDITOR'S REPORT TO THE MEMBERS OF KFP PLC

Report on the financial statements

As for the audit report in Figures 14.1 and 14.3

Directors' responsibilities for the financial statements

As for the audit report in Figures 14.1 and 14.3

Auditor's responsibilities

Our responsibility is to express an opinion on these financial statements based on our audit, having regard to the directors' duty to ensure that they give a true and fair view.   We conducted our audit in accordance with International Standards on Auditing (UK and Ireland).   Those standards require that we comply with ethical requirements and plan and perform the audit to obtain reasonable assurance as to whether the financial statements are free from material misstatement.

An audit involves performing procedures to obtain audit evidence about the amounts and disclosures in the financial statements.   The procedures selected depend on the auditor's judgment, including assessment of the risks of material misstatement of the financial statements, whether due to fraud or error.   In making those risk assessments, the auditor considers internal control relevant to the preparation and presentation of financial statements that give a true and fair view in order to design audit procedures that are appropriate in the circumstances, but not for the purpose of expressing an opinion on the effectiveness of internal control.   An audit also includes evaluating the appropriateness of accounting policies used and the reasonableness of accounting estimates made by the directors, as well as evaluating the overall presentation of the financial statements.   We believe the audit evidence we have obtained is sufficient and appropriate to provide a basis for our qualified audit opinion.

Basis for Qualified Opinion

The company's investment in Warbridge Ltd, the foreign associate acquired during the year and accounted for by the equity method, was carried at £57,978,000 on the balance sheet as at 30 June 20X1, and the company's share of Warbridge Ltd's net income of £7,465,000 is included in the company's income for the year then ended.   We were unable to obtain sufficient appropriate audit evidence about the carrying amount of the company's investment in Warbridge Ltd as at 30 June 20X1 and the company's share of Warbridge Ltd's net income for the year because we were denied access to the financial information, management, and the auditors of Warbridge Ltd.   Consequently, we were unable to determine whether any adjustments to these amounts were necessary.

Qualified Opinion

In our opinion, except for the effects of the matter described in the Basis for Qualified Opinion paragraph, the financial statements:
• give a true and fair view of the state of the group's and the parent company's affairs as at 30 June 20X1 and of the group's and the parent company's profit for the year then ended;
• have been properly prepared in accordance with IFRSs as adopted by the European Union; and
• have been prepared in accordance with the requirements of the Companies Act 2006 and, as regards the group financial statements, Article 4 of the IAS Regulation.

Report on other legal and regulatory requirements

Auditor's responsibilities

As for the audit report in Figures 14.1 and 14.3

Opinion

In our opinion:
• the part of the Directors' Remuneration Report to be audited has been properly prepared in accordance with the Companies Act 2006; and
• the information given in the Directors' Report is consistent with the financial statements.
• in respect solely of the company's investment in Warbridge Ltd, we were unable to obtain all the information and explanations that we considered necessary for the purpose of our audit.

Brittle & Fellows   Exeter
Registered auditor   United Kingdom

Peter Fisk
Senior Statutory Auditor   25 September 20X1

Source: Adapted from ISA 705: *Modifications to the opinion in the independent auditor's report*, Appendix, Illustration 3

Figure 14.6:   A disclaimer of opinion resulting from the auditor's inability to obtain sufficient appropriate audit evidence about a significant joint venture

---

INDEPENDENT AUDITOR'S REPORT TO THE MEMBERS OF BDJ PLC

Report on the financial statements

As for the audit report in Figures 14.1 and 14.3

Directors' responsibilities for the financial statements

As for the audit report in Figures 14.1 and 14.3

Auditor's responsibilities

Our responsibility is to express an opinion on these financial statements based on conducting the audit in accordance with International Standards on Auditing (UK and Ireland). Because of the matter described in the Basis for Disclaimer of Opinion paragraph, however, we were not able to obtain sufficient appropriate audit evidence to provide a basis for an audit opinion.

Basis for Disclaimer of Opinion

The company's investment in its joint venture Kentoff (Brazil) Ltd is carried at £835,479,000 on the company's balance sheet, which represents over 90% of the company's net assets as at 30 September 20X1. We were not allowed access to the management and the auditors of Kentoff Ltd. As a result, we were unable to determine whether any adjustments were necessary in respect of the company's proportional share of Kentoff Ltd's assets that it controls jointly, its proportional share of Kentoff Ltd's liabilities for which it is jointly responsible, its proportional share of Kentoff Ltd's income and expenses for the year, and the elements making up the statement of changes in equity and cash flow statement.

Disclaimer of Opinion

Because of the significance of the matter described in the Basis for Disclaimer of Opinion paragraph, we have not been able to obtain sufficient appropriate audit evidence to provide a basis for an audit opinion. Accordingly, we do not express an opinion on the financial statements.

Report on other legal and regulatory requirements

Auditor's responsibilities

As for the audit report in Figures 14.1 and 14.3

Opinion

In our opinion:
* the part of the Directors' Remuneration Report to be audited has been properly prepared in accordance with the Companies Act 2006; and
* the information given in the Directors' Report is consistent with the financial statements.
* in respect solely of the company's investment in its joint venture Kentoff (Brazil) Ltd:
  – we have not obtained all the information and explanations that we considered necessary for the purpose of our audit; and
  – adequate accounting records have not been maintained.

Swift & Speedy	Birmingham
Registered auditor	United Kingdom
Jonathan Swift	
Senior Statutory Auditor	20 December 20X1

Source: Adapted from ISA 705: *Modifications to the opinion in the independent auditor's report*, Appendix, Illustration 4

example report in Figure 14.3, but in Figures 14.4, 14.5 and 14.6 we have only presented the amended portions of the audit report that reflect the type of modification illustrated.

* Figure 14.3 illustrates a qualified opinion which has resulted from the misstatement of inventory. In the auditor's opinion, the misstatement is material but not pervasive to the financial statements.

- Figure 14.4 illustrates an adverse opinion which has arisen as a result of the non-consolidation of a subsidiary. In the auditor's opinion, this mis-statement is material and pervasive to the financial statements.
- Figure 14.5 illustrates a qualified opinion which has resulted from the auditor's inability to obtain sufficient appropriate audit evidence regarding an investment in a foreign affiliate. In the auditor's opinion, the matter is material but not pervasive to the financial statements.
- Figure 14.6 illustrates a disclaimer of opinion which has resulted from the auditor's inability to obtain sufficient appropriate audit evidence about the financial affairs of a joint venture investment that represents more than 90 per cent of the auditee's net assets. In the auditor's opinion, the effects of this matter are material and pervasive to the financial statements.

14.5.4 Auditor's actions when management limits the scope of the audit

In the event that an auditee's senior executives or directors impose a limitation on the scope of the audit after the audit engagement has been accepted, and the auditor considers it likely that it will result in the expression of a qualified, or disclaimer of, opinion, the auditor is to request that the limitation be removed. If it was imposed by senior executives and they refuse to remove it, the auditor should communicate with the directors (or, if the entity has one, the audit committee) about the matter (ISA 705, paras 13, 14).

If the limitation on the scope of the audit is still not removed, the auditor is required to determine whether alternative procedures can be performed so as to obtain sufficient appropriate audit evidence on which to base an unmodified opinion. If such procedures cannot be performed, ISA 705, para 15, requires the auditor to determine whether the possible effects of the scope limitation are:

(i) material but not pervasive to the financial statements, in which case a qualified audit opinion should be expressed; or

(ii) material and pervasive to the financial statements. In this case, the auditor is to:
- resign from the audit; or
- if resignation from the audit before issuing the auditor's report is not practicable, express a disclaimer of opinion.

ISA 705 explains that, where the auditor has substantially completed the audit, (s)he may decide to complete the audit to the extent possible and disclaim an opinion. In this event, the auditor should explain the limitation on the scope of the audit in the Basis for Disclaimer of Opinion paragraph. If the auditor chooses to resign from the audit, (s)he is required to communicate to the directors any misstatements identified during the portion of the audit conducted that would, in the auditor's opinion, have given rise to a qualified or adverse opinion (paras 16, A13).

In the event that the auditor resigns from the audit, the Companies Act 2006 provisions relating to the resignation of auditors apply, including the need to deposit a written notice of resignation at the company's registered office, together with a statement of circumstances connected with their ceasing to hold office, and to notify the appropriate authority, that is, the Financial Reporting Council's (FRC) Public Oversight Board or the auditor's Recognised Supervisory Body, depending on whether it is a 'major' or 'not major' audit (see Chapter 5, section 5.2.5).

14.6   EMPHASIS OF MATTER AND OTHER MATTER(S) PARAGRAPHS

As we noted in section 14.3, occasionally auditors consider that matters presented or disclosed within the financial statements, or elsewhere in the entity's annual report, are so important to users' understanding of the financial statements that they wish to draw attention to, or elaborate on, them. Such additional information is placed in an 'Emphasis of Matter' paragraph if it relates to matters within the financial statements, or in an 'Other Matter(s)' paragraph if it relates to matters disclosed outside of the financial statements.

14.6.1   Emphasis of Matter paragraphs

ISA 706: *Emphasis of Matter paragraphs and Other Matter(s) paragraphs in the independent auditor's report* explains the use of an emphasis of matter paragraph as follows:

> When the auditor determines it is necessary to draw users' attention to a matter presented or disclosed in the financial statements that, in the auditor's judgment, is of such importance that it is fundamental to the users' understanding of the financial statements, the auditor shall include an Emphasis of Matter paragraph in the auditor's report provided the auditor has obtained sufficient appropriate audit evidence that the matter is not materially misstated in the financial statements. Such a paragraph shall refer only to information presented or disclosed in the financial statements. (para 6)

Examples of situations when an Emphasis of Matter paragraph is appropriate include the following:

- when it is necessary for the auditor to issue a new auditor's report on amended financial statements as a result of the auditor becoming aware of a fact that existed at the date the auditor's report was signed which, if known then, would have caused the auditor to request the financial statements to be amended or to modify the auditor's opinion on the financial statements;[32]
- when the auditor has doubt about the ability of the entity to continue as a going concern but the matter is adequately disclosed in the financial statements;[33]
- when there is an uncertainty relating to the future outcome of an expected litigation or regulatory action;
- when application of a new accounting standard (for example, a new International Financial Reporting Standard) has had a pervasive effect on the financial statements in advance of its effective date (i.e., where early application is permitted);
- when a major catastrophe when has had, or continues to have, a significant effect on the entity's financial position.

When auditors use an Emphasis of Matter paragraph, they are required by ISA 706, para 7, to:

- use the heading 'Emphasis of Matter' (or other appropriate heading), and place the paragraph immediately following the opinion paragraph;
- make clear reference in the paragraph to the matter being emphasised and to where in the financial statements passage the relevant disclosures fully describing the matter can be found; and
- indicate that the auditor's report is not modified in respect of the matter emphasised.

An example audit report including an Emphasis of Matter paragraph that complies with the Companies Act 2006, ISA 700 (Revised) and ISA 706 is provided in Figure 14.7.

ISA 706 envisages that auditors should use Emphasis of Matter paragraphs sparingly, noting: "A widespread use of emphasis of matter paragraphs diminishes the effectiveness of the auditor's communication of such matters" (para A2).

---

[32] This 'subsequent event' circumstance is explained in Chapter 13, section 13.3.2.

[33] The auditor's reference to going concern uncertainties are explained in Chapter 13, section 13.4.

Figure 14.7: An unqualified audit opinion with an Emphasis of Matter paragraph referring to uncertainty about the outcome of a lawsuit

---

INDEPENDENT AUDITOR'S REPORT TO THE MEMBERS OF ETS PLC

Report on the financial statements

As for the audit report in Figures 14.1 and 14.3

Directors' responsibilities for the financial statements

As for the audit report in Figures 14.1 and 14.3

Auditor's responsibilities

Our responsibility is to express an opinion on these financial statements based on our audit, having regard to the directors' duty to ensure that they give a true and fair view. We conducted our audit in accordance with International Standards on Auditing (UK and Ireland). Those standards require that we comply with ethical requirements and plan and perform the audit to obtain reasonable assurance as to whether the financial statements are free from material misstatement.

An audit involves performing procedures to obtain audit evidence about the amounts and disclosures in the financial statements. The procedures selected depend on the auditor's judgment, including assessment of the risks of material misstatement of the financial statements, whether due to fraud or error. In making those risk assessments, the auditor considers internal control relevant to the preparation and presentation of financial statements that give a true and fair view in order to design audit procedures that are appropriate in the circumstances, but not for the purpose of expressing an opinion on the effectiveness of internal control. An audit also includes evaluating the appropriateness of accounting policies used and the reasonableness of accounting estimates made by the directors, as well as evaluating the overall presentation of the financial statements. We believe the audit evidence we have obtained is sufficient and appropriate to provide a basis for our audit opinion.

Opinion

In our opinion the financial statements:
- give a true and fair view of the state of the group's and the parent company's affairs as at 31 December 20X1 and of the group's and the parent company's profit for the year then ended;
- have been properly prepared in accordance with IFRSs as adopted by the European Union; and
- have been prepared in accordance with the requirements of the Companies Act 2006 and, as regards the group financial statements, Article 4 of the IAS Regulation.

Emphasis of matter

We draw attention to Note 25 to the financial statements which describes the uncertainty related to the outcome of the lawsuit filed against the company by Nelsonian Company Ltd. Our opinion is not qualified in respect of this matter.

Report on other legal and regulatory requirements

Auditor's responsibilities

As for the audit report in Figures 14.1 and 14.3

Opinion

As for the audit report in Figures 14.1 and 14.3

Rentoll and Spencer   Edinburgh
Registered auditor   United Kingdom

Harold Spencer
Senior Statutory Auditor   12 March 20X2

Source: Adapted from ISA 706; and APB (2007) Example 1, Appendix

14.6.2 Other Matter(s) paragraphs

Auditors may consider it appropriate to use the auditor's report to communicate information to users of the financial statements about matters, other than those presented or disclosed in the financial statements, that may be relevant to users' understanding of the financial statements or the audit. Such information is to be provided in a paragraph in the auditor's report headed 'Other Matter(s)' (or some other appropriate heading), which is to be placed "after the Opinion paragraph and any Emphasis of Matter paragraph, or elsewhere in the audit report of the content of the Other Matter(s) paragraph is relevant to other responsibilities" (ISA 706, para 8).

Examples of matters the auditor may wish to refer in an Other Matter(s) paragraph include the following:
- information in a document containing audited financial statements is materially inconsistent with those financial statements;
- a predecessor auditor audited the prior period's financial statements (and, hence, the comparative figures in the current financial period); the auditor should draw attention to this fact and state the type of opinion the predecessor auditor expressed in the audit report, the date of that report and, if it was modified, the reasons for the modification;
- in rare circumstances, the auditor may judge it necessary to explain why (s)he has been unable to resign from the engagement even though the possible effect of an inability to obtain sufficient appropriate audit evidence due to a scope limitation[34] imposed by management is pervasive.

We also noted in Chapter 13, section 13.6.2, that, if the auditor finds a misstatement in a listed company's annual report on its compliance with *The Combined Code on Corporate Governance* (FRC, 2006) and it is a matter the auditor is required to review, the auditor is to refer to the misstatement in the other matter(s) section of the audit report.

14.7 THE AUDIT REPORT – THE AUDITOR'S CHANCE TO COMMUNICATE

When considering the standard form of audit report, it should be remembered that this report is the auditor's primary opportunity to communicate with users of the financial statements. If the auditor's opinion is to provide credibility to the financial statements [statements prepared by the entity's management, which essentially report on their (i.e., management's) own performance], it is essential that financial statement users read and understand the audit report.

---

[34] Scope limitations are explained in section 14.4 above.

Yet, as is shown below, evidence from many parts of the English-speaking world suggests that, particularly until the 'expanded' (or 'long form')[35] audit report was adopted some two decades ago, this was not the case. Indeed, it was principally as a result of concern about the apparent ineffectiveness of the audit report as a means of communication that the former 'short form' standard audit report was replaced by an 'expanded' form of audit report.

An example of the short form audit report used in the UK prior to the adoption (in 1993)[36] of the expanded report, is presented in Figure 14.8. It can be seen from this Figure that the report is characterised by its brevity. It merely states that the accounts have been audited in accordance with auditing standards, they give a true and fair view of the company's and group's state of affairs at 31 December 1991, and the group's profit (or loss) and cash flows for the year then ended, and that they comply with the Companies Act 1985.

Figure 14.8: **Example of standard unqualified audit report used in the UK until 1993**

Report of the auditors

To the members of The Peninsular and Oriental Steam Navigation Company

We have audited the accounts on pages 27 to 49 in accordance with Auditing Standards.

In our opinion the accounts give a true and fair view of the state of affairs of the Company and the Group at 31 December 1991 and of the profit and cash flows of the Group for the year then ended and have been properly prepared in accordance with the Companies Act 1985.

London   KPMG Peat Marwick
24 March 1992   Chartered Accountants
                                                                              Registered Auditor

From the early 1970s, the apparent deficiencies of the short form audit report attracted considerable attention, particularly in the United States of America (USA), Canada, the UK, New Zealand and Australia. Studies by, for example, Lee and Tweedie (1975) in the UK and Wilton and Tabb (1978) in New Zealand, found that little more than 50 per cent of financial statement users read audit reports. Further, in the USA, the Commission on Auditors' Responsibilities (CAR; 1978; the Cohen Commission) found that the standard short form audit report (then in use) served to confuse rather than inform financial statement users. The Commission noted, for example, that "users are unaware of the limitations of the audit function and are confused about the distinction between the responsibilities of management and those of the auditor" (p. 71). Surveys conducted by researchers such as Lee (1970) in the UK, Beck (1973) in

---

[35] The equivalent of what is known in the UK as the 'expanded' audit report is referred to as the 'long form' report in countries such as the USA, Australia and New Zealand.

[36] The expanded audit report was adopted first, in the USA, in 1988.

Australia, the Canadian Institute of Chartered Accountants (CICA; 1988) in Canada, and Porter (1993) in New Zealand, provide support for the Cohen Commission's conclusions. These surveys found that a significant number of auditee representatives (directors, senior executives, chief accountants and internal auditors of companies), as well as financial statement users, believed that auditors are responsible for preparing auditees' financial statements, that they verify *every* transaction of the entity, and that a 'clean' audit report signifies the auditor guarantees that the financial statements are accurate and/or the reporting entity is financially secure.

Concerned about the apparent shortcomings of the short form audit report, and stimulated by the Cohen Commission's (CAR, 1978) observation that "the auditor's standard report is almost the only formal means used both to educate and inform users of financial statements concerning the audit function" (p. 71), professional accountancy bodies in most parts of the English-speaking world developed and adopted an expanded form of audit report. More specifically, since 1988, new audit report auditing standards prescribing the use of an expanded audit report have been promulgated by the American Institute of Certified Public Accountants (AICPA), the CICA, the Auditing Practices Board (APB; UK), the Australian Accounting Research Foundation (AARF), the New Zealand Society of Accountants (NZSA)[37] and the International Federation of Accountants (IFAC). In each case, unlike its predecessor short form report, the new expanded report included, *inter alia*:
- a statement explaining the respective responsibilities of the directors and auditor for the entity's financial statements;
- a brief description of the audit process;
- a statement that an audit is planned and performed so as to obtain sufficient appropriate audit evidence to provide reasonable assurance that the financial statements are free (or not free, as the case may be) of material misstatement, whether caused by fraud, other irregularity or error.

An example of the expanded form of audit report adopted in the UK in 1993 is presented in Figure 14.9. This shows the unqualified audit report issued by Ernst & Young on the 1995 financial statements of British Airways Plc.

The primary motive for the professional accountancy bodies adopting the expanded audit report was to educate financial statement users about the respective responsibilities of the directors and auditor for the financial statements, the audit process, and the level of assurance provided by the auditor's opinion. Studies by Kelly and Mohrweis (1989), Hatherly, Innes and Brown (1991), and Zachry (1991), among others, suggest that the expanded report has achieved some success in meeting its objectives. However, this has been at the

---

[37] The NZSA is now known as the New Zealand Institute of Chartered Accountants (NZICA).

Figure 14.9:   Example of the standard unqualified audit report adopted for use in the UK in 1993

Report of the auditors to the members of British Airways Plc

We have audited the accounts on Pages 16 to 47, which have been prepared under the historical cost convention as modified by the revaluation of certain fixed assets and on the basis of the accounting policies set out on Pages 20 to 22.

Respective responsibilities of Directors and auditors

As described above, the Company's Directors are responsible for the preparation of the accounts. It is our responsibility to form an independent opinion, based on our audit, on those accounts and to report our opinion to you.

Basis of opinion

We conducted our audit in accordance with Auditing Standards issued by the Auditing Practices Board. An audit includes examination, on a test basis, of evidence relevant to the amounts and disclosures in the accounts. It also includes an assessment of the significant estimates and judgements made by the Directors in the preparation of the accounts and of whether the accounting policies are appropriate to the Group's circumstances, consistently applied and adequately disclosed.

We planned and performed our audit so as to obtain all the information and explanations which we considered necessary in order to provide us with sufficient evidence to give reasonable assurance that the accounts are free from material misstatement, whether caused by fraud or other irregularity or error. In forming our opinion we also evaluated the overall adequacy of the presentation of information in the accounts.

Opinion

In our opinion the accounts give a true and fair view of the state of affairs of the Company and of the Group as at 31 March 1995 and of the profit of the Group for the year then ended and have been properly prepared in accordance with the Companies Act 1985.

Ernst & Young
Chartered Accountants
Registered Auditor
London
11 May 1995

cost of changing the audit report into a longer and more complex document. Further, questions have been raised, for example, by Alfano (1979), about the ease with which a financial statement user can determine whether or not the auditor has reservations about the financial statements, and the value of explaining *in the audit report* the responsibilities of the directors and auditors for the financial statements. To Alfano, this merely enables financial statement users to allocate blame if something is wrong. Additionally, commentators such as Elliott and Jacobson (1987) have questioned the ability of a few sentences in the audit report to convey adequately the essence of the audit process. Further, Epstein (1976) found that financial statement users "are not interested in the details of an audit" but "are looking for a seal of approval" (as reported, CAR, 1978, p. 164). As Alfano (1979) has expressed it: "the reader wants to know whether the statements are right or wrong" (p. 39) – a fact they could glean by merely glancing at the former short form report. Certainly, it seems pertinent to ask whether financial statement users require details of the auditor's and the directors' responsibilities for the financial statements, and a standard description of the audit process, in *every* audit report. Financial statement users need to be informed about these matters, but ways more appropriate than including it in every audit report could perhaps be found.[38] According to critics of the expanded audit report (such as those named above), including the information in the audit report detracts from fulfilment of the report's primary function, that is, conveying the auditor's opinion on the accompanying financial statements.

Notwithstanding the criticism levelled against the expanded audit report, since 1993 its wording has been amended to provide even more information. Comparison of the unqualified audit reports issued by Ernst & Young on British Airways' 1995 financial statements, and on BP's 2006 financial statements (presented in Figures 14.9 and 14.10, respectively), shows that the content of audit reports increased significantly over this period. The detail provided in the introductory, responsibilities and opinion paragraphs all increased but the greatest difference is in the detail provided about auditors' responsibilities. More specifically, unlike the standard audit report adopted for use in the UK in 1993 (reflected in Figure 14.9), the standard form report adopted in 2004 (reflected in Figure 14.10[39]) includes information explaining:

(i)   the matters on which auditors are required to express an opinion, including the truth and fairness of the financial statements and their compliance with the relevant Companies Act and IAS Regulation, and also the consistency of the directors' report (including the business review) with the financial statements;

(ii)   the matters on which auditors are required to report if the entity has not complied with relevant statutory and/or regulatory requirements (for example, if the entity has not disclosed required information relating to directors' remuneration and related party transactions) and if they have not received the information and explanations they required for the purposes of the audit;

(iii) auditors' responsibility with respect to the nine provisions of *The Combined Code on Corporate Governance* they are required to review. It also highlights certain corporate governance matters that lie outside auditors' responsibilities (for example, forming an opinion on the effectiveness of the group's corporate governance procedures or its risk and control procedures);

---

[38] As we observe in footnotes 18 and 20, the provisions of CA 2006, ss. 416 and 493, may render the disclosure of the directors' and auditors' responsibilities in companies' audit reports redundant in the UK. Where companies provide adequate explanations about the directors' and auditors' responsibilities for the financial statements in their annual reports or elsewhere that is readily accessible to financial statement users, such as the entity's website, the audit report merely needs to make reference to the location of the information that is provided elsewhere.

[39] This audit report complies with the Companies Act 1985 and ISA 700: *The auditor's report on financial statements* (2004) and, other than the insertion of the third paragraph in the introductory section, follows the wording recommended by the APB in Bulletin 2006/6, Appendix 1, Example 7 (APB, 2006).

Figure 14.10:   Example of the standard unqualified audit report adopted for use in the UK in 2004

Independent auditor's report to the members of BP p.l.c.

We have audited the consolidated financial statements of BP p.l.c. for the year ended 31 December 2006, which comprise the group income statement, the group balance sheet, the group cash flow statement, the group statement of recognized income and expense and the related notes 1 to 51.   These consolidated financial statements have been prepared under the accounting policies set out therein.

We have reported separately on the parent company financial statements of BP p.l.c. for the year ended 31 December 2006 and on the information in the Directors' Remuneration Report that is described as having been audited.

This report is made solely to the company's members, as a body, in accordance with Section 235 of the Companies Act 1985.   Our audit work has been undertaken so that we might state to the company's members those matters we are required to state to them in an auditors' report and for no other purpose.   To the fullest extent permitted by law, we do not accept or assume responsibility to anyone other than the company and the company's members as a body, for our audit work, for this report, or for the opinions we have formed.

Respective responsibilities of directors and auditors

The directors are responsible for preparing the Annual Report and the consolidated financial statements in accordance with applicable United Kingdom law and International Financial Reporting Standards (IFRS) as adopted by the European Union as set out in the Statement of directors' responsibilities in respect of the consolidated financial statements.

Our responsibility is to audit the consolidated financial statements in accordance with relevant legal and regulatory requirements and International Standards on Auditing (UK and Ireland).

We report to you our opinion as to whether the consolidated financial statements give a true and fair view and whether the consolidated financial statements have been properly prepared in accordance with the Companies Act 1985 and Article 4 of the IAS Regulation. We also report to you whether in our opinion the information given in the directors' report, including the business review, is consistent with the financial statements.

In addition we report to you if, in our opinion, we have not received all the information and explanations we require for our audit, or if information specified by law regarding directors' remuneration and other transactions is not disclosed.

We review whether the governance board performance report reflects the company's compliance with the nine provisions of the 2006 Combined Code Principles of Good Governance and Code of Best Practice specified for our review by the Listing Rules of the Financial Services Authority, and we report if it does not. We are not required to consider whether the board's statements on internal control cover all risks and controls, or form an opinion on the effectiveness of the group's corporate governance procedures or its risk and control procedures.

We read other information contained in the Annual Report and consider whether it is consistent with the audited consolidated financial statements. The other information comprises the Additional information for US reporting, the Supplementary information on oil and natural gas, the Directors' Report and the Governance: Board performance report. We consider the implications for our report if we become aware of any apparent misstatements or material inconsistencies with the consolidated financial statements. Our responsibilities do not extend to any other information.

Basis of audit opinion

We conducted our audit in accordance with International Standards on Auditing (UK and Ireland) issued by the Auditing Practices Board. An audit includes examination, on a test basis, of evidence relevant to the amounts and disclosures in the consolidated financial statements. It also includes an assessment of the significant estimates and judgements made by the directors in the preparation of the consolidated financial statements, and of whether the accounting policies are appropriate to the group's circumstances, consistently applied and adequately disclosed.

We planned and performed our audit so as to obtain all the information and explanations which we considered necessary in order to provide us with sufficient evidence to give reasonable assurance that the consolidated financial statements are free from material misstatement, whether caused by fraud or other irregularity or error.

In forming our opinion we also evaluated the overall adequacy of the presentation of information in the consolidated financial statements.

Figure 14.10: *Continued*

Opinion

In our opinion:

– The consolidated financial statements give a true and fair view, in accordance with IFRS as adopted by the European Union, of the state of the group's affairs as at 31 December 2006 and of its profit for the year then ended.

– The group financial statements have been properly prepared in accordance with the Companies Act 1985 and Article 4 of the IAS Regulation.

– The information given in the directors' report is consistent with the consolidated financial statements.

Separate opinion in relation to IFRS

As explained in Note 1 to the consolidated financial statements, the group, in addition to complying with its legal obligation to comply with IFRS as adopted by the European Union, has also complied with IFRS as issued by the International Accounting Standards Board. In our opinion the consolidated financial statements give a true and fair view, in accordance with IFRS, of the state of the group's affairs as at 31 December 2006 and of its profit for the year then ended.

Ernst & Young LLP
Registered auditor
London
23 February 2007

(iv) that auditors read specified other information in the annual report to identify any apparent misstatements or material inconsistencies with the financial statements but their responsibilities do not extend beyond the information specified. (In BP's case, Ernst & Young reported that it had read the additional information presented by BP for US reporting purposes, supplementary information relating to oil and natural gas, the directors' report, and the directors' corporate governance report.)

The additional information provided by Ernst & Young in the Opinion paragraph on the 2006 financial statements compared with that provided in 1995 reflects the additional matters on which auditors were legally required to express an opinion in 2006. Similarly, much of the additional information provided in the standard audit report adopted for use in the UK in 2004 reflects the additional responsibilities placed on auditors by the law, regulations or auditing standards since 1993 when the expanded form of the audit report was first adopted for use in the UK.

Before leaving Ernst & Young's report on BP's 2006 consolidated financial statements, we should note that the third paragraph in the introductory section of the report is not required by legislation, regulation or auditing standards. It has been included by Ernst & Young in an attempt to limit the parties to whom it may be liable should these financial statements, on which it has expressed an unqualified opinion, subsequently prove to be materially misstated.[40]

---

[40] In Chapter 16 we explore the other ways in other auditors have attempted to limit their liability.

From Figure 14.10 we can see that the audit report in use in the UK in 2006 is long and complex. Nevertheless, it provides readers with useful information about the auditor's responsibilities and the basis for the auditor's opinion. It should give users of the financial statements some understanding of what the audit entailed and the reliance they may (justifiably) place on the auditor's opinion. Further, the section headings reduce the report's complexity by providing guidance to readers about the content of the various sections; similarly, the heading for the Opinion paragraph signals whether the auditor's opinion is unqualified, qualified, adverse or a disclaimer of opinion. However, we should note that, while qualified, adverse, and disclaimers of opinion are clearly signalled as such in the Opinion paragraph heading, the same does not apply to an unqualified opinion; in this case, the heading is limited to 'Opinion'. In our view, financial statements users would benefit from an equally clear signal in the case of an unqualified audit opinion.

ISA 700 (Revised) seems to be an attempt by the International Auditing and Assurance Standards Board (IAASB) to clarify the information content of the standard audit report and to highlight the auditor's opinion on the financial statements.[41] Comparing Ernst & Young's audit report on BP's 2006 financial statements with the example audit report presented in Figure 14.1 [that complies with the Companies Act 2006 and ISA 700 (Revised)], we can see that the content overall is very similar but the ISA 700 (Revised) report has a two-part structure – the first relates to the audited financial statements and the second to auditors' other legal and regulatory responsibilities. Each part of the report contains an explanation of the auditor's responsibilities as they relate to the matters reported in that part, and the auditor's opinion on those matters.

Although the increased information provided in the standard audit report should aid users' understanding of an audit and the reliance they may place on the auditor's opinion, research conducted by the Audit Quality Forum's (AQF) working group on auditor reporting (AQF, 2007) found that financial statement users consider the standard audit report[42] to be:

> too boilerplate and overly standardised and . . . shareholders can feel excluded from what they perceive to be the "real" findings of the audit. . . . [T]he current format of the audit report is too long . . . with reports being virtually identical from one company to another and, consequently, most of the information [is] too generic to be of real use. . . . [D]espite the existence of wording within the audit report that provides the assurance that the annual accounts have been prepared in accordance with the relevant standards and show a true and fair view, the report does not clearly identify the key areas of audit focus that were addressed to arrive at these conclusions. (AQF, 2007, paras 25, 46)

---

[41] As we note in footnote 12, ISA 700 (Revised) [IFAC, 2006b) became effective for audit reports dated on or after 31 December 2006 but, at the time of writing, the APB had not adopted ISA 700 (Revised) for use in the UK. The standard audit report presented in Figure 14.10 remained current in the UK in 2008.

[42] The standard audit report reflected in Figure 14.10 was the subject of the research.

The research found that financial statement users want audit reports to be less standardised, more company-specific and more discursive. Specifically, they would like audit reports to provide:

- more information about emphases of matter, and reference to uncertainties and future risks;
- discussion of material issues encountered during the audit and how they were resolved;
- discussion of alternative accounting treatments considered, and the reasons for selecting the treatment adopted, where material;
- more information on material areas of judgment, and difficult, sensitive or contentious issues (AQF, 2007)

It is pertinent to observe that, as we will see in section 14.8 below, much of this information is reported by the auditor to the company's directors but neither legislation nor auditing standards require it to be reported to shareholders or other users of the company's financial statements.

The AQF's working group on auditor reporting found that financial statement users acknowledge that much of the standardised wording in the audit report "is necessary in order to provide clarification as to what auditors' responsibilities are and perhaps more importantly, in order to clarify what auditors both can and cannot do" (AQF, 2007, para 25). However, the other information they would like to see included in the audit report, as outlined above, brings us into the realm of 'free form' reporting, whereby each audit report is specifically prepared for the audit that has been performed. A move away from 'boilerplate, standardised wording' is likely to encourage financial statement users to read the audit report and to better understand the context and meaning of the auditor's opinion. However, free form reporting also has some significant disadvantages. These include the following:

- the absence of standardised wording may cause confusion for financial statement users regarding the auditor's precise meaning; it may "give rise to misunderstandings, unrealistic expectations, misplaced concerns and other problems derived from a lack of knowledge on the part of shareholders as compared to directors who have in depth knowledge as a result of running the business" (AQF, 2007, para 47);
- preparing each audit report individually would be time-consuming and costly for the auditors and may result in their inadvertent failure to meet all of their statutory and regulatory requirements;
- auditors are bound by their duty of confidentiality and this may prevent them from disclosing their discussions about company matters to anyone other than the directors;
- provision of additional information within the audit report, beyond that which is required by legislation, regulation or auditing standards, could extend auditors' exposure to liability;

- much of the information obtained by auditors may be commercially sensitive 'insider information' such that there is a risk of influencing the market value of the company by inappropriately making sensitive information more widely available.

According to the AQF working group, considerations of auditors' duty of confidentiality, 'insider trading' implications and potential extension of their exposure to liability result in auditors tending to be circumspect in what they say and how they say it (AQF, 2007, paras 22, 28).

As we note in footnote 38, the Companies Act 2006 (ss. 416 and 493) may result in the responsibilities of the directors and auditors for a company's financial statements being explained by the directors in the company's annual report. If this eventuates, there will be no need for the information also to be provided in the auditor's report. As a consequence, the content of the audit report could be reduced to a brief description of the information within the annual report that is subject to audit and the auditor's opinion on:
  (i) the financial statements; and
  (ii) other legal and regulatory matters on which the auditor is required to express an opinion.[43]
Such a report would be concise, and easily read and understood; it would also be akin to the short form audit report that prevailed until adoption of the extended form in 1988 in the USA and 1993 in the UK.

If a statement explaining the directors' and auditor's responsibilities for the financial statements is not included in a company's annual report, or if the statement does not provide sufficient detail for financial statement users to be clear about the parties' respective responsibilities and/or what the audit entailed, the information could be provided in an appendix to the audit report (AQF, 2007, para 53) or elsewhere that is readily accessible to financial statement users. This would enable the auditor's report *per se* to remain succinct, and to convey clearly the auditor's key messages about their opinion on the financial statements and their other legal and regulatory responsibilities. However, the APB (2007a) warns that ISA 700 (Revised) is prescriptive as regards the wording to be included in audit reports describing the directors' and auditor's responsibilities, and deviations or omissions from what is prescribed may preclude the auditor from stating that the audit has been conducted in accordance with ISAs (APB, 2007a, paras 4.16, 4.19).

---

[43] In this regard, the APB (2007a) has expressed the view that, in respect of the matters CA 2006 requires auditors to form an opinion but only to report on if something is amiss (for example, if adequate records have not been kept by the company or the auditor has not received all the information (s)he required for the purpose of the audit), it would be helpful to readers of the auditor's report if the auditor's opinion included, in applicable cases, a statement to the effect that there is nothing to report on the matters concerned (para 3.19).

14.8 AUDITORS' COMMUNICATION WITH THOSE CHARGED WITH GOVERNANCE

14.8.1 Importance and purpose of governance communications

In addition to issuing audit reports on the financial statements, auditors are required to communicate with those charged with their auditees' governance (i.e., their board of directors) on various aspects of the audit. ISA 260: *Communication with those charged with governance* provides guidance for auditors on these communications (which we refer to as 'governance communications'). It explains that they enable the auditor to:

(i) communicate to the directors the auditor's responsibilities in relation to the financial statement audit, and to provide an overview of the planned scope and timing of the audit;

(ii) obtain from the directors information relevant to the audit; for example, the directors may assist the auditor in understanding the entity and its environment, in identifying appropriate sources of audit evidence, and in providing information about specific transactions or events;

(iii) provide the directors with timely observations arising from the audit that are significant and relevant to their responsibility to oversee the financial reporting process – and thereby assist them to fulfil their responsibility for the financial statements and reduce the risk of material misstatement therein;

(iv) promote effective two-way communication between the auditor and the directors to enable a constructive working relationship, and mutual understanding about audit matters, to develop.

The fundamental principle of external auditing included in *The Auditors' Code* (APB, 2008) – Providing Value reflects some of these benefits of governance communications. It states:

> Auditors add to the reliability and quality of financial reporting; they provide to directors and officers constructive observations arising from the audit process; and thereby contribute to the effective operation of business capital markets and the public sector.

In cases where auditees have an audit committee, auditors usually communicate with that committee rather than with the full board of directors.[44] In this regard, ISA 260 observes:

> [C]ommunication with the audit committee, where one exists, has become a key element in the auditor's communication with those charged with governance. Good governance principles suggest that:

---

[44] In this section, wherever we use the term 'the directors', it should be read as 'the directors or, if the entity has one, the audit committee'. In this connection, it should be recalled that, under the provisions of *The Combined Code* (FRC, 2006), listed companies are required to have an audit committee or disclose that they do not have one and the reasons therefor.

- The auditor will be invited to regularly attend meetings of the audit committee.
- The chair of the audit committee and, when relevant, the other members of the audit committee, will liaise with the auditor periodically.
- The audit committee will meet the auditor without management [i.e., senior executives] present at least annually. (para A11)

However, the Standard (para A10) also notes that when auditors communicate with an audit committee (or other subgroup of the board of directors) they are required to determine whether and, if so, the extent to which, they also need to communicate with the full board. Factors affecting their decision include their assessment of how effectively and appropriately the audit committee communicates relevant information to the full board.

14.8.2 Matters to be communicated

Regarding the matters to be included in governance communications, ISA 260 conveniently groups them into the following four categories:
- (i) the auditor's responsibilities in relation to the financial statement audit;
- (ii) planned scope and timing of the audit;
- (iii) significant audit findings; and
- (iv) auditor independence.

We discuss each of these categories below.

(i) The auditor's responsibilities in relation to the financial statement audit

The auditor is required to communicate to the auditee's directors[45] that:

- the auditor is responsible for forming and expressing an opinion on the financial statements that have been prepared by, or whose preparation has been overseen by, the directors;
- the auditor is required to communicate to the directors significant matters arising from the audit of the financial statements that are relevant to the directors in overseeing the financial reporting process;
- the audit of the financial statements does not relieve the directors of their responsibility for the financial statements and the financial reporting process (ISA 260, paras 10, A13).

(ii) Planned scope and timing of the audit

ISA 260 requires the auditor to communicate to the directors an overview of the planned scope and timing of the audit. It notes that this communication may:

---

[45] ISA 260, para A13, notes that the auditor's responsibilities are often included in the audit engagement letter and providing the directors with a copy of that letter may be an appropriate way to communicate the auditor's responsibilities in respect of the financial statements. (Audit engagement letters are discussed in Chapter 8, section 8.3.)

(a) assist the directors to:
- better understand the consequences of the auditor's work,
- discuss with the auditor issues of risk and materiality,
- identify areas in which they wish the auditor to undertake additional work; and
(b) assist the auditor to better understand the entity and its environment (paras 11, A15).

However, the Standard (para A16) warns that care is needed not to provide too much detail about, for example, the nature and timing of audit procedures, as this may compromise the effectiveness of the audit. This is particularly the case when executives are members of the auditee's board of directors or, more especially, its audit committee.

The auditor's communication to the auditee's directors regarding the scope and timing of the audit generally includes matters such as the following:
- an outline of the general approach and overall scope of the work the auditor proposes to undertake, and the form of the reports the auditor expects to make;
- an indication of how the auditor proposes to address the significant risks of material misstatement in the financial statements, whether due to fraud or error;
- the auditor's approach to internal control relevant to the audit;
- application of the concept of materiality in the context of the audit;
- the extent, if any, to which the auditor will use the work of the auditee's internal auditors, and how the external and internal auditors can best work together in a constructive and complementary manner.

However, this communication is not a one-way process; it should involve a two-way interaction between the auditor and the directors to the mutual benefit of both parties. Auditors frequently find it useful to ascertain from, or discuss with, the directors matters such as:
- the directors' views about the entity's objectives and strategies, and related business risks that may result in material misstatements in the financial statements;
- matters the directors consider warrant particular attention during the audit, and any areas where they request additional work to be undertaken;
- any significant communications the entity has with regulators;
- other matters the directors consider may influence the audit of the financial statements;
- the attitudes, awareness, and actions of the directors concerning:
  - the entity's internal control and its importance in the entity, including how the directors oversee the effectiveness of internal control, and
  - the detection or possibility of fraud within the auditee;

- the directors' response to developments in, for example, legislation, accounting standards, corporate governance practices, listing rules, and other developments relevant to the entity's financial statements and annual report;
- the directors' response to previous communications from the auditor. If significant matters raised previously have not been dealt with effectively, the auditor needs to enquire why appropriate action has not been taken. (S)he should also consider raising the matter(s) again, in the current communication; otherwise, the directors may gain the impression that the matters are no longer of significance.

(iii) Significant audit findings

Various ISAs require the auditor to communicate significant findings of the audit to the auditee's directors. These include the following:

(a) qualitative aspects of the entity's accounting practices and financial reporting (ISA 260; *Communication with those charged with governance*, para 12a);

(b) significant difficulties, if any, encountered during the audit (ISA 260, para 12b);

(c) uncorrected misstatements (ISA 450; *Evaluation of misstatements identified during the audit*, paras 12, 13, A23; IAASB, 2008c);

(d) significant deficiencies in internal control identified during the audit (ISA 265: *Communicating deficiencies in internal control*);

We discuss each of the above matters in more detail below.

(e) significant matters, if any, arising from the audit that were discussed, or were the subject of correspondence, with senior executives. These may include, for example, business conditions affecting the entity, the entity's business plans and strategies that may affect the risk of material misstatement in the financial statements, and concerns about senior executives' consultations with other accountants on accounting or auditing matters (ISA 260: *Communication with those charged with governance*, paras 12c, A23);

(f) any matters related to fraud that, in the auditor's judgment, are relevant to the directors' responsibilities to oversee the financial reporting process. More specifically, ISA 240: *The auditor's responsibilities relating to fraud* ... (IAASB, 2006a) suggests that the matters discussed may include the following:
  - Concerns about the nature, extent and frequency of management's assessments of the controls in place to prevent and detect fraud and of the risk that the financial statements may be misstated.
  - A failure by management to appropriately address identified significant deficiencies in internal control, or to appropriately respond to an identified fraud.

- The auditor's evaluation of the entity's control environment, including questions regarding the competence and integrity of management.
- Actions by management [i.e., senior executives] that may be indicative of fraudulent financial reporting, such as management's selection and application of accounting policies that may be indicative of management's effort to manage earnings in order to deceive financial statement users by influencing their perceptions as to the entity's performance and profitability.
- Concerns about the adequacy and completeness of the authorization of transactions that appear to be outside the normal course of business. (para A63);

(g) any matters (other than those which are clearly inconsequential) involving non-compliance with laws and regulations that have a material effect on the financial statements or otherwise come to the auditor's attention during the course of the audit (ISA 250: *Consideration of laws and regulations in an audit of financial statements*, para 22; IAASB, 2008b);

(h) material uncertainties related to events and conditions that may cast significant doubt on the entity's ability to continue as a going concern and, more particularly, whether adherence to the going concern assumption is appropriate, and whether the relevant matters are adequately disclosed in the financial statements (ISA 570: *Going Concern*, para 23; IAASB, 2008e);

(i) significant matters identified during the audit regarding the entity's related party relationships and transactions. ISA 550: *Related parties*, para A50 (IAASB, 2008d), notes that communicating these matters enables the auditor to establish a common understanding with the directors about the nature and resolution of related party matters. Examples of significant related party matters include the following:
- non-disclosure (whether intentional or not) by senior executives to the auditor of related parties or significant related party transactions;
- identification of significant related party transactions that have not been appropriately authorised and approved, which may give rise to suspected fraud;
- disagreement with senior executives about accounting for, and disclosure of, significant related party transactions required by the applicable financial reporting framework;
- non-compliance with applicable laws or regulations prohibiting or restricting specific types of related party transactions;
- difficulties in confirming the identity of the party that ultimately controls the entity;

(j) any other audit matters warranting attention by the directors or audit committee that are significant to their oversight of the financial reporting process (ISA 260: *Communication with those charged with governances*, para 12d).

We now return to examine in more detail the first four significant audit findings listed about [(a) to (d)] that auditors are to communicate to the directors.

(a) *Qualitative aspects of accounting practices and financial reporting*: ISA 260, para A21, explains:

> Financial reporting frameworks ordinarily allow for the entity to make accounting estimates, and judgments about accounting policies and financial statement disclosures. Open and constructive communication about significant qualitative aspects of the entity's accounting practices may include comment on the acceptability of significant accounting practices.

Other matters likely to be discussed include:

- the appropriateness of accounting policies selected to the particular circumstances of the auditee. Where acceptable alternative accounting policies exist, the auditor may communicate to the directors the financial statement items that are affected by the choice of significant accounting policies and inform them of accounting policies used by similar entities;
- the selection of, and changes in, significant accounting policies (including the application of new accounting pronouncements) that have, or could have, a material effect on the entity's financial statements;
- the effect of the timing of transactions in relation to the reporting period in which they are recorded;
- the items for which accounting estimates are significant, the entity's process for making such estimates, the reasonableness of the accounting estimates included in the financial statements, the possibility of bias in accounting estimates, and disclosure of estimation uncertainty in the financial statements;
- the issues involved, and related judgments made, in formulating particularly sensitive financial statement disclosures such as those related to revenue recognition, remuneration, going concern, subsequent events and contingency issues;
- the potential effect on the financial statements of any significant risks, exposures and uncertainties, such as pending litigation, that are required to be disclosed in the financial statements;
- the extent to which the financial statements are affected by unusual transactions including non-recurring amounts recognised in the reporting period, and the extent to which such transactions are required to be separately disclosed in the financial statements;
- the factors affecting asset and liability carrying values, including the entity's bases for determining the useful economic lives of tangible and intangible assets. The communication may explain how factors affecting carrying values were selected and how alternative selections would have affected the financial statements (ISA 260, Appendix 2).

(b) *Significant difficulties encountered during the audit*: ISA 260, para A22, observes that significant difficulties encountered during the audit that should be communicated to the directors may include:

- significant delays in the auditor being provided with requested information;
- the unavailability of expected information;
- the unwillingness of senior executives to make, or provide to the auditor, their assessment of the entity's ability to continue as a going concern when requested;
- attempts by senior executives to place restrictions on the auditor; this may include the entity providing the auditor with an unnecessarily brief time within which to complete the audit.

ISA 260, para A22, notes that, in some circumstances, difficulties such as those outlined about may constitute a scope limitation that would lead to a modified audit report.

(c) *Uncorrected misstatements*: As we explain in Chapter 11, section 11.5, as the audit progresses, the auditor accumulates identified misstatements and communicates them to senior executives (such as the finance director and/or chief executive, or their equivalents) and requests that they be corrected. If the senior executives refuse to correct some or all of the misstatements on the grounds that their effect is immaterial, individually or in aggregate, to the financial statements as a whole, the auditor is to obtain written representations from the senior executives to this effect, together with a summary of the uncorrected misstatements.

As an element of the auditor's governance communication to the entity's directors, (s)he is required to inform the directors of the misstatements the senior executives have refused to correct, and their reasons for so doing. The auditor is to provide the written representations obtained from the senior executives on the matter, together with the summary of the unadjusted misstatements attached to, or included in, the executives' written representations. All material misstatements are to be identified individually. The auditor is required to request the directors to correct the uncorrected misstatements and discuss with them the reasons for, and implications of, a failure to correct misstatement. In so doing, the auditor is to have regard to the size and nature of the misstatement judged in the surrounding circumstances, and possible implications for future financial statements (ISA 450: *Evaluation of misstatements identified during the audit*, paras 12, A23; IAASB, 2008c). As discussed earlier in this chapter, an auditor cannot issue an unqualified audit report on financial statements that are materially misstated so, if the directors decline to correct misstatements the auditor judges to be material, the auditor will have little choice but to express a modified opinion.

Additionally, the auditor is required to communicate to the directors the effect of uncorrected misstatements in prior periods on relevant classes of transactions, account balances or disclosures, and to the financial statements as a whole, in the current period (ISA 450, para 13, IAASB, 2008c).

(d) *Significant deficiencies in internal control identified during the audit*: ISA 265: *Communicating deficiencies in internal control* defines an internal control deficiency and significant deficiency as follows:

> Deficiency in internal control – A control that is either missing or is designed, implemented or operated in such a way that it is unable to prevent, or detect and correct, misstatements in the financial statements on a timely basis. (para 6a)
>
> Significant deficiency – A deficiency or combination of deficiencies in internal control relevant to the audit that, in the auditor's professional judgment, is of sufficient importance to merit the attention of those charged with governance [i.e., the board of directors]. (para 6b)

The Standard (para A6) explains that the indicators of significant deficiencies include:
- Deficiencies in the control environment, such as:
  - Ineffective oversight of the financial reporting process by those charged with governance, especially in an environment with limited segregation of duties.
  - Identification of management fraud, whether or not material, that was not prevented by the entity's internal control.
- A deficiency in a control over a significant risk.
- Material misstatements detected by the auditor's procedures that were not identified by the entity's internal control.
- Restatement of previously issued financial statements to reflect the correction of a material misstatement due to error or fraud.

Prior to publication of ISA 260: *Communication with those charged with governance*, auditors routinely reported to their auditees' directors and/or senior executives material weaknesses (or, in ISA 265 terminology, significant deficiencies) in internal control discovered during an audit in a 'Management Letter'. In addition to noting the existence and effect of the internal control deficiencies, recommendations were made as to ways in which they might be rectified.

Management letters were usually provided at the conclusion of both the interim and the final audit. The interim letter, which reported internal control deficiencies discovered during the interim audit, was sent to senior executives (such as the chief executive and/or the finance director) or the audit committee as soon as possible after the interim audit so that the deficiencies could be rectified on a timely basis. The final management letter was frequently broader in nature than the interim letter and usually included comments on the conduct and findings of the audit as a whole. However, the main focus was generally on matters relating to the entity's accounting and internal control systems and/or its financial affairs, where the auditor considered improvements could be made.

The governance communication now required by ISA 260: *Communication with those charged with governance*, has developed from the former final management letter but, as can be seen from the matters discussed above, is much broader in scope than its predecessor. However, publication of ISA 265[46]: *Communicating deficiencies in internal control*, reflects the importance the auditing profession accords to auditors reporting internal control deficiencies to their auditees' managements, and the requirements of auditors in this regard are now much more explicit. As we indicate in Chapter 10, section 10.7, in general, auditors are required to communicate all deficiencies in internal control (other than those that are clearly trivial) identified during the audit to management (i.e., senior executives) at an appropriate level of responsibility on a timely basis. Although auditors usually indicate ways in which the deficiencies may be rectified, ISA 265 notes:

> Management may already be aware of deficiencies that the auditor has identified during the audit and may have chosen not to remedy them because of cost or other considerations. The responsibility for evaluating the costs and benefits of implementing remedial action rests with management. Accordingly, the requirement for the auditor to communicate deficiencies to management [i.e., senior executives] applies regardless of cost or other considerations that management may consider relevant in determining whether to remedy such deficiencies. (para A11)

In addition to reporting internal control deficiencies to appropriate executives within the entity, auditors are required to communicate significant deficiencies identified during the audit to the directors in writing on a timely basis. The written communication is to include:

- a description of the deficiencies and an explanation of their potential effects;
- sufficient information to enable the directors to understand the context of the communication. In particular, the auditor is to explain that:
  - the audit was not planned and performed with a view to identifying all deficiencies in internal control that might exist;
  - the matters reported are limited to those deficiencies identified during the audit that the auditor concluded should be reported to the directors; and

---

[46] The Exposure Draft of ISA 265 was published in December 2007. The final standard is expected to be issued by December 2008.

- the purpose of the audit was to express an audit opinion on the financial statements, and audit procedures have not been performed to obtain reasonable assurance, and no assurance is provided, on the effectiveness of internal control (ISA 265, paras 10, 11).

(iv) Auditor independence

For auditees that are listed companies, ISA 260: *Communication with those charged with governance* para 13, requires the auditor to communicate to their directors:

- confirmation that the engagement team, the audit firm and, if applicable, its related firms, have complied with relevant ethical requirements regarding independence;[47]
- all relationships between the firm, its related firms, and the entity that, in the auditor's professional judgment, may reasonably be thought to bear on independence;
- the total amount of fees the audit firm (and its related entities) has charged the client entity (and its related entities) for the provision of services during the reporting period, analysed into appropriate categories; for example, statutory audit services, further audit services, tax advisory services and other non-audit services. The categories are to be such as to enable the directors to assess the effect of the provision of services on the auditor's independence; and
- safeguards that have been applied to eliminate identified threats to independence or reduce them to an acceptable level.

These requirements underline the importance the auditing profession places on auditors being, and being seen to be, independent of their audit clients. They also accord with ISA 220: *Quality control for an audit of financial statements*, para 10 (IAASB, 2008a), which requires audit engagement partners to form a conclusion on compliance with the independence requirements that apply to the audit engagement. This includes identifying threats to independence and appropriate action taken to eliminate such threats or reduce them to an acceptable level. They similarly accord with provision C.3.2 of *The Combined Code on Corporate Governance* (FRC, 2006), which requires the audit committees of listed companies, *inter alia*, to keep under review the independence and objectivity of the company's auditors.

14.8.3 Form and frequency of communications

Although auditors are required to communicate with the directors as an element of all audits of companies' financial statements, the form, content and frequency of the communication varies widely – reflecting variations in the size,

---

[47] The ethical requirements are discussed in detail in Chapter 4.

complexity, organisation and nature of auditees, as well as in auditors' views about the importance of matters relevant to the audit. The larger and more complex the organisation, the more formal the governance communication is likely to be. To ensure there is no misunderstanding between the auditor and the directors regarding the governance communication(s), ISA 260: *Communication with those charged with governance*, para 14, requires auditors to communicate with the directors about the form, timing and expected general content of the communications.

Noting that effective communication may involve structured presentations and written reports as well as less structured communications, including discussions, ISA 260 specifies that, in general, auditors may communicate with the directors orally and/or in writing. However, the significant findings from the audit and statements relating to independence must be communicated in writing. Auditors also need to communicate in writing when, in their professional judgment, oral communication would not be adequate (ISA 260, paras 15, 16, A41).

When deciding the appropriate form of the communication (for example, whether to communicate orally or in writing, the extent of the detail or summarisation that is appropriate, and whether to adopt a structured or unstructured style), auditors consider factors such as:
- the significance of the matter being communicated;
- whether the matter has been satisfactorily resolved;
- whether the matter has been communicated previously to the directors by senior executives;
- the size, operating structure, control environment, and legal structure of the entity;
- the expectations of the directors and the frequency of ongoing contact and dialogue between the auditor and the directors;
- whether the membership of the board of directors or, more particularly, the audit committee has changed significantly (ISA 260, para A42).

Regarding the timing of communications, ISA 260 requires auditors to communicate with the directors "on a timely basis" (para 17). The Standard expands on this requirement, explaining:

> The appropriate timing for communications will vary with the circumstances of the engagement. Relevant circumstances include the significance and nature of the matter, and the action expected to be taken by those charged with governance. For example:
> - Communications regarding planning matters may often be made early in the audit engagement . . . .
> - It may be appropriate to communicate a significant difficulty encountered during the audit as soon as practicable if those charged with governance are able to assist the auditor to overcome the difficulty, or if it is likely to lead to a

modified opinion. Similarly, it may be appropriate to communicate significant deficiencies in the design, implementation or operating effectiveness of internal control that have come to the auditor's attention as soon as practicable.

- Communications regarding independence may be appropriate whenever significant judgments are made about threats to independence and related safeguards, for example, when accepting an engagement to provide non-audit services, and at a concluding discussion. A concluding discussion may also be an appropriate time to communicate findings from the audit, including the auditor's views about the qualitative aspects of the entity's accounting practices. (para A44)

The auditor's task is not complete when (s)he has communicated with the directors on all relevant matters. ISA 260, para 18, requires the auditor to evaluate whether the two-way communication between the auditor and the directors has been adequate for the purpose of the audit. Factors the auditor should take into consideration when making this evaluation include the following:

- the appropriateness and timeliness of actions taken by the directors in response to matters raised by the auditor;
- the apparent openness of the directors in their communications with the auditor;
- the willingness and capacity of the directors to meet with the auditor without senior executives present;
- the apparent ability of the directors to fully comprehend matters raised by the auditor. This may be reflected, for example, by the extent to which the directors ask probing questions and question recommendations made to them; and
- the difficulty the auditor experiences in reaching a mutual understanding with the directors about the form, timing and expected general content of the governance communications (para A46).

If, in the auditor's opinion, the two-way communication has not been adequate for the purpose of the audit, the auditor is to evaluate the effect, if any, on his or her assessment of the risks of material misstatement and ability to obtain sufficient appropriate audit evidence to express an opinion on the financial statements. Having made the evaluation, the auditor is required to "take appropriate action" (ISA 260, para 18).

When matters are communicated orally to the directors (for example, by a presentation by the audit partner and audit manager), the auditor is to document the matters, and when and to whom they were communicated. Where matters are communicated in writing, the auditor is required to include a copy of the communication in the audit working papers (ISA 260, para 19).

Governance communications, like the earlier management letters, are private communications between the auditor and the directors of the client entity. They constitute a valuable service to the client which, amongst other things, assists those responsible to improve the entity's internal control system and financial reporting process. With improvements in these regards, the auditor's confidence about the completeness, accuracy and validity of the accounting data may well increase, and thus the audit work required to form an opinion about the financial statements (and hence audit fees) may, in subsequent years, be reduced.

14.9 SUMMARY

In this chapter we have discussed the reports that auditors provide for users of audited financial statements and for those charged with the governance of reporting entities. We have examined the standard form of audit report used for companies in the UK and discussed the various types of audit opinion which may be expressed, and the circumstances in which each is appropriate. We have also considered differences between the expanded form of audit report and its short form predecessor. We have noted that the expanded report was introduced to reduce misconceptions about the auditor's (*vis-à-vis* the directors') responsibility for the financial statements, the level of assurance provided by the audit report, and the audit process. But we have also seen that the result has been a long and complex document which some commentators maintain is less effective than the former short form report in communicating the auditor's key message about the accompanying financial statements. However, notwithstanding the reservations of some commentators about the expanded audit report, we have observed that in recent years additional information about auditors' responsibilities has been included in the report.

In the final section of the chapter we have given some attention to auditors' communications to those charged with the governance of auditees. We have noted that the auditor's report to users of the financial statements is a statutory requirement whose content is largely defined by the Companies Act 2006 and ISA 700: *Forming an opinion and reporting on financial statements*. It is required to be filed at Companies House and thus is a public document.[48] Governance communications are, however, private communications between the auditor and the auditee's directors. They are designed to ensure that the directors have no misconceptions about their responsibility for the financial statements or about the scope and nature of the audit process, and that they are informed about key findings of the audit. The form and content of the communications vary widely according to the client and the particular circumstances encountered during the audit. However, in virtually all cases, one of the most important components of the governance communication is the section detailing the existence and effect of significant deficiencies in the financial reporting and

---

[48] Requirements regarding filing of audited financial statements, together with the audit report, are explained in Chapter 5, section 5.2.2.

internal control systems discovered during the audit and how these might be rectified. In reporting these and similar matters, auditors provide a valuable service to those charged with the governance of auditees, assisting them to improve their entity's financial reporting and internal control systems and other aspects of its financial affairs.

SELF-REVIEW QUESTIONS

14.1 List the elements the Companies Act 2006 requires auditors to refer to in their audit reports.

14.2 The auditor of a company is required to form and express an opinion on the truth and fairness of the company's financial statements. Explain briefly:
 (i) the meaning frequently given to the phrase 'true and fair' by lawyers;
 (ii) why this interpretation is not useful for preparers and auditors of financial statements;
 (iii) what is generally accepted by the accounting profession as being required for financial statements to provide the required true and fair view.

14.3 Describe briefly the format of the standard audit report currently in use in the United Kingdom (as reflected in Figure 14.10).

14.4 State the criteria ISA 700 requires to be met before an auditor may issue an unqualified audit report.

14.5 List three types of modified audit report and briefly explain the circumstances in which each is appropriate.

14.6 Explain briefly the difference between an 'Emphasis of Matter' paragraph and an 'Other Matter(s)' paragraph.

14.7 Explain briefly the ways in which the expanded audit report differs from its short form predecessor.

14.8 Explain briefly the difference between a standard audit report prepared in accordance with ISA 700 (2004) and ISA 700 (Revised; 2006).

14.9 Discuss briefly the advantages and disadvantages of:
 (i) a standard form of audit report compared to a 'free form' of report;
 (ii) a short form audit report compared to an expanded form of audit report.

14.10 Explain briefly the purpose, content and value of auditors' communications of audit matters to those charged with auditees' governance.

REFERENCES

Alfano, J.B. (1979). Making auditor's reports pure and simple. *CPA Journal* **46**(6), 37–41.

Arden QC, M. (1993). *The True and Fair Requirement* (Counsel's opinion). London: Accounting Standards Board [Also reprinted in Institute of Chartered Accountants in England and Wales. (1994). *Members' Handbook, volume 2*. Appendix to the Foreword (pp. 14–20)].

Auditing Practices Board (APB). (2006). *Auditor's Reports on Financial Statements in the United Kingdom*, Bulletin 2006/6. London: Financial Reporting Council.

Auditing Practices Board (APB). (2007). *The Auditor's Report: A Time for Change.* London: Financial Reporting Council.

Auditing Practices Board (APB). (2008). *The Auditing Practices Board – Scope and authority of pronouncements*. London: Financial Reporting Council.

Audit Quality Forum (AQF). (2007). *Fundamentals – Auditor Reporting* (Report of the working group on auditor reporting). London: Institute of Chartered Accountants in England and Wales (ICAEW).

Beck, C.W. (1973). The role of the auditor in modern society: An empirical appraisal. *Accounting and Business Research* **3**(10), 117–122.

Canadian Institute of Chartered Accountants (CICA). (1988). *Report of the Commission to Study the Public's Expectations of Audits* (Macdonald Commission). Toronto: CICA.

Commission on Auditors' Responsibilities (CAR). (1978). *Report, Conclusions and Recommendations* (The Cohen Commission). New York: AICPA.

Elliott, R.K., and Jacobson, P.D. (1987). The auditor's standard report: the last word or in need of change? *Journal of Accountancy* **164**(2), 72–78.

Epstein, M.J. (1976). The Corporate Shareholders' View of the Auditor's Report, in Commission on Auditors' Responsibilities. *Report, Conclusions and Recommendations*. New York: AICPA, p. 164.

European Union (EU). (2002). *Regulation (EC) No. 1606/2002 on the application of international accounting standards*. Brussels: European Parliament and Council.

European Union (EU). (2004). Directive *2004/019/EC of the European Parliament and of the Council on harmonisation of transparency requirements in relation to information about issuers whose securities are admitted to trading on a regulated market.* Brussels: European Parliament and Council.

European Union (EU). (2006). Directive *2006/43/EC of the European Parliament and of the Council on statutory audits of annual accounts and consolidated accounts* (8th Directive). Brussels: European Parliament and Council.

Financial Reporting Council (FRC). (2006). *The Combined Code on Corporate Governance*. London: FRC.

Financial Reporting Council (FRC). (2008, 19 May). *Relevance of the 'True and Fair' concept confirmed*. London: FRC.

Flint, D. (1980). *The Significance of the Standard of True and Fair View*. Invitation Research Lecture. New Zealand: New Zealand Society of Accountants.

Hatherly, D., Innes, J., and Brown, T. (1991). The expanded audit report: An empirical investigation. *Accounting and Business Research* **21**(84), 311–319.

Inflation Accounting Committee. (1975). *Report of the Inflation Accounting Committee* (Sandilands Committee). London: HMSO, CMND 6225.

International Auditing and Assurance Standards Board (IAASB). (2006a).[49] International Standard on Auditing (ISA) 240 (Redrafted): *The Auditor's Responsibilities Relating to Fraud in an Audit of Financial Statements*. New York: International Federation of Accountants.

International Auditing and Assurance Standards Board (IAASB). (2006b). International Standard on Auditing (ISA) 700 (Revised): *The Independent Auditor's Report on General Purpose Financial Statements*. New York: International Federation of Accountants.

International Auditing and Assurance Standards Board (IAASB). (2008a, June**). International Standard on Auditing (ISA) 220 (Redrafted): *Quality Control for an Audit of Financial Statements*. New York: International Federation of Accountants.

International Auditing and Assurance Standards Board (IAASB). (2008b). International Standard on Auditing (ISA) 250 (Redrafted): *Consideration of Laws and Regulations in an Audit of Financial Statements*. New York: International Federation of Accountants.

International Auditing and Assurance Standards Board (IAASB). (2008c, June**). International Standard on Auditing (ISA) 450 (Redrafted): *Evaluation of Misstatements Identified During the Audit*. New York: International Federation of Accountants.

International Auditing and Assurance Standards Board (IAASB). (2008d). International Standard on Auditing (ISA) 550 (Redrafted): *Related Parties*. New York: International Federation of Accountants.

International Auditing and Assurance Standards Board (IAASB). (2008e). International Standard on Auditing (ISA) 570 (Redrafted): *Going Concern*. New York: International Federation of Accountants.

Johnston, T.R., Edgar, G.C., and Hays, P.L. (1982). *The Law and Practice of Company Accounting in New Zealand* (6th Edition). Wellington: Butterworths.

Kelly, A.S., and Mohrweis, L.C. (1989). Bankers' and investors' perceptions of the auditor's role in financial statement reporting: the impact of SAS No. 58. *Auditing: A Journal of Practice & Theory* **Fall**.

Lee, T.A. (1970). The nature of auditing and its objectives. *Accountancy* **81**(920), 292–296.

Lee, T.A., and Tweedie, D.P. (1975). Accounting information: An investigation of private shareholder usage. *Accounting and Business Research* **5**(20), 280–291.

---

[49] The status of ISAs referred to in this chapter is explained in the Important Note following the Preface to this book.

Northey, J. (1965). *Recommendations for Company Law Reform*, Business Law Symposium.

Porter, B.A. (1990). True and fair view: an elusive concept. *Accountants' Journal* **69**(110), Editorial.

Porter, B.A. (1993). An empirical study of the audit expectation-performance gap. *Accounting and Business Research* **24**(93), 49–68.

Ryan, S.J.O. (1974). A true and fair view revisited. *Australian Accountant* **44**(1), 8–10, 14–16. (Commissioner for Corporate Affairs in New South Wales).

Statutory Instrument 2002 No. 1986: *The Directors' Remuneration Report Regulations 2002*.

Tweedie, D. (1983). True and fair rules. *The Accountant's Magazine* **87**(925), 424–428, 449.

Wilton, R.L., and Tabb, J.B. (1978, May). An investigation into private shareholder usage of financial statements in New Zealand. *Accounting Education* **18**, 83–101.

Zachry, B.R. (1991). Who understands audit reports? *The Woman CPA* **53**(2), 9–11.

ADDITIONAL READING

Alexander, D., and Jermakowicz, E. (2006). A true and fair view of the principles/rules debate. *Abacus* **42**(2), 132–164.

Audit Quality Forum. (2005). *Shareholder Involvement – Identifying the Audit Partner*. London: Institute of Chartered Accountants in England and Wales.

Clarke, F.L. (2006). Introduction: true and fair – *anachronism or quality criterion* par excellence? *Abacus* **42**(2), 129–131.

Dean, G., and Clarke, F. (2005) 'True and fair' and 'fair value' – accounting and legal will-o'-the-wisps. *Abacus* **41**(2), i–vii.

Evans, L. (2003). The true and fair view and the 'fair presentation' override of IAS1. *Accounting and Business Research* **33**(4), 311–325.

Flint, D. (1982). *A True and Fair View in Company Accounts*. Made available by the Institute of Chartered Accountants of Scotland (2007) at www.icas.org.uk.

Garcia-Benau, M.A., and Zorio, A. (2004). Audit reports on financial statements prepared according to IASB Standards: empirical evidence from the European Union. *International Journal of Auditing* **8**(3), 237–252.

Kirk, N. (2006). Perceptions of the true and fair view concept: an empirical investigation. *Abacus* **42**(2), 205–235.

Seidler, L.J. (1976). Symbolism and communication in the auditor's report. In Stettler, H.F., (Ed). *Auditing Symposium III*. University of Kansas: ToucheRoss/University of Kansas Symposium on Auditing Problems.

15 Legal Liability of Auditors

LEARNING OBJECTIVES

After studying the material in this chapter you should be able to:
- distinguish between auditors' statutory and common law duties;
- discuss auditors' contractual liability to their clients;
- discuss auditors' liability to third parties for negligence;
- explain how auditors' duty of care to third parties was extended by a series of cases starting in 1931 with *Ultramares* v *Touche* through to the 1980s with the cases of *Jeb Fasteners* and *Twomax Ltd*;
- explain the significance of the House of Lords' decision in the *Caparo* case (1990);
- describe how the law relating to auditors' liability to third parties has developed since the *Caparo* judgment;
- discuss the effect of out-of-court settlements.

15.1 INTRODUCTION

When an auditor[1] accepts an audit engagement, this gives rise to the assumption that the auditor undertakes to perform the audit in accordance with certain statutory and common law obligations. If these obligations are not met, in general, the auditor is liable to parties who suffer loss as a result. These parties include the client entity with whom the auditor has a contractual relationship, and may also include third parties who do not have a contractual relationship with the auditor but who, nevertheless, rely on the proper performance of the auditor's duties (more particularly, on the opinion expressed in the auditor's report).

In this chapter we address the issue of auditors' legal liability. More specifically, we examine auditors' contractual liability to their audit clients and trace the development of their liability to third parties. We then consider in some detail the House of Lords' decision in the *Caparo* case (1990). This remains the most influential case in the United Kingdom (UK) with respect to auditors' liability and is notable for reversing the trend towards extending auditors' liability to third parties and returning the law to where it stood some 30 years earlier. We also discuss some cases decided subsequent to *Caparo* and note how case law has, once again, gradually widened auditors' liability to third parties. Before closing the chapter we explore the effect of out-of-court settlements on the development of the law relating to auditors' liability and indemnity insurance.

15.2 OVERVIEW OF AUDITORS' LEGAL LIABILITY

15.2.1 Auditors' exposure to legal liability

As noted above, when an auditor accepts an audit engagement it is understood that (s)he agrees to perform the audit in accordance with certain statutory and common (or case) law obligations. If either of these sets of obligations is not met, the auditor is exposed to liability. Auditors' exposure to liability is depicted in Figure 15.1.

---

[1] As we note in Chapter 5, section 5.2.3, under the Companies Act 2006 (CA 2006), s. 1212, an individual or an audit firm may be appointed as 'the auditor'. The principles of legal liability apply equally in either case. If the audit firm is constituted as an ordinary partnership (as opposed to a limited liability partnership), which is usually the case, the partners are jointly and severally liable. This means they are liable jointly with the other partners of the firm for any damages awarded by a court against any one of the firm's partners; they are also liable individually to meet damages awarded against any of the firm's partners, should the other partners of the firm not be able to pay. However, under CA 2006, ss. 534–536, auditors' may (if the client agrees) limit their liability to their audit clients by means of limited liability agreements. We discuss these agreements and limited liability partnerships in Chapter 16.

Figure 15.1: Auditors' exposure to legal liability

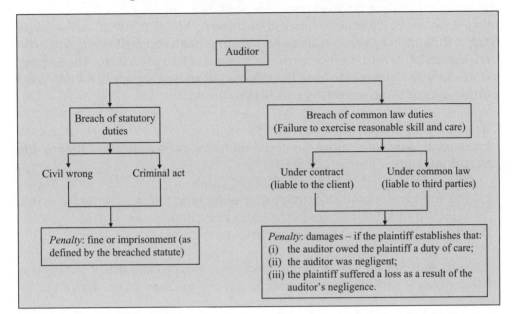

15.2.2 Breach of statutory duties

Some of the auditor's duties are specified by statute, for example, in the Companies Act 2006 (CA 2006) and the Theft Act 1968. If the auditor fails to perform these duties, the breach may constitute either:

- a civil wrong, whereby the client entity or some individual suffers loss as a result of the auditor failing to meet his or her statutory obligations; or
- a criminal act. This arises, for example, when an auditor deliberately signs a report knowing it to be false.

In either case, the maximum penalty the auditor will face (which will be in the form of a fine or imprisonment) is specified in the statute the auditor has breached. For example, under CA 2006, s. 1213, if the auditor of a company becomes ineligible during his or her term of office to hold the position of auditor, (s)he is required to vacate the position and inform the company in writing. Failure to give such written notice renders the auditor liable:

(a) on conviction on indictment, to a fine;
(b) on summary conviction, to a fine not exceeding the statutory maximum (£5,000 at the time CA 2006 received Royal Assent; CA 2006, Explanatory Notes, para 1443).

15.2.3 Breach of common law duties

In addition to statutory obligations which arise when an auditor agrees to perform an audit, a common law duty also arises, namely, a duty to perform the audit with reasonable skill and care appropriate to the circumstances. If the auditor fails to exercise reasonable skill and care, (s)he will be liable to make good any resultant loss suffered by those to whom a duty of care is owed. Such a duty of care may result from a contractual relationship or may arise under common law to parties outside a contractual arrangement. The circumstances in which the courts have held that auditors owe a duty of care to third parties are discussed in section 15.4 below.

The penalty for proven negligence (that is, failure to take due care) is the award of damages. However, before damages will be awarded against an auditor, the plaintiff must prove three facts, namely:
- the auditor owed him or her a duty of care;
- the auditor was negligent (that is, the auditor did not exercise a reasonable standard of skill and care in the particular circumstances); and
- the plaintiff suffered a loss as a result of the auditor's negligence.

Although these three requirements have been clearly established in law, two of them create difficulties for auditors as they are not static. These are as follows:

(i) What qualifies as negligence?[2]

As we note in Chapter 5 (section 5.3), Moffit J made it clear in the Australian case of *Pacific Acceptance Corporation Limited* v *Forsyth and Others* (1970) 92 WN (NSW) 29 that compliance with generally accepted auditing standards may not be enough to protect the auditor from being judged negligent. Moffit J observed that professional standards and practice must change over time to reflect changes in the economic and business environment. Although the courts are guided by professional standards and current best auditing practice, they will not be bound by them and, if the courts see fit, they will go beyond them. It is for the courts not the auditing profession to determine, in the light of society's norms of the time, what constitutes reasonable skill and care in the particular circumstances of the case.

---

[2] The concept of due care is discussed in Chapter 3, section 3.6.1. There we note that two significant characteristics of the concept are as follows:
  (i) the standard of 'reasonable skill, care and caution' has become more exacting over the past 100 or so years, as society, and more particularly the commercial and corporate worlds, have become more complex and dynamic;
  (ii) although Auditing Standards and other professional promulgations provide guidance to the court on what may reasonably be expected of auditors, it is up to the court, not the auditing profession, to determine whether an auditor has taken due care in any particular audit.

This leaves auditors in a difficult and unenviable position. Not only do they lack a clear standard to which they are expected to work (the standard of skill and care required of them varies over time and between different sets of circumstances) but, additionally, when the courts evaluate whether or not they have exercised the required standard of skill and care, it is with the wisdom of hindsight.

(ii) The parties to whom auditors owe a duty of care

As indicated in Figure 15.1, a duty of care may arise under either:

(a) *contract*, that is, as part of the contractual arrangement between the auditor and the client. This duty is generally clear-cut and does not give rise to uncertainty; or

(b) *common law*. This duty of care to third parties (that is, parties outside a contractual relationship) is imposed on auditors when the courts consider it reasonable and equitable to do so. As will be shown in section 15.4 below, between the early 1960s and the end of the 1980s, the parties to whom auditors were held to owe a duty of care were extended progressively. Then, as a result of the *Caparo* case, they were reduced significantly only to be broadened once more, at least to some extent, in post-*Caparo* cases. The various changes leave auditors unsure as to whom they are liable should they fail to exercise a reasonable standard of skill and care in the particular circumstances of the audit.

15.3 AUDITORS' CONTRACTUAL LIABILITY TO THEIR CLIENTS

15.3.1 Auditors' contractual duties

When an auditor accepts an audit engagement, (s)he contracts with the client to perform certain duties. Some of these are specified in legislation (such as CA 2006); others have been determined over the years by the courts as a result of various cases being brought against auditors. (Some of these cases are discussed in Chapter 5, section 5.3.) If the auditor does not perform his or her duties with a reasonable standard of skill and care and, as a consequence, the client[3] suffers a loss, then the auditor is liable to make good the loss suffered.

---

[3] It should be noted that 'the client' is the client entity, not the entity's shareholders or any other interested party.

An example of an auditor being held liable for breach of contractual duties is provided by the Australian case of *AWA Limited* v *Daniels, trading as Deloitte Haskins & Sells & Others* (1992) 10 ACLC 933. In this case, AWA's manager of foreign exchange operations, whilst appearing to trade profitability in foreign exchange dealings, in fact, caused AWA to incur a loss of A$50 million. The manager concealed the losses by various means, including unauthorised borrowing from a number of banks, allegedly on behalf of AWA. AWA sued the auditors for damages in breach of contract, claiming that the loss suffered was caused by Deloitte's failure to draw attention to serious deficiencies in the company's internal controls and accounting records, and for failing to qualify their audit reports.

Rogers C J found that Deloitte failed to perform their contractual duties in three ways. These are as follows:

(i)   It was clear that the books and records relevant to AWA's foreign exchange transactions were "inaccurate and inadequate" and "the auditors should have formed the opinion that proper accounting records had not been kept" (Rogers, C J at 959). They failed to fulfil this duty.

(ii) The auditors had doubts about the extent of the foreign exchange manager's authority to enter into foreign exchange transactions on behalf of AWA. In such circumstances, the auditors had a duty to make enquiries from an appropriate level of management. This, Deloitte failed to do.

(iii) Notwithstanding that the auditors had discussed the inadequate system of recording foreign exchange transactions with the general manager of AWA, they did nothing to ensure that the matter was dealt with urgently and effectively, nor did they ensure that it was referred to AWA's board of directors. Rogers C J held that simply identifying shortcomings and bringing them to the attention of management below board level is an insufficient discharge of an auditor's duty in cases where the auditor is aware that management fails to respond adequately. Management's failure to take action to rectify the position imposes on the auditor an obligation to inform the board. Further, this duty to report to the board is not discharged by relying on the possibility that the chief executive officer will have already done so.[4]

In the AWA case it was decided that the auditors had been negligent in the performance of their duties and that their negligence had contributed to the loss suffered by AWA. However, AWA's senior management was also found to have contributed to the company's loss by virtue of deficiencies in its system of internal controls and record keeping.

---

[4] As we note in Chapter 14, section 14.8, this responsibility is now made explicit in ISA 260: *Communication with those charged with governance* (IAASB, 2007).

Deloitte appealed the trial judge's ruling but the Court of Appeal upheld Rogers C J's findings.[5] Nevertheless, the Appeal Court gave greater weight than did the trial judge to the part played by AWA's management in the loss suffered by the company. Taking due cognisance of the contributory negligence of AWA's management, the Court of Appeal reduced the damages awarded against Deloitte from A$17 million to A$A6 million. In the Court of Appeal's view, the crux of Deloitte's negligence lay in their failure to give appropriate advice to the board of directors regarding (i) the absence of controls over the foreign exchange operations and (ii) the failure of senior management to respond to their (the auditors') warnings regarding the absence of controls (Shanahan, 1995, p. 214).

With respect to auditors' contractual liability to their clients, the *AWA* case is particularly interesting as it illustrates both:
- a breach of auditors' statutory duties [that is, their failure to qualify their audit report for the company's failure to maintain proper accounting records, as required by section 331E(2) of the Australian Corporations Law[6]]; and
- a breach of their common law duties [that is, their failure to make the necessary enquiries of AWA's senior management about matters of which they were uncertain (for example, the extent of the foreign exchange manager's authority), and their failure to report to the appropriate level of the entity's management (namely, the board of directors) serious deficiencies they had discovered in the entity's internal controls and record keeping].

The case is also interesting in that it illustrates the exercise by the court of the principle of contributory negligence.

The English case of *Sasea Finance Ltd v KPMG* [2000] 1 All ER 676; [2000] 1 BCLC 236; [2001] 1 All ER (D) 127 (May), similarly involved a breach of auditors' contractual obligations to their client. In this case, Sasea Finance Limited (SFL), an English registered company which was part of the Swiss-based Sasea group of companies, sued its auditor, KPMG, for the negligent conduct of its audit for the year ending 31 December 1989. The audit was completed and audit report signed in November 1990.

In 1992, the Sasea group collapsed and SFL went into liquidation. The affairs of the group were subject to criminal investigations and these revealed that the companies in the group had been vehicles for a massive fraud. SFL claimed that, had KPMG acted with reasonable skill and care, it would have

---

[5] *Daniels (formerly practising as Deloitte Haskins & Sells) v AWA Ltd*; 14 May 1995, (NSW) CA.

[6] This section contains the same provisions as section 498(2) of the UK Companies Act 2006.

taken such action that would have allowed SFL to avoid suffering four losses between September 1990 and early 1991 (of £2.4 m, £113,000, £458,000 and £8 m, respectively) which resulted from fraud and theft. KPMG contended that none of the losses was caused by any breach of contract or negligence on its part.

The High Court held that SFL's claims in respect of two of the losses (those of £2.4 m and £8 m, respectively) had insufficient bases to proceed to a trial, but it refused to strike out the other two claims. SFL appealed the Court's decision and KPMG cross-appealed. KPMG contended, amongst other things, that any negligence on its part was not the cause of the alleged losses.

The Court of Appeal overturned the High Court's decision and SFL's claim against KPMG for all four losses was reinstated. During the Court of Appeal hearing, Kennedy L J explained some aspects of auditors' duties. He stated:

> Where a firm of accountants accepts instructions to audit the accounts of a company for a fiscal year, its primary obligation is, within a reasonable time, to exercise an appropriate level of skill and care in reporting to the company's members on the accounts of the company stating, in their opinion, whether the accounts of the company give a true and fair view of the company's financial affairs.

He then went on to clarify auditors' duty to report significant facts to their clients, and to do so in a timely fashion. He said:

> If, for example, the auditors discover that a senior employee of the company has been defrauding the company on a grand scale and is in the position to go on doing so, then it would normally be the duty of the auditors to report what had been discovered to the management of the company at once, not simply when rendering the auditor's report weeks or months later.

He concluded that the present case was concerned with losses brought about by fraud or irregularities, the risk of which KPMG ought to have apprehended and reported. KPMG had a duty to warn the company's directors as soon as the fraud or irregularities had been detected.

It should be noted that, in order for contractual liability to be invoked, the aggrieved party must be a party to the contract. In the case of auditors appointed to perform a statutory audit under CA 2006, the contract is between the auditor and the company *per se*, not the company's shareholders as individuals. As the *AWA* and *Sasea* cases illustrate, if an auditor fails to perform his or her statutory duties, or fails to take due care in performing the audit, the client entity (in these cases, AWA Ltd and Sasea Finance Ltd) may sue for breach of contract. Should a shareholder wish to take action against the auditor(s), (s)he can do so only by exercising his or her rights as a third party under the common law (see section 15.4 below). However – worse news yet for a company's shareholders – as a result of the House of Lords' decision in the *Caparo* case (1990), even this avenue of relief for them as individuals is of doubtful availability (see section 15.4.2 below).

15.3.2 The importance of engagement letters

As we explain in Chapter 8, section 8.3, International Standard on Auditing (ISA) 210: *Agreeing the terms of audit engagements* (IAASB, 2008) requires auditors, upon their appointment, to prepare an engagement letter to clarify the terms of the contract. The engagement letter does not (indeed, cannot) excuse the auditor from performing his or her statutory or common law duties, or from performing those duties with a reasonable standard of skill and care appropriate to the circumstances of the audit. However, the letter can reduce to a minimum any misunderstanding between the client and the auditor with respect to the duties to be performed and the terms of the engagement.

Although engagement letters are important to clarify the terms of an audit engagement, as the United States (US) case of *1136 Tenants' Corporation* v *Max Rothenberg & Co* (1971) 319 NYS2d 1007 demonstrates, they are even more important when the engagement does not include an audit. In the *1136 Tenants' Corporation* case, a firm of certified public accountants was engaged to write up the books of a co-operative block of flats. It was successfully sued for negligence for not uncovering embezzlement by the managing agent. Damages were awarded against the accountants despite the fact that each set of accounts they submitted to the corporation was accompanied by a letter which began:

> Pursuant to our engagement, we have reviewed and summarised the statements of your managing agent, and other data submitted to us by the managing agent.

The letter concluded:

> The following statements were prepared from the books and records of the Corporation. No independent verifications were undertaken thereon ...

Additionally, the financial statements themselves were marked:

> Subject to comments in letter of transmittal ...

The accountants argued that the statement in the transmittal letter that "no independent verifications were undertaken" was sufficient warning to all users of the financial statements that they were unaudited. The court nevertheless found them to be guilty of negligence (Woolf, 1979, p. 263). Had the accountants clarified the scope of their engagement in an engagement letter and, more particularly, specified that no audit would be undertaken, they may well have avoided the costly position in which they found themselves.

15.4 LIABILITY TO THIRD PARTIES UNDER COMMON LAW

15.4.1 Development of auditors' duty of care to third parties – until the *Caparo* decision

As noted above, if auditors breach their statutory duties, or fail to perform their duties with reasonable skill and care, they may be held liable to make good any consequential loss suffered by their client. This liability arises as a result of the contractual relationship between the auditor and the client.

Over the past 40 or so years, the courts in the UK (and elsewhere) have held that auditors also owe a duty of care to certain third parties who suffer loss as a consequence of auditors failing to perform their duties with due care. Through a series of cases, beginning in 1931 in the US, when it was held that auditors' liability should be restricted to contractual relationships and not extended to third parties, the parties to whom auditors have been held to owe a duty of care were widened progressively. This trend was reversed with the *Caparo* decision in 1990. The relevant cases are summarised in Figure 15.2.

In 1931, in the US case of *Ultramares Corporation* v *Touche* (1931) 255 NY 170, it was held that auditors' liability can arise only under a contractual relationship. Cardozo J decided that it would be too much to impose on accountants a liability to third parties for financial loss as this may expose them to liability out of all proportion to the gravity of their actions. As Cardozo J expressed it (at 179):

> [It] may expose accountants to liability in an indeterminate amount for an indeterminate time to an indeterminate class.

In 1932, the English case of *Donoghue* v *Stevenson* (1932) AC 562 started the process of recognising a liability to parties outside a contractual relationship. This case involved a young man who purchased a bottle of ginger beer, complete with decomposed snail, and gave it to his girlfriend to drink. Not surprisingly, the girlfriend became ill. The court held that a duty of care is owed to third parties in circumstances where it can reasonably be foreseen that failure to take care may result in physical injury. Thus, this case established that liability may arise outside a contractual relationship in circumstances involving possible physical injury.

Nearly 20 years later, in the case of *Candler* v *Crane Christmas & Co.* [1951] 2 KB 164, the court confirmed that no duty of care is owed to third parties in the case of financial loss. In this case, the defendant firm of chartered accountants negligently prepared a set of financial statements for their clients,

Figure 15.2: Summary of significant cases relating to auditors' liability to third parties – up to and including *Caparo* v *Dickman* (1990)

Case	Key finding(s) of the case
1. *Ultramares Corporation* v *Touche* (1931) 255 NY 170 [US case]	Accountants' liability should not be extended to third parties. It can only arise under a contractual relationship.
2. *Donoghue* v *Stevenson* (1932) AC 562 [UK case]	A duty of care is owed to third parties in circumstances where it can reasonably be foreseen that failure to take care may result in physical injury.
3. *Candler* v *Crane Christmas & Co.* [1951] 2 KB 164 [UK case]	No duty of care is owed to third parties in the case of financial loss. Lord Denning's dissenting judgment indicated things to come. He considered that accountants owe a duty of care to any third party to whom they know the accounts are to be shown in order to induce him or her to invest money or to take some other action on them. He did not think that the duty could be extended to include strangers, i.e., persons of whom the auditor knows nothing at the time of the audit.
4. *Hedley Byrne & Co. Ltd* v *Heller & Partners* [1963] 2 All ER 575; [1964] AC 465 [UK case]	A duty of care is owed to third parties for financial loss where it can be shown that a 'special relationship' exists, i.e., where the provider of information knows, or ought to know, that a particular person is going to rely on the information for some specific purpose. The duty of care does not extend to strangers.
5. *Diamond Manufacturing Company* v *Hamilton* [1969] NZLR 609 [NZ case]	A 'special relationship' was said to exist because one of the auditors had been involved in negotiations with the investor; a duty of care therefore existed.
6. *MLC* v *Evatt* [1971] AC 793 [Australian case]	A 'special relationship' can arise only where the person giving the advice holds him or herself out to be an expert. (The *Hedley Byrne* principle was effectively narrowed.)
7. *Haig* v *Bamford* [1976] 3WWR331 (SC Can) [Canadian case]	No duty of care is owed to strangers. Auditors do not owe a duty of care to those whom, at the time of the audit, they are not aware will rely on the audited financial statements for a particular purpose.
8. *Anns* v *Merton London Borough Council* [1977] 2 All ER 492, [1978] AC 728 [UK case]	The requirement for a 'special relationship' was replaced by a 'relationship of proximity or neighbourhood', and the test of 'knowledge' that someone would rely on the advice given and may suffer loss as a result of a failure to take care, was replaced by one of 'reasonable foreseeability'. This case extended quite considerably the third parties to whom a duty of care is owed in cases involving non-physical injury.
9. *Scott Group Ltd* v *McFarlane* [1978] 1 NZLR 553 [NZ case]	A duty of care is owed by auditors who could or reasonably should foresee that a particular person or group of persons will rely on the audited financial statements for a particular type of investment decision. The *Hedley Byrne* principle of knowledge of reliance on the audited financial statements was replaced by a test of reasonable foreseeability. Attention was drawn to the fact that audited financial statements of companies become a matter of public record through filing with the Companies Office.
10. *Jeb Fasteners Ltd* v *Marks, Bloom & Co.* [1981] 3 All ER 289 [UK case]	Auditors owe a duty of care to any person or class of persons whom they do not know, but reasonably should foresee might rely on the audited financial statements when making investment decisions about the company. The case extended the *Scott Group* case from circumstances in which a takeover is reasonably foreseeable, to circumstances in which any form of financial support seems likely to be needed and reliance on audited financial statements could or should be expected.
11. *Twomax Ltd* v *Dickson McFarlane & Robinson* [1982] SC 113, [1983] SLT 98 [UK – Scottish case]	The duty of care owed by auditors to third parties established in the *Scott Group* case was extended to virtually anyone who can prove they relied on negligently audited financial statements when making an investment decision and suffered loss as a consequence.
12. *Caparo Industries plc* v *Dickman & Others* [1990] 1 All ER 568; [1990] 2 AC 605; [1990] 2 WLR 358, HL [UK case]	In the absence of special circumstances, auditors owe a duty of care only to (i) the audit-client company and (ii) the company's shareholders as a body. A duty of care is owed to third parties only when the three tests of foreseeability of damage, proximity of relationship, and fairness of imposing a duty are satisfied.

knowing that they would be shown to the third-party plaintiff for the purpose of making an investment decision. The investment failed and the plaintiff sued the accountants.

The majority of the court, re-iterating the fears expressed by Cardozo J in the *Ultramares* case, held that a duty of care is not owed to third parties in the case of financial loss. However, the dissenting judgment of Lord Denning signalled the way the law would develop in the future. He said:

> [Accountants] owe a duty, of course, to their employer and client and also, I think, to any third party to whom they themselves show the accounts or to whom they know their employer is going to show the accounts so as to induce him to invest money or to take some other action on them. But I do not think the duty can be extended still further so as to include strangers of whom they have heard nothing ...

Twelve years later, in *Hedley Byrne & Co. Ltd* v *Heller & Partners* [1963] 2 All ER 575, [1964] AC 465, the court accepted as correct the reasoning of Lord Denning in the *Crane Christmas* case. The *Hedley Byrne* case involved a telephone enquiry by a bank to a merchant bank (Heller & Partners Ltd) regarding the credit worthiness of a company for which Heller was banker. The bank communicated Heller's reply, that the company was "considered good for its normal business engagements" and in particular for a proposed advertising contract, to one of its customers (Hedley Byrne & Co. Ltd). The court held that a duty of care is owed to third parties where it can be shown that a 'special relationship' exists. Such a relationship will exist when the person giving the information knows, or ought to know, that another particular person is going to rely on the information for a specific purpose. However, the court emphasised that a duty of care does not extend to strangers; that is, persons of whom the person giving the information knows nothing at the time.

Hedley Byrne is a landmark decision in that it recognised third-party liability in a case involving financial loss. Until then, liability to third parties had been limited to situations involving physical injury.

The next two cases in the series helped to clarify the meaning of a 'special relationship'. In the New Zealand case of *Diamond Manufacturing Company* v *Hamilton* [1969] NZLR 609, a member of an audit firm showed the financial statements the firm had audited to another party, knowing that the statements would be used for an investment decision. The court held that the auditors were liable to the third party as a special relationship existed and, therefore, a duty of care was owed. The special relationship arose because one of the auditors was involved in the negotiations with the investor. However, the court confirmed that a duty of care did not extend to strangers.

In 1971, in the Australian case of *Mutual Life & Citizens' Assurance Co. Ltd* v *Evatt* [1971] AC 793, the circumstances in which a special relationship could arise were narrowed somewhat. This case involved an insurance agent who was negligent in giving financial advice at a social function. It was held that, in order for a special relationship to exist, the person giving the financial advice must not only know that someone is going to rely on the advice proffered but, further, he (or she) must be giving the advice in a professional capacity. The special relationship can only arise in circumstances where the person giving the advice holds him- or herself out to be an expert.

Five years later (and 12 years after the *Hedley Byrne* principle was established) a Canadian court, in *Haig* v *Bamford* [1976] 3WW R331 (SC Can), confirmed that in cases involving financial loss no duty of care is owed to a stranger: liability to third parties cannot arise in the absence of knowledge that a particular person will rely on the financial advice given (or the audited financial statements) for a specific purpose. This principle was to be tested in the UK just one year later.

The case of *Anns* v *Merton London Borough Council* [1977] 2 All ER 492, [1978] AC 728, involved the failure of a local authority to inspect a faulty building. The court held that the authority owed a duty of care to the occupants of the building. Although not involving auditors or accountants, this case is of singular importance to the extension of auditors' liability to third parties. It introduced a 'relationship of proximity or neighbourhood' in place of a 'special relationship', and replaced the test of 'knowledge' that someone would rely on the advice given and may suffer damage or loss as a result of failure to take care, with one of 'reasonable foreseeability'. The court provided a two-step approach as a guideline for determining whether or not a duty of care exists in particular circumstances. In the words of Lord Wilberforce:

> In order to establish whether a duty of care arises in a particular situation, two questions must be asked:
> 1. As between the alleged wrongdoer and the injured party there must be a relationship of proximity or neighbourhood, such that in the reasonable contemplation of the former, carelessness on his part may be likely to cause damage to the latter, in which case a *prima facie* duty of care arises.
> 2. If the question is answered affirmatively, it is necessary to consider whether there are any considerations which ought to negative, or to reduce or limit the scope of the duty or class of person to whom it is owed.

The principles enunciated in this case extended quite considerably the third parties to whom a duty of care is owed in circumstances involving non-physical injury. However, it is pertinent to note that it also brought the law in such cases into line with that obtaining in situations involving physical injury: the reasonable foreseeability test was established in circumstances involving physical injury in *Donoghue* v *Stevenson* in 1932 (*supra*).

The courts did not have long to wait before the *Anns* case's principles were applied in a case involving auditors. In the New Zealand case of *Scott Group Ltd* v *McFarlane* [1978] 1 NZLR 553, auditors failed to detect a basic double-counting error which resulted in assets being significantly overvalued. At the time of the audit, the defendant auditor had no knowledge that the plaintiff had any intention of making a takeover offer. However, the court held that the company's rich assets and low profits situation made it a prime target for takeover or merger and, therefore, the auditor should have foreseen that some person or group of persons was likely to rely on the audited financial statements to make such an offer.

Thus, this case extended the *Hedley Byrne* test of *knowledge* to one of *reasonable foreseeability* in situations involving audited financial statements. It established that a duty of care is owed by auditors who can, or should, reasonably foresee that a particular person or group of persons will rely on the audited financial statements when deciding whether to make a takeover offer. Applying the two-part *Anns* test for a duty of care to be recognised, Woodhouse J identified four factors which give rise to a *prima facie* duty of care in the case of auditors. These are as follows:

1. Auditors are professionals in the business of providing expert advice for reward. If they did not intend their audited accounts to be relied upon, their work would be pointless.
2. Confidence in the ability of a company to handle its commercial arrangements would disappear if the audit report authenticating the company's accounts could not be relied upon.
3. In ordinary circumstances there is no opportunity for a person to make any intermediate examination of the company's accounts, nor is it practicable for many persons to do so.
4. Auditors are aware that the audited accounts will be filed with the Companies Office and therefore they become a matter of public record; they are available to the public, and anyone interested in the company has direct access to them.

Considering whether there are any factors which might negate or limit the scope of auditors' duty of care or the persons to whom it is owed, Woodhouse J found the only argument in favour of negating liability was that raised by Cardozo J in *Ultramares* v *Touche* (supra) over 45 years earlier, namely, the fear that auditors may be exposed "to liability in an indeterminate amount for an indeterminate time to an indeterminate class". However, his Honour considered that this need not be a matter of concern because of the difficulty of bringing a successful action against auditors for negligence. To succeed in such an action, the plaintiff must prove:

- it is reasonable to expect the auditors to have anticipated that the plaintiff would act on the audited financial information;
- the plaintiff actually relied on the audited financial information; and
- the auditors' failure to take care when auditing the financial information was the cause of the plaintiff's loss.

Woodhouse J concluded:

> [The auditors] must be taken to have accepted . . . a duty to those persons whom they can reasonably foresee will need to use and rely on [the audited financial statements] when dealing with the Company in significant matters affecting the Company's assets and business.

The *Scott Group* decision was applied and extended in the UK case of *Jeb Fasteners Ltd* v *Marks Bloom & Co.* [1981] 3 All ER 289. In this case, the defendants conducted an audit for a company which they were aware was undergoing a liquidity crisis and needed to raise finance. The company's financial statements contained assets that were seriously overvalued, a fact the auditors failed to detect. The plaintiffs had reservations about the assets figure but nevertheless proceeded with the takeover. The court re-affirmed that the auditor owes a duty of care to any person or class of persons whom they do not know but should be able to reasonably foresee might rely on the audited financial statements when making an investment decision relating to the company. Woolf J, citing the *Scott Group* decision with approval, stated:

> When he audited the accounts, Mr Marks would not know precisely who would provide the financial support, or what form the financial support would take, and he certainly had no reason to know that it would be by way of takeover by the plaintiffs. However, this was certainly one foreseeable method, and it does not seem to me that it would be right to exclude the duty of care merely because it was not possible to say with precision what machinery would be used to achieve the necessary financial support. Clearly, any form of loan would have been foreseeable, including the raising of money by debenture and, while some methods of raising money were more obvious than others, and a takeover was not the most obvious method, it was certainly one method which was within the contemplation of Mr Marks.

Woolf J concluded that the auditors should have foreseen that a person might rely on the audited financial statements for the purpose of making an investment decision and that the person could, therefore, suffer loss if the accounts were inaccurate.

Analysing Mr Justice Woolf's judgment (above) it appears that, although the case involved a takeover, he extended the *Scott Group* decision from circumstances in which a takeover is reasonably foreseeable to circumstances in which any form of financial support seems likely to be needed, and reliance on audited financial statements can (or should) be expected.

In the Scottish case of *Twomax Ltd* v *Dickson, McFarlane & Robinson* [1982] SC 113, [1983] SLT 98, the facts are similar to those of the *Jeb Fasteners* case and Lord Stewart had little hesitation in applying Woolf J's judgment. He held that, although the auditors did not know the plaintiffs would rely on the audited financial statements to make an investment decision, they were aware that the auditee company (Kintyre Knitwear Ltd) needed capital. Given these circumstances, the auditors should have reasonably foreseen that some person (or group of persons) would rely on the audited financial statements and would suffer loss if they were inaccurate.

This case is significant because it confirmed the *Scott Group's* and *Jeb Fasteners'* extension of auditors' duty of care to third parties whom they do not know but should reasonably foresee might rely on the audited financial statements when making an investment decision relating to the reporting entity. But, further, unlike the plaintiffs in the *Scott Group* and *Jeb Fasteners* cases, the plaintiffs in the *Twomax* case were able to prove to the satisfaction of the court that they not only relied on the financial statements when making their investment decision but also suffered loss as a result of relying on those statements which had been audited negligently. As a consequence, damages were awarded against the defendant auditors.

Reviewing the cases outlined above, it is evident that between 1931 and 1983 the auditor's duty of care to third parties evolved from nothing to a very wide duty. Prior to 1963, influenced by the *Ultramares* case, auditors' liability was restricted to that arising under a contractual relationship. By the mid-1980s, auditors' duty of care extended to virtually anyone whom the auditors could, or should, reasonably foresee might rely on the audited financial statements when making an investment decision in respect of the reporting entity. When it is remembered that the audited financial statements of companies are filed with the Registrar of Companies and are readily available for public scrutiny, auditors' duty of care and their exposure to potential liability had become very wide indeed.

In this regard it is interesting to note the remarks of Savage (1981), made after the *Jeb Fasteners* but before the *Twomax* decision:

> [I]t is not beyond the bounds of possibility that a British Court might hold that an auditor owes a duty of care to anyone who consults audited accounts at the Companies Registry and sustains a loss as a result of a negligent audit. To that extent the Jeb decision only brings the law into line with the public's expectations. If the auditor carries out his work with reasonable care and competence . . . he

has nothing to fear.[7] If he fails to do so then, rightly, justice and equity demand that the law give remedy to those who have suffered as a direct result of his negligence. (p. 341)

Nevertheless, as is shown below, Savage's views were not shared by the House of Lords in the case of *Caparo Industries plc* v *Dickman & Others* [1990] 1 All ER 568; [1990] 2 AC 605; [1990] 2 WLR 358, HL. The Law Lords apparently felt the law had gone too far.

15.4.2 The *Caparo* decision

The facts of this case are briefly as follows. In June 1984 Caparo Industries plc (Caparo) purchased shares in Fidelity plc. Prior to the purchase (in May 1984), Fidelity's directors announced that the company's profits for the year were £1.3 million – well short of the forecast profit of £2.2 million. Nevertheless, relying on the audited financial statements, Caparo purchased more shares in Fidelity and, later in the year, made a successful takeover bid for the company.

Subsequent to the takeover, Caparo brought an action against the auditors (Touche Ross)[8] alleging that, notwithstanding the unqualified audit report, Fidelity's accounts were inaccurate; the reported pre-tax profit of £1.3 million should, in fact, have been a reported loss of £0.46 million. In bringing its action, Caparo claimed that Touche Ross, as auditors of Fidelity, owed a duty of care to investors and potential investors and, in particular, to Caparo, in respect of the audit of Fidelity's accounts. More particularly, Caparo asserted that:

- Touche Ross knew or ought to have known:
  - (a) that in March 1984 a press release had been issued stating that profits for the financial year would fall significantly short of £2.2 million;
  - (b) that Fidelity's price fell from 143 pence per share on 1 March 1984 to 75 pence per share on 2 April 1984; and
  - (c) that Fidelity required financial assistance;
- Touche Ross therefore ought to have foreseen that Fidelity was vulnerable to a takeover bid and that persons such as Caparo might well rely on

---

[7] This has been demonstrated in the case of *Lloyd Cheyham & Co. Ltd* v *Littlejohn & Co.* [1987] BCLC 303. This case established that:
  (i) Auditors are not required to do any more than a person can or should do for himself. A person is not entitled to place unwarranted reliance on the financial statements.
  (ii) Auditors who have performed good-quality audits and who have good, defensible working papers which show that their conclusions were justified on the basis of the evidence gathered are able to defend themselves.

[8] A 'former Big 8' auditing firm that merged with Deloitte (one of the current 'Big 4' firms). After the merger in 1996, the merged firm was known as Deloitte & Touche for a number of years in many parts of the world.

the accounts for the purpose of deciding whether to take over Fidelity and might well suffer loss if the accounts were inaccurate.

The Law Lords were unanimous in their decision that, in general, auditors do not owe a duty of care to individual shareholders or to potential investors. Rather, a duty of care is owed to the company's shareholders as a body. In reaching this decision, the Lords held that *Scott Group Ltd* v *McFarlane & Others* (supra), and the subsequent English and Scottish decisions which had relied on *Scott Group*, namely, *Jeb Fasteners Ltd* v *Marks Bloom & Co.* (supra) and *Twomax Ltd* v *Dickson, McFarlane & Robinson* (supra), had been decided wrongly.

Analysis of the House of Lords' decision in the *Caparo* case reveals that the Lords were concerned to ensure that the scope of liability arising in professional negligence cases is not extended beyond reasonable limits. They referred with considerable respect to Cardozo J's statement in the *Ultramares* case, namely, that auditors' liability should not be extended to the point where it may exist "in an indeterminate amount for an indeterminate time to an indeterminate class". Their concern is reflected in Lord Oliver's statement:

> To apply as a test of liability only the foreseeability of possible damage without some further control would be to create a liability wholly indefinite in area, duration and amount and would open up a limitless vista of uninsurable risk for the professional man.

Lord Bridge indicated what "further control" might be imposed before the court would find that auditors (and other professional advisors) owe a duty of care to those who rely upon their statements. He stated:

> [T]here should exist between the party owing the duty and the party to whom it is owed a relationship characterised by the law as one of proximity or neighbourhood and the situation should be one in which the court considers it fair, just and reasonable that the law should impose a duty of a given scope upon the one party for the benefit of the other.

Following from these (and other similar) lines of reasoning, the Lords considered that, in order to establish that a duty of care exists, a three-part test needs to be satisfied, namely:

- *reasonable foreseeability of damage*: When a person (A) makes a statement for another (B) (either an individual or a member of an identifiable class) to rely upon, A should be able to reasonably foresee that B might suffer loss if the statement is incorrect;
- *relationship of proximity*: With respect to the statement made, there must be a relationship of proximity between A and B. Such a relationship will exist if, when making the statement, A knew:

- that the statement would be communicated to B;
- that the statement would be communicated in relation to a particular transaction or a transaction of a particular kind;
- B would be very likely to rely on the statement when making a decision with respect to the transaction in question; and
- B acted on the statement to his or her detriment.

In determining whether there is a relationship of proximity between the parties, the court will determine whether the particular damage suffered by B is the kind of damage A was under a duty to prevent and whether there are circumstances from which the court can pragmatically conclude that a duty of care existed;

- *fairness*: The court must consider it fair, just and reasonable to impose a duty of care on A for the benefit of B.

Whilst recognising that audited financial statements might be used for a variety of purposes, including the making of investment decisions, the Lords were of the view that their primary purpose is to protect the interests of the company *per se*, and to enable shareholders and debenture holders to evaluate the quality of the stewardship exercised by the company's directors and "to exercise such powers as are vested in them by virtue of their respective propriety interests" (per Lord Oliver).[9] Their purpose is not to protect the interests of the general public or investors in particular who choose to use the financial statements for a particular purpose. The Law Lords saw the auditor's function within the context of this purpose of financial statements. Lord Oliver, for example, stated:

> It is the auditor's function to ensure, so far as possible, that the financial information as to the company's affairs prepared by the directors accurately reflects the company's position in order, first, to protect the company itself from the consequences of undetected errors ... and, secondly, to provide shareholders with reliable intelligence for the purpose of enabling them to scrutinise the conduct of the company's affairs and to exercise their collective powers to reward or control or remove those to whom that conduct has been confided.

Following from this view of the auditor's function, the Law Lords concluded that, in the absence of special circumstances, auditors owe a duty of care only

---

[9] It is interesting to compare this conclusion of the Law Lords with the objective of (audited) financial statements stated by the International Accounting Standards Board (IASB) in its *Framework for the preparation and presentation of financial statements* (IASB, 2001):

> The objective of financial statements is to provide information about the financial position, performance and changes in financial position of an entity that is useful to a wide range of users in making economic decisions. ... Those users who wish to assess the stewardship or accountability of management do so in order that they make economic decisions; these decisions may include, for example, whether to hold or sell their investment in the entity or whether to reappoint or replace the management. (paras 12, 14)

It is clear that the IASB envisages (audited) financial statements as being for the use of individual shareholders (and other users) for their economic decision-making rather than (or, possibly, as well as) for the shareholders as a body.

to (i) the company *per se* and (ii) the company's shareholders as a body. More particularly, in general, auditors do not owe a duty of care to individual shareholders or potential investors, irrespective of any reliance they may place on the audited financial statements for their investment decision(s). In order for a duty of care to arise, other than to the company or the shareholders as a body, the three-part test of foreseeability of damage, proximity of relationship, and fairness of imposing a duty of care must be satisfied.

This returned the law roughly to where it stood nearly 30 years earlier at the time of *Hedley Byrne* v *Heller & Partners* (supra). However, many commentators consider the reversal of the law to be unfortunate. Baxt (1990) for example notes that, as a result of the *Caparo* decision, both professional investors, such as Caparo, and ordinary individual investors are denied a possible avenue for relief when they suffer loss as a result of negligence on the part of auditors. He states:

> Clearly, we do not wish to see the prophecy come true of Chief Justice Cardozo, nor do we wish to identify any particular group of professionals as being more subject to liabilities than others. But some protection is needed for the investor in circumstances such as [*Caparo*], assuming (and this is important and tends to be overlooked in cases of this kind) that liability can be established. (Baxt, 1990, p. 18)

Picking up on the last point made by Baxt in the above quotation, he (Baxt, 1990), Gwilliam (1988) and others (including Woodhouse J in the *Scott Group* case) have emphasised the difficulty an investor faces in bringing a successful action against auditors. As noted in section 15.2 above, in order to do so, the investor must satisfy the court that:
- the auditor in question owed him or her a duty of care;
- the auditor was negligent in the performance of his or her duties;
- the investor suffered a loss as a result of relying on the negligently audited financial statements.

It seems that in the *Caparo* case the House of Lords, in seeking to ensure that auditors are not exposed to unbounded liability, focused on the first requirement (above). They appear to have given little attention to the third factor. Yet, as cases such as *Scott Group* and *Jeb Fasteners* have demonstrated, this is the most difficult factor to prove. Most investors would find it difficult to prove to the satisfaction of the court that audited financial statements provided the sole or main basis for an investment decision. As Baxt (1990) observes:

> There must be a number of factors that will influence a shareholder to buy more shares in a company for investment purposes – a comparative analysis of other companies' performances, the market reaction to the information about those companies, the individual shareholder's financial position, his/her interests and

needs, and a myriad of other individual factors. Each case will see different shareholders having to prove different things in order to show that the particular investment decision taken was based on the auditor's report, and that any loss is linked to the report, assuming further, that the report was negligent. (p. 9)

In the case of a large investor such as Caparo, it must surely be extremely difficult to prove reliance on negligently prepared audited financial statements. A large investor would almost certainly be expected to seek additional information from the company and elsewhere (that is, to undertake due diligence) before committing significant resources to the investment, such as occurs when a takeover offer is made.

15.4.3 Development of auditors' duty to third parties since the *Caparo* decision

As may be seen from Figure 15.3, since *Caparo* a number of cases relevant to auditors' duty of care to third parties have been decided in the UK.[10] Some of these, such as *Al-Saudi Banque & Others* v *Clark Pixley* [1990] Ch 313, have clarified aspects of the *Caparo* three-part test for a duty of care to be established; others, especially those in more recent years, such as *Independents' Advantage Insurance Co Ltd* v *Representatives of Michael Cook (deceased)* [2002] All ER (D) 151 (Nov); [2003] EWCA Civ 1103; [2003] All ER (D) 423 (Jul); [2004] PNLR 3 CA (as in fig. 15.3) have served to widen once more the parties to whom auditors may be held to owe a duty of care. In a number of the cases the judges have emphasised that the law in this area remains 'transitional', 'developing', 'in a state of flux' and 'facts-sensitive'.

The *Al-Saudi Banque* case (supra) helped to clarify what is required for a 'special relationship' to exist, such as to give rise to auditors owing a duty of care to third parties. The case involved a company whose business consisted of providing finance to overseas customers in exchange for bills of exchange. The company then used the bills of exchange (which constituted virtually all of the company's assets) to negotiate advances from the 10 plaintiff banks. In 1983 the company was compulsorily wound up and the bills of exchange were found to be worthless. The banks sued the auditors for negligence, alleging that they ought reasonably to have foreseen that the banks would rely on the auditors' reports when deciding whether to continue, renew or increase loans to the company, that they did so rely on the reports and were misled thereby. At the time of the relevant audit reports (1981 and 1982), seven of the plaintiff banks were existing creditors of the company but three were not.

---

[10] A number of cases have also been decided overseas. However, in the interests of keeping our discussion within reasonable bounds, we limit the cases discussed in section 15.4.3 to significant cases decided in the UK. In the first edition of this book we also discuss some 1990s cases in Australia and New Zealand. In some of these cases *Caparo* was followed, in others it was not.

Figure 15.3: Summary of significant UK cases since the *Caparo* ruling relating to auditors' liability to third parties

Case	Key finding(s) of the case
1. *Al-Saudi Banque & Others* v *Clark Pixley* [1990] Ch 313	The court applied *Caparo* and held that in order for auditors to owe a duty of care to a third party they must have given the third party a copy of their audit report, or know, or intend, that their audit report will be supplied to the third party.
2. *James McNaughton Papers Group Ltd.* v *Hicks Anderson & Co.* [1991] 1 All ER 134; [1990] BCC 891; (1991) 9 ACLC 3091	The court applied *Caparo* and held that when deciding whether a 'special relationship' exists, such as to give rise to a duty of care to a third party, the following need to be considered: 1. the purpose for which a statement is made; 2. the purpose for which it is communicated to the third party; 3. the relationship between the maker of the statement and the third party; 4. the size of the class to which the third party belongs; 5. the knowledge of the maker of the statement; and 6. the extent to which the third party relies on the statement or advice.
3. *Morgan Crucible Co plc* v *Hill Samuel Bank Ltd* [1991] Ch 295; [1991] 1 All ER 148; [1991] 2 WLR 655; [1991] BCLC 178; [1991] BCC 82; [1990] NLJR 1605	Applying *Caparo* the court held that if during a contested takeover bid financial advisors of the target company make express representations after an identified bidder has emerged, intending the bidder to rely on those representations, a relationship of proximity exists such that the financial advisors owe the bidder a duty of care not to be negligent in making representations which might mislead him.
4. *Berg Sons & Co. Ltd.* v *Mervyn Hampton Adams* [1993] BCLC 1045	The court applied, but effectively narrowed, the *Caparo* decision. It held: 1. For a company to succeed in an action against its auditors it must show the company or its shareholders were misled. 2. To establish that auditors owe a duty of care to a third party it must be shown that: (a) a specific relationship exists between the audit function and the transaction in relation to which reliance was placed on the audit report and (b) the case is brought within the period in which it is reasonably foreseeable that reliance may be placed on the audited financial statements.
5. *Galoo Ltd* v *Bright Grahame Murray* [1995] 1 All ER 16; [1994] 1 WLR 1360; [1994] 2 BCLC 492; [1994] BCC 319	Applying *Caparo* the court held that: 1. A plaintiff can claim for damages for breach of contract by an auditor only when the breach is the effective or dominant cause of his loss – not when the breach merely provides the opportunity to sustain a loss. 2. If an auditor is aware that a particular investor will rely on the audited financial statements for a particular share purchase or lending decision, and intends the bidder or lender to rely on them, a duty of care to the bidder or lender will arise.
6. *Henderson* v *Merrett Syndicates* [1995] 2 AC 145; [1994] 3 All ER 506; [1994] 3 WLR 761; [1994] NLJR 1204; [1994] 4 LRC 355	The House of Lords introduced 'assumption of responsibility' as an alternative to the three-part *Caparo* test in determining whether a professional advisor owed a duty of care to a third party. It also established that a professional advisor could owe a duty of care: 1. simultaneously to a party under a contractual relationship and to a third party; 2. to the same person under a contractual relationship and under the common law.
7. *ADT Ltd* v *BDO Binder Hamlyn* [1996] BCC 808	Binder Hamlyn was held to have assumed responsibility to a third party (ADT), and thus owed it a duty of care, because Binder Hamlyn's partner made (negligently prepared) oral representations to ADT, knowing the purpose for which the information was required and knowing that ADT would rely on it without independent enquiry.
8. *Coulthard & Ors* v *Neville Russell* (1998) PNLR 276; (1998) 1 BCLC 143; (1998) BCC 359	As a matter of principle, accountants can owe a duty of care to a client company's directors. However, whether a duty is owed in a particular case depends on the facts of the case and, in particular, on whether the accountants can be shown to have assumed responsibility to the directors.
9. *Siddell* v *Sydney Cooper & Partners* (1999) PNLR 511	The Court of Appeal emphasised that: 1. in the area of the liability of professional advisors, the law is in a state of transition or development; 2. there is a distinction between breaches of duty by professional advisors that cause another's loss and those that merely provide the opportunity to sustain a loss. The type of loss sustained is a question to be decided on the facts; 3. whether or not professional advisors owe a company's individual shareholders and directors a duty of care depends on the facts of the particular case.

Figure 15.3: *Continued*

10. *Bank of Credit & Commerce International (Overseas) Ltd, BCCI Holdings (Luxembourg) SA, and BCCI SAv Price Waterhouse & Ors, Ernst & Whinney & Ors* [1998] BCC 617; [1998] 15 LS Gaz R 32; [1998] 142 Sol Jo LB 86; [1998] 5 PNLR 564	A duty of care may be owed by the auditors of one company to another company where the business of the two companies is conducted as a single business. Leading decided cases considering the liability of professional advisors to third parties for financial loss had adopted two approaches: 1. the 'threefold test' – for a duty of care to be owed by an advisor to an advisee: (a) it must be foreseeable that if negligent advice is given, the recipient is likely to suffer damage, (b) there is a sufficient proximate relationship between the parties and (c) it is just and reasonable to impose the liability; 2. the 'voluntary assumption of responsibility test'. Factorsto be taken into account when deciding whether these tests have been met include: (i) the precise relationship between the advisor and advisee; (ii) the precise circumstances in which the advice came into existence and in which it was communicated to the advisee; (iii) the degree of reliance the advisor intended or should reasonably have anticipated would be placed on the accuracy of his advice by the advisee and the reliance in fact placed on it; (iv) the presence or absence of other advisors on whom the advisee would or could rely; (v) the opportunity, if any, given to the advisor to issue a disclaimer.
11. *Electra Private Equity Partners* v *KPMG Peat Marwick& Ors* [1999] All ER (D) 415; [2000] BCC 368; [2001] 1 BCLC 589	The Court of Appeal's decision indicates that: 1. when deciding whether auditors owe a duty of care to a third party, the court will consider factors such as: (i) the auditor's knowledge or foreseeability that the third party will rely on the audited financial statements for a particular decision, (ii) any direct communications between the auditor and the third party, (iii) whether the auditor believed the third party would receive independent advice and, if so, (iv) whether the auditor appreciated the advisor would rely on the audited financial statements in giving the advice; 2. the law in relation to the liability of professional advisors to third parties is in a state of development and transition; 3. the fact that a third party receives independent advice will not necessarily negate an auditor's duty of care to the third party.
12. *Barings plc* v *Coopers & Lybrand & Ors, Barings Futures (Singapore) Pte Ltd* v *Mattar & Ors* [2002] EWHC 461 (Ch); [2002] All ER (D) 309 (Mar); [2003] Lloyd's Rep IR 566	In circumstances where the auditor of a subsidiary forwards information to the parent company for use in the preparation of the consolidated financial statements, a duty of care may be owed by the auditor of the subsidiary to the parent company.
13. *Andrew* v *Kounnis Freeman* [1999] 2 BCLC 641 (CA); [1999] All ER (D) 553; [2000] Lloyd's PN 263	As a result of a letter from the Civil Aviation Authority (CAA) to Kounnis Freeman (KF), the latter knew or ought to have known that the CAA would rely on F plc's audited financial statements when deciding whether or not to renew F plc's licence to organise air travel. As a result, KF had assumed responsibility to the CAA and thus owed it a duty of care.
14. *Independents' Advantage Insurance Co Ltd* v *Representatives of Michael Cook (deceased)* [2002] All ER (D) 151 (Nov); [2003] EWCA Civ 1103; [2003] All ER (D) 423 (Jul); [2004] PNLR 3 CA	The auditors did not know (i) the identity of the party seeking to rely on their work or (ii) the purpose for which it would be relied upon; nor did they have any direct contact with the third party. Nevertheless, they were held to owe a duty of care to the third party on the grounds that they knew, or ought to have known, that Swift's audited financial statements would be relied upon when Swift applied to "one of a possible class of providers" for bonds and/or other securities. This case marks a distinct broadening of auditors' potential liability to third parties.
15. *Royal Bank of Scotland* v *Bannerman, Johnstone, Maclay* [2003] SC 125; [2005] CSIH 39	A duty of care to a third party may exist when the provider of information or advice knows that it will be passed to the third party for a specific purpose and the recipient is likely to rely on it for that purpose. Intention may support the existence of proximity between the auditor and the third party but it is not essential in every case. The absence of a disclaimer may point to an assumption of responsibility by the auditor.
16. *Equitable Life Assurance Society* v *Ernst & Young* [2002] EWHC 112 (Comm); [2003] 2 BCLC 603; [2003] EWHC 804; [2003] EWCA (Civ) 1114	This case demonstrates that: (i) in the area of auditors' liability to third parties, the law remains in a state of development and flux and sensitive to the facts of the case; (ii) the courts are concerned to limit the size of plaintiffs' claims against auditors. Equitable dropped its claim against the auditors early in the trial.
17. *Man Nutzfahzeuge AG and Ors* v *Freightliner Ltd and Ors* [2003] EWHC 2245; [2005] EWHC 2347 (Comm); [2007] EWCA (Civ) 910	The case provides further evidence of judges' reluctance to strike out cases involving auditor's liability to third parties because the cases are facts-sensitive and the law in the area 'is in development and not without difficulty'. It also shows that, when there is just cause, auditors can win cases brought against them.

Millet J held that the auditors did not owe the banks a duty of care:

- In respect of the three banks which were not existing creditors at the dates of the audit reports, the judge noted that the auditors had not reported directly to the banks and had not intended or known that the reports would be communicated to them. Even though it was foreseeable that a bank might ask a company for copies of its audited financial statements as a basis for making relevant loan decisions, the element of proximity necessary to find a duty of care was lacking.[11]
- Regarding the other seven banks, Millet J observed that, although their identities and amounts of exposure were known to the auditors when they signed their audit reports, their position was not comparable to that of the company's shareholders, to whom the auditors owed a statutory duty to report. As the auditors had not sent copies of their reports directly to the banks, or sent copies to the company with the intention or knowledge that they would be supplied to the banks, the auditors owed no duty of care to the plaintiffs.

This case suggested that, in order for auditors to owe a duty of care to a third party (or, more particularly, the audit client's bankers) they must either give a copy of their audit report to the third party or intend or know that their report will be supplied to that party. The case of *James McNaughton Papers Group Ltd* v *Hicks Anderson & Co* [1991] 1 All ER 134; [1990] BCC 891; (1991) ACLC 3091, indicated other factors the court will consider when deciding whether or not auditors owe a duty of care to a third party. In this case, James McNaughton Ltd was involved in the takeover of another company (MK). Draft accounts for use in the negotiations were prepared by Hicks Anderson and, at a meeting of the negotiators, a representative of that firm stated that MK was breaking even. After the takeover was completed, discrepancies were found in the draft accounts and MK was found to be insolvent. McNaughton sued the accountants for negligent preparation of the accounts and stated that, in proceeding with the takeover, they had relied on the accounts and the statement made at the negotiating meeting by the accountants' representative.

The court of first instance found that the accountants owed McNaughton Ltd a duty of care but this decision was reversed on appeal. The Court of Appeal, applying *Caparo*, held that when a statement or advice is acted upon by a person (C), other than the person intended by the giver of the statement or advice (A) to act on it, the factors to be considered in determining whether A owes C a duty of care include:

---

[11] This ruling is diametrically opposed to that of Chadwick L J, 13 years, later in the *Independents' Advantage* case (supra).

- the purpose for which the statement is made;
- the purpose for which the statement is communicated;
- the relationship between A, C and any relevant third party;
- the size of any class to which C belongs;
- the state of knowledge of A;
- the reliance by C on A's statement or advice.

Considering these factors, the court found that the accountants owed no duty of care to McNaughton Ltd in respect of the draft accounts because:
- the accounts were produced for MK and not McNaughton;
- the accounts were merely draft accounts and the accountants could not have reasonably foreseen that McNaughton would treat them as final accounts;
- the accountants did not take part in the negotiations;
- McNaughton was aware that MK was in a poor financial state and, thus, could have been expected to consult its own accountants;
- the statement made at the negotiating meeting was very general and did not affect the figures in the accounts. The accountants could not reasonably have foreseen that McNaughton would rely on the statement without further enquiry or advice.

The *McNaughton* case added to the *Al-Saudi* decision in that it provided guidance on the matters (other than knowledge or intention of reliance on the audit report) the court would consider when deciding whether or not auditors owe a duty of care to a third party. These include the purpose for which an audit report is prepared, the purpose for which it is communicated to a third party, and the extent to which the third party relies (or sensibly should rely) on the auditor's statement or advice.

Unlike the two cases cited above, *Morgan Crucible Co plc* v *Hill Samuel Bank Ltd* [1991] Ch 295; [1991] 1 All ER 148; [1991] 2 WLR 655; [1991] BCLC 178; [1991] BCC 82; [1990] NLJR 1605 provides an example of a case in which auditors (and other professional advisors) were held to owe a duty of care to a third party. On 6 December 1985, Morgan Crucible (MC) announced a takeover bid for First Castle Electronics plc (FCE). On 19 December 1985, FCE's chairman sent to FCE's shareholders the first of a number of circulars recommending that the takeover offer be rejected. Each circular, which was also issued as a press release by Hill Samuel Bank Ltd (HSB, the merchant bank advising FCE), referred to the company's audited financial statements for the years to 31 January 1984 and 1985 and its unaudited interim statements for the six months to 31 July 1985. A circular dated 24 January 1986 forecast a 38 per cent increase in pre-tax profits for the year to 31 January 1986. It also contained (i) a letter from FCE's auditors stating that the profit forecast had been properly compiled in accordance with FCE's stated accounting policies and (ii) a letter from HSB expressing the opinion that the forecast had been made after due and careful enquiry.

On 29 January 1986, MC increased its offer and this was accepted. MC subsequently found that FCE was worthless. MC sued the bank, the auditors and the directors of FCE, alleging that it was foreseeable that it would rely on the representations contained in the pre-bid financial statements and the profit forecast. MC claimed that FCE's accounting policies were flawed, its pre-bid financial statements were prepared negligently and its profit had been grossly overstated. It asserted that, had it known the true facts, it would not have made the takeover bid, let alone increased it.

The court of first instance, relying on *Caparo*, held that neither the financial advisors (in this case, HSB and the auditors) nor the directors of a target company in a contested takeover bid owe a duty of care to a known takeover bidder regarding the accuracy of profit forecasts, financial statements, and defence documents prepared for the purpose of contesting the bid. Such documents are prepared for the purpose of advising shareholders whether or not to accept the bid, not for the guidance of the bidder. Hence, there is insufficient proximity between the financial advisors and directors of the target company and the bidder to give rise to a duty of care.

The Court of Appeal reversed this decision. It held that if, during the course of a contested takeover bid, the financial advisors and directors of the target company make express representations after an identified bidder has emerged, intending that the bidder will rely on those representations, they owe the bidder a duty of care not to be negligent in making representations which might mislead him. In the instant case, the defendants intended the plaintiff to rely on the pre-bid financial statements and profit forecast for the purpose of deciding whether to make an increased bid, and the plaintiff did so rely. There was, therefore, a relationship of proximity between each of the defendants and the plaintiff such as to give rise to a duty of care.

The case of *Berg Sons & Co. Ltd* v *Mervyn Hampton Adams* [1993] BCLC 1045 focused primarily on auditors' duty of care to the auditee (that is, auditors' contractual duties) but it also explored, and to some extent further narrowed, auditors' duty of care to third parties. The case involved a small company all of whose shares were held by the sole executive director, his wife and his son. In 1985 the company was put into liquidation and the company's liquidator, together with a discount house which had provided Berg Sons & Co. with finance, sued the auditors for negligence. It was alleged that, as a consequence of the auditor's unqualified audit report on the company's 1982 financial statements, (i) the company was able to continue in business and borrow money which it had no prospect of repaying and (ii) the discount house discounted bills receivable which should have been shown in the financial statements as irrecoverable.

Hobhouse J found that the auditors were not negligent even though they had received unsatisfactory assurances from both the acceptor of certain bills and Mr Berg, and this should have prompted an audit report qualified on grounds of uncertainty. His Honour, following the reasoning of the Law Lords in *Caparo*, stated:

> [T]he purpose of the statutory audit is to provide a mechanism to enable those having a proprietary interest in the company ... to have access to accurate financial information about the company. Provided that those persons have that information, the statutory purpose is exhausted ... In the present case the ... plaintiffs have based their case not upon any lack of information on the part of the company's executive director but rather upon the opportunity that the possession of the auditor's certificate is said to have given for the company to continue to carry on business and borrow money from third parties. Such matters do not fall within the scope of the duty of the statutory auditor.

With respect to the auditors owing the company a duty of care, the court held that, in order for a company to bring a successful action against its auditors, it must show "that the company or its members were in some way misled or left in ignorance of some material fact" (per Hobhouse J). A 'one-man' company such as Berg Sons & Co. could never prove that it had been misled because its controlling director and shareholder would always know better than anyone else the true position of the company and its business.

The court also held that the auditors owed no duty of care to the discount house. Hobhouse J reaffirmed, but went beyond, the *Caparo* decision. He stated that, before a duty of care to third parties will arise, two criteria must be satisfied, namely:

1. there must be a specific relationship between the function the defendant has been requested to perform and the transaction for which the plaintiff relied on the proper performance of that function (in this case, between the statutory audit and the discounting of bills receivable);
2. the case must be brought within a limited period of the alleged negligence. There is only a limited period of time within which it would be reasonably foreseeable that a bank or discount house would rely upon a given set of audited financial statements.

Commenting on this decision of Hobhouse J in the *Berg* case, Davies (1992) pointed out:

> The effect of these additional limitations is to place such stringent restrictions on the circumstances in which the creditors of a company can sue its auditors that

it is now difficult to imagine any circumstances when such a claim could succeed arising out of the statutory audit function. (p. 4)

He also noted that, as a result of the *Berg Sons & Co.* judgment, it is most unlikely that a successful case can be brought in the UK against auditors by their small company audit clients or by such clients' creditors.

The case of *Galoo Ltd* v *Bright Grahame Murray* [1995] 1 All ER 16; [1994] 1 WLR 1360; [1994] 2 BCLC 492; [1994] BCC 319 served to confirm the difficulty a company's creditors will experience in trying to establish that a company's auditors owed them a duty of care. It also helped to clarify what the UK courts will accept (in the wake of the *Caparo* decision) as a 'special relationship' which may give rise to auditors owing a duty of care to a third party.

The facts of this case are briefly as follows. Hillsdown Holdings (HD) purchased 51 per cent of the shares in GM; GM, in turn, owned all of the shares in Galoo Ltd (GL). The acquisition agreement stated that the purchase price of the shares in GM was to be 5.2 times the net profit of GM, as reflected in the audited financial statements of GM and GL for the year ending December 1986. The financial statements were audited by Bright Grahame Murray and delivered by them to HD for the specific purpose of establishing the share price. Between 1987 and 1992, HD advanced £30 million in loans to GM and GL and, in 1991, purchased a further 44 per cent of shares in GM on terms set out in a supplemental share purchase agreement.

In 1992, HD, GM and GL sued the auditors claiming that the audited financial statements of GM and GL for the years 1985 to 1989, and the draft audited financial statements for 1990, contained substantial inaccuracies. In failing to discover or report the inaccuracies, the auditors had been negligent and in breach of the duties they owed to the plaintiffs. Had the auditors performed their duties with reasonable skill and care, the insolvency of GM and GL would have been revealed and they would have ceased trading immediately. They would not have accepted, or continued to accept, advances from HD, and HD would not have purchased shares in GM or made loans to GM and GL.

The Court of Appeal was asked to rule on whether there was a sustainable cause of action against the auditors. It found there was – but only in respect of HD's initial 51 per cent investment. The court held:

1. A plaintiff's claim that it had suffered loss by entering into a loan agreement did not give rise to any damages since the mere acceptance of a loan could not be described as a loss giving rise to damages. The mere acceptance by GM and GL of loans from HD in reliance on the auditors' statements did not give rise to any cause of action against the auditors.

2. A plaintiff is entitled to claim damages for breach of contract by the defendants where the breach is the effective or dominant cause of his loss – rather than merely providing him with the opportunity to sustain loss. Based on the facts in this case, the auditors' breach of duty clearly provided GM and GL with the opportunity to incur, and to continue to incur, trading losses, but it could not be said to have caused those losses.

3. The fact that it is foreseeable that a potential investor in a company might rely on a company's audited financial statements is not of itself sufficient to impose on the auditor a duty of care to the investor. However, if the auditor has been made aware that a particular identified bidder for shares or lender will rely on the audited financial statements, and the auditor intends the party to so rely, the auditor owes a duty of care to the identified party and may be liable in the event of any breach of this duty. In respect of the 1987 acquisition of shares in GM by HD, it is clear that the auditors knew the audited financial statements for the year to December 1986 would be relied upon by HD for calculating the purchase price of the shares and they were required to submit the audited financial statements to HD for that specific purpose. Thus, the auditors owed a duty of care to HD in that regard. However, with respect to HD's loans to GM and GL and additional shares purchased in GM, it was not alleged that the auditors either knew or intended that HD would rely on the audited financial statements of GM and GL when deciding whether to make the loans or when calculating the purchase price of the shares in GM under the supplemental share price agreement. Hence, no duty of care was owed by the auditors to HD in respect of the loans or the additional shares purchased.

From the post-*Caparo* cases reviewed above, it is evident that subsequent to *Caparo* it was (and, indeed remains) difficult for third parties to establish that auditors owed them a duty of care. To do so, they must show that the auditors knew, or intended, that they would place reliance on the audited financial statements for a specific transaction, that there is a nexus between the audit and the transaction, and that they brought their case against the auditors within a limited period of the auditors' alleged negligence. However, as the cases outlined below bear witness, in more recent years the courts have modified the *Caparo* decision to some extent and have recognised a duty of care to third parties in situations where strict application of the three-part *Caparo* test (reasonable foreseeability of damage, relationship of proximity, and fairness of imposing a duty) would have precluded such a duty being owed. The most significant modification of the *Caparo* ruling is the court's recognition of a duty of care arising when auditors (or other professional advisors) 'assume responsibility' to a third party. This principle was enunciated by the House of Lords in *Henderson* v *Merrett Syndicates* [1995] 2 AC 145; [1994] 3 All ER 506; [1994] 3 WLR 761; [1994] NLJR 1204; [1994] 4 LRC 355.

In the *Henderson* case the plaintiffs were Lloyd's Names[12] who were members of syndicates that were managed by the defendants. The plaintiffs fell into two groups:

(i) direct Names – Names who belonged to syndicates that were managed by the members' agents. Thus, the agents were both the members' and managing agents;[13]

(ii) indirect Names – Names who were placed by their members' agents with syndicates that were managed by other agents. The members' agents entered into sub-agency agreements with the managing agents of those syndicates.

The relationship between the Names, members' agents and managing agents was regulated by agency and sub-agency agreements. These gave the managing agent 'absolute discretion' in respect of underwriting business conducted on behalf of the Names but they also contained an implied term that the agents would exercise due care and skill in the exercise of their functions as managing agents.

Following very poor performance in the Lloyd's insurance market, the plaintiffs sued the defendants alleging they had been negligent in the conduct and management of the plaintiffs' syndicates. The key issues for the court to decide included the following:

(i) whether the members' (and managing) agents owed a common law duty of care to the direct Names, notwithstanding that a contractual relationship existed between them;

(ii) whether the managing agents appointed as sub-agents by the members' agents owed a duty of care to the indirect Names (who were third parties in respect of the sub-agency agreements);

(iii) whether the members' agents were responsible to the indirect Names for any failure on the part of the managing agents to whom they had delegated underwriting duties under the sub-agency agreements.

The court of first instance found in the plaintiffs' favour on all three questions. The defendants appealed the decision and, when the Court of Appeal dismissed their appeal, the defendants appealed to the House of Lords. The Law Lords also dismissed their appeal explaining their reasons as follows:

---

[12] Names are persons who underwrite (or accept the risks, and hence the financial consequences, attaching to) insurance contracts within the Lloyd's insurance market. As the potential liability attaching to an insurance contract can run into many millions of pounds sterling, the Names are organised in syndicates which operate as single entities to underwrite one or more insurance contract and also, in appropriate circumstances, to re-insure the syndicate against the risks attaching to insurance contracts they have accepted.

[13] Names are members of Lloyd's and each member has an agent (which, almost invariably, is a firm of professional insurance underwriters) who looks after their interests within the Lloyd's insurance market. Additionally, each syndicate has a managing agent (also a firm of professional insurance underwriters) who conducts the business of the syndicate.

1. Where a person assumes responsibility to perform professional services for another who relies on those services, the relationship between the parties is sufficient, in itself, to give rise to a duty by the person providing the services to exercise reasonable skill and care in so doing. Accordingly, the managing agents at Lloyd's owed a duty of care to the Names who were members of the syndicates they managed. By holding themselves out as possessing special expertise to advise the Names on the suitability of risks to be underwritten, on when and the extent to which re-insurance should be taken out, and on claims that should be settled, the agents clearly assumed responsibility towards the Names in their syndicates. Moreover, Names, as the managing agents well knew, placed implicit reliance on that expertise in that they gave authority to the managing agents to bind them (the Names) to contracts of insurance and re-insurance, and to the settlement of claims.

2. An assumption of responsibility by a person rendering professional services, coupled with reliance on those services by the person for whom they are rendered, can give rise to a common law duty of care irrespective of any contractual relationship between the parties. In the case of the direct Names, their contract with their members' agents did not operate to exclude the common law duty of care because an implied term of the agency agreements was that the agents would exercise due care and skill in the exercise of their functions as managing agents; that duty of care is no different from the duty of care owed by the managing agents to the Names under the common law. Likewise, the indirect Names were not prevented by the chain of contracts contained in the agency and sub-agency agreements from suing the managing agents under the common law. In particular, the fact that the managing agents had, with the consent of the indirect Names, assumed responsibility in respect of their managing activities to the members' agents under sub-agency agreements (thus, under contract) did not prevent the managing agents from also assuming responsibility in respect of the same activities to the indirect Names as third parties to those agreements.

Thus, in *Henderson* v *Merrett Syndicates*, the House of Lords recognised the criterion of 'assumption of responsibility' as an alternative to the three-part *Caparo* test to apply when determining whether or not a professional advisor (or professional services provider) owed a duty of care to a third party who relied on his or her advice (or services). The Law Lords also established that a professional advisor (or services provider) may simultaneously owe a duty of care to a party with whom the advisor has a contractual relationship and to a third party. Additionally, the fact that a person is in a contractual relationship with a professional advisor does not preclude that person from also being owed a common law duty of care by the advisor.

The court applied the criterion of 'assumption of responsibility' in *ADT Ltd* v *BDO Binder Hamlyn* [1996] BCC 808 to determine whether or not a professional advisor (in this case the auditor) owed a duty of care to a third party. Binder Hamlyn issued an unqualified audit report on the 1989 financial statements of Britannia Securities Group (BSG) – a company ADT Ltd was contemplating purchasing. In January 1990, a partner of Binder Hamlyn attended a meeting with a director of ADT and confirmed that BSG's 1989 audited financial statements showed a true and fair view of BSG's state of affairs. On the strength of this representation ADT purchased BSG for £105 million. It was subsequently found that BSG's true value was £40 million.

The question to be decided by the court was whether, as a result of the oral assurance given by Binder Hamlyn's partner to the ADT director in respect of BSG's audited financial statements, Binder Hamlyn had assumed responsibility to ADT and thus owed it a duty of care. May J held that Binder Hamlyn had assumed responsibility to ADT at the meeting in January 1990 when its partner gave (negligently prepared) information or advice directly to ADT, knowing the purpose for which it was required and knowing ADT would place reliance on it without further enquiry. The judge also noted that the defendants were negligent when conducting the 1989 audit; their standard of professional competence did not achieve that of ordinarily skilled auditors. The judge awarded damages against Binder Hamlyn of £65 million, the difference in the amount paid for BSG (£105 million) and its true value (£40 million).

Like the *ADT* case considered above, those of *Coulthard & Ors* v *Neville Russell* (1998) PNLR 276; (1998) 1 BCLC 143; (1998) BCC 359 and *Siddell* v *Sydney Cooper & Partners* (1999) PNLR 511 extended the *Caparo* decision by recognising that an accountant's duty of care is not limited to the company *per se* and the company's shareholders as a body, but may also be owed to the company's directors and shareholders as individuals. However, in each case, the court emphasised that whether or not a duty of care is owed by a professional advisor to a third party depends upon the particular circumstances of the case.

The *Coulthard* case involved Neville Russell's failure to advise its client company's directors that loan payments to a shell company, to pay for shares the company was purchasing in the parent company, might infringe s. 151 of the Companies Act 1985. The High Court judge refused to uphold Neville Russell's assertion that the plaintiff's action against it had insufficient legal grounds to proceed. Neville Russell appealed the decision but the Court of Appeal confirmed the lower court's ruling. The Court of Appeal held that, as a matter of principle, accountants can owe a duty of care to a client company's directors but whether or not a duty is owed in a particular case depends upon the facts of the case and, in particular, on whether it can be shown that the accountants had assumed responsibility to the directors.

In *Siddell* v *Sydney Cooper & Partners* (supra), the defendants (SCP) were the auditors and management accountants of a small, family-run company with four shareholders and directors (Mr and Mrs Siddell and Mr and Mrs Fellows). Following the departure of the company's finance director (Mrs Jefferies – the only 'outside' director) in 1992, irregularities were found in the accounting records. Soon afterwards the company, which had been thought to be profitable, went into receivership with a deficit of more than £1 million.

The plaintiffs sued SCP for breach of their duty of care to them as shareholders and directors. The court of first instance held that the plaintiffs' claim had insufficient legal grounds to proceed. Following *Caparo*, the judge held that auditors do not normally owe a duty of care to a company's shareholders. However, the plaintiffs appealed the decision and the Court of Appeal overturned the lower court's ruling. Mummery L J and Clarke L J explained their reasons as follows:

1. Where, as in the case of the liability of professional advisors, the law is in a state of transition or development, an order to disallow an action to proceed should not be made unless the court can be properly persuaded that the claim is bound to fail. This is not the position in this case.

2. The judge (in the court of first instance), relying on *Caparo* v *Dickman* (1990) and *Galoo Ltd* v *Bright Grahame Murray* (1994), disallowed the appellants' action to proceed on the basis that SCP owed them, as third parties, no duty of care. The judge also submitted that, as in *Caparo*, liability did not arise unless it could be shown that the advisors intended or knew that the third parties were personally relying on the services being provided to the company and there was actual reliance. Whilst accepting, for present purposes, these requirements for liability to arise (although noting that the law is in a state of transition or development), the facts in this case are very different from those in *Caparo*. SCP was not simply acting as auditor but was providing broader services to the company, including the preparation of quarterly and annual accounts and the giving of advice. Following *Henderson* v *Merrett Syndicates Ltd* (1995) 2 AC 145, it cannot be maintained that the existence of a contract between the parties necessarily precludes a co-extensive duty of care at common law (that is, to third parties).

3. The judge in the first court also disallowed the appellants' action to proceed on the basis that the alleged breaches of duty did not cause the appellants' loss but merely provided an opportunity to sustain loss. Only the former kind of loss is recoverable. It is for the court to decide, by applying common sense, which type of loss has been suffered. However,

it is important to note that the question of whether a particular loss has been caused by a breach of duty is a question of fact and, as such, an action should not be prevented from proceeding on this ground unless it is bound to fail. That is not the position in this case.

In the course of its judgment, the Court of Appeal noted:

> The principles upon which *Caparo* was based cannot be restricted to large companies [but] whether a duty of care [to third parties] exists depends upon all the circumstances of the particular case. Those circumstances will include the size of the company and the number and type of shareholders (or indeed directors) to whom the duty is said to be owed (as quoted in Scott, 1999).

By recognising that auditors (or accountants) may owe a duty of care to their client company's shareholders and/or directors as individuals, *Coulthard* v *Neville Russell* and *Siddell* v *Sydney Cooper & Partners* clearly extended the *Caparo* decision. However, the story does not end here. In the case of *Bank of Credit & Commerce International (Overseas) Ltd, BCCI Holdings (Luxembourg) SA*, and *BCCI SA* v *Price Waterhouse & Ors*, and *Ernst & Whinney & Ors* [1998] BCC 617, [1998] 15 LS Gaz R 32, [1998] 142 Sol Jo LB 86, [1998] 5 PNLR 564, the Court of Appeal held that the auditor of one company may owe a duty of care to another [third party] company. In this case, the court also took the opportunity to summarise the approaches to the liability of professional advisors for financial loss which had been adopted in leading cases where the issue had been considered.

The facts of the case are briefly as follows. On 5 July 1991, after evidence emerged of a long-standing, large-scale, global fraud, an international swoop (co-ordinated by the Bank of England) closed down the Bank of Credit & Commerce International (BCCI) group of companies. Until 1987, when BCCI was persuaded to engage Price Waterhouse (PW) as its sole auditors, it was able to obscure its worldwide fraudulent operations by engaging different auditors for its different banking subsidiaries. While Ernst & Whinney (E&W) acted as the auditors of BCCI Holdings (Luxembourg) SA and BCCI SA (located in Luxembourg), PW acted as auditors of BCCI (Overseas) (located in the Cayman Islands).

The liquidators of all three banks brought proceedings against PW [as auditors of all the banks for the years 1987, 1988 and 1989 and of BCCI (Overseas) prior to 1987] and E&W [as auditors of BCCI (Holdings) and BCCI SA prior to 1987] for negligently performed audits – audits that failed to detect massive frauds being perpetrated on BCCI's creditors and shareholders. In addition to suing PW for breach of its contractual duties, BCCI (Overseas) alleged that E&W also owed it a duty of care on the grounds that the business and operations of BCCI (Overseas) and BCCI SA (BCCI's two principal banking subsidiaries) were managed as if they were the business and operations of a single bank (Lascelles & Donkin, 1991).

In the trial court, Laddie J held that BCCI (Overseas)'s claim against E&W could not proceed. He said that, in order to proceed, BCCI (Overseas) had to show that E&W had provided it with information knowing or intending that BCCI (Overseas) would rely on it for a particular purpose, and that BCCI (Overseas) had in fact relied on the information for that purpose. (Expressed in terms of the *Caparo* ruling, it had to meet the requirements for a relationship of proximity to be established.) Laddie J ruled that BCCI (Overseas) had not succeeded in pleading a case that contained the required elements.

Upon appeal, the Court of Appeal overturned the decision. During its judgment, the court noted:

> The liability of accountants and of other professional advisors for economic loss caused by reason of their alleged negligence to persons other than their clients has been the subject of a substantial number of leading cases. In *Smith* v *Eric S Bush* (1990) 1 AC 83 "the threefold test" as to whether a duty of care is owed by an advisor to those who act on his advice was stated to be: (a) it must be foreseeable that if the advice is negligent the recipient is likely to suffer the kind of damage that has occurred; (b) there is a sufficient proximate relationship between the parties and (c) it is just and reasonable to impose the liability (Lord Griffiths at (1990) 1 AC 864H). To this test has been added "the voluntary assumption of responsibility test" referred to in *Henderson* v *Merrett Syndicate Ltd* (1995) 2 AC 145 by Lord Goff and extended from the principle underlying the decision in *Hedley Bryne* v *Heller and Partners Ltd* (1964) AC 465.

The court pointed out that the 'threefold test' and the 'assumption of responsibility test' indicated the criteria that had to be satisfied in order for liability to be attached to the appellants. It also noted that the authorities had provided guidance on factors to be taken into account in deciding whether these criteria had been met. These include:

(i)   the precise relationship between the advisor and advisee;

(ii) the precise circumstances in which the advice was given and in which it was communicated to the advisee, and whether the communication was made by the advisor or by a third party;

(iii) the degree of reliance the advisor intended or should reasonably have anticipated would be placed on the accuracy of the advice by the advisee and the reliance in fact placed on it;

(iv) the presence or absence of other advisors on whom the advisee would or could rely;

(v) the opportunity, if any, given to the advisor to issue a disclaimer.

The court also observed that decided cases concerning the liability of professional advisors to third parties had established that any development in the law in this area ought only to made incrementally (i.e., in small steps). It further noted:

> It needs to be borne in mind that . . . a barrier exists between an advisor and any person who is not his immediate client [i.e., a third party] which has to be overcome before the advisor can be said to owe a duty to that person, a barrier which will be all the stronger if that person is in receipt of independent advice. However, the reality in the present case is that any barrier between Ernst & Whinney and BCCI (Overseas) was a mere shadow. Overseas' and BCCI SA's banking activities were conducted as those of a single bank, such was the intermingling of their operations and the constant exchange of information between them. Ernst & Whinney were, in effect, the supervising auditors of both banks, as well as the auditors of BCCI Holdings (Luxembourg) SA.

The court held that, if the threefold test or the assumption of responsibility test were applied to the facts of the case, it would be quite wrong to dismiss the claims of BCCI (Overseas) against E&W on the grounds that they had no legal foundation.[14] However, the court noted that the facts of the case were very unusual and, therefore, the case ought not to be regarded as setting a precedent. Nevertheless, the court's decision is very significant in terms of auditors' liability to third parties as it shows that, in certain circumstances (such as where the business of two companies is conducted as if it were a single business), the court will recognise that the auditors of one company may owe a duty of care to another (third party) company.

Since the Court of Appeal's summary of the law relating to the liability of professional advisors (including auditors) to third parties for financial loss suffered as a result of the professional advisor's negligence, a number of other cases of note have reached the courts. We discuss seven of these below. The first is *Electra Private Equity Partners* v *KPMG Peat Marwick & Ors* [1999] All ER (D) 415; [2000] BCC 368; [2001] 1 BCLC 589. This case concerned venture capital fund managers who, in May 1992, invested IR£10 million in unquoted convertible loan stock and thereby acquired effective control of C plc, an Irish leasing company. Eighteen months later the plaintiffs lost all of their investment when C plc went into receivership.

The plaintiffs sought to recover their losses from two firms of accountants:
(i) KPMG – whom the plaintiffs had instructed to investigate and report on the suitability of the investment; and
(ii) SKC (an Irish partnership which was part of the KPMG International firm) – who as auditors of C plc had procured for, or concurred in C plc

---

[14] BCCI's liquidators originally filed claims against PW and E&W for $US11 billion (approximately £6.5 billion). However, in September 1998, PW and E&W agreed an out-of-court settlement with the liquidators for an amount reputed to be in the region of $US95 million to $US100 million (Nisse, 1999; Financial Times, 1998).

producing, to the plaintiffs prior to the investment its audited financial statements (complete with 'clean' audit report) for the year ending 29 February 1992.

Carnwath J disallowed Electra's claim against SKC from proceeding on the basis that, in order for a duty of care to arise to a third party, the claimant would need to show that the auditors had consciously assumed responsibility to the third party. The plaintiffs appealed the ruling and the Court of Appeal found in their favour. Reasons advanced by the court for its decision included the following:

1. The court's determination in a case such as the present might depend, in particular, on:
    (i) knowledge or foreseeability by the auditor that the potential investor would rely on the accuracy of the audited financial statements in deciding whether to invest – as distinct from insisting on audited reports and an unqualified auditor's report as a condition of investment;
    (ii) the fact and nature of any direct communications between the auditor and the potential investor;
    (iii) whether the auditor reasonably believed that the potential investor would obtain independent advice on the suitability of the investment; and
    (iv) if the auditor did so believe, whether he appreciated that the independent advisor would rely on his (the auditor's) figures for the purpose of advising the potential investor.

    The court held that Carnwath J had wrongly focused on a 'conscious assumption of responsibility' as the test for the existence of a duty of care and this could have resulted in too high a threshold for the plaintiffs. Electra's claim against SKC gave rise to a triable issue, namely, whether SKC knew or foresaw the purpose for which the plaintiffs required the audited financial statements, and whether they assumed responsibility for their accuracy by providing them to the plaintiffs in the alleged circumstances (i.e., for the purpose of making an investment decision).

2. The court should proceed with great caution in exercising its power to disallow cases from proceeding on the basis of the facts presented when:
    (i) all the facts are not known by the court;
    (ii) the facts, and the legal principles turning on them, are complex; and
    (iii) when the law, as in the instant case, is in a state of development.

    Actions by a third party against auditors and other professional advisors for negligence are notable examples of facts-sensitive cases where the law is still in a state of transition.

3. Carnwath J wrongly held that the involvement of KPMG as independent advisors was fatal to the plaintiffs' claimed duty of care by SKC. It was not necessary to the success of the claim that KPMG be acting as agents for Electra in their dealings with SKC. Further, there had been considerable direct contact between Electra and SKC. At the very least, it was arguable that such a tripartite relationship, particularly having regard to the close professional association between KPMG and SKC, created a 'special relationship' between the plaintiffs and SKC.

The *Electra* case seems to signal a loosening by the court of the strict principles enunciated in the *Caparo*, *Galoo* and *Henderson* v *Merrett Syndicates* cases and seems to indicate that, when the court considers it just and equitable (the third of the three-part *Caparo* test) to do so, it will find a way to hold that auditors (or other professional advisors) owe a duty of care to a third party. Such a process can be discerned in *Barings plc* v *Coopers & Lybrand & Ors, Barings Futures (Singapore) Pte Ltd* v *Mattar & Ors* [2002] EWHC 461 (Ch); [2002] All ER (D) 309 (Mar); [2003] Lloyd's Rep IR 566.

The *Barings* case (supra) or, more correctly, the portion of the case relevant to the theme of this section of the chapter, namely, auditors' liability to third parties, essentially turned on the question of whether Coopers & Lybrand Singapore (C&LS) owed a duty of care to Barings plc. During 1992 and 1993, Deloitte & Touche (D&T) were the auditors of Barings Futures (Singapore) Pte Ltd (BFS) – a subsidiary of Barings Securities Ltd (BSL), which was, in turn, an indirect subsidiary of Barings plc, a non-trading group holding company based in London. In 1994, D&T were replaced by C&LS as auditors of BFS. Coopers & Lybrand (C&L) were the auditors of both BSL and Barings plc throughout the relevant period. As auditors of BFS, D&T and C&LS were required to provide Barings plc's directors with consolidated schedules (and a copy of BFS's audit report) which the directors used in preparing the group's consolidated financial statements.

The Barings Group collapsed in February 1995 as a result of unauthorised, and heavily loss-making, speculative trading and gambling on movements in the Japanese stock market by Leeson, general manager of BFS. In 1996, the liquidators of the Barings Group sued C&L, C&LS, and the Singapore partners of D&T for £1 billion,[15] claiming that their negligent auditing of the group accounts (by C&L) and of BFS's accounts (by D&T and C&LS) was responsible for the collapse of the Barings Group in 1995. C&L, C&LS and D&T maintained that the collapse of the group was due to management failings and fraud, not to the

---

[15] As reported, for example, Perry, 2001b.

work of the auditors (Perry, 2001a). Irrespective of the outcome of that fundamental and overarching argument, at a more detailed level, C&LS and D&T challenged the claims brought against them by Barings plc and BFS, respectively.[16]

C&LS sought to have Barings plc's claim against it dismissed as having no legal foundation. The firm submitted that it owed a duty of care to BFS (its audit client) but not to Barings plc: any claim for damage suffered as a consequence of its negligence could only be claimed by the subsidiary that had suffered damage (i.e., BFS) and not by its shareholder (Barings plc). The information C&LS was required to supply to Barings plc was simply so that Barings plc's directors could comply with their legal obligation to prepare consolidated financial statements. The High Court found in favour of C&LS but Barings plc appealed its ruling.

Unlike the High Court, the Court of Appeal did not accept C&LS's arguments. Leggatt L J pointed out that at no time during the audit of BFS's consolidation schedules, prepared for the purpose of the group's consolidated financial statements, did the auditors detect or report the unauthorised trading of Leeson or the losses which resulted. On the contrary, those schedules showed BFS to be profitable. He cited with approval the decision in *George Fischer (Great Britain) Ltd* v *Multi Construction Ltd* [1995] 1 BCLC 260, where it was held that there was no legal principle preventing a holding company from recovering damages for loss in the value of its subsidiaries resulting directly from a breach of duty owed to it, as distinct from a duty owed to the subsidiaries themselves.

Leggatt L J also noted that C&LS could not have supposed that the only responsibility it assumed to Barings plc was to submit BFS's schedules in a form suitable for incorporation into the consolidated financial statements and that it did not matter whether they showed a true and fair view of BFS's financial affairs. His Honour observed that an auditor's task is to conduct the audit so as to make it probable that material misstatements in financial documents will be detected. That did not occur and C&LS had a case to answer. The Court of Appeal concluded that C&LS must have appreciated that its audit report and consolidated schedules would be used for the purpose of producing the consolidated financial statements. That was enough

---

[16] The portion of the case which addressed the question of whether D&T had sufficient grounds to negate claims brought against it by BFS did not concern auditors' liability to third parties. However, as the key issue in dispute was the reliance auditors may place on written representations, a topic we discuss in Chapter 13 (section 13.5), we have reported this portion of the case in an appendix to this chapter.

to establish that C&LS owed a duty of care to Barings plc in addition to that owed to BFS.[17]

According to Leggat L J, a critical point in this case was that Barings plc pleaded a direct relationship between it and C&LS arising from the circumstances in which work was done for, and information was supplied by, C&LS to Barings plc and its auditors in England (C&L) for the preparation of the group's accounts. This seems to limit future application of the decision to cases in which the facts are fairly similar. Nevertheless, as a result of the court's ruling in this case, it seems likely that where the auditor of a subsidiary forwards information to the parent company for use in the preparation of the group's consolidated financial statements, a duty of care will be owed, more or less routinely, by the auditor of the subsidiary to the parent company.

Auditors were similarly held to owe a duty of care to a third party in *Andrew* v *Kounnis Freeman* [1999] 2 BCLC 641 (CA); [1999] All ER (D) 553; [2000] Lloyd's PN 263, a case involving F plc, a company which organised air travel. Prior to renewing F's licence to organise air travel, the Civil Aviation Authority (CAA), in a letter dated 15 March 1996, notified F plc that it required, amongst other things, a copy of F plc's 1995 audited financial statements. The CAA also notified F plc's auditors, Kounnis Freeman (KF), of this requirement and that it additionally required the auditors to confirm certain matters. Following its 1995 audit of F plc's financial statements, KF wrote to the CAA confirming the relevant matters. Relying on F's 1995 audited financial statements and KF's confirmations, the CAA renewed F plc's licence. However, the company collapsed suddenly a few months later and the CAA was left to pay the return flights of stranded passengers. The CAA sued KF claiming that KF owed it a duty of care, that it was negligent in its audit of F plc's 1995 financial statements and that, as a consequence of that negligence, the CAA had suffered a loss.

KF sought to have the claim struck out on the basis that it did not owe the CAA a duty of care. However, the court of first instance refused to strike out the claim – a decision upheld by the Court of Appeal. Notwithstanding that

[17] Rather than pursue their case through the courts, in October 2001, C&L and C&LS (now part of PwC) reached an out-of-court settlement with the liquidators of the Barings Group for £65 million (Schlesinger, 2003). By October 2001, legal costs involved in the cases brought by the Barings Group against C&L, C&LS, and D&T had exceeded £100 million (Perry, 2002a). In addition to its out-of-court settlement, C&L was also to have been fined £1 million by the Accountants' Joint Disciplinary Scheme (which conducts independent disciplinary enquiries into cases referred to it by the Institutes of Chartered Accountants in England and Wales, and of Scotland). Upon appeal by C&L, the Appeal Tribunal reduced the fine to £250,000 but stated that C&L's belief that Leeson's trading activities "posed little (or no) risk to the Barings group, but yielded very good returns, is implausible and in our view, demonstrates a degree of ignorance of market reality that totally lacks credibility" (Perry, 2002b).

there was no contractual relationship between the CAA and KF, the court held that, as a result of the CAA's letter of 15 March 1995, KF knew, or ought to have known, that the CAA would rely on F plc's 1995 audited financial statements for the purpose of deciding whether to renew F plc's licence to organise air travel. In these circumstances, KF had assumed responsibility to CAA and thus owed it a duty of care.

The facts of *Independents' Advantage Insurance Company Ltd* v *Representatives of Michael Cook (deceased)* [2002] All ER (D) 151 (Nov); [2003] EWCA Civ 1103; [2003] All ER (D) 423 (Jul); [2004] PNLR 3 CA are similar to those of the *Kounnis Freeman* case (above) but, while the latter followed the ruling in *Henderson* v *Merrett Syndicates* and thus applied existing law, the *Independents'* case extended auditors' duty of care to third parties.

Swift Travel, a travel agent and tour operator, was a member of the Association of British Travel Agents (ABTA) and the International Air Transport Association (IATA). Under these Associations' rules, members are required to have in place a bond or other form of security in the Associations' favour. Independents' Advantage Insurance Co Ltd (Independent) provides bond facilities to travel agents to enable them to satisfy ABTA's and IATA's requirements.

Michael Cook was a partner in the firm which audited Swift's financial statements from 1995 to 1998. The audited financial statements were sent by Swift to ABTA and IATA, and also to Independent, in support of its applications to renew its membership of the Associations and bond facilities, respectively. Placing reliance on the audited financial statements, Independent provided and renewed bonds to Swift between 1996 and 1999 and, in late 1999, also provided Swift with a loan of £144,254. In March 2000, Swift went bankrupt and Independent lost £32,000 in respect of the bond and £144,254 in respect of the loan. Independent sued the auditors, arguing that they had conducted their audits negligently and that, but for the audited financial statements, it would not have provided finance to Swift. The auditors sought to have the claim struck out on the basis that they did not owe Independent a duty of care. However, both the court of first instance and the Appeal Court refused to support their position.

In the Court of Appeal, Chadwick L J relied heavily on the court's decision in the *Kounnis Freeman* case (supra). He was swayed by Independent's argument that, due to their experience in providing accountancy and audit services to travel agents (as well as several alleged conversations between Swift and an employee of the audit firm), the auditors knew, or ought to have known, that:

   (i) Swift obtained bond facilities from institutions such as Independent to
        satisfy the bond requirements of ABTA and IATA; and
   (ii) Swift's audited financial statements were provided to institutions such
        as Independent (and would be relied upon by them) to support applica-
        tions for bond facilities and other financial support.
The judge concluded that it was arguable that the auditors owed Independent
a duty of care when auditing Swift's financial statements.

Commenting on the *Independent* case, Simmons & Simmons (2003a) note that,
although the Court of Appeal relied on the judgment in the *Kounnis Freeman*
case, there are significant differences between the two cases. They note, in
particular, that in *Kounnis Freeman*:

1. ... the auditors knew the identity of the party seeking to rely on their work,
   the CAA. In contrast, the auditors in this case [i.e., the *Independent* case] did
   not know the identity of the provider of the bond facilities. This fact also
   distinguishes the case from ... *RBS* v *Bannerman* [see below] ... where the
   auditors knew of the involvement of RBS, the third party claiming to rely on
   the auditors' work.
2. ... there was direct contact between the CAA and the auditors. The CAA
   wrote a letter actually pointing out they would be relying on the financial
   statements which Kounnis Freeman were auditing. In this [the *Independent*]
   case, there was no such contact.
3. ... the auditors knew precisely why the CAA required input from the
   auditors. The CAA stated that it would only renew the company's licence on
   confirmation of various matters by the company's auditors. ... In such circumstances it is perhaps not surprising that the auditors were taken to have
   assumed a duty of care to the CAA. By way of contrast, in this case [i.e., the
   Independent] the auditors had no idea what precise use Independent would
   make of their work. Indeed, the judge accepted that Independent's requirements had not been communicated specifically or directly to the ... auditors.

   In the light of the above facts, it is difficult to see how it could be said that the
   auditors had assumed responsibility to Independent for their work. ... Of particular interest (and, to a degree, concern) is the judge's statement that, although
   the auditors did not know the identity of Independent, it was arguably sufficient
   that Independent was one of a "possible class of providers" of bonds and other
   securities on behalf of Swift to the Associations [ABTA and IATA]. That might
   be sufficient, the judge thought, for Independent to be within the range of proximity so as to give rise to a duty of care to them. Auditors often know, for
   example, that audited ... financial statements may be provided to banks financing
   the company being audited. Even without knowing the identity of the bank
   involved, could it be said, following the judge's conclusions in this case, that auditors owe a duty of care to a bank relying on their audit just because the auditors
   know that "banks" might rely on their work? (p. 2)

Considering the *Independent* case in the light of Simmons & Simmons' (2003a)
observations, it seems that, as an outcome of the judgment in *Independent*,

auditors' exposure to liability to third parties was edging towards that which existed prior to *Caparo*. However, potential relief for auditors[18] was offered as a result of *Royal Bank of Scotland* v *Bannerman Johnstone Maclay* [2003] SC 125; [2005] SCIH 39.

The *Bannerman* case concerns overdraft facilities and term loans provided by the Royal Bank of Scotland (RBS) to APC Limited. When APC failed the bank asserted:

(i) it made the loans after relying on the company's audited financial statements;

(ii) the auditors (Bannerman's firm) failed to exercise reasonable care when auditing the financial statements;

(iii) had the financial statements not contained the errors in question the bank would not have provided the loans;

(iv) the auditors were closely involved in the financial affairs of the company and were well aware of the bank's role in providing financial support;

(v) because of the terms of the company's overdraft facility letters, the auditors knew the audited financial statements would be passed to the bank and relied upon for the purpose of making lending decisions.

In these circumstances, the auditors owed RBS a duty of care in respect of the audited financial statements and were liable to it for the loss sustained.

The auditors sought to have the case struck out on the grounds that RBS had to show not only that an advisor knows the identity of the person to whom advice or information is to be communicated, the purpose thereof, and the person to whom it is given is likely to rely on it for the known purpose, but that it must also be the advisor's intention that the recipient should rely upon the information (i.e., the audited financial statements). In the Outer House of the Scottish Court of Session, Lord Macfadyen held, *inter alia*:

(i) the authorities established that proximity in relation to a duty of care in circumstances such as the present was determined by whether there had been an assumption of responsibility by the party sought to be made liable (i.e., the auditors); and

(ii) no disclaimer of responsibility had been made to the bank by the auditors such that an assumption of responsibility was denied.

As a consequence, it could not be argued that the auditors did not owe RBS a duty of care.

---

[18] In the form of a potential avenue to deny an 'assumption of responsibility' to a third party – and, hence, a duty of care.

The auditors appealed Lord Macfayden's decision but it was upheld by the Inner House of the Scottish Court of Session. The court noted that in some circumstances, in order to establish the relevant duty of care, it may be sufficient for the provider of information or advice to know that it will be passed to a known third party for a specific purpose and that the recipient is likely to rely on it for that purpose. Whilst intention, if present, may support the existence of proximity between the auditors and the third party, intention should not be seen as essential in every case. Following *Caparo*, what really matters is not the intention of the auditor but the auditor's actual or presumed knowledge that the information or advice is likely to be relied on by the third party. The Court also confirmed that a failure to disclaim responsibility to a third party can, in appropriate circumstances, be a factor pointing to an assumption of responsibility on the part of the auditor.

It is interesting to observe that, in the *BCCI* case (supra), one of the factors the court noted as needing to be taken into consideration when determining whether or not the threefold *Caparo* test or the 'assumption of responsibility' test had been met was whether the advisor (in this case, the auditor) had been given the opportunity to offer a disclaimer of responsibility. However, it is as a result of the ruling in the *Bannerman* case that, as we saw in Chapter 14, Figure 14.10, audit reports in the UK now generally include a disclaimer of responsibility paragraph.

The legal issues involved in our last two cases below are similar, and both resulted in a successful outcome for Ernst & Young (E&Y). However, in the first case, the plaintiffs dropped their claim against E&Y early in the trial so the legal issues were not fully explored; in the second case, the court found in E&Y's favour. The first case, that of *Equitable Life Assurance Society* v *Ernst & Young* [2002] EWCH 112 (comm); [2003] EWHC 804 (Comm); [2003] 2 BCLC 603; [2003] EWCA (Civ) 1114 is of particular interest as:

   (i)   it involves one of the largest claims ever brought against a firm of auditors (£3.75 billion);

   (ii) it indicates that the courts are concerned to limit such claims; and

   (iii) as in earlier cases noted above, the court emphasised that, in the area of professional advisors' duty of care to third parties the law, is in a state of development and flux and is facts-sensitive.

The case has its origins in *Equitable Life Assurance* v *Hyman* [2000] 3 All ER 961; [2000] 3 WLR 529, HL; [2000] 2 WLR 798, CA; [2002] 1 AC 408. In 1999, Equitable was unable to meet its obligation to pay holders of guaranteed annuity policies their guaranteed bonuses and it sought leave from the court to reduce the bonuses of non-guaranteed annuity policyholders in order to meet the shortfall of £1.5 billion. The court of first instance found in Equitable's favour but disaffected policyholders appealed the decision. The Court of Appeal reversed the lower court's ruling. Equitable appealed this decision but it was upheld by the House of Lords. The Law Lords ruled that Equitable was not entitled to distinguish between policyholders holding guaranteed, and those holding non-guaranteed, annuity policies. This decision left Equitable exposed to additional liabilities of £1.5 billion and, as a consequence, Equitable put itself up for sale. When no sale was achieved, it sued its auditor, Ernst & Young (E&Y), alleging that E&Y had breached its duty of care in the following ways:

(i) Equitable's 1998 and 1999 audited financial statements should have included substantial provisions in respect of the guaranteed annuity liability; and

(ii) its 1999 financial statements should have disclosed contingent liabilities and uncertainties in respect of the *Hyman* litigation.

Equitable claimed that E&Y's failure to exercise due care had resulted in it suffering:

(a) a diminution in the value of the business of £2.6 billion between 1998 and 2001; or

(b) alternatively, a lost opportunity (valued at £1.7 billion) to sell the business; and

(c) losses of £1.6 billion in 1997, tapering to £0.8 billion in 1999, through declaring unwarranted bonuses to policyholders (Simmons & Simmons, 2003b).

Not surprisingly, E&Y sought to have the claims struck out. In the High Court, Langley J struck out the first two claims on the grounds that, based on both the facts and the law, they were unlikely to succeed. However, he allowed Equitable's claim relating to its bonus declarations to proceed but restricted it to £500 million. Equitable appealed the ruling and the Court of Appeal found in Equitable's favour. Brooke L J concluded there were no grounds in the facts to dismiss the case but he limited the losses relating to the sale of the business to the loss of the opportunity to sell the business. He noted that the legal issues to be considered concern "the concepts which are used to limit the scope of the legal consequences of negligence or of legal responsibility for negligence" and, as these "continue to be in a state of development and flux, and sensitive to the facts", the court "had to show extra caution before disposing of them summarily" (Simmons & Simmons, 2003b, p. 1).

The key issue was whether E&Y owed a duty of care to Equitable to protect it from the losses claimed. E&Y argued that it did not do so as Equitable had never sought its advice about the desirability of selling the business or about its bonus declarations. Equitable, on the other hand, argued that it should have been protected from making inappropriate decisions (or from failing to make appropriate decisions) when it relied on its audited financial statements in the belief that they were free from material error. Brooke L J, after considering *Caparo* and subsequent relevant cases, concluded that the issue was one that turned on the particular facts of the case and that it could not be said that Equitable had no real prospect of persuading a court that E&Y owed it the duty to protect it from the harm Equitable had identified. He observed:

> When auditors undertake for a reward to perform services and are found to be negligent in the way they perform those services, the law does not require the client to ask for specific advice before it can recover damages for the foreseeable losses it later suffered. (as cited in Simmons & Simmons, 2003b, p. 2)

Thus, the Court of Appeal allowed Equitable's claims to proceed although the claims relating to the lost sale of the business were restricted to damages for the loss of a chance of achieving a sale. The bonus declaration claims were also allowed to stand in their entirety rather than being limited to £500 million (as ruled by Langley J in the lower court). The Court of Appeal expressed sympathy with E&Y's submission that the size of Equitable's claims was an unwarranted burden for a litigant to carry to trial but, having concluded that the claims could not be struck down, the Court of Appeal could not see how the claims could be limited to a certain amount (Simmons & Simmons, 2003b, p. 2).

The case went to trial in April 2005 with Equitable claiming £3.75 billion damages for losses it suffered as a consequence of E&Y's negligence. E&Y, in response, claimed the case was "over-lawyered, far-fetched and based on a claim that is no more than a theological assertion" (Bennett, 2005, p. 2). In September 2005, Equitable suddenly dropped its claim against E&Y. Its counsel, Milligan QC, told Langley J: "I would like to inform you that the claim by the Society [i.e., Equitable] against Ernst & Young has been settled on terms of the claim being discontinued and each party bearing its own costs" – costs reputed to be in the region of £30 million for each side (Pearson, 2005, p. 1). Hopgood QC, counsel for E&Y stated:

> At the end of this very long and costly and utterly pointless piece of litigation, which has culminated in the biggest climb down in English legal history, there is a salutary lesson to be learned for those thinking of suing auditors. It is simply this: bringing a hugely inflated claim for blood-curdling amounts of money in the hope that the sheer scale of the claim will force the defendant into making a substantial cash payment is misconceived. It has not worked against Ernst & Young in this claim and it will not work against Ernst & Young in the future. (as quoted, in Pearson, 2005, p. 1)

It was not long before Hopwood's words were put to the test in *Man Nutzfahzeuge AG and Ors* v *Freightliner Ltd and Ors* [2003] EWHC 2245; [2005]

EWHC 2347 (Comm); [2007] EWCA (Civ) 910. This case involved the sale by Western Star Truck (a Canadian company) of its subsidiary, ERF plc (a British truck maker), to Man (a German company) in March 2000. The settlement price of approximately £100 million was based on financial statements audited by E&Y that indicated ERF was making a small profit and had net assets of around £25 million.

In July 2001, Man discovered that ERF's financial controller, Ellis (who was heavily involved in the sale negotiations on behalf of Western Star) had been fraudulently manipulating ERF's accounts since 1996, and he had also made fraudulent misrepresentations during the due diligence process prior to the sale. Rather than making profits and holding net assets, ERF was making losses and had net liabilities of around £75 million. After the fraud was discovered, Man successfully sued Freightliner (the then owner of Western Star) for £350 million, for breaches of warranties given in the sale agreement and for fraudulent misrepresentations by Western Star's agent (i.e., Ellis), which allegedly had induced the sale (Sukhraj, 2007; Simmons & Simmons, 2003c).

Freightliner then sought to recoup its losses from E&Y, alleging that E&Y had negligently failed to detect the falsification of accounting records by Ellis with the result that the audited financial statements for 1998 and 1999 did not give a true and fair view of EFR's affairs. E&Y applied to the High Court to have the claim struck out on the grounds that it could not succeed because of the *Caparo* ruling (i.e., it owed no duty of care to Freightliner as a third party). It asserted that, in order for auditors' duty of care to be extended beyond *Caparo*, there had to be a clear assumption of responsibility by the auditors to the third party concerned and, in this case, there had been no such assumption (Simmons & Simmons, 2003d, p. 1).

However, Cooke J was not persuaded by E&Y's argument. He observed that "the issues of duty and causation which [arise in this case] are fact sensitive and inappropriate for determination on a summary basis.... [Further,] the areas of law [involved] are areas which are not only developing but also not free from difficulty" ([2003] EWHC at p. 2259). He concluded that there were real issues to be tried and that Freightliner had a real prospect of success.

The case was heard in the High Court in 2005. The trial judge (Moore Bick L J) found that, although E&Y admitted making errors in aspects of its audit of ERF's financial statements in the late 1990s, Freightliner's claims went far beyond the scope of E&Y's duties as auditor. E&Y did not owe Freightliner a duty of care and was not liable for the losses claimed. He noted that E&Y could not be held responsible for the use Ellis, acting as Western Star's agent, made of the audited financial statements in the negotiations surrounding ERF's sale to Man.

Freightliner appealed the court's decision but it was upheld by the Court of Appeal. It seemed that the case was at an end. E&Y claimed not to be surprised by the Court of Appeal's decision. Lisa Cameron, general counsel of E&Y, explained:

> We have stressed consistently since the beginning of this action that the case brought by Freightliner against Ernst & Young was unsustainable because it attempted to extend the recognised boundaries of an auditor's duties and responsibilities. (as cited in Sukhraj, 2007)

However, E&Y was not quite 'out of the woods'. In December 2007, Freightliner petitioned the House of Lords seeking leave to appeal the Court of Appeal's ruling. In January 2008, the House of Lords rejected Freightliner's petition and E&Y could breathe a sigh of relief; it was now certain of avoiding a possible £350 million liability (Sukhraj, 2008).

15.4.4 Synopsis of auditors' liability to third parties

From our review of cases decided in the post-*Caparo* era, it is evident that since the House of Lords' momentous decision in the *Caparo* case in 1990, which essentially returned the law relating to auditors' liability to third parties to where it had stood nearly 30 years earlier at the time of *Hedley Byrne* v *Heller & Partners* (supra), the courts have tended towards extending, once again, the parties to whom auditors are held to owe a duty of care. However, the judges' comments in the *Bannerman*, *Equitable* and *Freightliner* cases suggest that the tide may have turned once more in auditors' favour but, in any event, the law in the area remains uncertain and in a state of development and transition.

Whilst acknowledging the characteristics of uncertainty and change, some key factors of the law relating to the liability of auditors to third parties can be distilled from the cases we have reviewed. These are as follows:

1. In addition to the 'three-part *Caparo* test', the courts may apply the 'assumption of responsibility test' to determine whether or not an auditor owed a duty of care to a third party plaintiff in a particular case.
2. Although the law relating to the liability of auditors to third parties for economic loss is transitional and developmental, it will be developed only incrementally (i.e., in small steps).
3. In cases in which a third party has received independent advice, this will serve to strengthen the barrier between the auditor and the third party which will need to be overcome before the auditor will be held to owe a duty of care to the third party. However, the fact that a third party has received independent advice will not necessarily negate the auditor's duty of care to that party.

4. When a third party claims to have suffered financial loss as a consequence of the auditor's negligence, the court will evaluate the facts of the case to determine whether the auditor's negligence actually caused the loss or whether it merely provided an opportunity for the plaintiff to sustain a loss. Only the former type of loss will give rise to damages.

5. In order to succeed in a case alleging financial loss caused by an auditor's negligence, a third party must commence proceedings within the period in which it is reasonably foreseeable that reliance may be placed on the audited financial statements.

6. Whether or not an auditor will be held to owe a duty of care to one or more third parties in a particular case depends upon the facts of that case. The courts have demonstrated that, notwithstanding the *Caparo* decision, auditors may, in principle, be held to owe a duty of care to, *inter alia*, individual shareholders and directors of auditee companies, to a 'sister' subsidiary company and/or parent company of the auditee and to the auditors of the parent company and also to financial institutions who provide financial support to the auditee. However, in each of the cases where the auditor has been held to owe a duty of care to a third party, such as those noted above, the court has emphasised that its decision is case specific; that is, it applies only in the circumstances of the particular case being considered by the court.

7. It may be possible for auditors to disclaim responsibility to third parties by conveying that fact to relevant third parties.

Although we can identify these and other elements of the law relating to auditors' liability to third parties as it currently stands, a more general common theme may be discerned from the cases we have reviewed. This theme was given explicit recognition by the New Zealand Court of Appeal in *South Pacific Manufacturing Co Ltd* v *New Zealand Security Consultants & Investigations Ltd* [1992] 2 NZLR 282.[19] The court held that proper standards of care should be imposed on people who undertake tasks which require skill and judgment and on whom others are dependent. However, this must be balanced by the need to preserve a proper balance between the differing interests of people (such as the plaintiffs and defendants) going about their business or daily lives. The court concluded that, irrespective of whether judges follow the *Anns* rule (cited in section 15.4.1 above) or adopt a more conservative approach (such as that enunciated in *Caparo*) they essentially seek to decide whether it is just and reasonable that a duty of care should be imposed on one party for the benefit of another in the particular circumstances of the case before them.

---

[19] The case involved insurance assessors who reported suspected arson in two separate incidents of suspicious fires preceding insurance claims. The insured sued the assessors for preparing their reports negligently. The Court of Appeal was asked to decide whether a duty of care was owed by insurance assessors to the insured party.

15.5 THE EFFECT OF OUT-OF-COURT SETTLEMENTS

Woolf (1983) has observed that the development of the law relating to auditors' liability and, more particularly, auditors' common law liability to third parties has been hampered by the predisposition of the auditing profession to settle out of court. However, the issue is complex and is worthy of further examination.

As we noted in section 15.2.3 above, one of the major difficulties faced by auditors with respect to their liability for breach of their common law duties is that neither the parties to whom they owe a duty of care nor the requirements which constitute a reasonable standard of skill and care are static. This leaves auditors uncertain as to their legal obligations and may incline them towards going on the defensive, 'playing safe', and agreeing an out-of-court settlement with those who bring an action against them. Added to this are the enormous costs involved in lengthy court hearings – costs that are not limited to hefty legal fees[20] but also include the lost earnings of partners who spend days, if not weeks or months, in court, and the costs associated with damaged reputations resulting from allegations (whether justified or not) of negligent auditing. Given the legal uncertainties and high costs involved, it is not surprising that auditors are disposed to settle out of court – even in circumstances where they believe they may be able to successfully defend a case brought against them.[21,22] This action is encouraged by their indemnity insurers, who frequently pressure them to settle out of court as they consider this to be the least costly option.

Nevertheless, auditors' propensity to settle out of court has some serious adverse consequences for the profession. For example, it prevents the underlying legal

---

[20] As noted in footnote 17, by the time PwC reached an out-of-court settlement with the liquidators of the Barings Group, legal fees alone had exceeded £100 million.

[21] It will be interesting to see if Ernst & Young's success in the *Equitable Life* and *Freightliner* cases will encourage other auditors not to settle out of court. *Stone & Rolls Ltd (in liquidation)* v *Moore Stephens (a firm) & another* [2007] EWHC 1826 (Comm); [2007] All ER (D) 448 (Jul), a case brought by the liquidators of Stone & Rolls (S&R) against S&R's auditors (Moore Stephens: MS) for their negligent audits in 1996, 1997 and 1998 suggests this might be the result. In the court of first instance, Langley J struck out a compound interest claim against MS of £40.5 million and gave leave for MS to appeal against the rest of the £85.3 million claim. It has been reported that MS "would be vigorously defending the claim but hoped to get the rest of the audit negligence suit ... struck out" (Jetuah, 2007). Commenting on the *Moore Stephens* case, Rickard, a litigation expert, is reported as stating: "Auditors have been seen as deep pockets. Throughout the 90s, whenever there was a corporate collapse, there was a claim against the auditors. The Equitable Life case, amongst others, has changed all that. What Ernst & Young achieved, in facing Equitable down and waiting for its claims to be exposed as flimsy in court, has encouraged insurers and auditors to stand their ground" (as reported in Hawkes, 2007).

[22] A senior audit partner in one of the 'Big 4' firms observed to one of the authors that out-of-court settlements are analogous to proportional liability. He said:
> Audit firms are prepared to pay for harm they cause when they get it wrong [are negligent] but they are not prepared to foot the total bill for the harm suffered by a plaintiff when the auditee's management is also culpable. The amount paid by an audit firm in an out-of-court settlement usually represents the amount of harm for which the audit firm accepts responsibility.

We discuss proportional liability in Chapter 16, section 16.3.

issues with respect to auditors' liability from being resolved and thus it stifles clarification and development of the law in this area – an area which, as we have noted, is still in a state of transition and flux. It also causes indemnity insurance premiums to rise to unnecessarily high levels. As Woolf (1983) explained:

> Treating insurance as an escape leads to an increase (not a decrease) in the risks against which further insurance cover is then needed – and so on, until the premiums exceed, by a very substantial margin, the damages which would be awarded against us if the issues in question were tested in the courts. (p. 65)

A further damaging outcome is that, when news of an out-of-court settlement reaches the media headlines (which it inevitably does), it seems to signify to interested parties, and to the public at large, that the auditors concerned accept they are in the wrong and that they are unable to defend successfully the claims brought against them. It is arguable that, in general, this is more damaging to the reputation of the auditors involved, and to the auditing profession as a whole, than having the facts of the case exposed in court – and the possibility that the case will be decided in the auditors' favour.

Whatever the advantages and disadvantages of auditors settling out of court, decided cases have demonstrated that the courts will not impose an unfair burden on auditors. *Caparo*, and subsequent cases (including those discussed in section 15.4.3 above), shows that the courts have been concerned to limit the parties to whom auditors owe a duty of care so as not to leave them exposed to liability which is indeterminate in amount for an indeterminate time to an indeterminate class. Similarly, examples such as the *Littlejohn*[23] and *Equitable Life* cases may be cited to show that the courts have also been concerned to keep the standard of skill and care required of, and the amount of plaintiffs' claims against, auditors within reasonable bounds.

15.6 SUMMARY

In this chapter we have addressed the issue of auditors' legal liability. We have distinguished between a breach of auditors' statutory duties and a breach of their common law duties, and between auditors' contractual and third-party liability. We have also traced the development of auditors' duty of care to third parties and noted the effect of the *Caparo* ruling. We have further noted that, since *Caparo*, the law relating to auditors' liability to third parties has continued to evolve but the courts have been concerned to ensure that auditors are not exposed to an unreasonable liability burden.

In the final section of the chapter we have considered the effect of out-of-court settlements on the development of the law relating to auditors' liability,

---

[23] See footnote 7.

on auditors' indemnity insurance, and on auditors' (and the profession's) reputation. In the next chapter we discuss measures that both audit firms and the auditing profession as a whole have taken (and are taking) to try to reduce auditors' exposure to liability through the performance of consistently high-quality audits and other means.

SELF-REVIEW QUESTIONS

15.1 Distinguish briefly between a breach of auditors' statutory duties and a breach of their common law duties.

15.2 Distinguish briefly between auditors' contractual liability and their liability to third parties.

15.3 List the three facts a plaintiff must prove before a court will award damages against auditors for negligence.

15.4 Explain the position adopted in the case of *Ultramares* v *Touche* (1931) with respect to auditors' liability to third parties. What reason did the judge give for his decision in this case?

15.5 Explain briefly the significance of the decision in *Hedley Byrne & Co. Ltd* v *Heller & Partners* (1963) to the development of auditors' liability to third parties.

15.6 Explain the position adopted in the cases of *Jeb Fasteners* (1981) and *Twomax Ltd* (1983) with respect to auditors' liability to third parties.

15.7 Explain briefly the principles enunciated in the *Caparo* decision (1990) with respect to the parties to whom auditors are liable.

15.8 Identify the parties to whom auditors may be held to owe a duty of care as a result of the *Coulthard, Siddell, BCCI, Barings* and *Independents' Advantage* cases.

15.9 List seven factors of the law relating to the liability of auditors to third parties that have emerged from cases settled subsequent to the *Caparo* decision, and identify the common theme that can be discerned from the courts' decisions.

15.10 Explain briefly the impact of out-of-court settlements on:
    (i)   the development of the law as it relates to auditors' liability;
    (ii) auditors' professional indemnity insurance; and
    (iii) the reputation of the auditors concerned and, more generally, on the auditing profession.

REFERENCES

Baxt, R. (1990). Shutting the gate on shareholders in actions for negligence – the Caparo decision in the House of Lords. *Companies and Securities Forum*, pp. 2–12. CCH Australia Ltd.

Bennett, J. (2005, 22 September). Timeline: Equitable Life vs Ernst & Young. *Accountancy Age*, www.accountancyage.com/articles/print/2142678.

Davies, J. (1992). *Auditors' Liabilities: Who can sue now?* Unpublished paper written for Reynolds Porter Chamberlain, UK.

Financial Times. (1998, 19 November). PW Sued. *Financial Times*, p. 14.

Gwilliam, D. (1988). Making mountains out of molehills. *Accountancy*, **101**(1135), 22–23.

Hawkes, A. (2007, 19 July). The Moore Stephens case: a sense of déjà vu. *Accountancy Age*, www.accountancyage.com/articles/print/2194595.

International Accounting Standards Board (IASB). (2001). *Framework for the Preparation and Presentation of Financial Statements*. London: IASB.

International Auditing and Assurance Standards Board (IAASB). (2007).[24] International Standard on Auditing (ISA) 260 (Redrafted): *Communication with those charged with governance*. New York: International Federation of Accountants.

International Auditing and Assurance Standards Board. (2008). International Standard on Auditing (ISA) 210 (Redrafted): *Terms of audit engagements*. New York: International Federation of Accountants.

Jetuah, D. (2007, 2 August). Long wait for Moore Stephens. *Accountancy Age*, p. 2.

Lascelles, D., & Donkin, R. (1991, 8 July). The bank that liked to say yes. *Financial Times*, p. 10.

Nisse, J. (1999, 29 September). Pots of money appear on the horizon for BCCI's creditors. *The Times*.

Pearson, R. (2005, 22 September). Collapsed claim against Ernst & Young was 'blood-curdling'. *Accountancy Age*, www.accountancyage.com/articles/print/2142653.

Perry, M. (2001a, 31 July). Coopers' Barings settlement collapses. *Accountancy Age*.

Perry, M. (2001b, 11 October). Analysis – Battle of Barings rages on. *Accountancy Age*, www.accountancyage.com/accountancyage/news/2027704.

Perry, M. (2002a, 21 March). Barings' case against Deloitte set for May. *Accountancy Age*, www.accountancyage.com/accountancyage/news/2029348.

Perry, M. (2002b, 29 April). Coopers fined in Barings Disciplinary. *Accountancy Age*, www.accountancyage.com/accountancyage/news/2029722.

Savage, N. (1981). The auditor's legal responsibility to strangers? *The Accountant's Magazine* **85**(904), 338–341.

---

[24] The status of ISAs referred to in this chapter is explained in the Important Note following the Preface to this book.

Schlesinger, L. (2003, 18 June). Coopers paid £65m in Barings case. *Accountancy Age*, www.accountancyage.com/accountancyage/news/2033104.

Scott, A. (1999). Another Year in Court: 1998's key liability cases, *Accountancy* **123**(1266), 106.

Shanahan, J. (1995, 19 May). The AWA case: an auditor's view, reported in *Butterworths Corporation Law Bulletin* (Australian Corporation Law), No. 10, 213–214.

Simmons & Simmons. (2003a, January). *Professional Liability Bulletin*, Iss. 31, www.elexica.co.uk/newsletter.aspx?cat=60&id=173.

Simmons & Simmons. (2003b). *Auditors – Duty of care: Equitable Life Assurance Society v Ernst & Young*, www.elexica.com/briefdoc.aspx?cat=42&id=3069.

Simmons & Simmons. (2003c). *Case summary of Man Nutzfahrzeuge Aktienge-sellschaft and others v Freightliner Ltd*, www.elexica.com/briefdoc.aspx?cat=42&id=3201.

Simmons & Simmons. (2003d, November). Update on recent professional liability events. *Professional Liability Bulletin*, Iss. 42. www.elexica.com/newsletter.aspx?cat=60&id=337.

Sukhraj, P. (2007, 12 September). E&Y heads off £350m Freightliner claim. *Accountancy Age*, www.accountancyage.com/accountancyage/news/2198547.

Sukhraj, P. (2008, 24 January). E&Y claims victory in £350m case. *Accountancy Age*, www.accountancyage.com/articles/print/2207931.

Woolf, E. (1979). *Auditing Today*. London: Prentice-Hall.

Woolf, E. (1983). Auditing and staying out of court. *Accountancy* **94**(1074), 65–66.

ADDITIONAL READING

Erickson, M., Mayhew, B.W., & Felix Jr W.L. (2000). Why do audits fail? Evidence from Lincoln Savings and Loan. *Journal of Accounting Research* **38**(1), 165–194.

Institute of Chartered Accountants in England and Wales (ICAEW). (2005). *Audit Liability: claims by third parties*. London: ICAEW.

Kadous, K. (2000). The effects of audit quality and consequence severity on juror evaluations of auditor responsibility for plaintiff losses. *The Accounting Review* **75**(3), 327–341.

Khurana, I.K., & Raman, K.K. (2004). Litigation risk and the financial reporting credibility of Big 4 versus Non-Big 4 audits: evidence from Anglo-American countries. *The Accounting Review* **79**(2), 473–496.

Lowe, D.J., Reckers, P.M.J., & Whitecotton, S.M. (2002). The effects of decision-aid use and reliability on jurors' evaluations of auditor liability. *The Accounting Review* **77**(1), 185–203.

Pacini, C., Hillison, W., Alagiah, R., & Gunz, S. (2002). Commonwealth convergence toward a narrower scope of auditor liability to third parties for negligent misstatements. *Abacus* **38**(3), 425–464.

APPENDIX

Barings plc (in liquidation) v *Coopers & Lybrand & Ors, Barings Futures (Singapore) Pte Ltd (in liquidation)* v *Mattar & Ors* [2002] EWHC 461 (Ch); [2002] ALL ER (D) 309 (Mar); [2003] EWHC 1319 (Ch); [2003] All ER (D) 142 (Jun).

The facts of this case are as set out in Chapter 15, section 15.4.3. The part of the case reported here concerns the action brought by Barings Futures (Singapore) (BFS) against Deloitte & Touche (D&T) for negligent auditing in 1992 and 1993.

D&T sought to have BFS's action dismissed on the grounds that Jones, a qualified accountant and finance director of BFS at the relevant time, signed letters of representation addressed to D&T prior to the 1992 and 1993 audit reports being signed. D&T claimed that, when signing the audit reports, it had relied on statements in the letters, namely: there had been no irregularities involving employees that could have a material effect on the financial statements; the financial statements were free of material errors and omissions; transactions with related parties and losses on sale and purchase commitments had been properly recorded; BFS had recorded or disclosed all of its liabilities; and there had been no post-balance sheet events requiring adjustment to the financial statements.

D&T explained to the court that it routinely requires audit clients to provide a representation letter, signed by a suitably knowledgeable director or senior employee, before it will sign an unqualified audit report on the statutory accounts (and on which, in this case, its audit report on the consolidated schedules was dependent).[25]

It was undisputed that Jones had signed the letters but, unknown to D&T, his contact with BFS during the 1992 and 1993 accounting periods was so small that he had no relevant knowledge which would render him properly able to sign the letters. D&T claimed that had Jones not signed the letters it would not have issued an unqualified audit report and, had it refused to issue an unqualified report on the accounts, the subsequent damage to BFS would have been averted. Therefore, Jones' reckless signature was a cause of D&T's exposure to the claims of negligence made against it. Jones signed the letters as a director of BFS, in the course of acting as such a director. It followed that BFS was vicariously liable for the consequences. It also followed that D&T had a claim against BFS for the consequences of Jones' fraud. That claim mirrored the claim against D&T and so gave them an absolute defence of circuity.

---

[25] As we note in Chapter 13, section 13.5, auditors are now required by ISA 580: *Written Representations* (IAASB, 2008) to obtain written representations from their auditee's directors prior to completion of the audit.

The court held that Jones' action in signing the letters was not recklessly fraudulent. D&T had not proved to the court's satisfaction that when he signed the representation letters he did so:

(i) knowing that the statements in the letters were untrue, without honest belief in their truth, or with indifference as to whether or not they were true; or

(ii) knowing that he had no reasonable grounds for making the statements, without an honest belief that he had such grounds, or with indifference as to whether he had or not.

Hence, Evans-Lombe J ruled that, although the letters signed by Jones were inaccurate, D&T's claim should be dismissed and BFS's negligence claim against D&T for £200 million could proceed.

When BFS's case against D&T was heard in June 2003, Evans-Lombe J found that the audits conducted by D&T in 1992 and 1993 were negligent. However, the losses suffered by BFS as a result of Leeson's fraudulent trading on the Singaporean and Japanese financial markets were largely brought about by BFS's lack of control over Leeson. Indeed, so serious was BFS's contributory negligence that the damages to which BFS was entitled from D&T for the period from November 1992 to April 1994 was reduced by 50 per cent to 80 per cent (on an increasing scale) and, beyond April 1994, BFS alone was responsible for the losses it suffered as a result of Leeson's actions (Simmons & Simmons, 2003e). Evans-Lombe J held that D&T was responsible for about "£1.5m, a tiny fraction of the £200m claimed by the bank [BFS]" (Accountancy Age, 2003). Both parties appealed Evans-Lombe J's ruling but, in April 2004, shortly before the appeals were to be heard, the parties reached a final agreement whereby BFS would not enforce its claim against D&T and each party would bear its own cost of the appeals (Deloitte, 2004).

REFERENCES

Accountancy Age. (2003, 17 October). Deloitte fined £1.5m over Barings. *Accountancy Age*, www.managementconsultancy.co.uk/articles/print/2033955.

Deloitte. (2004, 27 April). *Statement on Behalf of Deloitte & Touche Singapore*, www. deloitte.com/dtt/press_release/0,1014.

International Auditing and Assurance Standards Board (IAASB). (2008). International Standard on Auditing (ISA) 580 (Redrafted): *Written Representations*. New York: International Federation of Accountants.

Simmons & Simmons. (2003e). *High Resolution – July 2003 Professional Liability: Auditors – Contributory Negligence of Management*, www.elexica.com/newsletter. aspx?cat=202id=749.

16 Avoiding and Limiting Auditors' Liability

LEARNING OBJECTIVES

After studying the material in this chapter you should be able to:
- describe and evaluate measures audit firms and engagement partners are required to implement in order to ensure that high quality audits are performed;
- explain the objectives, process and outcomes of monitoring/inspecting auditors' performance in the United Kingdom;
- discuss the advantages and disadvantages of:
  - limited liability companies,
  - limited liability partnerships,
  - limited liability agreements,
  - liability caps, and
  - proportionate liability
  as means of limiting auditors' liability.

The following publications are particularly relevant to this chapter:

- International Standard on Quality Control (ISQC) 1 (Redrafted): *Quality Control for Firms that Perform Audits and Reviews of Historical Financial Information, and Other Assurance and Related Services Engagements* (IFAC, June 2008)**[1]
- International Standard on Auditing (ISA) 220 (Redrafted): *Quality Control for an Audit of Financial Statements* (IFAC, June 2008)**

---

[1] The status of ISAs referred to in this chapter is explained in the Important Note following the Preface to this book.

16.1 INTRODUCTION

In Chapter 15 we reviewed a number of cases involving auditors who were sued by their clients and/or by third parties for (allegedly) performing their duties negligently (that is, without due skill and care). Although the 1990 *Caparo* decision reduced significantly the parties to whom auditors owe a duty of care and, thus, those who can succeed in an action against them, auditors continue to face staggering claims for damages. For example, as we note in Chapter 15, Price Waterhouse (PW) and Ernst & Young (E&Y) faced a claim of about £6.5 billion as a consequence of their (allegedly) negligent auditing of the failed Bank of Credit and Commerce International (BCCI) Group's financial statements;[2] Coopers & Lybrand (C&L), Coopers & Lybrand Singapore (C&LS) and Deloitte and Touche (D&T) faced a claim for £1 billion for their (allegedly) negligent auditing of the Barings Group's financial statements;[3] and E&Y faced a claim for £3.75 billion for (allegedly) failing to exercise due skill and care in its audits of Equitable Life Assurance Society's financial statements.[4]

However, not only has the size of claims against auditors been staggering; in some cases, the damages awarded against them by the courts have been enormous. For instance, in 1995, damages of £65 million were awarded against the former BDO Binder Hamlyn partnership for its negligent auditing of Britannia Security Group's 1989 financial statements.[5] Similarly, in 2004, $US10 million (about £6 million) were awarded against KPMG in the United States of America (USA), in the largest enforcement action brought by the Securities and Exchange Commission (SEC) against an audit firm, for "repeated audit failures in connection with [its] audits of Gemstar's financial statements . . .

---

[2] We also note that, in September 1998, PW and E&Y agreed a settlement with the liquidators of the BCCI Group for an amount reputed to be in the region of $US95 to $US100 million (see Chapter 15, footnote 14).

[3] We also note that, in October 2001, C&L and C&LS (now both part of PricewaterhouseCoopers) agreed a settlement with the liquidators of the Barings Group for £65 million. D&T faced a claim of £200 million for their (allegedly) negligent auditing of the accounts of Barings Futures Singapore Ltd (BFS) in 1992 and 1993. In 2003, the firm was ordered to pay damages of £1.5 million as its proportion of the loss suffered by BFS but, shortly before appeals against the ruling were heard, BFS and D&T agreed a settlement whereby BFS agreed not to enforce its claim again D&T and each side would bear its own costs (see Chapter 15, Appendix).

[4] As we note in Chapter 15, section 15.4.3, in September 2005, Equitable Life dropped its claim against E&Y.

[5] See Chapter 15, section 15.4.3.

from 1999 through 2002" (SEC, 2004).[6] Further, in February 2007, D&T's Italian firm was ordered to pay $130 million (£66 million) as:

> part of the $149 m that [D&T]...agreed to pay to settle lawsuits accusing it of helping former Parmalat management hide debt and inflate results, that led to it [i.e., Parmalat] filing for bankruptcy in December 2003. (Accountancy Age, 2007a)

Additionally, in July 2007, PricewaterhouseCoopers (PwC) agreed to pay $225 million (£120 million) to the shareholders of Tyco International as settlement for its (alleged) failure to uncover the massive fraud perpetrated by Kozlowski and Swartz (Tyco's chief executive and chief financial officer, respectively) during its audits of Tyco's financial statements in the late 1990s and early 2000s.[7] Similarly, in August 2007, D&T agreed to pay $165.6 million (£81 million) to its former client, Adelphia, once the USA's sixth biggest telecom company, in "one of the biggest settlements ever paid by an auditor to its former audit client" (Accountancy Age, 2007b).

Damages claims and settlements of a magnitude such as those cited above have prompted audit firms to call for, and adopt, ways to limit their liability. Of particular concern to the firms is the fact that damages claims bear no relationship to the size of the audit fee or the extent of the auditors' negligence.[8] However, notwithstanding the successful actions brought against auditors, as we observe in Chapter 15 (section 15.5), the courts have shown themselves reluctant to impose on auditors a standard of skill and care higher than that

---

[6] In its press release (SEC, 2004), the SEC reported that Stephen Cutler, its Director of Enforcement, stated:

> Our action today holds KPMG as a firm accountable for the audit failures of its partners. Sanctions in this case should reinforce the message that accounting firms must assume responsibility for ensuring that individual auditors properly discharge their special and critical gatekeeping duties. (p. 1)

The same press release reported that Randall Lee, Regional Director of the SEC's Pacific Regional office, said:

> This case illustrates the dangers of auditors who rely excessively on the honesty of management. KPMG's auditors repeatedly relied on Gemstar management's representations even when those representations were contradicted by their audit work. The auditors thus failed to abide by one of the core principles of public accounting – to exercise professional skepticism and care. (p. 1)

[7] PwC argued that the plaintiffs could not show that its conduct had led to the losses of the company's shareholders. In agreeing the settlement, a spokesman for PwC explained: "While PwC was prepared to continue to defend all aspects of its work in the litigation process, the cost of that defense and the size of the securities class action made settlement the sensible choice for the firm". However, the SEC banned PwC's engagement partner for the Tyco audits (Richard Scalzo) from auditing public companies. The SEC stated: "from 1999 on Mr Scalzo had good reason to doubt the honesty of Mr Kozlowski and Mr Swartz ... but did not pursue auditing procedures that could have uncovered the fraud" (Norris, 2007, p. 1). The PwC settlement was additional to the nearly $3 billion Tyco International's shareholders recovered as settlement of their claim against the company.

[8] As we note in Chapter 15, footnote 22, in general, when an audit firm reaches an out-of-court settlement with a plaintiff, the amount the firm is prepared to pay reflects the proportion of the harm suffered by the plaintiff the firm admits has been caused by its negligence.

generally regarded as appropriate by the auditing profession. It seems to follow that the most effective way for auditors to address the problem of their exposure to liability for negligence is to avoid it by performing high quality audits.

In this chapter we explore ways in which auditors may avoid or limit their exposure to liability. More specifically, we discuss measures implemented by audit firms, engagement partners and the auditing profession and/or regulators, which are designed to ensure that auditors perform consistently high quality audits. We also examine moves by audit firms to form limited liability companies (LLCs) or limited liability partnerships (LLPs) and the advantages and disadvantages of each. We also discuss the Companies Act 2006 provision which enables auditors to enter into limited liability agreements with their audit clients, and proposals to limit auditors' liability by means of imposing a liability cap or enshrining the principle of proportionate liability in legislation.

16.2 MAINTAINING HIGH QUALITY AUDITS

16.2.1 Importance of, and responsibility for, quality control

It is essential that auditors perform high quality audits not only to avoid exposure to liability but also, arguably more importantly, to fulfil adequately their function in society. In order to ensure that high quality audits are performed, quality control is needed.

In Chapter 3 (section 3.6.2) we discuss the concept of quality control and note that Flint (1988) explained the importance of quality control as follows:

> Auditors have both a legal duty and a professional obligation to work to the highest standards which can reasonably be expected to discharge the responsibility that is placed on them. . . . In a profession whose authority is dependent among other things on public confidence . . . a demonstrable concern, individually and collectively on the part of the members of the profession, to control and maintain the highest quality in its work, is a matter of basic principle. The basis of continuing public confidence and trust in professional competence is a belief that the standards of the members of the profession will be maintained and can be relied on. (pp. 159, 161)

The key issue is minimising the prospect of audit failure; that is, auditors failing to detect material misstatements in the financial statements, or failing to report those that are detected but not corrected by the auditee's directors. Flint explains, "this is what society in general, and those who rely on audit in particular, expect". He adds, "this is what the professional accountancy bodies as the regulatory authority[9] have an obligation to pursue in the public interest" (Flint, 1980, p. 64).

Whether it be prompted by concern for the public interest, concern for the interests of users of financial statements, concern about potential damage to the profession's reputation if poor quality audits are performed, or concern about possible exposure to legal liability (or a mixture of these factors), individual firms, the auditing profession and regulators have established procedures designed to ensure that all audits are performed to the highest standard.

Guidance on performing high quality audits is provided in International Standard on Quality Control (ISQC) 1: *Quality control for firms that perform audits and reviews of historical financial information* ... and International Standard on Auditing (ISA) 220: *Quality control for an audit of financial statements*. These standards emphasise that both audit firms and engagement partners have a responsibility for ensuring that high quality audits are performed. More specifically, ISQC 1 states (paras 17, A4):

> The firm shall establish policies and procedures designed to promote an internal culture based on the recognition that quality is essential in performing engagements ... The promotion of a quality-oriented internal culture depends on clear, consistent and frequent actions and messages from all levels of the firm's management that emphasize the firm's quality control policies and procedures, and the requirement to:
> (a) Perform work that complies with professional standards and regulatory and legal requirements; and
> (b) Issue reports that are appropriate in the circumstances.
> Such actions and messages encourage a culture that recognizes and rewards high quality work.

Along similar lines, ISA 220 asserts (paras 7, A2):

> The engagement partner shall take responsibility for the overall quality on each audit engagement to which that partner is so assigned. ... The actions of the engagement partner and appropriate messages to the other members of the engagement team emphasize:
> (a) The importance to audit quality of:
>   (i) Performing work that complies with professional standards and regulatory and legal requirements:

---

[9] As explained in Chapter 5 (section 5.2.3), only auditors registered with one of the five Recognised Supervisory Bodies [RSBs – the Institutes of Chartered Accountants in England and Wales (ICAEW), of Scotland (ICAS) and in Ireland (ICAI), the Associations of Chartered Certified Accountants (ACCA) and of Authorised Public Accountants (AAPA)] are eligible for appointment as company auditors in the UK. Further, the Financial Reporting Council (FRC) has overall responsibility for ensuring that the audits of major public interest entities in the United Kingdom (UK) are performed to a high standard. Hence, strictly speaking, in respect of auditing, the RSBs and FRC rather than the professional bodies constitute the 'regulatory authority' in the UK.

    (ii) Complying with the firm's quality control policies and procedures as applicable;

    (iii) Issuing auditor's reports that are appropriate in the circumstances; and

    (iv) The engagement team's ability to raise concerns without fear of reprisals; and

 (b) The fact that quality is essential in performing audit engagements.

In the next two sections, we first examine audit firms' responsibility for securing high quality audits and then that of engagement partners.

16.2.2 Audit firms' responsibility for securing high quality audits

ISQC 1, para 16, requires audit firms to establish systems of quality control that include:

> policies and procedures that address each of the following elements:
> (a) Leadership responsibilities for quality within the firm.
> (b) Relevant ethical requirements.
> (c) Acceptance and continuance of client relationships and specific engagements.
> (d) Human resources.
> (e) Engagement performance.
> (f) Monitoring.

Audit firms are also required to ensure that their quality control policies and procedures are documented and communicated to the firm's personnel. Regarding communication of the firm's policies and procedures, the Standard explains that the:

> communication may include a description of the quality control policies and procedures and the objectives they are designed to achieve, and the message that each individual has a personal responsibility for quality and is expected to comply with these policies and procedures. (para A3)

As may be seen from Figure 16.1, each of the elements to be addressed by audit firms' quality control policies and procedures (which are discussed below) makes a unique but complementary contribution towards ensuring high quality audit work.

(a) Leadership responsibilities for quality within the firm

ISQC 1 places ultimate responsibility for an audit firm's system of quality control with its chief executive officer or managing board of partners, depending on the firm's organisational structure (para 17). It also notes that promoting an internal culture based on quality within an audit firm may be achieved by measures such as ensuring:

    (i) performance evaluation, compensation and promotion of personnel within the firm reflect the firm's overriding commitment to quality; and

    (ii) those given operational responsibility for developing and implementing the firm's quality control system have sufficient and appropriate experience and ability, as well as the necessary authority, to assume that

Figure 16.1: Elements to be addressed by an audit firm's quality control system

Element	Contribution to securing high quality audit work
Leadership responsibilities within the audit firm	The firm's chief executive officer or managing board of partners is responsible for the firm's quality control system. The firm's commitment to quality should be reflected in performance evaluation, promotion and reward. Personnel with operational responsibility for developing and implementing quality control policies and procedures should have appropriate experience, ability and authority.
Relevant ethical requirements	Policies and procedures designed to ensure the firm and its personnel comply with relevant ethical requirements – especially those relating to independence.
Acceptance and continuance of client relationships and specific engagements	Policies and procedures designed to provide reasonable assurance that only appropriate clients and audit engagements are accepted.
Human resources	Responsibility for the quality of audit work performed during an engagement lies with the engagement partner but audit staff must have the necessary capabilities, competence and time to perform work assigned to them.
Engagement performance	Policies and procedures designed to ensure audit team members are properly briefed, comply with ethical and technical standards and receive adequate supervision and training. In appropriate cases, engagement quality control reviews of audits and their documentation are undertaken, including reviews of the audit team's significant judgments and conclusions.
Monitoring	Policies and procedures designed to provide reasonable assurance that the firm's quality control system is relevant, adequate, operating effectively and complied with in practice. Monitoring of the firm's quality control system includes inspection of a selection of completed engagements, the reporting of deficiencies uncovered and instigating corrective action.

responsibility. Such experience, ability and authority enable those responsible to identify and understand relevant quality control issues, and to develop and implement appropriate policies and procedures. A senior audit quality control partner should be assigned responsibilities that include developing, documenting, and communicating the firm's quality control policies and procedures to relevant people.

(b) Relevant ethical requirements

Each audit firm is required to: "establish policies and procedures designed to provide it with reasonable assurance that the firm and its personnel comply with relevant ethical requirements" (ISQC 1, para 19). ISQC 1 notes that the International Federation of Accountants' (IFAC's) *Code of ethics for professional accountants* (IFAC, 2006) specifies the relevant ethical requirements; however, independence is so crucial to audit engagements that ISQC 1 addresses this issue separately.

In respect of independence, ISQC 1 requires each audit firm to:

establish policies and procedures designed to provide it with reasonable assurance that the firm, its personnel and, where applicable, others subject to independence requirements[10] ... maintain [their] independence ... Such policies and procedures shall enable the firm to:

(a) Communicate its independence requirements to its personnel and, where applicable, others subject to them; and

(b) Identify and evaluate circumstances and relationships that create threats to independence, and to take appropriate action to eliminate those threats or reduce them to an acceptable level by applying safeguards ..., or, if considered appropriate, to withdraw from the engagement. (para 20)

Such policies and procedures shall require:

(a) Engagement partners to provide the firm with relevant information about client engagements, including the scope of services, to enable the firm to evaluate the overall impact, if any, on independence requirements;

(b) Personnel to promptly notify the firm of circumstances and relationships that create a threat to independence so that appropriate action can be taken; and

(c) The accumulation and communication of relevant information to appropriate personnel so that:

(i) The firm and its personnel can readily determine whether they satisfy independence requirements;

(ii) The firm can maintain and update its records relating to independence; and

(iii) The firm can take appropriate action regarding identified threats to independence. (para 21)

In addition to the above, audit firms are required by ISQC 1, paras 22–24:

(i) at least annually, to obtain written confirmation of compliance with their policies and procedures on independence from all relevant personnel within, or associated with, the firm;

(ii) to establish policies and procedures:

(a) designed to provide them with reasonable assurance that:

– they are notified promptly of breaches of independence requirements; and

– enable them to take appropriate action to resolve the situation;

(b) setting out:

– criteria for determining the need for safeguards to reduce the familiarity threat[11] to an acceptable level when using the same senior personnel on an audit engagement for a long period of time;

– for the audits of listed entities, requiring the rotation of the engagement partner and engagement quality control reviewer[12]

---

[10] For example, external experts used during the audit, and auditors of components (such as subsidiaries) of the audit client. The use of 'others' in an audit is explained in Chapter 7, section 7.5.1.

[11] The 'familiarity threat' is explained in Chapter 4, section 4.3(b).

[12] Engagement quality control reviews are discussed below and in Chapter 7, section 7.6.4.

after a period of not more than five years and also requiring that such partner not hold a position of responsibility in respect of that audit client for a period of five years.[13]

(c) Acceptance and continuance of client relationships and specific engagements

Audit firms are required to establish policies and procedures for evaluating the propriety of accepting a new or continuing client relationship and specific audit engagements (ISQC 1, para 25). Such policies and procedures should be designed to ensure the firm only accepts, or continues with, clients and engagements after considering:

(i)   the integrity of the (potential) client and the identity and business reputation of its owners, directors and senior managers;

(ii) the firm's competence to undertake the work, paying due regard to factors such as the firm's knowledge and experience of the (potential) audit client's business sector, any potential conflict with another client in the same sector, and the availability of audit staff with the required levels of capabilities, experience and time to conduct the audit;

(iii) whether it can comply with relevant ethical (especially independence) requirements.

Pre-engagement investigations and procedures for accepting new and continuing audit engagements are discussed in detail in Chapter 8, section 8.2.3.

(d) Human resources

Clearly, it is fundamental to the performance of audits that comply with professional standards and regulatory and legal requirements, and that result in the issuance of appropriate audit reports, to have sufficient audit engagement partners and audit staff with the required capabilities, competence and commitment to ethical principles. To achieve this, audit firms need to have effective recruitment procedures that help them to select individuals with integrity and the ability to develop the capabilities and competence needed to perform the

---

[13] ISQC 1 refers to rotation of the engagement partner being required: "after a specified period in compliance with relevant ethical requirements" (para 24). However, as we note in Chapter 4, section 4.3, in the UK, the Auditing Practices Board's (APB) Ethical Standard (ES) 3: *Long association with the audit engagement* requires, for listed company clients, that both the engagement partner and the engagement quality control reviewer be rotated after a period of not more than five years and that there be a five-year period during which these partners are not to hold a position of responsibility with the particular audit client.

firm's work, as well as appropriate policies and procedures for staff members' performance evaluation, career development, promotion and reward (ISQC 1, paras 30, A23).[14]

In addition to ensuring appropriate personnel are recruited and nurtured (so as to ensure the proper development of their capabilities and competence), care needs to be taken to ensure that appropriate engagement partners and audit staff are assigned to individual audit engagements. Responsibility for the conduct and quality of an audit engagement belongs to the engagement partner assigned to the engagement. However, it is not just a case of assigning engagement partners to audits. ISQC 1 explains that audit firms are to establish policies and procedures requiring that:

(a) The identity and role of the engagement partner are communicated to key members of client management and those charged with governance [i.e., the auditee's senior executives and directors];

(b) The engagement partner has the appropriate capabilities, competence, authority and time to perform the role; and

(c) the responsibilities of the engagement partner are clearly defined and communicated to that partner. (para 31)

Given that audit engagement partners are responsible for the conduct of audit work performed during individual audit engagements, they clearly have a pivotal role in securing high quality audits. The requirements cited above are designed to enable these partners to discharge their role satisfactorily. (We discuss the responsibilities of audit engagement partners in more detail in section 16.2.3 below.) However, it is not only engagement partners that need to be appropriately assigned to individual audits; as has been implied above; it is equally important to assign to engagements audit staff who have the capabilities, competence and time required to perform the audit work expected of them. More specifically, when assigning staff to audit engagements, audit firms need to consider staff members':

- understanding of, and practical experience with, engagements of a similar nature and complexity;
- understanding of professional standards and regulatory and legal requirements;
- technical knowledge and expertise, including knowledge of relevant information technology;
- knowledge of relevant industries in which the client operates;

---

[14] The importance of staffing audits with personnel who adhere to high ethical standards (especially integrity and objectivity), who are intelligent and who have the ability and willingness to learn is discussed in Chapter 7, section 7.5. We discuss the concept of competence and how it may be acquired in Chapter 3, section 3.3.2.

- ability to apply professional judgment; and
- understanding of the firm's quality control policies and procedures (ISQC 1, para A30).

(e) Engagement performance

In order to be reasonably assured that their audits are conducted to a consistently high standard, audit firms need policies and procedures that address issues such as the following:

- how audit teams are to be briefed about audit engagements so as to ensure they understand the objectives of the work assigned to them;
- the means of ensuring that audit team members comply with applicable ethical and auditing standards;
- how the supervision and training of audit team members is to be effected. This includes consideration of:
  - the capabilities and competence of audit team members, the time allocated to complete work assigned to them, their understanding of instructions, whether their work is conducted in accordance with the audit plan (or programme);[15]
  - how significant matters arising during the audit are to be addressed and, if necessary, the manner in which the audit plan is to be amended;
  - how matters for consultation, or consideration by more experienced audit team members, are to be identified and communicated;
- the appropriate documentation of audit work performed;
- the method, timing and extent of reviews of audit work performed and significant judgments made, and the documentation thereof.[16]

It needs to be remembered that audits are invariably conducted by audit teams, and it is of critical importance to securing high quality audits that more junior audit team members refer matters of which they are uncertain to more experienced members. It is similarly essential that senior audit team members consult with each other and/or specialists from within (or, when appropriate, outside) the audit firm whenever they encounter difficult or contentious issues. Recognising the importance of appropriate consultation to high quality audits, ISQC 1 requires audit firms to establish policies and procedures designed to provide them with reasonable assurance that:

  (a) Appropriate consultation takes place on difficult or contentious matters;
  (b) Sufficient resources are available to enable appropriate consultation to take place;

---

[15] Audit plans (or audit programmes) are discussed in Chapter 9, section 9.2.3.

[16] Requirements relating to the review of audit work are discussed in Chapter 7, section 7.5.3.

(c) The nature and scope of, and conclusions resulting from, such consultations are documented and are agreed by both the individual seeking consultation and the individual consulted; and

(d) Conclusions resulting from consultations are implemented. (para 36)

Another element of engagement performance that contributes to high quality audits is an independent review of audit engagements and their related documentation prior to the audit report being issued. As noted in Chapter 7 (section 7.6.4), the audits of all listed company clients, and those of other clients that meet the criteria specified by the audit firm,[17] are required to be reviewed by an independent engagement quality control reviewer.[18] According to ISQC 1 such a review is to:

> involve discussion with the engagement partner, a review of the financial statements or other subject matter information and the proposed [audit] report, and consideration of whether the proposed report is appropriate. It shall also involve a review of selected working papers relating to the significant judgments the engagement team made and the conclusions they reached. (para 38)

The Standard explains that matters the engagement quality control may consider include:

- Significant risks identified during the engagement and the responses to those risks.
- Judgments made, particularly with respect to materiality and significant risks.
- The significance and disposition of corrected and uncorrected misstatements identified during the engagement.
- The matters to be communicated to management and those charged with governance [or, more usually, the audit committee] and, where applicable, other parties such as regulatory bodies. (para A41)

For the audits of listed entities, the engagement quality control review is to consider, *inter alia*, the following matters:

(a) The engagement team's evaluation of the firm's independence in relation to the specific engagement;

(b) Whether appropriate consultation has taken place on matters involving differences of opinion or other difficult or contentious matters, and the conclusions arising from those consultations; and

(c) Whether working papers selected for review reflect the work performed in relation to the significant judgments and support the conclusions reached. (ISQC 1, para 39)

---

[17] In Chapter 7, section 7.6.4, we note that, when establishing criteria for audits to be subject to engagement quality control reviews, the factors audit firms should consider include:
- The nature of the engagement, including the extent to which it involves a matter of public interest.
- The identification of unusual circumstances or risks in an engagement or class of engagements.
- Whether laws or regulations require an engagement quality control review. (ISQC 1, para A40)

[18] Definitions of an 'engagement quality control review' and 'engagement quality control reviewer' are provided in Chapter 7, section 7.6.4.

The reviews are to be conducted in a timely manner at appropriate stages during the engagement so that significant matters can be promptly resolved to the reviewer's satisfaction before the audit report is signed. Their extent depends on factors such as whether the audit is of a listed entity, the complexity of the engagement, and the risk that the report might not be appropriate in the circumstances (ISQC 1, paras A42, A43).

As for all other elements of an audit, the engagement quality control review is to be properly documented. In particular, documentation is required confirming that:

(i)   the firm's procedures for engagement quality control reviews have been performed;

(ii) the review was completed before the audit report was issued; and

(iii) the reviewer is not aware of any unresolved matters that would cause him or her to believe that significant judgments made by the engagement team or the conclusions they reached were not appropriate (ISQC 1, para 43).

(f)   Monitoring

As indicated in Figure 16.1, an audit firm's quality control system should include policies and procedures designed to provide it with reasonable assurance that the system is relevant, adequate, operating effectively and complied with in practice. ISQC 1 (paras 49–55) specifies that such policies and procedures should include requiring:

(i)   one or more partners, or other person(s), with sufficient, appropriate experience and authority to be responsible for monitoring the firm's quality controls on an ongoing basis. (For convenience, we refer to such a person as the firm's audit compliance partner);

(ii) periodic (for example, annual) inspection of selected completed audit engagements by the audit compliance partner or another partner (or person) not associated with the audit engagements in question or their quality control reviews;

(iii) evaluation of the effect of any deficiencies uncovered by the monitoring process, and determination of whether they are:

    – 'one-off' in nature and thus do not indicate the firm's quality control system is unable to provide reasonable assurance that the firm's audits comply with professional standards and regulatory and legal requirements, and the audit reports issued are appropriate in the circumstances; or

    – systemic and thus require prompt corrective action;

    (iv) communication of deficiencies uncovered by the monitoring process to the engagement partner(s) concerned, and other relevant personnel, together with recommended corrective action(s). The latter may include one or more of the following:
- taking appropriate remedial action in relation to the relevant audit engagement and/or one or more members of the audit team;
- communicating the findings to those responsible for the firm's training and professional development;
- effecting changes to the firm's quality control (or other relevant) policies and procedures;
- taking disciplinary action against those who fail to comply with the firm's standards – especially those who repeatedly fail to do so;

    (v) at least annually, communicate the monitoring procedures performed and results obtained to the relevant engagement partners and other appropriate individuals within the firm, including the firm's chief executive officer or its managing board of partners. This enables those responsible, if the circumstances demand it, to instigate corrective action.

Audit firms should also establish policies and procedures designed to provide them with reasonable assurance that they deal appropriately with:
    (i)   complaints and allegations that work performed by the firm fails to comply with professional standards and regulatory and legal requirements;
    (ii) allegations of non-compliance with the firm's quality controls;
    (iii) deficiencies in the design or operation of the firm's quality control procedures, and/or non-compliance therewith by one or more individuals, identified during investigations of complaints and allegations;
    (iv) documenting complaints and allegations of sub-standard work by the firm or firm personnel, and the firm's response(s) thereto.
ISQC 1 notes that:

> As part of this process, the firm shall establish clearly defined channels for firm personnel to raise any concerns in a manner that enables them to come forward without fear of reprisals. (para 57)

16.2.3 Engagement partners' responsibility for securing high quality audits

Although the six elements of a firm's quality control system outlined above provide a structure for ensuring that high quality audits are performed by the firm, responsibility for the quality of an individual audit engagement is that of the engagement partner. The responsibility of this partner is limited in scope in that it is restricted to the particular audit engagement but, in respect of that engagement, it is all-embracing. The engagement partner has responsibility for the quality of all the audit work performed during the engagement, for ensuring compliance with the firm's quality control policies and procedures throughout the engagement, and for finalising and signing the audit report on behalf of the firm. Whilst acknowledging this overall responsibility for the audit engagement, ISA 220: *Quality control for an audit of financial statements* specifies six sets of duties relating to audit quality for which the engagement partner is particularly responsible, namely:

    (a) providing leadership for quality on the audit;

    (b) ensuring audit team members comply with relevant ethical requirements;

    (c) ensuring appropriate acceptance or continuance procedures are followed;

    (d) ensuring the audit team collectively has the appropriate capabilities, competence and time to complete the audit to the required standard;

    (e) the performance of audit work throughout the engagement;

    (f) documentation of the engagement.

These are summarised in Figure 16.2 and discussed below.

Figure 16.2: **Engagement partner's responsibilities for securing a high quality audit**

Responsibility	Contribution to securing a high quality audit
Leadership for quality on the audit	Emphasise the importance of, *inter alia*, the audit being conducted in accordance with professional standards, regulatory and legal requirements, and the firm's quality control policies and procedures.
Compliance with relevant ethical requirements	Ensure audit team members comply with ethical standards and that any threats to independence are identified and appropriate safeguards are applied.
Performance of acceptance or continuance procedures	Ensure the firm's procedures for accepting the audit engagement have been followed.
Adequacy of the audit team's capabilities, competence and time	Ensure that, collectively, the audit team and any external experts to be used on the audit have the capabilities, competence and time required to complete a high quality audit.
Performance of audit work during the engagement	Ensure audit work is appropriately directed, supervised and reviewed and that audit team members consult appropriate personnel when difficult or contentious issues are encountered.
Documentation of the engagement	Ensure audit work performed, issues relating to compliance with ethical standards, conclusions on compliance with independence and engagement acceptance requirements, and audit team consultations are properly documented.

(a) Leadership for quality on the audit

As noted above, the audit engagement partner is responsible for all aspects of the engagement. In order to ensure the audit is of high quality, the engagement partner is required to convey to members of the audit team, by setting an example and through communication, the importance of:

(i) performing work that complies with professional standards and regulatory and legal requirements;
(ii) complying with the firm's quality control policies and procedures;
(iii) issuing an audit report that is appropriate in the circumstances;
(iv) being able to raise concerns without fear of reprisals;
(v) the critical importance of quality in the performance of the audit (ISA 220, para A2).

(b) Compliance with relevant ethical requirements

A key responsibility of the audit engagement partner is ensuring that all members of the audit team comply with the profession's ethical requirements; that is, the fundamental principles of integrity, objectivity, professional competence and due care, confidentiality and professional behaviour.[19] However, ISA 220 highlights, in particular, the engagement partner's responsibility for assessing whether or not the audit engagement can be performed in an independent, objective manner – and whether it would be so perceived by an outside observer. If this independence cannot be assured, either the engagement should not be accepted (if the firm's independence is in doubt) or the proposed engagement partner and/or senior audit staff members whose objectivity may be questioned should not be used on the engagement. More specifically, ISA 220 requires the engagement partner to form a conclusion on the engagement's compliance with independence requirements. In forming this conclusion, the engagement partner is to:

(a) Obtain relevant information from the firm and, where applicable, network firms,[20] to identify and evaluate circumstances and relationships that create threats to independence;
(b) Evaluate information on identified breaches, if any, of the firm's independence policies and procedures to determine whether they create a threat to independence for the audit engagement; and
(c) Take appropriate action to eliminate such threats or reduce them to an acceptable level by applying safeguards.[21] (para 10)

---

[19] These principles, which are specified and explained in IFAC's *Code of ethics for professional accountants* and the APB's Ethical Standards, are discussed in Chapter 3.

[20] A network firm is defined as a firm that belongs to a network. A network is a larger structure:
    (i) That is aimed at cooperation, and
    (ii) That is clearly aimed at profit or cost-sharing or shares common ownership, control or management, common quality control policies and procedures, common business strategy, the use of a common brand name, or a significant part of professional resources. (ISA 220, para 6)

[21] Independence threats and safeguards are discussed in detail in Chapter 4.

(c) Performance of acceptance or continuance procedures

We noted in section 16.2.2(c) above that audit firms are responsible for establishing policies and procedures designed to ensure proper evaluation of the propriety of accepting new or continuing audit clients and specific audit engagements. However, ISA 220, para 11, requires audit engagement partners to be satisfied that their firm's procedures have been followed and that the resulting conclusion about accepting the audit engagement is appropriate. If the engagement partner becomes aware of information which, had it been known earlier, the firm would have declined the engagement, (s)he is required to communicate the information to the firm promptly so that appropriate action may be taken.

(d) Adequacy of the audit team's capabilities, competence and time

Like the decision to accept an audit client and particular engagement, assignment of the engagement partner and audit team members to an audit engagement is the responsibility of the audit firm. However, ISA 220, para 13, requires the engagement partner to be satisfied that, collectively, the engagement team and any external experts to be used on the audit have the appropriate capabilities, competence and time to perform the engagement in accordance with professional standards and regulatory and legal requirements, and to enable an appropriate audit report to be issued.[22]

(e) Performance of audit work during the engagement

As the audit engagement partner is responsible for all of the audit work performed during the engagement, it is evident that (s)he is responsible for ensuring the work is appropriately directed, supervised and reviewed. We discuss the direction, supervision and review of audit work in detail in Chapter 7, section 7.5, and will not repeat it here. However, in addition to ensuring the work of audit team members is properly directed, supervised and reviewed, audit engagement partners are required to be satisfied that:

(i) members of the audit team undertake appropriate consultation during the course of the engagement, both within the engagement team and, when appropriate, with others at an appropriate level within or outside the audit firm. Such consultation is particularly important when difficult or contentious matters are encountered during the audit;

(ii) the nature and scope of, and conclusions resulting from, such consultations are agreed with the party consulted;

---

[22] The capabilities and competence audit team members collectively require are explained in Chapter 7, section 7.5.2.

(iii) conclusions resulting from such consultations are implemented (ISA 220, para 17).

A further element of the engagement partner's responsibility for the quality of work performed during the audit of listed company clients, and of other clients where the audit firm considers it appropriate, is ensuring that the audit engagement is subject to an engagement quality control review. This requirement is discussed in greater detail in section 16.2.2(e) above.

(f) Documentation of the engagement

In earlier chapters we have emphasised that auditing standards require each step of the audit process to be fully and properly documented. However, in addition to ensuring that all audit work is properly documented, the engagement partner (and/or other appropriate members of the audit team) is required to document matters relating to the quality control responsibilities outlined above. More specifically, ISA 220 requires the following matters to be documented:

(a) Issues identified with respect to compliance with relevant ethical requirements and how they were resolved.

(b) Conclusions on compliance with independence requirements that apply to the audit engagement, and any relevant discussions with the firm that support these conclusions.

(c) Conclusions reached regarding the acceptance and continuance of client relationships and audit engagements.

(d) The nature and scope of, and conclusions resulting from, consultations undertaken during the course of the audit engagement. (para 24)

In order for audit firms to be assured that audits conducted by the firm are of a high quality, they need to ensure that all of the quality controls outlined above are implemented and adhered to on every audit engagement. As indicated in section 16.2.2(a) above, each audit firm is expected to appoint a senior audit quality control partner. In multi-office firms, these senior audit partners need to satisfy themselves (usually by visiting each office of their firm) that each office of the firm is adhering to the firm's quality control policies and procedures and performing high quality audits.

Where audit firms have a number of offices internationally, intra-firm quality control reviews may be conducted. These involve teams of about five senior audit partners, drawn from different countries, visiting various offices of the firm around the world to review the adequacy of, and level of compliance with, the firm's quality control procedures. Such reviews are internal to the firms concerned and are designed to ensure that the risk of members of the firm performing poor quality audits, and thus exposing the firm's partners to liability, is kept to a minimum. At the same time, ensuring that all offices of the firm (internationally) maintain an adequate and effective system of quality control helps to enhance the reputation of the firm for the professional quality of its audit work.

16.2.4 Regulators' monitoring of audit quality

In addition to audit firms developing, implementing and monitoring systems of quality control, in the United Kingdom (UK), as in countries such as the United States of America (USA), Canada, Australia, New Zealand and also in the European Union (EU), what we might call 'quality control monitoring mechanisms' have been introduced. Although different countries use varying titles for their monitoring schemes, they all have two key objectives, namely:

- to ensure auditors meet their obligation to society to perform work that meets the profession's standards and regulatory and legal requirements;
- to sustain public confidence in the auditing profession (and audit function) by demonstrating a concern for maintaining a high standard of audit work.

We explain in Chapter 5 (section 5.2.3) that in the UK and Ireland only registered auditors are eligible for appointment as company auditors. Such auditors may be individuals, or firms with a majority of individuals, who have qualified with a Recognised Qualifying Body and registered with a Recognised Supervisory Body (RSB). In order to become an RSB, a professional body must have rules and practices regarding, *inter alia*:

(i) auditors being fit and proper persons, performing audit work properly and with integrity, and not being appointed as auditors in circumstances where their independence may be compromised;
(ii) technical standards to be applied in audit work;
(iii) admitting, disciplining and excluding registered auditors;
(iv) ensuring registered auditors maintain an appropriate level of competence;
(v) investigating complaints, and meeting claims arising out of audit work (through holding professional indemnity insurance);
(vi) monitoring compliance with, and enforcing, the RSB's rules.

Thus, monitoring auditors' compliance with ethical and auditing standards and other rules is a condition of a professional body gaining RSB status – and has been since the RSBs were established in 1991.[23] Monitoring fulfils both a 'carrot' and a 'stick' function. It provides the opportunity for registered auditors to receive constructive advice on best practice, compliance issues and/or training needs; however, if a registered auditor is found not to be complying with auditing and ethical standards and other audit regulations, sanctions may result – including, the ultimate sanction of withdrawal of audit registration.

Each RSB is also required to participate in arrangements for:
   (i)   setting technical auditing standards and standards relating to auditors' integrity and independence;
   (ii) independent monitoring of the audits of listed companies and other entities in which there is major public interest;
   (iii) independent investigation, for disciplinary purposes, of public interest cases (i.e., those which raise, or appear to raise, important issues affecting the public interest).
Since its establishment in April 2004, the Financial Reporting Council (FRC) has had overall responsibility for these activities in the UK – a responsibility it discharges through its operating bodies, specifically, the Auditing Practices Board (APB), the Professional Oversight Board (POB) and the Accountancy Investigation and Discipline Board (AIDB), respectively, with input from, and working collaboratively with, the RSBs.

From the commencement of monitoring of registered auditors in 1991 until 2004, the monitoring function of the five RSBs recognised in the UK[24] was discharged by two units:
   (i)   the Joint Monitoring Unit (JMU), which monitored auditors registered with the Institutes of Chartered Accountants in England

---

[23] Regulation (and registration) of company auditors is a requirement of the EU 8th Directive on Company Law (EU, 2006). However, although monitoring of registered auditors has been required in the UK and Ireland since the early 1990s, it was not required by the EU 8th Directive until a revised EU 8th Directive was issued in 2006. All Member States were required to implement the provisions of the revised EU 8th Directive by 29 June 2008. These provisions include:
  [ensuring] all statutory auditors and audit firms are subject to a system of quality assurance which meets the following criteria:
  (a) the quality assurance system shall be ... independent of the reviewed statutory auditors and audit firms and subject to public oversight ...
  (d) the persons who carry out quality assurance reviews shall have appropriate professional education and relevant experience in statutory audit and financial reporting combined with specific training on quality assurance reviews; ...
  (f) the scope of the quality assurance review, supported by adequate testing of selected audit files, shall include an assessment of compliance with applicable auditing standards and independence requirements, of the quantity and quality of resources spent, of the audit fees charged and of the internal quality control system of the audit firm; ...
  (h) quality assurance reviews shall take place at least every six years; ... (EU 8th Directive, 2006, Article 29, para 1)

[24] The Institutes of Chartered Accountants in England and Wales (ICAEW), of Scotland (ICAS) and in Ireland (ICAI); and the Associations of Chartered Certified Accountants (ACCA) and of Authorised Public Accountants (AAPA).

and Wales (ICAEW), of Scotland (ICAS) and in Ireland (ICAI); and

(ii) the ACCA monitoring unit which monitored those registered with the Associations of Chartered Certified Accountants (ACCA) and of Authorised Public Accountants (AAPA).

The JMU was established as a limited company, jointly owned by the ICAEW (with an 80 per cent ownership share) and ICAS and ICAI (each with a 10 per cent ownership share). However, all JMU staff were ICAEW employees. The ACCA monitoring unit was established as a component of the ACCA's regulation and monitoring department.

Since 2005, largely as a result of changes to the EU 8th Directive, each of the three Institutes has established its own system for monitoring its registered auditors. In the UK, the ICAEW has established a Quality Assurance Directorate (QAD) to monitor the work of all of its members, including its registered auditors, and the former JMU staff transferred to the QAD. Similarly, ICAS has established its own audit monitoring unit. Auditors registered with the two Associations have continued to be monitored by the ACCA's monitoring unit. As required by the revised EU 8th Directive, the activities of these three monitoring units in the UK are overseen by the FRC's POB.[25]

Company auditors in Ireland may be registered with any one of six RSBs – the ACCA, ICAEW, ICAS, ICAI, the Institute of Certified Public Accountants in Ireland (ICPAI) and the Institute of Incorporated Public Accountants (IIPA). Auditors registered with the ACCA, ICAEW and ICAS are monitored by the monitoring units mentioned above. The other three RSBs each has its own audit monitoring unit but the ICAI has established an independent Chartered Accountants' Regulatory Board (CARB) with responsibility for regulating ICAI members (including the monitoring of the ICAI registered auditors). The monitoring activities of the six RSBs recognised in Ireland are overseen by the Irish Auditing and Accounting Supervisory Authority (IAASA) – an independent body established in January 2006 with responsibility for overseeing the accountancy profession in Ireland.[26] In effect, it is the Irish equivalent of the FRC in the UK.

---

[25] The revised EU 8th Directive provides:

All statutory auditors and audit firms shall be subject to public oversight. The system of public oversight shall be governed by non-practitioners who are knowledgeable in the areas relevant to statutory audit. ... Persons involved in the governance of the public oversight system shall be selected in accordance with an independent and transparent nomination procedure. The system of public oversight shall have the ultimate responsibility for the oversight of:

(a) the approval and registration of statutory auditors and audit firms;
(b) the adoption of standards on professional ethics, internal quality control of audit firms and auditing; and
(c) continuing education, quality assurance and investigative and disciplinary systems. (EU 8th Directive, Article 32, paras 2–4)

[26] Similarly, the FRC's POB oversees the monitoring activities of CARB in so far as they relate to the audits of UK companies by ICAI registered auditors.

In addition to the changes noted above, since 2004, monitoring (or, inspections, as they are called) of the audits of companies listed on the London Stock Exchange, and other entities in whose financial condition there is a major public interest, have been conducted by the Audit Inspection Unit (AIU) of the POB. These inspections complement the monitoring of registered auditors by the RSBs.

(i) Monitoring by the RSBs

The remit of the RSBs' monitoring units is to ascertain whether registered auditors are complying with the audit regulations.[27] Thus, their monitoring activities embrace registered auditors' compliance with, for example, auditing, ethical and quality control standards, and regulations relating to independence, maintaining professional competence and professional indemnity insurance. The focus of monitoring is the audit firm rather than individual auditors.[28] At 31 December 2006, there were nearly 9,240 registered audit firms in the UK and Ireland and a further 120 individual auditors were registered with the IIPA. However, the number and profile of firms registered with the ICAEW, ICAS and ICAI on the one hand, and the ACCA[29] and ICPAI on the other, differ markedly. Nearly 6,150 firms were registered with three Institutes of Chartered Accountants: about 53 per cent were sole practitioners, some 45 per cent had between two and 10 principals, and about two per cent had more than 10 principals. Of the Institutes' registered audit firms, 95 (about 1.5 per cent) had listed company clients, with the largest 13 firms, each with more than 50 principals, auditing approximately 52 per cent (and the largest 47 firms, with more than 10 principals, auditing nearly 86 per cent) of such companies.[30] By comparison, nearly 3,100 firms were registered with the ACCA and ICPAI; approximately 71 per cent were sole practitioners, 28 per cent had between two and 10 principals, and only six firms (all registered with the ACCA) had more than 10 principals. No ACCA registered auditors had listed company clients (POB, 2007; IAASA, 2007; AIU, 2007).

In general, the monitoring process, which is depicted in Figure 16.3, involves both desktop reviews and firm visits; however, monitoring by the ACCA and IIPA relies primarily on firm visits. The EU 8th Directive requires all

---

[27] The audit regulations are primarily derived from the criteria specified in the Companies Act 2006 which RSBs must meet in order to be recognised as RSBs. However, each RSB may impose additional requirements, as it sees fit, on its registered auditors.

[28] An exception to this is monitoring by the IIPA in Ireland, which registers individuals, rather than firms, as auditors.

[29] Auditors registered with the AAPA are included with those registered with the ACCA.

[30] According to the AIU: "The Big Four firms have a dominant market share in the audit of larger listed companies auditing 99% of the FTSE 100 and 97% of the FTSE 250" (POB, 2006, p. 13). For an explanation of 'FTSE 100' and 'FTSE 250' see footnote 54.

registered auditors to be subject to monitoring visits at least once every six years[31] but, where a firm is identified as possessing a number of risk factors, monitoring visits occur more frequently (generally between one and three years depending on the firm's level of risk). According to the IAASA (2007, p. 108), the risk factors that increase the likelihood of more frequent monitoring visits include the following:

- the number of audit clients;
- the type of audit clients, specifically, specialist or public interest (including listed) clients and clients in regulated industries such as credit institutions, pension funds, insurance brokers and investment firms;

Figure 16.3:   Generalised outline of the RSBs' monitoring process

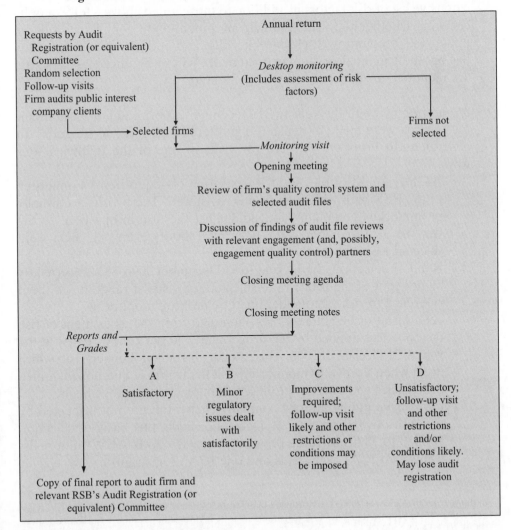

- the absence of, or out-of-date, procedures or the absence of specialist audit procedures when the firm has specialist clients;
- an indication of control problems within the firm;
- a history of complaints against the firm;
- failure to make an annual return (as required) to the relevant RSB;
- length of time since the last visit;
- deficiencies detected during the last monitoring visit.

(a) *Desktop reviews*: In general, registered audit firms are required to submit completed returns annually to their RSB. These are reviewed for any inconsistencies or omitted information and then subjected to a risk assessment. Some monitoring units, such as the ICAEW's QAD, have an extensive list of risk factors in addition to those noted above – for example, checking whether the firm conducts an annual audit compliance review, updates its accounting disclosure checklist and audit programme, and/or has an audit manual or similar document. Where significant risk factors are identified a risk report may be generated.

(b) *Monitoring visits*: In the year to 31 December 2006, a total of 1,249 monitoring visits were made to registered auditors in the UK and Ireland.[32] In general, audit firms are selected for visits in one of the following four ways:
- At the request of the Audit Registration (or equivalent) Committee of the RSB with which the firm is registered. These visits are usually prompted by complaints lodged against the firm in question. In the year to 31 December 2006, 93 firms (about seven per cent) were selected for visits on this basis.
- Random selection. In the year to 31 December 2006, 732 firms (nearly 59 per cent of the total) were selected for visits at random – without reference to risk factors identified by desktop monitoring.
- As a result of heightened risk (identified from the assessment of risk factors). This applied to 386 firms (nearly 30 per cent of visits) in the year to 31 December 2006. This category includes follow-up visits which occur when a previous monitoring visit to the firm in question identified deficiencies and the firm promised to implement improvements.
- Firms have public interest company clients but are not inspected by the AIU. In the year to 31 December 2006, this basis of selection applied to 38 firms (three per cent of visits) – 35 ICAEW audit registrants, two ICAI registrants and one ICAS registrant.

---

[32] In the year to 31 December 2006, 371 visits were made to ACCA audit registrants, 713 to ICAEW registrants, 68 to ICAS registrants, 33 to ICAI registrants, 59 to ICPAI registrants and five to IIPA registrants (POB, 2007; IAASA, 2007).

As may be seen from Figure 16.3, a monitoring visit begins with an opening meeting. At this meeting, the visiting reviewers discuss with the audit compliance partner[33] (and other audit partners who wish, or are requested by the reviewers or the firm, to be present), the firm's quality control policies and procedures – and compliance therewith. As noted in section 16.2.2(f) above, a key component of an audit firm's quality control system is 'monitoring' – internal monitoring by the firm to ensure, amongst other things, that the firm, its audit engagement partners and its audit staff are complying with auditing, ethical and quality control standards and other audit regulations. It is not, therefore, surprising that a significant element of a monitoring visit involves reviewing the firm's quality control monitoring process, deficiencies detected by the process and the remedial actions implemented.

During the opening meeting, the reviewers also discuss other elements of the firm's quality control system – including its policies and procedures that relate to client and engagement acceptance and continuance, the capabilities and competence of audit personnel, and audit engagement performance. The reviewers also identify the individual audit engagement files and other records they wish to review.

The reviewers then conduct a detailed review of the firm's quality control system and selected audit engagement files. At the time the audit file reviews are conducted, the reviewers discuss their findings with the relevant engagement partner(s) and any minor issues are clarified and resolved. Major points arising from the reviews are summarised in a closing meeting agenda. These points are usually expressed as actual or potential instances of non-compliance with auditing, ethical or quality control standards or other audit regulations resulting in risks to the firm's audit work. They are discussed in the overall context of the audit regulations.

At the conclusion of the visit, the reviewers meet with the audit compliance partner and other partners who wish, or are requested, to be present at a closing meeting. The partners give the firm's initial response to the issues identified by the reviewers and the reviewers' suggestions for improvement. The firm is usually requested to send typed notes of the closing meeting ('the closing meeting notes') to the relevant RSB's monitoring unit noting, in particular, its response to matters raised during the visit and how it plans to address them.

Upon receipt of the firm's closing meeting notes, the reviewers finalise their visit report. A copy of the final report is sent to the audit firm and also to the

---

[33] The partner responsible for monitoring the adequacy and effectiveness of the firm's quality control system; see section 16.2.2(f) above.

relevant RSB's Audit Registration (or equivalent) Committee. As indicated in Figure 16.3, monitoring visits result in one of the outcomes we have designated Grades A to D. The grades signify the following outcomes:

- *Grade A* – there are no regulatory issues to deal with;
- *Grade B* – any regulatory issues have been dealt with adequately in the firm's closing meeting notes and no further action is required. (However, information on the implementation of remedial action(s) agreed at the closing meeting may be required);
- *Grade C* – the findings of the reviewers are less than satisfactory and improvements are required. Depending on the severity of non-compliance with auditing, ethical or quality control standards, or other audit regulations, the audit firm may be required to provide information on the implementation of agreed improvements or follow-up visits may be arranged to ensure required remedial action has been taken. Additional restrictions or conditions may also be imposed; for example, the imposition of continuing education/training requirements for audit staff and/or partners, or a prohibition on the firm accepting new audit clients until required improvements have been made;
- *Grade D* – the findings of the reviewers are unsatisfactory and the relevant RSB's Audit Registration (or equivalent) Committee may take one of the following regulatory actions:
    - impose conditions such as requiring a follow-up visit to confirm that remedial action has been taken;
    - impose restrictions or conditions on the firm's registration such as prohibiting the acceptance of new audit clients for a specified period and/or until specified improvements have been made, or specifying that identified audit engagement partners are not to be given responsibility for audit engagements until they have undertaken further training;
    - in very serious cases, the suspension or withdrawal of audit registration.

The results of monitoring visits for the years 1992 to 2006 are presented in Figure 16.4 below.

As might be expected, the size of the team of reviewers and the time taken for monitoring visits varies with the size of audit firms. Some teams of reviewers may comprise just one member while others may have eight to 10 (or more) reviewers; similarly, while visits to single-office practitioners may be completed within one day on site, full monitoring visits to large firms may take 70 to 80 (or more) days. Additionally, as we noted earlier, audit firms with listed company clients or other public interest clients are subject to inspections by the POB's Audit Inspection Unit in addition to monitoring by their RSB.

Figure 16.4: Results of visits by the monitoring units 1992 to 2007[34]

Years: 1992–2006	92	93	94	95	96	97	98	99	00	01	02	03	04	05	06
ICAEW, ICAS and ICAI monitoring visits	No. 291	No. 312	No. 793	No. 1087	No. 1098	No. 1033	No. 937	No. 1066	No. 880	No. 957	No. 1081	No. 1030	No. 1099	No. 1023	No. 833
A and B Satisfactory	% 40	% 31	% 38	% 63	% 60	% 63	% 65	% 56	% 57	% 63	% 66	% 65	% 66	% 69	% 61
C Appropriate plans for improvement	-	58	48	22	24	26	28	33	32	25	25	22	21	24	27
D Restriction on audit registration	-	5	7	9	10	7	4	8	9	8	6	10	10	7	12
D Audit registration · withdrawn · surrendered	-	4 / 2	4 / 3	3 / 3	3 / 3	2 / 2	1 / 2	1 / 2	1 / 1	2 / 2	1 / 2	2 / 1	2 / 1		
Concerns about audit work or non-compliance with regulations	60	-	-	-	-	-	-	-	-	-	-	-	-	-	-
ACCA unit visits	No. 297	No. 409	No. 517	No. 394	No. 833	No. 717	No. 475	No. 535	No. 468	No. 605	No. 695	No. 456	No. 432	No. 462	No. 371
A and B Satisfactory	45	44	49	54	54	56	53	52	46	46	45	55	57	59	49
C Not satisfactory: C+ Revisit a low priority	27	27	21	16	17	12	12	13	15	18	13	10	13	14	17
C– Early revisit required	20	19	12	14	17	14	16	19	22	19	21	13	11	6	9
D Referred to Authorisation Committee	8	10	18	16	12	18	19	16	17	17	21	22	19	21	25

Source: ACCA and ICAEW, ICAS & ICAI, *Annual Reports to the DTI*, 1992 to 2004; POB, 2006.

(ii) Inspections by the Audit Inspection Unit (AIU)

Unlike the RSBs' monitoring units, which focus on registered auditors (primarily audit firms), the AIU focuses on the audits of entities with listed securities and those in whose financial condition there is a major public interest. The scope of the AIU is determined annually by the POB but, since 2004, it has included the following entities:

- all entities with listed securities (equity and debt);
- unquoted companies, groups of companies or limited liability partnerships in the UK which have either:
  - (a) turnover in excess of £500 million, or
  - (b) long-term liabilities in excess of £250 million and turnover in excess of £100 million;
- private sector pension schemes with either more than £1,000 million of assets or more than 20,000 members;

---

[34] As may be deduced from Figure 16.4, the grading system of the Institutes' and the ACCA's monitoring units differ slightly. Monitoring visits that are referred to the ACCA's Authorisation Committee are subject to regulatory action but details are not disclosed by the ACCA.

- Building Societies with assets exceeding £1,000 million;
- Open-ended Investment Companies and Unit Trusts managed by a fund manager with more than £1,000 million of UK funds under management (AIU 2005, 2006, 2007, 2008).

The AIU (2006, p. 4) explains which firms it inspects and the frequency of inspections:

> We undertake annual inspections of the Big Four firms [i.e., Deloitte & Touche, Ernst & Young, KPMG and PricewaterhouseCoopers]. There are currently only five other firms [i.e., Baker Tilly, BDO Stoy Hayward, Grant Thornton UK, PKF (UK) and RSM Robson Rhodes[35]] which audit a significant number of entities within our scope (the "Other Significant firms").[36] [These] firms will, in future, receive either a full inspection or a (shorter) interim inspection each year. The frequency with which full inspections of individual Other Significant firms are undertaken will reflect the nature of the entities within our scope audited by them ... [However, there will be] a minimum frequency for full inspections of every third year.
>
> For all other firms which fall within our scope, we will focus our inspection work on reviews of the small number of listed or other major public interest entities audited by them; we will rely, as appropriate, on reviews of their quality control systems and procedures undertaken by the monitoring unit of the professional body with which they are registered. We [will] review a sample of such audits for each of these firms on a three year cycle commencing in 2006/7.[37]

In the years to 31 March 2005, 2006 and 2007, the AIU reviewed, respectively, the audits of 27, 77 and 103 listed and other public interest entities (AIU, 2007, p. 3). It should be noted that the RSBs' monitoring units remain responsible for monitoring the audit work of auditors registered with them (including the Big Four and Other Significant firms) that lies outside the scope of the AIU.

While the remit of the RSBs' monitoring units is to ascertain whether registered auditors are complying with the audit regulations, that of the AIU is:

> to monitor the quality of auditing. ... By monitoring and promoting improvements in audit quality, [the AIU] contributes to the FRC's overall aim of promoting confidence in UK corporate reporting and governance. (AIU, 2006, p. 5)

Similarly, in accordance with their remit, the RSB monitoring units focus on registered auditors' compliance with auditing, ethical and quality control

---

[35] In July 2007, Grant Thornton UK and RSM Robson Rhodes merged to form the single firm of Grant Thornton UK.

[36] All of the Big Four and all but Baker Tilly of the Other Significant firms are registered with ICAEW; Baker Tilly is registered with ICAS.

[37] In 2006/7 the AIU carried out inspections at seven smaller firms (AIU, 2007, p. 2).

standards and other audit regulations. However, the AIU observes that its "responsibility extends beyond monitoring compliance with specific requirements of the UK regulatory framework and includes an assessment of the key audit judgments made" (AIU, 2006, p. 7).

The AIU inspections follow the same general process as the RSBs' monitoring unit visits. They include an opening meeting, a detailed review of the firm's system of quality control and selected engagement files, discussions with key audit partners (including the firm's audit compliance partner and relevant engagement partners and engagement quality control reviewers), a closing meeting and the preparation of inspection reports. Among other things, the inspectors examine:

- how the firm's commitment to quality and integrity is reflected in the basis on which partners are appointed, remunerated and promoted to more senior roles;
- the basis on which audit engagement partners and engagement quality control reviewers are appointed, and the firm's procedures for rotating key partners off major audits to mitigate familiarity threats;
- how the firm conducts its internal monitoring of audit engagements, the effectiveness of the process, its overall findings (and how these compare with those of the AIU inspectors) and any remedial action taken or planned by the firm;
- selected individual audit engagements; these are designed to assess the quality of each audit reviewed. The AIU explains:

> Our work programmes are structured around the requirements of Auditing Standards. They are tailored by each inspection team to ensure both that reviews are sufficiently focused on the major risk areas identified for each audit and that an appropriate level of coverage of the requirements of Auditing Standards is achieved across all reviews carried out at each firm. Our inspection teams challenge audit partners, where appropriate, regarding the basis on which key audit judgments were made. We believe that challenging audit judgments in this way is a key feature of an effective review of audit quality. (AIU, 2006, p. 8)

The inspection team prepares a detailed report on each audit engagement reviewed and this is provided to the audit team concerned and copied to senior management within the firm's audit practice. Additionally, a formal report is prepared for the audit firm setting out:

(a) key issues arising from the inspectors' review of:
  – the firm's quality control system, and
  – individual audit engagements;

(b) prioritised recommendations, the firm's responses thereto, and the firm's action plan to implement agreed improvements.

A copy of this report is sent to the RSB with which the relevant audit firm is registered.

The AIU also issues an annual public report setting out the overall findings and conclusions of its inspections.

Monitoring of UK audit firms by the Public Company Accounting Oversight Board (PCAOB[38])

Since 2004, firms in the UK that audit companies with securities listed on a stock exchange in the USA, or key subsidiaries of such companies, have been subject not only to monitoring by their RSB's monitoring unit and (probably) the AIU but also to inspections by the USA's PCAOB. Audit firms which are subject to monitoring by three separate sets of reviewers/inspectors, with each 'inspection' extending over, say, 60 or more days, are concerned about being 'over monitored' and the extent of senior partners' time which is devoted to this activity.[39] However, since 2006, some inspections of the Big Four and Other Significant firms have been conducted jointly by AIU and PCAOB staff (led by AIU staff) – a development which is expected to become more commonplace in the future. In relation to these joint inspections the AIU (2007) notes:

> We believe that effective co-operation with overseas audit regulators in the conduct of audit inspections, where appropriate, is in the interests of all parties involved including the firms themselves. It facilitates cost effective regulation and avoids unnecessary duplication of work. (p. 3)

16.2.5 Effectiveness of monitoring auditors' performance

As may be seen from Figure 16.4, the outcome of monitoring visits indicates that, in general, auditors' performance has improved since 1992. Perhaps not surprisingly, greatest improvement was noted in the early years (between 1992 and 1997) as audit firms became more acquainted with the standard of work required and more accustomed to having their performance monitored. However, the improvement appears to have levelled out and the proportion of monitoring visits resulting in a satisfactory outcome (Grades A and B) has remained fairly stable since the turn of the century.[40] This may partly be the result of the RSBs demanding rather higher standards now that the audit

---

[38] The PCAOB, established by the Sarbanes-Oxley Act of 2002, should not be confused with the UK's POB.

[39] Such concerns were expressed by senior audit partners of the Big Four firms during discussions with one of the authors. They also expressed concern that the extent of monitoring is resulting in an over-emphasis on audit compliance at the expense of audit judgment and that this seems to be resulting in audit staff being insufficiently willing and/or able to make appropriate audit judgments.

[40] The stability is more evident for ICAEW, ICAS and ICAI firms than for ACCA firms. In the latter case, the results vary quite markedly from one year to the next.

regulations are well known and the monitoring system is well established. However, in 2000, the ICAEW *et al.* cautioned:

> It is important to appreciate that, generally, different firms are visited each year. Thus it is not appropriate to talk in terms of changes in standards when comparing successive years. [Monitoring visit results show that] the large majority of firms are conducting audit work in accordance with the [audit] regulations and auditing standards or have appropriate plans to make improvements. ... Matters raised on a visit are mainly of a procedural nature and would not be critical to the audit opinion. Raising these issues with the firm contributes to the educational element of the visit. (ICAEW *et al.*, 2000, pp. 8–9)

Whatever the detailed outcomes of monitoring visits, the results of surveys conducted during the early years of monitoring in both the UK and USA indicate that, in general, monitoring of audit work has resulted in an overall improvement in its quality or, probably more precisely, its documentation. This improvement has been achieved primarily through improved quality control systems and documentation procedures (see, for example, Evers and Pearson, 1990; Wallace and Wallace, 1990; Fearnley and Page, 1992, 1993; Moizer, 1994). However, although most firms are found to have conducted their audits in accordance with auditing standards and audit regulations (see, for example, ICAEW *et al.*, 2004, p. 22), and the AIU has concluded that the quality of auditing in the UK is fundamentally sound (AIU, 2007, p. 6), the monitoring/inspection units have identified a number of commonly occurring deficiencies. These include the following:

- inadequate audit planning for specific engagements; some firms complete standard planning checklists and audit programmes without tailoring them to the needs of particular audit engagements or giving sufficient additional details of, for example, the approach adopted to key audit areas and/or identified significant risks;
- a lack of appreciation of the importance of evaluating and documenting the client's accounting system and relevant internal controls, and of gaining sufficient knowledge of the client's business, and the environment in which it operates, to be able to identify events, transactions and practices that may have a significant impact on the client's financial statements and/or the audit thereof;
- inadequate consideration of the risk of management override of internal controls;
- inadequate testing of profit and loss account balances, the existence and valuation of inventory (stock), and the completeness of creditors and related party disclosures;
- inappropriate reliance on analytical procedures which provide little or no substantive evidence;
- over-reliance on, and inadequate documentation of, management representations, especially in relation to the existence, ownership and condition

of fixed assets, ownership of inventory, and the collectability of debtors' balances;
- inadequate documentation of the rationale underlying key audit judgments, and of audit procedures performed and evidence gathered, especially in respect of:
  - identifying and assessing risks as a basis for planning the nature and extent of audit procedures,
  - assessment of clients' going concern status and compliance with relevant laws and regulations,
  - issues relating to fraud risks (including audit teams' fraud risk discussions), and subsequent events,
  - the materiality of unadjusted misstatements,
  - the competence and objectivity of experts whose work has been relied upon;
- inadequate documentation of:
  - analytical procedures performed during the planning and/or overall review stage of the audit,
  - determination of audit sampling methods and sample sizes,
  - review of audit work and, more particularly, how significant issues raised during the review were dealt with;
- inadequate (or no) documented evidence to indicate that audit quality is an overriding requirement within the firm or that audit quality issues and indicators constitute an important element in partner and staff appraisals and partner promotion processes;
- inadequate measures to ensure firms' quality control procedures are complied with throughout the audit;
- the provision of non-audit services that are prohibited by Ethical Standards; for example, some audit firms prepare clients' group cash flow statements and group tax accounting entries and disclosures;
- inadequate reporting to clients' audit committees of, for example:
  - significant matters that bear on audit firms' independence and objectivity,
  - how key risk areas communicated at the planning stage have been addressed, and the conclusions reached in relation thereto,
  - key issues arising during the audit,
  - identified unadjusted misstatements.

It is clear from the RSBs' annual reports to the Department of Trade and Industry (DTI)[41] that the monitoring units have uncovered numerous instances of non-compliance with auditing, ethical and quality control standards – and

---

[41] Since 2007 this Department has been renamed the Department of Business, Enterprise & Regulatory Reform.

generated innumerable suggestions for improvement. It also seems likely that the 'threat' of monitoring visits has motivated at least some practitioners to effect improvements in their quality control systems and auditing procedures. Further, when reporting on the effectiveness of their monitoring schemes, the RSBs have drawn attention to the large number of audit firms which received a less than satisfactory grade as the outcome of their initial monitoring visit (and hence were subject to a revisit) but which had 'cleaned up their act' before the follow-up visit. The RSBs have also noted that registered auditors who persist with defective performance are disciplined and, if necessary, excluded from the profession. In this regard it is pertinent to note that monitoring has resulted in the removal of a significant number of 'bad eggs' from the profession's nest and restricted the auditing activities of others. Between 1992 and 2004, 223 auditors registered with the ICAEW, ICAS or ICAI had their audit registration withdrawn, another 244 surrendered their registration following a monitoring visit, and a further 932 had restrictions imposed on them until required training and/or improvements in their performance had been effected (and verified through a follow-up visit). Examples of restrictions include prohibition on accepting new audit clients and precluding certain partners from appointment as audit engagement partners or, in some cases, from engaging in audit work (ICAEW *et al.*, 1992 to 2004).[42]

Given the improvement in auditors' compliance with auditing, ethical and quality control standards which monitoring appears to have brought, it may be asked why instances of auditor negligence still occur. In answer, commentators such as Wood and Sommer (1985), note that it is not known how many audit failures have been avoided as a result of auditors being required to conform to prescribed standards in the performance of their audit work. They also point out that monitoring cannot detect *all* audit work deficiencies and thus cannot prevent *all* undesirable events from occurring. Woodley (1991) echoed this theme when, on the eve of monitoring being introduced in the UK, he stated:

> It would be foolish to believe that there will be no audit failures in the future. No amount of monitoring can eliminate the possibility of errors of judgement or failures to follow laid down procedures. But ... the extra emphasis on quality control procedures, the possibility of a [monitoring] visit, and the dire consequences of failing to comply with the regulations [should] result in fewer audit failures in the future. (p. 61)

Additionally, as Wood and Sommer (1985), amongst others, have observed, although monitoring cannot prevent all audit errors from occurring, society

---

[42] In 2005 and 2006, respectively, another 67 and 93 audit firms registered with the ICAEW, ICAS or ICAI received a 'D' grade as the outcome of a monitoring visit. However, details are not available as to whether this resulted in the withdrawal or surrender of the firms' audit registration or the imposition of restrictions (POB, 2007).

has other checks in place to ensure that those responsible for causing harm to others as a result of sub-standard professional work do not go unpunished. For example, when questions of audit failure arise, authorities such as the Department of Business, Enterprise & Regulatory Reform (DBERR) in the UK and the Securities and Exchange Commission (SEC) in the USA investigate and, if justified, impose appropriate sanctions on the culprits. Further, as evidenced by cases such as those discussed in Chapter 15, in some instances, those harmed as a result of auditors' sub-standard work may seek redress through the courts.

16.3 PROPOSALS FOR LIMITING AUDITORS' LIABILITY

When investors and others suffer loss as a consequence of a company collapsing unexpectedly they seek to recover their loss from any hopeful avenue. Although a company's failure is frequently the result of mismanagement by (or, sometimes, the dishonesty of) its directors and/or senior executives, when the company fails, the fortunes of its directors often go with it. As a consequence, suing the directors is usually perceived as an option which is unlikely to bear fruit in the form of monetary recompense. However, auditors are known to carry indemnity insurance and, if any fault can be found with the way in which they performed their duties, they are often regarded as a potential source from which losses may be recouped. It is generally accepted that this 'deep pocket' syndrome has been a prime motivator in the large and increasing number of suits brought against auditors in recent decades in English-speaking countries, particularly in the USA, UK and Australia.

In some cases, as is noted in the Introduction to this chapter, auditors have faced enormous claims for damages amounting to many millions of pounds. Further, the damages awarded against auditors frequently bear no relation to the size of the audit fee or the extent of the auditors' negligence. The extent of such potential liability has caused some commentators, such as Hardcastle (1988), to conclude that there is a very real risk that it will result in a shortage of suitable people prepared to enter the auditing profession. Hardcastle states, for example:

> There is no doubt that, if current trends in litigation continue without check, the flow of people prepared to enter the professions will slow up and professional standards will fall, as the most able people come to regard a professional career as too risky. (p. 15)

Similar concerns were expressed by Pasricha (2002) when commenting on Ernst & Young (E&Y) becoming a limited liability partnership (LLP; such partnerships are discussed below). He observed:

Without our conversion to an LLP I could have seen a time in the future where it would have become difficult to attract the high calibre of person needed to become a partner in a professional services firm. (p. 12)

The potential liability burden auditors face has given rise to calls by auditing firms and others for auditors' liability to be limited in some way. The five main proposals which have been adopted or suggested are:
- (i) permitting auditors to form limited liability companies (LLCs);
- (ii) permitting auditors to form limited liability partnerships (LLPs);
- (iii) establishing a statutory or regulatory cap on auditors' liability;
- (iv) enshrining proportional liability (or contributory negligence) in statute law;
- (v) permitting auditors to make limited liability agreements with their clients.

We discuss each of these options below.

(i) *Limited liability companies (LLCs)*

Prior to the Companies Act 1989, a body corporate was precluded from being appointed as auditor. Audit firms had to exist as sole practitioners or partnerships. As noted in Chapter 15, under partnership law (which does not cover LLPs), all partners within a firm have joint and several liability. If a court awards damages against a partner in a non-LLP audit firm (or the firm reaches an out-of-court settlement with the plaintiffs) for an amount that exceeds the firm's indemnity insurance cover, the personal assets of the errant partner are used to make good the deficit. If there is still a shortfall, the personal assets of the other partners in the firm are called upon to rectify the deficiency. Thus, a particular partner may lose his or her personal assets as a consequence of negligence on the part of another partner in the firm – a partner whom (s)he may not even know if the firm is large and has many offices.

The Companies Act 1989 changed the law to permit audit firms to form limited liability companies (LLCs). In cases where firms take advantage of this option, to the extent that any damages awarded against the audit company (or out-of-court settlement agreed to by the company) exceed the company's insurance cover, the assets of the company are called upon to meet the damages claim. Additionally, the personal assets of the individual 'partner' (or, more correctly, shareholder/director) responsible for the negligence giving rise to the damages (or settlement) may be pursued through the corporate front and used to meet any deficiency. However, the personal assets of 'partners' not associated with the defective audit cannot be called upon.

Thus, incorporation benefits audit 'partners' (shareholder/directors) who are not themselves guilty of negligence in that their personal assets are safe from seizure to meet damages awarded to (or settlements agreed with) a successful plaintiff. However, it does not alter the fact that, if the damages awarded against the audit company exceed the company's indemnity insurance cover, the damages (or settlement) might still result in the company losing all of its assets (forcing the auditors out of business) and the successful plaintiffs not recovering all of their losses.[43]

Another argument raised against auditors forming LLCs is that auditors are members of a profession and, as such, they are accorded certain rights and privileges in society. As a consequence, they should not be permitted to hide behind a corporate front while retaining their professional status. One of the recognised hallmarks of a member of a profession is a preparedness to stand by the quality of his or her work and reputation as an individual. Although this argument has merit, as indicated above, incorporation does not result in the identity of the professional responsible for the audit being lost. The individual can still be traced through the corporate front in the event of failing to perform an audit without due skill and care.

Notwithstanding the apparent benefits of changing from a partnership to an LLC in terms of reduced exposure to potential liability, audit firms have demonstrated some reluctance to take advantage of this option. Only about 200 audit firms[44] have taken the incorporation route – including just one of the Big Four firms, namely, the audit section of KPMG which became KPMG Audit plc in 1996. The reasons for audit firms' reluctance to incorporate appear to be associated with company (compared with individual) tax and, more particularly, National Insurance, rules[45] and the requirement to produce an annual report – complete with audited financial statements which show a true and fair view of the audit company's financial position and its profit or loss for the year. It is also possible that some firms have reservations about whether an incorporated entity provides an appropriate environment within which professional services should be performed. Another possible reason may lie in the emergence of an attractive alternative – LLPs – which are, in the words of Davies (2001, p. 24):

---

[43] It should be recalled that, in order to be successful, plaintiffs must prove to the satisfaction of the court that, *inter alia*, they have suffered loss as a result of the auditor's negligence (i.e., they made an economic decision based on financial statements which the auditor audited without exercising due skill and care). The damages awarded by the court make good that loss suffered.

[44] Only six of the 60 largest accounting firms in the UK have become LLCs (Fisher, 2007). The six excludes KPMG Audit plc, which is a component of KPMG LLP.

[45] These rules result in the 'partners' (shareholders/directors) being subject to significantly higher taxes (or, more particularly, National Insurance contributions) than those to which they would be subject in a partnership.

a modern hybrid combining the internal flexibility of the partnership with the legal protection provided by the limited company.

(ii) Limited liability partnerships (LLPs)

LLPs were first accorded serious consideration as a possible means of reducing auditors' exposure to liability in 1996 – the year the auditing section of KPMG incorporated as KPMG Audit plc. E&Y and Price Waterhouse (PW),[46] perceiving that the disadvantages of LLCs outweighed their benefits, emerged as stalwart proponents of LLPs. As it seemed that the UK Government could not be persuaded to embrace the LLP notion, the two firms lobbied the Jersey Parliament. Their efforts were rewarded and, in May 1998, the Jersey Parliament enacted LLP law rendering it possible to establish LLPs in Jersey from September 1998.

Not surprisingly, the UK Government became concerned about the prospect of many UK professional firms (particularly accounting and legal firms) moving their 'Head Offices' to Jersey and setting up as LLPs there. In 1999, an LLP Bill was drafted and the DTI[47] "pledged that Limited Liability Partnerships would be up and running by 2000" (Kemeny, 1999). Howells, the then Minister of Consumer and Corporate Affairs, observed that the LLP Bill was "very important" and explained:

> One of the functions [of LLPs] will be to help partnerships attract new partners who have been fearful of taking up leadership roles because of unlimited liability. ... [However], in return for LLP status firms will be expected to offer greater disclosure in the form of filed audited annual accounts. If you have limited liability you have disclosure so that someone who deals with the firm can make an informed decision. (as quoted, Kemeny, 1999)

The Limited Liability Partnerships Act was enacted by the UK Parliament in 2000. Under this Act, businesses could register as LLPs from 6 April 2001; on that date, E&Y became the first organisation in the UK to be issued with an LLP certificate (Hinks, 2001b). Welcoming moves by E&Y to become the first firm to assume LLP status, Howells (Minister of Consumer and Corporate Affairs) stated:

> I know this new Act [Limited Liability Partnerships Act 2000] will be welcomed by many firms. ... It gives members the freedom to arrange their internal relationships as they wish while retaining the benefit of limited liability ... I am confident that the Act and [associated] Regulations strike the right balance between the interests of those who want to become Limited Liability Partnerships and those who will do business with them. (as quoted, Hinks, 2001a)

---

[46] Price Waterhouse merged with Coopers & Lybrand in 1998 to form PricewaterhouseCoopers.

[47] See footnote 41.

Compared with ordinary partnerships and LLCs, LLPs provide accounting (and other professional services) firms with four main advantages. These are as follows:

(a) *Limited liability*: This is probably the most important advantage as far as the large accountancy firms are concerned. As noted earlier, under partnership law, all partners are jointly and severally liable for losses caused by the negligence (or other wrongful acts or omissions) of any partner acting in the ordinary course of the partnership's business. Under the Limited Liability Partnerships Act 2000, partners (who are referred to as 'members') are able to limit their liability to the capital they invest in their firm (Loxton, 2001b). The importance of this advantage is reflected in two comments by Land, then Chairman of E&Y:

- The introduction of LLPs is an important step forward in beginning to provide a fair and reasonable measure of protection for businesses such as ours in an increasingly litigious society. (as quoted, Smith, 2001)
- I think it is easy for people to forget that in our profession ... there was real concern that, in an increasingly litigious environment, the law was unfair to us. The doctrine of joint and several liability is a pretty harsh doctrine. (as quoted, Hinks, 2001b)

(b) *The firm has a separate legal personality*: Under partnership law, a partnership does not have a legal personality; it exists as a network of relationships between individual partners. Each partner is an agent not of the firm but of the other partners. Under LLP law, the firm is established as a corporate body with a separate legal personality similar to that of an LLC. Each partner is an agent of the LLP in the same way as a director is an agent of his or her company (Davies, 2001, p. 24).

(c) *Taxation*: As we observed above, incorporation as an LLC is tax disadvantageous to the shareholder/directors of the company (partners of the 'converted' partnership). However, under LLP law members continue to be taxed as partners (that is, as individuals). Thus, while gaining the advantages of being a separate legal entity (as a corporate body), LLPs have the advantage over LLCs in that, for tax and National Insurance purposes, they are treated as businesses conducted by partners (Loxton, 2001a).

(d) *Internal flexibility*: LLPs are able to organise their management structure and internal affairs in any way they wish. As in ordinary partnerships, all members ('partners') are able to participate in the management of the LLP. There is no need to elect a board of directors or to comply with any of the other organisational requirements attaching to companies.

While there are distinct advantages to be gained by accounting firms converting to LLPs, there are also some disadvantages. These include the following:

(a) *Preparation of audited financial statements*: One of the 'costs' to accounting firms of becoming an LLP is that the provisions of the Companies Act 2006 regarding the preparation, audit and filing of annual financial statements apply to LLPs. Like LLCs, all LLPs are required to prepare annually, and to file with the Registrar of Companies, audited financial statements that give a true and fair view of the LLP's financial position and its profit or loss for the year. Additionally, where an LLP's profit exceeds £200,000 in any year, it must report the profit attributable to the member with the largest entitlement to profit under the firm's internal agreement.

However, just as the Companies Act's provisions relating to the preparation, audit and filing of financial statements apply to LLPs, so too do the exemptions. Thus, an LLP meeting the Companies Act's criteria to be classed as 'small'[48] is entitled to take advantage of the same limited reporting requirements as a small company. Further, any LLP with a turnover of no more than £5.6 million and a balance sheet total of no more than £2.8 million need not have its financial statements audited.

The reporting requirements applying to LLPs are viewed by some (for example, Davies, 2001) as onerous and as likely to be an obstacle to firms becoming LLPs. However, it is pertinent to observe that most accounting firms' clients are companies and these entities (which are probably less familiar with financial reporting and auditing requirements than the accounting firms) do not seem to find the reporting obligations too burdensome.

(b) *Consent of third parties may be required to transfer partnership loans and leases*: Where an existing partnership has, for example, a bank loan and/or overdraft, the partnership will need the bank's consent before the loan and/or overdraft can be transferred to an LLP. Further, because the liability of members of an LLP is limited, the bank's security is reduced when a partnership (with joint and several liability) converts to an LLP. Thus, the bank may require personal guarantees for the loan and/or overdraft from the LLP's members before granting its consent to the transfer. Similarly, if a partnership wishes to transfer a lease to an LLP, the landlord's consent will be required. As for the bank, because the landlord's security will be reduced by the transfer of the lease to an LLP, the LLP's members may be required to give personal guarantees in respect of the lease (Tutty, 2001).

(c) *Creditor safeguards are included in the Limited Liability Partnerships Act 2000*: The provisions of the Insolvency Act 1986 relating to a business

---

[48] To qualify as 'small', an LLP must meet any two of the following criteria: turnover of no more than £5.6 million, a balance sheet total of no more than £2.8 million, and no more than 50 employees.

trading when insolvent apply to LLPs. This means that, if an LLP goes into liquidation as a result of insolvency, its members may be personally liable for the debts of the LLP if they knew, or ought to have known, that their firm was heading for insolvency and did not take appropriate action (Davies, 2001). However, the 'bad news' for LLPs does not end here. As Davies (2001, p. 25) explains:

> [The Limited Liability Partnerships Act 2000 includes] a brand new provision for a liquidator to 'claw back' any withdrawal of funds made by a member of an LLP in the two-year period leading up to the firm's liquidation if, at the time of the withdrawal or as a result of it, he knew, or should have concluded that the firm could no longer pay its debts.

In addition to these disadvantages for audit firms forming LLPs is the (potential) disadvantage to innocent parties who suffer loss as a result of negligence (or other wrongdoing) by a member ('partner') of an LLP. If the loss suffered by a plaintiff exceeds the capital contribution of the member concerned and, his or her personal assets, then, to the extent of the shortfall, the consequences of the member's wrongdoing are borne by the plaintiff.[48] When it is remembered that the evidence suggests that plaintiffs do not succeed easily in actions brought against auditors (see Chapter 15, section 15.5), preventing those who are successful from recovering, in full, the amount lost as a result of auditors' negligence may be viewed as inequitable.

We noted earlier that, on 6 April 2001, E&Y became the first firm in the UK to become an LLP. On 3 May 2002, KPMG followed its example. As we have seen, the audit section of KPMG was incorporated as KPMG Audit plc in 1996 but the LLP covers all of KPMG's operations in the UK and embraces KPMG Audit plc as an element of the LLP. In May 2002, Lee reported that, since April 2001, "well over 1,000 LLPs have been registered at Companies House but take up among accountancy firms has been slow". However, he explains:

> I believe the apparent disinterest [in forming LLPs] is merely the consequence of two key factors that are delaying the inevitable. [Firstly,] most accountancy firms will only incorporate as an LLP at the start of an accounting period (typically 1 April or 1 May) and after the partners have made time to consider all relevant factors including the recommended creation and adoption of an appropriate members' agreement. . . . [Secondly] until a definitive SORP [Statement of Recommended Practice] is issued later this year, accountancy firms will not know for certain all of the implications of reflecting their results as an LLP. Last year's draft SORP, if adopted without any change, would have resulted in many firms reflecting increased taxable profits and future annuity obligations in the LLP accounts. (Lee, 2002, p. 12)

---

[48] Unlike in an ordinary partnership, the plaintiff does not have a right to call on the personal assets of members of an LLP who were not involved in the negligent audit (or other wrongdoing).

Just as Lee seems to think that accounting firms' conversion to LLPs is 'inevitable' (see above), Land (speaking as Chairman of E&Y) believes that "LLP status will become commonplace for professional services firms in the next few years" (as quoted, Smith, 2001). However, others appear to hold a contrary view. For example, Crofton-Martin [Senior tax partner of Pannell Kerr Forster (PKF), a middle-tier firm] observed that, although conversion to an LLP may be an attractive and effective option for large firms:

> the cost and management time involved ... may be disproportionately high for small partnerships.... Changing to LLP status is time-consuming and expensive due to financial accounting and administrative requirements. (as reported, Zea, 2001, p. 3)

A survey conducted in October 2001 by an accountancy support company, SWOT, provided support for Crofton-Martin's views; it found that "90% of high street [accountancy] partnerships are not planning to become LLPs" (as reported, Zea, 2001, p. 3). In July 2007, of the 60 largest accountancy firms in the UK, 25 had formed LLPs; this compares with six of the 60 that had incorporated as LLCs and 29 that had retained the standard partnership structure (Fisher, 2007).

(iii) Statutory or regulatory cap on auditors' liability

A widely discussed alternative to audit firms altering their legal form in order to secure limited liability, and one that is (understandably) favoured by audit firms (EU, 2007), is that of capping the liability (or specifying the maximum) to which auditors may be exposed. The capped amount may be stated as a formula, such as a multiple of the audit fee (for example, 10 times the fee) or as a fixed amount (for example, in Germany the limit for the audits of quoted companies is €4 million; for other clients it is €1 million).

This means of limiting auditors' liability possesses the advantages of simplicity, preventing (or reducing) the likelihood of auditors being forced out of business by a single negligently performed audit and, where the cap is set as a multiple of the audit fee, linking the size of the sanction associated with a negligently performed audit to the size of the reward resulting from the audit. However, as with LLCs and LLPs, limiting auditors' liability by means of a statutory or regulatory cap has some disadvantages. These include the following:

(a) *A decline in audit quality*: As the adverse consequences associated with sub-standard audit work are capped at a known level, auditors may be motivated to perform less audit work – thus reducing audit quality and increasing auditors' risk of allegations of negligence.

(b) *Inequity*: An innocent client or third party, who suffered loss as a consequence of auditors failing to perform their duties with reasonable skill and care, may be prevented from recovering the full amount of the loss suffered.

(c) Minimising the audit fee: If the cap is set at a multiple of the audit fee, auditors may be encouraged to minimise the fee in order to limit their exposure to liability. If cost-cutting measures were then adopted in an attempt to adjust audit work to the (minimal) audit fee, this may result in less audit work and, hence, in reduced audit quality.

In relation to (b) above, Pratt (1990, p. 78) points out that rather than an innocent party, who relies on an auditor's skill and professional judgment in good faith, bearing the cost of the auditor's negligence (as a consequence of the auditor's liability being limited), the audit firm should carry the burden. Indeed, to Pratt, a particularly strong argument against any form of limitation of auditors' liability is the ability of an audit firm to spread the risk of potential damages for negligence through professional indemnity insurance and/or increased audit fees. Pratt cites a Federal judge in the American case of *Rusch Factors* v *Levin* [1968] 284 F Supp. 85 in support of his argument. The judge asked:

> Why should an innocent reliant party be forced to carry the weighty burden of an accountant's professional malpractice? Isn't the risk of loss more easily distributed and fairly spread by imposing it on the accounting profession, which can pass the cost on to the entire consuming public? (as reported, Pratt, 1990, p. 79)

Against these views, audit firms would point to the decline in the capacity of the insurance market and their inability (particularly for the large firms) to secure – at any cost – the level of professional indemnity insurance they desire and need.

(iv) Enshrining contributory negligence (or proportional liability) in statute law

An alternative suggestion for limiting auditors' liability is that of giving statutory recognition to the principle of contributory negligence (or, equivalently, proportional liability). Under this principle, damages are awarded against those responsible for a plaintiff's loss in proportion to their responsibility for (or contribution to) that loss. For example, if a court held that a plaintiff's loss was caused equally by negligence on the part of the company's auditors and its directors, then the auditors and the directors would each be responsible for meeting half of the damages awarded.

At present in the UK, the law relating to negligence generally falls within the ambit of common (that is, court) law rather than statute law. The principle of contributory negligence (proportional liability) already exists within the common law but, to date, judges in the UK appear not to have applied it in cases involving auditors. Hence, it has been proposed that legislation be enacted requiring the courts, in any case involving auditors (or other professional groups to which it applies), to ascertain the extent of the auditors' negligence *vis-à-vis* that of any other party, for example, the auditees' directors, and apportioning blame, and hence damages, accordingly. Such legislation already exists in the USA and, as the *AWA* case discussed in Chapter 15 (section 15.3.1) shows, it is also in place in Australia.[50] Further, research conducted in the EU, investigating the preferences of various interest groups for alternative means of limiting auditors' liability, found that respondents from the investor, banker and company groups favoured proportional liability (EU, 2007).[51]

Proportionate liability offers significant advantages for auditors and plaintiffs alike. For example, in most cases, auditors are called upon to meet only part, rather than the full amount, of the damages awarded to a successful plaintiff. As a result, there is less likelihood of audit firms being forced out of business as a consequence of meeting damages settlements. Similarly, because damages awarded to a successful plaintiff are derived from more than one source (i.e., errant auditors and company directors), there is greater likelihood than under the alternative means of limiting auditors' liability of him or her recouping the full amount of the loss suffered. Although these benefits are clearly important, probably the single most important advantage of the principle of contributory negligence is the equity it introduces; it attempts to apportion damages against errant parties according to their proportion of (or contribution towards) the cause of the loss suffered by the plaintiff.

(v) Limited liability agreements

The Companies Act (CA) 2006 introduced provisions enabling auditors to enter into limited liability agreements with their audit clients. The Act explains that such an agreement:

> purports to limit the amount of liability owed to a company by its auditor in respect of any negligence, default, breach of duty or breach of trust, occurring in the course of the audit of accounts, of which the auditor may be guilty in relation to the company. (s. 534)

---

[50] Proportional liability was also applied in the portion of the *Barings* case discussed in the appendix to Chapter 15.

[51] As we note in Chapter 15, footnote 24, out-of-court settlements are, in effect, applications of the principle of proportional liability. In reaching the agreed settlement, the auditors implicitly acknowledge their portion of the 'blame' for losses suffered by a client or third party and agree the settlement on this basis. Notwithstanding the findings of the EU study that audit firms favour the statutory cap option for limiting their liability, in discussions with one of the authors, senior audit partners in a number of large and middle-tier firms expressed the view that proportional liability is the most equitable means of limiting auditors' liability.

However, in order to be valid, the agreement must meet three criteria. The agreement must:

(a) relate to only one financial year and specify the year in which it applies;

(b) be authorised by a resolution passed by the members of the company:
- before the company enters into the agreement, approving the agreement's principal terms;[52] or
- if after the agreement has been entered into, approving the agreement.

A private (but not a public) company may also pass a resolution before the company enters into the agreement, waiving the need for approval. The members of a company (whether private or public) may withdraw authorisation by passing a resolution to that effect before the company enters into the agreement or, if the agreement has been entered into, before the beginning of the financial year to which it relates;

(c) not limit the auditor's liability to less than an amount which is:
fair and reasonable in all the circumstances of the case having regard (in particular) to –
(a) the auditor's responsibilities under [CA 2006],
(b) the nature and purpose of the auditor's contractual obligations to the company, and
(c) the professional standards expected of him [or her]. (CA 2006, s. 537)

Additionally, the company must disclose in a note to its financial statements the fact that it has entered into a liability limitation agreement with its auditor, the principal terms of the agreement and the date of the members' resolution approving it (or, in the case of a private company, waiving the need for approval) (Simmons & Simmons, 2007).

The CA 2006, s. 535(4), specifies:
it is immaterial how a liability limitation agreement is framed. In particular, the limit on the amount of the auditor's liability need not be a sum of money, or a formula, specified in the agreement.

However, the Act does not provide guidance on how the amount that is 'fair and reasonable in the circumstances' might be arrived at.

In response to requests from both the auditing profession and market participants, in December 2007, the FRC published draft guidance on auditor liability agreements (FRC, 2007). According to the FRC:

---

[52] According to CA 2006, s. 536(4):
The "principal terms" of an agreement are terms specifying, or relevant to the determination of –
(a) the kind (or kinds) of acts or omissions covered,
(b) the financial year to which the agreement relates, or
(c) the limit to which the auditor's liability is subject.

The guidance aims to provide practical assistance to directors, auditors and shareholders on how to apply the new legislation. In particular it aims to:
- explain what is and is not allowed under the 2006 [Companies] Act;
- set out some of the factors that will be relevant when assessing the case for an agreement;
- explain what matters should be covered in an agreement . . . ; and
- explain the process to be followed for obtaining shareholder approval . . . (para 1.5)

The guidance does not attempt to determine whether particular arrangements will be considered "fair and reasonable". That is because every arrangement will need to be assessed in the context of the particular circumstances. That would ultimately be for the courts to decide in the event of a dispute. (para 1.7)

The provisions of CA 2006 became effective on 6 April 2008; nevertheless, in early 2007 some firms were reportedly discussing with their audit clients (for example, E&Y discussing with BP plc) the form the limitation of their liability might take (Sukhraj, 2007a). Initial reports suggested that a liability cap, set at some multiple of the audit fee and 'proportionality' were the most likely options (Simmons & Simmons, 2007). However, it seems that the pendulum has swung in favour of proportional liability. In October 2007, the director general of the Association of British Insurers (ABI), Stephen Haddrill, stated:

Government has proposed that the limit on auditors' liability should be proportionate to their responsibility. We agree with that. The Companies Act didn't enact the limit in these terms and some [in particular, the audit firms] are still talking of a fixed financial cap on a liability. We can't support that and we will red top any company[53] that agrees such a cap with their auditor. (as reported, Sukhraj, 2007b).

The National Association of Pension Funds (NAPF) has backed the ABI's position. Sukhraj (2007b) reports an NAPF spokesman as saying: "We are not in favour of capped liability. We are in favour of . . . proportional liability. We need a party to be liable for their portion of any loss". Conveying the significance of the ABI's and NAPF's stance on the issue, Sukhraj (2007b) notes that, between them, members of these associations control investment funds of more than £2,000 billion. According to informed lawyers, since the ABI gave its 'red top' warning, the FTSE 100 companies (the 100 largest companies listed on the London Stock Exchange)[54] have signalled that they are unlikely to agree to a fixed cap on their auditors' liability (Sukhraj, 2007c).

---

[53] A 'red top' is a serious governance warning given by the ABI (Sukhraj, 2007b).

[54] FTSE is an abbreviation of 'Financial Times Stock Exchange'. It is an independent company that originated as a joint venture between the *Financial Times* newspaper (FT) and the London Stock Exchange (LSE). FTSE has developed a wide array of share indices including the FTSE 100 (the 100 largest companies by market capitalisation listed on the LSE; these represent more than 80 per cent of the entire market capitalisation of the LSE) and the FTSE 250 (comprising the next 250 largest companies on the LSE; these companies represent about 15 per cent of the market capitalisation of the LSE).

It remains to be seen the extent to which companies will be willing to enter into limited liability agreements with their auditors and the manner in which auditors' liability will be limited. On the face of it, the statutory provisions seem to offer protection for auditors who perform sub-standard audits and the question arises as to why auditors who are negligent, or in breach of a duty or trust, should not be held fully liable for the adverse consequences of their deficient performance. However, if companies agree to limit their auditors' liability by means of proportional liability arrangements, then auditors will remain liable for the proportion of harm they cause any plaintiff – and they have a strong incentive to perform high quality audits and, thereby, avoid any liability!

It should be noted that the CA 2006 provisions only relate to limiting auditors' liability to their audit clients. It does not affect the ability of third parties to recover damages from an auditor under the common law if they can prove that: (i) the auditor owed them a duty of care, (ii) the auditor was negligent and (iii) they suffered a loss as a result of that negligence. Further, if a company enters into a limited liability agreement with its auditor, it must disclose the existence and principal terms of the agreement in its annual financial statements. As a result, the company's shareholders are informed and, if they object to the limitation of liability, they can sell their shareholding in the company.

Notwithstanding the discussions that are proceeding in the UK, the final form of limited liability agreements may, in fact, be determined by the EU. In accordance with the EU 8th Directive (2006), the European Commission engaged consultants, London Economics, to conduct a study of the impact of current auditor liability rules in the 27 EU Member States. The study's key findings (London Economics, 2006) are as follows.

    (a)   There is a wide range of auditor liability regimes within EU Member States. For example, in some countries (such as France) auditors owe a duty of care both to their clients and to third parties and auditors may not limit their liability. In other countries (such as Germany), auditors owe a duty of care to their clients but a duty to third parties is owed only in narrowly defined exceptional circumstances. In Germany, as in Belgium, Austria and Slovenia, auditors' exposure to liability is limited by means of a statutory cap.

    (b)   Despite assertions to the contrary, limiting auditors' liability is unlikely to result in complacency and reduced audit quality.

    (c)   Limiting auditors' liability is likely to lower the barriers to firms entering the audit market and thus reduce the concentration of audit supply.

    (d)   Liability indemnity insurance for large amounts has become less available to auditors in recent years.

(e) If limiting auditors' liability is adopted as EU policy, Member States may require some flexibility as regards the form of implementation.

In January 2007, McCreevy, the EU Internal Markets Commissioner, who has made it clear that he believes auditors' liability needs to be limited so as to ensure that another Big Four accounting firm does not collapse,[55] issued a Consultation Document (EU, 2007) seeking views on the following four possible approaches to limiting auditors' liability in the EU:

- a single monetary cap on auditors' liability set at EU level;
- a cap on liability depending on company size (based on market capitalisation);
- a cap on liability based on the size of the audit fee;
- proportionate liability.

As may be seen from Figure 16.5, responses to the Consultation Document tend to be polarised between the auditing profession (with some support from other respondents from Member States with an existing limitation of auditors' liability regime) and investors, bankers and companies – especially those from Member States with no current mechanism for limiting auditors' liability.

Figure 16.5: Summarised results of EU consultation on limiting auditors' liability

Views of auditing profession respondents and some other respondents from Member States with existing limited liability arrangements	Views of investor, banker and company respondents, especially those from Member States with no existing limited liability arrangements
Favour an EU-wide limitation on auditors' liability.	Oppose an EU-wide limitation on auditors' liability.
Believe that reform of auditors' liability could effectively protect against 'catastrophic losses' (i.e., losses that could result in the demise of another large auditing firm).	Reject the idea that catastrophic losses to auditing firms represent a real risk that should be addressed.
Limiting auditors' liability would reduce barriers to entry to the audit market and thus reduce market concentration.	Limiting auditors' liability is not an appropriate means by which to tackle the issue of audit market concentration.
There is no evidence of lower quality auditing in Member States in which auditors' liability is limited. The auditing profession believes that maintaining unlimited liability could lead to a decrease in audit quality as a result of 'defensive auditing'.	Limiting auditors' liability would have a negative impact on audit quality as there would be reduced incentive to conduct high quality audits.
Favour limitation based on a 'liability cap' or a combination of proportionate liability and a cap.	If a limitation of auditors' liability regime is to be adopted, proportionate liability is the preferred option.

Source: Adapted from *Summary Report, Consultation on Auditors' Liability* (EU, 2007)

---

[55] In 1998 the former Big Six firms was reduced to five with the merger of Price Waterhouse and Coopers & Lybrand; in 2002, Arthur Andersen collapsed following the Enron debacle.

16.4 SUMMARY

In this chapter we have explored the issue of how auditors' exposure to legal liability may be avoided or limited. More particularly, we have discussed measures individual audit firms may implement in order to ensure that audits conducted by the firm are of a consistently high standard. We have also examined the activities of the RSBs and the AIU in the UK that are designed to monitor the performance of registered auditors and the audits of public interest entities, respectively. Such monitoring seeks to ensure that audits are conducted in accordance with auditing, ethical and quality control standards and, in the case of the AIU inspections, that audit judgments are appropriate.

Additionally, we have discussed five means by which auditors' exposure to liability may be limited, namely, the incorporation of audit firms as LLCs or LLPs, the introduction of a statutory or regulatory cap on auditors' liability, statutory recognition of the principle of contributory negligence (or proportionate liability), and limited liability agreements between companies and their auditors. We have observed that, although the law has been changed to enable audit firms to form LLCs or LLPs, while each of the Big Four firms has formed an LLP, relatively few firms have taken advantage of this opportunity. We have also noted that, as a means of limiting auditors' liability, proportional liability has much to recommend it but, apart from its possible use as a basis for limited liability agreements, it has not (yet) found favour with the UK Government. This may well change if proportional liability is adopted as EU policy for limiting auditors' liability.

SELF-REVIEW QUESTIONS

16.1 List six elements of a good system of quality control for audit firms.

16.2 List six specific quality control responsibilities of audit engagement partners.

16.3 Explain briefly the rationale underlying the introduction of mechanisms designed to monitor auditors' performance.

16.4 Outline the key features of the general process of monitoring auditors' performance.

16.5 List two ways in which monitoring by the Recognised Supervisory Bodies (RSBs) and the Audit Inspection Unit (AIU) differ and give reasons to explain these differences.

16.6 Evaluate briefly the effectiveness of monitoring auditors' performance in the United Kingdom.

16.7 Given that systems of quality control have been established in audit firms and that auditors' performance is monitored by the RSBs, audit failures should be a thing of the past. Explain briefly:
   (a) why audit failures still occur; and
   (b) the checks which society has in place to ensure that auditors responsible for causing harm to others as a result of sub-standard work do not go unpunished.

16.8 List two advantages and two disadvantages of audit firms forming:
   (a) limited liability companies (LLCs); and
   (b) limited liability partnerships (LLPs).

16.9 List two advantages and two disadvantages of the introduction of:
   (a) a 'cap' on auditors' liability; and
   (b) contributory negligence (proportional liability).

16.10 Discuss briefly the statutory provisions enabling auditors to limit their liability and how they might be implemented.

REFERENCES

Accountancy Age. (2007a, 21 February). Deloitte ordered to pay £66 m in Parmalat settlement. *Accountancy Age*, www.accountancyage.com/articles/print/2183799.

Accountancy Age. (2007b, 6 August). Deloitte to pay £81 m over Adelphia collapse. *Accountancy Age*, www.accountancyage.com/articles/print/2195654.

Association of Chartered Certified Accountants (ACCA). (1992 to 2004 inclusive). *Annual Reports on Audit Regulation to the Secretary of State for Trade and Industry.* London: ACCA.

Audit Inspection Unit (AIU). (2005). *2004/5 Audit Quality Inspections: Public Report.* London: Financial Reporting Council.

Audit Inspection Unit (AIU). (2006). *2005/6 Audit Quality Inspections: Public Report.* London: Financial Reporting Council.

Audit Inspection Unit (AIU). (2007). *2006/7 Audit Quality Inspections: Public Report.* London: Financial Reporting Council.

Audit Inspection Unit (AIU). (2008). *Scope of Independent Inspection 2008/9.* London: Financial Reporting Council.

Davies, J. (2001, 27 March). Insight: LLPs – Safety in Numbers. *Accountancy Age*, pp. 24–25.

European Union (EU). (2006). *Directive 2006/43/EC of the European Parliament and Council on statutory audits of annual accounts and consolidated accounting.* Brussels: EU.

European Union (EU). (2007). *Summary Report, Consultation on Auditors' Liability.* Brussels: EU Directorate General for Internal Market and Services.

Evers, C.J., and Pearson, D.B. (1990, June). Lessons learned from peer review. *Singapore Accountant*, 19–23.

Fearnley, S., and Page, M. (1992). Counting the cost of audit regulation. *Accountancy* **109**(1181), 21–22.

Fearnley, S., and Page, M. (1993). Audit regulation – one year on. *Accountancy* **111**(1193), 59–60.

Financial Reporting Council (FRC). (2007). *FRC Working Group on Auditor Liability Limitation Agreements: Draft Guidance.* London: FRC.

Fisher, L. (2007). Boom boom. Firms are enjoying a second year of inflation-busting growth. *Accountancy* **140**(1367), 22–24.

Flint, D. (1980). Quality control policies and procedures – the prospect for peer review. *The Accountant's Magazine* **84**(884), 63–66.

Flint, D. (1988). *Philosophy and Principles of Auditing.* London: Macmillan.

Hardcastle, A. (1988). Going to the Government, cap in hand. *Accountancy* **101**(1133), 15–16.

Hinks, G. (2001a, 6 April). Howells welcomes E&Y into LLP fold. *Accountancy Age*, www.accountancyage. com/News/1120208.

Hinks, G. (2001b, 12 April). Ernst & Young is first LLP. *Accountancy Age*, p. 3.

Institute of Chartered Accountants in England and Wales (ICAEW), Institute of Chartered Accountants of Scotland (ICAS), Institute of Chartered Accountants in Ireland (ICAI). (1992 to 2004 inclusive). *Audit Regulation: Annual Reports to the DTI.* London: ICAEW, ICAS, ICAI.

International Federation of Accountants (IFAC). (2006). *Code of Ethics for Professional Accountants.* New York: IFAC.

Irish Auditing & Accounting Supervisory Authority (IAASA). (2007). *Annual Report 2006.* Dublin: IAASA.

Kemeny, L. (1999, 2 December). LLPs set for fast track through Parliament. *Accountancy Age*, p. 6.

Lee, M. (2002, 2 May). The debate: LLPs – Just delaying the inevitable. *Accountancy Age*, p. 12.

London Economics. (2006). *Study on the Economic Impact of Auditors' Liability Regimes (MARKT/2005/24/F0.* Final report to EC-DG Internal Market and Services. London: London Economics.

Loxton, L. (2001a, 7 March). Full steam ahead for LLPs. *Accountancy Age*, www. accountancyage.com/news/1118722.

Loxton, L. (2001b, 29 March). Limited Liability Partnerships 'normal' in five years. *Accountancy Age*, p. 1.

Moizer, P. (1994). *Review of Recognised Supervisory Bodies: A Report to the Department of Trade & Industry on the Audit Monitoring Process.* (Unpublished).

Norris, F. (2007, 7 July). PricewaterhouseCoopers to pay Tyco investors $225 million. *New York Times*, www.nytimes.com/2007/07/07/business/07tyco.

Pasricha, N. (2002, 1 May). The debate: LLPs – Changing nature of our business. *Accountancy Age*, p. 12.

Professional Oversight Board (POB). (2006). *Report to the Secretary of State for Trade and Industry. Year to 31 March 2006.* London: Financial Reporting Council.

Professional Oversight Board (POB). (2007). *Report to the Secretary of State for Business, Enterprise & Regulatory Reform. Year to 31 March 2007.* London: Financial Reporting Council.

Pratt, M.J. (1990). *External Auditing: Theory and Practice in New Zealand.* New Zealand: Longman Paul.

Securities and Exchange Commission (SEC). (2004, 20 Oct). *KPMG LLP and four auditors sanctioned for improper professional conduct in connection with Gemstar-TV Guide International Inc. audits.* Washington DC: SEC, Press Release 2004-147.

Simmons & Simmons. (2007, 22 August). *Audit liability*, www.elexica.com/briefdic. aspx?cat =42&id=6356.

Smith, P. (2001, 27 June). E&Y reaches LLP landmark. *Accountancy Age*, www. accountancyage.com/News/1122573.

Sukhraj, P. (2007a, 28 June). FTSE giants confirm audit liability cap discussions. *Accountancy Age*, www.accountancyage.com/accountancyage/news/2193043.

Sukhraj, P. (2007b, 11 October). Investors lay down law on liability caps. *Accountancy Age*, www.accountancyage.com/accountancyage/news/2200885.

Sukhraj, P. (2007c, 11 October). FTSE 100 and auditors in liability standoff. *Accountancy Age*, www.accountancyage.com/accountancyage/news/2200884.

Tutty, R. (2001, 29 March). Headstart: LLPs – Is an LLP the right choice for you? *Accountancy Age*, p. 26.

Wallace, W.A., & Wallace, J.J. (1990). Learning from peer review. *CPA Journal* **60**(5), 48–53.

Wood, A.M., & Sommer Jr, A.A. (1985). Statements in quotes. *Journal of Accountancy* **156**(5), 122–131.

Woodley, K. (1991). Introducing audit regulation. *Accountancy* **107**(1159), 60–61.

Zea, A. (2001, 4 October). LLPs too costly for small businesses. *Accountancy Age*, p. 3.

ADDITIONAL READING

Cahan, S.F., and Zhang, W. (2006). After Enron: auditor conservatism and ex-Andersen clients. *The Accounting Review* **81**(1), 49–83.

Favere-Marchesi, M. (2000). Audit quality in ASEAN. *The International Journal of Accounting* **35**(1), 121–149.

Fédération des Experts Comptables Européens (FEE). (2007). *Quality assurance arrangements across Europe.* Brussels: FEE.

Financial Reporting Council (FRC). (2008). *The Audit Quality Framework.* London: FRC.

Francis, J.R. (2004). What do we know about audit quality? *The British Accounting Review* **36**(4), 345–368.

Institute of Chartered Accountants in England and Wales (ICAEW). (1996). *Finding a Fair Solution. A Discussion paper on Professional Liability.* London: ICAEW.

Institute of Chartered Accountants in England and Wales (ICAEW). (2000). *Towards Better Auditing.* London: ICAEW, Audit and Assurance Faculty.

King, R.R., and Schwartz, R. (2000). An experimental investigation of auditors' liability: implications for social welfare and exploration of deviations from theoretical predictions. *The Accounting Review* **75**(4), 429–451.

O'Sullivan, N. (2000). The impact of board composition and ownership on audit quality: evidence from large UK companies. *British Accounting Review* **32**(4), 397–414.

Richards, I. (2004). *Bringing Audit back from the Brink (Auditor liability and the need to overhaul a key investor protection framework).* London: Morley Fund Management.

17 Environmental Management Systems and Audits

LEARNING OBJECTIVES

After studying the material in this chapter you should be able to:
- explain briefly the development of (internal) environmental audits;
- describe the key components of an environmental management system (EMS);
- outline the requirements for organisations to qualify for ISO 14001 and Europe's Eco-management and audit scheme (EMAS) certification and highlight the key differences between the two sets of requirements;
- explain the objective, scope and process of an environmental audit;
- outline the contents of (internal) environmental audit reports, environmental statements and environmental verification reports;
- discuss the professional requirements of environmental auditors;
- discuss the advantages and disadvantages to companies of having environmental audits.

The following publications are particularly relevant to this chapter:

- ISO 14001: *Environmental Management Systems* (International Organization for Standardization, 2004)
- *Eco-management and Audit Scheme* (EMAS) (Regulation (EC) No 761/2001 of the European Parliament and of the Council, 2001)[1]

---

[1] In this chapter we cite this Regulation as EMAS 2001.

17.1 INTRODUCTION

During the past 30 or so years, society's awareness of the need to take care of the environment and, more particularly, of the need for businesses to operate in an environmentally considerate manner has grown at a phenomenal rate. Society's level of concern about the environment today is reflected in the almost daily media reports about environmental issues. These cover, for example, industrial plants' chimneys belching forth clouds of unsightly, odorous and potentially dangerous gaseous wastes; reputedly harmful radioactive emissions from radio and mobile telephone masts; spillages of hazardous chemicals from tankers causing motorway closures and warnings to householders to keep doors and windows closed; and dire warnings about the harmful effects of greenhouse gas emissions. Society's concern is also reflected in the adoption of 'green policies' by all major political parties, in the emergence of formal environmental performance standards such as the International Standards Organization's ISO 14001: *Environmental management systems* and Europe's *Eco-management and audit scheme* (EMAS), and in the development of indices such as the FTSE4Good, the Dow Jones Sustainability Index, and the Carbon Disclosure Project's Climate Leadership Index.[2] The current position is succinctly conveyed by the British Safety Council (BSC) and Ethical Investments Research Services (EIRiS) as follows:

- With increased public awareness of environmental issues, stricter national and international legislation, and significant liabilities for non-compliance, the next five years will require all organisations to proactively manage their environmental impacts. (BSC, 2007, p. 1)

- Public concern about environmental degradation, climate change and water availability has grown in recent years. Protests, shareholder actions, investor pressure, regulation and the introduction of initiatives such as the European carbon emissions trading scheme have focused the attention of businesses onto these concerns. In recent years, there has been a steady expansion in the number of companies seeking to actively manage their environmental impacts as well as ongoing improvements in the standards of these efforts. (EIRiS, 2007, p. 53)

Since the early 1990s, companies in the United Kingdom (UK) and elsewhere have increasingly sought to demonstrate their concern for the environment by qualifying for recognised standards such as ISO 14001 and EMAS and/or publishing information about their efforts to manage their environmental impacts. However, the form of companies' reporting on their environmental performance varies widely – from brief statements in their annual reports to extensive, stand-alone environmental reports complete with photographs, graphs and other diagrammatic and pictorial representations of relevant information. Further, particularly since the turn of the century, as political, media and public

---

[2] These indices are explained in appendix to Chapter 18.

concern about environmental issues has broadened to include the exploitation of labour (especially 'sweatshops' and child labour), unfair trade practices, and other corporate responsibility issues, so companies (especially major public companies) have widened the coverage of their reports. The expanded reports first took the form of 'environmental and social' reports but these were quickly displaced by wide-ranging 'sustainability' (or 'corporate responsibility') reports, providing details of the relevant company's environmental, social and economic performance.

In the absence of universally accepted non-financial reporting standards, the range and quality of the information provided in environmental or sustainability reports differs significantly. The credibility of the information provided also differs markedly; some reports are not subject to any external assurance (or audit) and where they are assured, in the absence of generally accepted reporting and assurance standards, the level of assurance given on the reliability of the information varies widely.

In this chapter we focus on the emergence of environmental reporting and auditing and consider, in some detail, the requirements of ISO 14001 and EMAS. More specifically, we clarify some of the confusing terminology associated with environmental and sustainability reporting, and with environmental audits and assurance engagements, and then trace (albeit briefly) the development of environmental auditing. We also explain the key elements of environmental management systems and outline the objectives, scope and process of environmental audits. Additionally, we examine the reasons for companies reporting their environmental performance and the EMAS requirement for certified organisations to provide, annually, an externally verified environmental statement. Before concluding the chapter we explore the advantages and disadvantages attaching to environmental audits. In Chapter 18 we explore the development of, and key issues relating to, sustainability (or corporate responsibility) reporting and associated assurance engagements.

17.2 ENVIRONMENTAL REPORTING AND AUDITING: CLARIFYING THE JARGON

Considerable confusion exists in the environmental (or sustainability) reporting and auditing arena about the meaning of various terms. For example, some commentators use the term 'environmental reporting' to mean reporting about a company's performance in relation to certain environmental factors; others use the term to embrace the company's performance in respect of social (and also, in some cases, economic) as well as environmental matters. Lightbody (2000) reports similar confusion in respect of the term 'environmental audit'. She explains:

> At present [the term] is used both in practice and in the literature to refer to a wide range of environmental assessments and reviews.... For example, a recent publication jointly sponsored by IFAC [International Federation of Accountants] and AARF [Australian Accounting Research Foundation][3] referred to 'environmental audits' as including:
> - assessments of site contamination;
> - environmental impact assessments of planned investments;
> - environmental due diligence audits (pre-acquisition audits);
> - the audit of corporate environmental performance reports; and
> - the audit of the entity's compliance with environmental laws and regulations. (p. 152)

A review of these various types of audits reveals that most are internal audits – audits conducted for a company's directors or senior executives. However, the term also embraces "the audit of corporate environmental performance reports", which is similar in nature to the external audit of a company's financial statements. In order to ensure that we and our readers apply the same meaning to terms we use in this and the next chapter, we have drawn on EMAS 2001, ISO 14001 (1996),[4] and the Fédération des Experts Comptables Européens (FEE) Discussion paper: *Providing assurance on sustainability reports* (FEE, 2002) to define them as set out in Figure 17.1.

For the purposes of this and Chapter 18 we need to highlight the distinction between:

(a) an *environmental audit*, which is concerned with an organisation's environmental management system and its outcome in terms of environmental performance. Such an audit is conducted for *internal management purposes*; and

(b) an *assurance or verification engagement*, which is concerned with verifying (or providing assurance on) information about the organisation's environmental (and, usually, also its social and economic) performance. Such an engagement is designed to add credibility to the information provided for *parties external to the organisation*.

In this chapter we are concerned with environmental audits; we discuss assurance engagements in Chapter 18.

---

[3] Lightbody cites the relevant reference as: International Federation of Accountants (1995). *The audit profession and the environment.* Caulfield, Australia: Australian Accounting Research Foundation, p. 6.

[4] ISO 14001 was revised in 2004 but the meaning ascribed to defined terms remained unchanged.

Figure 17.1: **Definitions of terms associated with environmental and sustainability reporting and auditing**

Term	Definitions
Environment	Surroundings in which an organisation operates, including air, water, land, natural resources, flora, fauna, humans, and their interrelationships.
Environmental policy	An organisation's aims and principles with respect to its overall environmental performance. The policy provides a framework for action and for setting and reviewing environmental objectives and targets.
Environmental objective	An overall environmental goal, arising from the environmental policy, that an organisation sets itself to achieve, and which is quantifiable where practicable.
Environmental target	A detailed performance requirement, quantified where practicable, that is applicable to all or part(s) of an organisation. It arises from the environmental objectives, and needs to be set and met in order to achieve those objectives.
Environmental performance	The results of an organisation's management of its environmental aspects, that is, the interaction of its activities, products or services with the environment.
Environmental aspect	An element of an organisation's activities, products or services that can interact with the environment.
Environmental impact	Any change to the environment, whether adverse or beneficial, wholly or partially resulting from an organisation's activities, products or services.
Environmental management system (EMS)	The part of the organisation's overall management system that includes the organisational structure, planning activities, responsibilities, practices, procedures, processes and resources that are concerned with developing, implementing, achieving, reviewing and maintaining its environmental policy.
Environmental audit	A systematic, documented, periodic and objective evaluation of an organisation's EMS and environmental performance, and communication of the results of the process to the organisation's directors or senior executives. It is conducted with the aim of: (i) establishing the conformity of the organisation's EMS with the criteria set by the directors or senior executives; (ii) assessing compliance with the organisation's environmental policy and achievement of its environmental objectives and targets; (iii) facilitating improvement in the organisation's environmental performance.
Internal environmental auditor	An individual (or a team), internal or external to the organisation, who acts on behalf of the organisation's directors or senior executives. The individual or team possesses, individually or collectively, the competences required to conduct an environmental audit and is sufficiently independent of the activities audited to make an objective judgment.
Sustainability	The concept of meeting the needs of the present generation without compromising the ability of future generations to meet their own needs. It encompasses environmental, social and economic factors. A sustainability report contains disclosures about the sustainability performance of an organisation.
Environmental report	A report of an organisation dealing with the environmental dimension of sustainability.
Economic	The dimension of sustainability dealing with the economic impacts of an organisation, that is, the effects of the organisation's activities, products or services on the economy or economies in which it operates.
Social	The dimension of sustainability that relates to the human impacts of an organisation. These include the organisation's working conditions and community involvement.
Assurance or verification engagement	An engagement designed to provide assurance about, and thus to enhance the credibility of, information provided for external parties by an organisation's directors or senior executives.

17.3 DEVELOPMENT OF ENVIRONMENTAL AUDITING AND ENVIRONMENTAL MANAGEMENT SYSTEMS

17.3.1 Overview of development of environmental auditing

Environmental auditing is not new. Indeed, the International Chamber of Commerce (ICC, 1991) noted that Arthur D. Little, a firm of consultants in the United States of America (USA) specialising in environmental issues, has been conducting environmental audits around the world since the 1920s. However, unlike financial statement audits, these are audits of organisations' environmental phenomena that are conducted for the entities' management (directors and/or executives). Such audits have been defined as:

[A]management tool comprising a systematic, documented, periodic and objective evaluation of the performance of the organisation, management system and processes designed to protect the environment with the aim of:
  (i)   facilitating management control of practices which may have an impact on the environment;
  (ii) assessing compliance with the environmental policy, including environmental objectives and targets of the organisation. [EMAS, 2001, Article 2(l)]

The Confederation of British Industry (CBI) further explains that an environmental audit is:

The systematic examination of the interaction between any business operation and its surroundings. This includes all emissions to air, land and water; legal constraints; the effects on the neighbouring community, landscape and ecology; and the public's perception of the operating company in the local area. (CBI, 1990)

Despite their relatively long history, interest in environmental audits remained slight until the early 1980s. Since then they have burgeoned and today are fairly commonplace in major companies (particularly those in the extractive, manufacturing and chemicals sectors) throughout the industrialised world. Their rapid growth during the past couple of decades seems to be linked to two related stimuli – environmental catastrophes and regulation.

Since the 1970s catastrophes have caused immense harm to humans, the environment and property. They include, for example:
- dioxins released into the air by a chemical plant in Sevsoin, Italy in 1976 which harmed 250 people, including pregnant women (Natu, 1999, p. 133);
- a huge oil spill in the English Channel in 1978 when the super tanker *Amoco Cadiz* split into two. Much marine life was killed and the French coastline was badly polluted (Natu, 1999, p. 133);
- emissions of tons of toxic gas from the Union Carbide plant in Bhopal, India in 1984 which killed an estimated 3,800 people (Encyclopedia Britannica, 2002);
- radioactive material released into the atmosphere from the nuclear power station at Chernobyl, Ukraine, in 1986. "Beyond 32 immediate deaths,

several thousand radiation-induced illnesses and cancer deaths were expected in the long term" (Encyclopedia Britannica, 2002);

- a spillage of 10.9 million tons of crude oil from the super tanker *Exxon Valdez* when it ran aground a reef in Prince William Sound, South Alaska in 1989. The spillage had disastrous effects on marine life and coastal ecology in the Sound (Encyclopedia Britannica, 2002).

Disasters such as these, combined with the all too evident effects of climate change (in the form of severe droughts and floods, melting glaciers and ice caps, a rise in sea level, and changing – or disappearing – habitats for flora and fauna, etc.), which is attributed to greenhouse gas emissions, have caused a global outcry and demands that corporate activities be regulated so that organisations responsible for environmental damage are held accountable and made to suffer severe financial penalties or other sanctions.

Since the mid-1970s, industrialised nations have become more aware of the damage businesses (and individuals) can – and do – inflict on the environment and the need to implement preventative measures. Governments, first in the USA but rapidly followed by the UK, Continental Europe, Australia, New Zealand and elsewhere, have responded to society's concerns and pressure from environmental activists, and have introduced a wealth of laws and regulations designed to protect aspects of the environment. Such laws and regulations have had a major impact on businesses and how they conduct their activities. This has been noted by Roussey (1992), for example, who explains:

> Entities operating in this country [the US] are now subject to a growing number of environmental laws and regulations. As a result, these entities may be responsible for significant clean-up costs and liabilities if they have not appropriately disposed of hazardous wastes. They may also be liable for personal injury claims from employees and customers if there are toxic problems in the workplace or associated with their products. These concerns relate not only to the original owners, operators, or users of waste disposal sites, but they also relate to other third parties not originally associated with a contaminated site, or disposal at such a site. (pp. 47–48).

Of the plethora of laws and regulations which exist at both the Federal and State level in the USA, perhaps the most far-reaching and significant are the Congressional Comprehensive Environmental Response, Compensation and Liability Act 1980 (known as CERCLA or 'the Superfund' legislation) and the Superfund Amendment and Reauthorization Act 1986. In the European Union (EU) the key legislative provision, which applies to all Member States, was enacted as Article 130R of the Single European Act 1987. This states:

> 1. Action by the [European] Community relating to the environment shall have the following objectives:
>   (i)   to preserve, protect and improve the quality of the environment;
>   (ii) to contribute towards protecting human health;
>   (iii) to ensure a prudent rational utilization of natural resources.

2. Action by the Community relating to the environment shall be based on the principles that preventive action should be taken, that environmental damage should as a priority be rectified at source, and that the polluter should pay. Environmental protection requirements shall be a component of the Community's other policies.

Guided by this Article, Member States have enacted their own body of laws and regulations. In the UK, probably the most significant and far-reaching environmental legislation is enshrined in the Environmental Protection Act 1990. Vinten (1996) explains that this Act:

represents the beginning of the practical manifestation of the principle that the polluter pays. It also introduces the notion of integrated pollution control. Previously each component of the environment – air, land and water – had its own separate laws and systems of control. Now Her Majesty's Inspectorate of Pollution will control all releases [into the] air, water and land from most polluting industrial processes. . . . Companies have to . . . pay penalties for breaking the specified emission limits. There is a requirement for environmental impact assessments for new developments such as new shopping centres or factories. There is also a legal obligation to minimise waste production . . . Industries covered by the act have to apply for authorization to continue to operate, to make major changes to their plants, or to build new ones. Various bodies, such as the Health and Safety Executive, have to be consulted and then there has to be public advertisement in a local newspaper. Attempting to avoid compliance is a high risk strategy, with serious consequences for both the company and those within it. (pp. 15–16)

Since the mid-1980s, faced by the huge volume of highly complex environmental laws and regulations – and their company's exposure to liability should it wittingly or unwittingly breach one or more of them – company managements have increasingly adopted environmental (compliance) audits. These audits are designed to ensure that the company is complying with all relevant laws and regulations; they generally assess matters such as the company's compliance with:

- occupational health and safety requirements;
- emissions limits and other requirements attaching to a licence to operate;
- regulations governing the generation, storage and disposal of hazardous wastes;

and also its potential liability for the past disposal (on- and off-site) of hazardous substances.

During the late 1980s and early 1990s, as liability for contamination of land and other breaches of environmental law were held to attach not only to the perpetrator but also to third parties such as the purchaser of polluted land, environmental (due diligence) audits also came to be conducted in order to determine whether liability may attach to a transaction such as the purchase of property. Such environmental (due diligence) audits are now commonplace, as the costs of cleaning up contaminated land can run into many millions of pounds and the net to capture those who may be held responsible seems to be spread ever wider. Roussey (1992) reports that in the USA:

The courts have held four classes of parties responsible for clean-up of hazardous waste sites: (1) current owners and operators, (2) owners and operators at the time of the waste disposal, (3) hazardous waste generators, and (4) hazardous waste transporters. ... A recent court decision has also found lenders potentially responsible for the hazardous waste problems of borrowers. (p. 47)

These single transaction environmental (due diligence) audits are also important to ensure that projects can proceed as planned. Hamilton (1997), for example, reports a case where a group of friends purchased land (without an environmental audit) with the intention of finding a developer to build a block of luxury condominiums. They held the property for two years before they found a developer who was interested. Before signing the agreement, the developer's financial backers insisted on an environmental audit. During the audit, broken thermometers were found at the site and the soil was found to be contaminated with mercury and other toxic materials. Perhaps needless to say, the developer walked away from the project and the owners faced enormous clean-up costs, as well as the costs of trying to track down the previous owners to pin liability on them!

Although environmental audits were initially reactive and somewhat single focused in nature – designed to ensure compliance with relevant laws and regulations or to avoid liability or other adverse consequences attaching to a transaction, since the early 1990s they have become more proactive and wide-ranging in character. They are now regarded by many companies as a means of providing management with valuable information (especially where environmental management systems have been established) and of protecting and enhancing the company's reputation.[5]

17.3.2 Development and key features of environmental management systems (EMS)

The trend towards establishing environmental management systems was encouraged by the development of environmental performance certification schemes such as the British Standard (BS) 7750: *Specification for environmental management systems* [British Standards Institute (BSI) 1992], the International Standard ISO 14001: *Environmental management systems*, and Europe's *Eco-management and audit scheme* (EMAS). BS 7750 was introduced in 1992 as the world's first structured environmental management and audit scheme in which companies could seek certification. It was revised in 1994 but withdrawn in 1997 following the introduction of a similar scheme, ISO 14001, in 1996.[6] The development of ISO 14001, which was strongly influenced by BS 7750,

---

[5] The advantages for companies of conducting environmental audits are discussed in section 17.6.

[6] ISO 14001 was revised in 2004 but the meaning ascribed to defined terms remained unchanged.

resulted primarily from the 1992 Rio Earth Summit's international commitment to protect the environment across the world. According to the International Standards Organization (ISO), ISO 14001: "provides a framework for a holistic, strategic approach to the organizations's environmental policy, plans and actions" (iso.org, 2008, p. 1). Participation is voluntary and companies or parts thereof (such as individual sites, divisions or subsidiaries) in any economic sector, in any country, may apply for certification. ISO 14001 has been adopted by the European Committee of Standardisation as the European Standard for all Member States and is accepted as meeting the environmental management system requirements of EMAS.

EMAS was established in 1993 by European Regulation (EC) 1836/93; this was replaced in 2001 by European Regulation (EC) 761/2001 *Allowing voluntary participation by organisations in a Community eco-management and audit scheme (EMAS)*. The scheme was originally intended to be a compulsory environmental management and audit scheme applicable to specific industrial sites. However, faced by industry opposition, it was introduced as a voluntary scheme applicable to organisations (or parts thereof) of any size, in any economic sector, in any Member State of the European Union (EU) or European Economic Area (EEA).[7] According to the Europa and EMAS websites:

> EMAS is a management tool for companies and other organisations to evaluate, report and improve their environmental performance. . . . Its aim is to recognise and reward those organisations that go beyond minimum legal compliance and continuously improve their environmental performance. . . . Environmental management has become a core business issue for many organisations. Minimising the amount of waste that is produced, reducing energy consumption and making more efficient use of resources can all lead to financial cost savings, in addition to helping to protect and enhance the environment. (ec.europa.eu, 2007, emas. org, 2008)

EMAS and ISO 14001 both require registrants to be committed to:
    (i) continuous improvement in environmental performance; and
    (ii) compliance with applicable environmental laws and regulations.
Further, both schemes are structured around the operation of an environmental management system (EMS). As indicated in Figure 17.2, the starting point for establishing a system is an initial review. This enables an organisation (or part thereof) to gain a thorough understanding of the environmental impact of its activities, products and services, applicable environmental laws and regulations and existing environmental management practices. It also provides the 'base line' from which the entity can strive to improve its environmental performance.

---

[7] The EU comprises 27 Member States; the EEA comprises Iceland, Liechtenstein and Norway.

Figure 17.2 also indicates that an EMS comprises a set of elements that together facilitate companies achieving environmental performance improvements. These elements include the following:

(i) *An environmental policy*: this specifies the environmental principles promoted by the organisation's directors and senior executives and provides the framework for setting and reviewing environmental objectives and targets.

Figure 17.2:   Elements of an environmental management system (EMS)

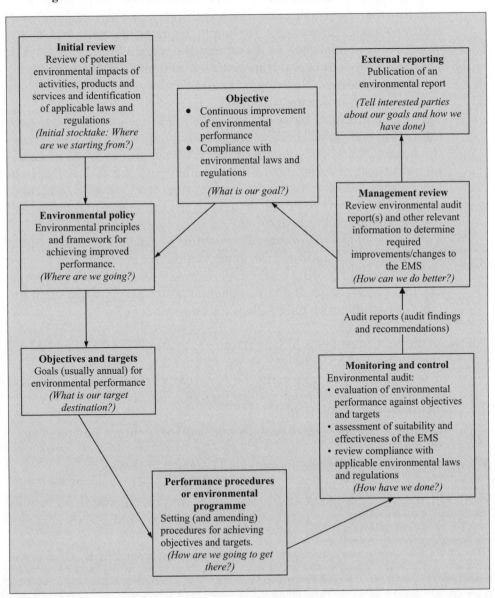

(ii) *Objectives and targets*: these are the specific goals (often set for the ensuing year) towards which environmental performance is to strive and against which performance can be evaluated.

(iii) *Performance procedures or an environmental programme*: this sets out the means by which the objectives and targets are to be achieved.

(iv) *A mechanism for monitoring and controlling environmental performance*: this constitutes the environmental audit by which (i) the company's environmental performance is evaluated against the set objectives and targets, (ii) the operation and effectiveness of the EMS is assessed, and (iii) the company's compliance with relevant environmental laws and regulations is reviewed. The audit generates one or more reports which are communicated to the company's board of directors, (or, if it has one, its environmental committee – a committee of the board) and/or senior executives. They report the audit findings and generally include recommendations for improvement.

(v) *Management review*: based on the audit report(s) and other relevant information, the board of directors (or other appropriate body) reviews the suitability and effectiveness of the EMS and achieved environmental performance. From this review, together with the auditors' recommendations, the directors and/or senior executives are able to identify and implement any required changes to the environmental policy and other elements of the EMS.

(vi) *Publication of an environmental report*: this is usually a summary of the key findings of the audit and recommendations for improvement that are included in the report(s) to the organisation's management. It informs external parties about the environmental performance of the organisation (or part thereof) and its plans for improvement.[8]

Although the elements of an EMS are required by both ISO 14001 and EMAS, organisations with EMAS certification are additionally required:

(i) to have their initial review (in the first year of registration), EMS and environmental audit (and results thereof), verified by an accredited environmental verifier; and

(ii) to publish annually an externally verified (or assured) environmental statement.

We discuss these requirements in sections 17.4 and 17.5, respectively.

Reviewing the components of an EMS, it is evident that environmental audits are crucial to the effective functioning of the system and achievement of

---

[8] The environmental report may constitute the company's external environmental report or it may be an element of a broader company environmental and social report, or corporate responsibility report (as described in Chapter 18). It may also be an environmental report on a single site or a component of the company. Further, the environmental report may be included in the company's annual report or be published as a stand-alone report.

improved environmental performance. They enable evaluation of the suitability and effectiveness of the EMS and appraisal of actual environmental performance against set objectives and targets. From this, opportunities for improvement in the design and operation of the system, and in the company's environmental performance, can be identified.

Although we have outlined the requirements for organisations wishing to gain ISO 14001 or EMAS registration, it seems that relatively few UK companies seek to do so, and some companies which formerly sought certification no longer do so.[9] For example, in 2002, J. Sainsbury, Shell, BP, Scottish Power, British Gas and British Energy were each EMAS and ISO 14001 certified. In 2007, a total of 44 UK companies (or components thereof) were included in the EMAS register (EMAS, 2007) but, of the 2002 registrants identified above, only Scottish Power was included.[10] It appears that many companies perceive greater benefits can be derived from inclusion in the FTSE4Good, Dow Jones Sustainability or other similar index. (These indices are discussed in Chapter 18.) Nevertheless, although they may not be seeking formal environmental performance certification, it is evident from their environmental (or corporate responsibility) reports that most major companies in the UK have either a full EMS or a well-developed environmental programme. It is also evident that although the primary motivator for environmental audits, at least until the mid-1990s, was seeking to avoid liability from arising – either through failure to comply with the "vast tomes of environmental legislation" (Economist, 1990, p. 19) or through unwittingly 'inheriting' liability through a transaction such as an acquisition, environmental audits today are generally wide-ranging and proactive in nature, and are designed to help organisations improve their environmental performance.

---

[9] Elsewhere in Europe, adoption of ISO 14001 and EMAS standards is high, particularly in Finland, Sweden, Germany, Denmark, France and Norway, where, according to EIRiS (2007):

strong public and governmental awareness of environmental issues historically has translated into companies demonstrating strong commitment to manage their environmental impacts. . . . Similarly in Japan a large proportion of companies have adopted ISO 14001 . . . [This] is partly due to the decision by [the Japanese] government to promote ISO 14001, encouraging take-up of the standard by the bulk of companies. ISO 14001 has been widely adopted by Japanese companies, principally as a way of providing customer assurance, and to avoid losing export business to certified firms elsewhere. (pp. 59–60)

[10] The 44 included two FTSE 350 (but no FTSE 100) companies, namely Biffa Waste Services Ltd and INVISTA (UK) Ltd. Scottish Power is no longer a FTSE 350 company as it has merged with Iberdrola but, as may be seen from Figure 17.3, components of Scottish Power remain EMAS and ISO 14001 certified.

FTSE is an abbreviation of 'Financial Times Stock Exchange'. It is an independent company that originated as a joint venture between the *Financial Times* newspaper (FT) and the London Stock Exchange (LSE). FTSE has developed a wide array of share indices, including the FTSE 100 (the 100 largest companies by market capitalisation listed on the LSE; these represent more than 80 per cent of the entire market capitalisation of the LSE); the FTSE 250 (comprising the next 250 largest companies on the LSE; these represent about 15 per cent of the market capitalisation of the LSE) and FTSE4Good. (The FTSE 350 is a combination of the FTSE 100 and FTSE 250 companies representing some 95 per cent of the market capitalisation of the LSE.)

In order to illustrate the nature of EMAS and ISO certification, Figure 17.3 depicts the EMAS and ISO 14001 certification of Scottish Power's environmental management systems in 2007.

Figure 17.3: 2007 EMAS and ISO 14001 certification of Scottish Power's environmental management systems

Environmental Management Systems

Our businesses operate Environmental Management Systems at three levels:
- Systems accredited to the EU Econ-Management and Audit Scheme (EMAS)
- Systems accredited to ISO 14001
- Systems compliant with ISO 14001, but not certified

Site	Type	EMAS	ISO 14001	Non-certified EMS
Atlantic Quay	Office			✓
Cathcart	Office			✓
Longannet	Coal Power Station	✓	✓	
Cockenzie	Coal Power Station		✓	
Rye House	CCGT Station		✓	
Damhead Creek	CCGT Station	✓	✓	
Shoreham	CCGT Station		✓	
Knapton	OC Gas Station		✓	
Hatfield	Gas Storage		✓	
Cruachan	Pumped Storage/Hydro Station		✓	
Galloway	Hydro-electric Scheme			✓
Lanark	Hydro-electric Scheme			✓
Windfarms	Windfarm Operations			✓
Daldowie	Sludge Drying Plant		✓	
Blackburn Mill	CHP Plant		✓	
Pilkington	CHP Plant		✓	
Warrington	Customer Service Centre			✓
Rhostyllen	Customer Service Centre			✓
Wrexham	Customer Service Centre			✓
Drakemire Drive	Office and Stores			✓
Falkirk	Customer Service Centre			✓
East Kilbride	Customer Service Centre			✓
Energy Networks			✓	

Source: www.scottishpower.com/uploads/EnergyManagementSystems

17.4 INTERNAL ENVIRONMENTAL AUDITS

The starting point for an internal environmental audit is definition of its objectives and scope, and identification of those who are to perform the audit. The objectives and scope of the audit are defined by management – generally the board of directors, a committee of the board (such as an audit or environmental issues committee), or senior executives. The audits are designed to meet management's needs.

The objective of the audit may be defined narrowly or broadly. It may be, for example:

- to ensure that the organisation is complying with applicable environmental laws and regulations (or even a subset of these – such as those relating to hazardous wastes);
- to evaluate the effectiveness of an existing waste control or waste treatment process or procedure;
- to identify the environmental impacts of current processes, products and services (with a view to identifying alternatives which are more 'environmentally friendly');
- to identify potential cost savings from waste minimisation and recycling of waste products;
- to identify ways to reduce materials, water and/or energy usage.

Alternatively, the objective may be broader, such as applies in the case of audits performed in accordance with the EMAS or ISO 14001 schemes. The objective may be, for instance:

- to ensure that the EMS is appropriate to the company's activities, products and services (and their environmental impacts) and is operating effectively;
- to ensure that environmental performance complies with the company's environmental policy and procedures, and also with applicable legal and regulatory requirements.

A particular audit may be one in a series of audits, or an element of an audit cycle, whereby all of the company's activities are audited over a period of time, such as three years.[11] However, whatever the time interval, and whether it be narrowly or broadly defined, the objective of an internal environmental audit almost invariably includes (implicitly or explicitly) the formulation of recommendations for improvement.

The scope of the audit (that is, its extent and boundaries in terms of factors such as the physical location(s), subject matter and organisational activities to be audited) is dependent on the audit objective(s). The audit may, for instance,

---

[11] For organisations with EMAS certification, EMAS 2001 Annex II explains:

Over a period of time all activities in a particular organisation shall be subject to an audit. The period of time taken to complete audits of all activities is known as the audit cycle. For small non-complex organisations, it may be possible to audit all activities at one time. For those organisations the audit cycle is the interval between these audits. ... The audit or audit cycle shall be completed ... at intervals no longer than 3 years. (paras 2.1, 2.9)

Companies registered with ISO 14001 are required to have "periodic environmental management system audits" (ISO 14001, para 4.5.3) but no timeframe is specified. However, the audit programme is required to include details of audit frequency (ISO 14001, Annex A, para. A.5.4). ISO 19011: *Environmental Management Systems Auditing* (ISO, 2002), provides guidelines for auditing environmental management systems and complements ISO 14001.

cover the entire organisation (a comprehensive audit), or focus on a department or process (an activity audit) or on one or more sites (a site audit). However, for every audit it is important that the scope, like the audit objective and expected audit outcomes, is clearly defined in writing and agreed with the director(s) or senior executive(s) requesting the audit. In particular, reference should be made to:

    (i)   the subject matter and activities to be covered by the audit;

    (ii) the environmental criteria to be established or used to evaluate performance;

    (iii) the period to be covered by the audit.

As for all other audits, in order to ensure objectivity and freedom from bias, it is important that all members of the audit team are independent of the subject matter and activities to be audited. It is also important that audit team members, individually or collectively, possess the necessary knowledge, skills and experience to achieve the audit objective(s). Because of the range of knowledge and skills that is required for environmental audits, most audit teams are interdisciplinary in nature. The audit team may comprise employees from the part of the organisation being audited, employees from other parts of the organisation, external consultants or auditors, or a combination thereof. Where internal staff are used, their independence from the subject(s) and activities to be audited is of particular importance. The audit objective(s) and scope determine the required size, knowledge, skills and experience of the audit team but, as Maltby (1995) points out:

> The environmental audit potentially requires a knowledge of the legal framework within which the company operates, and also of any forthcoming changes in the law, an understanding of the company's processes, raw materials, products, wastes and energy usage, the effects of each of these on the environment locally and globally, and the ability to suggest ways in which the company might change or improve what it does. Only the largest companies can afford to maintain all these skills permanently in-house. For this reason, it is likely that, whatever the form and purpose of environmental audits, most audit work will be carried out for companies by consultants. (p. 16)

The audit process is much the same as that for an external financial statement audit and it follows a similar set of logical steps, namely:

    (i)   gaining an understanding of the organisation, the subject matter and activity(ies) to be audited;

    (ii) planning the audit;

    (iii) collecting audit evidence;

    (iv) evaluating the evidence, forming conclusions and developing recommendations;

    (v) reporting the audit findings, conclusions and recommendations to the director(s) or senior executive(s) who requested the audit.

These steps are present in all environmental audits but their details vary according to the audit objective(s); for example, the details of a compliance audit will differ from those of a comprehensive or site audit. For purposes of illustration we describe below the steps that usually apply in a comprehensive audit.

(i) Gaining an understanding of the organisation, its environmental impact and its EMS

In order to gain a thorough understanding of the organisation, its environmental impact and its EMS, the audit team leader usually reviews all relevant documentation. This includes, for example, the company's environmental policy, specifications of environmental objectives and targets, procedures manual, staff training records (insofar as they relate to training in environment-related issues), regulatory requirements to which the company is subject, the findings and conclusions of previous environmental audits (whatever their objectives, whether broad or narrow), reports of management reviews of the environmental audit reports (including reports on the suitability and effectiveness of the EMS),[12] and records of accidents and emergencies and how they were dealt with.

The audit team members should also visit the company to meet key personnel and to familiarise themselves with such matters as organisational structure, the attitude of the directors, senior executives and employees to environmental issues, the organisation's functional areas (such as marketing, public relations, legal, production and finance), and its operating factors (such as process discharges – including air, water and noise; site tidiness; water, energy and materials usage; waste and recycling; and occupational health and safety).

(ii) Planning the audit

Based on their understanding of the organisation, its environmental impact and its EMS, the audit team can develop the audit strategy. This should specify, amongst other things:
  (a) the organisational, functional and operating units to be audited;
  (b) those elements of the organisation's EMS that are of high priority (because their effective operation is of particular importance to the effective operation of the entire EMS, or because past audits have identified significant problems, or for some other reason);

---

[12] As noted in section 17.3, management review of environmental audit reports and other relevant information is an integral element of the company's EMS.

(c) the procedures to be used for auditing the various elements of the EMS and the company's environmental performance, and responsibility for performing and reviewing these procedures (that is, devising the audit plan or programme);

(d) the dates and locations where the audit procedures are to be performed;

(e) the time to be taken for the audit as a whole and major segments thereof;

(f) a schedule of meetings to be held with the director(s) or senior executive(s) who requested the audit;

(g) the content and format of the audit report, its expected date of issue and the parties to whom it is to be distributed.

As for an external financial statement audit, the audit strategy and audit plan should be sufficiently flexible to allow changes to be made if such is deemed appropriate as information is gathered during the audit.

(iii) Collecting audit evidence

Sufficient appropriate audit evidence needs to be collected on which to base conclusions about:

(a) the suitability of the EMS to the company, its activities, products and services and their environmental impact; and

(b) the effectiveness of the system's operation and its ability to:
   – effect improved environmental performance, and
   – ensure compliance with relevant legal and regulatory requirements.

Similar to financial statement audits, the evidence is gathered by a variety of procedures including:

• *observation* of activities and conditions to evaluate whether these comply with the company's established EMS criteria;

• *enquiry* of relevant personnel (asking people about the activities they perform and whether they can identify ways in which their – or their area's – environmental performance could be improved);

• *acquiring information from outside sources* – for example, ascertaining measures used by other similar companies or industry norms that afford appropriate benchmarks for evaluating the company's environmental objectives and targets, or about alternative processes that result in less waste, reduced consumption of water and/or energy, or are otherwise more 'environmentally friendly' than those currently used by the company;

- *examination of records and documents* – for example, records of emissions, water and energy usage, waste created and disposed of, health and safety, and staff training;
- *analytical review* – for example, analysing the proportion of inputs to outputs of a process, and evaluating the extent and rate of change in the environmental impact of a particular activity, product or service from one period to the next;
- *tests of details* – for example, testing samples of records of factors such as energy and water usage, emissions, waste created and disposed of and so on, to evaluate whether recorded results correspond with actual results.

(iv) Evaluating the evidence, forming conclusions and developing recommendations

After the audit evidence has been gathered, the audit team should review the results of the audit procedures performed to ascertain whether sufficient appropriate evidence has been gathered for each audit segment and the audit as a whole on which to form conclusions about, for example:

- the suitability of the EMS for the organisation and its activities, products and services and their environmental impact;
- whether the environmental objectives and targets set for the period being audited have been reached or exceeded;
- whether the organisation has complied with all applicable environmental legal and regulatory requirements.

Any material instances of non-conformance with the EMS criteria and procedures should be evaluated to determine their nature (for example, whether they are isolated instances or systemic) and their effect. Additionally, opportunities for the organisation to improve its EMS or environmental performance should be determined and, where appropriate, formulated as recommendations.

(v) Reporting the audit findings, conclusions and recommendations

Before the audit report is prepared, the audit team generally holds a 'closing meeting' with the directors and/or senior executives responsible for the organisation's EMS, environmental performance, and compliance with environmental regulatory requirements, and also those responsible for the functions and activities audited. The purpose of the meeting is to present the audit findings in a factual manner and to ensure that those present understand and acknowledge the findings. It also provides an opportunity for the company's personnel to challenge or question the findings and for any misunderstandings or disagreements to be resolved.

Following the 'closing meeting' the audit report is prepared. It is normally addressed to the company's directors or senior executives who requested the audit and includes the following information:
- the agreed objectives and scope of the audit;
- identification of the functions and activities audited;
- identification of company personnel responsible for the functions and activities audited;
- the criteria against which the audit was conducted;
- the period covered by the audit and the dates of the audit;
- the audit findings, together with reference to supporting evidence;
- conclusions about:
    - the level of compliance with the company's environmental policy and procedures,
    - the company's environmental performance and progress,
    - the suitability of the EMS for the company, its activities, products and services and their environmental impacts,
    - the company's environmental objectives and targets,
    - the effectiveness of the EMS's operation,
    - the effectiveness and reliability of the company's arrangements for monitoring its environmental impacts,
    - the company's compliance with applicable legal and regulatory requirements;
- recommendations for corrective action, where appropriate, or for improvements to the company's EMS, its environmental performance and/or its compliance with applicable legal and regulatory requirements.

The report is also dated and signed by the audit team leader.

It should be recalled that companies (or parts thereof) with EMAS certification must, in addition to regular environmental audits which constitute an element of their EMS, have their initial review (in the first year of registration), EMS and environmental audit (and the results thereof) verified by an accredited environmental verifier. EMAS 2001, Annex V, para 5.5.2, requires the verification process to:

> involve examination of documentation, a visit to the organisation including, in particular, interviews with personnel, preparation of a report to the organisation's management and the organisation's solution of the issues raised by the report.

The environmental verifier's report to the organisation's management is required to specify:
(a) all issues relevant to the work carried out by the environmental verifier;
(b) the starting point of the organisation towards implementation of an environmental management system;
(c) in general, cases of nonconformity with the provisions of this Regulation [i.e., EMAS 2001], and in particular:

      – technical defects in the environmental review, or audit method, or environmental management system, or any other relevant process,

      – points of disagreement with the draft environmental statement, together with details of the amendments or additions that should be made to the environmental statement;[13]

(d) the comparison with the previous [environmental] statements and the performance assessment of the organisation. (EMAS 2001, Annex V, para 5.5.4)

To ensure that environmental verifiers are appropriately qualified, EMAS 2001, Article 4, requires all EU Member States to establish a system for the accreditation of environmental verifiers and for the supervision of their activities. Annex V further requires that, in order to qualify for accreditation, an individual or organisation must possess:

(a) knowledge and understanding of the Regulation [i.e., EMAS 2001], [and] the general functioning of environmental management systems ... ;

(b) knowledge and understanding of the legislative, regulatory and administrative requirements relevant to the activity subject to verification;

(c) knowledge and understanding of environmental issues, including the environmental dimension of sustainable development;

(d) knowledge and understanding of the technical aspects, relevant to environmental issues, of the activity subject to verification;

(e) understanding of the general functioning of the activity subject to verification in order to assess the appropriateness of the management system;

(f) knowledge and understanding of environmental auditing requirements and methodology;

(g) knowledge of information audit ([for the audit of the] Environmental Statement). (Annex V, para 5.2.1)

Additionally, environmental verifiers are to be independent, impartial and objective. Amongst other requirements they (and where the verifier is an organisation, its staff) are to be: "free of any commercial, financial or other pressures which might influence their judgment or endanger trust in their independence of judgment and integrity in relation to their activities". They are also required to: "have documented methodologies and procedures, including quality control mechanisms and confidentiality provisions, for the verification requirements of this Regulation" (Annex V, para 5.2.1).

In respect of the supervision of environmental verifiers, EMAS 2001, Annex V, para 5.3.1, requires the national accreditation bodies with which the particular accredited environmental verifier is registered, to ensure, at regular intervals not exceeding 24 months:

the environmental verifier continues to comply with the accreditation requirements and to monitor the quality of the verifications undertaken. Supervision

---

[13] The environmental statement is discussed in section 17.5.

may consist of office audit, witnessing in organisations, questionnaires, review of environmental statements validated by the environmental verifier and review of validation reports.

This system of 'supervision' is very similar to the 'monitoring' (or 'inspection') of registered auditors, undertaken by the Recognised Supervisory Bodies and Audit Inspection Unit, which we discussed in Chapter 16.

17.5 REASONS FOR COMPANIES REPORTING THEIR ENVIRONMENTAL PERFORMANCE

In June 2000, MacKay (2000) reported: "The number of companies publishing some sort of environmental report has increased exponentially over the last 10 years" (p. 1). Studies by Context (2006) and KPMG (2005)[14] reveal that this trend has continued but, since 2002, it has increased sharply and today is commonplace amongst major companies throughout the world. Remembering that most environmental reporting is undertaken voluntarily by companies, the question arises as to what prompts them to engage in this activity. A key reason is the regulatory framework within which they operate.

Legislation and regulations governing environmental and social performance, and the reporting of that performance, have a significant impact on companies. For example, companies (especially in the USA, but increasingly in the UK) are facing enormous actual or potential liabilities as a result of breaching environmental laws or regulations or through 'inheriting' them through transactions such as acquisitions. Beets and Souther (1999) (citing Chadwick, Rouse and Surma, 1993) reported the extent of these liabilities in the USA in 1993 as follows:

> The overall known environmental liability in the United States is currently estimated to be between 2 and 5 percent of the gross national product. Environmental cleanup costs under the Comprehensive Environmental Response, Compensation and Liability Act of 1980, or "Superfund", are approximately $500 billion and will take 40 to 50 years to complete. (p. 130)

Against such a background, it is understandable that current and potential shareholders are putting pressure on companies to report their environmental performance and policy.

Possibly as a response to the growing concern of investors, other stakeholders and society in general about companies' environmental performance and liabilities, regulatory and similar bodies are demanding or encouraging

---

[14] We examine some of the key findings of KPMG's triennial survey of corporate responsibility reports (KPMG, 2005) in Chapter 18, section 18.2.

companies to provide information about their environmental impact. In 1993, in the USA, for example, the Securities and Exchange Commission (SEC) prescribed increased, and more prominent, disclosure of existing and potential environment-related liabilities. In June 1994, SEC Commissioner Richard Roberts observed that increased public awareness of environmental issues had brought:

> increased pressure to bear on the SEC to ensure that publicly-held companies are disclosing in a full, fair, and timely manner the present and potential environmental costs of an economically material nature. My view is that the company owes this to the investing public. (as cited, Beets & Souther, 1999, p. 130)

Companies in the USA have also come under pressure from the Environmental Protection Agency (EPA) to make detailed environmental disclosures. Since 1998 companies in the oil, steel, metals, automobiles and paper industries have been required by the EPA to disclose in an Internet database:

> the number of plant inspections they underwent in the past two years, noncompliance ratings, dates and amounts of penalties imposed, the number of spills, pounds of materials spilled and any resulting injuries or deaths, a hazard rating for each factory based on the toxicity of the chemicals released, the ratio of pollution releases to production, the racial and income profiles of those living within three miles of each plant, and information from the Toxic Release Inventory. (Beets & Souther, 1999, pp. 130–131)

In Europe too, companies are facing increasing regulatory pressure to disclose environmental information. Since April 2005, the EU Accounts Modernisation Directive (AMD) has required all large and medium-size companies in the EU to provide a business risk review that includes information relating to environmental and social matters (EIRiS, 2007, p. 16). In the UK, the AMD requirements have been enacted in the Companies Act (CA) 2006, s. 417. All companies, other than those that qualify as 'small',[15] are required to include a business review in the directors' report within their annual report. CA 2006, s. 417, states:

> The business review must contain –
>   (a) a fair review of the company's business, and
>   (b) a description of the principal risks and uncertainties facing the company.
>
> The review required is a balanced and comprehensive analysis of –
>   (a) the development and performance of the company's business during the
>   financial year, and
>   (b) the position of the company's business at the end of that year,
> consistent with the size and complexity of the business.

---

[15] To qualify as 'small', companies must meet at least two of the following criteria: turnover of no more than £5.6 million, balance sheet total of no more than £2.8 million and no more than 50 employees.

In the case of a quoted company, the business review must, to the extent necessary for an understanding of the development, performance or position of the company's business, include –
   (a) the main trends and factors likely to affect the future development, performance and position of the company's business; and
   (b) information about –
      (i) environmental matters (including the impact of the company's business on the environment),
      (ii) the company's employees, and
      (iii) social and community issues,
      including information about any policies of the company in relation to those matters and the effectiveness of those policies....

Since the 1990s, investors in the UK (particularly institutional investors) have been urged by influential bodies such as the Association of British Insurers to pay due regard to companies' environmental, social and similar performance, in addition to financial indicators, when making their investment decisions. This, in turn, has put pressure on companies to disclose the relevant information. However, perhaps more significantly, in October 2001, the then prime minister (Tony Blair) called upon FTSE 350 companies[16] to voluntarily publish annual environmental reports (separate from their annual reports) by the end of 2001. In the event, only 43 did so (Fettis, 2002).[17] In the light of subsequent events, Blair's 'request' may be seen as a warning that, if companies did not voluntarily disclose environmental information, legislation would be enacted to force them to do so. Nevertheless, much of the environmental, social and other corporate responsibility information provided by UK companies goes well beyond the CA 2006 requirements and is provided voluntarily – either in stand-alone reports (variously titled) or within their annual reports, and the number of companies providing such information, and the extent of their disclosures, is increasing year after year. As we will see in Chapter 18, section 18.3, a significant (and growing) number of companies are also opting to have their published environmental information externally verified (or assured).

For companies (or components thereof) with EMAS accreditation, publishing environmental information, and having the information verified, is not voluntary. Instead, they are required to publish, annually, an externally verified environmental statement containing prescribed information. EMAS 2001, Annex III, explains:

   The aim of the environmental statement is to provide environmental information to the public and other interested parties regarding the environmental impact

---

[16] See footnote 10 for an explanation of FTSE 350.

[17] Just five years later, in 2006, 148 FTSE 350 (including 86 FTSE 100) companies produced stand-alone corporate responsibility (or similar) reports or provided a similar section of more than six pages in their annual reports (CorporateRegister.com, 2007).

and performance and the continual improvement of environmental performance of the organisation.... The minimum requirements for this information shall be as follows:

(a) a clear and unambiguous description of the organisation registering under EMAS and a summary of its activities, products and services ... ;

(b) the environmental policy and a brief description of the environmental management system of the organisation;

(c) a description of all the significant direct and indirect environmental aspects which result in significant environmental impacts of the organisation and an explanation of the nature of the impacts as related to these aspects;[18]

(d) a description of the environmental objectives and targets in relation to the significant environmental aspects and impacts;

(e) a summary of the data available on the performance of the organisation against its environmental objectives and targets with respect to its significant environmental impacts. The summary may include figures on pollutant emissions, waste generation, consumption of raw material, energy and water, noise ... The data should allow for year-by-year comparison to assess the development of the environmental performance of the organisation;

(f) other factors regarding environmental performance including performance against legal provisions with respect to their significant environmental impacts;

(g) the name and accreditation number of the environmental verifier and the date of validation.[19]

In order to meet EMAS certification requirements, the information published in the company's environmental statement must be:

validated by an environmental verifier as being:

(a) accurate and non-deceptive;

(b) substantiated and verifiable;

(c) relevant and used in an appropriate context or setting;

(d) representative of the overall environmental performance of the organisation;

(e) unlikely to result in misinterpretation;

(f) significant in relation to the overall environmental impact. (EMAS 2001, Annex III, para 3.5)

EMAS 2001 also specifies that the external environmental verifier is to check, *inter alia*, "the reliability, credibility and correctness of the data and information in the environmental statement" (Annex V, para 5.4.1).

As noted earlier, in 2007, 44 UK companies (or components thereof) were EMAS accredited and they all published externally verified environmental statements that comply with the above requirements.

---

[18] Definitions of environmental aspects and impacts, as defined by EMAS 2001, are included in Figure 17.1.

[19] The environmental statement is required to be verified by an accredited environmental verifier. The accreditation requirements are set out in EMAS 2001, Annex V, and explained in section 17.4 above.

17.6 ADVANTAGES AND DISADVANTAGES OF ENVIRONMENTAL AUDITS

17.6.1 Summary of advantages and disadvantages of environmental audits

Given that, at least in the UK at the present time, most internal environmental auditing, and external environmental reporting and verification, is undertaken voluntarily, the question arises as to why companies pursue these activities. Expressed slightly differently, what advantages may accrue to companies – and what disadvantages may result – as a consequence of them engaging in environmental auditing and reporting? As may be seen from Figure 17.4, we have identified eight advantages and three disadvantages resulting from internal environmental audits. We discuss the advantages and disadvantages attaching to external environmental reporting in Chapter 18, section 18.5.

Figure 17.4: Advantages and disadvantages resulting from internal environmental audits

Advantages	Disadvantages
(i) Avoidance (or minimisation) of environment-related liabilities	(i) Resources required to develop, implement and maintain an environmental auditing programme
(ii) More efficient operating processes (i.e., cost-savings)	(ii) Disruption caused when facilities are audited
(iii) Reduced insurance premiums	(iii) Adverse consequences of audits uncovering breaches of environmental legal regulatory requirements
(iv) Improved managerial decisions resulting in enhanced financial and environmental performance	
(v) Improved environmental management and enhanced environmental protection	
(vi) Improved risk management	
(vii) Satisfaction of customer requirements and enhanced customer relations	
(viii) Enhanced corporate image or reputation	

17.6.2 Advantages resulting from internal environmental audits

(i) Avoidance (or minimisation) of environment-related liabilities

Probably the most important advantage of internal environmental audits for companies is that they help to ensure they comply with the myriad of applicable environmental laws and regulations and thereby avoid (or at least minimise) financial penalties or other sanctions.

As we noted in section 17.3, many companies initially introduced environmental audits as a response to the ever-increasing volume and complexity of environmental regulations (and the increasing severity of penalties), and the resultant ease of inadvertently breaching them. Internal audits – whether conducted as focused environmental compliance audits or broader (comprehensive) environmental audits – enable companies to be alert to any compliance problems and thus to take appropriate corrective action in a timely manner. In some cases this may be limited to amending existing procedures or adopting new technologies (such as installing new plant or equipment to reduce emissions of toxic gases to permitted levels); in others it may involve taking costly remedial action – for example, cleaning up contaminated sites where hazardous waste has been dumped. By identifying potential compliance problems as soon as they arise, companies can avoid fines and other penalties for breaching regulatory requirements and the costs imposed by the court for remediation. It also avoids the adverse publicity and the consequential damage to the company's reputation that inevitably follows an environmental prosecution (Quality Network, 1996).

(ii)   More efficient operating processes (cost-savings)

One of the key objectives of internal environmental audits is ascertaining ways in which environmental management can be improved. This involves, among other things, reviewing current and alternative operating processes, and resource and energy sources (or types), in order to identify opportunities for cost-savings. These may be achieved through, for example, reduced resource and energy usage, and minimising waste with a consequential reduction in storage and disposal costs.

(iii)   Reduced insurance premiums

Quality Network (1996) points out that insurance companies are very aware of the risk that attaches to poor environmental performance by organisations they insure. Companies with a sound and effective EMS (in which environmental audits are an integral part; see section 17.3) are able to demonstrate to their insurers that they pose less risk. As a result, they are generally able to secure reduced insurance premiums. Indeed, according to Quality Network (1996), some insurance companies require an internal environmental audit of the insured organisation as a condition of agreeing insurance cover.

(iv)   Improved managerial decisions

All management decisions are made on the basis of available information and, all other things being equal, the more comprehensive and the higher the quality of relevant information, the better the decisions reached. Internal environmental audits generate a wealth of data that enhance the information on which management formulates decisions about, for example, resource allocation, products and services to be produced, operating processes, plant and equipment to acquire, procedures to be adopted in respect of the storage and disposal of hazardous wastes, and action to be taken in the event of, for instance, an environmental or health or safety emergency or disaster. These and similar decisions have a direct impact on the company's financial and non-financial performance. Hence, as commentators such as Bowman (1999) have noted: "Voluntary [internal] environmental audit is an integral part of good environmental management and good environmental management should be seen as good business" (p. 395). Given the avoidance of fines and costs of remediation through ensuring compliance with environmental laws and regulations, the cost-savings opportunities identified through environmental audits, and an improved basis for decision-making, it is not surprising that good environmental management results in enhanced financial, as well as environmental, performance.

Supporting the notion that good environmental management is good for business, Quality Network (1996) has observed that the financial performance of 'green portfolios' (that is, portfolios of companies that feature in indices such as FTSE4Good, signifying good environmental performance and ethical conduct) has "been good in comparison to more traditional investments" (p. 2).

(v) Improved environmental management and enhanced environmental protection

Where companies conduct environmental audits, it indicates a commitment by their directors and senior executives to environmental protection. It also signals a willingness by the directors and executives to give due consideration to the audit findings and to implement the accompanying recommendations which are designed to improve the company's environmental management system and environmental performance.

Further, the audits themselves generally have the effect of raising awareness within the organisation of environmental matters and, more specifically, the audit remit usually includes assessment of the suitability and adequacy of training programmes for company personnel with respect to environmental issues. Additionally, the audits facilitate comparison of environmental practices at various sites, divisions and, if applicable, subsidiaries of the company and, through their feedback and recommendations, help to ensure that best practices are adopted throughout the organisation. By these means, environmental audits help to improve companies' environmental management – and thereby enhance environmental protection.

(vi) Improved risk management

A recent development in the realm of environmental auditing is the use of these audits to evaluate potential business risks. Audits with this objective attempt to identify environmental issues that pose significant risk to continuing business operations. Such risks may be reflected in factors such as:

- major capital expenditure requirements – for example, for the purchase of new plant or equipment to reduce emissions to permitted levels, or the cost of cleaning up contaminated land, or removing asbestos from buildings;
- limitations on production – for instance, because products or processes and, in particular, resultant gaseous, liquids or solid wastes do not meet newly announced environmental or health and safety regulations, or other factors (Bowman, 1999).

(vii) Satisfaction of customer requirements and enhanced customer relations

The news media frequently report the concerns of various groups in society about matters such as the harmful effects of 'factory farming', the use of pesticides and chemical fertilizers to aid agricultural and horticultural production, 'over fishing' the oceans, and the removal of slow-regeneration hardwoods from tropical rainforests for building materials and furniture manufacture.

Increasingly, companies whose directors and senior executives are themselves sensitive to environmental issues, or who are aware of their customers' preferences in this regard, seek suppliers and sub-contractors who can demonstrate that they are good environmental citizens. Thus, 'supplier' and 'sub-contracting' companies which conduct environmental audits are well placed to reassure their customers of their commitment to good environmental management and performance.[20]

(viii) Enhancement of the company's image or reputation

A company's image and reputation may be enhanced through both conducting environmental audits and publishing independently verified information about its environmental performance. Where companies conduct environmental audits they are able to demonstrate their commitment to improved environmental performance. This in itself may enhance their image – or, alternatively, may help them counter (or mitigate) adverse publicity about their attitude to the environment.

---

[20] In this regard, the reasons cited for Japanese companies' adoption of ISO 14001 are relevant; see footnote 9.

However, companies are likely to be able to enhance their reputation more effectively if they report publicly on their environmental performance – particularly if their report is independently verified. Such reporting and verification may also translate into more tangible benefits in that, if the company is portrayed as being 'environmentally friendly', it may be favoured by environmentally concerned customers and investors. As Beets and Souther (1999) observe: "positive public relations . . . may accrue from issuing a verified environmental report; that is, 'being green' may have a positive impact on revenues and stock prices" (p. 135). We explore this advantage further in Chapter 18.

17.6.3 Disadvantages resulting from internal environmental audits

From Figure 17.4 it may be seen that we have identified three disadvantages attaching to internal environmental audits. We discuss these below.

(i) Resources required to develop, implement and maintain an environmental auditing programme

A significant disadvantage of internal environmental audits is their cost. To design, implement and maintain an environmental audit programme so that each function, process and site of the organisation is audited on a regular basis (at least once every three years for EMAS registrants) is a costly undertaking. As we noted in section 17.3 above, internal environmental audits may be conducted by personnel internal or external to the organisation. However, because of the range of skills required for environmental audits, it is beyond the resources of all but large companies to maintain an in-house audit team and the majority of companies rely on environmental consultants to perform their audits. But, irrespective of whether the audits are conducted by an internal or external team of environmental auditors, internal environmental audits are both time-consuming and costly.

(ii) Disruption caused when facilities are audited

Whatever function, process or site of a company is audited at a particular point in time, the activities of the facility are disrupted by the audit. The disruption is generally greatest during the on-site visit by the environmental audit team as personnel have their activities observed, are asked questions, or asked to locate and provide relevant documents and records – or their normal work routines are disrupted in some other way. However, the disruption is not limited to the period of the on-site visit but extends to the pre- and post-visit phases: work is disrupted during the preparation for the audit and when any resultant recommendations for improvement are implemented.

(iii) Adverse consequences of audits uncovering breaches of environmental legal and regulatory requirements

One of the most serious consequences of an environmental audit for an organisation is the possibility that the audit will uncover past or present breaches of environmental laws or regulations. Companies fear that regulators or third parties may impose liability for the previously unknown violations. Legal or regulatory breaches uncovered may not even be those of the company itself. For example, soil or groundwater on the company's property may have been contaminated by a previous owner but the present company may be faced with enormous remediation costs and, possibly, also claims for damages by third parties who have been harmed in some way by the contamination.

In the USA, the costs of audit discovery came to prominence in 1992 when Coors Brewing Company, based in Colorado, undertook a voluntary investigation of its volatile organic compound (VOC) emissions. As Volokh (1997, p. 28) explains:

> The investigation found that when beer is spilled during the making, packaging, and disposal process, large quantities of VOCs are released into the air. As the producer of about 20 million barrels of beer per year, Coors alone was releasing 650 to 750 tons of VOCs – about 17 times more than originally thought. [Coors voluntarily disclosed their finding to Colorado state officials]. . . . In July 1993, the Colorado Department of Health – allegedly under pressure from the federal EPA [Environmental Protection Agency] issued Coors a compliance order containing a $1.05 million civil penalty for violations of state pollution laws. The fine was also to include a to-be-determined-later "economic benefit payment" to the state for money the company had saved by not complying with the laws. . . . Coors argued that it was being unfairly punished for voluntarily revealing problems that both regulators and major brewers had missed[21], and warned that such fines would go a long way to discourage other companies from conducting self- [i.e., voluntary internal] audits. (Coors had already spent 18 months and $1.5 million conducting the study.) In February 1994, the fine was reduced. Coors agreed to pay a $100,000 fine and a $137,000 economic benefit payment.

The Coors' experience has prompted at least 24 states in the USA (including Colorado) to enact 'audit privilege' laws (Dailey and Bolduan, 1997). These states are keen to foster environmental protection and believe that companies are more likely to conduct voluntary environmental audits, and correct any discovered violations of environmental laws and regulations, if their audit findings will not be used as a basis for imposing sanctions upon them. In most states the audit privilege laws apply to "voluntary, internal and comprehensive environmental audits designed to identify past non-compliance and improve future compliance with state and federal environmental requirements" (Kass and McCarroll, 1995, p. 13). They generally have two components, namely:

---

[21] Official EPA figures had grossly underestimated brewing company emissions.

(a) a *privilege component* whereby neither information obtained as a result of the audit nor the audit documents are admissible as evidence against a company in administrative, civil or criminal proceedings;
(b) an *immunity component* whereby companies that find, report and correct environmental regulatory breaches are given immunity from sanctions. The company may be required to take certain steps to control or rectify environmental damage but punitive sanctions are outlawed (Volokh, 1997).

The Federal Environmental Protection Agency (EPA) has consistently been opposed to states' evidential privilege for environmental audits – contending that such privilege "invites secrecy' and weakens the states" power of environmental law enforcement (Morley, 1997; Dailey and Bolduan, 1997). The EPA has also made it clear that protection afforded by state audit privilege laws does not extend to violations of federal environmental laws (Sobnosky, 1999). This means that companies which report violations of federal environmental laws, discovered as a result of an environmental audit, remain liable to prosecution under the federal laws. This is a major concern for companies as many federal environmental laws embody a requirement for companies discovering violations of federal environmental regulations to report them to the EPA (or a state environmental agency acting for the EPA) – and provide severe penalties (including fines and imprisonment) for failure to do so (Dailey and Bolduan, 1997). Thus, companies are exposed to prosecution if they report violations of federal environmental laws – or if they violate the law by failing to report the violations.

Notwithstanding its opposition to state audit privilege laws, recognising the benefits of environmental audits in terms of enhanced environmental protection, in December 1995 the EPA issued a *Final Policy Statement* (EPA, 1995) which provides that, if companies meet all of the specified conditions, non-economic benefit penalties will not be imposed and the EPA will not refer cases for criminal prosecution. Morley (1997, p. 6) explains:

> The conditions [to be met] are the heart of the policy, and include the following:
> 1. The violation was discovered through a systematic procedure implemented by the company, such as an environmental audit or due diligence program.
> 2. The violation was identified voluntarily and not through a required monitoring program or pursuant to an [environmental protection] agency inspection or third party complaint; once identified, the violation was promptly disclosed.
> 3. The violation was expeditiously corrected.
> 4. The company agreed to take steps to prevent further violations.
> 5. Same or closely related violations have not occurred within a certain period in the past.

6. The company must co-operate and provide necessary information to determine whether the policy is applicable.

Although companies which meet the EPA's conditions gain some immunity from penalties they would otherwise incur as a consequence of breaching federal environmental laws, their violations are made public. These companies remain exposed to liability resulting from actions brought by non-governmental third parties (for example, organisations or individuals who suffer harm as a consequence of the company's breach of environmental regulations). Similarly, environmental activists are able to use information about companies' violations to generate negative publicity about the companies concerned.

In order to avoid the adverse consequences of having their reports of environmental regulation violations made public, some companies employ environmental lawyers to conduct their internal environmental audits and claim lawyer-client privilege (or confidentiality) to protect the audit findings from being placed in the public domain. Other companies, who use specialist environmental consultants, similarly try to prevent disclosure of their audit results through privilege by requiring the consultants to report the audit findings to the company's lawyers who then report them to the company (McKinney and Steadman, 1998).

As in the USA, companies in the UK are faced with something of a dilemma. If they demonstrate their commitment to good environmental management and conduct environmental audits, they risk prosecution in respect of any breaches of environmental laws and regulations the audit may uncover. If they do not conduct environmental audits, they risk prosecution in respect of violations they might have discovered and corrected that come to light in other ways – for example, through an inspection by an environmental regulatory agency, or another organisation or individual suffering consequential harm.

Environmentally oriented companies stress that the goal of environmental laws and regulations is to protect and enhance the environment rather than to collect fines; therefore the regulators should provide protection for companies that voluntarily conduct environmental audits and uncover, report and remedy violations of environmental regulations. They also argue that it is better for companies to allocate financial resources to remediation of damage caused by past or present breaches of environmental regulations than to defending prosecutions and paying hefty fines. Additionally, they observe that it is cost-effective for the regulators to focus their scarce resources on pursuing organisations that are habitually poor environmental performers rather than prosecuting those that demonstrate their commitment to good environmental management by conducting environmental audits and other similar means.

17.7 SUMMARY

In this chapter we have highlighted the importance of environmental issues for all companies, especially those in industrial sectors such as manufacturing, the extractive industries and chemicals which have (or are likely to have) a significant environmental impact. We have noted, in particular, that companies (like other organisations) are subject to a huge volume of highly complex environmental laws and regulations – and, also, that companies may gain significant advantages by incorporating environmental considerations into their business decisions.

We have traced the development of internal environmental audits from 'single issue' audits (such as compliance and due diligence audits) to 'comprehensive' audits – those covering organisations' environmental management systems and their environmental performance. Additionally, we have reviewed the objectives, scope and process of, and the reports associated with, internal environmental audits and, particularly for EMAS registered companies, external verification of (external) environmental statements or reports.

In the concluding section of the chapter we have discussed the advantages and disadvantages that may accrue to companies as a consequence of conducting (internal) environmental audits. Notwithstanding significant disadvantages that may result from such audits, many companies (and virtually all major companies in the UK and elsewhere) seem to find that developing environmental management systems and undertaking environmental audits makes good business sense.

SELF-REVIEW QUESTIONS

17.1 Define the following terms:
    (i)   environmental policy;
    (ii) environment management system;
    (iii) an internal environmental audit.

17.2 Explain briefly how the scope of internal environmental audits has developed over the past 30 or so years.

17.3 Outline the elements of an environmental management system.

17.4 Discuss briefly the objective and requirements of the ISO 14001 scheme and Europe's eco-management and audit scheme (EMAS), and list the key differences in the requirements of the two schemes.

17.5 Explain briefly the process for an internal environmental audit.

17.6 List the professional requirements for internal environmental auditors and identify the groups who may be equipped to undertake this work.

17.7 Outline the usual contents of:
      (i) an internal environmental audit report to management;
      (ii) a verification report attached to a company's environmental statement or report as required by EMAS.

17.8 Explain briefly the key reason(s) for companies reporting on their environmental performance.

17.9 Explain briefly eight advantages that may accrue to companies as a consequence of conducting internal environmental audits.

17.10 Explain briefly three disadvantages that companies may experience as a consequence of conducting internal environmental audits.

REFERENCES

Beets, S.D., & Souther, C.C. (1999). Corporate environmental reports: the need for standards and an environmental assurance service. *Accounting Horizons* **13**(2), 129–145.

Bowman, M. (1999). New legislative 'protection' of voluntary environmental audits: incentive or indictment. *Australian Business Law Review* **27**(5), 391–406.

British Safety Council (BSC). (2007). *Five Star Environmental Audit: Working together towards environmental sustainability.* London: British Safety Council.

British Standards Institute (BSI). (1992). *British Standard 7750: Specification for Environmental Management Systems.* London: BSI.

Chadwick, B., Rouse, R.W., & Surma, J. (1993, January). Perspectives on environmental accounting. *The CPA Journal*, 18–24.

Confederation of British Industry (CBI). (1990). *Narrowing the Gap: Environmental Auditing Guidelines for Business.* London: CBI.

Context. (2006). *Global Corporate Responsibility reporting trends: Reporting in Context 2006*, www.econtext.co.uk.

CorporateRegister.com. (2007). *Non-financial reporting status of the FTSE100: March 2007*, www.corporateregister.com/charts/FTSE.

Dailey, D.K., and Bolduan, L.M. (1997). Voluntary environmental audits: will Congress act? *Corporate Legal Times* **7**(73), 59.

Ec.europa.eu. (2007). *What is EMAS? Summary*, http://ec.europa.eu/environment/emas/about/summary_en.

Economist. (1990, 9 August). Managing greenly, *Economist* **316**(7671), 18–20.

EMAS. (2007). *Who participates in EMAS? EU register of organisations*, http://ec.europa.eu/environment/emas/about/participate/sites_en.

Emas.org. (2008). *Introducing EMAS*. www.emas.org.uk/aboutemas.intro.

Encyclopedia Britannica. (2002). *Britannica Ready Reference Encyclopedia*. Rugeley (UK): Focus Multimedia.

Environmental Protection Agency (EPA). (1995). *Final Policy Statement of Incentives for Self-Policing: Discovery, Disclosure, Correction and Prevention of Violation*, 60 Fed. Reg 66, 706. Washington: EPA.

Ethical Investment Research Services (EIRIS). (2007). *The State of Responsible Business: Global corporate response to environmental, social and governance (ESG) challenges*. London: Ethical Investment Research Services (EIRIS).

Fédération des Experts Comptables Européens (FEE). (2002). *FEE Discussion Paper Providing Assurance on Sustainability Reports*. Brussels: FEE.

Fettis, L. (2002, 20 June). FD's back environmental reports. *Accountancy Age*, p. 3.

Hamilton, E. (1997). The top ten pitfalls of environmental audits and how to avoid them. *Journal of Environmental Law & Practice* **4**(5), 29–35.

International Chamber of Commerce (ICC). (1991). *An ICC Guide to Effective Environmental Auditing*. Paris: ICC Publishing.

International Standards Organisation (ISO). (2002). *ISO 19011 Environmental Management Systems Auditing*. Geneva: ISO.

iso.org. (2008). *ISO 14000 Essentials*, www.iso.org/iso/iso_catalogue/managment_standards.

Kass, S.L., and McCarroll, J.M. (1995). Environmental audits: how they can help – and hurt – the corporation, *Directorship* **21**(9), 12–14.

KPMG. (2005). *KPMG International Survey of Corporate Responsibility Reporting 2005*. Amsterdam: KPMG Global Sustainability Services.

Lightbody, M. (2000). Environmental auditing: the audit theory gap. *Accounting Forum* **24**(2), 151–169.

MacKay, E. (2000, 14 June). Environmental reporting – creating the right environment. *Accountancy Age*, www.accountancyage.com/News/1103312, 1–3.

Maltby, J. (1995). Environmental audit: theory and practices, *Managerial Auditing Journal* **10**(8), 15–26.

McKinney, M.M., and Steadman, M.E. (1998). EPA challenges privilege issue in environmental self-audits. *CPA Journal* **68**(8), 9.

Morley, S.J. (1997). Environmental self-audit review: New EPA policy and self-audit privilege developments. *Journal of Environmental Law & Practice* **4**(4), 5–8.

Natu, A.V. (1999). Environmental audit – A tool for waste minimisation for small and medium scale dyestuff industries. *Chemical Business* **13**(9), 133–137.

Quality Network. (1996). *Benefits of eco-management systems*, www.quality.co.uk/eco/benefits.

Roussey, R.S. (1992). Auditing environmental liabilities. *Auditing: A Journal of Practice & Theory* **11**(1), 47–57.

Sobnosky, K.J. (1999). The value-added benefits of environmental auditing. *Environmental Quality Management* **9**(2), 25–32.

Vinten, G. (1996). The objectives of the environmental audit. *Environmental Management and Health* **7**(3), 12–21.

Volokh, A. (1997). Carrots over sticks. *Washington Monthly* **29**(6), 28–31.

ADDITIONAL READING

Canadian Institute of Chartered Accountants. (1992). *Environmental Auditing and the Role of the Accounting Profession.* Toronto: CICA.

Cobb, I., Collison, D., Power, D., and Stevenson, L. (2005). *FTSE4Good – perceptions and performance.* London: Association of Chartered Certified Accountants.

Fédération des Experts Comptables Européens (FEE). (2005). *Emissions Trading.* Brussels: FEE.

Institute of Chartered Accountants in England and Wales (ICAEW). (2004). *Sustainability: the role of accountants.* London: ICAEW.

Graham-Bryce, I. (1988). The approach to environmental auditing in the Royal Dutch/Shell Group of companies. In UNEP, *Industry and environment: Environmental auditing* (pp. 8–10). Paris: UNEP.

Gray, R., and Spence, C. (2007). *Social and Environmental Reporting and the business case.* London: Association of Chartered Certified Accountants.

Lewis, L. (2000). Environmental audits in local government: a useful means to progress in sustainable development. *Accounting Forum* **24**(3), 296–319.

World Commission on Environment and Development. (1987). *Our Common Future.* Oxford: Oxford University Press.

18 Corporate Responsibility Assurance Engagements

> **LEARNING OBJECTIVES**
>
> After studying the material in this chapter you should be able to:
> - briefly explain the development of corporate responsibility reporting since the early 1990s;
> - outline the motivations for companies to provide corporate responsibility information;
> - explain the objective, scope and process of corporate responsibility assurance engagements;
> - outline the contents of reports resulting from corporate responsibility assurance engagements;
> - discuss the professional requirements for performing assurance engagements and identify the professional groups which may be equipped to undertake such work;
> - explain the major difficulties facing corporate responsibility assurance providers;
> - discuss the advantages and disadvantages to companies of having their corporate responsibility reports externally assured;
> - discuss the relevance of environmental and similar matters to external financial statement auditors.

The following publications are particularly relevant to this chapter:

- International Standard on Assurance Engagements (ISAE) 3000: *Assurance Engagements other than Audits or Reviews of Historical Financial Information* (IFAC, 2004)
- *AA 1000 Assurance Standard* (Institute of Social and Ethical Accountability, 2003)[1]
- *Sustainability Reporting Guidelines (version 3.0)* (Global Reporting Initiative, 2006)
- International Auditing Standard (ISA) 250 (Redrafted): *The auditor's responsibilities relating to Laws and Regulations in an Audit of Financial Statements* (IFAC, 2008)[2]

---

[1] The Institute of Social and Ethical Accountability refers to itself, in its publications, as AccountAbility.

[2] The status of ISAs referred to in this chapter is explained in the Important Note following the Preface to this book.

18.1 INTRODUCTION

In Chapter 17 we noted the phenomenal increase in recent years in political, media and public concern about the environmental impact of companies' operations, products and services. We also noted that, since the late 1990s, many, especially major, companies in the United Kingdom (UK) and elsewhere have broadened their solely 'environmental reports' into 'environmental and social reports' and, more recently, into wide-ranging 'sustainability' or 'corporate responsibility reports', which provide information about the company's environmental, social and economic impacts.[3] We further observed that this change has been accompanied by an apparent decline in interest by major companies in seeking certification that signals their compliance with environmental standards such as the International Standards Organization's ISO 14001: *Environmental management systems* and Europe's *Eco-management and audit scheme* (EMAS). Instead, at least listed companies appear to perceive that greater benefit can be derived from qualifying for inclusion in indices such as the FTSE4Good, Dow Jones Sustainability Index and/or the Carbon Disclosure Project's Climate Disclosure Leadership Index.[4]

In the absence of universally accepted standards for reporting non-financial performance, both the quantity and quality of companies' disclosures about their environmental, social and economic impacts vary widely. Additionally, while some companies have their non-financial information (or parts thereof) independently assured (or 'audited'), others do not do so. Further, without generally accepted assurance standards, the level of assurance provided on the reliability of the disclosures (and thus their credibility) differs markedly.

In this chapter we explore corporate responsibility reporting and associated assurance engagements.[5] First, we consider the development of, and motivation for companies to engage in, corporate responsibility reporting. We then examine assurance engagements which are designed to provide credibility to companies' corporate responsibility disclosures. We also discuss the professional requirements for performing such engagements and identify the groups which may be equipped to undertake such work. Before concluding the chapter we explore the advantages and disadvantages accruing to companies as a consequence of providing assured sustainability performance information and

---

[3] 'Corporate responsibility reports' is the term that has emerged most recently and seems to describe most aptly the content of many major UK companies' reports of their non-financial performance. We therefore adopt this term for use in this chapter although, on occasion, we use it interchangeably with 'sustainability reports'.

[4] Information about these indices is provided in the appendix to this chapter.

[5] Definitions of relevant terms are provided in Chapter 17, Figure 17.1.

consider the relevance of environmental and similar matters to external financial statement audits.

18.2 DEVELOPMENT OF, AND MOTIVATIONS FOR, CORPORATE RESPONSIBILITY (OR SUSTAINABILITY) REPORTING

Many observers of sustainability reporting by companies, including for example MacKay (2000), Context (2006) and KPMG (2005), have noted that the number of companies providing environmental, social and similar information has increased exponentially since the early 1990s and today this type of reporting is commonplace amongst major companies throughout the world.

The extent and growth of, and changes in, such reporting are reflected in KPMG's 2005 triennial *International Survey of Corporate Responsibility Reporting*. This analyses trends in corporate responsibility (CR) reporting by the world's largest companies, including the largest 250 (by market capitalisation) of the Fortune 500 (F250), and largest 100 companies in each of 16 countries, including the UK (KPMG, 2005, p. 4). The survey found that CR reporting increased markedly between 2002 and 2005 and, although it increased in all 16 economic sectors covered by the survey, the change was particularly noticeable in the finance, securities and insurance sector – by far the largest sector represented in the F250 companies and the one most frequently cited as that not embracing CR concerns. Key findings of KPMG's survey reflecting these changes are presented in Figure 18.1.

Given the extent, and rapid growth, of corporate responsibility reporting, the question arises as to what prompts companies to engage in this activity. Three key factors may be identified: (i) business drivers, (ii) investor preferences and (iii) the regulatory framework. We briefly examine each of these below.

(i) Business drivers

The importance of business (or economic) reasons in motivating companies to engage in, and report, their corporate responsibility activities is highlighted by both Ethical Investment Research Services (EIRIS; 2007) and KPMG (2005). EIRiS notes, for example;

> For certain companies there is undoubtedly a positive financial case for adopting and enhancing responsible business practices. Companies may increase sales and profitability by increasing their appeal in the ethical consumer market. The numbers of consumers making ethical purchases is on the rise ... In addition, responsible business has the potential to improve financial performance by

Figure 18.1:   Changes in corporate responsibility reporting between 2002 and 2005

Corporate responsibility reports	2002		2005	
	No.	%	No.	%
F250 companies publishing CR information as a separate report[6]	112	45	129	52
Proportion of F250 companies with separate CR reports that had the information assured	32	29	39	30
UK's largest 100 companies publishing CR information in separate reports[7]	49	49	71	71
Proportion of UK's largest 100 companies with separate CR reports that had the information assured	26	53	38	54
Titles given to CR reports by F250 companies publishing separate reports:[8]				
Sustainability (environmental, social and economic) reports	16	14	88	68
Environmental and social reports	11	10	22	17
Environmental and health and safety reports	82	73	17	13
Social reports	3	3	2	2
Proportion of F250 companies in various economic sectors publishing CR reports:				
Chemicals and synthetics	5	100	5	100
Pharmaceutical	6	86	7	100
Utilities	11	58	11	92
Electronics and computers	21	48	21	91
Oil and gas	11	58	16	80
Automotive	11	73	17	85
Finance securities and insurance	67	24	63	57
Trade and retail	42	24	35	31

Source: KPMG, 2005, pp. 9, 13, 30, 31

delivering improvements in staff attitudes and productivity and enhancements to internal processes. Lowering operating costs can also be achieved alongside environmental performance improvements. As a straightforward example, cutting energy usage decreases both costs and CO_2 emissions. (EIRIS, 2007, p. 17)

Along similar lines, KPMG's 2005 triennial survey found:

[T]he most common driver for sustainability, as reported by 74 percent of the companies, is economic reasons.... [These] were either directly linked to increased shareholder value [identified by 39 per cent of companies] or market share [reported by 21 per cent] or indirectly linked through increased business opportunities, innovation, reputation and reduced risk.... Almost half of the

---

[6] In 2005, a further 32 (nealy 13 per cent) of the F250 companies included a CR report within their annual report. In 2002, no companies did so (KPMG, 2005, p. 9).

[7] None of the remaining 51 per cent (in 2002) or 29 per cent (in 2005) of companies provided CR information in their annual reports. Thus, major UK companies that published CR information did so in stand-alone reports.

[8] The change in report types in the UK may be illustrated by the titles of, for example, BT's and Scottish Power's reports. In 2003, 2004 and 2005, BT produced *Social and Environmental reports,* in 2006, a report entitled *Changing World: Sustained Values, Including BT's Social and environmental performance,* and in 2007, a *Sustainability Report.* Scottish Power produced *Environmental and Social Impact Reports* in 2003, 2004 and 2005, and *Corporate Responsibility Reports* in 2006 and 2007.

companies reported innovation and risk reduction as their main drivers. About half the companies also listed employee motivation as their driver for CR behavior, which is an indication of the 'war for talent' which is increasingly important in many companies in the [F]250. Only about a quarter of [companies] mentioned 'reputation/brand' [and nine per cent cited 'cost-savings'] as a driver for CR. (KPMG, 2005, p. 18)

(ii) Investor preferences

From the 'business drivers' identified above, it is evident that the impact on investors of environmental and other corporate responsibility activities is extremely important. This phenomenon was recognised by Gilmour and Caplan (2001), who reported:

> The global investor community has begun to develop a consensus view of the behaviour companies are expected to exhibit, and the kind of information they should report.... Analysts and investors are now asking about sustainability-related performance issues alongside financial measures. BP and Coca-Cola are two examples of large companies that faced questions on environmental and social issues at their recent annual general meetings. BP was asked about adapting to climate change, and Coca-Cola about the extent to which its bottles and cans could be recycled. (p. 44)

Globally, investor pressure on companies has been facilitated, and strengthened, by wider (and more probing) media coverage of corporate activities and access to the Internet. These developments have resulted in increased public awareness of corporate responsibility issues, and have facilitated high-profile environmental and other corporate responsibility campaigns by activists. "As a result, corporations are subjected to increased scrutiny, greater NGO [non-governmental organisations] pressure and more informed consumer attitudes" (EIRIS, 2007, p. 15). If companies are to curry favour with the public, and access funds from the growing pool of investors who wish to invest in 'environmentally friendly' and 'socially and ethically responsible' companies, they need to demonstrate to investors and other stakeholders that they are behaving in an environmentally, socially and ethically responsible manner. Thus, it is advantageous, at least for listed companies, to disclose relevant information to aid investors' decisions.

In response to investors' desire to invest in environmentally, socially and/or ethically responsible companies, 'ethical' or 'responsible' investment funds, and indices such as the FTSE4Good, Dow Jones Sustainability Index (DJSI) and/or the Carbon Disclosure Project's (CDP) Climate Disclosure Leadership Index (CDLI) have been established. In its 2007 report, EIRiS notes:

> The value of responsible investment funds under management has grown rapidly in the past ten years. Indeed, some have claimed that responsible investment has been the fastest growing financial instrument in the US and Europe over the past ten years. In addition, increasing numbers of mainstream investors are beginning

to incorporate consideration of ESG [environmental, social and governance] factors into their investment decisions. Consequently, companies are motivated to behave responsibly in order to access this growing volume of investment funds. (p. 19)

The amounts invested in responsible investment funds are staggering. In October 2007, companies included in the DJSI (World) had a total market capitalization of $US13 trillion (SAM, 2007). In Europe, in January 2006, funds invested in 'responsible investments' amounted to more than €1,313 billion (about £879 billion); in the UK alone, such investment exceeded €800 billion (about £536 billion) (EIRiS, 2007, p. 20). Companies' appreciation of the importance of attracting funds from those seeking to invest in 'responsible investments' is also reflected in the number of UK companies included in the FTSE4Good Global and UK Indices and/or the DJSI (World) and/or the CDLI in 2007. The relevant data are presented in Figure 18.2.

Figure 18.2:   Number of UK companies in the FTSE4Good Global and UK Indices, Dow Jones Sustainability Index (DJSI) and/or Carbon Disclosure Leadership Index (CDLI) 2007

Index	FTSE 100 Companies	FTSE 250 Companies	Total UK companies	Total companies in index
FTSE4Good UK Index	79	117	289	289
FTSE4Good Global Index	75	24	99	697
DJSI (World)	47	11	58	318
CDLI	20	0	20	68
FTSE4Good & DJSI (World) (not CDLI)	24	2	26	-
FTSE4Good & CDLI (not DJSI)	2	0	2	-
DJSI (World) & CDLI (not FTSE)	2	0	2	-
FTSE4Good & DJSI (World) & CDLI	16	0	16	-

Source: Data derived form FTSE4Good,[9] DJSI (2007), Innovest (2007)

(iii)   The regulatory framework

As we noted in Chapter 17, section 17.5, legislation and regulations governing environmental and social performance, and the reporting of that performance, have a significant impact on companies. In some cases, the regulatory framework impacts on corporate activities in such a manner that renders it beneficial to companies to make relevant disclosures to shareholders and

---

[9] The FTSE4Good data were provided by a correspondent from the FTSE Group's Responsible Investment Unit; according to the correspondent, it is "based on information on 20 November 2007".

other stakeholders. In other cases, legislation and/or regulations prescribe the environmental, social and similar information that companies are required to provide. (As we discussed this 'motivator' of sustainability performance reporting in some detail in Chapter 17, section 17.5, we will not consider it further here.)

18.3 CORPORATE RESPONSIBILITY ASSURANCE ENGAGEMENTS

18.3.1 Meaning of 'assurance engagements'

In section 18.2 we noted that most major companies in the UK report some sustainability performance information; in section 18.1 we observed that some companies have such information independently assured. We now turn our attention to the assurance engagements companies undertake in order for the sustainability information they provide for external parties to be accepted as reliable.

It is pertinent to note that we use the word 'assured' rather than 'audit' in relation to external environmental reporting. In FEE's view: "The term 'assurance' is preferable ... because it avoids confusion with terms such as 'audit' and 'verification' that have more specialised meanings" (FEE, 2002, para 19). In its Glossary, FEE (2002) defines 'assurance' as: "that which enhances the credibility of information". It defines 'audit' and 'verification' in the following terms:

Audit:	An assurance engagement in which the credibility of information is enhanced to a high level, for example a statutory audit of financial statements.
Verification:	A test of detail in which a matter is confirmed by reference to very persuasive evidence, such as checking a disclosure to third party documentation.

In the context of providing credibility to externally reported sustainability performance information, use of the term 'audit' is inappropriate as, in general, it is not possible to provide the implied high level of assurance. This stems from three main factors, namely:

- the lack of generally accepted criteria or standards for such reporting;
- the absence of generally accepted quantitative performance indicators, and the subjective and qualitative nature of much of the reported information;[10]

---

[10] Beets and Souther (1999) point out that even a term like water usage "can be defined differently from company to company and industry to industry" (p. 36).

- the lack of generally accepted assurance standards and the general absence of conclusive evidence.

These factors combine to generate a situation where, as Beets and Souther (1999) express it in relation to environmental reports:

> corporate environmental reports can disclose as much or as little information as corporations prefer in whatever format they prefer.... While some corporations genuinely want to be environmentally friendly and share information related to their efforts with the public, the absence of environmental reporting [and assurance] standards enables other corporations to publish "green glosses", i.e., attractive environmental reports that disseminate little useful information but are designed to enhance public relations.... Corporations may be especially tempted to publish few tangible details about their environmental efforts if their competitors' environmental programs and efforts are more substantive than their own. (pp. 136–137).

18.3.2 Emergence of reporting guidelines

Since 2000, the situation has changed to some extent as both reporting and assurance standards have been developed and these seem to be gaining acceptance by major companies around the world. The Global Reporting Initiative (GRI) has developed a comprehensive sustainability reporting framework and reporting guidelines. FEE (2001, p. 2) explains the origins and objectives of the GRI as follows:

> The GRI was originally convened in 1997 by CERES (Coalition for Environmentally Responsible Economies) in partnership with UNEP (United Nations Environment Programme) and has been developed by a steering committee representing a mix of stakeholders.... The GRI seeks to make sustainability reporting as routine and credible as financial reporting in terms of compatibility, rigour, and verifiability.... In June 2000 GRI published its [first] *Sustainability Reporting Guidelines* which have already formed the basis for a number of sustainability reports.

Version 2 of the Guidelines (G2) was published in 2002 and version 3 (G3) in 2006. In G3, the GRI (2006) explains:

> Sustainability reports based on the GRI Reporting Framework disclose outcomes and results that occurred within the reporting period in the context of the organization's commitments, strategy, and management approach.... The GRI Reporting Framework is intended to serve as a generally accepted framework for reporting on an organization's economic, environmental, and social performance. It is designed for use by organizations of any size, sector, or location. It ... contains general and sector-specific content that has been agreed by a wide range of stakeholders around the world to be generally applicable for reporting an organization's sustainability performance.
>
> The Sustainability Reporting Guidelines (the Guidelines) consist of Principles for defining report content and ensuring the quality of reported information. It also includes Standard Disclosures made up of Performance Indicators and other

disclosure items, as well as guidance on specific technical topics in reporting. (p. 3)

The Guidelines (GRI, 2006) identify four principles which determine the content of sustainability reports. These are as follows:

- *Materiality* – the report should include topics and performance indicators that reflect the organisation's significant economic, environmental, and social impacts or which are likely to affect the assessments and decisions of stakeholders (p. 8).
- *Stakeholder inclusiveness* – the reporting organisation should identify its stakeholders and explain in the report how it has responded to their reasonable expectations and interests (p. 10).
- *Sustainability context* – the organisation's performance should be reported in the wider context of sustainability (that is, meeting society's current needs without compromising the ability of future generations to meet their needs) (pp. 2, 11).
- *Completeness* – coverage of the material topics and performance indicators, and identification of the organisation's components that are covered by the report, should be sufficient to reflect the reporting organisation's significant economic, environmental, and social impacts and enable stakeholders to assess its performance during the reporting period (p. 12).

The GRI (2006) explains: "Application of these Principles with the Standard Disclosures, determines the topics and [Performance] Indicators to be reported" (p. 4).

The Guidelines also specify the following six principles that govern the quality of sustainability reporting.

- *Balance* – both positive and negative aspects of the organisation's performance should be reported to enable a reasoned assessment of its overall performance (p. 13).
- *Comparability* – issues and information should be selected, compiled, and reported consistently; the information should also be presented in a manner that enables stakeholders to analyse changes in the organisation's performance over time, and make comparisons of its performance with that of other organisations (p. 14).
- *Accuracy* – reported information should be sufficiently accurate and detailed to enable stakeholders to assess the organisation's performance (p. 15).
- *Timeliness* – reporting should occur on a regular schedule that enables information to be available in time for stakeholders to make informed decisions (p. 16).
- *Clarity* – information should be presented in a manner that renders it understandable and accessible to stakeholders (p. 16).

- *Reliability* – information should be gathered, recorded, compiled, analysed, and disclosed in a manner that facilitates its independent examination (p. 17).[11]

The principle of reliability brings us to assurance engagements. Although having corporate responsibility information assured is voluntary, as may be seen from Figure 18.1, KPMG's survey found that, in 2005, 39 (30 per cent) of the F250 companies, and 38 (54 per cent) of the 71 largest UK companies, which published separate corporate responsibility reports had their reports independently assured (KPMG, 2005, pp. 30, 31). Presumably, these companies believe it is cost-effective to have the credibility of the information provided in their reports enhanced in this way. This belief is reflected, at least to some extent, in the fact that most companies which have their corporate responsibility information independently assured engage in what FEE (2002) refers to as "stakeholder dialogue".[12] FEE (2002) explains that companies may undertake this activity in order to ascertain:

- what matters stakeholders want in a sustainability report (and whether past reports have met their needs)
- the levels at which matters become significant enough to be included [that is, materiality levels]
- what imprecision in measurement or degree of approximation is acceptable [that is, the tolerable error][13]
- what assurance, if any, stakeholders value. (para 160)

Unlike an external financial statement audit, where the objectives and scope are defined by statute and the level of assurance with respect to, *inter alia*, the truth and fairness of the financial statements must, by definition, be high, the objectives, scope and level of assurance to be provided by a corporate responsibility assurance engagement need to be specified by the company concerned.

---

[11] All sustainability reports prepared in accordance with GRI G3 are required to declare the level to which they have applied the GRI Reporting Framework. GRI (2006) explains:

[This] results in a clear communication about which elements of the GRI Reporting Framework have been applied in the preparation of a [sustainability] report.... [T]here are three levels in the system. They are titled C, B, and A. The reporting criteria found in each level reflects an increasing application or coverage [from C at the lowest level to A at the highest] of the GRI Reporting Framework. An organization can self-declare a "plus" (+) at each level (ex., C+, B+, A+) if they have utilized external assurance [i.e., + signifies that the report has been independently assured]. (p. 5)

From Ernst & Young's Assurance Statement on BP's Sustainability Report 2006 presented in Figure 18.3, it may be seen that BP declared an Application Level of C+.

[12] FEE (2002) defines stakeholders and stakeholder dialogue as follows:

Stakeholders: individuals or organisations that have, or could have, a non-trivial interest in a sustainable development decision of a company. The interest could be in influencing the decision or simply through being affected by the outcomes of a decision. For a company, stakeholders include: investors, government agencies, workers, suppliers, customers, and those potentially affected by environmental and other impacts. (para 155)

Stakeholder dialogue: Interaction between a company and its stakeholders to ascertain stakeholder views and communicate information relevant to stakeholders. (Glossary)

[13] Materiality levels and tolerable error are discussed in the context of external financial statement audits in Chapter 9, section 9.3.

In many companies where such engagements take place, the directors reach a decision about these matters as an outcome of stakeholder dialogue.

18.3.3 Development of assurance guidelines

Just as the GRI Guidelines emerged to assist organisations prepare their sustainability reports, so an Assurance Standard (AA1000) was developed by AccountAbility (AA)[14] in 2003 to assist assurance providers design and conduct their assurance assignments. According to AA:

> Assurance is an evaluation method that uses a specific set of principles and standards to assess the quality of a Reporting Organisation's subject matter, such as Reports, and the organisation's underlying systems, processes and competencies that underpin its performance. Assurance includes the communication of the results of this evaluation to provide credibility to the subject matter for its users.

> The *AA1000 Assurance Standard* [AA1000AS] is a generally applicable standard for assessing, attesting to, and strengthening the credibility and quality of organisations' sustainability Reporting, and their underlying processes, systems and competencies. (AA, 2003, p. 5)

The Standard covers the full range of organisational performance (i.e., sustainability performance) and applies to different types and sizes of organisation, and also to assurance providers from diverse geographical, cultural and social backgrounds. It adopts a forward-looking approach, designed to indicate the ability of organisations to carry out stated policies and goals, and to meet future standards and expectations (AA, 2003, pp. 5–6). The Standard comprises principles, public statements to be made by the assurance provider, and the assurance provider's competencies. AA (2003) explains:

> The *AA1000 Assurance Standard* supports Assurance (whether made public or not) of Reporting that adheres to specific standards and guidelines, and is customised by the Reporting Organisation. It is specifically designed to be consistent with, and to enhance, the Global Reporting Initiative Sustainability Reporting Guidelines, as well as other related standards. (p. 8)

Three principles underpin assurance engagements conducted in compliance with AA1000AS, namely, materiality, completeness and responsiveness. These principles, respectively, require assurance providers:

- to state whether the reporting organisation has included in its report the information about its sustainability performance required by its stakeholders to enable them to make informed judgments, decisions and actions (p. 14);
- to evaluate the extent to which the reporting organisation can identify and understand material aspects of its sustainability performance (p. 17);

---

[14] See footnote 1.

- to evaluate whether the reporting organisation has responded to stakeholder concerns, policies and relevant standards, and adequately communicated these responses in its report (p. 18).

It can be seen that these principles are closely aligned to those specified in the GRI's Guidelines outlined earlier.

In addition to adhering to these principles, AA1000AS requires assurance providers:

(a) to evaluate whether the reporting organisation has provided adequate evidence to support the information contained in the report (p. 21);

(b) to provide an assurance statement that includes (pp. 23–24):

    (i) a statement that the AA1000 Assurance Standard was used by the assurance provider and any special features about the application of the AA1000AS principles during the assurance process;

    (ii) a basic description of the work undertaken, the level of assurance pursued (including any differences in the levels applied in the assurance process), and the agreed criteria used during the assurance process;

    (iii) conclusions relating to the quality of the report and underlying organisational processes, systems and competencies. These must specify whether:

        - the report provides a fair and balanced representation of material aspects of the reporting organisation's performance for the period in question (i.e., materiality),
        - the organisation has an effective process in place for:
            – identifying and understanding activities, performance, impacts and stakeholder views (i.e., completeness), and
            – managing aspects of sustainability performance (including any significant weaknesses in the underlying organisational processes, systems and competencies) and responding to stakeholder views (i.e., responsiveness);

    (iv) a statement that the report can be used by the organisation's stakeholders (i.e., responsiveness);

    (v) additional commentary which:

        - highlights progress in both reporting and assurance since the last report;
        - provides suggestions for improvement in the next reporting cycle of matters such as the organisation's sustainability reporting, and its underlying processes, systems and competencies;

(c) to make information publicly available, in the assurance statement or related public documents, about their (i.e., the assurance provider's):

(i)   independence from the reporting organisation,
(ii) impartiality towards its stakeholders,
(iii) its own competencies.
(We discuss the ethical and competency requirements of assurance providers in section 18.4 below).

From Figures 18.3 and 18.4 it may be seen that Ernst & Young and Lloyd's Register Quality Assurance (LRQA) complied with the AA1000AS requirements in their assurance statements on BP's 2006 and BT's 2007 sustainability reports, respectively.

Another assurance standard with general application to corporate responsibility reports, and one with which registered auditors in the UK must comply if they undertake assurance engagements, is the International Standard on Assurance Engagements (ISAE) 3000: *Assurance engagements other than audits or reviews of historical financial information*. This encapsulates the key elements of the International Standards on Auditing and has sections addressing the following topics: ethical requirements, quality control, engagement acceptance and continuance, agreeing the terms of the engagement, planning and performing the engagement, using the work of an expert, obtaining evidence, considering subsequent events, documentation, and preparing the assurance report.

According to a Focus Report, these two assurance standards (that is, AA1000AS and ISAE 3000):

> provide valuable innovations in assurance [but use] differing language, method, development pathways, and institutional sources [which] have led to confusion on the part of assurance practitioners, organisations seeking assurance, and stakeholders. To overcome this confusion, AccountAbility (a standards developer) and KPMG Sustainability B.V. in the Netherlands (an assurance practitioner) have collaborated to determine whether these two international standards are consistent, complementary, or conflicting.

> Their study concluded that the two international assurance standards are not in conflict and are not substitutes, but rather are complementary. As such, sustainability assurance based on the combined use of AA1000AS and ISAE 3000 is likely to deliver enhanced results in approach, methodology, and conclusion, their communication, credibility, and ultimately the outcome in relation to stakeholder trust and behavior. (Anonymous, 2005, p. 6)

As for the internal environmental audits we discussed in Chapter 17, external assurance of sustainability disclosures proceeds in much the same way as an external financial statement audit. The assurance engagement must be planned and conducted so as to obtain sufficient appropriate evidence to express a conclusion with the desired level of assurance about the reliability of the information. It proceeds in a series of logically ordered steps, as follows.

Figure 18.3:   Ernst & Young LLP's Assurance statement on BP's Sustainability Report 2006

Independent assurance statement to BP management

BP Sustainability Report 2006 (the Report) has been prepared by the management of BP p.l.c., who are responsible for the collection and presentation of information within it. Our responsibility, in accordance with BP management's instructions, is to carry out a limited assurance engagement on the Report, in order to provide conclusions in relation to Materiality, Completeness and Responsiveness and also to include specific observations from our work in relevant sections of the Report.

Our responsibility in performing our assurance activities is to the management of BP p.l.c. only and in accordance with the terms of reference agreed with them. We do not therefore accept or assume any responsibility for any other purpose or to any other person or organization. Any reliance any such third party may place on the Report is entirely at its own risk.

What did we do to form our conclusions?

Our assurance engagement has been planned and performed in accordance with the Institute of Social and Ethical AccountAbility's AA1000 Assurance Standard and the International Federation of Accountants' ISAE3000. The Report has been evaluated against the following criteria:

– Adherence to the principles of Materiality, Completeness and Responsiveness as set out in the AA1000 Assurance Standard.

– The application of the Global Reporting Initiative G3 *Sustainability Reporting Guidelines* (the Guidelines).

In order to form our conclusions we undertook the steps outlined below.

1. Interviewed a selection of BP executives and senior managers to understand the current status of safety, social, ethical and environmental activities and progress made during the reporting period.
2. Reviewed BP's approach to stakeholder engagement through interviews and reviewing selected associated documentation. For more information on how we use stakeholder views in the design and delivery of our assurance process, please go to www.bp.com/external assurance.
3. Conducted a high-level benchmarking exercise of the material issues and areas of performance covered in the environmental and social report of BP's peers.
4. Reviewed a selection of external media reports and selected group-level documents relating to safety, social, ethical and environmental aspects of BP's performance, to test the coverage of topics within the Report.
5. Reviewed information or explanation about the Report's data, statements and assertions regarding BP's sustainability location performance. As part of this, undertook 12 location visits to give coverage across business segments, key material issues and the geographies in which BP operates. For more information on the locations visited and the process used for selection, please go to www.bp.com/external assurance.
6. Reviewed HSE, community investment and ethics dismissals data samples and processes to test whether they have been collected, consolidated and reported appropriately at group level and the locations visited. We also reviewed leadership diversity data at group level.
7. Reviewed BP's processes for determining material issues to be included in the Report.
8. Reviewed whether BP's reporting has applied the GRI G3 Guidelines to a level described on page 48.

Level of assurance

Our evidence gathering procedures have been designed to obtain a limited level of assurance on which to base our conclusions. The extent of evidence gathering procedures performed is less than that of a reasonable assurance engagement (such as a financial audit) and therefore a lower level of assurance is provided.

Limitations of our review

The scope of our work was limited to a sample of 12 visits from approximately 120 locations. Our stakeholder engagement activities were limited to attendance at two events.

Our review of data processes included the following data sets: HSE, community investment, ethics dismissals and group leadership diversity data. Our review of these data processes at operations level was limited to the 12 locations visited.

Our conclusions

On the basis of our review and in accordance with the terms of reference for our work, we provide the following conclusions on the Report in relation to each of the main AA1000 Assurance Standard's principles (Materiality, Completeness and Responsiveness) and in relation to the GRI G3 Guidelines. Our conclusions should be read in conjunction with the above section on 'What did we do to form our conclusions?'

Materiality

Has BP provided a balanced representation of material issues concerning BP's sustainability performance? Based on our review:

– With the exception of the subject area listed below, we are not aware of any material aspects concerning BP's sustainability performance that have been excluded from the Report.

– We consider that BP could have covered the following subject area in more depth in the Report:
  - Influencing the performance of joint ventures in relation to sustainability issues. Additional work has been undertaken to identify issues relating to joint ventures but content is still limited.

– Nothing has come to our attention that causes us to believe that BP management has not applied its processes for determining material issues to be included in the Report, as described in *Further Information* (page 48)

Figure 18.3: *Continnued*

Completeness
Does BP have complete information on which to base a judgement of what is material for inclusion in the Report?
Based on our review:
- We are not aware of any material issues excluded or misstatements made in relation to the information on which BP has made judgements in respect of the content of the Report.
- We are not aware of any material reporting units that have been excluded in BP management's review of safety, social, ethical and environmental performance.
- We have reviewed information or explanation on the statements on BP's sustainability activities presented in the Report and we are not aware of any misstatements in the assertions made.

HSE and community investment data
- We are not aware of any material reporting units that have been excluded from the group HSE or community investment data.
- Nothing has come to our attention that causes us to believe that HSE or community investment data has not been properly collated from information reported at operations level.
- We are not aware of any errors that would materially affect the group HSE or community investment data.

Ethics dismissals data
- With the exception of the exclusion of ethics dismissals data for the retail business, we are not aware of any excluded reporting units or other material omissions in relation to the ethics dismissals data.
- Nothing has come to our attention that causes us to believe that ethics dismissals data has not been properly collated from reporting units through the group's annual compliance and ethics reporting system.

Leadership diversity data
- Nothing has come to our attention that causes us to believe that leadership diversity data has not been collated properly from group-wide systems.

Responsiveness
How has BP responded to stakeholder concerns?
Based on our review, with the exception of the items listed above, we are not aware of any additional issues of stakeholder interest that are not currently included in the Report's scope and content.

GRI
Does the Report meet the requirements of the C+ application level of the GRI G3 Guidelines?
Based on our review, including consideration of the Report, BP's social and environmental web content and elements of the BP *Annual Report and Accounts 2006*, nothing has come to our attention that causes us to believe that BP management's assertion that their sustainability reporting meets the requirements of the C+ application level of the Guidelines is not fairly stated.

Selected observations on particular aspects of our engagement
Our observations and areas for improvement will be raised in a report to BP management. Selected observations are provided below.

Additional specific observations regarding progress made and areas for improvement can be found in the appropriate sections of the Report and at www.bp.com/sustainability. These observations do not affect our conclusions on the Report set out above.
- BP's process for determining material issues for inclusion within the Report has been further refined, providing more clarity about the selection of issues for print and online content.
- The Report explains that BP is using additional indicators to measure integrity management performance. BP should consider including such indicators in future reporting.
- Documentation of the greenhouse gas emissions data collection, assumptions and assurance activities was in place at the operational sites visited. However, as in previous years, the completeness of documentation to support other HSE parameters is varied.
- We have observed policies, programmes and discrete activities aimed at addressing issues raised through stakeholder engagement. Observations on progress in these activities are provided in several sections of the Report. It is recognized that the response taken is BP's judgement and may not always be consistent with the expectations of all stakeholders.

Our independence
As auditors to BP p.l.c., Ernst & Young are required to comply with the independence requirements set out in the Institute of Chartered Accountants in England & Wales (ICAEW) Guide to Professional Ethics. Ernst & Young's independence policies, which address and in certain places exceed the requirements of the ICAEW, apply to the firm, partners and professional staff. These policies prohibit any financial interests in our clients that would or might be seen to impair independence. Each year, partners and staff are required to confirm their compliance with the firm's policies.

We confirm annually to BP whether there have been any events, including the provision of prohibited services, that could impair our independence or objectivity. There were no such events or services in 2006.

Our assurance team
Our assurance team has been drawn from our global environmental and sustainability network, which undertakes similar engagements to this with a number of significant UK and international businesses.

Ernst & Young LLP
London
April 2007

Figure 18.4: LRQA's Assurance statement on BT's Sustainability Report 2007

LRQA Assurance Statement

SCOPE, CRITERIA AND OBJECTIVES OF THE ASSURANCE
Lloyd's Register Quality Assurance Limited (LRQA) was commissioned by BT Group plc (BT) to assure both its Changing World: Sustained Values 2007 printed report and its web-based Sustainability Report 2007 (the reports) for the financial year ending 31 March 2007. Both reports remain the responsibility of and have been approved by BT.

The assurance was undertaken against:
* Accountability's Assurance Standard AA1000 AS, 2003;
* Global Reporting Initiative Sustainability Reporting Guidelines (GRI), 2002;
* GRI Telecommunications Sector Supplement, July 2003.
The objectives of the Assurance were to review the materiality, completeness and responsiveness of the data and information presented in the reports and to check that these are accurate and represent BT's sustainability performance fairly.
Our assurance did not extend to data and information accessed through links that take the reader out of these reports. Where BT presented data and information obtained from a second party, LRQA corroborated only that data and information was transcribed accurately, or the correct reference was provided.

LRQA'S APPROACH
The assurance was undertaken as a sampling exercise and included interviews, data and information analysis and reviewed BT's:
* stakeholder engagement processes;
* understanding, response and reporting on material issues;
* output on materiality against our own independent analysis of stakeholder issues;
* use of sustainability performance data within its business decision-making processes;
* processes for setting performance indicators and for monitoring progress;
* data and information management systems;
* Sustainability Report 2007 to establish that it is in accordance with the GRI Guidelines;
* reporting of performance in accordance with the GRI Guidelines.
We also reviewed issues arising from accredited third party certification of BT's quality and environmental management systems which are undertaken by LRQA and deemed none to be material.

LEVEL OF ASSURANCE
Our approach has enabled us to achieve a reasonable level of assurance from our review.

LRQA'S FINDINGS AND CONCLUSIONS
Based on our review, our conclusions on the reports in relation to the AA1000 Assurance Standard and the GRI Guidelines are summarised below:

Materiality
BT has established an effective process for determining issues that are material to the business.
The reports include information that is material to stakeholders and these issues are considered during strategic decision making.
We are not aware of any material aspects concerning BT's sustainability performance that have been excluded from the report.

Completeness
The reports are complete in coverage of sustainability performance and there are processes in place for identifying, understanding and managing stakeholder issues and potential risks to the business.

Responsiveness
We are not aware of any additional issues of stakeholder interest that should be included in the reports.

Global Reporting Initiative
The content of the Sustainability Report 2007 is in accordance with the requirements of the GRI Guidelines including the Telecommunications Sector Supplement.

IMPROVEMENTS IDENTIFIED BY LRQA
Recommendations made in assurance statements by LRQA for previous BT corporate social responsibility reports have been addressed.
Following our review this year, we recommend that BT continues to improve on the collection of environmental data from the countries outside of the UK that provide limited data. In addition, a more formalised, monitored, programme for environmental data verification audits should be produced to ensure accuracy of data currently being provided.
Further recommendations on sustainability performance and reporting are included in our report on this assurance assignment to BT senior management.

CE Rosser
For and on behalf of LRQA, UK
This Assurance Statement is valid for one calendar year from the date of issue.

(i) Determining the acceptability of the engagement

Amongst other matters, the potential assurance provider needs to consider whether:

- the assurance team possesses the necessary multidisciplinary skills to undertake the engagement;
- there are adequate assurance team resources at appropriate locations to conduct the verification work within a reasonable time frame;
- assurance team members possess the necessary degree of independence from the client;
- the information to be assured is suitable for assurance and suitable criteria exist to enable the intended level of assurance to be achieved.

(ii) Agreeing with the client the subject matter, scope and terms of the engagement

The scope of a particular assurance engagement may be limited to less than the whole of the corporate responsibility report. As FEE (2002) explains:

> This may be because the company does not want assurance on all of the report (perhaps because of cost or other assurance providers being involved), or because there are limitations through lack of suitable criteria or evidence that preclude some matters being included. [Additionally], [f]or a given set of subject matter, the objectives of the assurance engagement may be restricted. For example: assurance may be given on the implementation of a policy, but not its enforcement; or on the operation of a system but not on the accuracy of performance indicators that depend on data from it. [Further], [f]or a given objective, a company may request in advance that the assurance provider does not employ the full range of possible evidence gathering procedures. For example, visits to sites may be restricted or stakeholder dialogue prevented. (paras 117–119)

When considering the assurance of corporate responsibility disclosures, we need to remember that, unlike external financial statement audits, companies are reporting, and having the relevant information assured, voluntarily. Nevertheless, where the scope of the engagement is limited to less than the full corporate responsibility report, or the procedures to be performed are restricted in some way, the assurance provider will need to assess whether sufficient appropriate evidence can be collected to support a conclusion and whether (s)he will be able to define sufficiently clearly for users of the report the parts that have been subject to external assurance.

(iii) Gaining a thorough understanding of the organisation and its corporate responsibility related affairs

Before commencing the engagement, the assurer needs to gain a thorough understanding of the client organisation, its environmental, social and other relevant regulatory requirements, the environmental impacts of its activities, products and services, its environmental policy, environmental management system (EMS), environmental objects and targets,[15] environmental audit programme and the results thereof, and environmental and social performance. This understanding is necessary in order to provide a context for evaluating the quality of the information that is to be assured.

(iv) Planning the engagement

Planning an assurance engagement includes defining the parts of the corporate responsibility report that are to be assured, identifying appropriate evaluation criteria, determining materiality levels, assessing the likelihood of the report containing material misstatements, and designing appropriate assurance procedures.

(v) Performing compliance procedures

Where the steps of 'gaining an understanding of the client company' and 'planning the engagement' have indicated the company's EMS and other management information systems are effective in preventing, or detecting and correcting, errors in the company's data or information, the assurer may plan to rely on the systems to generate reliable environmental, economic and social information. However, as in an external financial statement audit, irrespective of how reliable the company's systems may appear to be, before the assurer can place reliance on them, (s)he must test (i) the suitability of the systems' design to prevent, or detect and correct, material misstatements in the corporate responsibility information, and (ii) the effectiveness of the operation of the systems' internal controls throughout the reporting period.

(vi) Performing substantive procedures

As in a financial statement audit, analytical review and tests of details are used to test the completeness, accuracy and validity of the information in the parts of the organisation's corporate responsibility report that are subject to external assurance.

(vii) Conducting completion and review procedures

As in an external financial statement audit, 'completion and review' includes performing procedures such as:
- obtaining a management representation letter to support all significant representations made by management on which the external assurer is placing reliance;

---

[15] Environmental objects and targets, and other relevant terms, are defined in Chapter 17, Figure 17.1.

- reviewing the entire corporate responsibility report to check, in particular, that its overall presentation is not misleading and that the report is 'balanced'; that is, it fairly reflects both positive and negative aspects of the company's corporate responsibility performance;
- reviewing other information published by the company (including its financial statements) which may be inconsistent with its corporate responsibility disclosures.

(viii) *Issuing the assurance report to management*

There are no generally accepted standards governing an assurance report on corporate responsibility information. However, as we have seen, assurance providers who comply with AA1000AS are required to meet certain reporting requirements. Similarly, ISAE 3000 requires assurers complying with this standard to:

- conclude whether sufficient appropriate evidence has been obtained to support the conclusion expressed in the assurance report (para 45);
- provide a written assurance report that expresses the assurer's conclusion about the information contained in the corporate responsibility report (para 46);
- tailor the assurance report to the circumstances of the engagement. In the case of assurance reports on corporate responsibility information, the report is likely to include details of, *inter alia*, the terms of the engagement, the criteria used, findings relating to particular aspects of the engagement, and recommendations for improvement. Any findings and recommendations are to be clearly separated from the assurer's conclusions about the subject matter of the report and the wording used should make it clear that they do not affect the assurer's conclusion (para 48);
- provide a report that includes:
  (a) a title that clearly indicates the report is an independent assurance report;
  (b) the addressee; that is, the party to whom the assurance report is directed;
  (c) identification and description of the information being assured. This includes reference to the period covered by the assurance statement and, where the corporate responsibility report does not apply to the entire reporting organisation, the components of the organisation the report covers. An explanation should also be provided of the characteristics of the subject matter assured of which users of the sustainability information should be aware, and how such characteristics may influence the precision of the evaluation or measurement of the subject matter against the identified criteria (see below), or the persuasiveness of the available evidence;

(d) identification of the criteria against which the subject matter was evaluated or measured. This enables intended users to understand the basis of the assurer's conclusion. The assurance report may include the criteria or refer to a source where report users may access them readily;

(e) where appropriate, a description of any significant inherent limitation associated with the evaluation or measurement of the subject matter against the criteria;

(f) if the criteria used to evaluate or measure the subject matter are available only to specific intended users, or are relevant only to a specific purpose, a statement restricting the use of the assurance report to those intended users or that purpose. (As we noted earlier, AA1000AS requires the assurance provider to state in the assurance statement that the statement can be used by the reporting organisation's stakeholders);

(g) a statement identifying the party responsible for the subject matter information and stating that the assurer's role is to independently express a conclusion about that information;

(h) a statement that the engagement was performed in accordance with ISAE 3000;

(i) a summary of the work performed. This helps intended users to understand the nature of the assurance conveyed by the assurance report. As we noted in section 18.3.1, owing to the absence of generally accepted quantitative performance indicators and standards for reporting corporate responsibility information, and because much of the information is subjective and qualitative in nature, corporate responsibility report assurance providers are generally only able to provide a limited (not high) level of assurance. ISAE 3000 (para 49) suggests that, in such circumstances, the assurance provider should identify limitations on the nature, timing and extent of the evidence gathering procedures, and state that the procedures are more limited than for a reasonable assurance engagement (such as an audit of financial statements);

(j) the assurance provider's conclusion. Where the corporate responsibility report covers a number of different aspects, separate conclusions may be provided on each aspect. The assurer's conclusion should be expressed in the negative form; for example, "Nothing has come to our attention that causes us to believe that ethics dismissals data has not been properly collated from reporting units through the group's annual compliance and ethics reporting system" (Ernst & Young, BP Sustainability Report 2006; see Figure 18.3). If the assurance provider expresses other than an unqualified conclusion, the report should contain a clear description of the reasons therefor;

(k) the assurance report date. As for a financial statement audit report, the date informs intended users that the assurance provider has considered the effect on the subject matter information, and on the assurance report, of events that occurred up to that date;

(l) the name of the firm of the assurance provider and the location of the office of the assurer responsible for the engagement.

Reference to Figures 18.3 and 18.4 reveals that Ernst & Young's assurance statement on BP's 2006 Sustainability Report complies with the ISAE 3000 requirements but that provided by LRQA on BT's 2007 Sustainability Report does not do so. As Ernst & Young is a registered auditor in the UK, it is required to comply with ISAE 3000 when conducting an assurance engagement. However, LRQA is not a registered auditor so need not so comply.

18.4 PROFESSIONAL REQUIREMENTS TO PROVIDE ASSURANCE SERVICES

Having examined the assurance engagement process, and noted that both registered auditors (like Ernst & Young) and others (such as LRQA), who are not registered auditors, conduct assurance engagements, we need to consider the qualifications needed to provide assurance services.

The three key requirements for external assurers of corporate responsibility reports are independence, impartiality and competence. Unless assurers possess these three attributes, an assurance statement issued by them will do little to enhance the credibility of the information provided by the relevant companies. A review of assurance statements issued on corporate responsibility reports published by FTSE 100 companies reveals that, while some are assured by the major accountancy firms (like BP's 2006 report), the majority are assured by specialist consultants such as LRQA. MacKay (2000) highlights the strengths and weaknesses of each of these groups of professionals as follows:

> The Big Five[16] trade on their audit experience, their sophisticated audit methodologies and their global brands. The consultants trade on their specialisation in environmental consultancy and their environmental expertise. The Big Five employ environmental specialists and the consultants employ auditors.
>
> They both poach each other's staff and KPMG'S environmental audit division was augmented some years ago by a mass defection of environmental audit experts from a client – The Body Shop. . . . The consultants can . . . be relied on to use words such as correct, accurate and complete in their reports; auditors generally balk at saying anything stronger than "properly collated". . . . Whatever the reasons, . . . more environmental reports in the UK are verified by firms of consultants than by firms of auditors. (p. 2)

---

[16] Arthur Andersen, Deloitte, Ernst & Young, KPMG, and PricewaterhouseCoopers. Andersen's did not collapse until 2002 – after MacKay's statement.

If accounting firms (or, indeed, any qualified accountants who are members of a professional accounting body) provide assurance services, they are required to comply with the International Federation of Accountants' (IFAC) *Code of ethics for professional accountants* (2006).[17] As a consequence, they must meet the ethical and competence requirements relating to, *inter alia*, independence, objectivity, ethical conduct, competence and due care, discussed in earlier chapters of this book, whether or not they are registered auditors.

For others who provide assurance services, AA1000AS spells out relevant requirements. It first explains their importance in the following terms:

> The credibility of a Report's Assurance relies on the Assurance Provider's competencies, independence and impartiality, as well as the use of appropriate standards, including the *AA1000 Assurance Standard*. The Assurance Provider should aim to be independent of the Reporting Organisation and impartial with respect to the organisation's Stakeholders. Any interests that detract from this independence and impartiality need to be transparently declared by the Assurance Provider. (p. 25)

Compared with IFAC's *Code of ethics*, this statement may appear fairly permissive especially in terms of the required level of independence. However, the Standard also specifies that assurance providers must be:

(i) "demonstrably independent" from the relevant reporting organisation and any agreement with the organisation "must not dilute or unduly influence" their ability to fulfil their responsibility to the organisation's stakeholders (p. 25);

(ii) impartial in their dealings with the reporting organisation's stakeholders. This requires them to fulfil their assurance assignments without their "understanding, judgement or statements being unduly influenced" by the nature of their relationships with the organisation's stakeholders (p. 26).

Acknowledging the diversity of assurance providers and contexts within which they undertake assurance engagements, AA1000AS also requires assurance providers to make a public statement in respect of both their independence and impartiality for each assurance assignment. The statement is to include:

- a declaration of independence with respect to the reporting organisation;
- a declaration of impartiality with respect to stakeholder interests;
- the conflict of interest policies relating to employment relationships to which they adhere, including any professional codes of ethics, whether on a voluntary or mandatory basis;
- any recent ongoing or potential financial or commercial relationships they (or their firms) have with the reporting organisation; for example,

---

[17] Or their own professional body's equivalent of IFAC's *Code of ethics*.

fee-for-service engagements such as consultancy, research, other forms of accounting, assurance, or advice, and governance arrangements and/or ownership such as directorships or shareholdings (pp. 26, 27).

Regarding the competency of assurance providers, AA1000AS requires both assurance providers and reporting organisations to ensure that individuals involved in the assurance process are "demonstrably competent" (p. 27). Reporting organisations are also required to ensure that assurance providers are prepared to make information available to interested stakeholders about the competencies of the individuals involved in the assurance process. The competencies to be possessed, collectively, by members of the assurance team are to include:

- professional qualifications such as skills in handling quantitative data, training in aspects of assurance, knowledge of aspects of performance and impacts (for example, environmental impacts and human rights);
- experience in environmental, economic, social and ethical, and financial assurance;
- expertise covering key dimensions of the information to be assured and the organisation's context and stakeholders (p. 28).

The firms to which individuals performing assurance engagements belong are also required to "demonstrate adequate institutional competencies" (p. 28). These include:

- adequate oversight to ensure that assurance engagements conducted by the firm are performed "to the highest possible standards" and not compromised by commercial interests or inadequate competencies (p. 28). The oversight is to be provided through one or more mechanisms or processes; for example, an assurance oversight committee comprised of members not undertaking, or directly benefiting, from the assurance work in question;
- adequate understanding of the legal aspects of the assurance process, and adequate professional indemnity insurance;
- infrastructure to ensure the above requirements are met and that assurance-related material is retained in secure, long-term, storage.

18.5 ADVANTAGES AND DISADVANTAGES OF CORPORATE RESPONSIBILITY REPORTING AND ASSURANCE

18.5.1 Summary of advantages and disadvantages of corporate responsibility reporting and assurance

We have noted that publishing corporate responsibility (that is, environmental, economic, social and/or similar non-financial performance) information is now commonplace among major companies in the UK, as elsewhere, and that a significant number of companies also choose to have the information independently assured. This reporting (and assurance) is almost entirely voluntary and, therefore, it seems that the companies concerned perceive the benefits to be derived from the activity outweigh the costs. But what are the advantages and disadvantages that result from publishing assured corporate responsibility information? As may be seen from Figure 18.5, we have identified six advantages and three disadvantages. We first discuss the advantages, and then the disadvantages, in the two sub-sections below.[18]

18.5.2 Advantages of corporate responsibility reporting and assurance

(i) *Reduced risk of regulatory investigations relating to environmental matters*

For companies that publish comprehensive environmental information – reporting, for example, their environmental policy, environmental objectives and targets, achieved environmental performance measured against the targets, environmental audit programme, the effectiveness of controls within their environmental management system, and the level of their compliance with environmental laws and regulations – the implication is that they are environmentally aware, and candid about their environmental impact. Where the information is independently assured, this impression is

Figure 18.5: Advantages and disadvantages of corporate responsibility reporting and assurance

Advantages	Disadvantages
(i) Reduced risk of regulatory investigations relating to environmental matters	(i) Possible adverse consequences of reporting corporate responsibility information
(ii) Support for disclosures in the financial statements	(ii) Absence of generally accepted corporate responsibility reporting and assurance standards
(iii) Improvements in the environmental management system, internal controls and reporting systems	(iii) High costs of producing corporate responsibility reports and having them assured
(iv) Reduced risk of litigation for misrepresentation by users of published corporate responsibility information	
(v) Enhanced corporate image or reputation especially when the information is assured	
(vi) Improved investment decisions by investors and increased potential funding	

---

[18] It should be noted that some of the advantages and disadvantages pertain to disclosure and/or assurance of environmental information; others relate to disclosure and/or assurance of corporate responsibility information more generally.

strengthened.[19] It seems likely that such companies will attract less regulatory investigation in respect of their environmental performance, and are less likely to breach environmental regulatory requirements, than companies which do not issue informative environmental reports, whether as stand-alone, or within their annual, reports.

(ii)   Support for disclosures in the financial statements

Particularly for companies whose activities, products or services have a significant adverse environmental impact (such as companies in the extractive, chemicals and manufacturing industries), publishing independently assured environmental information can enhance the credibility of their published financial statements. For example, if a company has material environmental remediation liabilities (possibly resulting from the storage and/or disposal of hazardous waste contaminating large areas of the company's land at various locations on- and off-site), both the company's directors and its external auditor will be concerned about the appropriateness and adequacy of disclosures relating to the liabilities in the financial statements. The publication of independently assured information relating to the liabilities in the company's environmental (within or separate from a corporate responsibility or annual) report will help to assure both the directors and the auditor about the adequacy of the disclosures (Beets and Souther, 1999).

(iii)   Improvement in the environmental management system, internal controls and reporting systems

As a consequence of having their published environmental information independently assured, companies benefit from the expertise and experience of a competent, knowledgeable professional who is divorced from the day-to-day operation of the company's environmental management system and its procedures, controls and monitoring mechanisms. As part of their work, external assurance providers are likely to review the various elements of the company's environmental management system, identify weaknesses or opportunities for improvement, and make recommendations. Thus, as a by-product of having their external environmental reports externally assured, companies' environmental management systems, reporting mechanisms and performance may be improved. This, in turn, should enhance many of the advantages accruing to companies as a result of internal environmental audits, which we discuss in Chapter 17, section 17.6.

---

[19] However, we need to recall from Figure 18.1 that, in 2005, only 39 of the world's 250 largest companies, and 38 of the UK's largest 100 companies, had their corporate responsibility reports independently assured.

(iv) *Reduced risk of litigation for misrepresentation by users of published corporate responsibility information*

A reduced risk of litigation resulting from misrepresentation derives from companies having their corporate responsibility disclosures (or parts thereof) independently assured. Where companies publish (non-assured) corporate responsibility information they may believe it is complete, unbiased, and that it fairly represents the facts. However, without independent assurance of the relevant information, companies run the risk of inadvertently disclosing inaccurate or misleading information – and, hence, of being exposed to the risk of being sued (or subjected to other adverse actions) by parties who act in reliance on the corporate responsibility information provided and thereby suffer loss.

(v) *Enhancement of the company's image and reputation*

Especially in the current era of widespread concern within political and public arenas about the environmental impact of companies' operations and outputs, the health and safety of products and workplaces, fair trade, employment practices, and so on, companies may enhance their image and reputation by publishing independently assured corporate responsibility information. Reporting such information may also translate into more tangible benefits in that, if companies are portrayed as being environmentally, socially and ethically responsible, they may be favoured by customers and investors to whom these issues are important. As Beets and Souther (1999) observe in relation to environmental reporting: "positive public relations ... may accrue from issuing a verified environmental report; that is, 'being green' may have a positive impact on revenues and stock prices" (p. 135).

The independent assurance of corporate responsibility reports is important as, in its absence, some users of the reports may consider the information provided to be biased or otherwise unreliable. Some may go as far as regarding the disclosures as an exercise in public relations rather than reporting on responsible conduct. Independent verification of the information renders it more credible – and thus more useful – to users.

(vi) *Improved investment decisions by investors and increased potential funding*

Like management decisions, investors' decisions are based on available information and, all other things being equal, the more comprehensive and the higher the quality of the information, the better the decisions made. Thus, where companies publish corporate responsibility reports – particularly if these are externally assured – investors have additional information on which to base their investment decisions.

Further, the results of a number of studies of investor preferences indicate that many investors are concerned about companies' corporate responsibility performance and are more likely to invest in companies with a good track record for acting in an environmentally, socially and/or ethically responsible manner (see, for example, The Accountant, 1998; Investors Chronicle, 1998; Krumsiek, 1998). Hence, for companies with a good record, publishing information about their corporate responsibility performance may result in a rise in their share price (as demand for their shares increases) and in their increased ability to attract new capital. The importance to investors of 'ethical' or 'responsible' investments, and the importance to companies of being accepted as providing opportunities for such investment, is also reflected in the rapid growth of indices such as FTSE4Good, the Dow Jones Sustainability Index and the Carbon Disclosure Leadership Index since the turn of the 21st century.

18.5.3 Disadvantages of sustainability reporting and assurance

(i) *Possible adverse consequences of reporting corporate responsibility information*

A disadvantage accruing to companies that publish information about their corporate responsibility performance is that their reports need to be, and need to be accepted by users as, complete and balanced (that is, reporting both 'good' and 'bad' performance). However, if a company's report discloses detrimental environmental effects caused by its activities, products or services, or employment of child or 'sweatshop' labour, etc. that were not previously known, this may generate negative publicity and/or prompt an adverse reaction by customers, investors and/or regulators. It may, for example, trigger regulatory investigations and, possibly, litigation.

(ii) *Absence of generally accepted corporate responsibility reporting and assurance standards*

In the absence of generally accepted standards prescribing the information to be included in published corporate responsibility reports and defining how quantitative items are to be identified, measured and reported, the content, format and quality (in terms of completeness, accuracy and validity) of the reports varies widely. Similarly, without generally accepted assurance standards, the rigour of the assurance process to which the reports are subject varies markedly.

A further disadvantage for companies resulting from the absence of universally accepted corporate responsibility reporting standards is the potential for users of the reports to misinterpret statements made or data provided. Such misunderstanding may result in adverse consequences for the company concerned;

it may, for example, result in unjustified negative publicity or even in a court action alleging misrepresentation. Along similar lines, in the absence of generally accepted assurance standards, there is a danger that users of assured corporate responsibility reports may not properly understand the nature and level of the assurance provided. If informed users are familiar with externally audited financial statements, they may mistakenly conclude that a similar high level of assurance is provided by the assurance statement attached to corporate responsibility reports (FEE, 2002, para 236).

While the absence of generally accepted reporting and assurance standards remains a problem, as we have seen in earlier sections of this chapter, the GRI's Sustainability Reporting Standards and AccountAbility's AA1000 Assurance Standard are gaining acceptance by major companies in the UK and elsewhere and this trend can be expected to continue. Further, for companies in the UK that engage a registered auditor (or other professional accountant) to provide assurance on their corporate responsibility information, the assurance engagement is required to be conducted in accordance with ISAE 3000.

(iii) High costs of producing corporate responsibility reports and having them verified

A significant disadvantage for companies that publish assured corporate responsibility reports is the cost involved. Many companies that publish separate corporate responsibility reports produce a document that is nearly as 'thick' as their annual report and one which contains significantly more photographs, graphs and diagrams.[20] Such reports are extremely expensive to compile (in terms of gathering relevant information and data, deciding what to include and what to leave out, and how to present the material to be included). They are also expensive to publish, whether in hard copy or electronic form.[21] Companies that have their corporate responsibility reports independently assured also incur the costly professional fees of the assurance service providers.

Notwithstanding the financial resources that are consumed by publishing assured corporate responsibility reports, companies engage in this activity only if they believe those resources are used to good effect. By implication, these companies consider that the financial costs involved, together with the other

---

[20] This may be illustrated by BP's 2006 Sustainability Report with 54 pages and BT's 2007 Sustainability Report with 128 pages. The greater part of both of these reports consists of pictorial and diagrammatic material.

[21] A number of companies, such as J Sainsbury and BT, have sought to reduce the cost – as well as reducing the use of resources such as paper and ink – by publishing their reports only on the Internet.

disadvantages attaching to corporate responsibility reporting and assurance, are outweighed by the advantages to be gained: in other words, they believe the exercise makes good business sense.

18.6 RELEVANCE OF ENVIRONMENTAL ISSUES TO EXTERNAL FINANCIAL STATEMENT AUDITS

Although this and Chapter 17 are concerned, respectively, with external corporate responsibility reports and their assurance, and internal environmental audits, the primary focus of this book is external financial statement audits. It is, therefore, appropriate to consider the relevance of environmental and other corporate responsibility issues to external financial statement audits. That environmental matters are relevant to financial statement audits has been noted by commentators such as Owen (1992) and Collison (1996).[22] Owen (1992), for example, observes:

> [T]he fact that environmental issues, and particularly company shortcomings in response to these issues, have ever-increasing financial consequences for business means that the financial auditor must pay due regard to them now in the conduct of current statutory audits.

Collison (1996) further explains:

> A company's environmental policy and obligations and its reaction to environmental developments, such as the changing attitudes of consumers are clearly a concern to the financial auditor to the extent that they are material to the financial statements. (p. 328)

Reviewing the content of statutory financial statements, it could be argued justifiably that environmental, if not most corporate responsibility, issues impact, at least to some extent, on all aspects of the financial statements and their audit. However, the areas where they are probably of greatest significance for external auditors include the following:

(i) Gaining an understanding of the client, its environment, industry and business, and assessing its risks

Earlier in this chapter we have commented on:
- society's increasing awareness of environmental impact, product and workplace health and safety, employment practices and other similar issues;

---

[22] Given the extension of environmental reports, which were common in the 1990s, into wide-ranging corporate responsibility reports which are more usually produced by major companies today, it seems likely that, if Owen and Collison were commenting a little more than a decade later, their remarks would have been extended to 'sustainability' or 'corporate responsibility' issues rather than being limited to environmental matters.

- the increasing volume and complexity of laws and regulations relating to these issues; and
- the increasing importance of incorporating corporate responsibility considerations into business decisions.

Given these and similar factors, it is clearly important that auditors gain a thorough understanding of their clients':

– environmental, social and ethical policies,
– environmental impacts – resulting from their operations, products and services, and
– environmental, health and safety, and social (including employer) legal and regulatory obligations.

However, not only must auditors gain an understanding of the environmental and other corporate responsibility factors that affect their clients, they must also consider the relevance and impact of those factors when assessing their clients' financial, operational, business and other risks, and the impact of these risks on the financial statements.

(ii) Ascertaining audit clients' compliance with corporate responsibility related laws and regulations

As part of gaining an understanding of the client, International Standard on Auditing (ISA) 250: *The auditor's responsibilities relating to laws and regulations in an audit of financial statements* requires auditors to:

obtain a general understanding of:
(a) The legal and regulatory framework applicable to the entity and the industry or sector in which the entity operates; and
(b) How the entity is complying with that framework. (para 12)

In this and Chapter 17, we have noted that virtually all companies are, to a greater or lesser extent, subject to environmental and other corporate responsibility related laws and regulations. Such laws and regulations are components of the entity's 'regulatory framework' and, therefore, must be understood by the auditor. In order to obtain the required understanding, auditors may, for example, ascertain from the entity's directors and/or senior executives:

- the entity's policies and procedures regarding its, and its employees', compliance with applicable laws and regulations;
- the laws and regulations that may be expected to have a fundamental effect on the operations of the entity and its financial statements; and
- the policies or procedures adopted by the entity for identifying, evaluating and accounting for litigation claims.

Although auditors are required to obtain a general understanding of their clients' legal and regulatory frameworks and their compliance therewith, ISA 250, para 6, distinguishes the auditor's responsibilities in relation to the entity's compliance with:

(a) The provisions of those laws and regulations generally recognized to have a direct effect on ... the financial statements; and

(b) Other laws and regulations that do not have a direct effect on ... the financial statements, but compliance with which may be fundamental to the operating aspects of the business, to an entity's ability to continue its business, or to avoid material penalties ...; non-compliance with such laws and regulations may therefore have a material effect on the financial statements.

Environmental, health and safety, employment practices and other corporate responsibility related laws and regulations clearly fall within the latter category.

For organisations in industrial sectors such as chemicals, manufacturing and the extractive industries, environmental laws and regulations may well be "fundamental to the operating aspects of the business, to [the] entity's ability to continue its business or to avoid material penalties"[23] (ISA, 250, para 6). For audit clients for which environmental and other corporate responsibility laws and regulations are significant, auditors are required to make enquiries of the directors and/or senior executives as to whether the entity is in compliance with applicable laws and regulations, and also to inspect correspondence with relevant licensing or regulatory authorities, to help identify instances of non-compliance with laws and regulations that may have a material effect on the financial statements. They are also required to request the directors and/or senior executives to provide written representations confirming that all known actual or possible non-compliance with laws and regulations, whose effect should be considered when preparing the financial statements, have been disclosed to the auditor (ISA 250, paras 14, 16).

Thus, for audit clients for which environmental and other corporate responsibility laws and regulations are central to their ability to conduct their business, ascertaining their compliance (or, more pertinently, instances of non-compliance) with the applicable laws and regulations is an important element of an external financial statement audit.

---

[23] For example, in a waste disposal company, the terms of licences under which the company is allowed to dispose of hazardous waste are central to its ability to conduct its business. If the company should breach the terms of the licences, it is likely that it will be unable to continue in business.

(iii) Evaluating the adequacy of disclosures relating to contingent liabilities and the adequacy of provisions

If a company breaches environmental and/or other corporate responsibility related laws and regulations it is exposed to liabilities in the form of, for example, fines, damages and remediation costs (that is, costs to remedy any harm to the environment, property or people that result from the breach). In some cases the liabilities may be minor in relation to the financial affairs of the company but in others they may be of sufficient size to be material to the company's financial statements.

ISA 250 explains external auditors' responsibilities in these circumstances. It states:

> If the auditor becomes aware of information concerning an instance of non-compliance or suspected non-compliance with [relevant] laws or regulations, the auditor shall obtain:
> (a) An understanding of the nature of the act and the circumstances in which it has occurred; and
> (b) Further information to evaluate the possible effect on the financial statements. (para 18)

> Matters relevant to the auditor's evaluation of the possible effect on the financial statements include:
> - The potential financial consequences of possible non-compliance ... including for example, the imposition of fines, penalties, damages, threat of expropriation of assets, enforced discontinuance of operations, and litigation.
> - Whether the potential financial consequences require disclosure.
> - Whether the potential financial consequences are so serious as to call into question the fair presentation of the financial statements [that is, whether the going concern assumption is valid], or otherwise make the financial statements misleading. (para A14)

Where the potential financial consequences of one or more violations of corporate responsibility related legal or regulatory requirements are material to an audit client's financial statements, the auditor needs to evaluate the adequacy of disclosures relating to the associated contingent liabilities, both in terms of the likely amount involved and the explanation of the relevant circumstances.[24]

Additionally, for audit clients whose activities, processes, products or services have (or are likely to have) a significant impact on the environment, external

---

[24] It should be remembered that when an audit client has been prosecuted for non-compliance with laws or regulations and the resultant fine, damages, remediation costs, etc. have been settled by the regulatory authority or the court but are not yet paid, an actual liability exists and should be recorded as such in the financial statements. Contingent liabilities relate, amongst other things, to breaches of environmental laws or regulations which have been discovered but the resultant financial consequences are, as yet, uncertain as to their amount.

auditors need to evaluate the adequacy of their clients' insurance cover for the possible consequences of breaching environmental legal or regulatory requirements (including the associated legal costs) and for potential environment-related emergencies and disasters. Similarly, they need to evaluate the adequacy of their provisions in respect of these matters.

(iv)   Reviewing the valuation of fixed assets and inventory (stock)

Amongst other matters to which external auditors need to pay special regard for client entities for which environmental matters are particularly significant is the value of fixed assets – in particular land and buildings – and of inventory (stock) as shown in the pre-audited financial statements. The value of land may be altered dramatically by factors such as the discovery of hazardous waste, or contaminated soil or underground water, at any of the client's locations (anywhere in the world) irrespective of whether the hazardous waste was dumped, or the soil or water was contaminated by, the client or a previous occupier of the site(s) concerned.

Similarly, the value of buildings and plant may be altered by, for instance, the discovery that they breach health and safety or environmental regulations; for example, that the present arrangement for storage of waste poses a fire or health hazard, or radioactive or gaseous emissions exceed permitted levels. In some cases, violation of regulations may be caused by changes in the regulations themselves; for example, permitted levels of emissions may be reduced as a result of a regulatory change.[25] Whatever their cause, where buildings or plant (or, indeed, any other productive asset) breaks current or soon-to-be-implemented regulations, considerable capital expenditure may be required to bring existing assets into line with the required standards. Apart from affecting the value of the assets stated in the balance sheet, planned capital expenditure may give rise to commitments that need to be disclosed in the financial statements: the external auditor will need to review the adequacy of any such disclosures.

Along similar lines, for clients with products that have a significant influence on the environment or have health and safety implications, external auditors need to be alert to the fact that the value of inventory may be diminished, or items of inventory may be rendered obsolete (or even give rise to costs rather than revenues). This may arise, for example, from 'health hazard' issues,[26] or

---

[25] A pertinent example is afforded by the capping of companies' permitted greenhouse gas emissions during the first and second decade of the 21st century.

[26] A pertinent example of inventory rendered obsolete, and also giving rise to costs, is provided by the return of many millions of toys manufactured in China during 2007 which contained lead paint that exceeded permitted levels in the USA, EU, Australia and New Zealand and elsewhere.

through "environmental concerns, storage and disposal costs of environmentally-maligned materials and recycling commitments" (Collison, 1996, p. 32). The value of stock stated in the balance sheet may need to be adjusted accordingly.

18.7 SUMMARY

In this chapter we have explored aspects of corporate responsibility reporting – broadly based reports that provide environmental, social, economic and similar non-financial performance information. We have noted that, in order to enhance the credibility of such information, an increasing number of companies voluntarily submit it to independent assurance. Additionally, we have drawn attention to the recent emergence and rapid growth of 'ethical' or 'responsible investments' and associated indices such as the FTSE4Good, Dow Jones Sustainability Index and the Carbon Disclosure Leadership Index. These indices appear to be equally important to investors seeking to invest in such equity and to companies seeking inclusion in one or more index.

Much of the chapter is concerned with the objectives, scope and process of, and the reports associated with, external assurance engagements, and the professional requirements for those who provide assurance services. However, we have also discussed the advantages and disadvantages that may accrue to companies through engaging in corporate responsibility reporting and assurance. We observed that, notwithstanding the significant disadvantages that may result from companies pursuing this activity, many – and a rapidly growing number – of major companies in the UK and elsewhere appear to find that publishing independently assured corporate responsibility reports makes good business sense. In the final section of the chapter we have considered some of the ways in which corporate responsibility matters may impact the statutory audit of companies' financial statements.

SELF-REVIEW QUESTIONS

18.1 Define the following terms:
    (i)   an environmental report;
    (ii) a corporate responsibility report;
    (iii) a 'responsible (or ethical) investment index'.

18.2 Explain briefly the motivations for companies to engage in corporate responsibility reporting.

18.3 Outline the principles identified in the Global Reporting Initiative's Sustainability Reporting Guidelines (G3) that underpin:
    (i) the content of corporate responsibility reports; and
    (ii) the quality of the information provided.

18.4 (a) Explain briefly what is meant by an 'assurance engagement' in the context of corporate responsibility reporting;
    (b) Outline the professional requirements for providers of assurance services.

18.5 Explain briefly the three principles that underpin assurance engagements conducted in accordance with AccountAbility's AA1000 Assurance Standard.

18.6 Identify the key differences for:
    (i) qualified accountants, and
    (ii) others
in terms of the requirements they must meet when conducting an assurance engagement on a client's corporate responsibility report.

18.7 (a) Outline the content of an assurance statement prepared by a professional accounting firm which is attached to a corporate responsibility report the firm has assured.
    (b) Briefly explain how this report differs from one prepared in accordance with AA1000AS.

18.8 List and briefly explain six advantages that may accrue to companies as a consequence of publishing independently assured corporate responsibility reports.

18.9 List and briefly explain three disadvantages that companies may experience as a consequence of publishing independently assured corporate responsibility reports.

18.10 List four ways in which environmental factors may impact upon the statutory audit of companies' financial statements.

REFERENCES

Accountant, The. (1998, 14 April). Going green. *The Accountant*, 14.

Anonymous. (2005). Focus Report: Comparing sustainability reporting assurance standards. *Business and the Environment* **XVI**(6), 6–7.

Beets, S.D., and Souther, C.C. (1999). Corporate environmental reports: the need for standards and an environmental assurance service. *Accounting Horizons* **13**(2), 129–145.

Collison, D.J. (1996). The response of statutory financial auditors in the UK to environmental issues: A descriptive and exploratory case study. *British Accounting Review* **28**, 325–349.

Context. (2006). *Global Corporate Responsibility reporting trends: Reporting in Context 2006*, www.econtext.co.uk.

Dow Jones Sustainability Indexes (DJSI). (2007). *Components – DJSI World*, www.sustainability-index.com/07_htmle/data/djsiworld.

Ethical Investment Research Services (EIRIS). (2007). *The State of Responsible Business: Global corporate response to environmental, social and governance (ESG) challenges*. London: Ethical Investment Research Services (EIRIS).

Fédération des Experts Comptables Européens (FEE, November). (2001). *FEE Update on Sustainability Issues*. Brussels: FEE.

Fédération des Experts Comptables Européens (FEE). (2002). *FEE Discussion Paper Providing Assurance on Sustainability Reports*. Brussels: FEE.

Gilmour, G., and Caplan, A. (2001). Who cares? *Accountancy* **128**(1297), 44–45.

Innovest. (2007). *Carbon Disclosure Project Report 2007 Global FT500*. Toronto: Innovest Group.

International Federation of Accountants (IFAC). (2006). *Code of Ethics for Professional Accountants*. New York: IFAC.

Investors Chronicle. (1998). Survey – ethical investment: pensions with principles. *Investors Chronicle*, (17 July), 44.

KPMG. (2005). *KPMG International Survey of Corporate Responsibility Reporting 2005*. Amsterdam: KPMG Global Sustainability Services.

Krumsiek, B.J. (1998). The emergence of a new era in mutual find investing: socially responsible investing comes of age. *Journal of Investing*, (Winter), 84–99.

MacKay, E. (2000, 14 June). Environmental reporting – creating the right environment. *Accountancy Age*, www.accountancyage.com/News/1103312, 1–3.

Owen, D. (1992). *Green Reporting: Accountancy and the Challenge of the Nineties*. London: Chapman and Hall.

SAM. (2007). *Dow Jones Sustainability World Index (DJSI World)*, www.sustainability-index.com/djsi_pdf.

ADDITIONAL READING

Adams, C.A., and McNicholas, P. (2007). Making a difference: sustainability reporting, accountability and organisational change. *Accounting, Auditing & Accountability Journal* **20**(3), 382–402.

Confederation of British Industry (CBI). (1990). *Narrowing the Gap: Environmental Auditing*. London: CBI.

Fédération des Experts Comptables Européens. (FEE). (2006). *Key Issues in Sustainability Assurance – an overview*. Brussels: FEE.

International Auditing and Assurance Standards Board (IAASB). (2006). *Assurance Aspects of G3 – The Global Reporting Initiative's 2006 Draft sustainability guidelines*. New York: International Federation of Accountants (IFAC).

O'Dwyer, B., and Owen, D.L. (2005). Assurance statement practice in environmental, social and sustainability reporting: a critical evaluation. *The British Accounting Review* **37**(2), 205–229.

Owen, D.L., Swift, A., Humphrey, C., and Bowerman, M. (2000). The new social audits: accountability, managerial capture or the agenda of social champions? *The European Accounting Review* **9**(1), 81–98.

PricewaterhouseCoopers. (2007). *Business Review: has it made a difference? Narrative Reporting Survey 2007*. London: PricewaterhouseCoopers LLP.

World Commission on Environment and Development. (1987). *Our Common Future*. Oxford: Oxford University Press.

APPENDIX

BRIEF DESCRIPTIONS OF 'RESPONSIBLE INVESTMENT' INDICES

1. FTSE4GOOD

FTSE is an abbreviation of 'Financial Times Stock Exchange'. It is an independent company that originated as a joint venture between the *Financial Times* newspaper (FT) and the London Stock Exchange (LSE). The FTSE Group has developed 100,000 indices covering more than 48 countries and all major classes of assets. Among its indices are the FTSE4Good benchmark series – including the FTSE4Good Global, FTSE4Good UK, FTSE4Good USA, FTSE4Good Europe, and FTSE4Good Japan Indices.

The FTSE4Good Index series was launched in 2001 and includes companies that meet prescribed standards in three areas, namely:
  (i)   working towards environmental sustainability;
  (ii) developing positive relations with stakeholders;
  (iii) upholding and supporting universal human rights (Smile, 2007).
Any company in the various FTSE share indices that meet the prescribed criteria are included in the relevant FTSE4Good Benchmark index. However, FTSE4Good reports:

> In line with mainstream global SRI [Social Responsible Investor] thinking, a small number of sector exclusions have been applied:

- Tobacco Producers
- Companies manufacturing either whole, strategic parts, or platforms for nuclear weapons systems
- Companies manufacturing whole weapons systems
- Owners or operators of nuclear power stations. (p. 2)

In November 2007, the FTSE4Good Global Index included 697 companies; of these 99 were UK companies (75 were also FTSE 100 companies and 24 FTSE 250 companies).[27] USA companies accounted for about 46 per cent of the market capitalisation of companies included in the Index, and UK companies about 17 per cent. The next highest contributor was Japan; its companies accounted for about eight per cent of the market capitalisation represented by the Index. In November 2007 the FTSE4Good UK Index included a total of 289 companies; 79 of these were also FTSE 100 companies and 117 were FTSE 250 companies. (Seventy-five of the FTSE 100 companies were also included in the FTSE4Good Global Index but this applied to only 24 of the FTSE 250 companies.)[28]

FTSE has recognised that, in the current era of global concern about climate change, "investors, governments and wider society expect companies to take responsibility for identifying and reducing their climate change impacts" (FTSE4Good, 2007b). As a result, during 2008 and 2009, FTSE is phasing in climate change criteria for companies whose operations have a 'high' or 'medium' climate change impact (for example, general mining, airlines, electricity and delivery services), or whose products have a high climate change impact (for example, aerospace and automobiles). These companies must meet the climate change criteria (in addition to the three groups of criteria indicated above) if they wish to be a FTSE4Good company.

2. DOW JONES SUSTAINABILITY INDEX (DJSI)

The Dow Jones Sustainability Index (DJSI), launched in 1999, was the first global index tracking the financial performance of the leading sustainability-driven companies worldwide. It captures the top 10 per cent of the biggest 2,500 companies worldwide[29] based on long-term economic, environmental and social criteria (DJSI, 2007). Components are selected according to a systematic corporate sustainability assessment that identifies the sustainability leaders in each of 58 industry groups (SAM, 2007). In October 2007 the DJSI World

---

[27] See Chapter 17, footnote 10 for information about the FTSE 100 and FTSE 250 indices.

[28] The data on FTSE4Good companies were provided by a correspondent from the FTSE Group's Responsible Investment Unit in November 2007.

[29] This notwithstanding, in October 2007, there were 318 companies in the DJSI (world) (SAM, 2007).

index included 318 companies, of which 58 were UK companies (47 of the 58 were FTSE 100 companies and 13 were FTSE 250 companies) (data derived from www.sustainability-indexes.com).

3. CARBON DISCLOSURE LEADERSHIP INDEX (CDLI)

The Carbon Disclosure Project (CDP) was launched in 2002 as an independent non-profit-making organisation centred in the UK. It seeks to provide information to 315 major institutional shareholders around the world (with total assets under management of $US41 trillion). On behalf of these institutional investors, CDP seeks information from the world's largest companies (2,400 in 2007) about the commercial risks they face from, and opportunities presented by, climate change and greenhouse gas emissions. CDP also works with these companies to help them to ensure that an effective carbon emissions/reductions strategy is in place and is integral to their business (CDP, 2007a).

Since 2004, independent analysts from Innovest Strategic Value Advisors, who write the annual *Carbon Disclosure Project Global FT500* reports, grade the responses provided to CDP from the Fortune 500 (FT500) companies on the quality of their disclosures and rank companies within the Climate Disclosure Leadership Index (CDLI). In 2007, the index was:

> comprised of 68 F500 companies that show distinction in their responses to the Carbon Disclosure Project survey based on their reporting of greenhouse gas emissions and assessment of a company's climate change strategy.

CDP explains that Innovest ranks the FT500 companies included in the CDP survey on a 100-point scale and all companies which achieve a score of 85 or more are featured in the index (CDP, 2007b). In 2007, 20 UK (FTSE 100) companies were included in the CDLI (see Figure 18.1).

REFERENCES

Carbon Disclosure Project (CDP). (2007a). *Carbon Disclosure Project: About the Carbon Disclosure Project*, www.cdproject.net.

Carbon Disclosure Project (CDP). (2007b). *Carbon Disclosure Project: Climate Leadership Index (CLI) 2007*, www.cdproject.net/climateleaders2007.asp.

Dow Jones Sustainability Indexes (DJSI). (2007). *Overview*. www. sustainability-index. com/07/_htmle/indexes/overview.

FTSE4Good. (2007a). *FTSE4Good Index Series*. www.FTSE.com/FTSE4good.

FTSE4Good. (2007b). *FTSE4Good Climate Change Criteria*, www.FTSE.com/FTSE4good.

Smile. (2007). *Invest: FTSE4Good*. www. smile.co.uk.

Appendix
Summary of Steps in a Statutory
Financial Statement Audit

The steps in the audit process are depicted in the diagram on the next page.

Step 1 – Engagement procedures (see Chapter 8)

Before accepting appointment for a new or continuing audit engagement, auditors are required to conduct 'engagement procedures'; these include investigating the integrity of the client's directors and senior executives and ensuring that they (the auditors) are adequately independent and have the required capability, competence and time to complete the audit.

Step 2 – Appointment (see Chapter 5)

Company auditors are formally appointed (or reappointed) by the company's shareholders at their annual 'accounts meeting' (or, if a private company, at a meeting during the 'period for appointing auditors'). However, in practice, the company's directors usually arrange the appointment and this is ratified by the shareholders at the accounts meeting (or private company meeting).

Step 3 – Engagement letter (see Chapter 8)

At the commencement of the audit, an engagement letter is prepared by the auditor and sent to the client. This is to ensure there are no misunderstandings between the auditor and the client. The letter includes things such as:
- a statement emphasising that, under the Companies Act 2006, the financial statements are the responsibility of the auditee's directors and that the financial statements are required to give a true and fair view of the company's financial position and performance and comply with relevant legislation;[1]

---

[1] It should be noted that the Companies Act 2006 specifies that companies must prepare their financial statements in accordance with an applicable financial reporting framework [either International Financial Reporting Standards ('IAS accounts') or UK Generally Accepted Accounting Practice (UK GAAP: 'Companies Act accounts').

Summary of the audit process

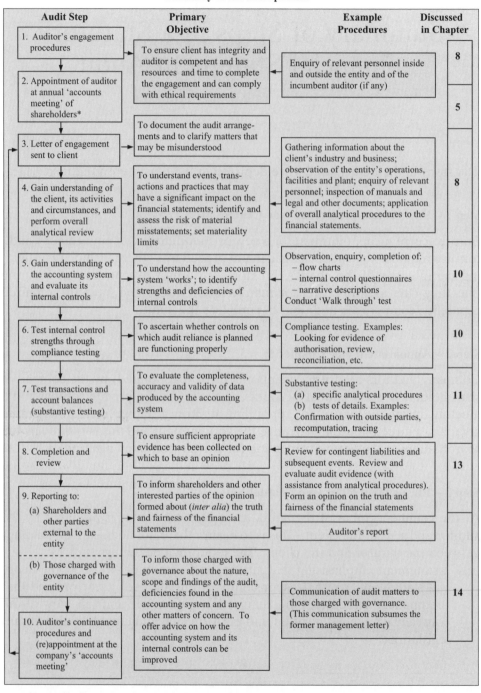

Audit Step	Primary Objective	Example Procedures	Discussed in Chapter
1. Auditor's engagement procedures	To ensure client has integrity and auditor is competent and has resources and time to complete the engagement and can comply with ethical requirements	Enquiry of relevant personnel inside and outside the entity and of the incumbent auditor (if any)	8
2. Appointment of auditor at annual 'accounts meeting' of shareholders*			5
3. Letter of engagement sent to client	To document the audit arrangements and to clarify matters that may be misunderstood	Gathering information about the client's industry and business; observation of the entity's operations, facilities and plant; enquiry of relevant personnel; inspection of manuals and legal and other documents; application of overall analytical procedures to the financial statements.	8
4. Gain understanding of the client, its activities and circumstances, and perform overall analytical review	To understand events, transactions and practices that may have a significant impact on the financial statements; identify and assess the risk of material misstatements; set materiality limits		
5. Gain understanding of the accounting system and evaluate its internal controls	To understand how the accounting system 'works'; to identify strengths and deficiencies of internal controls	Observation, enquiry, completion of: – flow charts – internal control questionnaires – narrative descriptions Conduct 'Walk through' test	10
6. Test internal control strengths through compliance testing	To ascertain whether controls on which audit reliance is planned are functioning properly	Compliance testing. Examples: Looking for evidence of authorisation, review, reconciliation, etc.	10
7. Test transactions and account balances (substantive testing)	To evaluate the completeness, accuracy and validity of data produced by the accounting system	Substantive testing: (a) specific analytical procedures (b) tests of details. Examples: Confirmation with outside parties, recomputation, tracing	11
8. Completion and review	To ensure sufficient appropriate evidence has been collected on which to base an opinion	Review for contingent liabilities and subsequent events. Review and evaluate audit evidence (with assistance from analytical procedures). Form an opinion on the truth and fairness of the financial statements	13
9. Reporting to: (a) Shareholders and other parties external to the entity	To inform shareholders and other interested parties of the opinion formed about (*inter alia*) the truth and fairness of the financial statements		
		Auditor's report	
(b) Those charged with governance of the entity	To inform those charged with governance about the nature, scope and findings of the audit, deficiencies found in the accounting system and any other matters of concern. To offer advice on how the accounting system and its internal controls can be improved	Communication of audit matters to those charged with governance. (This communication subsumes the former management letter)	14
10. Auditor's continuance procedures and (re)appointment at the company's 'accounts meeting'			

*As noted in Chapter 5, section 5.2.4, the Companies Act 2006 provides for all public companies to appoint their auditor for the following year at the annual 'accounts meeting' of shareholders; private companies may appoint their auditor without such a meeting during the 'period for appointing auditors'.

- a statement that the directors are responsible for ensuring the auditor has access to all of the company's books and records and is given any information and explanations (s)he requires;
- an indication of how the auditor will approach the audit and guidance on the approximate timing of the audit work to be done;
- a statement noting that the objective of the audit is to form an opinion on the truth and fairness of the financial information, not to detect fraud. However, it is also pointed out that audit procedures are designed to give reasonable assurance that any material fraud will be detected;
- the scope of the audit and the fact that it is not designed to detect significant deficiencies in the company's systems but that any such deficiencies which come to light will be reported to the directors;
- in appropriate cases, an explanation of the involvement of client personnel, other auditors or experts in certain aspects of the audit;
- a statement that the directors will be expected to provide written confirmation of certain oral representations expressed by them to the auditor during the course of the audit;
- the basis on which fees are to be computed and billed.

The auditor prepares two copies of the engagement letter. They are both sent to the client for signing; one is retained by the client, the other is returned to the auditor for inclusion in the audit file.

It should be noted that the engagement letter does not absolve the auditor from any statutory, common law or professional duties in relation to the audit. Its principal purpose is to clarify the role and scope of the audit and to confirm that the client entity's management[2] is aware of the nature of the audit engagement. It also outlines some administrative matters.

Step 4 – Understanding the client and overall analytical review (see Chapter 8)

It is essential that the auditor gains a thorough understanding of the client entity, its business, its operations, its industry and its key personnel. This understanding, *inter alia*:

- makes the auditor aware of any particular events, transactions or accounting practices which may have a significant impact on the financial statements;
- enables the auditor to identify and assess any circumstances which may increase the likelihood of misstatements being present in the (pre-audited) financial statements;

---

[2] Readers are reminded that, in this text, unless indicated otherwise we use the term 'management' to denote non-executive and executive directors and non-director senior executives (i.e., all directors and senior executives).

- provides a background against which evidence gathered during the course of the audit can be evaluated to see if it 'makes sense' and 'looks right'.

This understanding of the client is acquired primarily through the following procedures:
- visiting the client company, touring its premises and meeting key personnel (for example, the managing director, the finance director, and the marketing, production and human resources department managers);
- discussing with key personnel, in relation to the past year, the trading and financial position of the company, problems and successes experienced, and any significant changes in activities, accounting or personnel policies and procedures;
- reviewing the company's legal documents (including, for example, its Memorandum and Articles of Association, and any debenture trust deeds), policy and procedures manuals, and any significant commercial agreements (e.g., franchise and leasing agreements).

Gaining an understanding of the client also involves making an initial assessment of its financial affairs through overall analytical procedures. Primarily by means of examining meaningful relationships in the client's financial data through trend and ratio analysis, the auditor gains an understanding of the entity's financial position, the results of its operations and its cash flows, as presented in the financial statements. The results of this analysis are evaluated against the auditor's expectations, based on his or her understanding of the client's circumstances. Key indicators, such as net profit to sales, return on shareholders' funds, debt to equity ratio, and working capital ratio, are compared with the averages for these indicators in the client's industry (or business sector). Based on the auditor's knowledge of the client, its 'usual' position in its industry and any known exceptional circumstances, the auditor can assess whether the financial statement data 'look right', or whether it appears that there are errors in the data.

Based on the overall analytical review the auditor can assess:
- audit risk: the likelihood that material misstatements are present in the (pre-audited) financial statements;
- materiality limits: the amount of error the auditor is prepared to accept in individual financial statement account balances or other disclosures, and in the financial statements as a whole, before concluding that they are materially misstated. (A material misstatement is one which is likely to affect a decision or action of a reasonable user of the financial statements.)

Step 5 – Understanding the accounting system and evaluating its internal controls (see Chapter 10)

Before the auditor can assess the truth and fairness with which the financial statements portray the company's financial position and performance, (s)he must understand the accounting system and the controls which are 'built into' the system to prevent, or detect and correct, errors and irregularities in the accounting data (i.e., the internal accounting controls). The auditor must understand how the transactions data are captured, how they are processed through the accounting system, and how the data are 'converted' into financial information in the form of financial statements. (S)he also needs to know which personnel are responsible for performing what tasks.

The auditor gains this understanding of the accounting system primarily through:
- observation: observing various aspects of the client's accounting system;
- enquiry: asking questions of client personnel;
- completing a (or using a client-prepared) flow chart of the system;
- completing an Internal Control Questionnaire (ICQ). This usually consists of a list of questions which require 'yes', 'no' or 'not applicable' answers. The auditor completes this on the basis of observation and enquiry.

The flow chart and/or ICQ, together with any narrative descriptions of parts of the accounting system, are important audit documents and are kept in the audit file.

In order to test his or her understanding of the accounting system, the auditor conducts a 'walk through' test. For this test, one or two transactions are followed through the accounting system, from their recording on a source document (e.g., sales invoice) at the time the transaction takes place, through the journals, ledger, trial balance, etc., to their presentation in the financial statements (that is, as an element of account balances presented in the financial statements; e.g., as an element of 'Sales' and 'Debtors').

In addition to gaining knowledge of how the accounting system 'works', the auditor makes a preliminary evaluation of the system's internal controls. More specifically, the auditor identifies internal control 'strengths' and 'deficiencies'.

- *Strengths* are controls within the accounting system which, if operating properly, will prevent, or detect and correct, errors and irregularities.

- *Deficiencies* are aspects of the system which are susceptible to error or irregularities, but which lack a control (or an effective control) to prevent or detect such occurrences.

Based on the results of the overall analytical review and preliminary evaluation of the internal controls, the auditor can make decisions concerning the nature, timing and extent of audit procedures.

- *The nature of audit procedures* refers, for example, to whether the auditor will rely primarily on:
    - compliance tests: audit procedures designed to test whether the internal controls on which the auditor plans to rely to protect the integrity of the accounting data are functioning as intended (i.e., are being complied with), or
    - substantive tests: audit procedures designed to test the validity, completeness and accuracy of transactions and/or account balances.

    Both types of test are used in virtually every audit, but the emphasis on one or the other largely depends on the auditor's preliminary evaluation of the internal controls. Where internal controls are considered to be effective, greater reliance is placed on compliance testing than on substantive testing. Where internal controls are regarded as defective, the emphasis is on substantive tests. Because the auditor is required to express an opinion on the truth and fairness of the information presented in the financial statements, some substantive testing of that information *must* be undertaken in *every* audit.

    The 'nature of audit procedures' also refers to the procedures the auditor chooses from the alternatives available to accomplish a particular audit objective; for example, whether the auditor uses analytical procedures or tests of transactions to evaluate the accuracy, validity and completeness of the interest paid account balance.

- *The timing of audit tests* refers to whether (and the extent to which) the auditor conducts audit tests during an interim audit (that is, two or three months before the end of the financial year) rather than during the final audit (that is, around and shortly after the balance sheet date). Some testing must always be done during a final audit but, where internal controls are strong, some tests may be conducted earlier in the year. This enables the auditor to spread audit work more evenly throughout the financial year and to complete the final audit in a shorter period.

- *The extent of audit procedures* refers to the amount of evidence the auditor needs to gather before (s)he can be confident that the financial statements do or do not contain material misstatements and/or inadequate disclosures. In general, the more effective the internal controls in preventing, or detecting and correcting, errors, the more likely it is that the financial statements will be free from misstatement and, therefore, the less the evidence the auditor needs to gather in order to form an opinion that this is, in fact, the case.

**Step 6 – Testing internal control strengths through compliance testing
      (see Chapter 10)**

Before the auditor can rely on 'strengths' in the accounting system (i.e., effective internal controls) to prevent or detect errors in the accounting data, tests must be conducted to make sure that:
- these controls are, in fact, working effectively; and
- they have been so working throughout the financial year.

To illustrate a compliance test: one objective of internal controls is to ensure that all transactions are properly authorised. A control might be that, before any credit sale is made to a customer, it must be authorised by the credit manager. The credit manager is required to initial the sales invoice to indicate that the sale has been authorised. An audit procedure to test whether this control has been complied with is to examine duplicates of sales invoices for the credit manager's initials.

**Step 7 – Testing the validity, completeness and accuracy of transactions and account
      balances (substantive testing) (see Chapter 11)**

Because the auditor is required to express an opinion on whether or not the company's financial statements give a true and fair view of its financial position and performance and comply with relevant legislation, (s)he must always conduct some substantive tests. There are two main types of substantive tests:
  (i) substantive analytical procedures;
  (ii) tests of details.

(i)   Substantive analytical procedures: In these tests the relationships in accounting data are examined to determine the 'reasonableness' of individual account balances. For example, in order to verify the interest paid account balance, the auditor may ascertain the entity's average debt and average interest rate for the year. By applying the interest rate to the debt, an indication of the interest which should have been paid (or payable) during the year can be determined. By comparing the interest paid account balance with the calculated amount, the auditor can decide whether or not the recorded amount is 'reasonable'. If it is, in many cases, no further testing of this account will be performed. However, if it is not, then the disparity between the recorded and calculated amounts will need to be investigated.

(ii) Tests of details: In these tests, the validity, completeness and accuracy (as to amount, account classification, and reporting period) of transactions and account balances are examined. For example, the auditor may:
  - recompute items such as depreciation and allowance for bad debts, and reperform bank reconciliations, etc. This checks for arithmetical errors;

- trace transactions forwards from source documents to financial statements. This checks for completeness: to make sure all relevant transactions have been included in the financial statement account balances and that none has been 'lost' on its way through the system;
- trace transactions backwards from financial statements to source documents. This checks for validity: to make sure that account balances shown in the financial statements reflect the totals of genuine transactions;
- request confirmations from outside parties. For example, a sample of customers may be asked to confirm that they owed the client company the amount stated in the company's debtors' ledger account, and banks are asked to confirm the client's bank balances as at the balance sheet date;
- observe such items as inventory (stock). This usually includes attendance at the company's inventory count (or stocktake) when inventory is counted. However, it also includes observing the type and quality of inventory on hand in order to assess whether, and how much of it, is obsolete or substandard;
- inspection of documents such as marketable securities (for example, share certificates) and loan, lease or hire-purchase contracts.

Step 8 – Completion and review (see Chapter 13)

This step, which completes the evidence gathering and evaluation phase of the audit, comprises the following sub-steps:
  (i)   review for contingent liabilities and commitments;
  (ii) review for subsequent events before and after the audit report is signed;
  (iii) re-assessment of the validity of preparing the financial statements based on the going concern assumption;
  (iv) obtaining written representations from management;
  (v)   final review of the financial statements;
  (vi) evaluation of the audit evidence and working papers, and formation of the audit opinion.

(i)   *Review for contingent liabilities and commitments*: Before concluding the audit, the auditor must ascertain whether the entity has any contingent liabilities or commitments which should be disclosed in the financial statements.

- A *contingent liability* is a possible obligation which is expected to arise from a past event but which, at the balance sheet date, is uncertain as to existence or amount. An example is litigation for infringement of, say, environmental or product safety regulations. The outcome of the litigation will not be known until the case is heard in court.

- A *commitment* is a contractual undertaking; for example, an undertaking to purchase a certain amount of raw materials at a fixed price at a particular time in the future, or an agreement to lease or buy fixed assets, or to sell products or services, at an agreed price on a specified future date.

The auditor faces two major problems when reviewing for contingent liabilities and commitments:

(a) management may not wish to disclose these items in the financial statements;

(b) it is more difficult to discover unrecorded transactions and events than it is to evaluate recorded information.

However, financial statements are required to show a true and fair view of the reporting entity's state of affairs and this necessitates disclosure of any material contingent liabilities and commitments. Therefore, the auditor must attempt to ascertain whether they exist. This is accomplished primarily through:

- making enquiries of management;
- reviewing the minutes of directors' (or equivalent) meetings;
- reviewing correspondence files;
- reviewing audit working papers prepared during the course of the audit for information that may indicate a potential contingent liability;
- obtaining confirmation from the client's solicitor(s) regarding known, pending or expected liabilities or commitments.

(ii) ***Review for subsequent events***: The auditor is required to review transactions and events which occur during the period between the balance sheet date and the date of the audit report to see if an event has occurred which might affect the truth and fairness of the financial statements as at the balance sheet date. Two types of subsequent events may have occurred:

(a) Adjusting events: These are events which clarify conditions existing at the balance sheet date and/or which permit more accurate valuation of an account balance as at that date. For example, the commencement of bankruptcy proceedings against a major customer during the subsequent events period may indicate that his or her financial position was not sound at the balance sheet date. In this case, some adjustment to the Allowance for Bad Debts might be called for.

(b) Non-adjusting events: These are events which indicate conditions that have arisen subsequent to the balance sheet date. As these conditions do not affect the financial position or performance of the entity as at the balance sheet date, they should not be incorporated in the financial statements. However, where a non-adjusting post balance sheet event is material, it should be disclosed by way of a note to the financial statements so that users of the financial statements can gain a proper understanding of the entity's financial position and performance. An example of this type of event is a major expansion (or retraction) of the organisation, such as a purchase (or sale) of a subsidiary subsequent to the balance sheet date.

If the post balance sheet event is such that it brings into question the validity of the going concern concept (for example, as a consequence of a fire or flood occurring after the balance sheet date which results in a significant loss not covered by insurance), then it should be considered in the re-assessment of the going concern assumption.

(iii) ***Re-assessment of the validity of the going concern assumption***: In normal circumstances, financial statements are prepared on the basis of an assumption that the reporting entity will continue as a going concern for the foreseeable future. As part of their audits, auditors are required to consider whether adoption of this assumption is justified. Amongst other things, they are required to:

- make a preliminary assessment of the propriety of the client's adherence to the going concern assumption during the initial phase of the audit;
- plan and perform specific procedures to evaluate the directors'/senior executives' assessment of the client's going concern status and to identify indications that adoption of the going concern assumption may not be valid;
- consider and, if necessary, revise the preliminary going concern assessment;
- determine and document the extent of their (i.e., the auditors') concern (if any) about the company's ability to continue as a going concern.

If auditors believe that the company's ability to continue as a going concern is in question, they need to consider whether the relevant information is adequately disclosed in the financial statements. Where auditors believe the relevant matters are adequately disclosed (assuming the auditors are satisfied in all other respects), they are required to express an unqualified opinion. However, it is generally also appropriate for them to include an explanatory paragraph referring to the uncertainty in respect of the company's status as a going concern in an 'Emphasis of Matter' paragraph in the audit report. If auditors consider the relevant information is not adequately disclosed, they are required to express an 'except for' or 'adverse' audit opinion, as appropriate (see Step 9 below).

(iv) ***Obtaining written representations from management***: During the completion and review stage of the audit, auditors seek to have significant representations made by management in response to the auditor's enquiries, recorded in writing. Technically, these 'representation letters' are written by the client's directors (with input from other relevant parties) to the auditor but, in practice, they are normally prepared by the auditor and signed by the directors. They have two primary purposes, namely:

- to obtain evidence that the client's directors acknowledge their responsibility for the entity's financial statements and for making available complete information to the auditor; and
- to place on record management's (and other relevant parties') responses to enquiries by the auditor that relate to specific assertions about classes of transactions, account balances or other disclosures in the financial statements. These written representations ensure there is no misunderstanding between management and the auditor as to what was said – and provide management with an opportunity to correct any response the auditor has misinterpreted. They also ensure that management assumes responsibility for representations made to the auditor.

(v) ***Final review of the financial statements***: Towards the end of the completion and review phase of the audit, auditors:
   (a) perform analytical procedures;
   (b) evaluate the effect of uncorrected misstatements; and
   (c) conduct an overall review of the financial statements.

   (a) Analytical procedures: Analytical procedures are performed during the final review of the financial statements in order to identify any unusual fluctuations and/or unexpected results or relationships which are inconsistent with other audit evidence. If this occurs, the auditor is required to make enquiries of management about the findings and to evaluate management's responses in the light of the auditor's understanding of the entity and its environment, and audit evidence gathered during the audit. If management is unable to provide an adequate explanation of the findings, the auditor must perform additional audit procedures to resolve the matter.

(b) *Evaluate the effect of uncorrected misstatements*: As the audit progresses, the auditor accumulates all identified misstatements (other than those that are clearly trivial), distinguishing between those that are factual, judgmental and projected. These misstatements are communicated to the appropriate level of management (i.e., senior executives) with the request that they be corrected. If the senior executives refuse to correct some or all of the misstatements, the auditor refers them to the directors. If the directors support the stance of the senior executives, the auditor is required to obtain written representations from the directors stating that they believe the uncorrected misstatements are immaterial to the financial statements. However, although the directors may consider the uncorrected misstatements are immaterial to the financial statements, it is for the auditor to form an opinion as to whether this is, or is not, the case.

The auditor first evaluates whether the planning materiality and tolerable error thresholds determined during the planning stage of the audit (when the entity's actual financial results were not available) remain appropriate in the context of the entity's actual financial results. When the materiality levels have been confirmed or revised, the auditor evaluates whether the uncorrected misstatements are material, individually or in aggregate, to the financial statements. In determining whether or not the misstatements are material, the auditor is required to consider both their size and their nature.

(c) *Overall review of the financial statements*: During the completion and review stage of the audit, auditors evaluate the overall presentation of the financial statements and their conformity (or otherwise) with the applicable financial reporting framework. This involves, *inter alia*, evaluating whether the information presented in the individual financial statements and the notes thereto is properly classified and described, and whether the form, arrangement and content of the financial statements are appropriate.

(vi) **Evaluation of evidence, review of audit working papers and formation of the audit opinion**: Before reaching a final opinion on the audited financial statements, auditors are required to determine:
  (a) whether their assessment of the risks of material misstatement at the assertion level remains appropriate; and
  (b) whether sufficient appropriate audit evidence has been gathered in relation to each assertion in each class of transactions, account balance and disclosure in the various audit segments.

(a) Re-evaluation of risk assessment: Auditors need to re-evaluate their assessment of the risks of material misstatement at the assertion level at this stage of the audit because the results of audit procedures used to test the assertions in each class of transactions, account balance and disclosure, and/or the analytical procedures performed for the overall review of the financial statements may indicate the existence of a previously unidentified internal control deficiency or material misstatement. If this is the case, the auditor's risk assessment may need to be amended, and additional audit procedures planned and performed to address the newly assessed risk.

(b) Sufficient appropriate audit evidence: Before concluding the audit, the audit engagement partner must be satisfied that sufficient appropriate audit evidence has been obtained to support the audit opinion. In order to determine that sufficient appropriate audit evidence has been obtained, the engagement partner reviews the work conducted during the audit, as documented in the audit working papers, and holds discussions with audit team members as (s)he thinks appropriate. The audit working papers are reviewed to ensure, *inter alia*, that:

- sufficient appropriate audit evidence has been collected in each audit segment, and for the audit as a whole, on which to base an audit opinion;
- all audit work has been properly performed, documented and reviewed;
- conclusions reached in relation to specific audit objectives are consistent with the results obtained from the audit procedures performed;
- all questions and difficulties arising during the course of the audit have been resolved;
- the financial statements as a whole, and the assertions contained therein, are consistent with the auditor's knowledge of the entity's business and the results of audit procedures performed;
- the presentation of the financial statements (including their form, content and manner of disclosure) is appropriate.

On the basis of the review of the audit working papers, together with knowledge gained as the audit has progressed, the audit engagement partner forms an opinion as to whether or not the financial statements give a true and fair view of the reporting entity's state of affairs and financial performance and comply with the applicable financial reporting framework and Companies Act 2006.

For all but small audits a second audit partner, who has not been involved in the audit, usually reviews the audit working papers; for listed companies an engagement quality control review is required.

Before reaching a final conclusion as to the appropriate opinion to express in the audit report, auditors are required to review other information in documents which will be published along with the audited financial statements (such as the company's annual report). The auditor is to ensure the 'other information' is not inconsistent with the financial statements or materially misleading.[3]

Once the auditor is satisfied that sufficient appropriate audit evidence has been gathered and the audit has met other legal, regulatory and professional requirements, (s)he must form an opinion (based on the evidence collected and documented in the working papers) as to whether or not:
- the financial statements present a true and fair view of the company's financial position and performance;
- adequate accounting records have been kept by the company;
- returns adequate for the audit have been received from branches not visited by the auditors;
- the financial statements are in agreement with the underlying accounting records;
- the auditor has received all the information and explanations (s)he required for the purposes of the audit;
- the information given in the directors' report is consistent with the financial statements; and
- for quoted companies, the auditable portion of the directors' remuneration report complies with the Companies Act 2006.

Step 9 – Reporting (see Chapter 14)

The concluding step in the audit process is the preparation of reports addressed to:
- (i) the company's shareholders. (This report may also be read by other stakeholders external to the entity);
- (ii) those charged with the company's governance (i.e., the directors).

(i) ***Report to shareholders***: Auditors are required by the Companies Act 2006 to report to shareholders their opinion as to the truth and fairness of the company's financial statements and their compliance (or otherwise) with the applicable financial reporting framework and Companies Act 2006. The report may be unqualified or modified.

---

[3] Auditors are not required to review specifically the 'other information' for 'material misstatements of fact'; however, if anything comes to their attention while they are assessing whether or not the 'other information' is inconsistent with the financial statements, then they are required to discuss the matters with the directors and take other actions, as described in Chapter 13, section 13.6.2.

- An *unqualified audit report* indicates that, in the auditor's judgment, the financial statements give a true and fair view of the company's financial position and performance and comply with the applicable financial reporting framework and Companies Act 2006. The auditor may draw attention to matters directly related to the financial statements in an 'Emphasis of Matter' paragraph, or to matters not directly related to the financial statements in an 'Other Matter(s)' paragraph. These additional paragraphs do not affect the auditor's unqualified opinion on the financial statements.

- A *modified audit report* indicates that:
  – the auditor disagrees with the treatment or disclosure of a matter in the financial statements, or
  – there has been a limitation on the scope of the auditor's examination,

  and, in the auditor's opinion, the effect of matter with which (s)he disagrees, or the scope limitation, is material to the financial statements. Depending on the effect of the matter about which the auditor disagrees, or the limitation on the scope of the audit, on the audited financial statements, the auditor may express a qualified ('except for'), an adverse or a disclaimer of opinion.
  – If the matter is material but not pervasive to the financial statements, a qualified opinion will be expressed; that is, 'except for' the matter concerned the financial statements give a true and fair view and comply with the applicable financial reporting framework and Companies Act 2006.
  – If the effect of the matter about which the auditor disagrees is material and pervasive, such that the auditor concludes the financial statements do not give a true and fair view, an adverse opinion will be expressed.
  – If the limitation on the scope of the audit is material and pervasive, such that the auditor is not able to gather sufficient audit evidence on which to base an opinion, a disclaimer of opinion will be expressed.

(ii) **Report to the directors**: In addition to the auditor's report to shareholders, auditors are required to communicate audit matters to those charged with the company's governance (i.e., the directors or, more usually, if the auditee has one, its audit committee). In particular, they are required to communicate matters relating to:
  (i)   the auditor's responsibilities in relation to the financial statement audit;
  (ii) the planned scope and timing of the audit (in general terms);

(iii) significant audit findings; and

(iv) the auditor's independence.

The purpose of these communications (which occur at various times during the audit) is to:

- help ensure there is a mutual understanding between the auditor and the company's directors about the scope of the audit and the respective responsibilities of the auditor and directors;
- share relevant information that will assist the auditor and the directors fulfil their respective responsibilities; and
- provide the directors with constructive observations (and recommendations for improvement) arising from the audit process.

The content of the auditor's communication to those charged with governance varies quite widely in practice – depending on the auditor, the client and the circumstances. However, each of the above matters [(i) to (iv)] are invariably included. In relation to significant findings from the audit, matters frequently covered are as follows:

- qualitative aspects of the entity's accounting practices and financial reporting;
- significant difficulties, if any, encountered during the audit;
- uncorrected misstatements;
- any matters related to fraud that, in the auditor's judgment, are relevant to the directors' responsibilities to oversee the financial reporting process;
- any matters (other than those which are clearly inconsequential) involving non-compliance with laws and regulations that have a material effect on the financial statements or otherwise come to the auditor's attention during the course of the audit;
- material uncertainties related to events and conditions that may cast significant doubt on the entity's ability to continue as a going concern and, more particularly, whether adherence to the going concern assumption is appropriate, and whether the relevant matters are adequately disclosed in the financial statements;
- any other audit matters warranting attention by the directors or audit committee that are significant to their oversight of the financial reporting process.

This communication to those charged with the entity's governance has subsumed, and is broader in content than, the former 'management letter' but an important component of the communication (like the management letter) is commenting on any internal control deficiencies which have come to light during the audit, explaining the effect of these deficiencies, and recommending steps which could be taken to rectify them.

Index